BOLLINGEN SERIES XLI

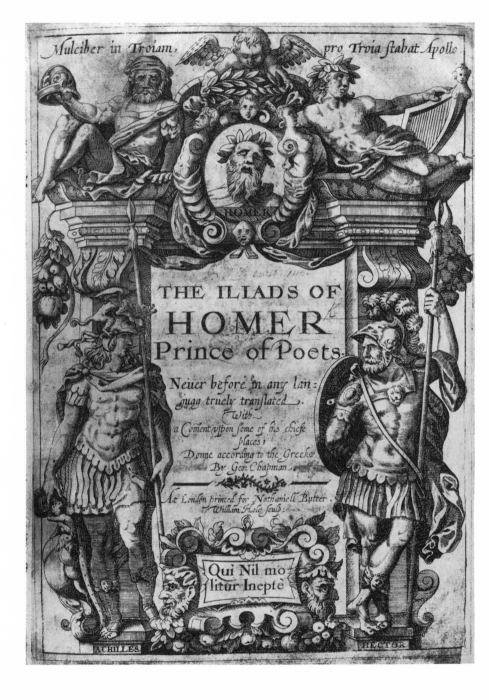

Mulciber in Troiam,   pro Troia ſtabat Apollo

HOMER

THE ILIADS OF
HOMER
Prince of Poets.

Neuer before in any lan-
guag truely tranſlated.
With
a Coment vpon ſome of his chiefe
places;
Donne according to the Greeke
By Geo: Chapman

At London printed for Nathaniell Butter.
William Hole ſculp:

Qui Nil mo-
litur Ineptè

ACHILLES   HECTOR

CHAPMAN'S HOMER

THE ILIAD

Edited, with Introduction and Glossary, by

ALLARDYCE NICOLL

With a New Preface by Garry Wills

BOLLINGEN SERIES XLI

PRINCETON UNIVERSITY PRESS

Princeton, New Jersey

Published by Princeton University Press,
41 William Street, Princeton, New Jersey 08540
In the United Kingdom: Princeton University Press,
Chichester, West Sussex

This is part one of the forty-first in a series of works sponsored by
and published for Bollingen Foundation

Library in Congress Cataloging-in-Publication Data
Homer.
[Iliad. English]
Chapman's Homer. Volume 1, The Iliad / edited, with introduction
and glossary by Allardyce Nicoll ; with a new preface by Garry
Wills.—1st Princeton pbk. ed.
p.   cm.
Originally published: Chapman's Homer. V. 1, The Iliad. New York :
Pantheon, 1956. (Bollingen series ; 41).
Includes bibliographical references.
ISBN 0–691–00236–3 (PB : acid-free paper)
1. Epic poetry, Greek—Translations into English.   2. Achilles
(Greek mythology)—Poetry.   3. Trojan War—Poetry.   I. Chapman,
George, 1559?–1634.   II. Nicoll, Allardyce, 1894–1976.   III. Title.
IV. Series: Bollingen series ; 41.
PA4025.A2C5 1998
883'.01–dc21   98–33505

Princeton University Press books are printed on acid-free paper
and meet the guidelines for permanence and durability of the
Committee on Production Guidelines for Book Longevity of the
Council on Library Resources
First Princeton Paperback Edition, 1998

http://pup.princeton.edu

Printed in the United States of America

3   5   7   9   10   8   6   4   2

CONTENTS

Preface to the Paperback Edition   vii
Preface   xv

The Iliad

Introduction   xix

Homer's Iliads

To the High Borne Prince of Men   3
To the Reader   7
The Preface to the Reader   14
The First Booke   23
   Commentarius   42
The Second Booke   46
   Commentarius   69
The Third Booke   73
   Commentarius   88
The Fourth Booke   91
The Fifth Booke   109
The Sixth Booke   136
The Seventh Booke   153
The Eighth Booke   166
The Ninth Booke   181
The Tenth Booke   200
The Eleventh Booke   215
The Twelfth Booke   238
The Thirteenth Booke   252
   Commentarius   275
The Fourteenth Booke   280
   Commentarius   294
The Fifteenth Booke   297
   Commentarius   319
The Sixteenth Booke   322
   Commentarius   346

Contents

The Seventeenth Booke   348
   Commentarius   368
The Eighteenth Booke   372
   Commentarius   389
The Nineteenth Booke   391
   Commentarius   403
The Twentieth Booke   405
The Twenty-First Booke   421
The Twenty-Second Booke   439
The Twenty-Third Booke   454
The Twenty-Fourth Booke   477
   [Commentary]   498

Seaven Bookes of the Iliades

To the Most Honored Earle Marshall   503
To the Reader   507
The First Booke   509
The Second Booke   526

Achilles' Shield

To the Most Honored Earle   543
To the Understander   548
Achilles' Shield   551

Glossary   559

PREFACE TO THE PAPERBACK EDITION

Garry Wills

To measure up to the *Iliad*'s greatness, a translator must find something in his or her own world that resonates deeply with the original's ethos. What was it in Chapman's time—that great period of Shakespeare and the English bible—that made his Homeric poem catch fire? It is usually said that Chapman imposed a Stoic framework on his poetry.[1] But that philosophy more often tugged against the spirit of the *Iliad* than opened new ways into it.

No, the consonance was between the semi-divine heroism of the *Iliad*'s warriors and Renaissance humanism. Elizabethan man, as the wonder of the universe, was sphered in cosmological symbols, like his queen rainbowed with stars in her ceremonial portraits.[2] Renaissance heroes were "stellified," as Alastair Fowler puts it, with a mix of science, magic, astronomy and theology.[3] Tycho Brahe's discovery of a "new star" in 1572 seemed to open fresh realms for man's intellectual mastery. The crushing weight of Hamlet's anguish can be measured by his closing off of that universe that was beckoning others to mingle with its constellations:

> This most excellent canopy, the air, look you, this brave o'erhanging firmament, this majestical roof fretted with golden fire—why, it appears no other thing to me than a foul and pestilent congregation of vapours. What a piece of work is man, how noble in reason, how infinite in faculty, in form and moving how express and admirable, in action how like an angel, in apprehension how like a god—the beauty of the world, the paragon of animals! And yet, to me, what is this quintessence of dust?

[1]See, for instance, Ennis Rees, *The Tragedies of George Chapman* (Harvard, 1954).
[2]Frances A. Yates, *Astraea: The Imperial Theme in the Sixteenth Century* (Ark Paperbooks, 1975), pp. 29–87.
[3]Alastair Fowler, *Time's Purpled Masquers: Stars and Afterlife in Renaissance English Literature* (Oxford, 1996).

The orthodoxy Hamlet is challenging with this black unbelief was expressed in an engraving for Robert Fludd's *History of the Double Cosmos,* where man's "microcosm" spans the whole "macrocosm."

That is the vision of heroes that flames from Chapman's *Iliad.* When he abbreviates a simile ("like Hesperus") to show a *causal* relation of man's acts and the stars, he is voicing the deepest belief of Renaissance humanism:

> And, at him, Achilles! His mind's fare
> Was fierce and mighty, his shield cast
> a sunlike radiance.
> Helm nodded and his [its] four plumes shook.
> And when he rais'd his lance,
> Up Hesp'rus rose 'mongst th'ev'ning stars.
> 22.272–75

When Priam sees Achilles blaze across the plain, he is not just *like* "Orion's dogstar," he *becomes* it (fall'n to earth):

> When aged Priam spied
> The great Greek come spher'd round with beams
> and show'ng as if the star
> Surnam'd Orion's hound—that springs
> in autumn and sends far
> Her radiance through a world of stars,
> of all whose beams his own
> Cast greatest splendor (the midnight
> that renders them most shown
> Then being their foil) and on their points
> cure-passing fevers then
> Come shaking down into the joints
> of miserable men—
> As *this* were fall'n to earth and shot
> above the fields his rays
> Now towards Priam.
> 22.22–30

The "cosmologizing" of man in the Renaissance made the easy communication between Homer's gods and his heroes something that Chapman could take with entire seriousness. The two worlds intersect, not least in the way gods provide a "mood music" for encounters in shadow or in dazzling light. There is a kind of divine meteorology that goes with the heroes' astrology. Zeus, whom Chapman calls "weather-wielder" (7.3), expresses his moods in clouds or sunbursts or lightning bolts, or in portents even direr:

[viii]

        – ◡ –

And from air's upper region
      did bloody vapors rain
For sad ostent much noble life
      should ere their times be slain.
           11.47–48

Earth and heaven are in a dialogue, expressive of the traffic between men and gods:

    The host set forth and pour'd his steel
        waves far out of the fleet.
    And, as from air the frosty North
        wind blows a cold thick sleet
    That dazzles eyes, flakes after flakes
        incessantly descending.
    So thick helms, curets [cuirasses], ashen darts
        and round shields, never ending,
    Flow'd from the navy's hollow womb.
        Their splendors gave heav'ns eye
    His beams again. Earth laugh'd
        to see her face so like the sky.
    Arms shin'd so hot, and she such clouds
        made with the dust she cast,
    She thunderd, feet of men and horse
        importun'd her so fast.
           19.347–54

And if gods and men share energies, so do men and animals, in the "Homeric similes." The Renaissance bestiary saw cosmic symbols in the animal world, a fact reflected in the zodiacal signs and the heraldic animals on noblemen's coats of arms. The interest in falconry gives a timely urgency to Hector's flight from a swooping Achilles:

        He fled in fear the hand
    Of that fear-master who, hawklike,
        air's swiftest passenger
    That holds a tim'rous dove in chase,
        and with command doth bear
    His fiery onset. The dove hastes.
        The hawk comes whizzing on,
    This way and that he turns and winds,

        – ◡ –

        and cuffs the pigeon
    And, till he trusses it, his great
        spir't lays hot charge on's wing—
    So urg'd Achilles Hector's flight . . .
          22.120–125

[ix]

Men on this scale are "stellified" even as they move to death. Zeus gives Hector special glory, knowing his end:

> And from his [Hector's] temples his bright helm
>
> > abhorred lightnings throws.
> For Jove, from forth the sphere of stars,
> > to his state put his own,
> And all the blaze of both the hosts
> > Confin'd in him alone.
> And all this was since, after this,
> > he had not long to live.
> This lightning flew before his death
> > which Pallas was to give.

Chapman shows a partiality to Hector, the doomed hero. His language, energetic everywhere, works itself to a thunderous climax at Hector's moment of greatest triumph, when he breaks through the rampart that protects the Achaean fleet.

> > Hector leaps
> Upon the port, from whose out-part
> > he tore a massy stone.
> Thick downward, upward edg'd, it was.
> > It was so huge an one
> That two vast yeomen of most strength
> > such as these times beget
>
> > ‒ ◡ ◡ ‒
>
> Could not from earth lift to a cart
> > Yet he did brandish it
> Alone (Saturnius made it light)
> > and, swinging it as nought,
> He came before the planky gates
> > that all for strength were wrought
> And kept the port. Two-fold they were
> > and with two rafters barr'd,
> High and strong-lock'd. He rais'd the stone;
> > bent to the hurl so hard,
> And made it with so main a strength,
> > that all the gates did crack,
> The rafters left them, and the folds
> > one from another brake.
> The hinges piecemeal flew, and through
> > the fervent little rock
> Thunder'd a passage. With his weight
> > th'inwall his breast did knock,
> And in rush'd Hector, fierce and grim
> > as any stormy night.
> His brass arms round about his breast

[x]

reflected terr'ble light.
Each arm, held up, held each a dart.
His presence call'd up all
The dreadful spir'ts his being held,
that to the threaten'd wall
None but the gods might check his way.
His eyes were furnaces
And thus he look'd back, called in all
All fir'd their courages
And in they flow'd. The Grecians fled.
Their fleet, now, and their fright,
Ask'd all their rescue. Greece went down.
Tumult was at its height.

I have marked one inverted accent in that passage (lift to, not lift to).
These inversions are common in Chapman, and vital to understand-
ing his metric inventiveness. They occur principally in two places. In
the first foot, as is common in all iambic lines, it is regular
("Thunder'd" in the passage above). It also occurs regularly after
the lines' most frequent pause (the "caesura").

So Ajax with his bead-hook leap'd

nimbly from ship to ship.

Such inversion gives the pattern Greeks called a choriamb (-ᴗᴗ-),
which can occur in almost any part of the line:

Far from the fleet / led to a place,

pure and exempt from blood.
8.431

Once one gets a feel for these inversions, and for the shifting, cae-
sura, the long Chapman line (the "fourteener") is recognized for
what it is, a highly flexible and expressive instrument. Here, for in-
stance, Apollo comes arrowing plague upon the army (irregular cae-
surae are marked //):

And, vex'd at heart, down from the tops
of steep heav'n stoop'd. // His bow
And quiver (cover'd round) // his hands

<pre>
         -   ᵕ   ᵕ   -
</pre>
did on his shoulders throw.
And of the angry deity
    the arrows, // as he mov'd,

<pre>
   -   ᵕ   ᵕ   -
</pre>
Rattled about him. // Like the night
    he rang'd the host and rov'd
(Athwart the fleet set) terribly.
    With his hord-loosing hand

<pre>
          -        ᵕ   ᵕ   -
</pre>
His silver bow twang'd // and his shafts
    did first the mules command
And swift hounds; // then the Greeks themselves
    his deadly arrows shot.
The fires of death went never out . . .

           1.43–50

The spelling and pronunciation of words must often be puzzled out, even from the best text, Allardyce Nicoll's. Peculiarities of Chapman include the trisyllabic "heroes," scanned to fit lines either as

<pre>
 - ᵕ -   ᵕ - ᵕ   ᵕ - ᵕ -
</pre>

heroes or heroes. (In the *Odyssey* we even get heroesses, 11.445). Other oddities—along with Chapman's heavily Latinate vocabulary—come from his reliance on three Latin books he used to explain Homer's Greek—Andreas Divus' translation of the epic into Latin hexameters, the accompanying commentary by "Spondanus" (Jean de Sponde), and the Greek-Latin *Lexicon* of Johannes Scapula. The latter book gave him his often fanciful etymologies.

    Chapman also uses the syntax of inflected languages like Greek or Latin, though English lacks an objective case that would make it clear, at a first look, that "bull" in this simile is the object, not the subject, of the verb "pulls":

And as a tortur'd bull
To Neptune brought for sacrifice,
    a troop of youngsters pull

<pre>
   -   ᵕ   ᵕ   -
</pre>
Down to the earth and drag him round
    about the hallow'd shore,
To please the wat'ry deity
    with forcing him to roar.
And forth he pours his utmost throat . . .

           12.353–57

The throaty roar of that last line shows what rewards lie in wait for those who get the knack of reading Chapman's challenging lines. The stretch and leap of the fourteener lifts the poem onto the superhuman level of Homer's warriors. The poet's moralizing disappears into wonder at the blaze of human energy and beauty. We become like the bloodless Trojan judges who are reanimated, despite their city's doom, when they look on the cause of it: Helen.

> And as, in well-grown woods, on trees
> cold-spiny grasshoppers
> Sit chirping and send noises out
> that scarce can pierce our ears
> For softness and their weak faint sounds,
> so—talking on the tow'r—
> These seniors of the people sat
> Who, when they saw the pow'r
> Of beauty in the queen ascend,
> e'en those cold-spir'ted peers,
> Those wise and almost wither'd men,
> found this heat in their years
> That they were forc'd (though whispering)
> to say, "What man can blame
> The Greeks and Trojans to endure,
> for so admir'd a dame
> So many mis'ries and so long?"
>   3.161–69

PREFACE

The present edition of Chapman's *Homer* has been designed rather for the general reader and for the student engaged in exploring the literature of the Elizabethan period than for the scholar. Every care has been taken to make the text as accurate as possible, and the original spelling has in general been preserved. On the other hand, the punctuation of the original, which certainly would have confused and puzzled the reader, has been abandoned, and an attempt has been made, wherever possible, to regularise the many conflicting forms which the Homeric character-names assumed in Chapman's hands. In addition, again with the object of aiding the reader, I have taken the liberty of making a few modifications in words liable to be misinterpreted. The principles adopted are outlined in the introduction, and all changes in the original text (apart from the punctuation) have been listed in the textual notes. In a similar way, the glossary is to be regarded merely as a guide to the general reader.

For the suggestion that this task deserved to be undertaken and that the *Iliads, Odysses,* and *Lesser Homerica* should be made available to students, I have to thank Mr. Huntington Cairns. I wish, also, to thank Dr. R. A. Foakes for assisting me in the double checking of the *Iliads,* and Dr. J. T. McCullen for similarly double checking *The Crowne of all Homers Workes.*

THE ILIAD

INTRODUCTION

1.

NO LENGTHY INTRODUCTION is required to a work so well known and so often discussed as Chapman's *Homer*. Even although there are hundreds who can freely quote Keats' famous lines for one who has read a few pages of the volume that inspired his sonnet, the fact that so many scholars have devoted careful attention to the merits and demerits of Chapman's endeavour would render a further detailed examination of its qualities entirely otiose. If we wish evaluating criticism we can turn to Coleridge and Arnold and Saintsbury; if we want a detailed analysis of its relationship to its original and of its stylistic features we can find all the information necessary in H. M. Regel's excellently painstaking study; if we seek for an understanding of its relationship to other poetic endeavours of its own time there are several modern scholars to grant us assistance.

All that is needed here is a brief preface, designed as a guide to the reader.

First, it should be emphasized that, although the poem itself consists of several strata laid down between the appearance of the *Seven Books* in 1598 and the publication of the complete *Iliads* of 1611, the only way to gain a true appreciation of Chapman's virtues is to read his work as Keats read it—gaining an understanding of its bold sweep and inspiring vigour in one uninterrupted perusal. If we but dip into it, if we read separate paragraphs, only the strangeness of the poet's style may be apparent; a vision of Chapman's truly tremendous achievement can come only when the entire *Iliads* is treated as a single work, to be read as a whole. One wonders if Keats gained his vision of deep-browed Homer by reciting the lines aloud. The probability is that he did, and certainly the true flavour of the Elizabethan poet's writing may be savoured best when his thundering words and mighty sentences are permitted to take shape on the tongue rather than remain mere literal symbols set on a printed page. There is rich organ music throughout, not only in these battle-scenes wherein the excitement of the translator matches Homer's own excitement, but in quieter passages as well—for example in the episode when Hector bids farewell to Andromache:

> In this fire must Hector's triall shine.
> Here must his country, father, friends be in him made divine.
> And such a stormy day shall come, in mind and soule I know,
> When sacred Troy shall shed her towres for teares of overthrow,
> When Priam, all his birth and powre, shall in those teares be drownd.
> But neither Troy's posteritie so much my soule doth wound—
> Priam, nor Hecuba her selfe, nor all my brothers' woes
> (Who, though so many and so good, must all be food for foes)—

As thy sad state, when some rude Greeke shall leade thee weeping hence,
These free dayes clouded and a night of captive violence
Loding thy temples, out of which thine eyes must never see
But spin the Greeke wives webs of taske and their Fetch-water be
To Argos, from Messeides, or clear Hyperia's spring—
Which (howsoever thou abhorst) Fate's such a shrewish thing
She will be mistris, whose curst hands, when they shall crush out cries
From thy oppressions (being beheld by other enemies)
Thus they will nourish thy extremes: 'This dame was Hector's wife,
A man that, at the warres of Troy, did breathe the worthiest life
Of all their armie.' This againe will rub thy fruitfull wounds
To misse the man that to thy bands could give such narrow bounds.
But that day shall not wound mine eyes: the solide heape of night
Shall interpose and stop mine eares against thy plaints and plight.

The vigour inherent in his lines is Chapman's greatest achievement. Pope chisels a cameo where the Elizabethan hammers out a vast piece of statuary. And the piece of statuary is at once a work inspired by the great Greek original and an independent poem. Too much perhaps has been said by some writers about Chapman's supposedly inadequate knowledge of the Homeric tongue. True, he has made some mistakes, and he is markedly careless in his use of proper names; but errors of this kind are comparatively few in his work, and we may well be prepared to agree that, in terms of his age at least, he possessed as complete a scholarly equipment as any translator might require. He understood his Homer, but —and this is the important point—he understood Homer in his own way. Perhaps we might even be prepared to go further and say that he understood Homer in his own ways, for there is clear evidence to show that as he proceeded with his endeavour he changed his attitude towards the heroes of the *Iliad*. From the very beginning he was inclined to interpret the poem morally and to see its chief figures as exempla; but, just as in his dramatic work he moved from admiration of Bussy D'Ambois and wonder at Byron to reverence for Clermont and Cato, so here his ideal altered during the passage of the years. When he published his *Seven Books* in 1598 his mind obviously was dominated by devotion to the "Achilleian virtues." Later, as he himself tells us, he gained a new vision when he turned to the last twelve books—"in which the first free light of my Author entred and emboldened me." One may guess that the chief result of seeing this "first free light" was a realisation that Achilles no longer could be esteemed the true ideal, that this ideal more nearly might be found in Hector or, better still, in the much-tried and wise Ulysses.

Concerning his own interests and attitudes Chapman never leaves us in doubt: one of the peculiarities of his *Iliads,* indeed, is the manner in which he is prepared to include in his text passages of individually inspired comment that one might well have considered more properly designed for an introduction or interpretative notes. Into his translation he inserts his own personality.

No doubt such identification of the translator with the characters in the original takes away from the *Iliads* its faithful mirroring of the authentic spirit of Homer, but without this we could not have its resounding vigour. We must be prepared to accept the one with the other and to recognise that Chapman, albeit with over-enthusiastic licence, has taken the only path a translating poet can travel: he has determined that it is his business to provide, not a word-for-word version of the original, but a poem that attempts to recreate the spirit of the original in an alien tongue. When he speaks of his 'English Homer' he does not mean simply 'Homer in English'; his words are to be interpreted literally and 'English Homer' is to be regarded as an independent exercise in the creative imagination. If on occasions he adds whole lines for which Homer gives him no authority, if continually he provides his own qualifying epithets (so that, for example, the Homeric 'Nestor' becomes 'the good old Nestor'), he is not to be blamed. This is merely part of his general endeavour, an integral and indeed necessary part of the work of art he has wrought.

Another thing that has sometimes been overstressed by Chapman's critics is the so-called 'difficulty' occasioned by his use of strange words. In fact, Chapman's verbal innovations are not as numerous as Shakespeare's, and few of them are likely to prevent a reader from understanding his meaning. More serious, perhaps, are his often involved sentences and particularly his characteristic treatment of relative clauses; but here an appreciation of certain basic peculiarities in his syntactical usage, easily gained from examination of a few key passages, makes an understanding of others relatively easy. Read slowly, the *Iliads* may seem 'difficult'; read rapidly, it presents surprisingly few stumbling blocks in the way of complete appreciation.

Nor should his metre form any bar to a modern appreciation of his work. The fourteener, it is true, is a relatively rare English measure except in ballad shape, and it may be confessed that easily it can degenerate into a jog-trot rhythm. Chapman's technical ability as a poet, however, is nowhere more clearly shown than in the manner by which he has avoided monotony in his long line. Despite the fact that he treats his metrical unit syllabically, refusing to allow himself the luxury of dactylic or anapæstic movements, his verses have variety in music. Although hardly so successful in the earlier versions of 1598, he has, at least in the later books, given us such diversity as takes away from any impression of metrical barrenness. In particular, there may be noted here his characteristic use of a spondaic effect—an effect that serves both to add to the dignity of his lines and to break the fourteener's trend towards a thumping rhythm. Examples crowd in upon us:—

> Our blacke saile; in it rowers put, in it fit sacrifice . . .
> But in his hands still. What then lifts thy pride in this so high? . . .
> Reins on thy passions and serve us. He answer'd: 'Though thy heart . . .
> O Gods! Our Greeke earth will be drown'd in just tears. Rapefull Troy . . .

The Iliad

As all men else do. Nor do thou encounter with thy crowne . . .
Have clos'd your Greeke eyes and so farre from their so loved home.

These examples are sufficient to demonstrate Chapman's use of this device: they demonstrate, too, that the poet sought so far as he could to vary his caesura. Another among the common weaknesses of the fourteener is that it splits so easily into an eight and a six. In his earliest versions Chapman finds it almost impossible to escape from this tendency, but it is obvious that, as he proceeded with the work, he gained mightily in technical mastery. Such lines as

The cry increases. I must needs the watchtower mount to see,

and

In his discourse, if first to take direct course to the King,

take us far away from the ballad measure, and from monotony.

In all, Chapman's *Iliads* must be accounted one of the major poetic achievements of an age rich in poetic achievement. Here is a poet's echo of a poet—an Elizabethan Englishman calling across the centuries to a Greek. Coleridge is fully justified in declaring that Chapman writes "as Homer might have written had he lived in England in the reign of Queen Elizabeth"; equally justified is a recent critic, Douglas Bush, when he says that

> if Homer could return from Elysium to read all the English renderings, he would surely find in Chapman his truest son, a man who has fed on lion's marrow; he would rejoice in such phrases as 'The sea had soakt his heart through,' and he might not disapprove of Chapman's moral emphasis.

Although he has had his adverse critics, early and late, and although we may discern certain failures in his vast endeavour, Chapman's fame has well withstood time's ravages: his *Iliads* are as vital today as they were for Shakespeare and for Keats. The verses printed on the title page of his *Odysses* have prophetic fire in them:

At mihi quod vivo detraxerit invida turba,
Post obitum duplici fœnore reddet honos.

2.

My aim in preparing the present edition of the *Iliads* has been to provide a text which, while maintaining the greatest possible fidelity to the original, may yet be acceptable to the general reader. At the same time, an attempt has been made to give in the textual notes such indication of Chapman's revisions as may enable the specialist student to see how the translation gradually was brought to its final state and to assess both the author's changing views and his technical development.

[xxii]

Introduction

As has been noted above, four separate texts in all have to be put under review:

A. First comes the volume containing seven books of the *Iliads*, entered in the Stationers' Register to T. Cooke on April 10, 1598, with the note 'expunctum per mandatum.' This appeared with the name of John Windet as the printer, the title page reading:

SEAVEN BOOKES

OF THE ILIADES OF

HOMERE, PRINCE
OF POETS,

℃ *Translated according to the Greeke, in iudgement*
of his best Commentaries

by

George Chapman Gent.

Scribendi recte, sapere est & principium & fons.
[Device: a clenched fist and motto: EX
AVARITIA BELLVM]
LONDON.

Printed by *John Windet,* and are to be solde at
the signe of
the Crosse-keyes, neare *Paules* wharffe.
1598.

A wretched piece of printing, with wildly erratic punctuation, it can hardly have been reviewed by the author, and the list of 'faultes' on the last page notes only some few among the hundreds of glaring errors in the text.

The volume includes an epistle dedicatory addressed to the Earl of Essex and a short preface 'To the Reader,' preceding the translations of Books 1, 2, 7, 8, 9, 10 and 11. Each book has at its head a long and a short 'Argument,' but there are no commentaries or marginalia. (The copy used for this edition is that in the British Museum, C.39. d.46.)

B. The same year, 1598, saw the appearance of a partial translation of Book 18, under the title of *Achilles Shield:*

[xxiii]

The Iliad

ACHILLES

SHIELD

Translated as the other seuen Bookes
*of Homer, out of his eighteenth
booke of Iliades.*
By *George Chapman* Gent.

[Device: a clenched fist and motto:
CONTRAHIT AVARITIA BELLVM]

LONDON

Imprinted by Iohn Windet, and are to be sold
*at Paules Wharfe, at the signe of the
Crosse Keyes.*
1598.

Since Chapman has here decided—for what reason we cannot tell—to render the Homeric lines into rimed decasyllabic verse instead of into the fourteeners of the *Seaven Bookes,* this work represents a kind of aberration, but, despite the fact that its wording is entirely different from that of the later text, it obviously must have some consideration here. It includes an epistle dedicatory addressed to the Earl Marshal (the Earl of Essex), a note 'To the understander,' and (at the end) a poem addressed to Thomas Harriot. (The copy used for this edition is that in the British Museum, C.39. d.54.)

C.   On November 14, 1608, the Stationers' Register has an assignment of the *Seaven Bookes* from Windet to Samuel Macham, evidently preparatory to the issuing of a new volume containing twelve books:

HOMER

Prince of Poets:

*Translated accord-
ing to the Greeke,
in
twelue Bookes of
his* Iliads,

By
Geo: Chapman

[motto: *Qui Nil
molitur Ineptè*]
At London printed for Samuel Macham. Will: Hole sculp.

[xxiv]

Introduction

The title page was engraved and signed by William Hole; it shows two standing figures, labelled *'Achilles'* and *'Hector'* respectively; above, in a medallion, is a head of Homer, on each side of which is a reclining figure, with an inscription across the page—*'Mulciber in Troiam: pro Troia stabat Apollo.'* For his text Chapman here used, with revisions, the seven books already issued in *A* and added renderings of Books 3, 4, 5, 6 and 12. The volume is prefaced by verses addressed to Prince Henry, verses addressed 'To the Reader' and a sonnet to Queen Anne. At the end are sixteen sonnets—to the Duke of Lennox, the Lord Chancellor (Lord Ellesmere), the Lord Treasurer (the Earl of Salisbury), the Earl of Suffolk, the Earl of Northampton. Lady Arabella Stuart, the Countess of Bedford, the Earl of Sussex, the Earl of Pembroke, the Earl of Montgomery, Lord Lisle, Lord Wotton, the Earl of Southampton, the Earl of Arundell, Lady Wrothe and the Countess of Montgomery. (The copy used for this edition is that in the British Museum, C.39. g.24.)

D. Finally, the whole twenty-four books were entered for publication on April 8, 1611, and, as printed by Richard Field, were published with another engraved title page, similar in design to that of *C:*

THE ILIADS OF

HOMER

Prince of Poets.

*Neuer before in any lan-
guag truely translated.*

*With
a Coment vppon some of his chiefe
places;
Donne according to the Greeke*

By Geo: Chapman.

*At London printed for Nathaniell Butter.
William Hole sculp:*

Here the prefatory matter of *C* is reprinted, together with a sonnet anagram addressed to Prince Henry, a 'Preface to the Reader,' a short essay 'Of Homer' and a list of 'Faults escaped.' While Books 1 and 2 are presented in an entirely new version, the earlier renderings of Books 3 to 12 are reproduced, with some revisions, from *C*. To these are added new translations of Books 13 to 24. Throughout, marginal comments are provided, and a 'Commentarius' follows each of Books 1, 2, 3, 13, 14, 15, 16, 17, 18 and 19. A prose comment at the close of the text declares that the whole of Books 13 to 24 was rendered by

[xxv]

the author within a period of fifteen weeks, and this comment concludes with a Latin prayer. At the end of the volume are sixteen sonnets (increased to eighteen in some copies)—thirteen reprinted from *C* (those to Lady Arabella Stuart and Lord Wotton being omitted), one other (to the Earl of Arundell) presented in a revised version and two added (to the Lord of Walden and Sir Thomas Howard). A brief anagram is appended to the sonnet addressed to the Lord Treasurer. Some copies of this volume also include an additional leaf with sonnets to Viscount Cranborne and Viscount Rochester.

The printing of the text in the complete *Iliads* is uniformly good and we may imagine that the author took some considerable care with it. Even so, however, Chapman was forced to give his list of 'Faults escaped,' while a copy of the volume has been recorded by Richard Hooper containing a few author's corrections in the prefatory matter. Examination of three copies—that in the British Museum (1348. k. 15) and two in my own possession—has revealed no variations save on signatures E3 recto and verso, M3 verso and Z4 verso; in the first, the variants are of no textual importance; in the second, a passage later altered is given in the *C* version; in the third, the only deviation is in the gloss, where '*Patroclus*' is the reading of one of my own copies, and '*Patroclus body*' that of the British Museum copy.

On November 2, 1614, Nathaniel Butter entered the twenty-four books of the *Odysses,* and these, together with the *Iliads,* made up a new volume:

THE

WHOLE WORKS

OF

HOMER;

PRINCE OF POETTS

In his Iliads, and
Odysses.

Translated according to the Greeke,

By

Geo: Chapman.

De Ili: et Odiss:
Omnia ab his: et in his sunt omnia:
siue beati
Te decor eloquij, seu rerũ pondera
tangunt   Angel: Pol:
At London printed for Nathaniell Butter.
William Hole sculp:

[xxvi]

Introduction

The new volume contains what evidently were the unsold sheets of *D,* to-gether with the twenty-four books of the *Odysses.* Before it was published, Prince Henry had died and a rather mediocre engraved plate was inserted with two mourning columns, a sonnet to the Prince's memory and a brief set of verses (in Latin and English) 'Ad Famam.' Much more important is the handsome engraved portrait of Chapman, evidently paid for by some friend whose initials are I. M. or J. M. As the date here is given as 'M. DC. XVI,' we must assume (unless 'M. DC. XIV' was meant) that the 'Whole Works' did not appear until two years after the entry in the Stationers' Register.

These four texts are all that need be considered. In earlier modern editions of the *Homer,* allusion is made to a 'second folio,' but this re-print—a line-by-line copy of *D*—is certainly of considerably later date (probably between 1635 and 1640). As the variants recorded by Richard Hooper fully indicate, its deviations from the *D* version have no authori-tative value.

In the present edition, all the complimentary sonnets, together with the introductory anagram, have been omitted, since they have little or no bear-ing on the text and in any case have recently been reprinted by Phyllis B. Bartlett in her *Poems of George Chapman.* On account of the interesting critical matter, however, the verses to Prince Henry and to the reader are included here. The basic text follows *D,* with the original spelling in gen-eral retained. Comparison of the *Iliads* with Chapman's other poems seems to indicate that most of the spelling forms here are his own, and conse-quently, quite apart from the fact that any attempt at modernisation is apt to involve difficulties with some riming words, there is ample justification for retaining these forms. At the same time, since the meticulously exact reproduction of all Elizabethan printing and spelling peculiarities inevi-tably sets up a barrier between the original and a modern reader, certain changes have been silently made:

1. Long ſ has been levelled under short *s;* the *u-v* usage has been brought into accordance with modern practice; and, in similar manner, *j* has been substituted for *i.* (No *j* forms, it may be noted, appear in the original, except in some Latin quotations.) It should be noted, however, that Chapman's usual spelling of 'Troian—Troians' appears here as 'Troyans.'
2. Since Chapman never has the spelling 'than' for the comparative and since this word, in the form of 'then,' is of frequent occurrence alongside of 'then' in a time sense, I have altered 'then' to 'than' in all comparative clauses. Similarly 'least' has been altered to 'lest,' when the context requires the latter sense, and 'to' to 'too.'
3. The quotations from Greek are given, without comment, as in modern texts, with appropriate accents.

4. Chapman's use of proper names presents a problem. There are some definite mistakes and numerous strange forms, while throughout inconsistencies occur. In general, where the metre would not be injured, I have sought to bring these names as close as possible to the usual current transliterations of the Greek originals, but all changes are recorded in the Textual Notes. For words with œ-oe and æ-ae the particular form adopted in any individual line has been determined by the metre.

5. The punctuation of the original is interesting, but at the same time hopelessly confusing: apparently the printer has spattered his own stops over Chapman's own habitually heavy pointing, with the result that in many passages the sense is seriously obscured.

The following lines, selected entirely at random from the original text, will demonstrate that any attempt faithfully to reproduce the punctuation of the folio would have placed a barrier between Chapman and his readers:—

> He met, then issuing the flood; with all intent of flight,
> *Lycaon,* (*Dardan Priams* sonne;) whom lately in the night,
> He had surprisde; as in a wood, of *Priams,* he had cut,
> The greene armes of a wild figge tree; to make him spokes to put
> In Naues of his new chariot. An ill then, all unthought,
> Stole on him in *Achilles* shape, who tooke him thence, and brought
> To well-built *Lemnos,* selling him, to famous *Iasons* sonne:
> From whom, a guest then, in his house; (*Imbrius Eetion*)
> Redeem'd at high rate, and sent home, t'*Arisba;* whence he fled,
> And saw againe his fathers court: eleuen daies banquetted,
> Amongst his friends; the twelfth god thrust, his haplesse head againe
> In t'hands of sterne *Æacides;* who now must send him slaine,
> To *Plutos* Court; and gainst his will.

The only course open for an editor who wishes to do more than merely reprint the original in type-facsimile is to introduce his own punctuation—and this I have done. Although an attempt has been made, by the use both of brackets and of dashes, to preserve the effect of Chapman's characteristic bracketed parentheses, it may be noted that in my punctuation I have deliberately kept the stops light, believing that only thus can Chapman's vigorous flow of verse properly be interpreted.

6. This punctuation includes the indicating of speeches (by means of single quotation marks) and the insertion of the possessive apostrophe. In the original no speeches are so marked, nor are possessives thus designated. All other apostrophes (e.g. in verbal forms such as 'retir'd') are reproduced from the original text, un-

Introduction

less deviation from that text is indicated in the notes. After some
hesitation, I have changed Chapman's verbal 'Ile' and 'ile' to
'I'le,' in order to avoid confusion with 'Ile' or 'ile,' meaning 'isle.'
7. A problem presents itself to an editor in the use of italics through-
out the volume. In the earlier books, proper names of persons are
usually italicised, but names of towns, countries and races (e.g.
Troy, Greece, Phrygian) are, in general, not. Later, however, but
with no absolute regularity, the printer tends to use italics for the
second group as well as for the first. In view of this uncertainty in
usage, I have felt myself justified in disregarding completely the
use of italics in roman content and of roman in italic content. All
passages of Latin quotation are, however, rendered in roman (these
only occur in the commentaries and marginalia, which are normally
printed in italic).
8. Throughout those books provided with a commentary Chapman
has occasionally indicated by an a, b or c passages on which he has
penned notes. These indications, however, are so erratic that they
have been silently omitted and, instead, line references have been
added in the 'Commentarius' itself.
9. Here, as in the *Odysses* and the 'Homeric Hymns,' the headings
and tail lines of the books or separate verses do not reproduce
typographically the use in the original texts of upper- and lower-
case forms.

Apart from these exceptions, all changes introduced into the text are
cited in the Textual Notes, so that a specialist reader who so desires should
have no difficulty in reconstructing from the present edition the forms
(except for italicised words and punctuation) assumed by the original.

Emendations have been kept to a minimum. A few obvious corrections
have been made in passages that clearly are faulty and one or two new
readings are suggested. Where any of these had already been suggested by
G. G. Loane,* the debt is acknowleged in the Textual Notes. The only
large body of alterations is with respect to Greek names. Chapman's usage
here is erratic, particularly when the vowels *y* and *i* are involved. An at-
tempt has been made to regularise these, but owing to the facts a) that
sometimes he coins his own proper names out of adjectival and other Greek
forms, and b) that occasionally his names cannot be altered without de-
stroying the rhythm of the lines in which they occur, several of his ab-
normalities have had perforce to remain. All changes made are duly noted.

Since the final *Iliads* is the end result of a series of revisions, I have indi-
cated, in the Textual Notes, the basic sources of each book. Thus '*A, C, D*'
means that the first version of 1598 was reproduced with variations in the

* 'Misprints in Chapman's Homer' (*Notes and Queries*, clxxiii, Dec. 4 and 25,
1937, 394–402 and 453–5); 'Queries from Chapman's *Iliad*' (*Notes and Queries*,
clxxi, Oct. 10, 1936, 261–2).

edition of 1609 and that, in turn, revised for the edition of 1611; '*C, D*' indicates that the earlier version of the book was issued in 1609 and formed the basis of the 1611 text. As has been noted, Books 1 and 2 in the 1598 volume, together with *Achilles Shield,* are independent versions and these accordingly are printed as an appendix, with, however, the omission of the verses addressed to Harriot. It should be observed that, while the Textual Notes record all variations in the *D* text, only substantive variations in the *A* and *C* texts are listed; no note has been taken of differences in spelling.

In the Glossary an endeavour has been made briefly to outline some of the interest attaching to Chapman's vocabulary. Primarily, this glossary is designed for the purpose of giving the reader a guide to Chapman's writing but, in addition, note is taken of words or meanings which apparently he first introduced. No attempt has been made to register every word, but most of Chapman's peculiarities in vocabulary have, it is hoped, been noted.

While interest would have attached to a careful listing of all passages wherein the translator has deviated from, or added to, his original, such a catalogue of variations would have occupied far too much space; and accordingly in the Commentary I have restricted myself to interpretation of some difficult lines and to occasional discussion of Chapman's indebtedness to the Spondanus edition of Homer which he used as his basic text.

[Attention is drawn to the fact that the prose passages in this edition do not correspond in lining to the lining of the original texts.]

Homer's Iliads

TO THE

HIGH BORNE PRINCE OF MEN,

HENRIE THRICE

Royall Inheritor to the United Kingdoms

of Great BRITTAINE, &c.

Since perfect happinesse, by Princes sought,
Is not with birth borne, nor Exchequers bought,
Nor followes in great Traines, nor is possest
With any outward State, but makes him blest
That governes inward, and beholdeth theare   5
All his affections stand about him bare,
That by his power can send to Towre, and death,
All traitrous passions, marshalling beneath
His justice his meere will, and in his minde
Holds such a scepter as can keepe confinde   10
His whole life's actions in the royall bounds
Of Vertue and Religion, and their grounds
Takes in to sow his honours, his delights
And complete empire—You should learne these rights,
Great Prince of men, by Princely presidents.   15
Which here, in all kinds, my true zeale presents
To furnish your youth's groundworke and first State,
And let you see one Godlike man create
All sorts of worthiest men, to be contriv'd
In your worth onely, giving him reviv'd   20
For whose life Alexander would have given
One of his kingdomes; who (as sent from heaven,
And thinking well that so divine a creature
Would never more enrich the race of Nature)
Kept as his Crowne his workes, and thought them still   25
His Angels, in all power to rule his will;
And would affirme that Homer's poesie
Did more advance his Asian victorie
Than all his Armies. O! tis wondrous much

[3]

(Though nothing prisde) that the right vertuous touch   30
Of a well-written soule to vertue moves.
Nor have we soules to purpose if their loves
Of fitting objects be not so inflam'd.
How much, then, were this kingdome's maine soule maim'd
To want this great inflamer of all powers   35
That move in humane soules? All Realmes but yours
Are honor'd with him, and hold blest that State
That have his workes to reade and contemplate—
In which Humanitie to her height is raisde,
Which all the world (yet none enough) hath praisde.   40
Seas, earth and heaven he did in verse comprise,
Out-sung the Muses and did equalise
Their king Apollo, being so farre from cause
Of Princes' light thoughts that their gravest lawes
May finde stuffe to be fashiond by his lines.   45
Through all the pompe of kingdomes still he shines
And graceth all his gracers. Then let lie
Your Lutes and Viols, and more loftily
Make the Heroiques of your Homer sung;
To Drums and Trumpets set his Angel's tongue;   50
And with the Princely sport of Haukes you use
Behold the kingly flight of his high Muse,
And see how like the Phœnix she renues
Her age and starrie feathers in your sunne—
Thousands of yeares attending, everie one   55
Blowing the holy fire and throwing in
Their seasons, kingdomes, nations that have bin
Subverted in them; lawes, religions, all
Offerd to Change and greedie Funerall,
Yet still your Homer lasting, living, raigning,   60
And proves how firme Truth builds in Poet's faining.
  A Prince's statue, or in Marble carv'd
Or steele or gold, and shrin'd (to be preserv'd)
Aloft on Pillars or Pyramides,
Time into lowest ruines may depresse;   65
But, drawne with all his vertues in learn'd verse,
Fame shall resound them on Oblivion's herse
Till graves gaspe with her blasts and dead men rise.
No gold can follow where true Poesie flies.
  Then let not this Divinitie in earth,   70
Deare Prince, be sleighted as she were the birth
Of idle Fancie, since she workes so hie,
Nor let her poore disposer (Learning) lie

Stil bed-rid. Both which being in men defac't,
In men (with them) is God's bright image rac't: 75
For as the Sunne and Moone are figures given
Of his refulgent Deitie in Heaven,
So Learning and her Lightner, Poesie,
In earth present his fierie Majestie.
Nor are Kings like him since their Diademes   80
Thunder and lighten and project brave beames,
But since they his cleare vertues emulate—
In Truth and Justice imaging his State,
In Bountie and Humanitie since they shine,
Than which is nothing (like him) more divine—   85
Not Fire, not Light, the Sunne's admired course,
The Rise nor Set of Starres, nor all their force
In us and all this Cope beneath the Skie,
Nor great Existence, term'd his Treasurie—
Since not for being greatest he is blest,   90
But being Just, and in all vertues best.
   What sets his Justice and his Truth best forth,
Best Prince, then use best—which is Poesie's worth;
For as great Princes, well inform'd and deckt
With gracious vertue, give more sure effect   95
To her perswasions, pleasures, reall worth,
Than all th' inferiour subjects she sets forth,
Since there she shines at full, hath birth, wealth, state,
Power, fortune, honor, fit to elevate
Her heavenly merits—and so fit they are   100
Since she was made for them and they for her—
So Truth, with Poesie grac't, is fairer farre,
More proper, moving, chaste and regular
Than when she runnes away with untruss't Prose;
Proportion, that doth orderly dispose   105
Her vertuous treasure and is Queene of Graces,
In Poesie decking her with choicest Phrases,
Figures and numbers, when loose Prose puts on
Plaine letter-habits, makes her trot upon
Dull earthly businesse (she being meere divine),   110
Holds her to homely Cates and harsh hedge-wine,
That should drinke Poesie's Nectar; everie way
One made for other, as the Sunne and Day,
Princes and vertues. And, as in a spring
The plyant water, mov'd with any thing   115
Let fall into it, puts her motion out
In perfect circles, that move round about

[5]

The gentle fountaine, one another raising;
So Truth and Poesie worke, so Poesie, blazing
All subjects falne in her exhaustlesse fount,   120
Works most exactly, makes a true account
Of all things to her high discharges given,
Till all be circular and round as heaven.
    And lastly, great Prince, marke and pardon me—
As in a flourishing and ripe fruite Tree   125
Nature hath made the barke to save the Bole,
The Bole the sappe, the sappe to decke the whole
With leaves and branches, they to beare and shield
The usefull fruite, the fruite it selfe to yeeld
Guard to the kernell, and for that all those   130
(Since out of that againe the whole Tree growes):
So in our Tree of man, whose nervie Roote
Springs in his top, from thence even to his foote
There runnes a mutuall aide through all his parts,

The soule.   All joyn'd in one to serve his Queene of Arts,   135
In which doth Poesie like the kernell lie
Obscur'd, though her Promethean facultie
Can create men and make even death to live—
For which she should live honor'd, Kings should give
Comfort and helpe to her that she might still   140
Hold up their spirits in vertue, make the will
That governes in them to the power conform'd,
The power to justice—that the scandals storm'd
Against the poore Dame, clear'd by your faire Grace,
Your Grace may shine the clearer. Her low place   145
Not shewing her, the highest leaves obscure.
Who raise her, raise themselves; and he sits sure
Whom her wing'd hand advanceth, since on it
Eternitie doth (crowning Vertue) sit.
All whose poore seed, like violets in their beds,   150
Now grow with bosome-hung and hidden heads.
For whom I must speake (though their Fate convinces
Me, worst of Poets) to you, best of Princes.

By the most humble and faithfull implorer for all
the graces to your highnesse eternised   155
by your divine Homer,
GEO. CHAPMAN.

TO THE READER

Lest with foule hands you touch these holy Rites
    And with prejudicacies too prophane
Passe Homer in your other Poets' sleights,
    Wash here. In this Porch to his numerous Phane,
Heare ancient Oracles speake and tell you whom   5
    You have to censure. First then Silius heare,
Who thrice was Consull in renowned Rome,
    Whose verse, saith Martiall, nothing shall out-weare.

SILIUS ITALICUS, LIB. 13.

He in Elysium having cast his eye   10
    Upon the figure of a Youth whose haire,
With purple Ribands braided curiously,
    Hung on his shoulders wondrous bright and faire,
Said: 'Virgine, what is he whose heavenly face
    Shines past all others, as the Morne the Night,   15
Whom many marvelling soules from place to place
    Pursue and haunt with sounds of such delight?
Whose countenance (wer't not in the Stygian shade)
    Would make me, questionlesse, beleeve he were
A verie God?' The learned Virgine made   20
    This answer: 'If thou shouldst beleeve it here,
Thou shouldst not erre. He well deserv'd to be
    Esteem'd a God, nor held his so-much breast
A little presence of the Deitie;
    His verse comprisde earth, seas, starres, soules at rest;   25
In song the Muses he did equalise,
    In honour Phœbus. He was onely soule,
Saw all things spher'd in Nature, without eyes,
    And raisde your Troy up to the starrie Pole.'
Glad Scipio, viewing well this Prince of Ghosts,   30
    Said: 'O if Fates would give this Poet leave
To sing the acts done by the Romane Hoasts,
    How much beyond would future times receive
The same facts made by any other knowne?
    O blest Æacides! to have the grace   35
That out of such a mouth thou shouldst be showne
    To wondring Nations as enricht the race

Of all times future with what he did know.
    Thy vertue with his verse shall ever grow.'

Now heare an Angell sing our Poet's Fame,   40
Whom Fate for his divine song gave that name.

                ANGELUS POLITIANUS, IN NUTRICIA.
More living than in old Demodocus
    Fame glories to waxe yong in Homer's verse.
And as, when bright Hyperion holds to us   45
    His golden Torch, we see the starres disperse
And every way flie heaven, the pallid Moone
    Even almost vanishing before his sight:
So with the dazling beames of Homer's Sunne
    All other ancient Poets lose their light.   50
Whom when Apollo heard, out of his starre,
    Singing the godlike Acts of honor'd men
And equalling the actuall rage of warre
    With onely the divine straines of his pen,
He stood amaz'd and freely did confesse   55
    Himselfe was equall'd in Mæonides.

Next, heare the grave and learned Plinie use
His censure of our sacred Poet's Muse.

                PLIN. NAT. HIST. LIB.7. CAP.29.
    Turnd into verse, that no Prose may come neare Homer.   60

Whom shall we choose the glorie of all wits,
    Held through so many sorts of discipline
And such varietie of workes and spirits,
    But Grecian Homer, like whom none did shine
For forme of worke and matter? And because   65
    Our proud doome of him may stand justified
By noblest judgements and receive applause
    In spite of envie and illiterate pride,
Great Macedon, amongst his matchlesse spoiles
    Tooke from rich Persia (on his Fortunes cast),   70
A Casket finding (full of precious oyles)
    Form'd all of gold, with wealthy stones enchac't,
He tooke the oyles out, and his nearest friends
    Askt, in what better guard it might be usde?
All giving their conceipts to severall ends,   75
    He answerd: 'His affections rather chusde

[8]

An use quite opposite to all their kinds,
  And Homer's bookes should with that guard be serv'd,
That the most precious worke of all men's minds
  In the most precious place might be preserv'd.'   80

Idem. lib.17. cap.5.
Idem. lib.25. cap.3.

The Fount of wit was Homer, Learning's Syre,
  And gave Antiquitie her living fire.

Volumes of like praise I could heape on this,
  Of men more ancient and more learn'd than these,
But since true Vertue enough lovely is   85
  With her owne beauties, all the suffrages
Of others I omit, and would more faine
  That Homer for himselfe should be belov'd,
Who everie sort of love-worth did containe.
  Which how I have in my conversion prov'd   90
I must confesse I hardly dare referre
  To reading judgements, since so generally

*Of Translation, and
the naturall difference
of Dialects necessarily
to be observed in it.*

Custome hath made even th' ablest Agents erre
  In these translations: all so much apply
Their paines and cunnings word for word to render   95
  Their patient Authors, when they may as well
Make fish with fowle, Camels with Whales engender,
  Or their tongues' speech in other mouths compell.
For even as different a production
  Aske Greeke and English, since, as they in sounds   100
And letters shunne one forme and unison,
  So have their sense and elegancie bounds
In their distinguisht natures, and require
  Onely a judgement to make both consent
In sense and elocution, and aspire   105
  As well to reach the spirit that was spent
In his example, as with arte to pierce
  His Grammar and etymologie of words.

Ironicè.

But as great Clerkes can write no English verse
  Because (alas! great Clerks) English affords,   110
Say they, no height nor copie—a rude toung
  (Since 'tis their Native)—but in Greeke or Latine
Their writs are rare, for thence true Poesie sprong—
  Though them (Truth knowes) they have but skil to chat-in
Compar'd with that they might say in their owne,   115
  Since thither th' other's full soule cannot make
The ample transmigration to be showne
  In Nature-loving Poesie: so the brake
That those Translators sticke in that affect

[9]

Their word-for-word traductions (where they lose   120
   The free grace of their naturall Dialect
     And shame their Authors with a forced Glose)

The necessarie
nearenesse of
translation to the
example.

I laugh to see—and yet as much abhorre
   More licence from the words than may expresse
     Their full compression and make cleare the Author.   125
   From whose truth if you thinke my feet digresse
Because I use needfull Periphrases,
   Read Valla, Hessus, that in Latine Prose
And Verse convert him; read the Messines
   That into Tuscan turns him, and the Glose   130
Grave Salel makes in French as he translates—
   Which (for th' aforesaide reasons) all must doo—
And see that my conversion much abates
   The licence they take, and more showes him too,
Whose right not all those great learn'd men have done   135
   (In some maine parts) that were his Commentars.
But (as the illustration of the Sunne
   Should be attempted by the erring starres)
They fail'd to search his deepe and treasurous hart.
   The cause was since they wanted the fit key   140

The power of nature
above Art in Poesie.

Of Nature, in their down-right strength of Art,
   With Poesie to open Poesie—
Which in my Poeme of the mysteries
   Reveal'd in Homer I will clearely prove,
Till whose neere birth suspend your Calumnies   145
   And farre-wide imputations of selfe love.
Tis further from me than the worst that reades,
   Professing me the worst of all that wright,
Yet what, in following one that bravely leades,
   The worst may show, let this proofe hold the light.   150
But grant it cleere: yet hath detraction got
   My blinde side in the forme my verse puts on—
Much like a dung-hill Mastife that dares not
   Assault the man he barkes at, but the stone
He throwes at him takes in his eager jawes   155
   And spoyles his teeth because they cannot spoyle.
The long verse hath by proofe receiv'd applause
   Beyond each other number, and the foile
That squint-ey'd Envie takes is censur'd plaine:
   For this long Poeme askes this length of verse,   160
Which I myselfe ingenuously maintaine
   Too long our shorter Authors to reherse.

Our English language
above all others for
Rhythmicall Poesie.

And for our tongue, that still is so empayr'd
   By travailing linguists, I can prove it cleare
That no tongue hath the Muses' utterance heyr'd   165
   For verse, and that sweet Musique to the eare
Strooke out of rime, so naturally as this.
   Our Monosyllables so kindly fall
And meete, opposde in rime, as they did kisse;
   French and Italian, most immetricall,   170
Their many syllables in harsh Collision
   Fall as they brake their necks, their bastard Rimes
Saluting as they justl'd in transition,
   And set our teeth on edge, nor tunes nor times
Kept in their falles. And, me thinkes, their long words   175
   Shew in short verse as in a narrow place
Two opposites should meet with two-hand swords
   Unweildily, without or use or grace.
Thus having rid the rubs and strow'd these flowers
   In our thrice sacred Homer's English way,   180
What rests to make him yet more worthy yours?
   To cite more prayse of him were meere delay
To your glad searches for what those men found
   That gave his praise, past all, so high a place;
Whose vertues were so many and so cround   185
   By all consents Divine, that not to grace
Or adde increase to them the world doth need
   Another Homer but even to rehearse
And number them. They did so much exceed,
   Men thought him not a man, but that his verse   190
Some meere celestiall nature did adorne;
   And all may well conclude it could not be
That for the place where any man was borne,
   So long and mortally could disagree
So many Nations as for Homer striv'd,   195
   Unlesse his spurre in them had bene divine.
Then end their strife and love him (thus reviv'd)
   As borne in England: see him over-shine
All other-Countrie Poets: and trust this—
   That whose-soever Muse dares use her wing   200
When his Muse flies, she will be truss't by his,
   And show as if a Bernacle should spring
Beneath an Eagle. In none since was seene
   A soule so full of heaven as earth's in him.
O! if our moderne Poesie had beene   205
   As lovely as the Ladie he did lymne,

What barbarous worldling, groveling after gaine,
    Could use her lovely parts with such rude hate
As now she suffers under every swaine?
    Since then tis nought but her abuse and Fate   210
That thus empaires her, what is this to her
    As she is reall, or in naturall right?
But since in true Religion men should erre
    As much as Poesie, should th' abuse excite
The like contempt of her Divinitie?   215
    And that her truth and right saint-sacred Merites
In most lives breed but reverence formally,
    What wonder is't if Poesie inherits
Much lesse observance, being but Agent for her
    And singer of her lawes, that others say?   220
Forth then, ye Mowles, sonnes of the earth, abhorre her;
    Keepe still on in the durty vulgar way,
Till durt receive your soules, to which ye vow;
    And with your poison'd spirits bewitch our thrifts.
Ye cannot so despise us as we you.   225
    Not one of you above his Mowlehill lifts
His earthy Minde, but, as a sort of beasts,
    Kept by their Guardians, never care to heare
Their manly voices, but, when in their fists
    They breathe wild whistles and the beasts' rude eare   230
Heares their Curres barking, then by heapes they flie
    Headlong together—so men beastly given
The manly soule's voice (sacred Poesie
    Whose Hymnes the Angels ever sing in heaven)
Contemne and heare not; but when brutish noises   235
    (For Gaine, Lust, Honour, in litigious Prose)
Are bellow'd-out and cracke the barbarous voices
    Of Turkish Stentors, O! ye leane to those
Like itching Horse to blockes or high May-poles,
    And breake nought but the wind of wealth, wealth, All   240
In all your Documents; your Asinine soules
    (Proud of their burthens) feele not how they gall.
But as an Asse that in a field of weeds
    Affects a thistle and falles fiercely to it,
That pricks and gals him, yet he feeds and bleeds—   245
    Forbeares a while and licks, but cannot woo it
To leave the sharpnes, when (to wreake his smart)
    He beates it with his foote, then backward kickes
Because the Thistle gald his forward part,
    Nor leaves till all be eate, for all the prickes,   250

[12]

Then falles to others with as hote a strife,
  And in that honourable warre doth waste
The tall heate of his stomacke and his life:
  So, in this world of weeds you worldlings taste
Your most-lov'd dainties, with such warre buy peace,   255
  Hunger for torment, vertue kicke for vice;
Cares for your states do with your states increase,
  And, though ye dreame ye feast in Paradise,
Yet Reason's Day-light shewes ye at your meate—
  Asses at Thistles, bleeding as ye eate.   260

THE PREFACE
TO THE READER

Of all bookes extant in all kinds, Homer is the first and best. No
one before his, Josephus affirmes, nor before him, saith Velleius
Paterculus, was there any whom he imitated, nor after him any that
could imitate him. And that Poesie may be no cause of detraction
from al the eminence we give him, Spondanus (preferring it to all   5
Arts and sciences) unanswerably argues and proves. For to the glory
of God and the singing of his glories (no man dares deny) man was
chiefly made. And what art performes this chiefe end of man with so
much excitation and expression as Poesie—Moses, David, Salomon,
Job, Esay, Jeremy, &c. chiefly using that to the end abovesaid? And   10
since the excellence of it cannot be obtained by the labor and art of
man (as all easily confesse it), it must needs be acknowledged a divine
infusion. To prove which in a word this distich in my estimation
serves something nearely:

> Great Poesie, blind Homer, makes all see   15
> Thee capable of all Arts, none of thee.

For out of him, according to our most grave and judicial Plutarch,
are all Arts deduced, confirmed or illustrated. It is not therefore the
world's vilifying of it that can make it vile, for so we might argue
and blaspheme the most incomparably sacred. It is not of the world   20
indeed, but (like Truth) hides it selfe from it. Nor is there any such
reality of wisdome's truth in all humane excellence as in Poets'
fictions—that most vulgar and foolish receipt of Poeticall licence
being of all knowing men to be exploded (accepting it as if Poets
had a tale-telling priviledge above others), no Artist being so strictly   25
and inextricably confined to all the lawes of learning, wisedome and
truth as a Poet. For were not his fictions composed of the sinewes and
soules of all those, how could they defie fire, iron, and be combined
with eternitie? To all sciences, therefore, I must still (with our learned
and ingenious Spondanus) preferre it, as having a perpetuall   30
commerce with the divine Majesty, embracing and illustrating al his
most holy precepts and enjoying continuall discourse with his thrice
perfect and most comfortable spirit. And as the contemplative life is
most worthily and divinely preferred by Plato to the active, as much
as the head to the foote, the eye to the hand, reason to sence, the   35
soule to the bodie, the end it selfe to all things directed to the end,

quiet to motion and Eternitie to Time, so much preferre I divine
Poesie to all worldly wisedome. To the onely shadowe of whose
worth, yet I entitle not the bold rimes of everie Apish and impudent
Braggart (though he dares assume anything); such I turne over to the 40
weaving of Cobwebs, and shall but chatter on molehils (farre under
the hill of the Muses) when their fortunat'st selflove and ambition
hath advanced them highest. Poesie is the flower of the Sunne and
disdains to open to the eye of a candle. So kings hide their treasures
and counsels from the vulgar—ne evilescant, saith our Spondanus. 45
We have example sacred enough that true Poesie's humility, poverty
and contempt are badges of divinity, not vanity. Bray then, and
barke against it, ye Wolf-fac't wordlings, that nothing but honours,
riches and magistracie, nescio quos turgidè spiratis *(that I may use*
the words of our friend still) qui solas leges Justinianas crepatis; 50
paragraphum unum aut alterum, pluris quàm vos ipsos facitis &c.
I for my part shall ever esteeme it much more manly and sacred in this
harmelesse and pious studie to sit till I sinke into my grave than
shine in your vainglorious bubbles and impieties—al your poore
policies, wisedomes and their trappings at no more valuing than a 55
musty Nut. And much lesse I wey the frontlesse detractions of some
stupide ignorants that, no more knowing me than their owne beastly
ends, and I ever (to my knowledge) blest from their sight, whisper
behind me vilifyings of my translation—out of the French affirming
them, when both in French and all other languages but his owne our 60
with-all-skill-enriched Poet is so poore and unpleasing that no man
can discerne from whence flowed his so generally given eminence and
admiration. And therefore (by any reasonable creature's conference
of my sleight comment and conversion) it will easily appeare how I
shunne them and whether the originall be my rule or not. In which 65
he shall easily see I understand the understandings of all other
interpreters and commenters in places of his most depth, importance
and rapture. In whose exposition and illustration if I abhorre from
the sence that others wrest and racke out of him, let my best detractor
examine how the Greeke word warrants me. For my other fresh fry, 70
let them fry in their foolish gals—nothing so much weighed as the
barkings of puppies or foisting hounds, too vile to thinke of our
sacred Homer or set their prophane feete within their lives' lengths
of his thresholds. If I faile in something, let my full performance in
other some restore me—haste spurring me on with other necessities. 75
For as at my conclusion I protest, so here at my entrance, lesse than
fifteene weekes was the time in which all the last twelve books were
entirely new translated—no conference had with any one living in al
the novelties I presume I have found. Only some one or two places
*I have shewed to my worthy and most learned friend, **M. Harriots**,* 80

[15]

*for his censure how much mine owne weighed: whose judgement and
knowledge in all kinds I know to be incomparable and bottomlesse—
yea, to be admired as much as his most blameles life and the right
sacred expence of his time is to be honoured and reverenced. Which
affirmation of his cleare unmatchednesse in all manner of learning I*   85
*make in contempt of that nastie objection often thrust upon me:—
that he that will judge must know more than he of whom he judgeth,
for so a man should know neither God nor himself. Another right
learned, honest and entirely loved friend of mine, M. Robert Hews,
I must needs put into my confest conference touching Homer, though*   90
*very little more than that I had with M. Harriots. Which two, I
protest, are all, and preferred to all. Nor charge I their authorities
with any allowance of my generall labour, but onely of those one or
two places which for instances of my innovation, and how it shewed
to them, I imparted. If any taxe me for too much periphrasis or*   95
*circumlocution in some places, let them reade Laurentius Valla and
Eobanus Hessus, who either use such shortnesse as cometh nothing
home to Homer, or, where they shun that fault, are ten parts more
paraphrastical than I. As, for example, one place I will trouble you
(if you please) to conferre with the originall and one interpreter for*   100
*all. It is in the end of the third booke, and is Helen's speech to Venus
fetching her to Paris from seeing his cowardly combat with
Menelaus—part of which speech I will here cite:*

> Οὔνεκα δὴ νῦν δῖον Ἀλέξανδρον Μενέλαος
> Νικήσας, &c.   105

*For avoiding the common reader's trouble here, I must referre the
more Greekish to the rest of the speech in Homer, whose translation
ad verbum by Spondanus I will here cite, and then pray you to
conferre it with that which followeth of Valla:*

> Quoniam verò nunc Alexandrum Menelaus   110
> Postquam vicit, vult odiosam me domum abducere,
> Propterea verò nunc dolum (ceu dolos) cogitans advenisti?
> Sede apud ipsum vadens, deorum abnega vias,
> Neque unquam tuis pedibus revertaris in cœlum,
> Sed semper circa eum ærumnas perfer, et ipsum serva   115
> Donec te vel uxorem faciat, vel hic servam, &c.

Valla thus:

> Quoniam victo Paride, Menelaus me miseram est reportaturus
> ad lares, ideo tu, ideo falsa sub imagine venisti, ut me
> deciperes ob tuam nimiam in Paridem benevolentiam; eò   120
> dum illi ades, dum illi studes, dum pro illo satagis, dum
> illum observas atque custodis, deorum commercium reliquisti,

nec ad eos reversura es ampliùs; adeò (quantum suspicor)
aut uxor eius efficieris, aut ancilla, &c.

Wherein note if there be any such thing as most of this in Homer; 125
yet only to expresse (as he thinkes) Homer's conceipt for the more
pleasure of the reader he useth this overplus dum illi ades, dum illi
studes, dum pro illo satagis, dum illum observas atque custodis,
deorum commercium reliquisti. *Which (besides his superfluitie) is*
utterly false. For where he saith, reliquisti deorum commercium, 130
Helen saith, Θεῶν δ' ἀπόιειπε κελεύθους, *deorum autem abnega, or*
abnue, vias, ἀπειπεῖν (vel ἀποειπεῖν *as it is used poetically*) *signifying*
denegare *or* abnuere; *and Helen (in contempt of her too much*
observing men) bids her renounce heaven and come live with Paris
till he make her his wife or servant—scoptically or scornefully 135
speaking it, which both Valla, Eobanus and all other interpreters
(but these ad verbum*) have utterly mist. And this one example I*
thought necessarie to insert here to shew my detractors that they have
no reason to vilifie my circumlocution sometimes when their most
approved Grecians, Homer's interpreters, generally hold him fit to 140
be so converted. Yet how much I differ, and with what authoritie, let
my impartiall and judiciall reader judge—alwaies conceiving how
pedanticall and absurd an affectation it is in the interpretation of
any Author (much more of Homer) to turn him word for word,
when (according to Horace and other best lawgivers to translators) 145
it is the part of every knowing and judiciall interpreter not to follow
the number and order of words but the materiall things themselves,
and sentences to weigh diligently, and to clothe and adorne them
with words and such a stile and forme of Oration as are most apt
for the language into which they are converted. If I have not turned 150
him in any place falsly (as all other his interpreters have in many
and most of his chiefe places); if I have not left behind me any of
his sentence, elegancie, height, intention and invention; if in some
few places (especially in my first edition, being done so long since
and following the common tract) I be somthing paraphrasticall and 155
faulty—is it justice in that poore fault (if they will needs have it so)
to drowne all the rest of my labour? But there is a certaine envious
Windfucker, that hovers up and downe, laboriously engrossing al the
aire with his luxurious ambition and buzzing into every eare my
detraction—affirming I turne Homer out of the Latine onely, &c— 160
that sets all his associates and the whole rabble of my maligners on
their wings with him to beare about my empaire and poyson my
reputation. One that, as he thinkes, whatsoever he gives to others he
takes from himselfe, so whatsoever he takes from others he addes to
himselfe. One that in this kinde of robberie doth like Mercurie, that 165

[17]

stole good and supplied it with counterfeit bad still. One like the
two gluttons, Philoxenus and Gnatho, that would still emptie their
noses in the dishes they loved that no man might eate but themselves.
For so this Castrill, with too hote a liver and lust after his owne
glorie, and to devoure all himself, discourageth all appetites to the   170
fame of another. I have stricken: single him as you can. Nor note I
this to cast any rubbes or plashes out of the particular way of mine
owne estimation with the world, for I resolve this with the wilfully
obscure:

Sine honore vivam, nulloque numero ero.   175

Without men's honors I will live, and make
No number in the manlesse course they take.

But to discourage (if it might be) the generall detraction of
industrious and well-meaning vertue, I know I cannot too much
diminish and deject my selfe; yet that passing little that I am, God   180
onely knowes—to whose ever-implored respect and comfort I onely
submit me. If any further edition of these my sillie endevors shall
chance, I will mend what is amisse (God assisting me) and amplifie
my harsh Comment to Homer's farre more right and mine owne
earnest and ingenious love of him. Notwithstanding, I know the   185
curious and envious will never sit downe satisfied. A man may go
over and over till he come over and over, and his paines be onely
his recompence: every man is so loded with his particular head, and
nothing in all respects perfect but what is perceived by few. Homer
himselfe hath met with my fortune in many maligners, and   190
therefore may my poore selfe put up without motion. And so little I
will respect malignitie and so much encourage my selfe with mine
owne knowne strength and what I finde within me of comfort and
confirmance (examining my selfe throughout with a farre more
jealous and severe eye than my greatest enemie, imitating this: 195

Judex ipse sui totum se explorat ad unguem, &c.)—

that after these Iliads *I will (God lending me life and any meanest*
meanes) with more labour than I have lost here and all uncheckt
alacritie dive through his Odysses. *Nor can I forget here (but with*
all heartie gratitude remember) my most ancient, learned and right   200
noble friend M. Richard Stapilton, first most desertfull mover in
the frame of our Homer. For which (and much other most ingenious
and utterly undeserved desert) God make me amply his requiter and
be his honorable familie's speedy and full restorer. In the meane
space, I intreate my impartiall and judiciall Reader that all things   205
to the quicke he will not pare, but humanely and nobly pardon
defects, and if he find anything perfect receive it unenvied.

[18]

Of Homer

Of his countrey and time the difference is so infinite amongst all writers that there is no question (in my conjecture) of his antiquitie beyond all. To which opinion the nearest I will cite: Adam Cedrenus placeth him under David's and Solomon's rule, and the destruction of Troy under Saul's; and of one age with Solomon, Michael Glycas Siculus affirmeth him. Aristotle (in tertio de Poetica) affirmes he was borne in the Ile of Io, begot of a Genius, one of them that used to dance with the Muses, and a virgine of that Ile, comprest by that Genius, who being quicke with child (for shame of the deed) came into a place called Ægina, and there was taken of theeves and brought to Smyrna, to Mæon King of the Lydians, who for her beautie maried her: after which, she walking neare the flood Meletes, on that shore being overtaken with the throwes of her deliverie she brought foorth Homer, and instantly died. The infant was received by Mæon and brought up as his owne till his death, which was not long after. And, according to this, when the Lydians in Smyrna were afflicted by the Æolians and thought fit to leave the citie, the Captaines by a Herald willing all to go out that would and follow them, Homer (being a little child) said he would also ὁμηρεῖν *(that is, sequi), and of that (for Melesigenes, which was his first name) he was called Homer. These Plutarch.*

The varieties of other reports touching this I omit for length, and in place thereof thinke it not unfit to insert something of his praise and honour amongst the greatest of all Ages—not that our most absolute of himselfe needs it, but that such autenticall testimonies of his splendor and excellence may the better convince the malice of his maligners.

First, what kind of person Homer was, saith Spondanus, his statue teacheth, which Cedrenus describeth. The whole place we will describe that our relation may hold the better coherence, as Xylander converts it. Then was the Octagonon at Constantinople consumed with fire, and the Bath of Severus that bore the name of Zeuxippus, in which there was much varietie of spectacle and splendor of Arts, the workes of all Ages being conferred and preserved there of Marble, Rockes, Stones and Images of Brasse, to which this onely wanted— that the soules of the persons they presented were not in them. Amongst these masterpeeces and all-wit-exceeding workmanships stood Homer as he was in his age, thoughtfull and musing, his hands

5

10

15

20

25

30

35

[19]

folded beneath his bosome, his beard untrimmed and hanging downe,
the haire of his head in like sort thinne on both sides before, his 40
face with age and cares of the world (as these imagine) wrinkled and
austere, his nose proportioned to his other parts, his eyes fixt or
turned up to his eyebrowes, like one blind (as it is reported he was)
not born blind (saith Velleius Paterculus—which he that imagins,
saith he, is blind of all senses). Upon his under coate he was attired 45
with a loose robe and at the base beneath his feet a brazen chaine
hung. This was the statue of Homer which in that conflagration
perished. Another renowned statue of his, saith Lucian in his
Encomion *of Demosthenes, stood in the temple of Ptolemy, on the*
upper hand of his own statue. Cedrenus likewise remembreth a 50
Library in the Pallace of the king at Constantinople that contained
a thousand a hundred and twentie bookes, amongst which there was
the gut of a Dragon of an hundred and twentie foote long in which,
in letters of gold, the Iliads *and* Odysses *of Homer were inscribed,*
which miracle in Basiliscus the Emperour's time was consumed 55
with fire.

For his respect amongst the most learned Plato in Ione *calleth*
him ἄριστον καὶ θειότατον τῶν ποιητῶν, Poetarum omnium et
præstantissimum et divinissimum; *in* Phædone, θεῖον ποιητὴν,
divinum Poetam; *and in* Theætetus, Socrates *citing diverse of the* 60
most wise and learned for confirmation of his there held opinion (as
Protagoras, Heraclitus, Empedocles, Epicharmus and Homer) who,
saith Socrates, against such an armie, being all led by such a Captaine
as Homer, dares fight or resist, but he will be held ridiculous? This
for Scaliger and all Homer's envious and ignorant detractors. Why 65
therefore Plato in another place banisheth him with all other Poets
out of his Common-wealth, dealing with them like a Politician
indeed—use men and then cast them off—though Homer he thinks fit
to send out crowned and annointed, I see not, since he maketh still
such honorable mention of him and with his verses (as with precious 70
Jemmes) everie where enchaceth his writings. So Aristotle continually
celebrateth him. Nay, even amongst the Barbarous not onely Homer's
name but his Poems have bene recorded and reverenced. The Indians,
saith Ælianus var.hist.lib.12.cap.48, *in their owne tongue had*
Homer's Poems translated and sung—nor those Indians alone but the 75
kings of Persia. And amongst the Indians (of all the Greek Poets
Homer being ever first in estimation) whensoever they used any
divine duties according to the custome of their housholds and
hospitalities, they invited ever Apollo and Homer. Lucian in his
Encomion *of Demosthenes affirmeth all Poets celebrated Homer's* 80
birth day and sacrificed to him the first fruites of their verses: so
Thersagoras answereth Lucian he used to do himselfe. Alex. Paphius,

saith Eustathius, delivers Homer as borne of Egyptian Parents,
Dmasagoras being his father and Æthra his mother, his nurse being
a certaine Prophetesse and the daughter of Oris, Isis' Priest, from   85
whose breasts, oftentimes, honey flowed in the mouth of the infant—
after which, in the night, he uttered nine severall notes or voices
of fowles, viz. of a Swallow, a Peacocke, a Dove, a Crow, a Partrich,
a Red-shank, a Stare, a Blackebird and a Nightingale; and being a
little boy was found playing in his bed with nine Doves. Sibylla being 90
at a feast of his Parents was taken with sodaine furie and sung verses
whose beginning was Δμασαγόρα πολύνιχε—polynice signifying much
victorie—in which song also she called him μεγάκλεα, great in glorie, and
στεφανίτην, signifying gyrlond-seller, and commanded him to build
a temple to the Pegridarii, that is to the Muses. Herodotus affirmes   95
that Phæmius (teaching a publicke schoole at Smyrna) was his
maister, and Dionysius in his 56th. oration saith Socrates was Homer's
scholler. In short, what he was his workes shew most truly, to which,
if you please, go on and examine him.

THE FIRST BOOKE

of

HOMER'S ILIADS

THE ARGUMENT

Apollo's Priest to th' Argive fleete doth bring
Gifts for his daughter, prisoner to the King;
For which her tenderd freedome he intreats.
But, being dismist with contumelious threats,
At Phœbus' hands, by vengefull prayer, he seekes   5
To have a plague inflicted on the Greekes.
Which had, Achilles doth a Councell cite,
Emboldning Calchas, in the King's despite,
To tell the truth why they were punisht so.
From hence their fierce and deadly strife did grow.   10

Æacides, sirname of *For wrong in which Æacides so raves*
Achilles, being the *That Goddesse Thetis (from her throne of waves*
grand child of Æacus. *Ascending heaven) of Jove assistance wonne,*
To plague the Greekes by absence of her Sonne,
And make the Generall himselfe repent   15
To wrong so much his Armie's Ornament.
This found by Juno, she with Jove contends,
Till Vulcan with heaven's cup the quarrell ends.

Another Argument

Alpha, the prayer of Chryses, sings:
The Armie's plague: the strife of Kings.

His proposition and Achilles' banefull wrath resound, O Goddesse, that imposd
invocation. Infinite sorrowes on the Greekes, and many brave soules losd
From breasts Heroique—sent them farre, to that invisible cave
That no light comforts; and their lims to dogs and vultures gave.

Atrides, sirname of To all which Jove's will gave effect; from whom first strife   5
Agamemnon, being   begunne
son to Atreus. Betwixt Atrides, king of men, and Thetis' godlike Sonne.

[23]

What God gave Eris their command, and op't that
    fighting veine?
Jove's and Latona's Sonne, who, fir'd against the king of men
For contumelie showne his Priest, infectious sicknesse sent
To plague the armie; and to death, by troopes, the souldiers   10
    went.

Narration.

Occasiond thus: Chryses, the Priest, came to the fleete to buy,
For presents of unvalued price, his daughter's libertie—
The golden scepter and the crowne of Phœbus in his hands
Proposing—and made suite to all, but most to the Commands

Agamemnon and
Menelaus, called the
Atrides, being brothers,
and both sonnes to
Atreus.

Of both th' Atrides, who most rulde. 'Great Atreus' sonnes,'   15
    said he,
'And all ye wel-griev'd Greekes, the Gods, whose habitations be
In heavenly houses, grace your powers with Priam's razed towne,
And grant ye happy conduct home! To winne which
    wisht renowne

Chryses, the Priest
of Apollo, to the
Atrides and other
Greekes.

Of Jove, by honouring his sonne (farre-shooting Phœbus), daine
For these fit presents to dissolve the ransomeable chaine   20
Of my lov'd daughter's servitude.' The Greekes entirely gave
Glad acclamations, for signe that their desires would have
The grave Priest reverenc'd, and his gifts of so much
    price embrac'd.
The Generall yet bore no such mind, but viciously disgrac'd

Agamemnon's
contumelious repulse
of Chryses.

With violent termes the Priest, and said: 'Doterd, avoid our   25
    fleete,
Where lingring be not found by me, nor thy returning feete
Let ever visite us againe, lest nor thy Godhead's crowne
Nor scepter save thee. Her thou seekst I still will hold mine owne
Till age defloure her. In our court at Argos (farre transferd

See my bed made,
it may be englisht:
the word is
ἀντιόωσαν
which signifies
contra stantem,
as standing of one
side, opposite to
another on the
other side, which
yet others translate
capessentem, et
adornantem; which,
since it showes
best to a reader,
I follow.

From her lov'd countrie) she shall plie her web, and see   30
    prepard
(With all fit ornaments) my bed. Incense me then no more,
But (if thou wilt be safe) be gone.' This said, the sea-beate shore
(Obeying his high will) the Priest trod off with haste and feare.
And, walking silent till he left farre off his enemie's eare,
Phœbus (faire-haird Latona's sonne) he stird up with a vow   35
To this sterne purpose: 'Heare, thou God that bear'st the
    silver bow,
That Chrysa guard'st, rulest Tenedos with strong hand,
    and the round
Of Cilla most divine dost walke! O Smintheus, if crownd
With thankfull offerings thy rich Phane I ever saw, or fir'd
Fat thighs of oxen and of goates to thee, this grace desir'd   40

[24]

Vouchsafe to me: paines for my teares let these rude Greekes repay,

The prayer of Chryses to Apollo.

Forc'd with thy arrowes.' Thus he praid, and Phœbus heard him pray

And, vext at heart, downe from the tops of steepe heaven stoopt: his bow,

And quiver coverd round, his hands did on his shoulders throw,

And of the angrie deitie the arrowes as he mov'd   45

Ratl'd about him. Like the night he rang'd the host and rov'd

(Athwart the fleete set) terribly; with his hard-loosing hand

His silver bow twang'd, and his shafts did first the Mules command,

Apollo sends the plague among the Greekes.

And swift hounds; then the Greekes themselves his deadly arrowes shot.

The fires of death went never out; nine daies his shafts flew hot   50

About the armie, and the tenth Achilles cald a court

Juno.

Of all the Greeks: heaven's white-arm'd Queene (who everywhere cut short

Beholding her lov'd Greeks by death) suggested it: and he

Achilles to Agamemnon.

(All met in one) arose and said: 'Atrides, now I see

We must be wandering againe, flight must be still our stay   55

(If flight can save us now), at once sicknesse and battell lay

Such strong hand on us. Let us aske some Prophet, Priest, or prove

Some dreame interpreter (for dreames are often sent from Jove)

Why Phœbus is so much incenst; if unperformed vowes

He blames in us, or Hecatombs; and if these knees he bowes   60

To death may yeeld his graves no more, but offering all supply

Of savours burnt from lambes and goates avert his fervent eye

And turne his temperate.' Thus he sate: and then stood up to them

Calchas the Prophet.

Calchas, sirnam'd Thestorides, of Augures the supreme;

He knew things present, past, to come, and rulde the Equipage   65

Of th'Argive fleete to Ilion, for his Prophetique rage

Given by Apollo; who, well seene in th'ill they felt, proposd

Calchas to Achilles.

This to Achilles: 'Jove's belov'd, would thy charge see disclosd

The secret of Apollo's wrath? Then covenant, and take oth

To my discoverie, that with words and powrefull actions both   70

Thy strength will guard the truth in me, because I well conceive

That he whose Empire governs all, whom all the Grecians give

Confirm'd obedience, will be mov'd—and then you know the state

Of him that moves him. When a king hath once markt
    for his hate
A man inferior, though that day his wrath seemes to digest   75
Th'offence he takes, yet evermore he rakes up in his brest
Brands of quicke anger till revenge hath quencht to his desire
The fire reserved. Tell me then, if, whatsoever ire
Suggests in hurt of me to him, thy valour will prevent?'

Achilles to Calchas.   Achilles answerd: 'All thou know'st speake, and be   80
    confident:
For by Apollo, Jove's belov'd (to whom performing vowes,
O Calchas, for the state of Greece thy spirit Prophetique showes
Skils that direct us) not a man of all these Grecians here
(I living and enjoying the light shot through this flowrie
    sphere)
Shall touch thee with offensive hands—though Agamemnon be   85
The man in question, that doth boast the mightiest Emperie
Of all our armie.' Then tooke heart the Prophet unreprov'd

Calchas discovers And said: 'They are not unpaid vowes, nor Hecatombs,
to the Greekes the   that mov'd
cause of their plague. The God against us: his offence is for his Priest empair'd
By Agamemnon, that refusd the present he preferd   90
And kept his daughter. This is cause why heaven's farre-darter
    darts
These plagues amongst us, and this still will emptie in
    our hearts
His deathfull quiver uncontaind till to her loved sire
The blacke-eyd damsell be resign'd, no redemptorie hire
Tooke for her freedome, not a gift, but all the ransome quit,   95
And she convaide, with sacrifice, till her enfranchisd feete
Treade Chrysa under: then the God (so pleasd) perhaps
    we may
Move to remission.' Thus he sate: and up the great in sway,
Heroique Agamemnon, rose, eagerly bearing all,
His mind's seate overcast with fumes; an anger generall   100
Fill'd all his faculties; his eyes sparckl'd like kindling fire—
Which sternly cast upon the Priest, thus vented he his ire:

Agamemnon, incenst,   'Prophet of ill! For never good came from thee towards me—
to Calchas. Not to a word's worth. Evermore thou tookst delight to be
Offensive in thy Auguries; which thou continuest still,   105
Now casting thy prophetique gall and vouching all our ill
(Shot from Apollo) is imposd since I refusd the prise
Of faire Chryseis' libertie—which would in no worth rise
To my rate of her selfe, which moves my vowes to have her
    home,

Past Clytemnestra loving her, that grac't my nuptiall roome   110
With her virginitie and flowre. Nor aske her merits lesse
For person, disposition, wit and skill in housewiferies.
And yet, for all this, she shall go, if more conducible
That course be than her holding here. I rather wish the weale
Of my lov'd armie than the death. Provide yet, instantly,   115
Supplie for her, that I alone of all our royaltie
Lose not my winnings: tis not fit, ye see all, I lose mine
Forc't by another—see as well some other may resigne
His Prise to me.' To this replied the swift-foote God-like sonne

Achilles to
Agamemnon.
Of Thetis thus: 'King of us all, in all ambition   120
Most covetouse of all that breathe, why should the great-soul'd
          Greekes
Supply thy lost prise out of theirs? Nor what thy avarice seekes
Our common treasurie can find, so little it doth guard
Of what our rac'd towns yeelded us—of all which, most is shar'd
And given our souldiers, which againe to take into our hands   125
Were ignominious and base. Now then, since God commands,
Part with thy most-lov'd prise to him: not any one of us
Exacts it of thee, yet we all, all loss thou sufferst thus
Will treble, quadruple in gaine when Jupiter bestowes
The sacke of well-wall'd Troy on us—which by his word he   130
          owes.'

Agamemnon to
Achilles.
          'Do not deceive your selfe with wit,' he answerd, 'God-like
          man,
Though your good name may colour it; tis not your swift
          foote can
Outrunne me here; nor shall the glosse set on it with the God
Perswade me to my wrong. Wouldst thou maintaine in
          sure abode
Thine owne prise and sleight me of mine? Resolve this: 135
          if our friends
(As fits in equitie my worth) will right me with amends,
So rest it; otherwise, my selfe will enter personally
On thy prise, that of Ithacus or Ajax for supply;
Let him on whom I enter rage. But come, we'le order these
Hereafter, and in other place. Now put to sacred seas   140
Our blacke saile; in it rowers put, in it fit sacrifise;
And to these I will make ascend my so much envied prise,
Bright-cheekt Chryseis. For conduct of all which we must chuse
A chiefe out of our counsellors. Thy service we must use,
Idomeneus—Ajax, thine, or thine, wise Ithacus,   145
Or thine, thou terriblest of men, thou sonne of Peleus—

[27]

Which fittest were that thou mightst see these holy acts
    performd
For which thy cunning zeale so pleades, and he whose bow thus
    stormd
For our offences may be calmd.' Achilles with a frowne

Achilles to
Agamemnon.

Thus answerd: 'O thou impudent! of no good but thine owne   150
Ever respectfull—but of that with all craft covetous—
With what heart can a man attempt a service dangerous,
Or at thy voice be spirited to flie upon a foe,
Thy mind thus wretched? For my selfe, I was not injur'd so
By any Troyan that my powers should bid them any blowes.   155
In nothing beare they blame of me. Phthia, whose bosome
    flowes
With corne and people, never felt empaire of her increase
By their invasion; hils enow and farre-resounding seas
Powre out their shades and deepes betweene. But thee, thou
    frontlesse man,
We follow and thy triumphs make with bonfires of our bane—   160
Thine and thy brother's vengeance sought (thou dog's eyes)
    of this Troy
By our exposd lives—whose deserts thou neither dost employ
With honour nor with care. And now thou threatst to force
    from me
The fruite of my sweate, which the Greekes gave all; and
    though it be
(Compar'd with thy part then snatcht up) nothing—nor   165
    ever is
At any sackt towne—but of fight (the fetcher-in of this)
My hands have most share; in whose toyles when I have
    emptied me
Of all my forces, my amends in liberalitie
(Though it be little) I accept and turne pleasd to my tent—
And yet that little thou esteemst too great a continent   170
In thy incontinent avarice. For Phthia therefore now
My course is, since tis better farre than here endure that thou
Shouldst still be ravishing my right, draw my whole treasure drie

Agamemnon to
Achilles.

And adde dishonor.' He replied: 'If thy heart serve thee, flie.
Stay not for my cause; others here will aid and honor me.   175
If not, yet Jove I know is sure; that counsellor is he
That I depend on. As for thee, of all our Jove-kept kings
Thou still art most my enemie; strifes, battles, bloodie things
Make thy blood-feasts still. But if strength, that these moods
    build upon,

Flow in thy nerves, God gave thee it, and so tis not   180
    thine owne
But in his hands still. What then lifts thy pride in this so hie?
Home with thy fleete and Myrmidons. Use there their Emperie;
Command not here. I weigh thee not, nor meane to magnifie
Thy rough-hewne rages, but in stead I thus farre threaten thee:
Since Phœbus needs will force from me Chryseis, she shall go;   185
My ships and friends shall waft her home. But I will imitate so
His pleasure that mine owne shall take, in person, from thy tent
Bright-cheekt Briseis, and so tell thy strength how eminent
My powre is, being compar'd with thine—all other making feare
To vaunt equalitie with me, or in this proud kind beare   190

Achilles angrie with   Their beards against me.' Thetis' sonne at this stood vext.
Agamemnon.   His heart
Bristled his bosome and two waies drew his discursive part—
If, from his thigh his sharpe sword drawne, he should
    make roome about
Atrides' person, slaughtring him, or sit his anger out
And curb his spirit. While these thoughts striv'd in his bloud   195
    and mind

Pallas.   And he his sword drew, downe from heaven Athenia stoopt
    and shind
About his temples, being sent by th'Ivorie-wristed queene
Saturnia, who out of her heart had ever loving bene
And carefull for the good of both. She stood behind, and tooke
Achilles by the yellow curles, and onely gave her looke   200
To him apparance—not a man of all the rest could see.
He, turning backe his eye, amaze strooke everie facultie,
Yet straight he knew her by her eyes, so terrible they were

Achilles to Pallas.   Sparkling with ardor, and thus spake: 'Thou seed of Jupiter,
Why com'st thou? To behold his pride, that bosts our Emperie?   205
Then witnesse, with it, my revenge, and see that insolence die

Pallas to Achilles.   That lives to wrong me.' She replied: 'I come from heaven to see
Thy anger settled, if thy soule will use her soveraigntie
In fit reflection. I am sent from Juno, whose affects
Stand heartily inclind to both. Come, give us both respects   210
And ceasse contention. Draw no sword. Use words, and such
    as may
Be bitter to his pride, but just. For, trust in what I say,
A time shall come when thrice the worth of that he forceth now
He shall propose for recompence of these wrongs. Therefore

Achilles Palladi,   throw
hoc est, rationi   Reines on thy passions, and serve us.' He answerd: 'Though   215
obsequitur.   my heart

[29]

Burne in just anger, yet my soule must conquer th'angrie part
And yeeld you conquest. Who subdues his earthly part
    for heaven,
Heaven to his prayres subdues his wish.' This said, her charge
    was given
Fit honor. In his silver hilt he held his able hand
And forc't his broad sword up. And up to heaven did reascend   220
Minerva, who in Jove's high roofe that beares the rough shield
    tooke
Her place with other deities. She gone, againe forsooke
Patience his passion, and no more his silence could confine

His wrath, that this broad language gave: 'Thou ever steep't
    in wine,
Dog's face, with heart but of a Hart, that nor in th'open eye   225
Of fight dar'st thrust into a prease, nor with our noblest lie
In secret ambush. These works seeme too full of death for thee.
Tis safer farre, in th'open host, to dare an injurie
To any crosser of thy lust. Thou subject-eating king,
Base spirits thou governst—or this wrong had bene the last   230
    fowle thing
Thou ever author'dst. Yet I vow, and by a great oath sweare,
Even by this scepter—that, as this never againe shall beare

Greene leaves or branches, nor increase with any growth his sise,
Nor did since first it left the hils and had his faculties
And ornaments bereft with iron, which now to other end   235
Judges of Greece beare and their lawes receiv'd from Jove
    defend
(For which my oath to thee is great), so, whensoever need
Shall burne with thirst of me thy host, no prayres shall
    ever breed
Affection in me to their aid, though well-deserved woes
Afflict thee for them, when to death man-slaughtring Hector   240
    throwes
Whole troopes of them, and thou torment'st thy vext mind
    with conceit
Of thy rude rage now and his wrong, that most deserv'd
    the right
Of all thy armie.' Thus he threw his scepter gainst the ground,
With golden studs stucke, and took seate. Atrides' breast was
    drownd

In rising choler. Up to both sweet-spoken Nestor stood,   245
The cunning Pylian Orator whose tongue powrd foorth a flood
Of more-than-hony-sweet discourse: two ages were increast
Of diverse-languag'd men, all borne in his time and deceast

In sacred Pylos, where he reignd amongst the third-ag'd men.
He (well seene in the world) advisd, and thus exprest it then: 250

'O Gods! Our Greeke earth will be drownd in just teares;
rapefull Troy,
Her king and all his sonnes will make as just a mocke and joy
Of these disjunctions, if of you, that all our host excell
In counsell and in skill of fight, they heare this. Come, repell
These yong men's passions. Y'are not both (put both your   255
yeares in one)
So old as I: I liv'd long since and was companion
With men superior to you both, who yet would ever heare

My counsels with respect. My eyes yet never witnesse were,
Nor ever will be, of such men as then delighted them—
Perithous, Exadius and god-like Polypheme,   260
Ceneus and Dryas prince of men, Ægean Theseus,
A man like heaven's immortals formd, all, all most vigorous
Of all men that even those daies bred, most vigorous men,
and fought
With beasts most vigorous, mountain beasts (for men in strength
were nought
Matcht with their forces), fought with them, and bravely   265
fought them downe.
Yet even with these men I converst, being cald to the renowne
Of their societies, by their suites, from Pylos farre, to fight
In th'Apian kingdome; and I fought, to a degree of might
That helpt even their mights, against such as no man now
would dare
To meete in conflict. Yet even these my counsels still   270
would heare,
And with obedience crowne my words. Give you such palme
to them—
Tis better than to wreath your wraths. Atrides, give not streame
To all thy powre, nor force his prise, but yeeld her still his owne,
As all men else do. Nor do thou encounter with thy crowne,
Great sonne of Peleus, since no king that ever Jove allowd   275
Grace of a scepter equals him. Suppose thy nerves endowd
With strength superior, and thy birth a verie Goddesse gave,
Yet he of force is mightier since what his owne nerves have
Is amplified with just command of many other. King of men,
Command thou then thy selfe, and I with my prayres will   280
obtaine
Grace of Achilles to subdue his furie; whose parts are
Worth our intreatie, being chiefe checke to all our ill in warre.'

'All this, good father,' said the king, 'is comely and good right.

[31]

But this man breakes all such bounds; he affects, past all men,
    height;
All would in his powre hold, all make his subjects, give to all   285
His hote will for their temperate law—all which he never shall
Perswade at my hands. If the Gods have given him the great stile
Of ablest souldier, made they that his licence to revile
Men with vile language?' Thetis' sonne prevented him,
    and said:

Achilles to
Agamemnon.

    'Fearefull and vile I might be thought if the exactions laid   290
By all meanes on me I should beare. Others command to this:
Thou shalt not me—or, if thou dost, farre my free spirit is
From serving thy command. Beside, this I affirme (affoord
Impression of it in thy soule) I will not use my sword
On thee or any for a wench, unjustly though thou tak'st   295
The thing thou gav'st; but all things else that in my ship thou
    mak'st
Greedie survey of, do not touch without my leave—or do
Adde that act's wrong to this that these may see that outrage
    too:
And then comes my part: then be sure thy bloud upon my lance
Shall flow in vengeance.' These high termes these two   300
    at variance
Usd to each other, left their seates, and after them arose

The Grecian councell
dissolved.

The whole court. To his tents and ships, with friends and
    souldiers, goes
Angrie Achilles. Atreus' sonne the swift ship lancht and put
Within it twentie chosen row'rs; within it likewise shut
The Hecatomb, t'appease the God. Then causd to come abord   305

Chryseis sent to her
father.

Faire cheekt Chryseis. For the chiefe, he in whom Pallas pourd
Her store of counsels, Ithacus, aboord went last, and then
The moist waies of the sea they saild. And now the king
    of men
Bad all the hoast to sacrifice. They sacrific'd and cast
The offall of all to the deepes; the angrie God they grac't   310
With perfect Hecatombs—some buls, some goates along the
    shore
Of the unfruitfull sea inflam'd. To heaven the thicke fumes
    bore
Enwrapped savours. Thus though all the politique king
    made shew
Respects to heaven, yet he himselfe all that time did pursue
His owne affections. The late jarre, in which he thunderd   315
    threats
Against Achilles, still he fed, and his affections' heats

The First Booke

Thus vented to Talthybius and grave Eurybates,
Heralds and ministers of trust to all his messages:

Agamemnon to Talthybius and Eurybates his Heralds.

'Haste to Achilles' tent, where take Briseis' hand and bring
Her beauties to us. If he faile to yeeld her, say your king   320
Will come himselfe with multitudes that shall the horribler
Make both his presence and your charge that so he dares
deferre.'

This said, he sent them with a charge of hard condition.
They went unwillingly and trod the fruitlesse sea's shore. Soone
They reacht the navie and the tents in which the quarter lay   325
Of all the Myrmidons, and found the chiefe Chiefe
in their sway
Set at his blacke barke in his tent. Nor was Achilles glad
To see their presence, nor themselves in any glorie had
Their message, but with reverence stood and fear'd th'offended
king—
Askt not the dame nor spake a word. He yet, well knowing   330
the thing

Achilles' Princely receipt of the Heralds.

That causd their coming, grac'd them thus: 'Heralds, ye
men that beare
The messages of men and Gods, y'are welcome, come ye neare.
I nothing blame you, but your king. Tis he, I know, doth send
You for Briseis: she is his. Patroclus, honourd friend,
Bring foorth the damsell, and these men let leade her   335
to their Lord.
But, Heralds, be you witnesses, before the most ador'd,
Before us mortals and before your most ungentle king,
Of what I suffer—that, if warre ever hereafter bring
My aide in question, to avert any severest bane
It brings on others, I am scusde to keepe my aide in wane,   340
Since they mine honour. But your king, in tempting
mischiefe, raves,
Nor sees at once by present things the future—how like waves
Ils follow ils, injustices, being never so secure
In present times, but after-plagues, even then, are seene as sure.
Which yet he sees not and so sooths his present lust—   345
which, checkt,
Would checke plagues future, and he might, in succouring
right, protect
Such as fight for his right at fleete. They still in safetie fight
That fight still justly.' This speech usd, Patroclus did the rite

Briseis led to Agamemnon.

His friend commanded and brought forth Briseis from her tent,
Gave her the heralds, and away to th'Achive ships they went.   350

[33]

She, sad, and scarce for griefe could go. Her love all friends
    forsooke
And wept for anger. To the shore of th'old sea he betooke
Himselfe alone and, casting forth upon the purple sea
His wet eyes and his hands to heaven advancing, this sad plea

Achilles to Thetis.   Made to his mother: 'Mother, since you brought me forth   355
    to breath
So short a life, Olympius had good right to bequeath
My short life honor; yet that right he doth in no degree,
But lets Atrides do me shame and force that prise from me
That all the Greekes gave.' This with teares he utterd,
    and she heard,
Set with her old sire in his deepes, and instantly appeard   360
Up from the gray sea like a cloud, sate by his side, and said:

Thetis to Achilles.   'Why weepes my sonne? What grieves thee? Speake,
    conceale not what hath laid
Such hard hand on thee: let both know.' He (sighing like
    a storme)

Achilles to Thetis.   Replied: 'Thou dost know. Why should I things knowne
    againe informe?
We marcht to Thebes, the sacred towne of King Eetion,   365
Sackt it and brought to fleete the spoile, which everie
    valiant sonne
Of Greece indifferently shar'd. Atrides had for share
Faire-cheekt Chryseis, after which his priest that shoots so farre,
Chryses, the faire Chryseis' sire, arriv'd at th'Achive fleete
With infinite ransome to redeeme the deare imprison'd feete   370
Of his faire daughter. In his hands he held Apollo's crowne
And golden scepter, making suite to everie Grecian sonne
But most the sonnes of Atreus (the others' orderers).
Yet they least heard him; all the rest receiv'd with
    reverend eares
The motion, both the Priest and gifts gracing and holding   375
    worth
His wisht acceptance. Atreus' sonne yet (vext) commanded forth
With rude termes Phœbus' reverend Priest, who, angrie,
    made retreat
And prayd to Phœbus, in whose grace he standing passing great,
Got his petition. The God an ill shaft sent abrode
That tumbl'd downe the Greekes in heapes. The host had   380
    no abode
That was not visited. We askt a Prophet that well knew
The cause of all, and from his lips Apollo's prophecies flew,
Telling his anger. First my selfe exhorted to appease

The angerd God, which Atreus' sonne did at the heart
    displease,
And up he stood, usde threats, performd. The blacke-eyd   385
    Greeks sent home
Chryseis to her sire and gave his God a Hecatome;
Then for Briseis to my tents Atrides' Heralds came
And tooke her, that the Greekes gave all. If then thy
    powres can frame
Wreake for thy sonne, affoord it; scale Olympus and implore
Jove (if by either word or fact thou ever didst restore   390
Joy to his greev'd heart) now to helpe. I oft have heard
    thee vant
In court of Peleus that alone thy hand was conversant
In rescue from a cruell spoile the blacke-clowd-gathering Jove,

*Neptune, Juno and
Pallas, confederates in
the binding of Jupiter.*

Whom other Godheads would have bound (the powre whose
    pace doth move
The round earth, heaven's great Queene and Pallas)   395
    to whose bands
Thou cam'st with rescue, bringing up him with the hundred
    hands

*The fiction of
Briareus.*

To great Olympus, whom the Gods call Briareus, men
Ægæon, who his sire surpast and was as strong againe
And in that grace sat glad by Jove. Th'immortals stood
    dismaid
At his ascension and gave free passage to his aid.   400
Of all this tell Jove. Kneele to him, embrace his knee and pray
(If Troy's aide he will ever deigne) that now their forces may
Beate home the Greeks to fleete and sea, embruing
    their retreat
In slaughter, their pains paying the wreake of their proud
    Soveraign's heart—
And that farre-ruling king may know from his poore souldiers'   405
    harms
His owne harme fals, his owne and all in mine, his best
    in arms.'

Thetis to Achilles.

    Her answer she powr'd out in teares: 'O me, my sonne,'
    said she,
'Why brought I up thy being at all, that brought thee forth
    to be
Sad subject of so hard a fate? O would to heaven that, since
Thy fate is little and not long, thou mightst without offence   410
And teares performe it. But to live thrall to so sterne a fate
As grants thee least life, and that least so most unfortunate,

Grieves me t'have given thee any life. But what thou
    wishest now
(If Jove will grant) I'le up and aske. Olympus crownd
    with snow
I'le clime; but sit thou fast at fleete, renounce all warre,   415
    and feed
Thy heart with wrath and hope of wreake—till which come,
    thou shalt need

Jupiter's feast with   A little patience. Jupiter went yesterday to feast
the Æthiops.   Amongst the blamelesse Æthiops in th'Ocean's deepned breast,
All Gods attending him; the twelfth high heaven againe he sees,
And then his brasse-pav'd court I'le skale, cling to his   420
    powrefull knees,
And doubt not but to winne thy wish.' Thus made she her
    remove
And left wrath tyring on her sonne for his enforced love.

Navigation to Chrysa.   Ulysses, with the Hecatomb, arriv'd at Chrysa's shore;
And when amids the haven's deepe mouth they came to
    use the oare
They straite stroke saile, then rold them up and on the   425
    hatches threw.
The top mast to the kelsine then with haleyards downe
    they drew,
Then brought the ship to Port with oares, then forked anchor
    cast
And gainst the violence of stormes for drifting made her fast.
    All come ashore, they all exposd the holy Hecatomb
To angrie Phœbus, and with it Chryseis welcomd home   430
Whom to her sire wise Ithacus, that did at th'altar stand,
For honour led, and (spoken thus) resignd her to his hand:

Ulysses to Chryses.   'Chryses, the mightie king of men, great Agamemnon, sends
Thy lov'd seed by my hands to thine, and to thy God commends
A Hecatomb which my charge is to sacrifice, and seeke   435
Our much-sigh-mixt-woe his recure, invokt by everie Greeke.'
    Thus he resignd her, and her sire receiv'd her highly joyd.
About the well-built altar then they orderly emploide
The sacred offring, washt their hands, tooke salt cakes, and
    the Priest

Chryses' prayer to   (With hands held up to heaven) thus praid: 'O thou that   440
Apollo for appeasing   all things seest,
the plague.   Fautour of Chrysa, whose faire hand doth guardfully dispose
Celestiall Cilla, governing in all powre Tenedos,
O heare thy Priest, and as thy hand, in free grace to my prayers,

[36]

Shot fervent plague-shafts through the Greekes, now hearten
    their affaires
With health renewd and quite remove th'infection   445
    from their blood.'
  He praid: and to his prairs againe the God propitious stood.

The sacrifice.
All, after prayre, cast on salt cakes, drew back, kild, flaid the
    beeves,
Cut out and dubd with fat their thighes, faire drest with
    doubled leaves,
And on them all the sweet-breads prickt. The Priest
    with small sere wood
Did sacrifice, powr'd on red wine, by whom the yong men   450
    stood

The banquet.
And turnd (in five ranks) spits; on which (the legs on those)
    they eate
The inwards, then in giggots cut the other fit for meate
And put to fire, which (rosted well) they drew.
    The labour done,
They serv'd the feast in, that fed all to satisfaction.
  Desire of meate and wine thus quencht, the youths crownd   455
    cups of wine,
Drunke off and fild againe to all. That day was held divine
And spent in Pæans to the Sunne, who heard with pleased eare,

The evening.
When whose bright chariot stoopt to sea and twilight
    hid the cleare.
All soundly on their cables slept even till the night was worne;

The morning.
And, when the Lady of the light, the rosie-fingerd morne,   460
Rose from the hils, all fresh arose and to the campe retir'd.
Apollo with a fore-right wind their swelling barke inspir'd.
The top-mast hoisted, milke-white sailes on his round breast
    they put.
The Misens strooted with the gale, the ship her course did cut
So swiftly that the parted waves against her ribs did rore,   465
Which coming to the campe, they drew aloft the sandie shore,
Where laid on stocks, each souldier kept his quarter as before.
  But Peleus' sonne, swift-foote Achilles, at his swift ships sate,
Burning in wrath, nor ever came to Councels of estate
That make men honord, never trod the fierce embattaild field,   470
But kept close and his lov'd heart pin'd—what fight and
    cries could yeeld
Thirsting, at all parts, to the hoast. And now since first he told
His wrongs to Thetis twelve faire mornes their ensignes
    did unfold.

[37]

Jupiter and the other
Gods from the
Æthiops.

And then the everliving Gods mounted Olympus, Jove
First in ascension. Thetis then remembred well to move   475
Achilles' motion, rose from sea, and by the morne's first light
The great heaven and Olympus climbd, where, in supremest
    height

Jupiter.

Of all that many-headed hill, she saw the farre-seene sonne
Of Saturne set from all the rest, in his free seate alone.
Before whom (on her owne knees falne) the knees of Jupiter   480
Her left hand held, her right his chinne, and thus she did prefer

Thetis' prayer
to Jupiter.

Her sonne's petition: 'Father Jove, if ever I have stood
Aidfull to thee in word or worke, with this implored good
Requite my aide: renowne my sonne, since in so short a race
(Past others) thou confin'st his life. An insolent disgrace   485
Is done him by the king of men: he forc't from him a prise
Wonne with his sword. But thou, O Jove, that art most strong,
    most wise,
Honour my sonne for my sake. Adde strength to the
    Troyans' side
By his side's weaknesse in his want, and see Troy amplifide
In conquest so much, and so long, till Greece may give againe   490
The glorie reft him, and the more illustrate the free raigne
Of his wrongd honour.' Jove at this sate silent: not a word
In long space past him. Thetis still hung on his knee, implor'd
The second time his helpe, and said: 'Grant or deny my suite.
Be free in what thou doest. I know thou canst not sit   495
    thus mute
For feare of any. Speake, denie, that so I may be sure
Of all heaven's Goddesses tis I that onely must endure
Dishonor by thee.' Jupiter, the great cloud-gatherer, griev'd
With thought of what a world of griefs this suite askt, being
    atchiev'd,

Jove to Thetis.

Sweld, sigh'd, and answerd: 'Works of death thou urgest.   500
    O, at this
Juno will storme and all my powers inflame with contumelies.
Ever she wrangles, charging me in eare of all the Gods
That I am partiall still, that I adde the displeasing oddes
Of my aide to the Ilians. Be gone then, lest she see.
Leave thy request to my care. Yet, that trust may hearten thee   505
With thy desire's grant, and my powre to give it act approve
How vaine her strife is, to thy praire my eminent head
    shall move—
Which is the great signe of my will with all th'immortall states—
Irrevocable, never failes, never without the rates

Of all powers else: when my head bowes, all heads bow   510
    with it still
As their first mover, and gives powre to any worke I will.'
    He said, and his blacke eyebrows bent; above his
        deathlesse head
Th'Ambrosian curls flowed. Great heaven shooke, and both
    were severed,
Their counsels broken. To the depth of Neptune's
    kingdome div'd
Thetis from heaven's height. Jove arose, and all the Gods   515
    receiv'd
(All rising from their thrones) their sire, attending to his court.
None sate when he rose; none delaid the furnishing his port
Till he came neare; all met with him and brought him
    to his throne.
    Nor sate great Juno ignorant, when she beheld alone
Old Nereus' silver-footed seed with Jove, that she had brought 520
Counsels to heaven; and straight her tongue had teeth in it,
    that wrought

Juno to Jupiter.   This sharpe invective: 'Who was that, thou craftiest counsellor
Of all the Gods, that so apart some secret did implore?
Ever, apart from me, thou lov'st to counsell and decree
Things of more close trust than thou thinkst are fit t'impart   525
    to me.
What ever thou determin'st, I must ever be denied
The knowledge of it, by thy will.' To her speech, thus replied
Jupiter to Juno.   The Father both of men and Gods: 'Have never hope to know
My whole intentions, though my wife. It fits not,
    nor would show
Well to thine owne thoughts; but what fits thy woman's   530
    eare to heare,
Woman nor God shall know before it grace thine eare.
Yet, what, apart from men and Gods, I please to know, forbeare
T'examine or enquire of that.' She with the cowe's faire eyes,
Juno's replie.   Respected Juno, this returned: 'Austere king of the skies,
What hast thou utterd? When did I, before this time, enquire   535
Or sift thy counsels? Passing close you are still. Your desire
Is serv'd with such care that I feare you can scarce vouch
    the deed
That makes it publike, being seduc't by this old sea-God's seed
That could so early use her knees, embracing thine. I doubt
The late act of thy bowed head was for the working out   540
Of some boone she askt, that her sonne thy partiall hand
    would please

[39]

With plaguing others.' 'Wretch!' said he, 'Thy subtle jelousies
Are still exploring; my designes can never scape thine eye,
Which yet thou never canst prevent. Thy curiositie
Makes thee lesse car'd for at my hands, and horrible the end   545
Shall make thy humor. If it be what thy suspects intend,
What then? Tis my free will it should—to which let way
    be given
With silence. Curbe your tongue in time, lest all the Gods
    in heaven
Too few be, and too weake, to helpe thy punisht insolence
When my inaccessible hands shall fall on thee.' The sence   550
Of this high threatning made her feare, and silent
    she sate downe,
Humbling her great heart. All the Gods in court of Jove
    did frowne
At this offence given, amongst whom heaven's famous Artizan,

Ephaistus, in his mother's care this comely speech began:
    'Beleeve it, these words will breed wounds beyond our   555
    powres to beare
If thus for mortals ye fall out. Ye make a tumult here
That spoiles our banquet. Evermore worst matters put
    downe best.
But, mother, though your selfe be wise, yet let your sonne
    request
His wisdome audience. Give good termes to our lov'd father
    Jove,
For feare he take offence againe, and our kind banquet prove   560
A wrathfull battell. If he will, the heavenly lightner can
Take you and tosse you from your throne, his power Olympian
Is so surpassing. Soften then with gentle speech his splene
And drinke to him. I know his heart will quickly
    downe againe.'

    This said, arising from his throne, in his lov'd   565
    mother's hand
He put the double-handeld cup, and said: 'Come, do not stand
On these crosse humors. Suffer, beare, though your great
    bosome grieve,
And lest blowes force you—all my aide not able to relieve
Your hard condition, though these eyes behold it and
    this heart
Sorrow to thinke it. Tis a taske too dangerous to take part   570
Against Olympius. I my selfe the proofe of this still feele:
When other Gods would faine have helpt, he tooke me by
    the heele

The First Booke

The fall of Vulcan.

And hurld me out of heaven. All day I was in falling downe;
At length in Lemnos I strooke earth; the likewise falling Sunne
And I together set. My life almost set too, yet there   575
The Sintii cheard and tooke me up.' This did to laughter cheare
White-wristed Juno, who now tooke the cup of him and smil'd.

Vulcan skinker to the Gods.

The sweete-peace-making draught went round, and lame
    Ephaistus fild
Nectar to all the other Gods. A laughter never left
Shooke all the blessed deities to see the lame so deft   580
At that cup service. All that day, even till the Sunne
    went downe,
They banqueted and had such cheere as did their wishes crowne.

Apollo touches his harpe at the banquet and the Muses sing to it.

Nor had they musicke lesse divine; Apollo there did touch
His most sweete harpe, to which with voice the Muses
    pleasd as much.
But when the Sun's faire light was set, each Godhead
    to his house   585
Addrest for sleepe, where everie one with art most curious
(By heaven's great both-foote-halting God) a severall roofe
    had built.
Even he to sleepe went by whose hand heaven is with
    lightning guilt,
High Jove, where he had usd to rest when sweet sleepe
    seisd his eyes.
By him the golden-thron'd Queene slept, the Queene   590
    of deities.

COMMENTARIUS

Since I dissent from all other Translators and Interpreters that
ever assaid exposition of this miraculous Poeme, especially where the
divine rapture is most exempt from capacitie in Grammarians
meerely and Grammaticall Criticks, and where the inward sense or
soule of the sacred Muse is onely within eye-shot of a Poeticall   5
spirit's inspection (lest I be prejudiced with opinion to dissent of
ignorance or singularity) I am bound by this briefe Comment to shew
I understand how all other extants understand, my reasons why I
reject them and how I receive my Author. In which labour, if where
all others find discords and dissonances I prove him entirely   10
harmonious and proportionate; if where they often alter and flie his
originall I at all parts stand fast and observe it; if where they mixe
their most pitiful castigations with his praises I render him without
touch and beyond admiration; (though truth in her verie nakednesse
sits in so deepe a pit that from Gades to Aurora, and Ganges, few   15
eyes can sound her) I hope yet those few here will so discover and
confirme her that the date being out of her darkenesse in this morning
of our Homer, he shall now gird his Temples with the Sunne and be
confest (against his good friend) nunquam dormitare. But how all
Translators, Censors or Interpretors have slept and bene dead to his   20
true understanding, I hope it will neither cast shadow of arrogance
in me to affirme nor of difficultie in you to beleeve if you please to
suspend censure and diminution till your impartiall conference of
their paines and mine be admitted. For induction and preparative
to which patience and perswasion, trouble your selves but to know   25
this:— This never-enough-glorified Poet (to vary and quicken his
eternal Poem) hath inspired his chiefe persons with different spirits,
most ingenious and inimitable characters, which not understood, how
are their speeches, being one by another as conveniently and
necessarily knowne as the instrument by the sound? If a Translator   30
or Interpreter of a ridiculous and cowardly described person (being
deceived in his character) so violates and vitiates the originall to
make his speech grave and him valiant, can the negligence and
numbnesse of such an Interpreter or Translator be lesse than the
sleepe and death I am bold to sprinckle upon him? Or could I do   35
lesse than affirme and enforce this, being so happily discovered? This
therfore (in his due place) approved and explaned, let me hope my
other assumpts will prove as conspicuous.

[42]

This first and second booke I have wholly translated againe, the
seventh, eighth, ninth and tenth bookes deferring still imperfect,   40
being all Englished so long since and my late hand (overcome with
labour) not yet rested enough to refine them. Nor are the wealthie
veines of this holy ground so amply discovered in my first twelve
labours as my last, not having competent time nor my profit in his
mysteries being so ample as when, driving through his thirteenth   45
and last books, I drew the main depth and saw the round coming of
this silver bow of our Phœbus, the cleare scope and contexture of his
worke, the full and most beautifull figures of his persons. To those
last twelve, then, I must referre you for all the chiefe worth of my
cleare discoveries. And in the meane space I intreate your acceptance   50
of some few new touches in these first—not perplexing you in first or
last with anything handled in any other Interpreter further than I
must conscionably make congression with such as have diminisht,
mangled and maimed my most worthily most tendered Author.

[3] Ἀΐδι προΐαψεν : ἀΐδης *(being compounded ex à privativa, and*   55
εἴδω, video) *signifies* locus tenebricosus, *or (according to Virgil)* sine
luce domus; *and therefore (different from others) I so convert it.*

[4] Κύνεσσιν, οἰωνοῖσι τε πᾶσι (Διὸς, &c.) *is the vulgar reading, which*
I reade: Κύνεσσιν οἰωνοῖσι τε (πᾶσι Διὸς δ'ετελείετο βουλὴ) *because*
πᾶσι, *referd to* κύνεσσιν &c., *is redundant and idle—to the miseries*   60
of the Greekes by Jove's counsell, grave and sententious.

[5] Ἐξ οὗ δὴ τὰ πρῶτα &c. ex quo quidem primum. *Here our*
common readers would have tempore *understood because* βουλὴ
(to which they thinke the Poet must otherwise have reference) is the
feminine gender. But Homer understands Jove, as in ταυ, *verse*   65
273, he expounds himselfe in these words— ἀλλά ποθι Ζεὺς &c.
which Pindarus Thebanus *in his Epitome of these*
Iliads rightly observes in these verses:—

> Conficiebat enim summi sententia Regis,
> Ex quo contulerant discordi pectore pugnas   70
> Sceptriger Atrides, et bello clarus Achilles.

[21] Ἐπευφήμησαν Ἀχαιοί, comprobarunt Græci, *all others turne*
it, but, since ἐπευφημέω *signifies properly* fausta acclamatione do
significationem approbationis, *I therefore accordingly convert it,*
because the other intimates a comprobation of all the Greekes by word,   75
which was not so, but onely by inarticulate acclamations or showtes.

[37] Ἀμφιβέβηκας : ἀμφιβεβάω *signifies properly* circumambulo, *and*
onely metaphoricè, protego, *or* tueor, *as it is alwaies in this place*
translated; which suffers alteration with me since our usuall phrase

[43]

of walking the round in townes of garrison, for the defence of it,   80
fits so well the propertie of the originall.

[197] Πρὸ γὰρ ἧκε θεὰ λευκώλενος ῞Ηρη: Præmiserat enim Dea alba
ulnis Juno. *Why Juno should send Pallas is a thing not noted by any.*
I therefore answer: because Juno is Goddesse of state. The allegory
therefore in the Prosopopœia both of Juno and Pallas is that   85
Achilles for respect to the state there present the rather used that
discretion and restraint of his anger. So in divers other places, when
state is represented, Juno procures it: as in the eighteenth booke for
the state of Patroclus his fetching off Juno commands the Sunne to
go downe before his time, &c.   90

[359] ῞Ως φάτο δακρυχέων. Sic dixit lachrymans, &c. *These teares*
are called by our Commentors unworthie and fitter for children or
women than such an Heroe as Achilles, and therefore Plato is cited in
3. de Repub. *where he saith* ᾽Ορθῶς ἄρα, &c. Meritò igitur clarorum
virorum ploratus è medio tolleremus, &c. *To answer which,*   95
and justifie the fitnesse of teares generally (as they may be occasioned)
in the greatest and most renowmed men (omitting examples of Virgil's
Æneas, Alexander the Great, &c.) I oppose against Plato onely one
president of great and most perfect humanitie (to whom infinitely
above all other we must prostrate our imitations) that shed teares,   100
viz. our All-perfect and Almightie Saviour, who wept for Lazarus.
This, then, leaving the fitnesse of great men's teares generally utterly
unanswerable, these particular teares of unvented anger in Achilles
are in him most naturall, teares being the highest effects of greatest
and most fierie spirits either when their abilities cannot performe   105
to their wils or that they are restrained of revenge, being injured,
out of other considerations—as now the consideration of the state and
gravitie of the counsell and publike good of the armie curbd Achilles.
Who can denie that there are teares of manlinesse and magnanimitie
as well as womanish and pusillanimous? So Diomed wept for curst   110
heart when Apollo strooke his scourge from him and hindered his
horse race, having bene warned by Pallas before not to resist the
Deities and so his great spirits being curbed of revenge for the wrong
he received then. So when not-enough-vented anger was not to be
exprest enough by that teare-starting affection in couragious and   115
fierce men, our most accomplisht expressor helpes the illustration in a
Simile of his fervour in most fervent-spirited fowles, resembling the
wrathfull fight of Sarpedon and Patroclus to two Vultures fighting
and crying on a rocke, which thus I have afterwards Englished and
here for example inserted: 120

[44]

Downe jumpt he from his chariot; downe leapt his foe as light.
And as on some far-seeing rocke a cast of Vultures fight,
Flie on each other, strike and trusse, part, meete and then
    sticke by,
Tugge both with crooked beakes and seres, crie, fight, and
    fight and cry—
So fiercely fought these angrie kings, &c.   125

Wherein you see that crying in these eagerlie fought fowles (which
is like teares in angrie men) is so farre from softnesse or faintnesse
that to the superlative of hardinesse and courage it expresseth both.
Nor must we be so grosse to imagine that Homer made Achilles or
Diomed blubber or sob &c., but in the verie point and sting of their   130
unvented anger shed a few violent and seething-over teares. What
Asse-like impudence is it then for any meerely vaineglorious and
selfe-loving puffe, that everie where may reade these inimitable
touches of our Homer's maisterie, any where to oppose his arrogant
    and ignorant castigations—when he should rather (with his much 135
        better understander Spondanus) submit where he oversees
            him faulty, and say thus: Quia tu tamen hoc voluisti,
                sacrosanctæ tuæ authoritati per me
                        nihil detrahetur.

The End of the First Booke

THE SECOND BOOKE
of
HOMER'S ILIADS

THE ARGUMENT

Jove cals a vision up from Somnus' den
To bid Atrides muster up his men.
The king (to Greekes dissembling his desire)
Perswades them to their countrie to retire.
By Pallas' will Ulysses stayes their flight   5
And wise old Nestor heartens them to fight.
They take their meate; which done, to armes they goe
And march in good array against the foe.
So those of Troy, when Iris, from the skie,
Of Saturn's sonne performs the Ambassie.   10

Another Argument

Beta *the dreame and Synod cites,*
And Catalogues the navall knights.

Jupiter carefull in performing his vow to Thetis.	The other Gods and knights at armes all night slept. Onely Jove Sweet slumber seisd not: he discourst how best he might approve His vow made for Achilles' grace and make the Grecians find His misse in much death. Al waies cast, this counsel serv'd his mind
	With most allowance—to dispatch a harmefull dreame to greet 5 The king of men, and gave this charge: 'Go to the Achive fleet,
Jupiter cals up a vision.	Pernicious dreame, and, being arriv'd in Agamemnon's tent, Deliver truly all this charge. Command him to convent His whole hoast arm'd before these towres, for now Troy's broad-waid towne
	He shall take in: the heaven-housd Gods are now indifferent 10 growne; Juno's request hath wonne them; Troy, now under imminent ils, At all parts labours.' This charge heard, the vision straight fulfils,

The ships reacht and Atrides' tent, in which he found him laid,
Divine sleepe powrd about his powres. He stood above his head
Like Nestor (grac'd of old men most) and this did intimate: 15

   'Sleepes the wise Atreus' tame-horse sonne? A counsellour
     of State
Must not the whole night spend in sleepe, to whom the
     people are
For guard committed and whose life stands bound to so
     much care.
Now heare me then, Jove's messenger, who, though farre off
     from thee,
Is neare thee yet in ruth and care, and gives command by me 20
To arme thy whole hoast. Thy strong hand the broad-waid
     towne of Troy
Shall now take in. No more the Gods dissentiously imploy
Their high-housd powers; Juno's suite hath wonne them all
     to her,
And ill fates over-hang these towres, addrest by Jupiter.
Fixe in thy mind this, nor forget to give it action when 25
Sweet sleepe shall leave thee.' Thus he fled and left the king
     of men

Repeating in discourse his dreame and dreaming still, awake,
Of powre not readie yet for act. O foole, he thought to take
In that next day old Priam's towne, not knowing what affaires
Jove had in purpose, who prepar'd (by strong fight) sighes 30
     and cares
For Greekes and Troyans. The dreame gone, his voice still
     murmured
About the king's eares, who sate up, put on him in his bed
His silken inner weed, faire, new, and then in hast arose,
Cast on his ample mantle, tied to his soft feet faire shoes;
His silver-hilted sword he hung about his shoulders, tooke 35
His father's scepter, never staind, which then abroad he shooke

And went to fleete. And now great heaven Goddesse Aurora
     scall'd,
To Jove and all Gods bringing light, when Agamemnon call'd
His heralds, charging them aloud to call to instant Court
The thicke-haird Greekes. The heralds call'd, the Greekes made 40
     quicke resort.
The Councell chiefly he composd of old great-minded men
At Nestor's ships, the Pylian king. All there assembled then,

Thus Atreus' sonne begunne the Court: 'Heare, friends, a
     dreame divine

[47]

Amids the calme night in my sleepe did through my shut eyes
    shine
Within my fantasie. His forme did passing naturally   45
Resemble Nestor: such attire, a stature just as hie.
He stood above my head and words thus fashiond did relate:

Agamemnon tels his   "Sleepes the wise Atreus' tame-horse sonne? A counsellor of
vision.   state

Must not the whole night spend in sleepe, to whom the people are
For guard committed and whose life stands bound to so much   50
    care.
Now heare me then, Jove's messenger, who, though farre off
    from thee,
Is neare thee yet in love and care, and gives command by me
To arme thy whole hoast. Thy strong hand the broad-waid
    towne of Troy
Shall now take in. No more the Gods dissentiously imploy
Their high-housd powres; Saturnia's suite hath wonne them all   55
    to her
And ill fates over-hang these towres, addrest by Jupiter.
Fixe in thy mind this." This exprest, he tooke wing and away,
And sweet sleepe left me. Let us then by all our meanes assay
To arme our armie. I will first (as farre as fits our right)
Trie their addictions and command with full-sail'd ships our   60
    flight,
Which if they yeeld to, oppose you.' He sate, and up arose
Nestor, of sandy Pylos king, who (willing to dispose
Their counsell to the publicke good) proposd this to the State:

Nestor to the Greekes.   'Princes and Counsellors of Greece, if any should relate
This vision but the king himselfe, it might be held a tale   65
And move the rather our retraite; but since our Generall
Affirmes he saw it, hold it true and our best meanes make
To arme our armie.' This speech usde, he first the Councell brake.
The other scepter-bearing States arose too, and obeyd
The people's Rector. Being abroad, the earth was overlaid   70

Simile.   With flockers to them that came forth. As when of frequent Bees
Swarmes rise out of a hollow rocke, repairing the degrees
Of their egression endlesly with ever rising new
From forth their sweet nest, as their store, still as it faded, grew
And never would ceasse, sending forth her clusters to the spring   75
They still crowd out so—this flocke here, that there, belabouring
The loaded flowres: so from the ships and tents the armie's store
Troopt to these Princes and the Court along th'unmeasur'd
    shore—

[48]

The Second Booke

Fame, Jove's
Ambassadresse.

Amongst whom Jove's Ambassadresse, Fame, in her vertue shin'd
Exciting greedinesse to heare. The rabble, thus inclin'd,   80
Hurried together. Uprore seisd the high Court; earth did grone
Beneath the setling multitude; tumult was there alone.
Thrice three voiciferous heralds rose to check the rout and get
Eare to their Jove-kept Governors, and instantly was set
That huge confusion: every man set fast, and clamor ceast.   85
Then stood divine Atrides up and in his hand comprest

The scepter of
Agamemnon.

His scepter, th'elaborate worke of fierie Mulciber,
Who gave it to Saturnian Jove, Jove to his messenger,
His messenger (Argicides) to Pelops, skild in horse,
Pelops to Atreus, chiefe of men; he, dying, gave it course   90
To Prince Thyestes, rich in heards, Thyestes to the hand
Of Agamemnon renderd it and, with it, the command
Of many Iles and Argos all. On this he, leaning, said:

Agamemnon to the
Greekes.

'O friends, great sonnes of Danaus, servants of Mars, Jove laid
A heavie curse on me, to vow, and binde it with the bent   95
Of his high forehead, that (this Troy of all her people spent)
I should returne, yet now to mocke our hopes built on his vow
And charge ingloriously my flight, when such an overthrow
Of brave friends I have authored. But to his mightiest will
We must submit us, that hath raz't, and will be razing still,   100
Men's footsteps from so many townes; because his power is most,
He will destroy most. But how vile such and so great an hoast
Will shew to future times, that, matcht with lesser numbers farre,
We flie, not putting on the crowne of our so long-held warre—
Of which there yet appeares no end! Yet should our foes and we   105
Strike truce and number both our powers—Troy taking all
        that be
Her arm'd inhabitants, and we in tens should all sit downe
At our truce banquet, everie ten allow'd one of the towne
To fill his feast-cup, many tens would their attendant want—
So much I must affirme our power exceeds th'inhabitant.   110
But their auxiliarie bands, those brandishers of speares
(From many cities drawne), are they that are our hinderers,
Not suffering well-raisd Troy to fall. Nine yeares are ended now
Since Jove our conquest vow'd, and now our vessels rotten grow,
Our tackling failes, our wives, yong sonnes, sit in their doores   115
        and long
For our arrivall, yet the worke that should have wreakt our
        wrong
And made us welcome lies unwrought. Come then, as I bid, all
Obey and flie to our lov'd home, for now, nor ever, shall
Our utmost take in broad-waid Troy.' This said, the multitude

[49]

Was all for home, and all men else that what this would conclude   120
Had not discoverd. All the crowd was shov'd about the shore,

Simile.

In sway like rude and raging waves rowsd with the fervent blore
Of th'East and South winds when they breake from Jove's
    clouds and are borne
On rough backs of th'Icarian seas, or like a field of corne
High growne that Zephyr's vehement gusts bring easily   125
    underneath
And make the stiffe-upbristl'd eares do homage to his breath—
For even so easily with the breath Atrides' usde was swaid
The violent multitude. To fleet, with showts and disaraid,
All rusht, and with a fogge of dust their rude feete dimd
    the day.
Each cried to other: 'Cleanse our ships! Come, lanch, aboord,   130
    away!'
The clamor of the runners home reacht heaven, and then,
    past fate,
The Greekes had left Troy had not then the Goddesse of estate

Juno to Pallas.

Thus spoke to Pallas: 'O foule shame, thou untam'd seed of Jove,
Shall thus the sea's broad backe be charg'd with these our
    friends' remove,
Thus leaving Argive Helen here, thus Priam grac't, thus Troy,   135
In whose fields farre from their lov'd owne (for Helen's sake)
    the joy
And life of so much Grecian birth is vanisht? Take thy way
T'our brasse-arm'd people, speake them faire, let not a man obey
The charge now given, nor lanch one ship.' She said, and
    Pallas did
As she commanded. From the tops of heaven's steepe hill she slid   140
And straight the Greekes' swift ships she reacht. Ulysses (like
    to Jove
In gifts of counsell) she found out, who to that base remove
Stird not a foote nor toucht a ship, but griev'd at heart to see
That fault in others. To him close the blue-eyd deitie
Made way and said: 'Thou wisest Greeke, divine Laertes' sonne,   145
Thus flie ye homewards to your ships? Shall all thus
    headlong runne?
Glorie to Priam thus ye leave, glorie to all his friends,
If thus ye leave her here for whom so many violent ends
Have closd your Greeke eyes and so farre from their
    so loved home!
Go to these people; use no stay; with faire termes overcome   150
Their foule endevour; not a man a flying saile let hoice.'
    Thus spake she, and Ulysses knew twas Pallas by her voice,

Ranne to the runners, cast from him his mantle, which his man
And Herald, grave Eurybates the Ithacensian,
That followd him tooke up. Himselfe to Agamemnon went,   155
His incorrupted scepter tooke, his scepter of descent,
And with it went about the fleete. What Prince or man of name
He found flight-given he would restraine with words of
        gentlest blame:

Ulysses' temper in   'Good sir, it fits not you to flie or fare as one afraid.
restraining the flight.   You should not onely stay your selfe but see the people staid.   160
You know not clearely (though you heard the king's words)
        yet his mind.
He onely tries men's spirits now, and whom his trials find
Apt to this course he will chastise. Nor you, nor I, heard all
He spake in councell, nor durst preasse too neare our Generall
Lest we incent him to our hurt. The anger of a king   165
Is mightie; he is kept of Jove and from Jove likewise spring
His honors, which, out of the love of wise Jove, he enjoyes.'
Thus he the best sort usd; the worst, whose spirits brake out
        in noise,
He cudgeld with his scepter, chid, and said: 'Stay, wretch,
        be still
And heare thy betters. Thou art base, and both in   170
        powre and skill
Poore and unworthie, without name in counsell or in warre.
We must not all be kings. The rule is most irregularre
Where many rule. One Lord, one king propose to thee; and he
To whom wise Saturn's sonne hath given both law and Emperie
To rule the publicke is that king.' Thus, ruling, he restrain'd   175
The hoast from flight, and then againe the Councell was
        maintain'd
With such a concourse that the shore rung with the tumult
        made,
As when the farre-resounding sea doth in his rage invade
His sandie confines, whose sides grone with his involved wave
And make his owne breast eccho sighes. All sate and   180
        audience gave.
Thersites onely would speake all. A most disordered store
Of words he foolishly powrd out, of which his mind held more
Than it could manage—anything with which he could procure
Laughter he never could containe. He should have yet bene
        sure
To touch no kings. T'oppose their states becomes not jesters'   185
        parts.
Thersites' description.   But he the filthiest fellow was of all that had deserts

In Troy's brave siege: he was squint-eyd and lame of
    either foote,
So crooke-backt that he had no breast, sharpe-headed, where
    did shoote
(Here and there sperst) thin mossie haire. He most of all envide

Achilles. Ulysses and Æacides, whom still his splene would chide,   190
Nor could the sacred king himselfe avoid his saucie vaine—
Against whom—since he knew the Greekes did vehement hates
    sustaine
(Being angrie for Achilles' wrong)—he cried out, railing thus:

Thersites to   'Atrides, why complainst thou now? What wouldst thou
Agamemnon.   more of us?
Thy tents are full of brasse and dames: the choice of all   195
    are thine—
With whom we must present thee first when any townes resigne
To our invasion. Wantst thou then (besides all this) more gold
From Troy's knights to redeeme their sonnes, whom to be
    dearely sold
I or some other Greeke must take? Or wouldst thou yet againe
Force from some other Lord his prise to sooth the lusts   200
    that raigne
In thy encroching appetite? It fits no Prince to be
A Prince of ill and governe us, or leade our progenie
By rape to ruine. O base Greekes, deserving infamie
And ils eternall! Greekish girls, not Greekes ye are! Come, flie
Home with our ships. Leave this man here to perish with his   205
    preys
And trie if we helpt him or not. He wrong'd a man that weys
Farre more than he himselfe in worth. He forc't from Thetis'
    sonne
And keepes his prise still. Nor think I that mightie man hath
    wonne
The stile of wrathfull worthily. He's soft, he's too remisse,
Or else, Atrides, his had bene thy last of injuries.'   210
    Thus he the people's Pastor chid; but straight stood up to him
Divine Ulysses, who with lookes exceeding grave and grim

Ulysses to Thersites. This bitter checke gave: 'Ceasse, vaine foole, to vent thy
    railing vaine
On kings thus, though it serve thee well. Nor thinke thou canst
    restraine
With that thy railing facultie their wils in least degree—   215
For not a worse of all this hoast came with our king than thee
To Troy's great siege. Then do not take into that mouth of thine
The names of kings, much lesse revile the dignities that shine

[52]

In their supreme states, wresting thus this motion for our home
To sooth thy cowardise, since our selves yet know not what   220
    will come
Of these designments—if it be our good to stay or go.
Nor is it that thou standst on: thou revil'st our Generall so
Onely because he hath so much, not given by such as thou
But our Heroes. Therefore this thy rude veine makes me vow
(Which shall be curiously observ'd) if ever I shall heare   225
This madnesse from thy mouth againe, let not Ulysses beare
This head nor be the father cald of yong Telemachus
If to thy nakednesse I take and strip thee not, and thus
Whip thee to fleete from Councell—send with sharpe stripes
    weeping hence
This glory thou affectst to raile.' This said, his insolence   230
He setl'd with his scepter, strooke his backe and shoulders so
That bloody wales rose. He shrunke round and from his eyes
    did flow
Moist teares, and, looking filthily, he sate, feard, smarted, dried
His blubberd cheekes, and all the preasse (though griev'd to be
    denied
Their wisht retrait for home) yet laught delightsomely, and   235
    spake
Either to other: 'O ye Gods, how infinitely take
Ulysses' vertues in our good! Author of Counsels, great
In ordering armies, how most well this act became his heate
To beate from Councell this rude foole! I thinke his sawcie spirit
Hereafter will not let his tongue abuse the soveraigne merit,   240
Exempt from such base tongues as his.' Thus spake the people.
    Then
The citie-razer Ithacus stood up to speake againe,
Holding his Scepter. Close to him gray-eyd Minerva stood,
And like a herald silence causd, that all the Achive brood
(From first to last) might heare and know the counsell, when   245
    (inclind

Ulysses to
Agamemnon and the
people.

To all their good) Ulysses said: 'Atrides, now I find
These men would render thee the shame of all men,
    nor would pay
Their owne vowes to thee when they tooke their free and
    honord way
From Argos hither, that till Troy were by their brave hands rac't
They would not turne home—yet like babes and widowes now   250
    they hast
To that base refuge. Tis a spite to see men melted so
In womanish changes—though tis true that if a man do go

[53]

Onely a moneth to sea and leave his wife farre off and he,
Tortur'd with winter's stormes and tost with a tumultuous sea,
Growes heavy and would home. Us then, to whom the   255
    thrice-three yeare
Hath fild his revoluble orbe since our arrivall here
I blame not to wish home much more. Yet all this time to stay
(Out of our judgements) for our end, and now to take our way
Without it were absurd and vile. Sustaine then, friends, abide
The time set to our object, trie if Calchas prophecied   260
True of the time or not. We know ye all can witnesse well
(Whom these late death-conferring fates have faild to
    send to hell)
That when in Aulis all our fleet assembl'd with a freight
Of ils to Ilion and her friends, beneath the faire growne height
A Platane bore, about a fount whence christall water flow'd   265
And neare our holy altar, we upon the Gods bestow'd
Accomplisht Hecatombs, and there appear'd a huge portent—
A Dragon with a bloody skale, horride to sight, and sent
To light by great Olympius, which, crawling from beneath
The Altar, to the Platane climbd and ruthlesse crasht to death   270
A Sparrowe's yong, in number eight, that in a top-bow lay
Hid under leaves; the dam the ninth, that hoverd every way
Mourning her lov'd birth, till at length the Serpent,
    watching her,
Her wing caught and devourd her too. This dragon, Jupiter
(That brought him forth) turnd to a stone; and made a   275
    powrefull meane
To stirre our zeales up, that admir'd when of a fact so cleane
Of all ill as our sacrifice so fearfull an ostent
Should be the issue. Calchas then thus prophecied the event:
"Why are ye dumbe strooke, faire-haird Greekes? Wise Jove
    is he hath showne
This strange ostent to us. Twas late, and passing lately done,   280
But that grace it foregoes to us for suffering all the state
Of his apparence (being so slow) nor time shall end, nor fate.
As these eight Sparrowes and the dam (that made the ninth)
    were eate
By this sterne Serpent, so nine yeares we are t'endure the heate
Of ravenous warre and in the tenth take in this broad-waid   285
    towne."
  Thus he interpreted this signe, and all things have their
    crowne
As he interpreted till now. The rest then to succeed
Beleeve as certaine. Stay we all till that most glorious deed

Of taking this rich towne our hands are honord with.' This said,
The Greekes gave an unmeasur'd shout, which backe the ships   290
    repaid
With terrible ecchoes, in applause of that perswasion
Divine Ulysses usd—which yet held no comparison

Nestor to the Greeks. With Nestor's next speech, which was this: 'O shamefull thing!
    Ye talke
Like children all, that know not warre. In what aire's region
    walke
Our oathes and covenants? Now I see the fit respects of men   295
Are vanisht quite, our right hands given, our faiths, our
    counsels vaine,
Our sacrifice with wine—all fled in that prophaned flame
We made to bind all. For thus still we vaine perswasions frame
And strive to worke our end with words, not joyning
    stratagemes
And hands together, though thus long the powre of our   300
    extremes
Hath urg'd us to them. Atreus' sonne, firme as at first howre
    stand!
Make good thy purpose. Talke no more in counsels, but
    command
In active field. Let two or three that by themselves advise
Faint in their crowning: they are such as are not truly wise.
They will for Argos ere they know if that which Jove hath said 305
Be false or true. I tell them all that high Jove bowd his head
As first we went aboord our fleet, for signe we should confer
These Troyans their due fate and death—almightie Jupiter
All that day darting forth his flames in an unmeasur'd light
On our right hand. Let therefore none once dreame of coward   310
    flight
Till (for his owne) some wife of Troy he sleepes withall, the rape
Of Helen wreaking and our sighes enforc't for her escape.
If any yet dare dote on home, let his dishonor'd hast
His blacke and well-built barke but touch, that (as he first
    disgrac't
His countrie's spirit) fate and death may first his spirit let go. 315
But be thou wise, king; do not trust thy selfe but others. Know
I will not use an abject word: see all thy men arraid
In tribes and nations that tribes, tribes, nations may nations
    aid—
Which doing, thou shalt know what chiefs, what souldiers
    play the men
And what the cowards, for they all will fight in severall then,   320

Easie for note. And then shalt thou, if thou destroist not Troy,
Know if the prophecie's defect, or men thou dost employ
In their approv'd arts want in warre, or lacke of that brave heate
Fit for the ventrous spirits of Greece, was cause to thy defeate.'

Agamemnon to Nestor.   To this the king of men replied: 'O father, all the sonnes   325
Of Greece thou conquerst in the strife of consultations.
I would to Jove, Athenia and Phœbus, I could make
(Of all) but ten such Counsellers! Then instantly would shake
King Priam's citie, by our hands laid hold on and laid wast.
But Jove hath orderd I should grieve, and to that end hath cast   330
My life into debates past end. My selfe and Thetis' sonne
(Like girles) in words fought for a girle, and I th'offence
    begunne.
But if we ever talke as friends, Troy's thus deferred fall
Shall never vexe us more one houre. Come then, to victles all
That strong Mars all may bring to field! Each man his lance's   335
    steele
See sharpned well, his shield well-lin'd, his horses meated well,
His chariot carefully made strong, that these affaires of death
We all day may hold fiercely out. No man must rest or breath.
The bosomes of our targatiers must all be steept in sweate;
The lancier's arme must fall dissolv'd; our chariot horse with   340
    heate
Must seeme to melt. But if I find one souldier take the chase,
Or stirre from fight, or fight not still fixt in his enemies' face,
Or hid a shipboord, all the world for force nor price shall save
His hated life—but fowles and dogs be his abhorred grave.'

Simile.   He said; and such a murmure rose as on a loftie shore   345
The waves make when the South wind comes and tumbles
    them before
Against a rocke growne neare the strand, which diversly beset
Is never free, but here and there with varied uprores beat.
  All rose then, rushing to the fleete, perfum'd their tents,
    and eate,
Each offring to th'immortall Gods and praying to scape th'heate   350
Of warre and death. The king of men an Oxe of five yeares'
    spring
T'almightie Jove slue, call'd the Peeres—first Nestor; then the
    king
Idomeneus; after them th'Ajaces and the sonne
Diomed. Of Tydeus; Ithacus the sixth, in counsell Paragon
To Jove himselfe. All these he bad, but at-a-martiall-crie   355
Good Menelaus, since he saw his brother busily
Employd at that time, would not stand on invitation

[56]

But of himselfe came. All about the offring overthrowne
Stood round, tooke salt-cakes, and the king himselfe thus praid
    for all:
  'O Jove, most great, most glorious, that in that starrie hall   360
Sit'st drawing darke clouds up to aire, let not the Sunne go
    downe,
Darknesse supplying it, till my hands the Pallace and the towne
Of Priam overthrow and burne, the armes on Hector's brest
Dividing, spoiling with my sword thousands (in interest
Of his bad quarrell) laid by him in dust and eating earth.'   365
  He pray'd. Jove heard him not, but made more plentifull
    the birth
Of his sad toiles; yet tooke his gifts. Prayres past, cakes on they
    threw.
The Oxe then (to the altar drawne) they kill'd, and from him
    drew
His hide, then cut him up, his thighes (in two hewne)
    dubd with fat,
Prickt on the sweat-breads, and with wood, leavelesse and   370
    kindl'd at
Apposed fire, they burne the thighes; which done, the inwards,
    slit,
They broild on coales, and eate. The rest, in giggots cut,
    they spit,
Roast cunningly, draw, sit and feast. Nought lackt to leave alaid
Each temperate appetite. Which serv'd, Nestor began, and said:

Nestor to Agamemnon.
  'Atrides, most grac't king of men, now no more words allow,   375
Nor more deferre the deed Jove vowes. Let heralds summon now
The brasen-coted Greekes, and us range everie where the host
To stirre a strong warre quickly up.' This speech no sillable lost.
The high-voic't heralds instantly he charg'd to call to armes
The curld-head Greeks. They call'd. The Greeks straight   380
    answerd their alarmes.
The Jove-kept kings, about the king all gatherd, with their aide
Rang'd all in tribes and nations. With them the gray-eyd maide
Great Ægis (Jove's bright shield) sustain'd, that can be
    never old,
Never corrupted, fring'd about with serpents forg'd of gold—
As many as suffisde to make an hundred fringes worth   385
A hunderd oxen, everie snake, all sprawling, all set forth
With wondrous spirit. Through the host with this the Goddesse
    ranne
In furie, casting round her eyes, and furnisht everie man
With strength, exciting all to armes and fight incessant. None

Now lik't their lov'd homes like the warres. And as a fire upon   390
A huge wood on the heights of hils that farre off hurles his
    light,
So the divine brasse shin'd on these, thus thrusting on for fight.
Their splendor through the aire reacht heaven. And as about
    the flood
Cayster, in an Asian meade, flockes of the airie brood
(Cranes, Geese or long-neckt Swans) here, there, proud of their   395
    pinions flie
And in their fals lay out such throats that with their spiritfull
    crie
The meddow shrikes againe: so here these many-nation'd men
Flow'd over the Scamandrian field from tents and ships.
    The din
Was dreadfull that the feete of men and horse beate out of
    earth.
And in the florishing meade they stood thicke as the odorous   400
    birth
Of flowres or leaves bred in the spring, or thicke as swarmes
    of flies
Throng then to sheep-cotes when each swarme his erring wing
    applies
To milke deawd on the milke-maids' pailes—all eagerly disposd
To give to ruine th'Ilians. And as in rude heapes closd
Though huge Goate heards are at their food the Goate-heards   405
    easly yet
Sort into sundry heards, so here the Chiefes in battell set,
Here tribes, here nations, ordring all. Amongst whom shin'd
    the king,
With eyes like lightning-loving Jove, his forehead answering,
In breast like Neptune, Mars in waste; and as a goodly Bull
Most eminent of all a heard, most strong, most masterfull,   410
So Agamemnon Jove that day made overheighten clere
That heaven-bright armie and preferd to all th'Heroes there.

Invocation.
    Now tell me, Muses, you that dwell in heavenly roofes (for you
Are Goddesses, are present here, are wise and all things know—
We onely trust the voyce of fame, know nothing), who   415
    they were
That here were captains of the Greeks—Commanding Princes
    here?
The multitude exceed my song, though fitted to my choice
Ten tongues were, hardned pallats ten, a breast of brasse, a voyce
Infract and trump-like. That great worke, unlesse the seed
    of Jove

(The deathlesse Muses) undertake, maintaines a pitch above   420
All mortall powers. The Princes, then, and navie that did bring
Those so inenarrable troopes and all their soyles I sing.

THE CATALOGUE OF THE GRECIAN
SHIPS AND CAPTAINES.

The Bœotian   Peneleus and Leitus, all that Bœotia bred,
captaines.   Arcesilaus, Clonius and Prothoenor led;
The places in Bœotia.   Th'inhabitants of Hyria and stonie Aulida,   425
Schœne, Scole, the hilly Eteon and holy Thespia,
Of Græa and great Mycalesse that hath the ample plaine,
Of Harma and Ilesius, and all that did remaine
In Eryth and in Eleon, in Hylen, Peteona,
In faire Ocalea and the towne, well-builded, Medeona,   430
Copas, Eutresis, Thisbe that for Pigeons doth surpasse,
Of Coroneia, Haliart that hath such store of grasse—
All those that in Platæa dwelt, that Glisa did possesse
And Hypothebs whose wel-built wals are rare and fellowlesse,
In rich Onchestus' famous wood, to watrie Neptune vow'd   435
And Arne, where the vine-trees are with vigorous bunches
    bow'd—
With them that dwelt in Midea and Nisa most divine,
All those whom utmost Anthedon did wealthily confine.

The navie of the   From all these coasts in generall full fiftie saile were sent
Bœotians fiftie.   And sixscore strong Bœotian youths in everie burthen went.   440
     But those who in Aspledon dwelt, and Minyan Orchomen,
Ascalaphus and   God Mars his sonnes did leade (Ascalaphus and Ialmen),
Ialmenus, sonnes of   Who in Azidon Actor's house did of Astyoche come:
Mars.   The bashfull Maide, as she went up into the higher roome,
     The warre-god secretly comprest. In safe conduct of these   445
Their navie 30.   Did thirtie hollow-bottom'd barkes divide the wavie seas.
The Phocensian   Brave Schedius and Epistrophus the Phocian captaines were,
captains Schedius and   Naubolida Iphitus' sonnes, all-proofe gainst any feare.
Epistrophus.   With them the Cyparissians went, and bold Pythonians,
     Men of religious Crisa's soyle, and fat Daulidians,   450
Panopæans, Anemores and fierce Hyampolists,
And those that dwell where Cephisus casts up his silken mists,
Their fleet 40.   The men that faire Lilæa held neare the Cephisian spring—
All which did fortie sable barkes to that designement bring.
About th'entoyld Phocensian fleete had these their saile   455
    assignde
And neare to the sinister wing the arm'd Bœotians shinde.

Ajax, Oileus captaines   Ajax the lesse, Oileus' sonne, the Locrians led to warre—
of the Locrians.   Not like to Ajax Telamon, but lesser man by farre.

[59]

Little he was, and ever wore a breastplate made of linne,
But for the manage of his lance he generall praise did winne. 460

The dwellers of Calliarus, of Bessa, Opoen,
The youths of Cynus, Scarphis and Augias, lovely men
Of Tarphis and of Thronius, neare flood Boagrius' fall

Twise twentie martiall barkes of these lesse Ajax saild withall.
Who neare Eubœa's blessed soile their habitations had, 465
Strength-breathing Abants who their seats in sweet Eubœa
    made,
The Histiæans rich in grapes, the men of Chalcida,
The Cerinths bordring on the sea of rich Eretria,
Of Dion's highly-seated towne, Carystus, and of Styre,

All these the Duke Elphenor led, a flame of Mars his fire 470
Surnam'd Chalcodontiades, the mightie Abants' guide,
Swift men of foot whose broad-set backes their trailing haire
    did hide,
Well-seene in fight, and soone could pierce with farre
    extended darts
The breast-plates of their enemies and reach their dearest hearts.

Fortie blacke men of warre did saile in this Elphenor's charge. 475

    The souldiers that in Athens dwelt, a citie builded large,
The people of Erechtheus, whom Jove-sprung Pallas fed,
And plentious-feeding Tellus brought out of her flowrie bed.
Him Pallas plac't in her rich Fane, and everie ended yeare
Of Buls and Lambes th'Athenian youths please him with 480
    offrings there.

Mightie Menestheus, Peteus' sonne, had their devided care.
For horsemen and for targatiers none could with him compare,
Nor put them into better place, to hurt or to defend,
But Nestor (for he elder was) with him did sole contend.

With him came fiftie sable saile. And out of Salamine 485
Great Ajax brought twelve saile that with th'Athenians did
    combine.
   Who did in fruitfull Argos dwell or strong Tiryntha keepe,
Hermion, or in Asinen whose bosome is so deepe,
Trœzena, Eion, Epidaure, where Bacchus crownes his head.

Ægina, and Maseta's soyle, did follow Diomede 490
And Sthenelus, the deare-lov'd sonne of famous Capaneus,
Together with Euryalus, heire of Mecisteus,
The king of Talaeonides—past whom in deeds of warre
The famous souldier Diomed of all was held by farre.

Fourescore blacke ships did follow these. The men faire 495
    Mycene held,
The wealthy Corinth, Cleon that for beautious sight exceld,

The Myceneans. *Their townes.*	Aræthyrea's lovely seate, and in Ornia's plaine,
	And Sicyona, where at first did king Adrastus raigne
	High-seated Gonoessa's towers, and Hyperesius,
	That dwelt in fruitfull Pellenen, and in divine Ægius 500
	With all the sea-side borderers, and wide Helice's friends,
Agamemnon captaine. *Ships 100.*	To Agamemnon everie towne her native birth commends
	In double fiftie sable barks. With him a world of men
	Most strong and full of valure went, and he in triumph then
	Put on his most resplendent armes, since he did overshine 505
	The whole heroique host of Greece in power of that designe.
The Lacedæmonians *and their townes.*	Who did in Lacedæmon's rule th'unmeasur'd concave hold,
	High Pharis', Sparta's, Messe's towers, for doves so much extold,
	Bryseia's and Augia's grounds, strong Laa, Œtylon,
	Amyclas, Helos' harbor-towne that Neptune beats upon, 510
Menelaus captaine. *Ships 60.*	All these did Menelaus leade (his brother that in cries
	Of warre was famous). Sixtie ships convaid these enemies
	To Troy in chiefe, because their king was chiefly injur'd there
	In Helen's rape, and did his best to make them buy it deare.
The Pylians and their *townes.*	Who dwelt in Pylos' sandie soyle, and Arene the faire, 515
	In Thryon, neare Alpheus' flood, and Æpy full of aire,
	In Cyparisseus, Amphigen and little Pteleon,
	The towne where all the Iliots dwelt, and famous Dorion,
	Where all the Muses (opposite in strife of Poesie
Thamyris deprived of *sight and Poesie by* *the Muses.*	To ancient Thamyris of Thrace) did use him cruelly— 520
	He coming from Eurytus' court, the wise Oechalian king—
	Because he proudly durst affirme he could more sweetly sing
	Than that Pierean race of Jove, who (angry with his vant)
	Bereft his eye-sight and his song that did the eare enchant
Nestor captaine. *Ships 90.*	And of his skill to touch his Harpe disfurnished his hand. 525
	All these in ninetie hollow keeles grave Nestor did command.
The Arcadians and *their towns.*	The richly blest inhabitants of the Arcadian land
	Below Cyllene's mount that by Æpytus' tombe did stand,
	Where dwell the bold neare-fighting men who did in Pheneus
	live,
	And Orchomen, where flockes of sheepe the shepheards 530
	clustering drive,
	In Rhipe and in Stratie, the faire Mantinean towne,
	And strong Enispe, that for height is ever weather-blowne,
	Tegea, and in Stymphelus, Parrhasia strongly wall'd,
Agapenor their leader. *Ships 60.*	All these Ankæus' sonne to field, king Agapenor, call'd.
	In sixtie barks he brought them on, and everie barke well-mand 535
	With fierce Arcadians skild to use the utmost of a band.
	King Agamemnon on these men did well-built ships bestow
	To passe the gulfie purple sea, that did no sea rites know.

The Epians and their townes. Ships 40.	They who in Hyrmin, Buprasis and Elis did remaine,
	What Olen's Cliffes, Aleisius and Myrsin did containe, 540
	Were led to warre by twise two Dukes and each ten ships did bring,
	Which many venterous Epians did serve for burthening.
Captaines Amphimachus, Thalpius, Diores, Polyxinus.	Beneath Amphimachus his charge and valiant Thalpius,
	Sonne of Eurytus Actor one, the other Cteatus';
	Diores Amaryncides the other did imploy, 545
	The fourth divine Polyxinus, Agasthenes his joy.
Dulichians. Meges captaine.	The king of faire Augeiades, who from Dulichius came
	And from Echinaus' sweet Iles, which hold their holy frame
	By ample Elis' region, Meges Phylides led,
	Whom Duke Phyleus, Jove's belov'd, begat and whilome fled 550
	To large Dulichius for the wrath that fir'd his father's breast.
Ships 40. The Cephaleans and their towns.	Twise twentie ships with Ebon sailes were in his charge addrest.
	The war-like men of Cephale, and those of Ithaca,
	Woody Neritus, and the men of wet Crocylia,
	Sharpe Ægilipa, Samos' Ile, Zacynthus sea-enclosd, 555
	Epirus, and the men that hold the Continent opposd,
Ulysses captaine. Ships 12.	All these did wise Ulysses leade, in counsell Peere to Jove.
	Twelve ships he brought, which in their course vermilion sternes did move.
The Ætolians their captaines and townes. Thoas captaine.	Thoas, Andræmon's wel-spoke sonne, did guide th'Ætolians well,
	Those that in Pleuron, Olenon and strong Pylene dwell, 560
	Great Chalcis that by sea-side stands, and stony Calydon—
	For now no more of Œneus' sonnes surviv'd; they all were gone;
	No more his royall selfe did live, no more his noble sonne,
	The golden Meleager; now their glasses all were run—
	All things were left to him in charge, the Ætolians' Chiefe 565 he was,
Ships 40. The Cretans, their townes and Captaines.	And fortie ships to Troyan warres the seas with him did passe.
	The royall souldier Idomen did leade the Cretans stout,
	The men of Knossus and the towne Gortyna, wall'd about,
	Of Lyctus' and Miletus' towres, of white Lycastus' state,
	Of Phæstus and of Rhytius, the cities fortunate, 570
Idomeneus. A hundred cities in Crete.	And all the rest inhabiting the hundred townes of Crete,
	Whom warre-like Idomen did leade, copartner in the fleete
Ships 80.	With kil-man Merion. Eightie ships with them did Troy invade.
	Tlepolemus Heraclides, right strong and bigly made,
	Brought nine tall ships of warre from Rhodes, which hautie 575 Rhodians mand
	Who dwelt in three dissever'd parts of that most pleasant land;
	Which Lindus and Ialysus were, and bright Camirus, cald.

Tlepolemus
Commander of the
Rhodians.
Ships 9.
Townes.

Tlepolemus commanded these, in battell unappald,
Whom faire Astyoche brought forth, by force of Hercules
Led out of Ephyr with his hand, from river Sellees,   580
When many townes of princely youths he leveld with the
        ground.
Tlepolem (in his father's house, for building much renownd,
Brought up to head-strong state of youth) his mother's brother
        slue,
The flowre of armes, Licymnius, that somewhat aged grew,
Then straight he gathred him a fleete, assembling bands of men,   585
And fled by sea to shun the threats that were denounced then
By other sonnes and nephewes of th'Alciden fortitude.
He in his exile came to Rhodes, driven in with tempests rude.
The Rhodians were distinct in tribes, and great with Jove
        did stand,
The king of men and Gods, who gave much treasure to   590
        their land.

The Symæans.
Nireus their Chiefe,
fairest of all the
Greekes but Achilles.
Ships 3.

Nireus, out of Syma's haven three wel-built barkes did bring—
Nireus, faire Aglaia's sonne and Charopus' the king.
Nireus was the fairest man that to faire Ilion came
Of all the Greekes, save Peleus' sonne, who past for generall
        frame,
But weake this was, not fit for warre, and therefore few   595
        did guide.

The Calydneians and
other Ilanders. Their
Chiefe Phidippus and
Antiphus.

Ships 30.
The Pelasgians,
Thessalians,
Myrmydons.

Who did in Casus, Nisyrus and Crapathus abide,
In Co, Eurypylus his towne, and in Calydna's soyles,
Phidippus and bold Antiphus did guide to Troyan toyles,
The sonnes of crowned Thessalus, deriv'd from Hercules,
Who went with thirtie hollow ships well ordred to the seas.   600
    Now will I sing the sackfull troopes Pelasgian Argos held,
That in deepe Alus, Alope and soft Trachina dweld,
In Phthia and in Hellade, where live the lovely dames,
The Myrmidons, Hellenians and Achives robd of Fames,

Achilles their
Captaine.
Ships 50.

All which the great Æacides in fiftie ships did leade.   605
But these forgat warre's horride voice because they lackt their
        head
That would have brought them bravely foorth; but now at fleete
        did lie
That wind-like user of his feet, faire Thetis' progenie,
Wroth for bright-cheekt Briseis' losse, whom from Lyrnessus'
        spoiles
(His owne exploit) he brought away as trophee of his toiles   610
When that towne was depopulate. He sunke the Theban towres,
Myneta and Epistrophus; he sent to Pluto's bowres

[63]

Who came of great Euenus' race, great Selepiades.
Yet now he idely lives enrag'd, but soone must leave his ease.

Phylacei and their townes.

Of those that dwelt in Phylace and flowrie Pyrason,   615
The wood of Ceres, and the soyle that sheepe are fed upon,
Iton and Antron, built by sea, and Pteleus full of grasse,

Protesilaus captaine.

Protesilaus, while he liv'd, the worthie captaine was,
Whom now the sable earth detaines. His teare-torne-faced spouse
He wofull left in Phylace, and his halfe-finisht house.   620
A fatall Dardane first his life of all the Greekes bereft
As he was leaping from his ship; yet were his men unleft
Without a Chiefe, for though they wisht to have no other man
But good Protesilay their guide, Podarces yet began
To governe them, Iphiclus' sonne, the sonne of Phylacus,   625
Most rich in sheepe, and brother to short-liv'd Protesilaus—
Of yonger birth, lesse, and lesse strong, yet serv'd he to direct
The companies, that still did more their ancient Duke affect.

Ships 40.

Twise twentie jettie sailes with him the swelling streame
            did take.

The Phereians and their towns.

But those that did in Pheres dwell, at the Bœbeian lake,   630
In Bœbe and in Glaphyra, Iolcus builded faire,

Eumelus captaine. Ships 18.

In thrise six ships to Pergamus did through the seas repaire
With old Admetus' tender sonne, Eumelus, whom he bred
Of Alcest, Pelias' fairest child of all his femall seed.

The Methonians and their borderers. Their chiefe Philoctetes left maimed at Lemnos.

The souldiers that before the siege Methone's vales did hold,   635
Thaumacie, flowrie Melibœ and Olizon the cold,
Duke Philoctetes governed, in darts of finest sleight.
Seven vessels in his charge convaid their honorable freight,
By fiftie rowers in a barke, most expert in the bow.
But he in sacred Lemnos lay, brought miserably low   640

Medon, Oileus' base sonne, captaine in Philoctetes' place.

By torment of an ulcer growne with Hydra's poyson'd bloud,
Whose sting was such Greece left him there, in most impatient
            moode.
Yet thought they on him at his ship and chusde to leade his men
Medon, Oileus' bastard sonne, brought forth to him by Rhen.

The Triccians, Ithomeneians and Œchalians, whose captaines were Podalirius and Machaon. Ships 30.

From Tricce, bleake Ithomen's cliffes and hapless Œchaly,   645
Eurytus' citie, rul'd by him in wilfull tyranny,
In charge of Æsculapius' sonnes, physition highly praisd,
Machaon, Podalirius, were thirtie vessels raisd.

The Ormenians, with their borderers.

Who neare Hyperia's fountaine dwelt and in Ormenius,
The snowy tops of Titanus and in Asterius,   650

Their captaine Eurypylus. Ships 40.

Euæmon's sonne Eurypylus did leade into the field,
Whose townes did fortie blacke-saild ships to that encounter
            yeeld.

Argissæans with their borderers.

Who Gyrton and Argissa held, Orthen and Elon's seate,
And chalkie Oloossone, were led by Polypœte,
The issue of Perithous, the sonne of Jupiter.   655

Meneptolemus their chiefe and Leonteus. Ships 40.

Him the Athenian Theseus' friend Hippodamy did beare
When he the bristled savages did give Ramnusia
And drave them out of Pelius, as farre as Æthica.
He came not single, but with him Leonteus, Coron's sonne,
An arme of Mars, and Coron's life Cæneus' seed begunne.   660

The Cyphians, Enians, Peræbians. Their chiefe Guneus. Ships 22.

Twise twentie ships attended these. Guneus next did bring
From Cyphus twentie saile and two, the Enians following
And fierce Peræbi that about Dodona's frozen mold
Did plant their houses, and the men that did the medowes hold
Which Titaresius deckes with flowers and his sweet current   665
     leades
Into the bright Peneius, that hath the silver heads,
Yet with his admirable streame doth not his waves commixe
But glides aloft on it like oyle, for tis the floud of Styx,
By which th'immortall Gods do sweare. Tenthredon's honor'd
     birth,

The Magnets. Prothous their chiefe. Ships 40.

Prothous, led the Magnets forth, who neare the shadie earth   670
Of Pelius and Peneion dwelt. Fortie revengefull saile
Did follow him. These were the Dukes and Princes of availe
That came from Greece. But now the man that overshin'd
     them all,
Sing Muse, and their most famous Steeds to my recitall call
That both th'Atrides followed. Faire Pheretiades   675

Eumelius had the best mares of the armie.

The bravest mares did bring by much. Eumelius manag'd these.
Swift of their feete as birds of wings, both of one haire did shine,
Both of an age, both of a height, as measur'd by a line,
Whom silver-bow'd Apollo bred in the Pierean meade,
Both slicke and daintie, yet were both in warre of wondrous   680
     dread.

Ajax Telamonius the strongest Greeke next Achilles. Achilles the best horse.

Great Ajax Telamon for strength past all the Peeres of warre
While vext Achilles was away, but he surpast him farre.
The horse that bore that faultlesse man were likewise past
     compare.
Yet lay he at the crookt-stern'd ships, and furie was his fare
For Atreus' sonne's ungracious deed. His men yet pleasd their   685
     hearts
With throwing of the holed stone, with hurling of their darts
And shooting fairely on the shore. Their horse at chariots fed
On greatest parsly and on sedge that in the fens is bred.
His Princes' tents their chariots held, that richly coverd were.

His Princes, amorous of their Chiefe, walkt storming here   690
    and there
About the host and scorn'd to fight: their breaths as they did
    passe
Before them flew as if a fire fed on the trembling grasse.
Earth under-gron'd their high-raisd feet, as when offended Jove,
In Arime, Typhoeus with ratling thunder drove
Beneath the earth. In Arime men say the grave is still   695
Where thunder tomb'd Typhoeus, and is a monstrous hill.
And as that thunder made earth grone, so gron'd it as they past,
They trode with such hard-set-downe steps, and so exceeding
    fast.

Iris to the Troyans,   To Troy the rainbow-girded dame right heavie newes relates
from Jove.   From Jove (as all to Councell drew in Priam's Pallace gates),   700
Resembling Priam's sonne in voice, Polites swift of feet—
In trust whereof (as Sentinell to see when from the fleet
The Grecians sallied) he was set upon the loftie brow
Of aged Æsyetes' tombe; and this did Iris show:

Iris to Priam.   'O Priam, thou art alwaies pleasd with indiscreet advise,   705
And fram'st thy life to times of peace, when such a warre
    doth rise
As threats inevitable spoyle. I never did behold
Such and so mightie troupes of men, who trample on the mold
In number like Autumnus' leaves, or like the marine sand,
All ready round about the walles to use a ruining hand.   710
Hector, I therefore charge thee most this charge to undertake.
A multitude remaine in Troy will fight for Priam's sake
Of other lands and languages. Let everie leader then
Bring forth, well arm'd into the field, his severall bands of men.'
    Strong Hector knew a deitie gave charge to this assay.   715
Dismist the Councell straight, like waves clusters to armes
    do sway.
The ports are all wide open set. Out rusht the troopes in
    swarmes,
Both horse and foote. The citie rung with suddaine-cryed
    alarmes.

Batieiæ tumulus.   A Columne stands without the towne that high his head
    doth raise,
A little distant in a plaine trod downe with divers waies,   720
Which men do Batieia call but the immortals name
Myrine's famous sepulcher, the wondrous active dame.
Here were th'Auxiliarie bands that came in Troy's defence,
Distinguisht under severall guides of speciall excellence.

[66]

Hector Generall of
the Troyans.
The catalogue of
other captaines.

Dardans, and Æneas
their captaine.

The Duke of all the Troyan power great helme-deckt   725
    Hector was,
Which stood of many mightie men well-skild in darts of brasse.
Æneas of commixed seed (a goddesse with a man—
Anchises with the Queene of love) the troopes Dardanian
Led to the field. His lovely Sire in Ida's lower shade
Begat him of sweet Cyprides. He solely was not made   730
Chiefe leader of the Dardan powers: Antenor's valiant sonnes,

Archelochus.
Acamas.

Archelochus and Acamas, were joyn'd companions.
    Who in Zelia dwelt beneath the sacred foote of Ide,
That drinke of blacke Æsepus' streame, and wealth made full
    of pride,

The Aphnii.
Pandarus their leader.
Adrestians.

Their Chiefe Adrestus,
and Amphius.

The Aphnii, Lycaon's sonne, whom Phœbus gave his bow,   735
Prince Pandarus did leade to field. Who Adrestinus owe
(Apæsus' citie, Pityæ and mount Tereies)
Adrestus and stout Amphius led, who did their Sire displease—
Merops Percotius, that exceld all Troy in heavenly skill
Of futures-searching prophesie—for much against his will   740
His sonnes were agents in those armes: whom since they disobeyd
The Fates, in letting slip their threds, their hastie valures staid.

Percosians, Sestians,
Abidens, Arisbeians,
led by Asius.

    Who in Percotes, Practius, Arisbe did abide,
Who Sestus and Abydus bred, Hyrtacides did guide—
Prince Asius Hyrtacides that through great Selees' force   745
Brought from Arisbe to that fight the great and fierie horse.

The Pelasgians.
Their chiefe
Hippothous and
Pylæus.

    Pylæus and Hippothous the stout Pelasgians led.
Of them Larisa's fruitfull soyle before had nourished.
These were Pelasgian Lethus' sonnes, sonne of Teutamidas.

The Thracians.
Their chief Pirous and
Acamas.
Euphemus Capt. of the
Ciconians.
Pyræchmes
Commander of the
Pæons.

    The Thracian guides were Pirous and valiant Acamas   750
Of all that the impetuous flood of Hellespont enclosd,
Euphemus the Ciconian troopes in his command disposd,
Who from Trœzenius Ceades right nobly did descend.
    Pyræchmes did the Pæons rule that crooked bowes do bend;
From Axius out of Amydon he had them in command—   755
From Axius whose most beautious streame still overflowes the
    land.

Pylæmen captain of
the Paphlagonians.

    Pylæmen with the well-arm'd heart the Paphlagonians led,
From Enes, where the race of mules fit for the plough is bred.
The men that broad Cytorus' bounds and Sesamus enfold,
About Parthenius' loftie floud, in houses much extold,   760
From Cromna and Ægialus, the men that armes did beare,
And Erythinus situate high, Pylæmen's soldiers were.

Halizonians, their
captaine Epistrophus
and Dius.

    Epistrophus and Dius did the Halizonians guide,
Far-fetcht from Alybe, where first the silver mines were tride.

The Mysians.
Ennomus and Chromis.

Chromis and Augur Ennomus the Mysians did command,   765
Who could not with his auguries the strength of death withstand,
But suffred it beneath the stroke of great Æacides
In Xanthus, where he made more soules dive to the Stygian seas.

The Phrygians.
Their Chiefes Phorcys
and Ascanius.

Phorcys and faire Ascanius the Phrygians brought to warre,
Well-train'd for battell, and were come out of Ascania farre.   770
With Mesthles and with Antiphus, Talæmen's sonnes, did fight

The Mæonians.
Antiphus and Mesthles
captaines.

The men of Mæon whom the fenne Gygæa brought to light
And those Mæonians that beneath the mountaine Tmolus sprong.

The Caribæ and
Milesians led by
Amphimachus and
Nastes.

The rude unletterd Caribæ that barbarous were of tongue
Did under Nastes' colours march, and young Amphimachus',   775
Nomion's famous sonnes, to whom the mountaine Phthirorus
That with the famous wood is crown'd, Miletus, Mycales
That hath so many loftie markes for men that love the seas,
The crooked-armd Meander, bow'd with his so snakie flood,
Resign'd for conduct the choice youth of all their martiall   780
    brood.
The foole Amphimachus to field brought gold to be his wracke,
Proude-girle-like that doth ever beare her dowre upon her
    backe—
Which wise Achilles markt, slue him and tooke his gold in strife

The Lycians, whose
Commanders were
Sarpedon and Glaucus.

At Xanthus' floud. So little death did feare his golden life.
Sarpedon led the Lycians, and Glaucus unreprov'd,   785
From Lycia and the gulfie flood of Xanthus farre remov'd.

COMMENTARIUS

[72] Ἠΰτε ἔθνεα, &c. Sicut examina prodeunt apum frequentium, &c. *In this Simile, Virgil (using the like in imitation) is preferd to Homer—with what reason I pray you see. Their ends are different, Homer intending to expresse the infinite multitude of souldiers everie where dispersing, Virgil, the diligence of builders. Virgil's* 5 *Simile is this:* I Æneid:

Qualis apes æstate nova per florea rura
Exercet sub sole labor; cum gentis adultos
Educunt fœtus; aut cum liquentia mella
Stipant; et dulci distendunt Nectare cellas; 10
Aut onera accipiunt venientum; aut, agmine facto,
Ignavum fucos pecus à præsepibus arcent;
Fervet opus, redolentque thymo fragrantia mella.

Now, compare this with Homer's but in my translation, and judge if to both their ends there be any such betternesse in Virgil's, but that 15 *the reverence of the scholler due to the maister (even in these his maligners) might well have contain their lame censures of the Poeticall furie from these unmannerlie and hatefull comparisons. Especially since Virgil hath nothing of his owne, but onely elocution— his invention, matter and forme being all Homer's, which laid by a* 20 *man, that which he addeth is onelie the worke of a woman, to netifie and polish. Nor do I, alas! but the formost ranke of the most ancient and best learned that ever were, come to the field for Homer, hiding all other poets under his ensigne. Hate not me, then, but them, to whom, before my booke, I referre you. But much the rather I insist* 25 *on the former Simile, for the word* ἰλαδὸν, *catervatim or confertim, which is noted by Spondanus to containe all the* ἀπόδοσις, *reddition or application of the comparison, and is nothing so. For though it be all the reddition Homer expresseth, yet he intends two speciall parts in the application more, which he leaves to his judicial reader's* 30 *understanding, as he doth in all his other Similes, since a man may pervially (or as he passeth) discerne all that is to be understood. And here, besides the throngs of souldiers exprest in the swarmes of Bees, he intimates the infinite number in those throngs or companies issuing from fleete so ceaslesly that there appeared almost no end of* 35 *their issue; and, thirdly, the everie where dispersing themselves. But Spondanus would excuse Homer for expressing no more of his*

[69]

application, with affirming it impossible that the thing compared and
the comparison should answer in all parts, and therefore alledges the
vulgar understanding of a Simile, which is as grosse as it is vulgar, 40
that a similitude must uno pede semper claudicare—*his reason for it*
as absurd as the rest, which is this: si ea inter se omnino responderent,
falleret illud axioma, nullum simile est idem, *as though the generall*
application of the compared and the comparison would make them
anything more the same or all one, more than the swarmes of Bees 45
and the throng of souldiers are all one or the same, for answering
most aptly. But that a Simile must needs halt of one foote still showeth
how lame vulgar tradition is, especially in her censure of Poesie.
For who at first sight will not conceive it absurd to make a Simile,
which serves to the illustration and ornament of a Poeme, lame of a 50
foote and idle? The incredible violence suffered by Homer in all
the rest of his most inimitable Similes, being exprest in his place, will
abundantly prove the stupiditie of this tradition—and how injuriously
short his interpreters must needs come of him in his streight and
deepe places, when in his open and faire passages they halt and 55
hang backe so.

[275] Τὸν μὲν ἀρίζηλον θῆκεν Θεός, &c. hunc quidem clarum (*or*
illustrem) fecit Deus, *as it is by all translated—wherein I note the*
strange abuse (as I apprehend it) of the word ἀρίζηλος, *beginning*
here and continuing wheresoever it is found in these Iliads. It is 60
by the transition of ζ *into* δ *in derivation, according to the Doricke,*
for which cause our Interpreters will needs have Homer intend
ἀρίδηλος, *which is* clarus *or* illustris, *when he himselfe saith* ἀρίζηλος,
which is a compound of ἀρι, *which is* valde, *and* ζῆλος, *and*
signifies quem valde æmulamur, *or* valde æmulandus, *according* 65
to Scapula. But because ζῆλος *is most authentically expounded*
impetus mentis ad cultum divinum, *that exposition I follow in this*
place, and expound Τὸν μὲν ἀρίζηλον θῆκεν Θεός hunc quidem
magnum impulsum ad cultum divinum fecit Deus, *because he turned*
so sodainly and miraculously the Dragon to a stone. To make it 70
ἀρίδηλον *and say* clarum *or* illustrem fecit Deus qui ostendit *or*
ostenderat (*which followes in the verse*) *and saith thus much in our*
tongue: 'God that shewed this, made it cleare,' is verie little more than
'God that shewed this, shewed it.' One way it observes the word
(betwixt which and the other you see what great difference) and is 75
faire, full, grave; the other alters the originall, and is uglie, emptie,
idle.

[355] Αὐτόματος δέ οἱ ἦλθε βοὴν ἀγαθὸς Μενέλαος, &c. Spontaneus
autem ei venit voce bonus Menelaus—*and some say* bello strenuus
Menelaus—*which is farre estranged from the mind of our Homer,* 80

βοὴ *signifying* vociferatio *or* clamor, *though some will have it* pugna, ex consequenti *because fights are often made with clamor. But in* bello strenuus (*unlesse it be ironically taken*) *is here straind beyond sufferance and is to be expounded* vociferatione bonus Menelaus, *which agreeth with that part of his character in the next booke,*   85 *that telleth his maner of utterance or voice—which is* μαλὰ λιγέως, valde stridulè *or* arguto cum stridore, λιγέως *being commonly and most properlie taken in the worse part, and signifieth shrillie, or noisefullie, squeaking, howsoever in the vulgar conversion it is in that place most grosselie abused. To the consideration whereof,*   90 *being of much importance, I referre you in his place, and in the meane time shew you that in this first and next verse Homer (speaking scoptically) breakes open the fountaine of his ridiculous humor following, never by anie interpreter understood, or touched at, being yet the most ingenious conceited person that any man can shew in*   95 *any heroicall Poeme, or in any Comicke Poet. And that you may something perceive him, before you reade him too in his severall places, I will, as I can, in haste give you him here together as Homer at all parts presents him, viz. simple, wel-meaning, standing still affectedlie on telling truth; small, and shrill-voiced (not sweet or eloquent,*   100 *as some most against the haire would have him); short-spoken after his countrie the Laconicall manner, yet speaking thicke and fast; industrious in the field and willing to be emploied, and (being* mollis Bellator *himselfe) set still to call to everie hard service the hardiest; even by the wit of Ajax plaid upon, about whom he*   105 *would still be diligent; and what he wanted of the martiall furie and facultie himselfe that he would be bold to supplie out of Ajax— Ajax and he to any for blowes, Antilochus and he for wit (Antilochus, old Nestor's sonne, a most ingenious, valiant and excellentlie formed person); sometimes valiant or daring (as what coward is not?),*   110 *sometimes falling upon sentence and good matter in his speeches (as what meanest capacitie doth not?). Nor useth our most inimitable Imitator of nature this crosse and deformed mixture of his parts more to colour and avoid too broad a taxation of so eminent a person than to follow the true life of nature, being often or alwaies exprest*   115 *so disparent in her creatures. And therefore the decorum that some poore Criticks have stood upon, to make fooles alwaies foolish, cowards at all times cowardly, &c. is farre from the variant order of nature, whose principles being contrary, her productions must needes containe the like opposition.*   120

But now to the first— αὐτόματος δέ οἱ ἦλθε, *&c.* Spontaneus autem ei venit, &c.—*about which a passing great peece of worke is pickt out by our greatest Philosophers, touching the unbidden coming of Menelaus to supper or Counsell, which some commend, others*

[71]

condemne in him; but the reason why he staid not the invitement,   125
rendered immediatly by Homer, none of them will understand—viz.
Ἠίδεε γὰϱ ϰατὰ θυμὸν, *&c.* sciebat enim in animo quantum frater
laborabat, *of which verse his interpreters crie out for the expunction,*
onely because it was never entered in their apprehension, which I
more than admire (for the easinesse of it) so freely offering it selfe   130.
to their entertainment, and yet using the hoofe of Pegasus, onely
with a touch breaking open (as abovesaid) the fountaine of his humor.
For thus I expound it (laying all againe together, to make it plaine
enough for you): Agamemnon, inviting all the chiefe Commanders
to supper, left out his brother, but he, seeing how much his brother   135
was troubled about the dreame, and busied, would not stand upon
invitement but came of himselfe. And this being spoken Scopticè,
or by way of irrision, argueth what manner of man he made of him.
Ineptus enim (*as it is affirmed in Plutarch,* I Symposium *and second*
question) fuit Menelaus, et locum dedit proverbio, qui ad consilium   140
dandum accessisset non vocatus. *And to this place he had reference,*
because a Councell of warre was to be held at this supper. And here,
I say, Homer opened the veine of his simplicitie, not so much
in his going unbidden to supper and Counsell as in the
reason for it ironically rendered—that he knew his   145
brother was busie, &c. And yet that addition,
without which the very sence of our Poet
is not safe, our interpreters would have
raced.

The End of the Second Booke

THE THIRD BOOKE
of
HOMER'S ILIADS

THE ARGUMENT

Paris (betwixt the Hoasts) to single fight
(Of all the Greekes) dares the most hardie knight.
King Menelaus doth accept his brave,
Conditioning that he againe should have
Faire Helena, with all she brought to Troy 5
If he subdu'd, else Paris should enjoy
Her and her wealth in peace. Conquest doth grant
Her deare wreath to the Grecian combattant,
But Venus to her champion's life doth yeeld
Safe rescue and conveyes him from the field 10
Into his chamber, and for Helen sends,
Whom much her lover's foule disgrace offends.
Yet Venus for him still makes good her charmes,
And ends the second combat in his armes.

Another Argument

Gamma the single fight doth sing
Twixt Paris and the Spartan king.

When every least Commander's will best souldiers had obaide
And both the hosts were rang'd for fight, the Troyans would have
   fraid
The Greeks with noises, crying out in coming rudely on;

The Troyans   At all parts like the Cranes that fill with harsh confusion
compared to Cranes.   Of brutish clanges all the aire and in ridiculous warre 5
(Eschuing the unsufferd stormes shot from the winter's starre)
Visite the Ocean and conferre the Pygmei souldiers' death.

The silent assalt of   The Greeks charg'd silent and like men bestow'd their thriftie
the Greekes.   breath
In strength of far-resounding blowes, still entertaining care

Of either's rescue when their strength did their engagements   10
    dare.
And as upon a hil's steepe tops the South wind powres a cloud
To shepheards thanklesse, but by theeves, that love the night,
    allowd,
A darknesse letting downe that blinds a stone's cast off men's
    eyes,
Such darknesse from the Greeks' swift feet (made all of dust)
    did rise.
But ere sterne conflict mixt both strengths, faire Paris stept   15
    before
The Troyan host. Athwart his backe a Panther's hide he wore,
A crooked bow and sword, and shooke two brazen-headed darts,
With which well-arm'd, his tongue provok't the best of Grecian
    hearts
To stand with him in single fight. Whom when the man,
    wrong'd most
Of all the Greekes, so gloriously saw stalke before the host,   20
As when a Lion is rejoyc't (with hunger halfe forlorne)
That finds some sweet prey (as a Hart, whose grace lies
    in his horne,
Or Sylvane Goate) which he devours, though never so pursu'd
With dogs and men, so Sparta's king exulted when he view'd
The faire-fac'd Paris so exposde to his so thirsted wreake—   25
Whereof his good cause made him sure. The Grecian front did
    breake
And forth he rusht, at all parts arm'd, leapt from his chariot
And royally prepar'd for charge. Which seene, cold terror shot

Paris flieth at sight   The heart of Paris, who retir'd as headlong from the king
of Menelaus.   As in him he had shund his death. And as a hilly spring   30

Simile.   Presents a serpent to a man full underneath his feete,
Her blew necke (swolne with poison) raisd and her sting out,
    to greet
His heedlesse entrie, sodainely his walke he altereth,
Starts backe amaz'd, is shooke with feare and lookes as pale
    as death;
So Menelaus Paris scar'd, so that divine-fac't foe   35
Shrunke in his beauties. Which beheld by Hector, he let go

Hector to Paris.   This bitter checke at him. 'Accurst, made but in beautie's
    skorne!
Impostor! woman's man! O heaven, that thou hadst neare
    bene borne
Or (being so manlesse) never liv'd to beare man's noblest state,
The nuptiall honor! Which I wish, because it were a fate   40

Much better for thee than this shame. This spectacle doth make
A man a monster. Harke how lowd the Greekes laugh, who
    did take
Thy faire forme for a continent of parts as faire. A rape
Thou mad'st of Nature, like their Queene. No soule, an
    emptie shape
Takes up thy being, yet how spight to everie shade of good   45
Fils it with ill! For as thou art, thou couldst collect a brood
Of others like thee and, farre hence, fetch ill enough to us—
Even to thy father: all these friends make those foes mocke
    them thus
In thee, for whose ridiculous sake so seriously they lay
All Greece and Fate upon their necks. O wretch! not dare   50
    to stay
Weake Menelaus? But twas well, for in him thou hadst tried
What strength lost beautie can infuse, and with the more griefe
    died
To feele thou robdst a worthier man, to wrong a souldier's right.
Your Harp's sweet touch, curld lockes, fine shape and gifts
    so exquisite
Given thee by Venus would have done your fine Dames little   55
    good
When bloud and dust had ruffled them, and had as little stood
Thy selfe in stead. But what thy care of all these in thee flies
We should inflict on thee our selves. Infectious cowardise
(In thee) hath terrified our host, for which thou well deserv'st
A coate of Tomb-stone, not of steele—in which for forme thou   60
    serv'st.'
        To this thus Paris spake (for forme, that might inhabit heaven):

Paris to Hector.

'Hector! Because thy sharpe reproofe is out of justice given,
I take it well; but though thy heart (inur'd to these affrights)
Cuts through them as an axe through Oke, that, more usd, more
    excites
The workman's facultie whose art can make the edge go farre,   65
Yet I (lesse practisd than thy selfe in these extremes of warre)
May well be pardond though lesse bold. In these your worth
    exceeds,
In others, mine. Nor is my mind of lesse force to the deeds
Requir'd in warre, because my forme more flowes in gifts of
    peace.
Reproach not therefore the kind gifts of golden Cyprides.   70
All heav'n's gifts have their worthie price, as little to be scorn'd
As to be wonne with strength, wealth, state—with which to be
    adorn'd

Some men would change state, wealth or strength. But if your
    martiall heart
Wish me to make my challenge good, and hold it such a part
Of shame to give it over thus, cause all the rest to rest   75
And twixt both hosts let Sparta's king and me performe our best
For Helen and the wealth she brought, and he that overcomes,
Or proves superiour any way in all your equall doomes,
Let him enjoy her utmost wealth, keepe her or take her home—
The rest strike leagues of endlesse date and heartie friends   80
    become,
You dwelling safe in gleby Troy, the Greekes retire their force
T'Achaia, that breeds fairest Dames, and Argos, fairest horse.'
    He said, and his amendsfull words did Hector highly please,
Who rusht betwixt the fighting hoasts and made the Troyans
    cease
By holding up in midst his lance. The Grecians noted not   85
The signall he for parle usde, but at him fiercely shot,
Hurld stones, and still were levelling darts. At last the king of
    men,

Agamemnon restraines
the fight against
Hector.

Great Agamemnon, cried alowd: 'Argives! for shame, containe!
Youths of Achaia! shoot no more! The faire-helm'd Hector
    showes

Hector to the Greekes
and Troyans.

As he desir'd to treate with us.' This said, all ceast from blowes,   90
And Hector spake to both the hosts: 'Troyans! and hardie
    Greekes!
Heare now what he that stird these warres for their cessation
    seekes.
He bids us all, and you, disarme, that he alone may fight
With Menelaus for us all, for Helen and her right,
With all the dowre she brought to Troy; and he that wins   95
    the day,
Or is in all the art of armes superiour any way,
The Queene, and all her sorts of wealth, let him at will enjoy:
The rest strike truce, and let love seale firme leagues twixt
    Greece and Troy.'
    The Greeke host wondred at this Brave. Silence flew
    every where.

Menelaus to both
the armies.

At last spake Sparta's warlike king: 'Now also give me eare,   100
Whom griefe gives most cause of replie. I now have hope to free
The Greekes and Troyans of all ils they have sustaind for me
And Alexander, that was cause I stretcht my splene so farre.
Of both, then, which is nearest fate, let his death end the warre:
The rest immediatly retire and greet all homes in peace.   105
Go then (to blesse your champion, and give his powers successe)

Fetch for the Earth and for the Sunne (the Gods on whom
    ye call)
Two lambes, a blacke one and a white, a femall and a male,
And we another for our selves will fetch and kill to Jove.
To signe which rites bring Priam's force, because we   110
    well approve
His sonnes perfidious, envious (and out of practisd bane
To faith, when she beleeves in them) Jove's high truce
    may prophane.
All yong men's hearts are still unstaid, but in those
    wel-weigh'd deeds
An old man will consent to passe; things past and what succeeds
He lookes into, that he may know how best to make his way   115
Through both the fortunes of a fact, and will the worst obay.'
    This granted, a delightfull hope both Greekes and
      Troyans fed
Of long'd-for rest from those long toyles their tedious warre
    had bred.
Their horses then in ranke they set, drawne from their
    chariots round,
Descend themselves, tooke off their armes and plac't them   120
    on the ground
Neare one another—for the space twixt both the hosts was small.

Hector sendeth for   Hector two heralds sent to Troy that they from thence might call
Priam.   King Priam, and to bring the lambes to rate the truce
    they swore.
But Agamemnon to the fleete Talthybius sent before
To fetch their lambe, who nothing slackt the royall charge   125
    was given.

Iris to Helen.   Iris the raine-bow then came downe, Ambassadresse from
    heaven,
To white-arm'd Helen. She assum'd at every part the grace
Of Helen's last love's sister's shape, who had the highest place
In Helen's love, and had to name Laodice, most faire
Of all the daughters Priam had, and made the nuptiall paire   130
With Helicaon, royall sproute of old Antenor's seed.
She found Queene Helena at home, at worke about a weed
Wov'n for her selfe: it shin'd like fire, was rich and full of sise,
The worke of both sides being alike, in which she did comprise
The many labors warlike Troy and brasse-arm'd Greece endur'd 135
For her faire sake, by cruell Mars and his sterne friends procur'd.
Iris came in in joyfull haste, and said: 'O come with me,
Lov'd Nymph, and an admired sight of Greekes and Troyans see,
Who first on one another brought a warre so full of teares

[77]

(Even thirstie of contentious warre). Now everie man forbeares   140
And friendly by each other sits, each leaning on his shield,
Their long and shining lances pitcht fast by them in the field.
Paris and Sparta's king alone must take up all the strife
And he that conquers onely call faire Helena his wife.'
    Thus spake the thousand-colour'd Dame, and to her mind   145
      commends

Helen's desire to see her first husband and friends.

The joy to see her first espousd, her native tow'rs and friends,
Which stir'd a sweet desire in her, to serve the which she hi'd,
Shadow'd her graces with white veiles and (though she tooke
    a pride
To set her thoughts at gaze and see, in her cleare beautie's flood,
What choice of glorie swum to her yet tender womanhood)   150
Season'd with teares her joyes, to see more joyes the more offence
And that perfection could not flow from earthly excellence.
    Thus went she forth and tooke with her her women most
      of name,
Æthre, Pittheus' lovely birth, and Clymene, whom fame
Hath for her faire eyes memorisd. They reacht the Scæan towrs,   155
Where Priam sat to see the fight with all his Counsellours,
Panthous, Lampus, Clytius and stout Hicetaon,
Thimœtes, wise Antenor and profound Ucalegon—
All grave old men, and souldiers they had bene, but for age
Now left the warres; yet Counsellors they were exceeding sage.   160

Old men and their weake utterance most aptly compared to Grashoppers and their singing.

And as in well-growne woods, on trees, cold spinie Grashoppers
Sit chirping and send voices out that scarce can pierce our eares
For softnesse and their weake faint sounds; so (talking on
    the towre)
These Seniors of the people sate, who, when they saw the powre
Of beautie in the Queene ascend, even those cold-spirited   165
    Peeres,

Helen's beautie moves even the oldest.

Those wise and almost witherd men, found this heate in
    their yeares
That they were forc't (though whispering) to say: 'What man
    can blame
The Greekes and Troyans to endure, for so admir'd a Dame,
So many miseries, and so long? In her sweet countenance shine
Lookes like the Goddesses'. And yet (though never so divine)   170
Before we boast, unjustly still, of her enforced prise
And justly suffer for her sake, with all our progenies,
Labor and ruine, let her go: the profit of our land
Must passe the beautie.' Thus, though these could beare so fit
    a hand
On their affections, yet when all their gravest powers were usde   175

[78]

They could not chuse but welcome her, and rather they accusde
The gods than beautie. For thus spake the most fam'd
    King of Troy:

Priam cals Helen to
informe him of the
Greeke Princes.

'Come, loved daughter, sit by me, and take the worthy joy
Of thy first husband's sight, old friends' and Princes' neare
    allyed,
And name me some of these brave Greekes, so manly beautified.   180
Come: do not thinke I lay the warres, endur'd by us, on thee:
The gods have sent them, and the teares in which they swumme
    to me.
Sit then, and name this goodly Greeke, so tall and broadly spred,
Who than the rest that stand by him is higher by the head—
The bravest man I ever saw, and most majesticall;   185
His onely presence makes me thinke him king amongst them all.'

Helen to Priam.

    The fairest of her sexe replyed: 'Most reverend fath'r in law,
Most lov'd, most fear'd, would some ill death had seizd me
    when I saw
The first meane why I wrong'd you thus! That I had never lost
The sight of these my ancient friends, of him that lov'd   190
    me most,
Of my sole daughter, brothers both, with all those kindly mates
Of one soyle, one age, borne with me, though under different
    fates!
But these boones envious starres denie. The memorie of these
In sorrow pines those beauties now that then did too much
    please,
Nor satisfie they your demand, to which I thus replie—   195
That's Agamemnon, Atreus' sonne, the great in Emperie,
A king whom double royaltie doth crowne, being great
    and good;
And one that was my brother in law when I contain'd my blood
And was more worthie—if at all I might be said to be,
My Being being lost so soone in all that honour'd me!'   200

Priam's admiration of
Agamemnon.

    The good old King admir'd, and said: 'O Atreus'
        blessed sonne!
Borne under joyfull destinies, that hast the Empire wonne
Of such a world of Grecian youths as I discover here!
I once marcht into Phrygia, that many vines doth beare,
Where many Phrygians I beheld well-skild in use of horse,   205
That of the two men, like two Gods, were the commanded force—
Otreus and great Mygdonus, who in Sangarius' sands
Set downe their tents, with whom my selfe (for my
    assistant bands)
Was numbred as a man in chiefe. The cause of warre was then

Th'Amazon dames that in their facts affected to be men.   210
In all, there was a mightie powre, which yet did never rise
To equall these Achaian youths that have the sable eyes.'
  Then (seeing Ulysses next) he said: 'Lov'd daughter,
          what is he
That lower than great Atreus' sonne seemes by the head to me,
Yet in his shoulders and big breast presents a broader show?   215
His armor lies upon the earth: he up and downe doth go
To see his souldiers keepe their rankes and ready have
          their armes,
If in this truce they should be tried by any false alarmes.
Much like a well-growne Bel-weather or feltred Ram he shewes
That walkes before a wealthie flocke of faire white-fleeced   220
          Ewes.'
  High Jove and Leda's fairest seed to Priam thus replies:

Ulysses described.

'This is the old Laertes' sonne, Ulysses, cald the wise,
Who, though unfruitfull Ithaca was made his nursing seate,
Yet knowes he everie sort of sleight, and is in counsels great.'

*Antenor to Helen by
way of digression.*

  The wise Antenor answerd her: ''Tis true, renowmed dame,   225
For, some times past, wise Ithacus to Troy a Legate came
With Menelaus, for your cause. To whom I gave receit
As guests and welcom'd to my house with all the love I might.
I learn'd the wisdomes of their soules and humors of their blood.
For, when the Troyan Councell met and these together stood,   230
By height of his broad shoulders had Atrides eminence,
Yet, set, Ulysses did exceed and bred more reverence.
And when their counsels and their words they wove
          in one, the speech
Of Atreus' sonne was passing lowd, small, fast, yet did not reach
To much, being naturally borne Laconicall, nor would   235
His humor lie for any thing or was (like th'other) old.
But when the prudent Ithacus did to his counsels rise,
He stood a little still, and fixt upon the earth his eyes,
His scepter moving neither way, but held it formally,
Like one that vainely doth affect. Of wrathfull qualitie   240
And franticke (rashly judging him) you would have said he was,

*Ulysses' wisdome
admirably illustrated
by similitude.*

But when out of his ample breast he gave his great voice passe
And words that flew about our eares like drifts of winter's snow,
None thenceforth might contend with him, though nought
          admird for show.'
  The third man aged Priam markt was Ajax Telamon,   245
Of whom he askt: 'What Lord is that so large of limme and bone,
So raisd in height, that to his breast I see there reacheth none?'
  To him the Goddesse of her sexe, the large-veild Helen, said:

[80]

Ajax Telamon the Grecian bulwarke. Idomeneus king of Crete.

'That Lord is Ajax Telamon, a Bulwarke in their aide.
On th'other side stands Idomen, in Crete of most command,   250
And round about his royall sides his Cretane captaines stand.
Oft hath the warlike Spartan King given hospitable due
To him within our Lacene court, and all his retinue.
And now the other Achive Dukes I generally discerne,
All which I know, and all their names could make thee   255
    quickly learne.
Two Princes of the people yet I no where can behold,

Castor and Pollux, brothers to Helen.

Castor, the skilfull knight on horse, and Pollux uncontrold
For all stand-fights and force of hand—both at a burthen bred
My naturall brothers. Either here they have not followed
From lovely Sparta, or, arriv'd within the sea-borne fleet,   260
(In feare of infamie for me) in broad field shame to meet.'
    Nor so: for holy Tellus' wombe inclosd those worthy men,

The heralds prepare for the compact.

In Sparta, their beloved soyle. The voicefull heralds then
The firme agreement of the Gods through all the citie ring.
Two lambs and spirit-refreshing wine (the fruit of earth)   265
    they bring
Within a Goateskin bottle closd. Idæus also brought
A massie glittering boll and cups, that all of gold were wrought—

Idæus to Priamus.

Which bearing to the king, they cride: 'Sonne of Laomedon!
Rise, for the wel-rode Peeres of Troy and brasse-arm'd Greekes
    in one
Send to thee to descend to field, that they firme vowes   270
    may make.
For Paris and the Spartan king must fight for Helen's sake
With long-arm'd lances, and the man that proves victorious,
The woman and the wealth she brought shall follow to his
    house;
The rest knit friendship and firme leagues; we safe in Troy
    shall dwell,
In Argos and Achaia they, that do in dames excell.'   275
    He said, and Priam's aged joints with chilled feare did shake.
Yet instantly he bad his men his chariot readie make.
Which soone they did, and he ascends. He takes the reines,
    and guide
Antenor cals, who instantly mounts to his royall side.
And through the Scæan ports to field the swift-foote horse   280
    they drive.
And when at them of Troy and Greece the aged Lords arrive,
From horse, on Troy's well-feeding soyle, twixt both the hosts
    they go,
When straight up rose the king of men; up rose Ulysses too.

The heralds in their richest cotes repeate (as was the guise)
The true vowes of the Gods, term'd theirs since made before   285
   their eyes.
Then in a cup of gold they mixe the wine that each side brings,
And next powre water on the hands of both the kings of kings.
Which done, Atrides drew his knife, that evermore he put
Within the large sheath of his sword, with which away he cut
The wooll from both fronts of the lambs, which (as a rite   290
   in use
Of execration to their heads that brake the plighted truce)
The heralds of both hosts did give the Peeres of both. And then,
With hands and voice advanc't to heaven, thus prayd the
      king of men:

*Agamemnon
himselfe prayes.*

   'O Jove, that Ida dost protect, and hast the titles wonne,
Most glorious, most invincible! And thou all-seeing Sunne,   295
All-hearing, all recomforting! Floods! Earth! And powers
   beneath,
That all the perjuries of men chastise even after death!
Be witnesses and see perform'd the heartie vowes we make!
If Alexander shall the life of Menelaus take,
He shall from henceforth Helena, with all her wealth, retaine,   300
And we will to our houshold Gods hoyse saile and home againe.
If by my honourd brother's hand be Alexander slaine,
The Troyans then shall his forc't Queene, with all her wealth,
   restore
And pay convenient fine to us and ours for evermore.
If Priam and his sonnes denie to pay this, thus agreed,   305
When Alexander shall be slaine, for that perfidious deed,
And for the fine, will I fight here till dearely they repay
By death and ruine the amends that falshood keepes away.'

*The contract is
confirmed.*

   This said, the throtes of both the lambs cut with his royall
      knife,
He laid them panting on the earth till (quite depriv'd of life)   310
The steele had robd them of their strength. Then golden cups
   they cround
With wine out of a cisterne drawne—which powr'd upon the
   ground,
They fell upon their humble knees to all the deities
And thus pray'd one of both the hosts, that might do sacrifice:

*Now one praies
whose office was
to do sacrifice.*

   'O Jupiter, most high, most great, and all the deathlesse   315
   powers!
Who first shall dare to violate the late sworne oaths of ours,
So let the bloods and braines of them, and all they shall produce,
Flow on the staind face of the earth—as now, this sacred juice.

And let their wives with bastardise brand all their future race.'
Thus praid they; but with wisht effects their prayrs Jove   320
    did not grace.

When Priam said: 'Lords of both hoasts! I can no longer stay
To see my lov'd sonne trie his life, and so must take my way
To winde-exposed Ilion. Jove yet, and heaven's high States,
Know onely which of these must now pay tribute to the Fates.'

    Thus, putting in his coach the lambs, he mounts and reines   325
    his horse,
Antenor to him; and to Troy both take their speedie course.

    Then Hector, Priam's Martiall sonne, stept forth and
    met the ground
(With wise Ulysses) where the blowes of combat must resound.
Which done, into a helme they put two lots, to let them know
Which of the combattants should first his brasse-pil'd javeline   330
    throw—
When all the people standing by, with hands held up to heaven,
Pray'd Jove the conquest might not be by force or fortune given,
But that the man who was in right the author of most wrong
Might feele his justice and no more these tedious warres prolong,
But, sinking to the house of death, leave them (as long before)   335
Linkt fast in leagues of amitie, that might dissolve no more.

    Then Hector shooke the helme that held the equall doomes
    of chance,
Look't backe, and drew; and Paris first had lot to hurle his lance.
    The souldiers all sat downe enrank't, each by his armes and
    horse,
That then lay downe and cool'd their hoofes. And now   340
    th'allotted course

Bids faire-haird Helen's husband arme, who first makes fast
    his greaves
With silver buckles to his legs; then on his breast receives
The curets that Lycaon wore (his brother), but made fit
For his faire bodie; next, his sword he tooke and fastned it
(All damaskt) underneath his arme; his shield then, grave and   345
    great
His shoulders wore, and on his head his glorious helme he set,
Topt with a plume of horse's haire, that horribly did dance
And seem'd to threaten as he mov'd. At last he takes his lance,
Exceeding big and full of weight, which he with ease could use.

    In like sort, Sparta's warlike king himselfe with armes   350
    indues.
Thus arm'd at either armie both, they both stood bravely in,
Possessing both hosts with amaze—they came so chin to chin

And with such horrible aspects each other did salute.
  A faire large field was made for them, where wraths (for
    hugenesse) mute

The combat.

And mutuall, made them mutually at either shake their darts   355
Before they threw. Then Paris first with his long javeline parts.
It smote Atrides' orbie Targe but ranne not through the brasse,
For in it (arming well the shield) the head reflected was.
  Then did the second combattant applie him to his speare,
Which ere he threw, he thus besought almightie Jupiter: 360

*Menelaus prayeth to
Jove.*

  'O Jove! vouchsafe me now revenge, and that my enemie
(For doing wrong so undeserv'd) may pay deservedly
The paines he forfeited, and let these hands inflict those paines
By conquering, ay, by conquering dead, him on whom life
    complaines—
That any now, or any one of all the brood of men   365
To live hereafter, may with feare from all offence abstaine
(Much more from all such foule offence) to him that was his
    host
And entertain'd him as the man whom he affected most.'
  This said, he shooke and threw his lance, which strooke
    through Paris' shield
And with the strength he gave to it, it made the curets yeeld,   370
His coate of Maile, his breast and all, and drave his intrailes in,
In that low region where the guts in three small parts begin.
Yet he, in bowing of his breast, prevented sable death.
This taint he follow'd with his sword, drawne from a silver
    sheath,
Which (lifting high) he strooke his helme full where his plume   375
    did stand,

*Menelaus' sword
breaketh.*
Menelaus at Jupiter.

On which it peece-meale brake and fell from his unhappie hand.
At which he sighing stood and star'd upon the ample skie
And said: 'O Jove, there is no God given more illiberally
To those that serve thee than thy selfe! Why have I pray'd
    in vaine?
I hop't my hand should have reveng'd the wrongs I still   380
    sustaine
On him that did them, and still dares their foule defence pursue:
And now my lance hath mist his end, my sword in shivers flew,
And he scapes all.' With this, againe he rusht upon his guest
And caught him by the horse-haire plume that dangl'd on his
    crest,
With thought to drag him to the Greekes—which he had surely   385
    done
And so (besides the victorie) had wondrous glorie wonne

[84]

(Because the needle-pointed lace with which his helme was tied
Beneath his chin, and so about his daintie throte implyed,
Had strangl'd him), but that in time the Cyprian seed of Jove
Did breake the string with which was lin'd that which the   390
     needle wove
And was the tough thong of a Steere—and so the victor's palme
Was (for so full a man at armes) onely an emptie helme.
That then he swong about his head and cast among his friends,
Who scrambled and took't up with shouts. Againe then
       he intends

To force the life blood of his foe and ranne on him amaine   395
With shaken javeline, when the Queene that lovers loves againe

Venus' rapture of   Attended, and now ravisht him from that encounter quite
Paris from Menelaus. With ease, and wondrous sodainly—for she (a Goddesse) might.
This place Virgil   She hid him in a cloud of gold and never made him knowne
imitateth.   Till in his chamber (fresh and sweet) she gently set him downe,   400
And went for Helen, whom she found in Scæa's utmost height,
To which whole swarmes of citie Dames had climb'd to see the
     sight.

Venus like Græa   To give her errand good successe, she tooke on her the shape
to Helen.   Of beldam Græa who was brought by Helen in her rape
From Lacedæmon and had trust in all her secrets still,   405
Being old, and had (of all her maids) the maine bent of her will,
And spun for her the finest wooll. Like her, love's Empresse
     came,
Puld Helen by the heavenly veile, and softly said: 'Madame,
My Lord cals for you. You must needs make all your kind haste
     home.
He's in your chamber, stayes and longs, sits by your bed. Pray   410
     come.
Tis richly made, and sweet; but he, more sweet, and lookes so
     cleare,
So fresh and movingly attir'd that (seeing) you would sweare
He came not from the dustie fight but from a courtly dance,
Or would to dancing.' This she made a charme for dalliance,
Whose vertue Helen felt, and knew (by her so radiant eyes,   415
White necke and most enticing breasts) the deified disguise.

Helen chideth   At which amaz'd, she answerd her: 'Unhappie Deitie!
Venus.   Why lov'st thou still in these deceipts to wrap my phantasie?
Or whether yet (of all the townes given to their lust beside
In Phrygia or Mæonia) com'st thou to be my guide,   420
If there (of divers-languag'd men) thou hast (as here in Troy)
Some other friend to be my shame—since here thy latest joy,
By Menelaus now subdu'd, by him shall I be borne

Home to his Court and end my life in triumphs of his scorne?
And to this end would thy deceits my wanton life allure.　　425
Hence, go thy selfe to Priam's sonne, and all the wayes abjure
Of Gods or Godlike-minded Dames, nor ever turne againe
Thy earth-affecting feet to heaven, but for his sake sustaine
Toiles here. Guard, grace him endlesly, till he requite thy grace
By giving thee my place with him; or take his servant's place　　430
If all dishonourable wayes your favours seeke to serve
His never-pleasd incontinence. I better will deserve
Than serve his dotage now. What shame were it for me to feed
This lust in him? All honour'd Dames would hate me for
　　the deed.
He leaves a woman's love so sham'd, and showes so base a　　435
　　mind,
To feele nor my shame nor his owne. Griefes of a greater kind
Wound me than such as can admit such kind delights so soone.'
　　The Goddesse (angrie that, past shame, her meere will was
　　　not done)

Venus terrifies Helen.

Replied: 'Incense me not, you wretch, lest (once incenst) I leave
Thy curst life to as strange a hate as yet it may receive　　440
A love from me, and lest I spread through both hosts such despite
For those plagues they have felt for thee that both abjure thee
　　quite
And (setting thee in midst of both) turne all their wraths
　　on thee
And dart thee dead—that such a death may wreake thy wrong
　　of me.'
　　This strooke the faire Dame with such feare it tooke her　　445
　　　speech away,
And (shadowed in her snowy veile) she durst not but obay;
And yet (to shun the shame she fear'd) she vanisht undescride
Of all the Troyan Ladies there, for Venus was her guide.

Helen followeth Venus from the port.

　　Arriv'd at home, her women both fell to their worke in hast,
When she, that was of all her sexe the most divinely grac't,　　450
Ascended to a higher roome, though much against her will,
Where lovely Alexander was, being led by Venus still.
The laughter-loving Dame discern'd her mov'd mind by her
　　grace,

Venus' mirth with Helen.

And (for her mirth sake) set a stoole full before Paris' face
Where she would needs have Helen sit, who (though she durst　　455
　　not chuse
But sit) yet lookt away, for all the Goddesse' powre could use,
And usd her tongue too, and to chide whom Venus sooth'd
　　so much,

[86]

*Helen's bitter
reproofe of Paris.*

And chid too, in this bitter kind: 'And was thy cowardise such
(So conquerd) to be seene alive? O would to God thy life
Had perisht by his worthy hand to whom I first was wife!   460
Before this, thou wouldst glorifie thy valour and thy lance
And, past my first Love's, boast them farre. Go once more,
    and advance
Thy braves against his single power: this foile might fall by
    chance.
Poore conquerd man! Twas such a chance as I would not advise
Thy valour should provoke againe. Shun him, thou most   465
    unwise,
Lest next, thy spirit sent to hell, thy bodie be his prise.'

Paris to Helen.

    He answerd: 'Pray thee, woman, ceasse to chide and grieve
    me thus.
Disgraces will not ever last: looke on their end—on us
Will other Gods, at other times, let fall the victor's wreath,
As on him Pallas put it now. Shall our love sinke beneath   470
The hate of fortune? In love's fire let all hates vanish. Come,
Love never so inflam'd my heart—no, not when (bringing home
Thy beautie's so delicious prise) on Cranae's blest shore
I long'd for and enjoyd thee first.' With this, he went before,
She after, to the odorous bed. While these to pleasure yeeld,   475

*Menelaus seeketh
for Paris through
the troopes.*

Perplext Atrides, savage-like, ran up and downe the field
And every thickest troope of Troy and of their farre-cald aid
Searcht for his foe, who could not be by any eye betraid—
Nor out of friendship (out of doubt) did they conceale his sight,
All hated him so like their deaths and ow'd him such despight.   480

*Agamemnon to
both the armies.*

    At last thus spake the king of men: 'Heare me, ye men of Troy,
Ye Dardans and the rest, whose powers you in their aides employ.
The conquest on my brother's part ye all discerne is cleare.
Do you then Argive Helena, with all her treasure, here
Restore to us and pay the mulct that by your vowes is due: 485
Yeeld us an honourd recompence and all that should accrue
To our posterities confirme, that when you render it
Our acts here may be memorisd.' This all Greekes else thought fit.

COMMENTARIUS

[121] Ἶρις δ' αὖθ' Ἑλένη &c. Iris autem Helene, &c. *Elegantly and most aptly (saith Spondanus) is Helen called by Homer to the spectacle of this single fight, as being the chiefe person in cause of all the action. The chiefe end of whose coming yet, enviously and most vainly, Scaliger's Criticus taxeth—which was her relation to* 5 *Priam of the persons he noted there—jesting (with his French wit) at this Greeke Father and fount of all wit for making Priam to seek now of their names and knowledges, when nine yeares together they had lien there before. A great peece of necessitie to make him therefore know them before when there was no such urgent occasion before to* 10 *bring Priam to note them, nor so calme a convenience in their ordered and quiet distinction! But let his criticisme in this be weighed with his other faults found in our maister—as for making lightning in winter before snow or raine, which the most ignorant upland peasant could teach him out of his observations. For which yet his* 15 *Criticus hath the project impudence to taxe Homer, most falsly repeating his words too, saying* Ubi ningit, *when he saith* τεύχων ἢ πολὺν ὄμβρον &c. parans, *or* struens, vel multum imbrem, immensamve grandinem, vel nivem—*preparing, or going about, those moist impressions in the aire, not in present act with them.* 20 *From this, immediatly and most rabidly he ranges to Ulysses' reprehension for killing the woers with his bow, in the* Odysses. *Then to his late vomit againe in the* Iliads *the verie next word, and envieth Achilles' horse for speaking (because himselfe would have all the tong), when, in sacred writ, Balaam's Asse could have taught* 25 *him the like hath bene heard of. Yet now to the* Odysses *againe with a breath, and challengeth Ulysses' ship for suffering Neptune to turne it to a rocke. Here is strange laying out for a maister so curiously methodicall! Not with what Graces, with what Muses, we may aske he was inspired, but with what Harpyes, what Furies,* 30 *putting the* putidum mendacium *upon Homer?* Putidus, ineptus, frigidus, puerilis (*being termes fitter for a scold or a bawd than a man softened by learning) he belcheth against him whom all the world hath reverenced and admired as the fountaine of all wit, wisdome and learning. What touch is it to me, then, to beare spots* 35 *of depravations, when my great maister is thus muddily dawb'd with it? But who ever saw true learning, wisdome or wit vouchsafe mansion in any proud, vaineglorious and braggartly spirit, when their chiefe act and end is to abandon and abhorre it? Language, reading,*

[88]

habite of speaking or writing in other learning I grant in this reviler 40
great and abundant, but in this Poesie redundant I affirme him and
rammish. To conclude, I will use the same words of him that he of
Erasmus (in calce Epinomidos)—*which are these (as I convert it): 'Great*
was his name, but had bene futurely greater, would himselfe have bene
lesse; where now, bold with the greatnesse of his wit, he hath 45
undertaken the more with much lesse exactnesse; and so his confidence
set on by the renowne of his name hath driven him headlong,' &c.

[162] ’Οπα λειριόεσσαν ἱεῖσι, Vocem suavem emittunt, *saith the*
Interpreter (intending the Grashoppers, to whom he compareth the
old Counsellors), but it is here to be expounded, vocem teneram, 50
not suavem (λειριόεις *in this place signifying* tener), *for Grashoppers*
sing not sweetly, but harshly and faintly, wherein the weake and
tender voices of the old Counsellors is to admiration exprest. The
Simile Spondanus highly commends as most apt and expressive, but
his application in one part doth abuse it, in the other right it—and 55
that is to make the old men resemble Grashoppers for their cold and
bloodlesse spininesse, Tython being for age turned to a Grashopper
—but where they were grave and wise Counsellors, to make them
garrulous, as Grashoppers are stridulous, that application holdeth
not in these old men, though some old men are so. These being 60
Εσθλοὶ ἀγορηταὶ, boni et perite concionatores—*the word* ἐσθλὸς
signifying frugi *also, which is temperate or full of al moderation,*
and, so, farre from intimating any touch of garrulitie. Nor was the
conceit of our Poet by Spondanus, or any other, understood in this
Simile. 65

[234] ’Επιτροχάδην ἀγόρευε, succinctè concionabatur Menelaus.
He spake succinctly, or compendiously, say his interpreters, which is
utterly otherwise, in the voice ἐπιτροχάδην *signifying* velociter,
properly, modo eorum qui currunt—*he spake fast, or thicke.*
παῦρα μὲν, *&c. few words yet he used,* ἀλλὰ μάλα λιγέως, sed 70
valde acutè *they expound it, when it is* valde stridulè, *shrilly, smally*
or alowd, λιγέως *(as I have noted before) being properly taken*
in the worse part and, accordingly expounded, maketh even with
his simple character at all parts—his utterance being noisefull, small
or squeaking, an excellent pipe for a foole. Nor is the voice or 75
manner of utterance in a man the least key that discovereth his
wisedome or folly. And therefore worth the noting is that of Ulysses
in the second booke, that he knew Pallas by her voice.
ἐπεὶ οὐ πολύμυθος, quoniam non garrulus, *or* loquax, *being borne*
naturally Laconical, which agreeth not the lesse with his fast or 80
thicke speaking, for a man may have that kind of utterance, and yet
few words.

[235] Οὐδ' ἀφαμαρτοεπὴς, Neque in verbis peccans, *say the Commentors, as though a foole were perfectly spoken; when the word here hath another sence and our Homer a farre other meaning,* 85 *the words being thus to be expounded,* neque mendax erat—*he would not lie by any meanes, for that affectedly he stands upon hereafter. But to make a foole* non peccans verbis *will make a man nothing wonder at any peccancie or absurditie in men of meere language.* 90

You see, then, to how extreme a difference and contrarietie the word and sence lie subject, and that without first finding the true figures of persons in this kind presented it is impossible for the best linguist living to expresse an Author trulie, especially any Greeke author, the language being so differently significant—which, not 95 *judicially fitted with the exposition, that the place (and coherence with other places) requireth, what a motley and confused man a translator may present! As now they do all of Menelaus, who, wheresoever he is called* 'Αρηίφιλος *is there untrulie translated* bellicosus—*but* cui Mars est carus, *because he might love the warre,* 100 *and yet be no good warriour, as many love many exercises at which they will never be good; and Homer gave it to him for another of his peculiar Epithets, as a vainglorious affectation in him rather than a solid affection.*

And here haste makes me give end to these new Annotations, 105 *deferring the like in the next nine bookes for more breath and encouragement, since time (that hath ever opprest me) will not otherwise let me come to the last twelve, in which the first free light of my Author entred and emboldened me—where so manie rich discoveries importune my poore expression that I feare rather to* 110 *betraie them to the world than expresse them to their price. But how soever envy and prejudice stand squirting their poison through the eyes of my Readers, this shall appeare to all competent apprehensions—I have followed the Originall with authenticall expositions (according to the proper signification of the word in his* 115 *place, though I differ therein utterly from others), I have rendred all things of importance with answerable life and height to my Authour (though with some periphrasis, without which no man can worthilie translate anie worthie Poet). And since the translation it selfe and my notes (being impartially conferred) amplie approove this, I will* 120 *still be confident in the woorth of my paines, how idlely and unworthily soever I be censured. And thus to the last twelve*

Books (leaving other horrible errors in his other Interpreters unmoved) with those free feet that entred me, I haste, sure of nothing but my labour.

The End of the Third Booke

THE FOURTH BOOKE
of
HOMER'S ILIADS

THE ARGUMENT

The Gods in Counsell at the last decree
That famous Ilion shall expugned be;
And that their owne continued faults may prove
The reasons that have so incensed Jove,
Minerva seekes, with more offences done　　　　　　5
Against the lately injur'd Atreus' sonne,
(A ground that clearest would make sene their sinne)
To have the Lycian Pandarus beginne.
He (gainst the Truce with sacred covenants bound)
Gives Menelaus a dishonour'd wound.　　　　　　10
Machaon heales him. Agamemnon then
To mortall warre incenseth all his men.
The battels joyne and in the heate of fight
Cold death shuts many eyes in endlesse night.

Another Argument

In Delta *is the Gods' Assise;*
The Truce is broke; warres freshly rise.

The Gods in
Counsel at Jove's
Court.
Hebe fils Nectar.

Within the faire-pav'd Court of Jove, he and the Gods conferd
About the sad events of Troy—amongst whom ministerd
Blest Hebe Nectar. As they sate and did Troy's towres behold,
They drank, and pledg'd each other round, in full-crownd
　　　cups of gold.
The mirth at whose feast was begun by great Saturnides　　5
In urging a begun dislike amongst the Goddesses,
But chiefly in his solemne Queene, whose splene he was disposd
To tempt yet further—knowing well what anger it inclosd,

Jove's mirth with
his wife and
daughter Pallas.

And how wives' angers should be usd. On which (thus pleasd)
　　he playd:
　　'Two Goddesses there are that still give Menelaus ayd,　　10

[91]

And one that Paris loves. The two that sit from us so farre
(Which Argive Juno is and she that rules in deeds of warre)
No doubt are pleasd to see how well the late-seene fight did
    frame—
And yet (upon the adverse part) the laughter-loving Dame
Made her powre good too for her friend—for though he were   15
    so neare
The stroke of death in th'other's hopes she took him from
    them cleare.
The conquest yet is questionlesse the martiall Spartan king's.
We must consult then what events shall crowne these future
    things—
If warres and combats we shall still with even successes strike,
Or (as impartiall) friendship plant on both parts. If ye like   20
The last, and that it will as well delight as meerely please
Your happie Deities, still let stand old Priam's towne in peace
And let the Lacedæmon king againe his Queene enjoy.'
   As Pallas and heaven's Queene sat close, complotting ill to
    Troy,
With silent murmures they receiv'd this ill-lik't choice from   25
    Jove,
Gainst whom was Pallas much incenst, because the Queene
    of Love
Could not without his leave relieve, in that late point of death,
The sonne of Priam, whom she loath'd. Her wrath yet fought
    beneath
Her supreme wisedome, and was curb'd: but Juno needs must
    ease

Juno angry with
Jupiter.

Her great heart with her readie tongue, and said: 'What words   30
    are these,
Austere and too much Saturn's sonne? Why wouldst thou render
    still
My labours idle, and the sweat of my industrious will
Dishonor with so little power? My chariot horse are tir'd
With posting to and fro for Greece, and bringing banes desir'd
To people-mustring Priamus and his perfidious sonnes;   35
Yet thou protectst and joynst with them, when each just Deitie
    shuns.
Go on, but ever go resolv'd all other Gods have vow'd
To crosse thy partiall course for Troy in all that makes it proud.'
   At this the cloud-compelling Jove a farre-fetcht sigh let flie,

Jupiter to Juno.

And said: 'Thou Furie, what offence of such impietie   40
Hath Priam or his sonnes done thee, that with so high a hate

Thou shouldst thus ceaslesly desire to raze and ruinate
So well a builded towne as Troy? I thinke (hadst thou the
    powre)
Thou wouldst the ports and farre-stretcht wals flie over and
    devoure
Old Priam and his issue quicke, and make all Troy thy feast,　45
And then at length I hope thy wrath and tired spleene
    would rest—
To which run on thy chariot, that nought be found in me
Of just cause to our future jarres. In this yet strengthen thee
And fixe it in thy memorie fast—that, if I entertaine
As peremptorie a desire to levell with the plaine　　　　　50
A citie where thy loved live, stand not betwixt my ire
And what it aimes at, but give way when thou hast thy desire,
Which now I grant thee willingly, although against my will.

Troy most loved　For not beneath the ample Sunne and heaven's starre-bearing hill
of Jupiter of all　There is a towne of earthly men so honour'd in my mind　　55
other cities.　As sacred Troy, nor of earth's kings as Priam and his kind,
Who never let my altars lacke rich feast of offrings slaine
And their sweet savours—for which grace I honor them againe.'

Three cities　　Drad Juno, with the Cowe's faire eyes, replyed: 'Three townes
deare to Juno.　　there are
Of great and eminent respect both in my love and care—　　60
Mycene, with the brode high waies, and Argos, rich in horse,
And Sparta—all which three destroy, when thou envi'st their
    force.
I will not aid them nor maligne thy free and soveraigne will,
For if I should be envious and set against their ill,
I know my envie were in vaine since thou art mightier farre.　65
But we must give each other leave, and winke at either's warre.
I likewise must have powre to crowne my workes with wished end,
Her deadly hate　Because I am a Deitie and did from thence descend
to Troy.　Whence thou thy selfe and th'elder borne: wise Saturne was
    our Sire.
And thus there is a two-fold cause that pleads for my desire,　70
Being sister, and am cal'd thy wife—and more, since thy
    command
Rules all Gods else, I claime therein a like superiour hand.
All wrath before then now remit, and mutually combine
In either's Empire—I, thy rule, and thou, illustrate mine.
So will the other Gods agree and we shall all be strong.　　75
And first (for this late plot) with speed let Pallas go among
The Troyans and some one of them entice to breake the truce

[93]

By offering in some treacherous wound the honourd Greekes' abuse.'
The Father both of men and Gods agreed, and Pallas sent,

Jupiter to Pallas.

With these wing'd words, to both the hosts: 'Make all haste, and invent   80
Some meane by which the men of Troy, against the truce agreed,
May stirre the glorious Greekes to armes, with some inglorious deed.'
Thus charg'd he her with haste that did, before, in hast abound,

Pallas fals from heaven like a Comet.

Who cast her selfe from all the heights with which steepe heaven is crownd.
And as Jove, brandishing a starre (which men a Comet call),   85
Hurls out his curled haire abrode, that from his brand exhale
A thousand sparkes (to fleets at sea and everie mightie host
Of all presages and ill haps a signe mistrusted most):
So Pallas fell twixt both the Camps and sodainly was lost—
When through the breasts of all that saw she strooke a strong amaze,   90
With viewing in her whole descent her bright and ominous blaze,
When straight one to another turn'd, and said: 'Now thundring Jove
(Great Arbiter of peace and armes) will either stablish love
Amongst our nations or renue such warre as never was.'
Thus either armie did presage when Pallas made her passe   95
Amongst the multitude of Troy—who now put on the grace
Of brave Laodocus, the flowre of old Antenor's race,
And sought for Lycian Pandarus, a man that, being bred
Out of a faithlesse familie, she thought was fit to shed
The blood of any innocent and breake the covenant sworne.   100
He was Lycaon's sonne, whom Jove into a Wolfe did turne
For sacrificing of a child, and yet in armes renownd
As one that was inculpable. Him Pallas standing found
And round about him his strong troopes that bore the shadie shields.
He brought them from Æsepus' flood, let through the Lycian   105
fields;

Pallas to Pandarus, perswading him to breake the truce.

Whom standing neare, she whispred thus: 'Lycaon's warlike sonne,
Shall I despaire at thy kind hands to have a favour done?
Nor dar'st thou let an arrow flie upon the Spartan king?
It would be such a grace to Troy, and such a glorious thing,
That everie man would give his gift, but Alexander's hand   110
Would loade thee with them, if he could discover from his stand

His foe's pride strooke downe with thy shaft, and he himselfe
ascend
The flaming heape of funerall. Come, shoote him, princely
friend;
But first invoke the God of light, that in thy land was borne
And is in archer's art the best that ever sheafe hath worne—   115
To whom a hundred first-ew'd lambes vow thou in holy fire
When safe to sacred Zelia's towres thy zealous steps retire.'
 With this the mad-gift-greedie man Minerva did perswade,

*The description
of Pandarus his bow.*

Who instantly drew forth a bow most admirably made
Of th'antler of a jumping Goate bred in a steepe upland,   120
Which Archer-like (as long before he tooke his hidden stand,
The Evicke skipping from a rocke) into the breast he smote
And headlong feld him from his cliffe. The forehead of the Gote
Held out a wondrous goodly palme that sixteene branches
brought,
Of all which (joynd) an usefull bow a skilfull Bowyer wrought,   125
Which pickt and polisht, both the ends he hid with hornes of
gold.
And this bow (bent) he close laid downe and bad his souldiers
hold
Their shields before him, lest the Greekes (discerning him)
should rise
In tumults ere the Spartan king could be his arrowe's prise.
Meane space with all his care he chusd, and from his quiver   130
drew,
An arrow fetherd best for flight and yet that never flew—
Strong-headed and most apt to pierce. Then tooke he up his bow
And nockt his shaft—the ground whence all their future griefe
did grow—
When (praying to his God the Sunne, that was in Lycia bred
And king of Archers, promising that he the blood would shed   135
Of full an hundred first-fallen lambes, all offred to his name
When to Zelia's sacred wals from rescu'd Troy he came)

*Virgil useth these
verses. Pandarus'
draught and shoote.*

He tooke his arrow by the nocke and to his bended brest
The Oxy sinew close he drew even till the pile did rest
Upon the bosome of the bow, and, as that savage prise   140
His strength constraind into an Orb, (as if the wind did rise)
The coming of it made a noise, the sinew-forged string
Did give a mightie twang, and forth the eager shaft did sing
(Affecting speedinesse of flight) amongst the Achive throng.
Nor were the blessed heavenly powres unmindfull of thy   145
wrong,

Menelaus hurt.

O Menelaus, but in chiefe Jove's seed, the Pillager,

[95]

Stood close before and slackt the force the arrow did confer,
With as much care and little hurt as doth a mother use
And keepe off from her babe, when sleepe doth through his
    powers diffuse
His golden humor, and th'assaults of rude and busie flies   150
She still checks with her carefull hand—for so the shaft she plies
That on the buttons made of gold which made his girdle fast,
And where his curets double were, the fall of it she plac't.
And thus much proofe she put it to: the buckle made of gold,
The belt it fastned, bravely wrought, his curets' double fold,   155
And, last, the charmed plate he wore, which helpt him more
    than all
And gainst all darts and shafts bestowd was to his life a wall.
So (through all these) the upper skin the head did onely race,
Yet foorth the blood flow'd which did much his royall person
    grace,
And shew'd upon his Ivorie skin as doth a purple dye   160
Laid (by a Dame of Caria, or lovely Mæony)
On Ivorie, wrought in ornaments to decke the cheeks of horse,
Which in her mariage roome must lie, whose beauties have
    such force
That they are wisht of many knights, but are such precious things
That they are kept for horse that draw the chariots of kings—   165
Which horse (so deckt) the chariotere esteemes a grace to him.
Like these (in grace) the blood upon thy solid thighes did swim,
O Menelaus, downe thy calves and ankles to the ground—
For nothing decks a souldier so as doth an honour'd wound.
Yet (fearing he had far'd much worse) the haire stood up   170
    on end
On Agamemnon, when he saw so much blacke blood descend.
And stifned with the like dismay was Menelaus too,
But (seeing th'arrowe's stale without, and that the head did go
No further than it might be seene) he cald his spirits againe;
Which Agamemnon marking not (but thinking he was slaine),   175
He grip't his brother by the hand and sigh't as he would breake,
Which sigh the whole host tooke from him, who thus at last did
    speake:

*Agamemnon's
complaint and
feare of his
brother's hurt.*

    'O dearest brother, is't for this? That thy death must be
    wrought,
Wrought I this truce? For this hast thou the single combat
    fought
For all the armie of the Greekes? For this hath Ilion sworne   180
And trod all faith beneath their feet? Yet all this hath not worne
The right we challeng'd out of force; this cannot render vaine

Our stricken right hands, sacred wine nor all our offrings slaine.
For though Olympius be not quicke in making good our ill,
He will be sure, as he is slow, and sharplier prove his will.   185
Their owne hands shall be ministers of those plagues they
    despise,
Which shall their wives and children reach, and all their
    progenies.
For both in mind and soule I know that there shall come a day
When Ilion, Priam, all his powre, shall quite be worne away,
When heaven-inhabiting Jove shall shake his fierie shield at all   190
For this one mischiefe. This, I know, the world cannot recall.
But be all this, all my griefe still for thee will be the same,
Dear brother, if thy life must here put out his royall flame.
I shall to sandie Argos turne with infamie my face,
And all the Greekes will call for home; old Priam and his race   195
Will flame in glorie, Helena, untoucht, be still their pray;
And thy bones in our enemies' earth our cursed fates shall lay;
Thy Sepulcher be troden downe; the pride of Troy desire
(Insulting on it): "Thus, O thus, let Agamemnon's ire
In all his acts be expiate, as now he carries home   200
His idle armie, emptie ships, and leaves here overcome
Good Menelaus!" When this Brave breakes in their hated breath,
Then let the broade earth swallow me and take me quicke to
    death.'

Menelaus to
Agamemnon.

   'Nor shall this ever chance,' said he, 'and therefore be of
    cheare,
Lest all the armie (led by you) your passions put in feare.   205
The arrow fell in no such place as death could enter at.
My girdle, curets doubled here, and my most trusted plate,
Objected all twixt me and death, the shaft scarce piercing one.'

Agamemnon to
Menelaus.

'Good brother,' said the king, 'I wish it were no further gone,
For then our best in medicines skild shall ope and search the   210
    wound,
Applying balmes to ease thy paines, and soone restore thee
    sound.'

Agamemnon sends
Talthybius for
Machaon.

This said, divine Talthybius he cald, and bad him haste
Machaon (Æsculapius' sonne, who most of men was grac't
With Physick's soveraigne remedies) to come and lend his hand
To Menelaus, 'shot by one well-skild in the command   215
Of bow and arrowes, one of Troy or of the Lycian aid,
Who much hath glorified our foe and us as much dismaid.'
   He heard, and hasted instantly, and cast his eyes about
The thickest squadrons of the Greekes to find Machaon out.

He found him standing guarded well with well-arm'd men of   220
    Thrace,

Talthybius to
Machaon.

With whom he quickly joynd, and said: 'Man of Apollo's race!
Haste—for the king of men commands—to see a wound imprest
In Menelaus (great in armes) by one instructed best
In th'art of archerie, of Troy or of the Lycian bands,
That them with such renowne adornes, us with dishonor   225
    brands.'
    Machaon much was mov'd with this, who with the herald flew
From troope to troope alongst the host, and soone they came in
    view
Of hurt Atrides, circled round with all the Grecian kings,

Machaon draws the
arrow.

Who all gave way; and straight he drawes the shaft, which forth
    he brings
Without the forkes; the girdle then, plate, curets, off he   230
    pluckes
And viewes the wound; when first from it the clotterd blood he
    sucks,
Then medicines wondrously composd the skilfull Leech applyed,
Which loving Chiron taught his Sire, he from his Sire had tryed.
    While these were thus employd to ease the Atrean martialist,

The Troyans
renew the fight.

The Troyans arm'd and charg'd the Greekes: the Greekes   235
    arme and resist.
Then not asleepe nor maz'd with feare, nor shifting off the
    blowes,
You could behold the king of men; but in full speed he goes

Agamemnon marshals
his armie.

To set a glorious fight on foote; and he examples this
With toyling (like the worst) on foote, who therefore did
    dismisse
His brasse-arm'd chariot and his steeds with Ptolemæus' sonne   240
(Sonne of Piraides), their guide, the good Eurymedon—
'Yet,' said the king, 'attend with them, lest wearinesse should
    seise
My lims, surcharg'd with ordering troopes so thicke and vast
    as these.'
    Eurymedon then rein'd his horse that trotted neighing by;
The king a foot-man, and so scowres the squadrons orderly.   245

Agamemnon to the
Greekes.

    Those of his swiftly-mounted Greekes that in their armes
    were fit,
Those he put on with chearfull words, and bad them not remit
The least sparke of their forward spirits because the Troyans
    durst
Take these abhord advantages, but let them do their wurst—
For they might be assur'd that Jove would patronise no lies,   250

And that, who with the breach of truce, would hurt their
    enemies
With vultures should be torne themselves, that they should raze
    their towne,
Their wives and children at their breasts led vassals to their
    owne.
    But such as he beheld hang off from that increasing fight,
Such would he bitterly rebuke, and with disgrace excite: 255

Agamemnon to the
negligent souldiers.

'Base Argives, blush ye not to stand, as made for Buts to darts?
Why are ye thus discomfited like Hinds that have no harts,
Who, wearied with a long-run field, are instantly embost,
Stand still, and in their beastly breasts is all their courage lost?
And so stand you strooke with amaze, nor dare to strike a   260
    stroke.
Would ye the foe should nearer yet your dastard splenes provoke,
Even where on Neptune's fomie shore our navies lie in sight,
To see if Jove will hold your hands and teach ye how to fight?'
    Thus he (commanding) rang'd the host, and (passing many
    a band)
He came to the Cretensian troopes, where all did armed stand   265
About the martiall Idomen, who bravely stood before
In vantguard of his troopes, and matcht for strength a savage
    Bore,
Meriones (his chariotere) the Rereguard bringing on—
Which seene to Atreus' sonne, to him it was a sight alone,
And Idomen's confirmed mind with these kind words he seekes: 270

Agamemnon to
Idomen.

'O Idomen! I ever lov'd thy selfe past all the Greekes,
In warre, or any worke of peace, at table, every where:
For when the best of Greece besides mixe ever, at our cheere,
My good old ardent wine with small, and our inferiour mates
Drinke even that mixt wine measur'd too, thou drinkst without 275
    those rates
Our old wine neate, and evermore thy boll stands full like mine,
To drinke still when and what thou wilt. Then rowse that heart
    of thine,
And whatsoever heretofore thou hast assum'd to be,
This day be greater.' To the king in this sort answerd he:

Idomen to
Agamemnon.

'Atrides, what I ever seem'd, the same at everie part   280
This day shall shew me at the full, and I will fit thy hart.
But thou shouldst rather cheare the rest, and tell them they in
    right
Of all good warre must offer blowes and should begin the fight
(Since Troy first brake the holy truce) and not endure these
    braves,

To take wrong first and then be dar'd to the revenge it craves— 285
Assuring them that Troy, in fate, must have the worse at last,
Since first, and gainst a truce, they hurt, where they should have
    embrac't.'
  This comfort and advice did fit Atrides' heart indeed,
Who still through new-raisd swarmes of men held his laborious
    speed,
And came where both th'Ajaces stood—whom, like the last, he 290
    found
Arm'd, caskt and readie for the fight. Behind them, hid the
    ground
A cloud of foot, that seem'd to smoke. And as a Goteheard spies

How the troopes
of Ajax stood.

On some hil's top, out of the Sea, a rainie vapour rise,
Driven by the breath of Zephyrus, which (though farre off
    he rest)
Comes on as blacke as pitch and brings a tempest in his 295
    breast—
Whereat he, frighted, drives his heards apace into a den:
So (darkning earth with darts and shields) shew'd these with
    all their men.
  This sight with like joy fir'd the king, who thus let forth
    the flame

Agamemnon to the
Ajaces.

In crying out to both the Dukes: 'O you of equall name
I must not cheare. Nay, I disclaime all my command of you: 300
Your selves command with such free minds and make your
    souldiers shew
As you nor I led, but themselves. O would our father Jove,
Minerva and the God of light would all our bodies move
With such brave spirits as breathe in you! Then Priam's loftie
    towne
Should soone be taken by our hands, for ever overthrowne.' 305

Nestor's art in
ordering his
souldiers.

  Then held he on to other troopes, and Nestor next beheld
(The subtle Pylian Orator) range up and downe the field,
Embattelling his men at armes and stirring all to blowes,
Points everie legion out his Chiefe, and every Chiefe he showes
The formes and discipline of warre. Yet his Commanders were 310
All expert and renowmed men. Great Pelagon was there,
Alastor, manly Chromius and Hæmon worth a Throne,
And Bias that could armies leade. With these he first put on
His horse troopes with their chariots. His foote (of which he
    chusde
Many, the best and ablest men, and which he ever usde 315
As rampire to his generall powre) he in the Rere disposd.
The slouthfull and the least of spirit he in the midst inclosd,

That such as wanted noble wils base need might force to stand.
His horse troopes (that the Vantgard had) he strictly did
    command
To ride their horses temperatly, to keepe their rankes and shun   320
Confusion, lest their horsemanship and courage made them run
(Too much presum'd on) much too farre, and (charging so
    alone)
Engage themselves in th'enemie's strength, where many fight
    with one:
'Who his owne chariot leaves to range, let him not freely go,
But straight unhorse him with a lance, for tis much better so: 325
And with this discipline,' said he, 'this forme, these minds,
    this trust,
Our Ancestors have walles and townes laid levell with the dust.'
    Thus prompt, and long inur'd to armes, this old man did
    exhort,
And this Atrides likewise tooke in wondrous chearefull sort,

Agamemnon to
Nestor.
And said: 'O Father! would to heaven that as thy mind   330
    remaines
In wonted vigor, so thy knees could undergo our paines!
But age, that all men overcomes, hath made his prise on thee,
Yet still I wish that some young man, growne old in mind,
    might be
Put in proportion with thy yeares, and thy mind (young in age)
Be fitly answerd with his youth—that still where conflicts rage   335
And young men usd to thrust for fame, thy brave exampling
    hand
Might double our young Grecian spirits and grace our whole
    Command.'

Nestor to
Agamemnon.
    The old knight answer'd: 'I my selfe could wish, O Atreus'
    sonne,
I were as young as when I slue brave Ereuthalion.
But Gods at all times give not all their gifts to mortall men.   340
If then I had the strength of youth, I mist the Counsels then
That yeares now give me, and now yeares want that maine
    strength of youth.
Yet still my mind retaines her strength (as you now said the
    sooth)
And would be where that strength is usd, affoording counsels
    sage
To stirre youths' minds up: tis the grace and office of our age.   345
Let yonger sinewes, men sprong up whole ages after me
And such as have strength, use it, and as strong in honour be.'

[101]

The king (all this while comforted) arriv'd next where he
    found
Well-rode Menestheus (Peteus' sonne) stand still, invirond round
With his well-train'd Athenian troopes; and next to him he   350
    spide
The wise Ulysses, deedlesse too, and all his bands beside
Of strong Cephalians—for as yet th'alarme had not bene heard
In all their quarters, Greece and Troy were then so newly stird
And then first mov'd (as they conceiv'd), and they so lookt about
To see both hoasts give proofe of that they yet had cause to   355
    doubt.
    Atrides (seeing them stand so still and spend their eyes
    at gaze)

Agamemnon to
Ulysses and
Menestheus.

Began to chide: 'And why,' said he, 'dissolv'd thus in a maze,
Thou sonne of Peteus, Jove-nurst king, and thou in wicked
    sleight
A cunning souldier, stand ye off? Expect ye that the fight
Should be by other men begun? Tis fit the formost band   360
Should shew you there: you first should front who first lifts
    up his hand.
First you can heare when I invite the Princes to a feast,
When first, most friendly and at will, ye eate and drinke the best:
Yet in the fight most willingly ten troopes ye can behold
Take place before ye.' Ithacus at this his browes did fold   365

Ulysses to
Agamemnon.

And said: 'How hath thy violent tongue broke through thy
    set of teeth,
To say that we are slacke in fight and to the field of death
Looke others should enforce our way—when we were busied
    then
(Even when thou spak'st) against the foe to cheare and leade our
    men?
But thy eyes shall be witnesses (if it content thy will   370
And that, as thou pretendst, these cares do so affect thee still).
The father of Telemachus (whom I esteeme so deare
And to whom as a Legacie I'le leave my deeds done here)
Even with the formost band of Troy hath his encounter dar'd,
And therefore are thy speeches vaine and had bene better   375
    spar'd.'
    He, smiling, since he saw him mov'd, recall his words, and
    said:

Agamemnon to
Ulysses.

'Most generous Laertes' sonne, most wise of all our aid,
I neither do accuse thy worth more than thy selfe may hold
Fit (that inferiours thinke not much, being slacke, to be
    controld),

Nor take I on me thy command, for well I know thy mind   380
Knowes how sweet gentle counsels are, and that thou standst
  enclind,
As I my selfe, for all our good. On, then: if now we spake
What hath displeasd, another time we full amends will make—
And Gods grant that thy vertue here may prove so free and brave
That my reproofes may still be vaine and thy deservings grave.'   385
  Thus parted they, and forth he went, when he did leaning find
Against his chariot, neare his horse, him with the mightie mind,
Great Diomedes (Tydeus' sonne) and Sthenelus, the seed
Of Capaneus, whom the king seeing likewise out of deed,

*Agamemnon chideth
Diomed.*

Thus cried he out on Diomed: 'O me! in what a feare   390
The wise great warriour, Tydeus' sonne, stands gazing everie
  where
For others to begin the fight! It was not Tydeus' use
To be so danted, whom his spirit would evermore produce,
Before the formost of his friends, in these affaires of fright,
As they report that have beheld him labour in a fight.   395
For me, I never knew the man, nor in his presence came;
But excellent above the rest he was in generall fame.

*The historie of
Tydeus.*

And one renowm'd exploit of his I am assur'd is true:
He came to the Mycenian Court without armes and did sue
At Godlike Polynices' hands to have some worthie aid   400
To their designes that gainst the wals of sacred Thebes were
  laid.
He was great Polynices' guest, and nobly entertaind,
And of the kind Mycenian state what he requested gaind
In meere consent; but when they should the same in act approve
(By some sinister prodigies held out to them by Jove)   405
They were discourag'd. Thence he went and safely had his passe
Backe to Asopus' flood, renowm'd for Bulrushes and grasse.
Yet once more, their Ambassadour, the Grecian Peeres addresse
Lord Tydeus to Eteocles, to whom being given accesse,
He found him feasting with a crew of Cadmians in his hall—   410
Amongst whom, though an enemie and onely one to all,
To all yet he his challenge made at everie Martiall feate,
And easly foild all, since with him Minerva was so great.
The ranke-rode Cadmians (much incenst with their so foule
  disgrace)
Lodg'd ambuscados for their foe in some well-chosen place   415
By which he was to make returne. Twise five and twentie men,
And two of them great captaines too, the ambush did containe.
The names of those two men of rule were Mæon, Hæmon's
  sonne,

[103]

And Polyphontes, Keepe-field cald, the heire of Autophon,
By all men honord like the Gods. Yet these and all their   420
    friends
Were sent to hell by Tydeus' hand and had untimely ends—
He trusting to the aid of Gods, reveald by Augurie,
Obeying which one Chiefe he sav'd and did his life apply
To be the heavie messenger of all the others' deaths;
And that sad message (with his life) to Mæon he bequeaths.   425
So brave a knight was Tydeus—of whom a sonne is sprong
Inferiour farre in martiall deeds, though higher in his tongue.'
    All this Tydides silent heard, aw'd by the reverend king;
Which stung hote Sthenelus with wrath, who thus put forth his
    sting:

Sthenelus' rough
speech to
Agamemnon.

    'Atrides! when thou know'st the truth, speake what thy   430
        knowledge is,
And do not lie so. For I know, and I will bragge in this,
That we are farre more able men than both our fathers were.
We tooke the seven-fold ported Thebes when yet we had not
    there
So great helpe as our fathers had, and fought beneath a wall
Sacred to Mars, by helpe of Jove and trusting to the fall   435
Of happie signes from other Gods, by whom we tooke the towne
Untoucht—our fathers perishing there by follies of their owne.
And therefore never more compare our fathers' worth with ours.'

Diomed rebukes
Sthenelus.

        Tydides frownd at this, and said: 'Suppresse thine anger's
            pow'rs,
Good friend, and heare why I refrain'd. Thou seest I am not   440
    mov'd
Against our Generall, since he did but what his place behov'd,
Admonishing all Greekes to fight; for if Troy prove our prise,
The honor and the joy is his. If here our ruine lies,
The shame and griefe for that as much is his in greatest kinds.
As he then his charge, weigh we ours—which is our dantlesse   445
    minds.'
        Thus from his chariot (amply arm'd) he jumpt downe to the
            ground.
The armor of the angrie king so horribly did sound,
It might have made his bravest foe let feare take downe his
    braves.

Simile.

And as when with the West-wind's flawes, the sea thrusts up
    her waves
One after other, thicke and high, upon the groning shores,   450
First in her selfe lowd (but opposd with banks and Rocks)
    she rores

[104]

And (all her backe in bristles set) spits everie way her fome:
So (after Diomed) instantly the field was overcome
With thicke impressions of the Greekes and all the noise
    that grew
(Ordring and chearing up their men) from onely leaders flew.   455

The silence of the Greeke fight.

The rest went silently away, you could not heare a voice,
Nor would have thought in all their breasts they had one in
    their choice—
Their silence uttering their awe of them that them contrould,
Which made ech man keep bright his arms, march, fight still
    where he should.

The Troyans compared to Ewes.

The Troyans (like a sort of Ewes pend in a rich man's fold,   460
Close at his dore till all be milkt, and never baaing hold,
Hearing the bleating of their lambs) did all their wide host fill
With showts and clamors, nor observ'd one voice, one baaing
    still
But shew'd mixt tongs from many a land of men cald to their
    aid.

Mars for the Troyans, Pallas for the Greekes. Discord the sister of Mars. Virgil the same of Fame.

Rude Mars had th'ordring of their spirits—of Greeks, the   465
    learned Maid.
But Terror follow'd both the hosts, and Flight, and furious
    Strife,
The sister and the mate of Mars, that spoile of humane life.
And never is her rage at rest: at first she is but small,
Yet after (but a little fed) she growes so vast and tall
That while her feet move here in earth, her forhead is in   470
    heaven.
And this was she that made even then both hosts so deadly given.
Through every troope she stalkt and stird rough sighes up as
    she went;
But when in one field both the foes her furie did content
And both came under reach of darts, then darts and shields
    opposd
To darts and shields, strength answerd strength. Then swords   475
    and targets closd
With swords and targets, both with pikes; and then did tumult
    rise
Up to her height; then conqueror's boasts mixt with the
    conquerd's cries;
Earth flow'd with blood. And as from hils, raine waters headlong
    fall
That all waies eate huge Ruts which, met in one bed, fill a vall
With such a confluence of streames that on the mountaine   480
    grounds,

Farre off, in frighted shepheards' eares the bustling noise
    rebounds:
So grew their conflicts, and so shew'd their scuffling to the eare,
With flight and clamor still commixt, and all effects of feare.
    And first renowm'd Antilochus slew (fighting in the face

Antilochus slue
Echepolus.

Of all Achaia's formost bands, with an undanted grace)   485
Echepolus Thalysiades. He was an armed man
Whom, on his haire-plum'd helmet's crest, the dart first smote,
    then ran
Into his forehead and there stucke, the steele pile making way
Quite through his skull: a hastie night shut up his latest day.
His fall was like a fight-rac't towre, like which, lying there   490
    dispred,

Elephenor drawing
off the body of
Echepolus is slaine
by Agenor.

King Elephenor (who was sonne to Chalcodon and led
The valiant Abants), covetous that he might first possesse
His armes, laid hands upon his feet, and hal'd him from the
    preasse
Of darts and Javelins hurld at him. The action of the king
When (great in heart) Agenor saw, he made his Javeline sing   495
To th'other's labor, and, along as he the trunke did wrest,
His side (at which he bore his shield in bowing of his breast)
Lay naked and receiv'd the lance: that made him lose his hold
And life together—which, in hope of that he lost, he sold.
But for his sake the fight grew fierce. The Troyans and their   500
    foes
Like wolves on one another rusht, and man for man it goes.

Ajax slaies
Simoisius.

    The next of name that serv'd his fate, great Ajax Telamon
Preferd so sadly. He was the heire to old Anthemion
And deckt with all the flowre of youth, the fruit of which
    yet fled
Before the honourd nuptiall torch could light him to his bed.   505
His name was Simoisius—for, some few yeares before,
His mother, walking downe the hill of Ida by the shore
Of Sylver Simois to see her parents' flocks, with them
She (feeling sodainely the paines of child-birth) by the streame
Of that bright river brought him forth; and so (of Simois)   510
They cald him Simoisius. Sweet was that birth of his
To his kind parents, and his growth did all their care employ.
And yet those rites of pietie that should have bene his joy
To pay their honourd yeares againe in as affectionate sort
He could not graciously performe, his sweet life was so short,   515
Cut off with mightie Ajax' lance. For as his spirit put on,
He strooke him at his breast's right pappe quite through his
    shoulder bone,

And in the dust of earth he fell that was the fruitfull soyle
Of his friends' hopes; but where he sow'd, he buried all his
    toyle.

Simile.
And as a Poplar shot aloft, set by a river side,   520
In moist edge of a mightie fenne, his head in curls implide
But all his bodie plaine and smooth; to which a Wheel-wright
    puts
The sharpe edge of his shining axe and his soft timber cuts
From his innative roote, in hope to hew out of his bole
The Fell'ffs, or out-parts of a wheele that compasse in the   525
    whole,
To serve some goodly chariot; but (being bigge and sad
And to be hal'd home through the bogs) the usefull hope he had
Sticks there, and there the goodly plant lies withring out his
    grace—
So lay, by Jove-bred Ajax' hand, Anthemion's forward race,
Nor could through that vast fen of toiles be drawne to serve   530
    the ends
Intended by his bodie's pow'rs, nor cheare his aged friends.

Antiphus, one of
Priam's sonnes.
    But now the gay-arm'd Antiphus (a sonne of Priam) threw
His lance at Ajax through the preasse, which went by him
    and flew
On Leucus, wise Ulysses' friend. His groine it smote, as faine
He would have drawne into his spoile the carkasse of the   535
    slaine—
By which he fell, and that by him. It vext Ulysses' heart,
Who thrust into the face of fight, well-arm'd at everie part,
Came close and lookt about to find an object worth his lance;
Which when the Troyans saw him shake and he so neare
    advance,
All shrunke. He threw and forth it shin'd, nor fell but where   540
    it feld.
His friend's griefe gave it angrie powre and deadly way it held

Democoon, Priam's
base sonne, slaine
by Ulysses.
Upon Democoon, who was sprung of Priam's wanton force,
Came from Abydus and was made the maister of his horse.
Through both his temples strooke the dart; the wood of one
    side shewd,
The pile out of the other lookt; and so the earth he strewd,   545
With much sound of his weightie armes. Then backe the
    formost went;
Even Hector yeelded. Then the Greekes gave worthie clamors
    vent,
Effecting then their first dumbe powers. Some drew the dead
    and spoild;

Some followed, that in open flight Troy might confesse it foild.

Apollo excites the
Troyans.

Apollo (angrie at the sight) from top of Ilion cride: 550
'Turne head, ye well-rode Peeres of Troy, feed not the
    Grecians' pride.
They are not charm'd against your points—of steele nor Iron
    fram'd:
Nor fights the faire-haird Thetis' sonne, but sits at fleet inflam'd.'

Pallas encourageth
the Greeks.

    So spake the dreadfull God from Troy. The Greekes, Jove's
       noblest seed
Encourag'd to keepe on the chace, and where fit spirit did need 555
She gave it, marching in the midst. Then flew the fatall howre
Backe on Diores, in returne of Ilion's sun-burnd powre—

Diores.

Diores Amaryncides, whose right leg's ankle bone
And both the sinewes with a sharpe and handfull-charging
    stone

Pirus.

Pirus Imbrasides did breake, that led the Thracian bands   560
And came from Ænos. Downe he fell and up he held his hands
To his lov'd friends; his spirit wingd, to flie out of his breast.
With which not satisfied, againe Imbrasides addrest
His Javeline at him and so ript his navill that the wound
(As endlesly it shut his eyes) so (opend) on the ground   565
It powr'd his entrailes. As his foe went then suffisd away,
Thoas Ætolius threw a dart, that did his pile convay

Pirus slaine by
Thoas.

Above his nipple through his lungs, when (quitting his sterne
    part)
He closd with him and, from his breast first drawing out his dart,
His sword flew in and by the midst it wip't his bellie out—   570
So tooke his life, but left his armes. His friends so flockt about
And thrust forth lances of such length before their slaughterd
    king,
Which, though their foe were big and strong and often brake
    the ring
Forg'd of their lances, yet (enforc't) he left th'affected prise.
The Thracian and Epeian Dukes laid close with closed eyes   575
By either other, drownd in dust: and round about the plaine,
All hid with slaughterd carkasses, yet still did hotely raigne
The martiall planet—whose effects had any eye beheld
Free and unwounded (and were led by Pallas through the field
To keepe off Javelins and suggest the least fault could be   580
    found)
He could not reprehend the fight, so many strew'd the ground.

The End of the Fourth Booke

THE FIFTH BOOKE

of

HOMER'S ILIADS

THE ARGUMENT

King Diomed (by Pallas' spirit inspir'd
With will and powre) is for his acts admir'd.
Meere men, and men deriv'd from Deities,
And Deities themselves he terrifies;
Addes wounds to terrors; his inflamed lance   5
Drawes blood from Mars and Venus. In a trance
He casts Æneas with a weightie stone:
Apollo quickens him and gets him gone.
Mars is recur'd by Pæon, but by Jove
Rebuk't for authoring breach of humane love.   10

Another Argument

In Epsilon *heaven's blood is shed*
By sacred rage of Diomed.

Pallas inspires
and glorifies
Diomed.
Then Pallas breath'd in Tydeus' sonne—to render whom
    supreame
To all the Greekes at all his parts she cast a hoter beame
On his high mind, his body fild with much superiour might
And made his compleate armor cast a farre more complete light.
From his bright helme and shield did burne a most unwearied   5
    fire,
This simile
likewise Virgil
learns of him.
Like rich Autumnus' golden lampe, whose brightnesse men
    admire
Past all the other host of starres when with his chearefull face
Fresh washt in loftie Ocean waves he doth the skies enchase.
    To let whose glory lose no sight, still Pallas made him turne
Where tumult most exprest his powre and where the fight did   10
    burne.
Dares, Priest of
Mulciber, or Vulcan.
    An honest and a wealthie man inhabited in Troy,
Dares, the Priest of Mulciber, who two sons did enjoy,

[109]

Idæus and bold Phegeus, well seene in everie fight.

*Idæus and
Phegeus both
against Diomed.*

These (singl'd from their troopes and horst) assaild Minerva's
    knight,
Who rang'd from fight to fight on foote. All hasting mutuall   15
    charge
(And now drawne neare), first Phegeus threw a javeline swift
    and large,
Whose head the king's left shoulder tooke but did no harme
    at all.
Then rusht he out a lance at him that had no idle fall

*Phegeus slaine.
Idæus flies.*

But in his breast stucke twixt the paps and strooke him from
    his horse.
Which sterne sight when Idæus saw (distrustfull of his force   20
To save his slaughterd brother's spoile) it made him headlong
    leape
From his faire chariot and leave all—yet had not scap't the
    heape
Of heavie funerall if the God, great president of fire,
Had not (in sodaine clouds of smoke, and pittie of his Sire
To leave him utterly unheird) given safe passe to his feet.   25
He gone, Tydides sent the horse and chariot to the fleet.
   The Troyans seeing Dares' sonnes one slaine, the other fled,
Were strooke amaz'd. The blew-eyd maide (to grace her Diomed
In giving free way to his power) made this so ruthfull fact
A fit advantage to remove the warre-God out of act,   30
Who rag'd so on the Ilian side. She grip't his hand and said:

Pallas to Mars.

'Mars, Mars, thou ruinor of men, that in the dust hast laid
So many cities and with blood thy Godhead dost disteine,
Now shall we ceasse to shew our breasts as passionate as men
And leave the mixture of our hands, resigning Jove his right   35
(As rector of the Gods) to give the glorie of the fight
Where he affecteth, lest he force what we should freely yeeld?'
He held it fit, and went with her from the tumultuous field,
Who set him in an nearby seate on brode Scamander's shore.

*Mars leaves the
field and Troy flies.*

He gone, all Troy was gone with him; the Greekes drave all   40
    before
And everie Leader slue a man. But first the king of men
Deserv'd the honor of his name and led the slaughter then

*Agamemnon slaies
Odius.*

And slue a Leader, one more huge than any man he led,
Great Odius, Duke of Halizons. Quite from his chariot's head
He strooke him with a lance to earth as first he flight addrest.   45
It tooke his forward-turned backe and lookt out of his breast:
His huge trunk sounded, and his armes did eccho the resound.

Idomeneus slaies Phæstus.

Idomeneus to the death did noble Phæstus wound,
The sonne of Meon-Borus that from cloddie Tarne came,
Who (taking chariot) tooke his wound and tumbl'd with the   50
     same
From his attempted seate. The lance through his right shoulder
     strooke
And horrid darknesse strooke through him. The spoile his
     souldiers tooke.

Menelaus slaies Scamandrius.

Atrides Menelaus slue (as he before him fled)
Scamandrius, sonne of Strophius, that was a huntsman bred—
A skilfull huntsman, for his skill Diana's selfe did teach   55
And made him able with his dart infallibly to reach
All sorts of subtlest savages which many a wooddie hill
Bred for him and he much preserv'd, and all to shew his skill.
Yet not the dart-delighting Queene taught him to shun this dart,
Nor all his hitting so farre off (the mastrie of his art).   60
His backe receiv'd it, and he fell upon his breast withall.
His bodie's ruine and his armes so sounded in his fall
That his affrighted horse flew off and left him, like his life.

Meriones slue Phereclus, an excellent Architect.

Meriones slue Phereclus, whom she that nere was wife
Yet Goddesse of good housewives held in excellent respect   65
For knowing all the wittie things that grace an Architect
And having pow'r to give it all the cunning use of hand.
Harmonides, his sire, built ships and made him understand
(With all the practise it requir'd) the frame of all that skill.
He built all Alexander's ships, that authord all the ill   70
Of all the Troyans and his owne, because he did not know
The Oracles advising Troy (for feare of overthrow)
To meddle with no sea affaire but live by tilling land.
This man Meriones surprisd and drave his deadly hand
Through his right hip. The lance's head ran through the region 75
About the bladder, underneath th' in-muscles and the bone.
He (sighing) bow'd his knees to death and sacrific'd to earth.

Pedæus slain by Phylides.

Phylides staid Pedæus' flight, Antenor's bastard birth,
Whom vertuous Theano his wife (to please her husband) kept
As tenderly as those she lov'd. Phylides neare him stept   80
And in the fountaine of the nerves did drench his fervent lance
At his head's backe-part, and so farre the sharpe head did
     advance
It cleft the Organe of his speech and th' Iron (cold as death)
He tooke betwixt his grinning teeth and gave the aire his
     breath.

Eurypylus slaies Hypsenor.

Eurypylus, the much renowm'd and great Euæmon's sonne,   85
Divine Hypsenor slue, begot by stout Dolopion

And consecrate Scamander's Priest. He had a God's regard
Amongst the people. His hard flight the Grecian followed hard,
Rusht in so close that with his sword he on his shoulder laid
A blow that his arme's brawne cut off; nor there his vigor staid   90
But drave downe and from off his wrist it hewd his holy hand,
That gusht out blood, and downe it dropt upon the
    blushing sand.
Death with his purple finger shut, and violent fate, his eyes.
    Thus fought these; but, distinguisht well, Tydides so implies
His furie that you could not know whose side had interest   95

*Diomed compared
to a torrent.*

In his free labours, Greece or Troy. But as a flood increast
By violent and sodaine showres let downe from hils, like hils
Melted in furie, swels and fomes, and so he overfils
His naturall channell that besides both hedge and bridge
    resignes
To his rough confluence, farre spread, and lustie flourishing   100
    vines
Drownd in his outrage: Tydeus' sonne so over-ran the field,
Strew'd such as flourisht in his way and made whole squadrons
    yeeld.
    When Pandarus, Lycaon's sonne, beheld his ruining hand
With such resistlesse insolence make lanes through everie band,

*Pandarus wounds
Diomed.*

He bent his gold-tipt bow of horne and shot him rushing in   105
At his right shoulder where his armes were hollow. Foorth
    did spin
The blood and downe his curets ranne. Then Pandarus
    cried out:
'Ranke-riding Troyans, now rush in! Now, now, I make
    no doubt
Our bravest foe is markt for death. He cannot long sustaine
My violent shaft, if Jove's faire Sonne did worthily constraine   110
My foot from Lycia.' Thus he brav'd, and yet his violent shaft
Strooke short with all his violence. Tydides' life was saft,
Who yet withdrew himselfe behind his chariot and steeds
And cald to Sthenelus: 'Come, friend, my wounded shoulder
    needs
Thy hand to ease it of this shaft.' He hasted from his seate   115
Before the coach and drew the shaft. The purple wound
    did sweate
And drowne his shirt of male in blood, and as it bled he praid:

*Diomed's prayer
to Pallas.*

    'Heare me, of Jove Ægiochus thou most unconquerd maid!
If ever in the cruell field thou hast assistfull stood
Or to my father or my selfe, now love and do me good.   120
Give him into my lance's reach that thus hath given a wound

[112]

To him thou guardst, preventing me, and brags that never more
I shall behold the chearefull Sunne.' Thus did the king implore.
The Goddesse heard, came neare and tooke the wearinesse
    of fight
From all his nerves and lineaments, and made them fresh   125
    and light,

Pallas encourageth Diomed.

And said: 'Be bold, O Diomed. In everie combat shine.
The great shield-shaker Tydeus' strength (that knight, that Sire
    of thine)
By my infusion breaths in thee. And from thy knowing mind
I have remov'd those erring mists that made it lately blind,
That thou maist difference Gods from men. And therefore   130
    use thy skill
Against the tempting Deities, if any have a will
To trie if thou presum'st of that, as thine, that flowes from them,
And so assum'st above thy right. Where thou discern'st a beame
Of any other heavenly power than she that rules in love
That cals thee to the change of blowes, resist not, but remove.   135
But if that Goddesse be so bold (since she first stird this warre)
Assault and marke her from the rest with some infamous scarre.'
    The blew-eyd Goddesse vanished, and he was seene againe
Amongst the foremost, who before though he were prompt
    and faine
To fight against the Troyans' powers, now on his spirits were   140
    cald

Diomed made thrise so strong as before by Pallas.

With thrise the vigor. Lion-like, that hath bene lately gald
By some bold sheapheard in a field where his curld flockes
    were laid,
Who tooke him as he leapt the fold—not slaine yet but appaid
With greater spirit, comes againe, and then the shepheard hides
(The rather for the desolate place) and in his Coate abides,   145
His flockes left guardlesse, which, amaz'd, shake and shrinke
    up in heapes;
He (ruthlesse) freely takes his prey and out againe he leapes:
So sprightly, fierce, victorious, the great Heroe flew
Upon the Troyans, and at once he two Commanders slew,

Hypenor and Astynous slaine by Diomed.

Hypenor and Astynous. In one his lance he fixt   150
Full at the nipple of his breast: the other smote betwixt
The necke and shoulder with his sword, which was so well
    laid on
It swept his arme and shoulder off. These left, he rusht upon
Abas and Polyeidus, of old Eurydamas
The haplesse sonnes, who could by dreames tell what would   155
    come to passe,

Yet when his sonnes set forth to Troy, the old man could not
    read
By their dreames what would chance to them, for both were
    stricken dead
By great Tydides. After these, he takes into his rage
Xanthus and Thoon, Phænops' sonnes borne to him in his age—
The good old man even pin'd with yeares, and had not one   160
    sonne more
To heire his goods. Yet Diomed tooke both and left him store
Of teares and sorowes in their steeds since he could never see
His sonnes leave those hote warres alive: so this the end must be

Egregium
πάθος

Of all his labours; what he heapt to make his issue great
Authoritie heird and with her seed fild his forgotten seate.   165
Then snatcht he up two Priamists that in one chariot stood,

Simile of a Lyon
otherwise applied
than before.

Echemmon and faire Chromius. As feeding in a wood
Oxen or steeres are, one of which a Lyon leapes upon,
Teares downe and wrings in two his necke, so sternely
        Tydeus' sonne
Threw from their chariot both these hopes of old Dardanides,   170
Then tooke their armes and sent their horse to those that ride
    the seas.
    Æneas (seeing the troopes thus tost) brake through the
    heate of fight
And all the whizzing of the darts to find the Lycian knight
Lycaon's sonne, whom having found he thus bespake the Peere:

Æneas to
Pandarus.

    'O Pandarus, where's now thy bow, thy deathfull arrowes   175
    where,
In which no one in all our host but gives the palme to thee,
Nor in the Sun-lov'd Lycian greenes that breed our Archerie
Lives any that exceeds thy selfe? Come, lift thy hands to Jove
And send an arrow at this man (if but a man he prove
That winnes such God-like victories and now affects our host   180
With so much sorrow, since so much of our best blood is lost
By his high valour). I have feare some God in him doth threat,
Incenst for want of sacrifice: the wrath of God is great.'

Pandarus to
Æneas.

    Lycaon's famous sonne replyde: 'Great Counsellor of Troy,
This man so excellent in armes I think is Tydeus' joy.   185
I know him by his fierie shield, by his bright three-plum'd caske
And by his horse: nor can I say if or some God doth maske
In his apparance or he be (whom I nam'd) Tydeus' sonne;
But without God the things he does (for certaine) are not done;
Some great Immortall that conveyes his shoulders in a clowd   190
Goes by and puts by everie dart at his bold breast bestowd,
Or lets it take with little hurt; for I my selfe let flie

[114]

A shaft that shot him through his armes, but had as good
  gone by—
Yet which I gloriously affirm'd had driven him downe to hell.
Some God is angrie, and with me, for farre hence, where I dwell 195
My horse and Chariots idle stand with which some other way
I might repaire this shamefull misse. Eleven faire chariots stay
In old Lycaon's Court, new made, new trimd to have bene gone,
Curtaind and Arrast under-foote, two horse to every one,
That eate white Barly and blacke Otes and do no good at all; 200
And these Lycaon (that well knew how these affaires would fall)
Charg'd (when I set downe this designe) I should command
  with here
And gave me many lessons more, all which much better were
Than any I tooke forth my selfe. The reason I laid downe
Was but the sparing of my horse, since in a sieged towne 205
I thought our horse-meate would be scant, when they were
  usd to have
Their mangers full. So I left them and like a lackey slave
Am come to Ilion confident in nothing but my bow,
That nothing profits me. Two shafts I vainly did bestow
At two great Princes but of both my arrowes neither slew, 210
Nor this nor Atreus' yonger sonne: a little blood I drew
That serv'd but to incense them more. In an unhappie starre
I therefore from my Armorie have drawne those tooles of warre,
That day when for great Hector's sake to amiable Troy
I came to leade the Troyan bands. But if I ever joy 215
(In safe returne) my Countrie's sight, my wive's, my lofty towres,
Let any stranger take this head if to the firie powres
This bow, these shafts, in peeces burst (by these hands) be
  not throwne—
Idle companions that they are to me and my renowne.'

Æneas to Pandarus.

Æneas said: 'Use no such words, for any other way 220
Than this they shall not now be usd. We first will both assay
This man with horse and chariot. Come then, ascend to me,
That thou maist trie our Troyan horse how skild in field
  they be,
And in pursuing those that flie, or flying, being pursude,
How excellent they are of foote: and these (if Jove conclude 225
The scape of Tydeus againe and grace him with our flight)
Shall serve to bring us safely off. Come, I'le be first shall fight:
Take thou these faire reines and this scourge. Or (if thou wilt)
  fight thou
And leave the horses' care to me.' He answered: 'I will now

[115]

Pandarus fights and
Æneas guideth the
chariot.

Descend to fight; keepe thou the reines, and guide thy selfe   230
    thy horse,
Who with their wonted manager will better wield the force
Of the impulsive chariot, if we be driven to flie,
Than with a stranger—under whom they will be much more shye,
And (fearing my voice, wishing thine) grow restie, nor go on
To beare us off, but leave engag'd for mightie Tydeus' sonne   235
Themselves and us. Then be thy part thy one-hov'd horses'
    guide,
I'le make the fight, and with a dart receive his utmost pride.'
    With this the gorgious chariot both (thus prepar'd) ascend
And make full way at Diomed; which noted by his friend,

'Mine owne most loved Mind,' said he, 'two mightie men   240
    of warre
I see come with a purposd charge; one's he that hits so farre
With bow and shaft, Lycaon's sonne: the other fames the brood
Of great Anchises and the Queene that rules in Amorous
    blood—
Æneas, excellent in armes. Come up and use your steeds
And looke not warre so in the face, lest that desire that feeds   245
Thy great mind be the bane of it.' This did with anger sting
The blood of Diomed, to see his friend, that chid the king
Before the fight, and then preferd his ablesse and his mind
To all his ancestors in fight, now come so farre behind—

Diomed now finds
time to make
Sthenelus see better
his late rebuke of
Agamemnon.

Whom thus he answerd: 'Urge no flight, you cannot please   250
    me so.
Nor is it honest, in my mind, to feare a coming foe,
Or make a flight good, though with fight. My powers are yet
    entire
And scorne the help-tire of a horse. I will not blow the fire
Of their hote valours with my flight, but cast upon the blaze
This body borne upon my knees. I entertaine amaze?   255
Minerva will not see that shame. And since they have begun,
They shall not both elect their ends; and he that scapes
    shall runne,
Or stay and take the other's fate. And this I leave for thee—
If amply wise Athenia give both their lives to me,
Reine our horse to their chariot hard, and have a speciall heed   260
To seise upon Æneas' steeds, that we may change their breed
And make a Grecian race of them that have bene long of Troy.
For these are bred of those brave beasts which, for the lovely Boy
That waits now on the cup of Jove, Jove, that farre-seeing God,
Gave Tros the king in recompence—the best that ever trod   265
The sounding Center underneath the Morning and the Sunne.

[116]

Anchises stole the breed of them, for where their Sires did runne
He closely put his Mares to them, and never made it knowne
To him that heird them, who was then the king Laomedon.
Sixe horses had he of that race, of which himselfe kept foure   270
And gave the other two his sonne; and these are they that scoure
The field so bravely towards us, expert in charge and flight.
If these we have the power to take, our prize is exquisite,
And our renowne will farre exceed.' While these were talking
    thus,
The fir'd horse brought th'assailants neare, and thus spake   275
    Pandarus:

Pandarus to Diomed.

    'Most suffering-minded Tydeus' sonne, that hast of warre
    the art,
My shaft, that strooke thee, slue thee not; I now will prove
    a dart.'
This said, he shooke, and then he threw, a lance, aloft
    and large,
That in Tydides' curets stucke, quite driving through his targe.
Then braid he out so wild a voice that all the field might heare: 280
'Now have I reacht thy root of life, and by thy death shall beare
Our praise's chiefe prize from the field.' Tydides undismaid
Replide: 'Thou err'st, I am not toucht: but more charge
    will be laid
To both your lives before you part: at least the life of one
Shall satiate the throate of Mars.' This said, his lance was gone.   285
Minerva led it to his face, which at his eye ranne in,
And, as he stoopt, strooke through his jawes, his tong's roote
    and his chinne.

Diomed slaies
Pandarus.

Downe from the chariot he fell, his gay armes shin'd and rung,
The swift horse trembled, and his soule for ever charm'd his
    tongue.
Æneas with his shield and lance leapt swiftly to his friend,   290
Affraid the Greekes would force his trunke; and that he did
    defend,
Bold as a Lyon of his strength. He hid him with his shield,
Shooke round his lance, and horribly did threaten all the field
With death, if any durst make in. Tydides raisd a stone,
With his one hand, of wondrous weight, and powr'd it mainly on   295

Æneas being
sonne to Anchises.

The hip of Anchisiades, wherein the joynt doth move
The thigh—tis cald the huckle bone—which all in sherds
    it drove,
Brake both the nerves, and with the edge cut all the flesh away.
It staggerd him upon his knees, and made th'Heroe stay
His strooke-blind temples on his hand, his elbow on the earth.   300

And there this Prince of men had died if she that gave him birth

(Kist by Anchises on the greene, where his faire oxen fed,
Jove's loving daughter) instantly had not about him spred
Her soft embraces, and convaid within her heavenly vaile
(Usd as a rampier gainst all darts, that did so hote assaile)   305
Her deare-lov'd issue from the field. Then Sthenelus in hast
(Remembring what his friend advisd) from forth the preasse
    made fast
His owne horse to their chariot, and presently laid hand

Upon the lovely-coated horse Æneas did command,
Which bringing to the wondring Greekes he did their guard   310
    commend
To his belov'd Deipylus, who was his inward friend
And (of his equals) one to whom he had most honor showne,
That he might see them safe at fleete. Then stept he to his owne,
With which he chearefully made in to Tydeus' mightie race.
He (madde with his great enemie's rape) was hote in desperate   315
    chase
Of her that made it, with his lance (arm'd lesse with steele
    than spight),
Well knowing her no Deitie that had to do in fight—
Minerva his great patronesse, nor she that raceth townes,
Bellona, but a Goddesse weake and foe to men's renownes.

Her (through a world of fight) pursude, at last he over-tooke,   320
And (thrusting up his ruthlesse lance) her heavenly veile he
    strooke
(That even the Graces wrought themselves at her divine
    command)
Quite through, and hurt the tender backe of her delicious hand.
The rude point piercing through her palme, forth flow'd th'
    immortall blood
(Blood such as flowes in blessed Gods, that eate no humane   325
    food

Nor drinke of our inflaming wine, and therefore bloodlesse are
And cald immortals). Out she cried, and could no longer beare
Her lov'd sonne, whom she cast from her; and in a sable clowd
Phœbus (receiving) hid him close from all the Grecian crowd,
Lest some of them should find his death. Away flew Venus then,   330
And after her cried Diomed: 'Away, thou spoile of men,
Though sprung from all-preserving Jove! These hote encounters
    leave!
Is't not enough that sillie Dames thy sorceries should deceive
Unlesse thou thrust into the warre and rob a souldier's right?
I thinke a few of these assaults will make thee feare the fight,   335

Where ever thou shalt heare it nam'd.' She, sighing, went
    her way

Iris rescues Venus.

Extremely griev'd, and with her griefes her beauties did decay,
And blacke her Ivorie bodie grew. Then from a dewy mist
Brake swift-foot Iris to her aide from all the darts that hist
At her quicke rapture; and to Mars they tooke their plaintife   340
    course,
And found him on the fight's left hand, by him his speedie horse
And huge lance lying in a fogge. The Queene of all things faire

Venus to Mars.
χρυσάμπυκας
ἤτεεν ἵππους

Her loved brother on her knees besought with instant prayre
His golden-ribband-bound-man'd horse to lend her up to
    heaven,
For she was much griev'd with a wound a mortall man had   345
    given—
Tydides, that gainst Jove himselfe durst now advance his arme.

*Mars lends his
horse to Venus.*

  He granted, and his chariot (perplext with her late harme)
She mounted, and her wagonnesse was she that paints the aire.
The horse she reind, and with a scourge importun'd their repaire
That of themselves out-flew the wind, and quickly they ascend   350
Olympus, high seate of the Gods; th' horse knew their journie's
    end,
Stood still, and from their chariot the windie-footed Dame
Dissolv'd and gave them heavenly food; and to Dione came
Her wounded daughter, bent her knees. She kindly bad her
    stand;
With sweet embraces helpt her up, strok't her with her soft   355
    hand;

*Dione, mother of
Venus, to Venus.*

Call'd kindly by her name, and askt: 'What God hath bene
    so rude,
Sweet daughter, to chastise thee thus—as if thou wert pursude
Even to the act of some light sinne, and deprehended so?
For otherwise each close escape is in the Great let go.'

Venus to Dione.

  She answerd: 'Haughtie Tydeus' sonne hath bene so insolent,   360
Since he whom most my heart esteemes of all my lov'd descent
I rescu'd from his bloodie hand. Now battell is not given
To any Troyans by the Greekes, but by the Greekes to heaven.'

Dione to Venus.

  She answerd: 'Daughter, thinke not much, though much it
    grieve thee: use
The patience, whereof many Gods examples may produce   365
In many bitter ils receiv'd, as well that men sustaine
By their inflictions as by men repaid to them againe.

*Mars bound in
chaines by Otus
and Ephialtes.*

Mars sufferd much more than thy selfe by Ephialtes' powre
And Otus', Aloeus' sonnes, who in a brazen towre
(And in inextricable chaines) cast that warre-greedie God;   370

[119]

Where twise six months and one he liv'd, and there the period
Of his sad life perhaps had closd if his kind step-dame's eye,
Faire Erebœa, had not seene, who told it Mercurie,
And he by stealth enfranchisd him, though he could scarce enjoy
The benefite of franchisment, the chaines did so destroy   375
His vitall forces with their weight. So Juno sufferd more
When with a three-forkt arrowe's head Amphitryon's sonne
    did gore
Her right breast past all hope of cure. Pluto sustain no lesse
By that selfe man, and by a shaft of equall bitternesse,
Shot through his shoulder at hell gates, and there (amongst   380
    the dead,
Were he not deathlesse) he had died, but up to heaven he fled
(Extremely tortur'd) for recure, which instantly he wonne

Pæon, Phisition   At Pæon's hand with soveraigne Balme—and this did Jove's
to the Gods.   great sonne,

ἐπιφώνημα   Unblest, great-high-deed-daring man, that car'd not doing ill,
That with his bow durst wound the Gods. But by Minerva's   385
    will
Thy wound the foolish Diomed was so prophane to give,
Not knowing he that fights with heaven hath never long to live.
And for this deed he never shall have child about his knee
To call him father, coming home. Besides, heare this from me,
Strength-trusting man: though thou be strong and art in   390
    strength a towre,
Take heed a stronger meet thee not, and that a woman's powre
Containes not that superiour strength, and lest that woman be
Adrastus' daughter, and thy wife, the wise Ægiale,
When (from this houre not farre) she wakes, even sighing
    with desire
To kindle our revenge on thee with her enamouring fire,   395
In choosing her some fresh young friend and so drowne all
    thy fame
Wonne here in warre in her Court-peace and in an opener
    shame.'
  This said, with both her hands she cleansd the tender backe
    and palme
Of all the sacred blood they lost; and, never using Balme,
The paine ceast, and the wound was cur'd of this kind Queene   400
    of love.
  Juno and Pallas seeing this, assaid to anger Jove
And quit his late-made mirth with them about the loving Dame
With some sharpe jest, in like sort built upon her present
    shame.

Pallas to Jove.

Grey-eyd Athenia began, and askt the Thunderer,
If (nothing moving him to wrath) she boldly might preferre   405
What she conceiv'd to his conceipt; and (staying no reply)
She bade him view the Cyprian fruite he lov'd so tenderly,
Whom she thought hurt, and by this meanes—intending to
    suborne
Some other Ladie of the Greekes (whom lovely veiles adorne)
To gratifie some other friend of her much-loved Troy,   410

Scopticè.

As she embrac't and stird her blood to the Venerean joy,
The golden claspe those Grecian Dames upon their girdles weare
Tooke hold of her delicious hand and hurt it, she had feare.

Jove to Venus.

    The Thunderer smil'd and cald to him love's golden
    Arbitresse,
And told her those rough workes of warre were not for her   415
    accesse:
She should be making mariages, embracings, kisses, charmes—
Sterne Mars and Pallas had the charge of those affaires in armes.
    While these thus talkt, Tydides' rage still thirsted to atchieve
His prise upon Anchises' sonne, though well he did perceive
The Sunne himselfe protected him: but his desires (inflam'd   420
With that great Troyan Prince's blood and armes so highly
    fam'd)
Not that great God did reverence. Thrise rusht he rudely on,
And thrise betwixt his darts and death the Sunne's bright target
    shone.
But when upon the fourth assault (much like a spirit) he flew,
The far-off-working Deitie exceeding wrathfull grew,   425

Apollo to Diomed.

And askt him: 'What? Not yeeld to Gods? Thy equals learne
    to know:
The race of Gods is farre above men creeping here below.'
    This drave him to some small retreite; he would not tempt
    more neare
The wrath of him that strooke so farre, whose powre had now
    set cleare

Apollo beares
Æneas to Troy.

Æneas from the stormie field within the holy place   430
Of Pergamus, where to the hope of his so soveraigne grace
A goodly Temple was advanc't, in whose large inmost part
He left him, and to his supply enclin'd his mother's heart
Latona, and the dart-pleasd Queene, who cur'd and made
    him strong.
    The silver-bow'd faire God then threw in the tumultuous   435

The Image of
Æneas.

    throng
An Image that in stature, looke and armes he did create

Like Venus' sonne—for which the Greekes and Troyans made
  debate,
Laid lowd strokes on their Ox-hide shields and bucklers easly
  borne:
Which error Phœbus pleasd to urge on Mars himselfe in scorne:

Apollo to Mars.

  'Mars, Mars,' said he, 'thou plague of men, smeard with the   440
  dust and blood
Of humanes and their ruin'd wals, yet thinks thy God-head good
To fright this Furie from the field, who next will fight with Jove?
First, in a bold approch he hurt the moist palme of thy Love,
And next (as if he did affect to have a Deitie's powre)
He held out his assault on me.' This said, the loftie towre   445
Of Pergamus he made his seate, and Mars did now excite
The Troyan forces, in the forme of him that led to fight

*Mars like
Acamas to the
sons of Priam.*

The Thracian troopes, swift Acamas: 'O Priam's sonnes,' said he,
'How long the slaughter of your men can ye sustaine to see?
Even till they brave ye at your gates? Ye suffer beaten downe   450
Æneas, great Anchises' sonne, whose prowesse we renowne
As much as Hector's. Fetch him off from this contentious prease.'
  With this, the strength and spirits of all his courage did
    increase;

*Sarpedon reproves
Hector.*

And yet Sarpedon seconds him with this particular taunt
Of noble Hector: 'Hector, where is thy unthankfull vaunt   455
And that huge strength on which it built—that thou and thy
  allies
With all thy brothers (without aid of us or our supplies,
And troubling not a citizen) the Citie safe would hold?
In all which, friends' and brothers' helps I see not, nor am told
Of any one of their exploits. But (all held in dismay   460
Of Diomed, like a sort of dogs that at a Lion bay
And entertaine no spirit to pinch), we (your assistants here)
Fight for the towne, as you helpt us: and I (an aiding Peere,
No Citizen, even out of care that doth become a man
For men and children's liberties) adde all the aide I can—   465
Not out of my particular cause; far hence my profit growes,
For far hence Asian Lycia lies, where gulfie Xanthus flowes,
And where my lov'd wife, infant sonne and treasure nothing
  scant
I left behind me, which I see those men would have that want,
And therefore they that have, would keepe. Yet I (as I would   470
  lose
Their sure fruition) cheere my troupes and with their lives
  propose
Mine owne life both to generall fight and to particular cope

With this great souldier—though (I say) I entertaine no hope
To have such gettings as the Greeks, nor feare to lose like Troy.
Yet thou (even Hector) deedlesse standst, and car'st not to   475
     employ
Thy towne-borne friends, to bid them stand, to fight and save
     their wives—
Lest as a Fowler casts his nets upon the silly lives
Of birds of all sorts, so the foe your walls and houses hales
(One with another) on all heads, or such as scape their fals
Be made the prey and prize of them (as willing overthrowne)   480
That hope not for you with their force: and so this brave-built
     towne
Will prove a Chaos. That deserves in thee so hote a care
As should consume thy dayes and nights to hearten and prepare
Th' assistant Princes, pray their minds to beare their far-brought
     toiles
To give them worth with worthy fight; in victories and foiles   485
Still to be equall; and thy selfe (exampling them in all)
Need no reproofes nor spurs. All this in thy free choice should
     fall.'
     This stung great Hector's heart: and yet, as every generous
     mind
Should silent beare a just reproofe and shew what good they find
In worthy counsels, by their ends put into present deeds,   490
Not stomacke, nor be vainly sham'd, so Hector's spirit proceeds,
And from his Chariot (wholly arm'd) he jumpt upon the sand,
On foote so toiling through the hoast, a dart in either hand,
And all hands turn'd against the Greeks. The Greeks despisde
     their worst
And (thickning their instructed powres) expected all they durst. 495
     Then with the feet of horse and foote the dust in clouds
     did rise.

Simile from the And as in sacred floores of barnes upon corne-winowers flies
husbandman, The chaffe, driven with an opposite wind, when yellow Ceres
expressing notably. dites,
Which all the Diters' feet, legs, armes, their heads and shoulders
     whites:
So lookt the Grecians gray with dust, that strooke the solide   500
     heaven,
Raisd from returning chariots and troupes together driven.
Each side stood to their labours firme: fierce Mars flew through
     the aire
And gatherd darknesse from the fight, and, with his best affaire,
Obeyd the pleasure of the Sunne, that weares the golden sword,

Who bad him raise the spirits of Troy, when Pallas ceast   505
    t'afford
Her helping office to the Greeks; and then his owne hands
    wrought,

*Apollo brings
Æneas from his
Temple to field
cured.*

Which (from his Phane's rich chancell, cur'd) the true Æneas
    brought,
And plac't him by his Peeres in field—who did (with joy) admire
To see him both alive and safe and all his powers entire,
Yet stood not sifting how it chanc't—another sort of taske   510
Than stirring th' idle sive of newes did all their forces aske,
Inflam'd by Phœbus, harmfull Mars, and Eris, eagrer farre.
The Greekes had none to hearten them; their hearts rose
    with the warre;
But chiefly Diomed, Ithacus and both th' Ajaces usde
Stirring examples and good words: their owne fames had   515
    infusde
Spirit enough into their blouds to make them neither feare
The Troyans' force nor Fate it selfe, but still expecting were,
When most was done, what would be more. Their ground
    they stil made good,

Simile.

And (in their silence and set powers) like faire still clouds they
    stood,
With which Jove crownes the tops of hils in any quiet day,   520
When Boreas and the ruder winds (that use to drive away
Aire's duskie vapors, being loose, in many a whistling gale)
Are pleasingly bound up and calme, and not a breath exhale:
So firmely stood the Greeks, nor fled for all the Ilians' ayd.
    Atrides yet coasts through the troupes, confirming men so   525
    stayd:
'O friends,' said he, 'hold up your minds; strength is but
    strength of will;
Reverence each other's good in fight, and shame at things
    done ill.
Where souldiers shew an honest shame, and love of honour lives
That ranks men with the first in fight, death fewer liveries gives
Than life, or than where Fame's neglect makes cow-herds fight   530
    at length.
Flight neither doth the bodie grace nor shewes the mind hath
    strength.'
He said, and swiftly through the troupes a mortall Lance did
    send,
That reft a standard-bearer's life, renownd Æneas' friend,

*Pergasides slain
by Agamemnon.*

Deicoon Pergasides, whom all the Troyans lov'd
As he were one of Priam's sonnes. his mind was so approv'd   535

[124]

In alwayes fighting with the first. The Lance his target tooke,
Which could not interrupt the blow that through it cleerly strooke
And in his bellie's rimme was sheath'd beneath his girdle-stead.
He sounded falling, and his armes with him resounded, dead.

*Orsilochus and
Crethon slain by
Æneas.*

Then fell two Princes of the Greeks, by great Æneas' ire,   540
Diocleus' sonnes, Orsilochus, and Crethon, whose kind Sire
In bravely-builded Phere dwelt, rich, and of sacred bloud.
He was descended lineally from great Alphæus' floud,

*The pedigree of
Orsilochus.*

That broadly flowes through Pylos' fields: Alphæus did beget
Orsilochus, who in the rule of many men was set: 545
And that Orsilochus begat the rich Diocleus:
Diocleus sire to Crethon was and this Orsilochus.
Both these, arriv'd at man's estate, with both th' Atrides went
To honor them in th' Ilian warres; and both were one way sent
To death as well as Troy, for death hid both in one blacke   550
  houre.

Simile.

As two yong Lions (with their dam, sustaind but to devoure)
Bred on the tops of some steepe hill and in the gloomie deepe
Of an inaccessible wood, rush out and prey on sheepe,
Steeres, Oxen, and destroy men's stals so long that they come
  short
And by the Owner's steele are slaine: in such unhappie sort   555
Fell these beneath Æneas' powre. When Menelaus view'd
(Like two tall fir-trees) these two fall, their timelesse fals he
  rew'd,
And to the first fight where they lay a vengefull force he tooke.
His armes beat backe the Sunne in flames; a dreadfull Lance he
  shooke;
Mars put the furie in his mind that by Æneas' hands   560
(Who was to make the slaughter good) he might have strewd
  the sands.

*Antilochus'
voluntary care of
Menelaus, and their
charge of Æneas.*

Antilochus (old Nestor's sonne) observing he was bent
To urge a combat of such ods, and knowing the event
Being ill on his part, all their paines (alone sustaind for him)
Er'd from their end, made after hard and tooke them in the   565
  trim
Of an encounter; both their hands and darts advanc't and
  shooke,
And both pitcht in full stand of charge—when suddenly the
  looke
Of Anchisiades tooke note of Nestor's valiant sonne
In full charge too, which two to one made Venus' issue shunne
The hote adventure, though he were a souldier well approv'd.   570

Then drew they off their slaughterd friends, who given to their
    belov'd,
They turnd where fight shewd deadliest hate, and there mixt
    with the dead
Pylæmen, that the targatiers of Paphlagonia led,
A man like Mars; and with him fell good Mydon that did guide

His chariot, Atymnus' sonne. The Prince Pylæmen died   575
By Menelaus; Nestor's joy slue Mydon; one before,
The other in the chariot. Atrides' lance did gore
Pylæmen's shoulder in the blade; Antilochus did force
A mightie stone up from the earth, and (as he turnd his horse)

Strooke Mydon's elbow in the midst; the reines of Ivorie   580
Fell from his hands into the dust; Antilochus let flie
His sword withall, and (rushing in) a blow so deadly layd
Upon his temples that he gron'd, tumbl'd to earth, and stayd
A mightie while preposterously (because the dust was deepe)
Upon his necke and shoulders there, even till his foe tooke   585
    keepe
Of his prisde horse and made them stirre; and then he prostrate
    fell.

His horse Antilochus tooke home. When Hector had heard tell
(Amongst the uprore) of their deaths, he laid out all his voice
And ran upon the Greeks: behind came many men of choice,
Before him marcht great Mars himselfe, matcht with his femall   590
    mate,
The drad Bellona. She brought on (to fight for mutuall Fate)
A tumult that was wilde and mad: he shooke a horrid Lance
And now led Hector, and anon behind would make the chance.
   This sight when great Tydides saw, his haire stood up on end,
And him whom all the skill and powre of armes did late attend   595

Now like a man in counsell poore, that (travelling) goes amisse,
And (having past a boundlesse plaine) not knowing where he is,
Comes on the sodaine where he sees a river rough and raves
With his owne billowes ravished into the king of waves,
Murmurs with fome, and frights him backe: so he, amazd,   600
    retirde,
And thus would make good his amaze: 'O friends, we all admirde
Great Hector as one of himselfe, well-darting, bold in warre,
When some God guards him still from death and makes him
    dare so farre.
Now Mars himselfe (formd like a man), is present in his rage,
And therefore whatsoever cause importunes you to wage   605
Warre with these Troyans, never strive, but gently take your rod,
Lest in your bosomes, for a man, ye ever find a God.'

As Greece retirde, the power of Troy did much more forward
    prease,

And Hector two brave men of warre sent to the fields of peace—
Menesthes and Anchialus; one chariot bare them both.   610
Their fals made Ajax Telamon ruthfull of heart and wroth,
Who lightned out a lance that smote Amphius Selages,
That dwelt in Pæsos, rich in lands, and did huge goods possesse,
But Fate to Priam and his sonnes conducted his supply:
The Javelin on his girdle strooke and pierced mortally   615
His bellie's lower part; he fell. His armes had lookes so trim
That Ajax needs would prove their spoile; the Troyans powrd
    on him
Whole stormes of Lances, large and sharpe, of which a number
    stucke
In his rough shield; yet from the slaine he did his Javelin plucke,
But could not from his shoulders force the armes he did affect,   620
The Troyans with such drifts of Darts the body did protect.
And wisely Telamonius fear'd their valorous defence,
So many and so strong of hand stood in with such expence
Of deadly prowesse, who repeld (though big, strong, bold he
    were)
The famous Ajax, and their friend did from his rapture beare.   625
    Thus this place, fild with strength of fight in th' armie's other
        prease,
Tlepolemus, a tall big man, the sonne of Hercules,
A cruell destinie inspir'd with strong desire to prove

Jove's son
Sarpedon, and
Tlepolemus his
nephew, son to
Hercules, draw to
encounter.

Tlepolemus to
Sarpedon.

Encounter with Sarpedon's strength, the sonne of Cloudy Jove;
Who, coming on to that sterne end, had chosen him his foe.   630
Thus Jove's great Nephew and his sonne 'gainst one another go.
Tlepolemus (to make his end more worth the will of Fate)
Began, as if he had her powre, and shewd the mortall state
Of too much confidence in man with this superflous Brave:
'Sarpedon, what necessitie, or needlesse humor drave   635
Thy forme to these warres—which in heart I know thou doest
    abhorre?
A man not seene in deeds of armes, a Lycian counsellor—
They lie that call thee sonne to Jove, since Jove bred none so
    late.
The men of elder times were they that his high powre begat,
Such men as had Herculean force. My father Hercules   640
Was Jove's true issue; he was bold, his deeds did well expresse
They sprung out of a Lion's heart. He whilome came to Troy
(For horse that Jupiter gave Tros, for Ganymed his boy)
With six ships onely and few men, and tore the **Citie downe,**

Left all her broad wayes desolate, and made the horse his   645
    owne.
For thee, thy mind is ill disposde, thy bodie's powers are poore,
And therefore are thy troopes so weake: the souldier evermore
Followes the temper of his chiefe, and thou pull'st downe a side.
But say thou art the sonne of Jove, and hast thy meanes supplide
With forces fitting his descent—the powers that I compell   650
Shall throw thee hence, and make thy head run ope the gates
    of hell.'

Sarpedon to
Tlepolemus.

    Jove's Lycian issue answerd him: 'Tlepolemus, tis true
Thy father holy Ilion in thát sort overthrew.
Th' injustice of the king was cause, that where thy father had
Usde good deservings to his state he quitted him with bad.   655
Hesione, the joy and grace of king Laomedon,
Thy father rescude from a whale and gave to Telamon
In honourd Nuptials—Telamon, from whom your strongest
    Greeke
Boasts to have issude; and this grace might well expect the like,
Yet he gave taunts for thanks, and kept, against his oath,   660
    his horse.
And therefore both thy father's strength and justice might
    enforce
The wreake he tooke on Troy. But this and thy cause differ farre;
Sonnes seldome heire their fathers' worths; thou canst not make
    his warre.
What thou assum'st from him is mine, to be on thee imposde.'
    With this, he threw an ashen dart, and then Tlepolemus   665
    losde
Another from his glorious hand. Both at one instant flew,
Both strooke, both wounded; from his necke, Sarpedon's
    Javelin drew

Sarpedon slaughters
Tlepolemus.

The life-bloud of Tlepolemus; full in the midst it fell,
And what he threatned, th' other gave—that darknesse, and
    that hell.

Himselfe sore hurt
by Tlepolemus.

Sarpedon's left thigh tooke the Lance; it pierc't the solide   670
    bone
And with his raging head ranne through; but Jove preserv'd
    his sonne.
The dart yet vext him bitterly, which should have bene puld out,
But none considerd then so much, so thicke came on the rout
And fild each hand so full of cause to plie his owne defence.
Twas held enough (both falne) that both were nobly caried   675
    thence.
    Ulysses knew the events of both and tooke it much to hart

Ulysses' valour.

That his friend's enemie should scape; and in a twofold part
His thoughts contended, if he should pursue Sarpedon's life
Or take his friend's wreake on his men. Fate did conclude this strife,
By whom twas otherwise decreed than that Ulysses' steele   680
Should end Sarpedon. In this doubt, Minerva tooke the wheele
From fickle Chance and made his mind resolve to right his friend
With that bloud he could surest draw. Then did Revenge extend
Her full powre on the multitude. Then did he never misse.
Alastor, Halius, Chromius, Noemon, Prytanis,   685
Alcander and a number more he slue, and more had slaine
If Hector had not understood, whose powre made in amaine
And strooke feare through the Grecian troupes, but to Sarpedon gave

Sarpedon to Hector.

Hope of full rescue, who thus cried: 'O Hector! helpe and save
My body from the spoile of Greece, that to your loved towne   690
My friends may see me borne, and then let earth possesse her owne
In this soyle for whose sake I left my countrie's; for no day
Shall ever shew me that againe, nor to my wife display
(And yong hope of my Name) the joy of my much thirsted sight:
All which I left for Troy, for them let Troy then do this right.'   695
   To all this Hector gives no word, but greedily he strives
With all speed to repell the Greekes and shed in floods their lives,
And left Sarpedon: but what face soever he put on
Of following the common cause, he left this Prince alone
For his particular grudge, because so late he was so plaine   700
In his reproofe before the host, and that did he retaine.
How ever, for example sake, he would not shew it then,
And for his shame too, since twas just. But good Sarpedon's men
Venturd themselves, and forc't him off and set him underneath
The goodly Beech of Jupiter, where now they did unsheath   705
The Ashen lance; strong Pelagon, his friend, most lov'd, most true,
Enforc't it from his maimed thigh—with which his spirit flew

Sarpedon in a trance.

And darknesse over-flew his eyes, yet with a gentle gale,
That round about the dying Prince coole Boreas did exhale,
He was reviv'd, recomforted, that else had griev'd and dyed.   710
   All this time, flight drave to the fleet the Argives, who applyed
No weapon gainst the proud pursuite, nor ever turnd a head,
They knew so well that Mars pursude, and dreadfull Hector led.
Then who was first, who last, whose lives, the Iron Mars did seise,

[129]

And Priam's Hector? Helenus, surnam'd Œnopides;   715
Good Teuthras, and Orestes, skild in managing of horse;
Bold Œnomaus, and a man renownd for martiall force,
Trechus, the great Ætolian Chiefe; Oresbius, that did weare
The gawdy Myter, studied wealth extremely, and dwelt neare
Th' Atlantique lake Cephisides, in Hyla, by whose seate   720
The good men of Bœotia dwelt. This slaughter grew so great
It flew to heaven. Saturnia discernd it, and cried out
To Pallas: 'O unworthy sight, to see a field so fought,
And breake our words to Sparta's king, that Ilion should be
        rac't
And he returne reveng'd, when thus we see his Greekes   725
        disgrac't
And beare the harmfull rage of Mars! Come, let us use our care
That we dishonor not our powers.' Minerva was as yare
As she at the despight of Troy. Her golden-bridl'd steeds
Then Saturn's daughter brought abrode, and Hebe she proceeds
T' addresse her chariot; instantly she gives it either wheele,   730

Juno's chariot.   Beam'd with eight Spokes of sounding brasse. The Axle-tree
        was steele,
The Felffes, incorruptible gold, their upper bands of brasse,
Their matter most unvallued, their worke of wondrous grace.
The Naves in which the Spokes were driven were all with
        silver bound;
The chariot's seate two hoopes of gold and silver strengthned   735
        round,
Edg'd with a gold and silver fringe; the beame that lookt before
Was massie silver, on whose top geres all of gold it wore
And golden Poitrils. Juno mounts and her hote horses rein'd,
That thirsted for contention and still of peace complaind.

Pallas armed.   Minerva wrapt her in the robe, that curiously she wove   740
With glorious colours as she sate on th' Azure floore of Jove,
And wore the armes that he puts on, bent to the tearefull field.

Ægis (Jove's shield)   About her brode-spred shoulders hung his huge and horrid
described.   shield,
Fring'd round with ever-fighting Snakes; through it was drawne
        to life
The miseries and deaths of fight; in it frownd bloodie Strife;   745
In it shin'd sacred Fortitude; in it fell Pursuit flew;
In it the monster Gorgon's head, in which (held out to view)
Were all the dire ostents of Jove. On her big head she plac't
His foure-plum'd glittering caske of gold, so admirably vast
It would a hundred garrisons of souldiers comprehend.   750
Then to her shining chariot her vigorous feet ascend,

And in her violent hand she takes his grave, huge, solid lance,
With which the conquests of her wrath she useth to advance
And overturne whole fields of men, to shew she was the seed
Of him that thunders. Then heaven's Queene (to urge her 755
   horses' speed)
Takes up the scourge, and forth they flie; the ample gates of
   heaven
Rung, and flew open of themselves, the charge whereof is given
(With all Olympus and the skie) to the distinguisht Howres,
That cleare or hide it all in clowds, or powre it downe in
   showres.
This way their scourge-obeying horse made haste, and soone 760
   they wonne
The top of all the topfull heavens, where aged Saturn's sonne
Sate severd from the other Gods. Then staid the white-arm'd
   Queene
Her steeds, and askt of Jove, if Mars did not incense his spleene
With his foule deeds in ruining so many and so great
In the Command and grace of Greece, and in so rude a heate. 765
At which (she said) Apollo laught and Venus, who still sue
To that mad God for violence that never justice knew;
For whose impietie she askt, if, with his wished love,
Her selfe might free the field of him? He bade her rather move
Athenia to the charge she sought, who usd of old to be 770
The bane of Mars, and had as well the gift of spoile as he.
   This grace she slackt not, but her horse scourg'd, that in
   nature flew
Betwixt the cope of starres and earth. And how farre at a view
A man into the purple Sea may from a hill descrie,
So farre a high-neighing horse of heaven at everie jumpe 775
   would flie.
   Arriv'd at Troy, where, broke in curls, the two floods mixe
   their force,
Scamander and bright Simois, Saturnia staid her horse,
Tooke them from chariot, and a clowd of mightie depth diffusd
About them; and the verdant bankes of Simois produc'd
(In nature) what they eate in heaven. Then both the Goddesses 780
Marcht like a paire of timorous Doves, in hasting their accesse
To th' Argive succour. Being arriv'd where both the most and
   best
Were heapt together (shewing all like Lyons at a feast
Of new slaine carkasses, or Bores beyond encounter strong),
There found they Diomed; and there midst all th' admiring 785
   throng

The three Howrs, Guardians of heaven gates.

How farre a heavenly horse took at one reach or stroke in galloping or running; wherein Homer's mind is farre from being exprest in his Interpreters, al taking it for how far Deities were borne from the earth: when instantly they came downe to earth: τόσσον ἐπιθρῴσκουσι &c. tantum uno saltu conficiunt, vel, tantum subsultim progrediuntur deorum altizoni equi, &c. *uno being understood, and the horses' swiftnes highly exprest. The sence otherwise is senslesse and contradictorie.*

Ἀμβροσίην *is the originall word, which Scaliger taxeth, very learnedly, asking how the horse came by it on those bankes, when the text tels*

*him Simois
produced it: being
willing to expresse
by Hyperbole the
delicacie of that
soile. If not, I
hope the Deities
could ever
command it.*

Saturnia put on Stentor's shape, that had a brazen voice
And spake as lowd as fiftie men—like whom she made a noise
And chid the Argives: 'O ye Greekes—in name and outward rite
But Princes onely, not in act—what scandall, what despight
Use ye to honor? All the time the great Æacides   790
Was conversant in armes, your foes durst not a foote addresse
Without their ports, so much they feard his lance that all
    controld—
And now they out-ray to your fleete.' This did with shame make
    bold
The generall spirit and powre of Greece, when (with particular
    note
Of their disgrace) Athenia made Tydeus' issue hote.   795
She found him at his chariot, refreshing of his wound
Inflicted by slaine Pandarus; his sweat did so abound,
It much annoid him underneath the brode belt of his shield,
With which, and tired with his toile, his soule could hardly yeeld
His bodie motion. With his hand he lifted up the belt   800
And wip't away that clotterd blood the fervent wound did melt.
Minerva leand against his horse, and neare their withers laid

Pallas to Diomed.

Her sacred hand; then spake to him: 'Beleeve me, Diomed,
Tydeus exampl'd not himselfe in thee his sonne; not Great,
But yet he was a souldier; a man of so much heate   805
That in his Ambassie for Thebes, when I forbad his mind
To be too ventrous, and when Feasts his heart might have
    declind
(With which they welcom'd him), he made a challenge to the
    best,
And foild the best. I gave him aide, because the rust of rest
(That would have seisd another mind) he sufferd not, but usd   810
The triall I made like a man, and their soft feasts refusd.
Yet when I set thee on, thou faint'st; I guard thee, charge,
    exhort
That (I abetting thee) thou shouldst be to the Greekes a Fort,
And a dismay to Ilion; yet thou obey'st in nought—
Affraid, or slouthfull, or else both. Henceforth renounce   815
    all thought

Diomed to Pallas.

That ever thou were Tydeus' sonne.' He answerd her:
    'I know
Thou art Jove's daughter, and for that in all just dutie owe
Thy speeches reverence: yet affirme ingenuously that feare
Doth neither hold me spiritlesse, nor sloth. I onely beare
Thy charge in zealous memorie, that I should never warre   820
With any blessed Deitie, unlesse (exceeding farre

The limits of her rule) the Queene that governs Chamber sport
Should preasse to field; and her thy will enjoynd my lance
    to hurt.
But he whose powre hath right in armes I knew in person here
(Besides the Cyprian Deitie) and therefore did forbeare,   825
And here have gatherd in retreit these other Greekes you see

Pallas againe.

With note and reverence of your charge.' 'My dearest mind,'
    said she,
'What then was fit is chang'd. Tis true, Mars hath just
    rule in warre,

What unjust
warre is.

But just warre; otherwise he raves, not fights. He's alterd
    farre;
He vow'd to Juno and my selfe that his aide should be usd   830
Against the Troyans, whom it guards; and therein he abusd
His rule in armes, infring'd his word, and made his
    warre unjust.
He is inconstant, impious, mad. Resolve then; firmly trust
My aide of thee against his worst, or any Deitie.
Adde scourge to thy free horse, charge home: he   835
    fights perfidiously.'
    This said, as that brave king, her knight, with his
    horse-guiding friend
Were set before the chariot (for signe he should descend.
That she might serve for wagonnesse) she pluckt the
    waggoner backe,
And up into his seate she mounts. The Beechen tree did cracke
Beneath the burthen, and good cause, it bore so huge a   840
    thing—
A Goddesse so repleate with powre, and such a puissant king.
    She snatcht the scourge up and the reines, and shut
    her heavenly looke
In hel's vast helme from Mars his eyes: and full careere
    she tooke
At him, who then had newly slaine the mightie Periphas,
Renown'd sonne to Ochesius, and farre the strongest was   845
Of all th' Ætolians; to whose spoile the bloodie God was run.
But when this man-plague saw th' approch of God-like
    Tydeus' sonne,
He let his mightie Periphas lie, and in full charge he ran

The combat of
Mars and Diomed.

At Diomed, and he at him. Both neare, the God began
And (thirstie of his blood) he throwes a brazen lance that beares 850
Full on the breast of Diomed, above the reines and geres;
But Pallas tooke it on her hand and strooke the eager lance
Beneath the chariot. Then the knight of Pallas doth advance,

And cast a Javeline off at Mars; Minerva sent it on,

That (where his arming girdle girt) his bellie graz'd upon   855
Just at the rim, and rancht the flesh. The lance againe he got,
But left the wound; that stung him so, he laid out such a
    throat,
As if nine or ten thousand men had bray'd out all their breaths
In one confusion, having felt as many sodaine deaths.
The rore made both the hosts amaz'd. Up flew the God   860
    to heaven,
And with him was through all the aire as blacke a tincture
    driven
(To Diomed's eyes) as when the earth, halfe chok't with
    smoking heate
Of gloomie clouds that stifle men and pitchie tempests' threat,
Usherd with horrid gusts of wind; with such blacke vapors
    plum'd

Mars flew t' Olympus and brode heaven, and there his   865
    place resum'd.
Sadly he went and sate by Jove, shew'd his immortall blood
That from a mortall-man-made wound powrd such an
    impious flood,

And (weeping) powr'd out these complaints: 'O Father,
    stormst thou not
To see us take these wrongs from men? Extreme griefes we
    have got
Even by our owne deepe counsels held for gratifying them;   870
And thou (our Councel's President) conclud'st in this extreme
Of fighting ever, being ruld by one that thou hast bred,
One never well but doing ill, a girle so full of head
That, though all other Gods obey, her mad moods must
    command
By thy indulgence, nor by word nor any touch of hand   875
Correcting her. Thy reason is she is a sparke of thee,
And therefore she may kindle rage in men gainst Gods, and she
May make men hurt Gods, and those Gods that are (besides)
    thy seed.
First in the palm's height Cyprides, then runs the impious deed
On my hurt person; and could life give way to death in me,   880
Or had my feete not fetcht me off, heaps of mortalitie
Had kept me consort.' Jupiter, with a contracted brow,

Thus answerd Mars: 'Thou many minds, inconstant changling
    thou,
Sit not complaining thus by me, whom most of all the Gods
(Inhabiting the starrie hill) I hate, no periods   885

Being set to thy contentions, brawles, fights, and pitching
  fields,
Just of thy mother Juno's moods, stiffe-neckt and never yeelds,
Though I correct her still and chide, nor can forbeare offence,
Though to her sonne. This wound I know tasts of her
  insolence.
But I will prove more naturall, thou shalt be cur'd because   890
Thou com'st of me; but hadst thou bene so crosse to sacred
  lawes,
Being borne to any other God, thou hadst bene throwne
  from heaven
Long since as low as Tartarus, beneath the Giants driven.'
  This said, he gave his wound in charge to Pæon, who applied
Such soveraigne medicines that as soone the paine   895
  was qualified
And he recur'd. As nourishing milke, when runnet is put in,
Runs all in heapes of tough thicke curd, though in his
  nature thin:
Even so soone his wounds' parted sides ran close in his recure—
For he (all deathlesse) could not long the parts of death
  endure.

Hebe attires Mars. Then Hebe bath'd, and put on him fresh garments, and he sate 900
Exulting by his Sire againe, in top of all his state.
So (having from the spoiles of men made his desir'd remove)
Juno and Pallas reascend the starrie Court of Jove.

The End of the Fifth Booke

THE SIXTH BOOKE

of

HOMER'S ILIADS

THE ARGUMENT

The Gods now leaving an indifferent field,
The Greekes prevaile, the slaughterd Troyans yeeld.
Hector (by Helenus' advice) retires
In haste to Troy and Hecuba desires
To pray Minerva to remove from fight   5
The sonne of Tydeus, her affected knight
And vow to her (for favour of such price)
Twelve Oxen should be slaine in sacrifice.
In meane space, Glaucus and Tydides meete
And either other with remembrance greet   10
Of old love twixt their fathers, which enclines
Their hearts to friendship, who change armes for signes
Of a continu'd love for either's life.
Hector, in his returne, meets with his wife
And taking in his armed armes his sonne,   15
He prophecies the fall of Ilion.

Another Argument

In Zeta, *Hector Prophecies,*
Prayes for his sonne, wils sacrifice.

    The stern fight freed of al the Gods, conquest with
        doubtful wings
Flew on their lances: everie way the restlesse field she flings
Betwixt the floods of Simois and Xanthus, that confin'd
All their affaires at Ilion and round about them shin'd.
    The first that weigh'd downe all the field of one particular side   5
Was Ajax, sonne of Telamon, who like a bulwarke plide
The Greekes' protection and of Troy the knottie orders brake,
Held out a light to all the rest and shew'd them how to make
Way to their conquest: he did wound the strongest man
        of Thrace,

[136]

The tallest and the biggest set, Eussorian Acamas; 10
His lance fell on his caske's plum'd top in stooping; the
fell head
Drave through his forehead to his jawes; his eyes Night
shadowed.

Tydides, alias
Diomed (being son
to Tydeus).

    Tydides slue Teuthranides Axylus that did dwell
In faire Arisbe's well-built towres. He had of wealth a Well
And yet was kind and bountifull: he would a traveller pray 15
To be his guest; his friendly house stood in the brode high way,
In which he all sorts nobly usd—yet none of them would stand
Twixt him and death, but both himselfe and he that had
command
Of his faire horse, Calesius, fell livelesse on the ground.
Euryalus, Opheltius and Dresus dead did wound, 20
Nor ended there his fierie course, which he againe begins
And ran to it succesfully upon a paire of twins,
Æsepus and bold Pedasus, whom good Bucolion
(That first cald father, though base borne, renowm'd
Laomedon)
On Nais Abarbarea got, a Nymph that (as she fed 25
Her curled flocks) Bucolion woo'd and mixt in love and bed.
Both these were spoild of armes and life by Mecistiades.
    Then Polypœtes for sterne death Astyalus did seise;
Ulysses slue Percosius; Teucer, Aretaon;
Antilochus (old Nestor's joy) Ablerus; the great sonne 30
Of Atreus and king of men, Elatus, whose abode
He held at upper Pedasus where Satnius' river flow'd.
The great Heroe Leitus staid Phylacus in flight
From further life; Eurypylus, Melanthius reft of light.
    The brother to the king of men Adrestus tooke alive, 35
Whose horse (affrighted with the flight) their driver
now did drive
Amongst the low-growne Tamricke trees, and at an arme of one
The chariot in the draught-tree brake, the horse brake
loose and ron
The same way other flyers fled, contending all to towne.
Himselfe close at the chariot wheele upon his face was throwne 40
And there lay flat roll'd up in dust. Atrides inwards drave,
And (holding at his breast his lance) Adrestus
sought to save
His head by losing of his feet and trusting to his knees,
On which the same parts of the king he hugs and offers fees
Of worthie value for his life, and thus pleades their receipt: 45

This Virgil imitates.   'Take me alive, O Atreus' sonne, and take a worthie weight

Of brasse, elaborate iron and gold; a heape of precious things
Are in my father's riches hid, which (when your servant brings
Newes of my safetie to his eares) he largely will divide
With your rare bounties.' Atreus' sonne thought this   50
   the better side
And meant to take it, being about to send him safe to fleete—
Which when (farre off) his brother saw, he wing'd his royall feet

And came in threatning, crying out: 'O soft heart;
   what's the cause
Thou spar'st these men thus? Have not they observ'd
   these gentle lawes
Of mild humanitie to thee with mightie argument   55
Why thou shouldst deale thus? In thy house and with
   all president
Of honord guest-rites entertaind? Not one of them shall flie
A bitter end for it from heaven, and much lesse (dotingly)
Scape our revengefull fingers: all, even th' infant in the wombe
Shall tast of what they merited and have no other tombe   60
Than razed Ilion, nor their race have more fruite than the dust.'
This just cause turnd his brother's mind, who violently thrust
The prisoner from him, in whose guts the king of men imprest
His ashen lance, which (pitching downe his foote
   upon the brest
Of him that upwards fell) he drew. Then Nestor spake to all: 65

  'O friends and household men of Mars, let not your pursuit fall
With those ye fell for present spoile; nor (like the king of men)
Let any scape unfeld: but on, dispatch them all and then
Ye shall have time enough to spoile.' This made so strong
   their chace
That all the Troyans had bene housd and never turnd a face   70
Had not the Priamist Helenus (an Augure most of name)

Will'd Hector and Æneas thus: 'Hector! Anchises' fame!
Since on your shoulders, with good cause, the weightie
   burthen lies
Of Troy and Lycia (being both of noblest faculties
For counsell, strength of hand, and apt to take chance   75
   at her best
In every turne she makes) stand fast and suffer not the rest
(By any way searcht out for scape) to come within the ports,
Lest (fled into their wives' kind armes) they there be made
   the sports
Of the pursuing enemie: exhort and force your bands
To turne their faces, and, while we employ our ventur'd hands 80
(Though in a hard condition) to make the other stay,

[138]

Hector, go thou to Ilion and our Queene mother pray
To take the richest robe she hath, the same
    that's chiefly deare
To her Court fancie, with which Jemme (assembling more
    to her
Of Troy's chiefe Matrones) let all go (for feare of all our fates)   85
To Pallas' temple, take the key, unlocke the leavie gates,
Enter and reach the highest towre where her Palladium stands,
And on it put the precious veile with pure and reverend hands
And vow to her (besides the gift) a sacrificing stroke
Of twelve fat Heifers of a yeare that never felt the yoke   90
(Most answering to her maiden state) if she will pittie us,
Our towne, our wives, our yongest joyes, and him that
    plagues them thus
Take from the conflict, Diomed, that Furie in a fight,
That true sonne of great Tydeus, that cunning Lord of Flight,
Whom I esteeme the strongest Greeke—for we have never fled   95
Achilles (that is Prince of men and whom a Goddesse bred)
Like him, his furie flies so high and all men's wraths commands.'
    Hector intends his brother's will, but first through
    all his bands
He made quicke way, encouraging and all to feare affraide:
All turnd their heads and made Greece turne. Slaughter   100
    stood still dismaid
On their parts, for they thought some God, falne from the
    vault of starres,
Was rusht into the Ilians' aide, they made such dreadfull warres.

Hector to the Troyans.

    Thus Hector, toyling in the waves and thrusting backe
    the flood
Of his ebb'd forces, thus takes leave: 'So, so, now runs
    your blood
In his right current. Forwards now, Troyans and farre-cald   105
    friends!
Awhile hold out till, for successe to this your brave amends,
I haste to Ilion and procure our Counsellours and wives
To pray and offer Hecatombs for their states in our lives.'

How Hector left the field.

    Then faire-helm'd Hector turnd to Troy and (as he
    trode the field)
The blacke Bul's hide that at his backe he wore about   110
    his shield
(In the extreme circumference) was with his gate so rockt
That (being large) it (both at once) his necke and
    ankles knockt.

[139]

The encounter of
Diomed and Glaucus.

And now betwixt the hosts were met Hippolochus' brave sonne
Glaucus, who in his verie looke hope of some wonder wonne,
And little Tydeus' mightie heire, who, seeing such a man   115
Offer the field (for usuall blowes), with wondrous words began:

Diomed to Glaucus.

  'What art thou, strongst of mortall men, that putst
    so farre before,
Whom these fights never shew'd mine eyes? They have bene
    evermore
Sonnes of unhappie parents borne that came within the length
Of this Minerva-guided lance and durst close with the strength   120
That she inspires in me. If heaven be thy divine abode
And thou a Deitie, thus inform'd no more with any God
Will I change lances. The strong sonne of Dryas did not live
Long after such a conflict dar'd, who godlesly did drive
Nysæus' Nurses through the hill made sacred to his name   125
And cald Nyseius; with a goade he puncht each furious dame
And made them every one cast downe their greene
    and leavie speares.
This th' homicide Lycurgus did, and those ungodly feares
He put the Froes in seised their God. Even Bacchus he did drive
From his Nyseius, who was faine (with huge exclaimes) to dive   130
Into the Ocean: Thetis there in her bright bosome tooke
The flying Deitie, who so feard Lycurgus' threats he shooke.
For which the freely-living Gods so highly were incenst
That Saturn's great sonne strooke him blind and with his
    life dispenc't
But small time after—all because th' immortals lov'd him not,   135
Nor lov'd him since he striv'd with them. And his end
    hath begot
Feare in my powres to fight with heaven. But if the
    fruits of earth
Nourish thy bodie and thy life be of our humane birth,
Come neare that thou maist soone arrive on that life-bounding
    shore

Glaucus his
worthie answer to
Diomed, and his
pedegree drawne
even from
Sisyphus.

To which I see thee hoise such saile.' 'Why dost thou   140
    so explore,'
Said Glaucus, 'of what race I am, when like the race of leaves
The race of man is, that deserves no question? Nor receives
My being any other breath. The wind in Autumne strowes
The earth with old leaves; then the Spring the woods with
    new endowes—
And so death scatters men on earth, so life puts out againe   145
Man's leavie issue. But my race, if (like the course of men)

Thou seekst in more particular termes, tis this (to many
    knowne):—
  'In midst of Argos, nurse of horse, there stands a walled towne

*The historie of
Bellerophon.*

Ephyré, where the Mansion house of Sisyphus did stand,
Of Sisyphus Æolides, most wise of all the land.   150
Glaucus was sonne to him and he begat Bellerophon,
Whose bodie heaven endued with strength and put a beautie on
Exceeding lovely. Prœtus yet his cause of love did hate
And banisht him the towne: he might—he ruld the Argive state;
The vertue of the one Jove plac't beneath the other's powre.   155
His exile grew since he denied to be the Paramour
Of faire Anteia, Prœtus' wife, who felt a raging fire
Of secret love to him; but he, whom wisedome did inspire
As well as prudence (one of them advising him to shunne
The danger of a Princesse' love, the other not to runne   160
Within the danger of the Gods, the act being simply ill),
Still entertaining thoughts divine, subdu'd the earthly still.
She (rul'd by neither of his wits) preferd her lust to both
And (false to Prœtus) would seeme true with this abhorr'd
    untroth:

Bellerophontis
literæ. Ad Eras.
*This long speech
many Critickes
taxe as untimely,
being (as they take
it) in the heate of
fight. Hier. Vidas
(a late observer)
beinge eagrest
against Homer,
whose ignorance in
this I cannot but
note and prove to
you: for (besides
the authority and
office of a Poet to
vary and quicken
his Poem with
these episods,
somtimes beyond
the leasure of their
actions) the
Critick notes not
how far his
forerunner prevents
his worst as far,
and sets downe his*

"Prœtus, or die thy selfe," said she, "or let Bellerophon die.   165
He urg'd dishonour to thy bed, which since I did denie
He thought his violence should grant—and sought thy shame
    by force."
The king, incenst with her report, resolv'd upon her course
But doubted how it should be runne: he shund his death direct
(Holding a way so neare not safe) and plotted the effect   170
By sending him with letters seald (that, opened, touch his life)
To Rheuns, King of Lycia and father to his wife.
He went, and happily he went: the Gods walkt all his way.
And being arriv'd in Lycia, where Xanthus doth display
The silver ensignes of his waves, the king of that brode land   175
Receiv'd him with a wondrous free and honourable hand.
Nine daies he feasted him and kild an Oxe in every day
In thankfull sacrifice to heaven for his faire guest, whose stay
With rosie fingers brought the world the tenth wel-welcomd
    morne.
And then the king did move to see the letters he had borne   180
From his lov'd sonne in law, which seene, he wrought thus
    their conten's:
Chimæra the invincible he sent him to convince—
Sprung from no man but meere divine; a Lyon's shape before,
Behind a dragon's, in the midst a Gote's shagg'd forme
    she bore,

*speech at the
sodain and strange
turning of the
Troyan field, set
on a litle before
by Hector—and that
so fiercely it made
an admiring stand
among the
Grecians, and
therein gave fit
time for these
great captaines to
utter their
admirations—the
whole field in
that part being
to stand like their
Commanders. And
then how full of
decorum this
gallant shew and
speech was to sound
understandings I
leave onely to such
and let our
Cricks go cavill.*

Sarpedon's birth.

And flames of deadly fervencie flew from her breath and eyes. 185
Yet her he slue: his confidence in sacred prodigies
Renderd him victor. Then he gave his second conquest way
Against the famous Solymi, when (he himselfe would say,
Reporting it) he enterd on a passing vigorous fight.
His third huge labour he approv'd against a woman's spight   190
That fild a field of Amazons: he overcame them all.
Then set they on him slie Deceipt when Force had such a fall.
An ambush of the strongest men that spacious Lycia bred
Was lodg'd for him—whom he lodg'd sure: they never raisd
        a head.
    'His deeds thus shewing him deriv'd from some Celestiall race, 195
The king detaind and made amends with doing him the grace
Of his faire daughter's Princely gift, and with her
        (for a dowre)
Gave halfe his kingdome, and to this the Lycians on did powre
More than was given to any king—a goodly planted field,
In some parts thicke of groves and woods, the rest rich crops   200
        did yeeld.
This field the Lycians futurely (of future wandrings there
And other errors of their Prince in the unhappie Rere
Of his sad life) the Errant cald. The Princesse brought him
        forth
Three children (whose ends griev'd him more, the more they
        were of worth),
Isander and Hippolochus and faire Laodamy,   205
With whom even Jupiter himselfe left heaven it selfe to lie
And had by her the man at armes Sarpedon, cald divine.
The Gods then left him (lest a man should in their glories
        shine)
And set against him: for his sonne Isandrus (in a strife
Against the valiant Solymi) Mars reft of light and life;   210
Laodamia (being envied of all the Goddesses)
The golden-bridle-handling Queene, the maiden Patronesse,
Slue with an arrow. And for this he wandred evermore
Alone through his Aleian field and fed upon the core
Of his sad bosome, flying all the loth'd consorts of men.   215
Yet had he one surviv'd to him of those three childeren,
Hippolochus, the root of me, who sent me here with charge
That I should alwaies beare me well and my deserts enlarge
Beyond the vulgar lest I sham'd my race, that farre exceld
All that Ephyre's famous towres or ample Lycia held.   220
This is my stocke, and this am I.' This cheard Tydides' heart,

Who pitcht his speare downe, leand and talkt in this
    affectionate part:
  'Certesse, in thy great Ancestor and in mine owne thou art

*Diomed's answer
to Glaucus.*

A guest of mine right ancient. King Œneus twentie daies
Detaind with feasts Bellerophon, whom all the world did praise; 225
Betwixt whom mutuall gifts were given: my Grandsire gave
    to thine
A girdle of Phœnician worke, impurpl'd wondrous fine;
Thine gave a two-neckt Jugge of gold which, though I use
    not here,
Yet still it is my gemme at home. But if our fathers were

Φρένας ἐξέλετο Ζεὺς,
Mentem ademit
Jupiter, *the text
hath it: which
onely I alter of
all Homer's
originall, since
Plutarch against
the Stoicks excuses
this supposed
folly in Glaucus—
Spondanus likewise
encouraging my
alterations, which
I use for the
loved and simple
Nobility of the
free exchange in
Glaucus, contrarie
to others that for
the supposed folly
in Glaucus turnd
his change into a
Proverb—*χρύσεα
χαλκείων,
golden for brazen.

Familiar or each other knew, I know not, since my sire   230
Left me a child at siege of Thebes, where he left his life's fire.
But let us prove our Grandsires' sonnes and be each others'
    guests.
To Lycia when I come, do thou receive thy friend with feasts;
Peloponnesus with the like shall thy wisht presence greet.
Meane space shun we each other here, though in the preasse 235
    we meet.
There are enow of Troy beside, and men enough renownd,
To right my powres, whom ever heaven shall let my lance
    confound.
So are there of the Greeks for thee; kill who thou canst;
    and now
For signe of amitie twixt us and that all these may know
We glorie in th' hospitious rites our Grandsires did commend, 240
Change we our armes before them all. From horse then both
    descend,
Joyne hands, give faith and take.' And then did Jupiter elate
The mind of Glaucus, who, to shew his reverence to the state
Of vertue in his grandsire's heart and gratulate beside
The offer of so great a friend, exchang'd (in that good pride) 245
Curets of gold for those of brasse that did on Diomed shine—
One of a hundred Oxens' price, the other but of nine.
  By this had Hector reacht the ports of Scæa and the tow'rs.
About him flockt the wives of Troy, the children, paramours,
Enquiring how their husbands did, their fathers, brothers, loves. 250
  He stood not then to answer them, but said: 'It now behoves
Ye should go all t' implore the aide of heaven in a distresse
Of great effect and imminent.' Then hasted he accesse

Priam's Court.

To Priam's goodly builded Court, which round about was runne
With walking porches, galleries, to keepe off raine and Sunne. 255
Within, of one side, on a rew, of sundrie colourd stones,
Fiftie faire lodgings were built out for Priam's fiftie sonnes,

And of as faire sort for their wives; and in the opposite view
Twelve lodgings of like stone, like height, were likewise built
    arew,
Where with their faire and vertuous wives twelve Princes, sons 260
    in law
To honourable Priam, lay. And here met Hecuba
(The loving mother) her great sonne, and with her needs must be
The fairest of her femall race, the bright Laodice.

Hecuba to Hector.   The Queene grip't hard her Hector's hand and said: 'O
    worthiest sonne,
Why leav'st thou field? Is't not because the cursed nation 265
Afflict our countrimen and friends? They are their mones
    that move
Thy mind to come and lift thy hands (in his high towre) to
    Jove.
But stay a little that my selfe may fetch our sweetest wine
To offer first to Jupiter, then that these joynts of thine
May be refresht—for (wo is me) how thou art toyld and spent! 270
Thou for our citie's generall state, thou for our friends farre
    sent,
Must now the preasse of fight endure, now solitude to call
Upon the name of Jupiter, thou onely for us all.
But wine will something comfort thee, for to a man dismaid,
With carefull spirits, or too much with labour overlaid, 275
Wine brings much rescue, strengthning much the bodie and
    the mind.'

Hector to Hecuba.   The great Helme-mover thus receiv'd the authresse of his
    kind:
'My royall mother, bring no wine, lest rather it impaire
Than helpe my strength and make my mind forgetfull of
    th' affaire
Committed to it. And (to poure it out in sacrifice) 280
I feare with unwasht hands to serve the pure-liv'd Deities;
Nor is it lawfull, thus imbrew'd with blood and dust, to prove
The will of heaven or offer vowes to clowd-compelling Jove.
I onely come to use your paines (assembling other Dames,
Matrons and women honourd most with high and vertuous 285
    names)
With wine and odors, and a robe most ample, most of price
And which is dearest in your love, to offer sacrifice
In Pallas' temple, and to put the precious robe ye beare
On her Palladium, vowing all twelve Oxen of a yeare
Whose necks were never wrung with yoke shall pay her Grace 290
    their lives

[144]

If she will pittie our sieg'd towne, pittie our selves, our wives,
Pittie our children, and remove from sacred Ilion
The dreadfull souldier Diomed. And when your selves are gone
About this worke, my selfe will go to call into the field
(If he will heare me) Helen's love, whom would the earth   295
    would yeeld
And headlong take into her gulfe even quicke before mine eyes,
For then my heart, I hope, would cast her lode of miseries.
Borne for the plague he hath bene borne and bred to the deface
(By great Olympius) of Troy, our Sire and all our race.'
    This said, grave Hecuba went home and sent her maids about   300
To bid the Matrones; she her selfe descended and searcht out
(Within a place that breath'd perfumes) the richest robe
    she had,
Which lay with many rich ones more, most curiously made
By women of Sidonia, which Paris brought from thence,
Sailing the brode Sea when he made that voyage of offence   305
In which he brought home Helena. That robe, transferd so farre
(That was the undermost) she tooke: it glitterd like a starre:
And with it went she to the Fane with many Ladies more,
Amongst whom faire-cheekt Theano unlockt the folded dore,
Chaste Theano, Antenor's wife and of Cisseus' race,   310
Sister to Hecuba, both borne to that great king of Thrace.
Her th' Ilians made Minerva's Priest, and her they followed all
Up to the Temple's highest towre, where on their knees they fall,
Lift up their hands and fill the Fane with Ladies' pitious cries.
Then lovely Theano tooke the veile and with it she implies   315

*Theano, Minerva's
Priest and
Antenor's wife,
prayes to Pallas.*

The great Palladium, praying thus: 'Goddesse of most renowne
In all the heaven of Goddesses! great guardian of our towne!
Reverend Minerva! breake the lance of Diomed, ceasse his grace,
Give him to fall in shamefull flight, headlong and on his face,
Before our ports of Ilion—that instantly we may   320
Twelve unyok't Oxen of a yeare in this thy Temple slay
To thy sole honor. Take their bloods and banish our offence,
Accept Troy's zeale, her wives, and save our infants' innocence.'
    She praid, but Pallas would not grant. Meane space was
    Hector come
Where Alexander's lodgings were, that many a goodly roome   325
Had built in them by Architects of Troy's most curious sort,
And were no lodgings, but a house; nor no house, but a Court—
Or had all these containd in them; and all within a towre,
Next Hector's lodgings and the king's. The lov'd of heaven's
    chiefe powre
(Hector) here entred. In his hand a goodly lance he bore,   330

Ten cubits long; the brasen head went shining in before,
Helpt with a burnisht ring of gold. He found his brother then
Amongst the women, yet prepar'd to go amongst the men.
For in their chamber he was set trimming his armes, his shield,
His curets, and was trying how his crooked bow would yeeld   335
To his streight armes. Amongst her maids was set the Argive
    Queene,
Commanding them in choisest workes. When Hector's eye
    had seene
His brother thus accompanied, and that he could not beare
The verie touching of his armes but where the women were,
And when the time so needed men, right cunningly he chid.   340
That he might do it bitterly, his cowardise he hid
(That simply made him so retir'd) beneath an anger, faind
In him by Hector, for the hate the citizens sustaind
Against him for the foile he tooke in their cause, and againe
For all their generall foiles in his. So Hector seemes to plaine   345
Of his wrath to them for their hate and not his cowardise
As that were it that shelterd him in his effeminacies
And kept him in that dangerous time from their fit aid in fight:
For which he chid thus: 'Wretched man! so timelesse is thy
    spight
That tis not honest, and their hate is just gainst which it bends.   350
Warre burns about the towne for thee; for thee our slaughterd
    friends
Besiege Troy with their carkasses, on whose heapes our high wals
Are overlookt by enemies; the sad sounds of their fals
Without are eccho'd with the cries of wives and babes within—
And all for thee. And yet for them thy honor cannot win   355
Head of thine anger. Thou shouldst need no spirit to stirre up
    thine
But thine should set the rest on fire, and with a rage divine
Chastise impartially the best that impiously forbeares.
Come forth, lest thy faire towers and Troy be burnd about
    thine eares.'
Paris acknowledg'd (as before) all just that Hector spake,   360
Allowing justice, though it were for his injustice sake;
And where his brother put a wrath upon him by his art,
He takes it (for his honor's sake) as sprung out of his hart,
And rather would have anger seeme his fault than cowardise.
And thus he answerd: 'Since with right you joynd checke with   365
    advise
And I heare you, give equall eare. It is not any spleene
Against the Towne (as you conceive) that makes me so unseene,

Hector dissembles the cowardise he finds in Paris, turning it as if he chid him for his anger at the Troyans for hating him being conquered by Menelaus, when it is for his effeminacie; which is all paraphrasticall in my translation.

Paris to Hector.

[146]

But sorrow for it, which to ease and by discourse digest
(Within my selfe) I live so close; and yet, since men might wrest
My sad retreat like you, my wife (with her advice) inclinde   370
This my addression to the field, which was mine owne free minde
As well as th' instance of her words: for, though the foyle were
    mine,
Conquest brings forth her wreaths by turnes. Stay then this
    hast of thine
But till I arme, and I am made a consort for thee streight:
Or go—I'le overtake thy haste.' Helen stood at receipt   375
And tooke up all great Hector's powers t' attend her heavie
    words,
By which had Paris no reply: this vent her griefe affords:

*Helen's ruthfull
complaint to
Hector.*

  'Brother (if I may call you so, that had bene better borne
A dog than such a horride Dame as all men curse and scorne,
A mischiefe-maker, a man-plague), O would to God the day   380
That first gave light to me had bene a whirlwind in my way,
And borne me to some desert hill, or hid me in the rage
Of earth's most far-resounding seas, ere I should thus engage
The deare lives of so many friends: yet, since the Gods have
    beene
Helplesse foreseers of my plagues, they might have likewise   385
    seene
That he they put in yoke with me, to beare out their award,
Had bene a man of much more spirit, and, or had noblier dar'd
To shield mine honour with his deed or with his mind had
    knowne
Much better the upbraids of men, that so he might have showne
(More like a man) some sence of griefe for both my shame and   390
    his.
But he is senslesse, nor conceives what any manhood is,
Nor now, nor ever after will; and therefore hangs, I feare,
A plague above him. But come neare, good brother, rest
    you here
Who (of the world of men) stands charg'd with most unrest
    for me
(Vile wretch) and for my Lover's wrong—on whom a destinie   395
So bitter is imposde by Jove that all succeeding times
Will put (to our un-ended shames) in all men's mouthes our
    crimes.'

Hector to Helen.

  He answerd: 'Helen, do not seeke to make me sit with thee.
I must not stay, though well I know thy honourd love of me.
My mind cals forth to aid our friends, in whom my absence   400
    breeds

Longings to see me—for whose sakes importune thou to deeds
This man by all meanes, that your care may make his owne
    make hast
And meete me in the open towne, that all may see at last
He minds his lover. I my selfe will now go home and see
My houshold, my deare wife and sonne, that little hope of me.   405
For, sister, tis without my skill if I shall ever more
Returne and see them, or to earth her right in me restore.
The Gods may stoupe me by the Greekes.' This said, he went
    to see
The vertuous Princesse, his true wife, white-arm'd Andromache.
She (with her infant sonne and maide) was climb'd the towre,   410
    about
The sight of him that fought for her, weeping and crying out.
Hector, not finding her at home, was going forth, retir'd,
Stood in the gate, her woman cald and curiously enquir'd
Where she was gone, bad tell him true if she were gone to see
His sisters or his brothers' wives, or whether she should be   415
At Temple with the other Dames t' implore Minerva's ruth.
  Her woman answerd: since he askt and urg'd so much
    the truth,
The truth was she was neither gone to see his brothers' wives,
His sisters, nor t' implore the ruth of Pallas on their lives,
But she (advertisde of the bane Troy sufferd and how vast   420
Conquest had made her selfe for Greece), like one distraught,
    made hast
To ample Ilion with her sonne and Nurse, and all the way
Mournd and dissolv'd in teares for him. Then Hector made
    no stay
But trod her path and through the streets (magnificently built)
All the great Citie past and came where (seeing how bloud   425
    was spilt)
Andromache might see him come, who made as he would passe
The ports without saluting her, not knowing where she was.
She, with his sight, made breathlesse hast to meet him, she,
    whose grace
Brought him withall so great a dowre, she that of all the race
Of King Eetion onely liv'd—Eetion whose house stood   430
Beneath the mountaine Placius, environd with the wood
Of Theban Hypoplace, being Court to the Cilician land.
She ran to Hector and with her (tender of heart and hand)
Her sonne borne in his Nurse's armes, when like a heavenly signe
Compact of many golden starres the princely child did shine,   435
Whom Hector cald Scamandrius but whom the towne did name

Astyanax because his sire did onely prop the same.
Hector, though griefe bereft his speech, yet smil'd upon his joy.
Andromache cride out, mixt hands and to the strength of Troy

Andromache's
passion to Hector.

Thus wept forth her affection: 'O noblest in desire,   440
Thy mind, inflam'd with others' good, will set thy selfe on fire,
Nor pitiest thou thy sonne, nor wife, who must thy widdow be
If now thou issue: all the field will onely run on thee.
Better my shoulders underwent the earth than thy decease,
For then would earth beare joyes no more—then comes the   445
    blacke increase
Of griefes (like Greeks on Ilion). Alas, what one survives
To be my refuge? One blacke day bereft seven brothers' lives
By sterne Achilles; by his hand my father breath'd his last;

Thebes a most
rich citie of Cilicia.

His high-wald rich Cilician Thebes sackt by him and laid wast.
The royall bodie yet he left unspoild—Religion charm'd   450
That act of spoile—and all in fire he burnd him compleat arm'd,
Built over him a royall tombe, and to the monument
He left of him th' Oreades (that are the high descent
Of Ægis-bearing Jupiter) another of their owne
Did adde to it and set it round with Elms: by which is showne   455
(In theirs) the barrennesse of death; yet might it serve beside
To shelter the sad Monument from all the ruffinous pride
Of stormes and tempests, usde to hurt things of that noble kind.
The short life yet my mother liv'd he sav'd, and serv'd his mind
With all the riches of the Realme, which not enough esteemd,   460
He kept her prisoner, whom small time but much more wealth
    redeemd,
And she in sylvane Hypoplace Cilicia rul'd againe,
But soone was over-rul'd by death—Diana's chast disdaine
Gave her a Lance and tooke her life. Yet all these gone from me
Thou amply renderst all: thy life makes still my father be,   465
My mother, brothers—and besides thou art my husband too,
Most lov'd, most worthy. Pitie then, deare love, and do not go,
For, thou gone, all these go againe: pitie our common joy,
Lest (of a father's patronage, the bulwarke of all Troy)
Thou leav'st him a poore widdowe's charge: stay, stay then,   470
    in this Towre
And call up to the wilde Fig-tree all thy retired powre,
For there the wall is easiest seal'd and fittest for surprise:
And there th' Ajaces, Idomen, th' Atrides, Diomed thrise
Have both survaid and made attempt—I know not if induc'd
By some wise Augure, or the fact was naturally infusd   475

Hector to
Andromache.

Into their wits or courages.' To this great Hector said:
'Be well assur'd, wife, all these things in my kind cares are waid:

[149]

But what a shame and feare it is to thinke how Troy would
    scorne
(Both in her husbands and her wives, whom long-traind gownes
    adorne)
That I should cowardly flie off! The spirit I first did breath   480
Did never teach me that—much lesse since the contempt of death
Was settl'd in me and my mind knew what a Worthy was,
Whose office is to leade in fight and give no danger passe
Without improvement. In this fire must Hector's triall shine.
Here must his country, father, friends be in him made divine.   485
And such a stormy day shall come, in mind and soule I know,
When sacred Troy shall shed her towres for teares of overthrow,
When Priam, all his birth and powre, shall in those teares
    be drownd.
But neither Troy's posteritie so much my soule doth wound—
Priam, nor Hecuba her selfe, nor all my brothers' woes   490
(Who, though so many and so good, must all be food for foes)—
As thy sad state, when some rude Greeke shall leade thee
    weeping hence,
These free dayes clouded and a night of captive violence
Loding thy temples, out of which thine eyes must never see
But spin the Greeke wives webs of taske and their   495
    Fetch-water be

*The names of two
fountaines, of which
one in Thessaly,
the other neer
Argos, or, according
to others, in
Peloponnesus
or Lacedæmon.*

To Argos, from Messeides, or cleare Hyperia's spring—
Which (howsoever thou abhorst) Fate's such a shrewish thing
She will be mistris, whose curst hands, when they shall crush
    out cries
From thy oppressions (being beheld by other enemies)
Thus they will nourish thy extremes: "This dame was Hector's   500
    wife,
A man that, at the warres of Troy, did breathe the worthiest life
Of all their armie." This againe will rub thy fruitfull wounds
To misse the man that to thy bands could give such narrow
    bounds.
But that day shall not wound mine eyes: the solide heape of
    night
Shall interpose and stop mine eares against thy plaints and   505
    plight.'
    This said, he reacht to take his sonne, who (of his armes afraid,
And then the horse-haire plume, with which he was so overlaid,
Nodded so horribly) he clingd backe to his nurse and cride.
Laughter affected his great Sire, who doft and laid aside
His fearfull Helme, that on the earth cast round about it light.   510
Then tooke and kist his loving sonne and (ballancing his weight

Hector's prayer for his sonne.

In dancing him) these loving vowes to living Jove he usde
And all the other bench of Gods: 'O you that have infusde
Soule to this Infant, now set downe this blessing on his starre.
Let his renowne be cleare as mine, equall his strength in warre, 515
And make his reigne so strong in Troy that yeares to come
    may yeeld
His facts this fame (when, rich in spoiles, he leaves the conquerd
    field
Sowne with his slaughters): "These high deeds exceed his father's
    worth."
And let this eccho'd praise supply the comforts to come forth
Of his kind mother with my life.' This said, th' Heroicke Sire 520
Gave him his mother, whose faire eyes fresh streames of love's
    salt fire
Billow'd on her soft cheekes to heare the last of Hector's speech,
In which his vowes comprisde the summe of all he did beseech
In her wisht comfort. So she tooke into her odorous brest
Her husband's gift; who (mov'd to see her heart so much 525
    opprest)
He dried her teares and thus desir'd: 'Afflict me not, deare wife,
With these vaine griefes. He doth not live that can disjoyne
    my life
And this firme bosome but my Fate—and Fate, whose wings can
    flie?
Noble, ignoble, Fate controuls: once borne, the best must die.
Go home and set thy houswifrie on these extremes of thought, 530
And drive warre from them with thy maids: keep them from
    doing nought.
These will be nothing: leave the cares of warre to men and mee,
In whom (of all the Ilian race) they take their high'st degree.'
  On went his helme; his Princesse home, halfe cold with
    kindly feares,
When every feare turnd backe her lookes, and every looke 535
    shed teares,
Fo-slaughtering Hector's house soone reacht; her many women
    there
Wept all to see her: in his life great Hector's funerals were—
Never lookt any eye of theirs to see their Lord safe home,
Scap't from the gripes and powers of Greece. And now was
    Paris come

Paris overtakes Hector. His simile, high and expressive, which Virgil almost word for word hath translated, 12. Æn.

From his high towres, who made no stay when once he had 540
    put on
His richest armour, but flew forth; the flints he trod upon
Sparkled with luster of his armes; his long-ebd spirits now flowd

The higher for their lower ebbe. And as a faire Steed, proud
With ful-given mangers, long tied up and now (his head-stall
    broke)
He breakes from stable, runnes the field and with an ample   545
    stroke
Measures the center, neighs and lifts aloft his wanton head,
About his shoulders shakes his Crest, and where he hath bene fed
Or in some calme floud washt or (stung with his high plight)
    he flies
Amongst his femals, strength puts forth, his beautie beautifies,
And like Life's mirror beares his gate—so Paris from the towre   550
Of loftie Pergamus came forth; he shewd a Sun-like powre
In cariage of his goodly parts, addrest now to the strife,
And found his noble brother neere the place he left his wife.

Paris to Hector.   Him (thus respected) he salutes: 'Right worthy, I have feare
That your so serious haste to field my stay hath made forbeare,   555

Hector to Paris.   And that I come not as you wish.' He answerd: 'Honourd man,
Be confident, for not my selfe nor any others can
Reprove in thee the worke of fight—at least not any such
As is an equall judge of things, for thou hast strength as much
As serves to execute a mind very important. But   560
Thy strength too readily flies off: enough will is not put
To thy abilitie. My heart is in my mind's strife sad
When Troy (out of her much distresse she and her friends
    have had
By thy procurement) doth deprave thy noblesse in mine eares.
But come, hereafter we shall calme these hard conceits of theirs   565
When (from their ports the foe expulst) high Jove to them hath
    given
Wisht peace, and us free sacrifice to all the powers of heaven.'

The End of the Sixth Booke

THE SEVENTH BOOKE

of

HOMER'S ILIADS

THE ARGUMENT

Hector, by Helenus' advice, doth seeke
Adventurous combat on the boldest Greeke.
Nine Greeks stand up, Acceptants every one,
But lot selects strong Ajax Telamon.
Both with high honor stand th' important fight   5
Till Heralds part them by approched night.
Lastly, they grave the dead: the Greeks erect
A mightie wall their Navie to protect:
Which angers Neptune. Jove, by haplesse signes
In depth of night, succeeding woes divines.   10

Another Argument

In Eta, *Priam's strongest sonne*
Combats with Ajax Telamon.

These next foure bookes have not my last hand, and because the rest (for a time) will be sufficient to employ your censures, suspend them of these: spare not the other.

This said, brave Hector through the ports with Troy's
    bane-bringing Knight
Made issue to th' insatiate field, resolv'd to fervent fight.
And as the weather-wielder sends to Sea-men prosperous gales
When with their sallow-polisht Oares, long lifted from their fals,
Their wearied armes, dissolv'd with toyle, can scarce strike   5
    one stroke more,
Like those sweet winds appear'd these Lords to Troyans tir'd
    before.
Then fell they to the works of death. By Paris' valour fell
King Areithous' haplesse sonne, that did in Arne dwell,
Menesthius, whose renown'd Sire a Club did ever beare
And of Phylomedusa gat (that had her eyes so cleare)   10
This slaughterd issue. Hector's dart strooke Eioneus dead;
Beneath his good steele caske it pierc't above his gorget-stead.
Glaucus, Hippolochus his sonne, that led the Lycian crew,

Iphinous-Dexiades with sodaine Javelin slew
As he was mounting to his horse; his shoulders tooke the speare   15
And ere he sate, in tumbling downe, his powres dissolved were.

Pallas to the
Grecian ayd:
Apollo to the
Troyan.

When gray-eyd Pallas had perceiv'd the Greekes so fall in fight,
From high Olympus' top she stoopt and did on Ilion light.
Apollo (to encounter her) to Pergamus did flie,
From whence he (looking to the field) wisht Troyans victorie.   20
At Jove's broad Beech these godheads met, and first Jove's sonne
    objects:

Apollo to Pallas.

'Why, burning in contention thus, do thy extreme affects
Conduct thee from our peacefull hill? Is it to oversway
The doubtfull victorie of fight and give the Greeks the day?
Thou never pitiest perishing Troy, yet now let me perswade   25
That this day no more mortall wounds may either side invade.
Hereafter, till the end of Troy they shall apply the fight
Since your immortall wils resolve to overturne it quite.'

Pallas to Apollo.

Pallas replide: 'It likes me well; for this came I from heaven.
But to make either army ceasse, what order shall be given?'   30

His reply.

He said: 'We will direct the spirit that burnes in Hector's brest
To challenge any Greeke to wounds, with single powers imprest;
Which Greeks (admiring) will accept and make some one
    stand out
So stout a challenge to receive with a defence as stout.'
It is confirmd, and Helenus (King Priam's loved seed)   35
By Augurie discernd th' event that these two powres decreed,

Helenus, Priam's
sonne and a
Prophet, to Hector.

And, greeting Hector, askt him this: 'Wilt thou be once advisde?
I am thy brother, and thy life with mine is evenly prisde.
Command the rest of Troy and Greece to ceasse this publicke
    fight
And what Greeke beares the greatest mind to single strokes   40
    excite.
I promise thee that yet thy soule shall not descend to fates;
So heard I thy survivall cast by the celestiall States.'
Hector with glad allowance gave his brother's counsell eare
And (fronting both the hoasts) advanc't, just in the midst,
    his speare.
The Troyans instantly surcesasse; the Greeks Atrides staid.   45

The combat prepared.

The God that beares the silver Bow and warre's triumphant
    Maide
On Jove's Beech like two Vultures sat, pleasd to behold both
    parts
Flow in to heare, so sternly arm'd with huge shields, helmes and
    darts.

[154]

Simile.

And such fresh horror as you see driven through the wrinkled
    waves
By rising Zephyr, under whom the sea growes blacke and raves— 50
Such did the hastie gathering troupes of both hoasts make to
    heare;
Whose tumult settl'd, twixt them both thus spake the challenger:

*Hector to both
hoasts.*

'Heare, Troyans and ye well-arm'd Greeks, what my strong
    mind (diffusde
Through all my spirits) commands me speake. Saturnius
    hath not usde
His promist favour for our truce, but (studying both our ils) 55
Will never cease till Mars, by you, his ravenous stomacke fils
With ruin'd Troy or we consume your mightie Sea-borne fleet.
Since then the Generall Peeres of Greece in reach of one voice
    meete,
Amongst you all whose breast includes the most impulsive mind,
Let him stand forth as combattant, by all the rest designde. 60
Before whom thus I call high Jove to witnesse of our strife,
If he with home-thrust iron can reach th' exposure of my life
(Spoiling my armes) let him at will convey them to his tent,
But let my body be returnd, that Troy's two-sext descent
May waste it in the funerall Pile: if I can slaughter him 65
(Apollo honoring me so much) I'le spoile his conquerd lim
And beare his armes to Ilion, where in Apollo's shrine
I'le hang them as my trophies due; his body I'le resigne
To be disposed by his friends in flamie funerals
And honourd with erected tombe where Hellespontus fals 70
Into Ægæum and doth reach even to your navall rode—
That when our beings in the earth shall hide their period,
Survivers, sailing the blacke sea, may thus his name renew:

Epitaphium per
anticipationem.

"This is his monument whose bloud long since did fates embrew,
Whom, passing farre in fortitude, illustrate Hector slew." 75
This shall posteritie report, and my fame never die.'
    This said, dumbe silence seiz'd them all: they shamed to denie
And fear'd to undertake. At last, did Menelaus speake,

Menelaus chides.
O vere Phrygiæ,
neque enim
Phryges—*saith his
imitator.*

Checkt their remisnesse and so sigh'd as if his heart would breake:
'Aye me, but onely threatning Greeks, not worthy Grecian 80
    names!
This more and more, not to be borne, makes grow our huge
    defames,
If Hector's honorable proofe be entertaind by none.
But you are earth and water all, which (symboliz'd in one)
Have fram'd your faint unfirie spirits! Ye sit without your harts,
Grosly inglorious! But my selfe will use acceptive darts 85

And arme against him, though you thinke I arme gainst too
    much ods;
But conquest's garlands hang aloft amongst th' immortall gods.'
  He arm'd and gladly would have fought; but, Menelaus, then
By Hector's farre more strength thy soule had fled th' abodes
    of men,
Had not the kings of Greece stood up and thy attempt   90
    restraind—
And even the king of men himselfe that in such compasse raign'd,
Who tooke him by the bold right hand and sternly pluckt
    him backe:

*Agamemnon wiser
than his brother.*

'Mad brother, tis no worke for thee: thou seekst thy wilfull
    wracke.
Containe, though it despite thee much, nor for this strife engage
Thy person with a man more strong and whom all feare   95
    t' enrage—
Yea, whom Æacides himselfe in men-renowning warre
Makes doubt t' encounter, whose huge strength surpasseth thine
    by farre.
Sit thou then by thy regiment: some other Greeke will rise
(Though he be dreadlesse and no warre will his desires suffice
That makes this challenge to our strength) our valours to   100
    avow;
To whom, if he can scape with life, he will be glad to bow.'
  This drew his brother from his will, who yeelded, knowing
    it true,
And his glad souldiers tooke his armes: when Nestor did pursue
The same reproofe he set on foote, and thus supplide his turne:

*Nestor to the
Greeks.*

'What huge indignitie is this! how will our country mourne!   105
Old Peleus, that good king, will weepe, that worthy counsellor,
That trumpet of the Myrmidons, who much did aske me for
All men of name that went to Troy: with joy he did enquire
Their valour and their towardnesse, and I made him admire.
But that ye all feare Hector now, if his grave eares shall heare,   110
How will be lift his hands to heaven and pray that death may
    beare

*O si præteritos
referat mihi Jupiter
annos, Qualis eram,
&c.*

His grieved soule into the deepe! O would to heaven's great
    King,
Minerva and the God of light, that now my youthfull spring
Did flourish in my willing veines as when at Pheia's towres,
About the streames of Jardanus, my gather'd Pylean powres   115
And dart-employed Arcadians fought neere raging Celadon!
Amongst whom first of all stood forth great Ereuthalion,
Who th' armes of Areithous wore—brave Areithous—

And (since he still fought with a club) sirnam'd Clavigerus:
All men and faire-girt Ladies both for honour cald him so.   120
He fought not with a keepe-off speare or with a farre-shot bow,
But with a massie club of iron he brake through armed bands;
And yet Lycurgus was his death, but not with force of hands.
With sleight (encountring in a lane where his club wanted sway)
He thrust him through his spacious waste, who fell and   125
          upwards lay,
In death not bowing his face to earth: his armes he did despoile,
Which iron Mars bestowd on him; and those in Mars his toile
Lycurgus ever after wore, but when he aged grew,
Enforc't to keepe his peacefull house, their use he did renew
On mightie Ereuthalion's lims, his souldier, loved well;   130
And with these Armes he challeng'd all that did in Armes excell.
All shooke and stood dismaid; none durst his adverse champion
          make.
Yet this same forward mind of mine of choice would undertake
To fight with all his confidence; though yongest enemie
Of all the armie we conduc't, yet I fought with him, I.   135
Minerva made me so renownd, and that most tall strong Peere
I slue; his big bulke lay on earth, extended here and there
As it were covetous to spread the center every where.
O that my youth were now as fresh and all my powers as sound!
Soone should bold Hector be impugn'd! Yet you that most are   140
          crownd
With fortitude of all our hoast, even you me thinkes are slow,
Not free and set on fire with lust t' encounter such a foe.'

*Nine Princes stand
up to answer Hector.*

     With this, nine royall Princes rose: Atrides for the first;
Then Diomed; th' Ajaces then, that did th' encounter thirst;
King Idomen and his consort, Mars-like Meriones;   145
Euæmon's sonne Eurypylus; and Andræmonides,
Whom all the Grecians Thoas cald, sprong of Andræmon's
          blood;
And wise Ulysses—every one proposd for combat stood.

*Lots advised by
Nestor for the
combattant.*

     Againe Gerenius Nestor spake: 'Let lots be drawne by all;
His hand shall helpe the wel-armd Greeks on whom the lot   150
          doth fall,
And to his wish shall he be helpt, if he escape with life
The harmfull danger-breathing fit of this adventrous strife.'
     Each markt his lot and cast it in to Agamemnon's caske.
The souldiers praid, held up their hands and this of Jove
          did aske
(With eyes advanc't to heaven): 'O Jove, so leade the Herald's   155
          hand,

[157]

That Ajax or great Tydeus' sonne may our wisht champion
    stand,
Or else the King himselfe that rules the rich Mycenian land!'
    This said, old Nestor mixt the lots. The foremost lot survaid
With Ajax Telamon was sign'd, as all the souldiers praid:
One of the Heralds drew it forth, who brought and shewd it   160
    round,
Beginning at the right hand first, to all the most renownd.
None knowing it, every man denide; but when he forth did passe

The lot fals to
Ajax.

To him which markt and cast it in, which famous Ajax was,
He stretcht his hand and into it the Herald put the lot,
Who (viewing it) th' inscription knew; the Duke denied not,   165
But joyfully acknowledg'd it, and threw it at his feet,

He to the Greeks.

And said: 'O friends, the lot is mine, which to my soule is sweet,
For now I hope my fame shall rise in noble Hector's fall.
But whilst I arme my selfe, do you on great Saturnius call,
But silently, or to your selves, that not a Troyan heare—   170
Or openly (if you thinke good) since none alive we feare.
None with a will, if I will not, can my bold powers affright,
At least for plaine fierce swinge of strength, or want of skill
    in fight;
For I will well prove that my birth and breed in Salamine
Was not all consecrate to meate or meere effects of wine.'   175
    This said, the wel-given souldiers prayed; up went to heaven
    their eyne:
'O Jove, that Ida doest protect, most happie, most divine,
Send victorie to Ajax' side; fame grace his goodly lim.
Or (if thy love blesse Hector's life and thou hast care of him)
Bestow on both like power, like fame.' This said, in bright   180
    armes shone

Ajax armed, and
his dreadful manner
of approch to the
combat.

The good strong Ajax, who, when all his warre attire was on,
Marcht like the hugely figur'd Mars when angry Jupiter
With strength, on people proud of strength, sends him forth to
    inferre
Wreakfull contention, and comes on with presence full of feare:
So th' Achive rampire, Telamon, did twixt the hoasts appeare;   185
Smil'd, yet of terrible aspect; on earth with ample pace
He boldly stalkt, and shooke aloft his dart with deadly grace.
It did the Grecians good to see, but heartquakes shooke the
    joynts
Of all the Troyans. Hector's selfe felt thoughts with horrid points
Tempt his bold bosome; but he now must make no   190
    counterflight,
Nor (with his honour) now refuse, that had provokt the fight.

[158]

*The shield of Ajax
like a tower.*

Tychius the currier
Hinc illud:
Dominus clypei
septemplicis Ajax.

Ajax came neare; and like a towre his shield his bosome bard,
The right side brasse, and seven Oxehides within it quilted hard.
Old Tychius, the best currier that did in Hyle dwell,
Did frame it for exceeding proofe, and wrought it wondrous   195
    well.
With this stood he to Hector close, and with this Brave began:
'Now, Hector, thou shalt clearly know, thus meeting man to man,
What other leaders arme our hoast besides great Thetis' sonne,
Who with his hardie Lion's heart hath armies overrunne.
But he lies at our crookt-sternd fleet, a Rivall with our King   200
In height of spirit; yet to Troy he many knights did bring
Coequall with Æacides, all able to sustaine
All thy bold challenge can import. Begin, then; words are vaine.'

Hector to Ajax.

    The Helme-grac't Hector answerd him: 'Renowned Telamon,
Prince of the souldiers came from Greece, assay not me,   205
    like one
Yong and immartiall, with great words as to an Amazon dame.
I have the habit of all fights, and know the bloudie frame
Of every slaughter. I well know the ready right-hand charge;
I know the left, and every sway of my securefull targe.
I triumph in the crueltie of fixed combat fight,   210
And manage horse to all designes. I thinke then with good right
I may be confident as farre as this my challenge goes,
Without being taxed with a vaunt borne out with emptie showes.
But (being a souldier so renownd) I will not worke on thee
With least advantage of that skill I know doth strengthen me,   215
And so with privitie of sleight winne that for which I strive,
But at thy best (even open strength) if my endevours thrive.'

The combat.

    Thus sent he his long Javelin forth. It strooke his foe's huge
    shield
Neere to the upper skirt of brasse, which was the eighth it held.
Sixe folds th' untamed dart strooke through, and in the   220
    seventh tough hide
The point was chekt. Then Ajax threw: his angry Lance did
    glide
Quite through his bright orbicular targe, his curace, shirt
    of maile,
And did his manly stomack's mouth with dangerous taint assaile;
But in the bowing of himselfe blacke death too short did strike.
Then both to plucke their Javelins forth encountred Lion-like,   225
Whose bloudie violence is increast by that raw food they eate,
Or Bores, whose strength wilde nourishment doth make so
    wondrous great.
Againe Priamides did wound, in midst, his shield of brasse,

Yet pierc't not through the upper plate—the head reflected was;
But Ajax (following his Lance) smote through his target quite   230
And stayd bold Hector rushing in. The Lance held way outright
And hurt his necke: out gusht the bloud, yet Hector ceast not so

Saxis pugnant.

But in his strong hand tooke a Flint (as he did backwards go)
Blacke, sharpe and big, layd in the field. The sevenfold targe
     it smit
Full on the bosse, and round about the brasse did ring with it.   235
But Ajax a farre greater stone lift up and (wreathing round,
With all his bodie layd to it) he sent it forth to wound
And gave unmeasur'd force to it: the round stone broke within

Hector strooke on
his knees.

His rundled target: his lov'd knees to languish did begin,
And he leand, stretcht out on his shield; but Phœbus raisd him   240
     streight.
Then had they layd on wounds with swords, in use of closer fight,
Unlesse the Heralds (messengers of Gods and godlike men),
The one of Troy, the other Greece, had held betwixt them then
Imperiall scepters, when the one (Idæus grave and wise)
Said to them: 'Now no more, my sonnes: the Soveraigne of   245
     the skies
Doth love you both: both souldiers are, all witnesse with good
     right.
But now night layes her mace on earth; tis good t' obey the
     night.'

Ajax to Idæus.

'Idæus,' Telamon replide, 'to Hector speake, not me.
He that cald all our Achive Peeres to station fight, twas he.
If he first ceasse, I gladly yeeld.' Great Hector then began: 250

Hector to Ajax.

     'Ajax, since Jove to thy big forme made thee so strong a man
And gave thee skill to use thy strength so much that for thy
     speare
Thou art most excellent of Greece, now let us fight forbeare.
Hereafter we shall warre againe till Jove our Herald be,
And grace with conquest which he will: heaven yeelds to night,   255
     and we.
Go thou and comfort all thy Fleet, all friends and men of thine,
As I in Troy my favourers, who in the Fane divine
Have offerd Orisons for me. And come, let us impart
Some ensignes of our strife, to shew each other's suppled hart—

Hector gives Ajax
a sword; Ajax,
Hector a girdle.
Both which gifts
were afterward
cause of both their
deaths.

That men of Troy and Greece may say: "Thus their high   260
     quarrell ends:
Those that, encountring, were such foes, are now (being
     separate) friends." '
He gave a sword whose handle was with silver studs through
     driven,

Scabard and all, with hangers rich. By Telamon was given
A faire well-glossed purple waste. Thus Hector went to Troy,
And after him a multitude fild with his safetie's joy,   265
Despairing he could ever scape the puissant fortitude
And unimpeached Ajax' hands. The Greeks like joy renude
For their reputed victorie and brought him to the King,

*Sacrifice for
victorie. Virgil
imit.*

*Convivium à
sacrificio.*

Who to the great Saturnides preferd an offering.
An Oxe that fed on five faire springs they fleyd and quartred   270
    him
And then (in peeces cut) on spits they rosted every lim,
Which neatly drest, they drew it off: worke done, they fell to
    feast.
All had enough, but Telamon the King fed past the rest
With good large peeces of the chine. Thus, thirst and hunger
    staid,
Nestor (whose counsels late were best) vowes new, and first   275
    he said:

*Nestor to the
Greeks.*

'Atrides and my other Lords, a sort of Greeks are dead
Whose blacke bloud neare Scamander's streame inhumane Mars
    hath shed:
Their soules to hell descended are. It fits thee then, our King,
To make our souldiers ceasse from warre, and by the day's first
    spring
Let us our selves, assembled all, the bodies beare to fire,   280
With Mules and Oxen, neare our fleet, that when we home retire
Each man may carrie to the sonnes of fathers slaughterd here
Their honourd bones: one tombe for all for ever let us reare,
Circling the pile without the field; at which we will erect
Wals and a raveling that may safe our fleet and us protect.   285
And in them let us fashion gates, solid and bard about,
Through which our horse and chariots may well get in and out.
Without all, let us dig a dike, so deepe it may availe
Our forces gainst the charge of horse and foote that come
    t' assaile:
And thus th' attempts, that I see swell in Troy's proud heart,   290
    shall faile.'
    The Kings do his advice approve. So Troy doth Court convent
At Priam's gate in th' Ilian tower, fearfull and turbulent.

*Antenor's counsell
to the Troyans.*

Amongst all, wise Antenor spake: 'Troyans and Dardan friends
And Peeres assistants, give good eare to what my care commends
To your consents for all our good. Resolve: let us restore   295
The Argive Helen, with her wealth, to him she had before.
We now defend but broken faiths. If, therefore, ye refuse,
No good event can I expect of all the warres we use.'

He ceast, and Alexander spake, husband to th' Argive Queene:

'Antenor, to mine eares thy words harsh and ungracious beene. 300
Thou canst use better if thou wilt, but if these truly fit
Thy serious thoughts, the Gods, with age, have reft thy graver
    wit.
To war-like Troyans I will speake. I clearly do denie
To yeeld my wife, but all her wealth I'le render willingly,
What ever I from Argos brought, and vow to make it more— 305
Which I have readie in my house, if peace I may restore.'
    Priam, sirnam'd Dardanides (godlike in counsels grave)
In his sonne's favour well advisde, this resolution gave:

'My royall friends of every state, there is sufficient done,
For this late counsell we have cald, in th' offer of my sonne. 310
Now then let all take needfull food; then let the watch be set,
And everie court of guard held strong. So when the morne
    doth wet
The high-raisd battlements of Troy, Idæus shall be sent
To th' Argive fleet and Atreus' sonnes t' unfold my sonne's intent,
From whose fact our contention springs; and (if they will) 315
    obtaine
Respit from heate of fight, till fire consume our souldiers slaine.
And after, our most fatall warre let us importune still
Till Jove the conquest have disposd to his unconquer'd will.'
    All heard and did obey the king, and (in their quarters all
That were to set the watch that night) did to their suppers fall. 320

Idæus in the morning went and th' Achive Peeres did find
In counsell at Atrides' ship: his audience was assignd,
And in the midst of all the kings the vocall Herald said:

    'Atrides, my renowned king and other kings his aid
Propose by me, in their commands, the offers Paris makes 325
(From whose joy all our woes proceed). He princely undertakes
That all the wealth be brought from Greece (would he had died
    before!)
He will (with other added wealth) for your amends restore.
But famous Menelaus' wife he still meanes to enjoy,
Though he be urg'd the contrarie by all the Peeres of Troy. 330
And this besides I have in charge, that, if it please you all,
They wish both sides may ceasse from warre, that rites of funerall
May on their bodies be performd that in the fields lie slaine,
And after, to the will of Fate, renue the fight againe.'
    All silence held at first: at last Tydides made reply: 335

'Let no man take the wealth, or Dame; for now a child's
    weake eye
May see the imminent blacke end of Priam's Emperie.'

This sentence, quicke and briefly given, the Greeks did all
    admire.

Agamemnon to
Idæus.

Then said the King: 'Herald, thou hear'st in him the voice entire
Of all our Peeres to answer thee for that of Priam's sonne.   340
But, for our burning of the dead, by all meanes I am wonne
To satisfie thy king therein, without the slendrest gaine
Made of their spoiled carkasses; but freely (being slaine)
They shall be all consumd with fire—to witnesse which I cite
High-thundring Jove, that is the king of Juno's bed's delight.' 345
    With this, he held his scepter up to all the skie-thron'd powres;
And grave Idæus did returne to sacred Ilion's towres
Where Ilians and Dardanians did still their counsels plie,
Expecting his returne. He came and told his Legacie.
All whirlewind-like assembled then; some, bodies to transport, 350
Some to hew trees. On th' other part, the Argives did exhort
Their souldiers to the same affaires. Then did the new-fir'd
    Sunne
Smite the brode fields, ascending heaven, and th' Ocean
    smooth did runne:
When Greece and Troy mixt in such peace, you scarce could
    either know.
Then washt they off their blood and dust, and did warme   355
    teares bestow
Upon the slaughterd and in Carres conveid them from the field.
Priam commanded none should mourne, but in still silence yeeld
Their honord carkasses to fire and onely grieve in heart.
All burnd, to Troy Troy's friends retire, to fleet the Grecian part.
Yet doubtfull night obscur'd the earth, the day did not   360
    appeare,
When round about the funerall pile the Grecians gatherd were.
The pile they circled with a tombe and by it raisd a wall,
High towres to guard the fleet and them; and in the midst of all
They built strong gates through which the horse and chariots
    passage had.
Without the rampire a brode dike, long and profound,   365
    they made,
On which they Pallesados pitcht: and thus the Grecians wrought.
Their huge workes in so little time were to perfection brought
That all Gods, by the Lightner set, the frame thereof admir'd,
Mongst whom the earthquake-making God this of their King
    enquir'd:

Neptune to Jupiter.

'Father of Gods, will any man, of all earth's grassie sphere,   370
Aske any of the Gods' consents to any actions there,

[163]

If thou wilt see the shag-haird Greekes with headstrong labours
    frame
So huge a worke and not to us due offrings first enflame?
As farre as white Aurora's dewes are sprinkled through the aire,
Fame will renowne the hands of Greece for this divine affaire: 375
Men will forget the sacred worke the Sunne and I did raise
For king Laomedon; bright Troy and this will beare the praise.'

Jove to Neptune.   Jove was extremely mov'd with him, and said: 'What words
    are these,
Thou mightie shaker of the earth, thou Lord of all the seas?
Some other God, of farre lesse powre, might hold conceipts   380
    dismaid

The fortification
that in the twelfth
Booke is razed.

With this rare Grecian stratageme, and thou rest well apaid;
For it will glorifie thy name as farre as light extends,
Since, when these Greekes shall see againe their native soile
    and friends,
(The bulwarke battred) thou maist quite devoure it with thy
    waves
And cover (with thy fruitlesse sands) this fatall shore of   385
    graves—
That what their fierie industries have so divinely wrought
In raising it, in razing it thy powre will prove it nought.'
   Thus spake the Gods among themselves: set was the fervent
    Sunne;
And now the great worke of the Greeks was absolutely done.
Then slue they Oxen in their tents, and strength with food   390
    reviv'd,

A fleete of wine of
a thousand tun sent
by Euneus, King of
Lemnos, Jason's son.

When out of Lemnos a great fleete of odorous wine arriv'd,
Sent by Euneus, Jason's sonne, borne of Hypsipyle.
The fleete containd a thousand tunne, which must
    transported be
To Atreus' sons, as he gave charge, whose merchandize it was.
The Greeks bought wine for shining steele, and some for   395
    sounding brasse,
Some for Oxe hides, for Oxen some, and some for prisoners.
A sumptuous banquet was prepar'd, and all that night the Peeres
And faire-haird Greeks consum'd in feast. So Troyans and their
    aide.
And all the night Jove thunderd lowd: pale feare all thoughts
    dismaide.
While they were gluttonous in earth, Jove wrought their banes   400
    in heaven.
They pourd full cups upon the ground and were to offrings
    driven

[164]

In stead of quaffings, and to drinke none durst attempt before
In solemne sacrifice they did almightie Jove adore.
Then to their rests they all repaird: bold zeale their feare
    bereav'd:
And sodaine sleepe's refreshing gift securely they receiv'd.   405

The End of the Seventh Booke

THE EIGHTH BOOKE

of

HOMER'S ILIADS

THE ARGUMENT

When Jove to all the Gods had given command
That none to either host should helpfull stand,
To Ida he descends, and sees from thence
Juno and Pallas haste the Greeks' defence,
Whose purpose his command, by Iris given,   5
Doth intervent: then came the silent Even,
When Hector chargde fires should consume the night,
Lest Greeks in darkenesse tooke suspected flight.

Another Argument

In Theta *gods a Counsell have,*
Troy's conquest, glorious Hector's Brave.

Periphrasis of the
Morning.

The chearfull Ladie of the light, deckt in her saffron robe,
Disperst her beames through every part of this enflowred globe,
When thundring Jove a Court of Gods assembled by his will
In top of all the topfull heights that crowne th' Olympian hill.

Jove to the bench
of Deities.

He spake, and all the Gods gave eare: 'Heare how I stand   5
   inclind—
That God nor Goddesse may attempt t' infringe my soveraigne
   mind,
But all give suffrage, that with speed I may these discords end.
What God soever I shall find indevour to defend
Or Troy or Greece, with wounds to heaven he (sham'd) shall
   reascend;

Virgil maketh this
likewise his place,
adding, Bis patet in
præceps, tantum
tenditque sub
umbras, &c.

Or (taking him with his offence) I'le cast him downe as deepe   10
As Tartarus (the brood of night) where Barathrum doth steepe
Torment in his profoundest sinks, where is the floore of brasse
And gates of iron; the place for depth as farre doth hell surpasse
As heaven (for height) exceeds the earth: then shall he know
   from thence

[166]

How much my power, past all the Gods, hath soveraigne   15
   eminence.

Homer's golden chaine.

Indanger it the whiles and see let downe our golden chaine,
And at it let all Deities their utmost strengths constraine
To draw me to the earth from heaven: you never shall prevaile
Though with your most contention ye dare my state assaile.
But when my will shall be disposd to draw you all to me,   20
Even with the earth it selfe and seas ye shall enforced be.
Then will I to Olympus' top our vertuous engine bind
And by it everie thing shall hang by my command inclind.
So much I am supreme to Gods, to men supreme as much.'
The Gods sat silent and admir'd, his dreadfull speech was such.   25

Pallas to Jove.

   At last his blue-eyd daughter spake: 'O great Saturnides,
O Father, O heaven's highest King, well know we the excesse
Of thy great power compar'd with all. Yet the bold Greekes'
   estate
We needs must mourne, since they must fall beneath so hard
   a fate.
For if thy grave command enjoyne, we will abstaine from fight,   30
But to afford them such advice as may relieve their plight
We will (with thy consent) be bold, that all may not sustaine
The fearefull burthen of thy wrath and with their shames be
   slaine.'

Jove to Pallas.

He smil'd and said: 'Be confident: thou art belov'd of me.
I speake not this with serious thoughts, but will be kind   35
   to thee.'

Jove's horse.

   This said, his brasse-hov'd winged horse he did to chariot bind,
Whose crests were fring'd with manes of gold, and golden
   garments shin'd
On his rich shoulders; in his hand he tooke a golden scourge,
Divinely fashiond, and with blowes their willing speed did urge

Jove descends to Ida.

Midway betwixt the earth and heaven. To Ida then he came,   40
Abounding in delicious springs and nurse of beasts untame,
Where (on the mountaine Gargarus) men did a Fane erect
To his high name, and altars sweet: and there his horse he
   checkt,
Dissolv'd them from his chariot, and in a cloud of jeate
He coverd them, and on the top tooke his triumphant seate,   45
Beholding Priam's famous towne and all the Fleet of Greece.

Jove's prospect.
Both hosts arme.

The Greeks tooke breakfast speedily, and arm'd at everie peece—
So Troyans, who, though fewer farre, yet all to fight tooke armes:
Dire need enforc't them, to avert their wives' and children's
   harmes.
All gates flew open: all the host did issue, foote and horse,   50

In mightie tumult: straite one place adjoynd each adverse force.
Then shields with shields met, darts with darts, strength against
    strength opposd.
The bosse-pik't targets were thrust on and thunderd as they
    closd
In mightie tumult: grone for grone and breath for breath
    did breath
Of men then slaine and to be slaine: earth flowd with fruits   55
    of death.
While the faire morning's beautie held, and day increast in
    height,
Their Javelins mutually made death transport an equall freight.
But when the hote Meridian point bright Phœbus did ascend,

Anceps victoria.
The Meridian libra

Then Jove his golden Ballances did equally extend,
Jovis Aurea. Virgil   And, of long-rest-conferring death, put in two bitter fates   60
transtulit Macrobius 5.   For Troy and Greece; he held the midst: the day of finall dates
Fell on the Greeks: the Greeks' hard lots sunke to the flowrie
    ground,
The Troyans' leapt as high as heaven. Then did the claps resound

Jove's thunder
amongst the
Grecians.

Of his fierce thunder: lightning leapt amongst each Grecian
    troope:
The sight amaz'd them: pallid feare made boldest stomacks   65
    stoope.
Then Idomen durst not abide: Atrides went his way,
And both th' Ajaces: Nestor yet against his will did stay
(That grave Protector of the Greekes), for Paris with a dart
Enrag'd one of his chariot horse: he smote the upper part
Of all his skull, even where the haire that made his foretop   70
    sprung.
The hurt was deadly, and the paine so sore the courser stung
(Pierc't to the braine) he stampt and plung'd: one on another
    beares,
Entangled round about the beame. Then Nestor cut the geres
With his new-drawne authentique sword. Meanewhile the firie
    horse
Of Hector brake into the preasse with their bold ruler's force.   75
Then good old Nestor had bene slaine had Diomed not espied,
Who to Ulysses, as he fled, importunately cried:

Diomed to Ulysses.

'Thou that in counsels dost abound, O Laertiades,
Why flyest thou? why thus cowardlike shunst thou the honourd
    prease?
Take heed thy backe take not a dart: stay, let us both intend   80
To drive this cruell enemie from our deare aged friend.'
    He spake, but warie Ithacus would find no patient eare,

The Eighth Booke

*Ulysses flies and
Diomed alone steps
to the rescue of
Nestor.*

But fled forthright, even to the fleet. Yet, though he single were,
Brave Diomed mixt amongst the fight, and stood before the
   steeds
Of old Neleides, whose estate thus kingly he areeds: 85
  'O father, with these youths in fight thou art unequall plac't;
Thy willing sinewes are unknit; grave age pursues thee fast;
And thy unruly horse are slow. My chariot therefore use
And trie how readie Troyan horse can flie him that pursues,
Pursue the flier and every way performe the varied fight.   90
I forc't them from Anchises' sonne, well-skild in cause of flight.
Then let my Squire leade hence thy horse: mine thou shalt guard,
   whilst I
(By thee advanc't) assay the fight, that Hector's selfe may trie
If my lance dote with the defects that faile best minds in age
Or find the palsey in my hands that doth thy life engage.'   95
  This noble Nestor did accept, and Diomed's two friends,
Eurymedon, that valour loves, and Sthenelus ascends
Old Nestor's coach: of Diomed's horse Nestor the charge
   sustains,
And Tydeus' sonne took place of fight. Neleides held the rains
And scourg'd the horse, who swiftly ran direct in Hector's face, 100

*Diomed charges
Hector.*

Whom fierce Tydides bravely charg'd: but he, turnd from the
   chace,
His javeline Eniopeus smit, mightie Thebæus' sonne,
And was great Hector's chariotere: it through his breast
   did runne
Neare to his pappe: he fell to earth: backe flew his frighted
   horse:
His strength and soule were both dissolv'd. Hector had deepe 105
   remorse
Of his mishap, yet left he him and for another sought.
Nor long his steeds did want a guide, for straight good fortune
   brought
Bold Archeptolemus, whose life did from Iphitus spring.
He made him take the reines and mount: then soules were set
   on wing;
Then high exploits were undergone: then Troyans in their 110
   wals
Had bene infolded like meeke Lambs, had Jove winkt at their
   fals,
Who hurld his horrid thunder forth and made pale lightnings
   flie
Into the earth before the horse that Nestor did applie.

[169]

A dreadfull flash burnt through the aire that savourd
    sulphure-like,
Which downe before the chariot the dazled horse did strike.   115
The faire reines fell from Nestor's hand, who did (in feare)
    intreate
Renownd Tydides into flight to turne his furie's heate.

Nestor to Diomed.   'For knowest thou not,' said he, 'our aide is not supplide from
    Jove?
This day he will give fame to Troy, which when it fits his love
We shall enjoy: let no man tempt his unresisted will,   120
Though he exceed in gifts of strength, for he exceeds him still.'

Diomed to Nestor.   'Father,' replied the king, 'tis true, but both my heart and soule
Are most extremely griev'd to thinke how Hector will controule
My valour with his vants in Troy—that I was terror-sicke
With his approch: which when he boasts, let earth devoure me   125
    quicke.'

Nestor to Diomed.   'Ah warlike Tydeus' sonne,' said he, 'what needlesse words
    are these?
Though Hector should report thee faint and amorous of thy
    ease,
The Troyans nor the Troyan wives would never give him trust—
Whose youthfull husbands thy free hand hath smotherd so
    in dust.'
   This said, he turn'd his one-hov'd horse to flight, and troope   130
    did take,
When Hector and his men with showts did greedie pursute make
And pour'd on darts that made aire sigh. Then Hector did
    exclame:

Hector's brave to   'O Tydeus' sonne, the kings of Greece do most renowne thy
Diomed.   name
With highest place, feasts and full cups—who now will do thee
    shame.
Thou shalt be like a woman usd, and they will say: "Depart,   135
Immartiall minion, since to stand Hector thou hadst no hart."
Nor canst thou scale our turrets' tops, nor leade the wives to
    fleet
Of valiant men, that wifelike fear'st my adverse charge to meet.'
   This two waies mov'd him, still to flie or turne his horse
    and fight.
Thrice thrust he forward to assault, and every time the fright   140
Of Jove's fell thunder drave him backe, which he proposd for
    signe

Hector to his   (To shew the change of victorie) Troyans should victors shine.
friends.   Then Hector comforted his men: 'All my adventrous friends,

Be men, and of your famous strength thinke of the honourd
 ends.
I know benevolent Jupiter did by his becke professe   145
Conquest and high renowne to me, and to the Greeks distresse.
O fooles, to raise such silly forts, not worth the least account
Nor able to resist our force! With ease our horse may mount
Quite over all their hollow dike. But when their fleet I reach,
Let Memorie to all the world a famous bonfire teach: 150
For I will all their ships inflame, with whose infestive smoke
(Feare-shrunke and hidden neare their keels) the conquerd
 Greeks shall choke.'

The names of   Then cherisht he his famous horse: 'O Xanthus, now,' said he,
Hector's horse. 'And thou Podargus, Æthon too, and Lampus, deare to me,
Make me some worthy recompence for so much choice of 155
 meate
Vinum equis. Given you by faire Andromache—bread of the purest wheate
And with it (for your drinke) mixt wine, to make ye wished
 cheare—
Still serving you before my selfe (her husband young and deare).
Pursue and use your swiftest speed, that we may take for prise
Nestor's shield al The shield of old Neleides, which Fame lifts to the skies, 160
of gold. Even to the handles telling it to be of massie gold.
And from the shoulders let us take of Diomed the bold
The royall curace Vulcan wrought with art so exquisite.
These if we make our sacred spoile, I doubt not but this Night
Even to their navie to enforce the Greekes' unturned flight.' 165
  This Juno tooke in high disdaine and made Olympus shake
As she but stird within her throne, and thus to Neptune spake:
Juno to Neptune. 'O Neptune, what a spite is this! Thou God so huge in power,
Afflicts it not thy honor'd heart to see rude spoile devoure
These Greekes that have in Helice and Ægæ offred thee 170
So many and such wealthie gifts let them the victors be?
If we that are the aids of Greece would beate home these of Troy
And hinder brode-eyd Jove's prowd will, it would abate his joy.'
Neptune to Juno. He (angrie) told her she was rash, and he would not be one,
Of all the rest, should strive with Jove, whose power was 175
 matcht by none.
Whiles they conferd thus, all the space the trench containd
 before
(From that part of the fort that flankt the navie-anchoring shore)
Was fild with horse and targateirs who there for refuge came,
By Mars-swift Hector's power engagde: Jove gave his strength
 the fame,
And he with spoilefull fire had burnt the fleet if Juno's grace 180

[171]

Had not inspirde the king himselfe to run from place to place
And stirre up everie souldier's powre to some illustrous deed.

*Agamemnon's
labor in ranging
his armie.*

First visiting their leaders' tents, his ample purple weed
He wore to shew all who he was; and did his station take
At wise Ulysses' sable barkes, that did the battell make   185
Of all the fleet; from whence his speech might with more ease
    be driven
To Ajax' and Achilles' ships, to whose chiefe charge were given
The Vantguard and the Rereguard both—both for their force
    of hand
And trustie bosomes. There arriv'd, thus urg'd he to withstand

*Agamemnon's
exprobration of
the Greeks.*

Th' insulting Troyans: 'O what shame, ye emptie-hearted   190
    Lords,
Is this to your admired formes? where are your glorious words,
In Lemnos vaunting you the best of all the Grecian host?
"We are the strongest men," ye said, "we will command the most,
Eating most flesh of high-hornd beeves and drinking cups full
    crownd,
And everie man a hundred foes, two hundred, will confound."   195
Now all our strength, dar'd to our worst, one Hector cannot
    tame,
Who presently with horrid fire will all our fleet inflame.

*Apostrophe ad
Jovem.*

O Father Jove, hath ever yet thy most unsuffred hand
Afflicted with such spoile of soules the king of any land,
And taken so much fame from him?—when I did never faile   200
(Since under most unhappie starres this fleet was under saile)
Thy glorious altars, I protest; but above all the Gods
Have burnt fat thighs of beeves to thee, and praid to race
    th' abodes
Of rape-defending Ilians. Yet grant, almightie Jove,
One favour, that we may at least with life from hence remove,   205
Not under such inglorious hands the hands of death imploy,
And where Troy should be stoopt by Greece, let Greece fall
    under Troy.'
    To this even weeping king did Jove remorsefull audience
    give,
And shooke great heaven to him for signe his men and he
    should live.

*Jove casts off his
Eagle on the Greeks'
right hand, that
truss't a Hinde calfe.*

Then quickly cast he off his hawke, the Eagle, prince of aire,   210
That perfects his unspotted vowes, who seisd in her repaire
A sucking hinde calfe, which she truss't in her enforcive seeres,
And by Jove's altar let it fall amongst th' amazed peeres,
Where the religious Achive kings with sacrifice did please
The authour of all Oracles, divine Saturnides.   215

Now, when they knew the bird of Jove, they turnd couragious
    head—
When none (though many kings put on) could make his vaunt,
    he led

Diomed.

Tydides to renewd assault, or issued first the dike,
Or first did fight; but farre the first, stone-dead his lance
    did strike
Arm'd Agelaus, by descent surnam'd Phradmonides.   220
He turn'd his readie horse to flight, and Diomed's lance did seise
His backe betwixt his shoulder blades and lookt out at his brest.
He fell, and his armes rang his fall. Th' Atrides next addrest
Themselves to fight, th' Ajaces next with vehement strength
    endude:
Idomeneus and his friend, stout Merion, next pursude,   225
And after these Eurypylus, Euæmon's honord race:
The ninth, with backward-wreathed bow, had little Teucer place.

Teucer serving
under Ajax' shield.

He still fought under Ajax' shield, who sometimes held it by
And then he lookt his object out and let his arrow flie,
And whomsoever in the preasse he wounded, him he slue,   230
Then under Ajax' seven-fold shield he presently withdrew.
He far'd like an unhappie child that doth to mother run
For succour, when he knowes full well he some shrewd turne
    hath done.
What Troyans then were to their deaths by Teucer's shafts
    imprest?
Haplesse Orsilochus was first, Ormenus, Ophelest,   235
Dætor and hardie Chromius and Lycophon divine,
And Amopaon, that did spring from Polyæmon's line,
And Melanippus—all on heapes he tumbled to the ground.
The king rejoyc't to see his shafts the Phrygian ranks confound,

Agamemnon to
Teucer.

Who straight came neare and spake to him: 'O Teucer,   240
    lovely man,
Strike still so sure, and be a grace to everie Grecian
And to thy father Telamon, who tooke thee kindly home
(Although not by his wife, his sonne) and gave thee foster roome,
Even from thy childhood. Then to him, though far from hence
    remov'd,
Make good fame reach, and to thy selfe I vow what shall   245
    be prov'd—
If he that dreadfull Ægis beares and Pallas grant to me
Th' expugnance of wel-builded Troy, I first will honour thee
Next to my selfe with some rich gift and put it in thy hand—
A three-foot vessell that for grace in sacred Fanes doth stand,
Or two horse and a chariot, or else a lovely Dame   250

[173]

That may ascend on bed with thee and amplifie thy name.'

*Teucer to
Agamemnon.*

Teucer right nobly answerd him: 'Why, most illustrate king,
I being thus forward of my selfe, dost thou adjoyne a sting?
Without which, all the power I have I ceasse not to imploy,
For from the place where we repulst the Troyans towards Troy 255
I all the purple field have strew'd with one or other slaine.
Eight shafts I shot, with long steele heads, of which not one
    in vaine.
All were in youthfull bodies fixt, well-skild in warre's constraint.
Yet this wild dog, with all my aime, I have no power to taint.'
This said, another arrow forth from his stiffe string he sent 260
At Hector, whom he long'd to wound: but still amisse it went.
His shaft smit faire Gorgythion, of Priam's princely race,
Who in Æsyme was brought forth (a famous towne in Thrace)
By Castianira, that for forme was like celestiall breed.

Virgil in Pallante
imitatus est.

And as a crimson Poppie flower, surcharged with his seed 265
And vernall humors falling thicke, declines his heavie brow;
So of one side his helmet's weight his fainting head did bow.
Yet Teucer would another shaft at Hector's life dispose,
So faine he such a marke would hit; but still besides it goes.
Apollo did avert the shaft: but Hector's charioteere 270
Bold Archeptolemus he smit as he was rushing neere
To make the fight: to earth he fell, his swift horse backe did flie,
And there were both his strength and soule exilde eternally.
Huge griefe, for Hector's slaughterd friend, pincht-in his
    mightie mind,
Yet was he forc't to leave him there, and his void place resignd 275
To his sad brother that was by, Cebriones; whose eare
Receiving Hector's charge, he straight the weightie reines
    did beare,
And Hector from his shining coach (with horrid voice) leapt on

*Hector with a
stone at Teucer.*

To wreake his friend on Teucer's hand, and up he tooke
    a stone
With which he at the Archer ran, who from his quiver drew 280
A sharpe-pild shaft and nockt it sure. But in great Hector flew
With such fell speed that in his draught he his right shoulder
    strooke
Where twixt his necke and breast the joynt his native closure
    tooke.
The wound was wondrous full of death; his string in sunder
    flees;
His nummed hand fell strengthlesse downe, and he upon 285
    his knees.
Ajax neglected not to aid his brother thus deprest,

But came and saft him with his shield; and two more friends,
    addrest
To be his aide, tooke him to fleet—Mecisteus, Echius' son,
And gay Alastor. Teucer sigh'd for all his service done.
    Then did Olympius with fresh strength the Troyan powers   290
    revive,
Who to their trenches once againe the troubled Greekes
    did drive.
Hector brought terror with his strength, and ever fought before.
As when some highly-stomackt hound, that hunts a sylvan Bore
Or kingly Lion, loves the hanch and pincheth oft behind,
Bold of his feet, and still observes the game to turne inclind,   295
Not utterly dissolv'd in flight—so Hector did pursue,
And whosoever was the last, he ever did subdue.
They fled, but when they had their dike and Pallesados past,
(A number of them put to sword) at ships they staid at last.
Then mutuall exhortations flew; then all, with hands and eyes   300
Advanc't to all the Gods, their plagues wrung from them
    open cries.

Hector's terrible   Hector, with his fowre rich-man'd horse, assaulting alwaies róde;
aspect.   The eyes of Gorgon burnt in him and warre's vermilion God.
The Goddesse that all Goddesses for snowie armes out-shin'd
Thus spake to Pallas, to the Greeks with gracious ruth inclin'd: 305
Juno to Pallas.   'O Pallas, what a griefe is this! Is all our succour past
To these our perishing Grecian friends—at least, withheld at last,
Even now, when one man's violence must make them perish all
In satisfaction of a Fate so full of funerall?
Hector Priamides now raves, no more to be indur'd,   310
That hath alreadie on the Greeks so many harmes inur'd.'
    The azure Goddesse answerd her: 'This man had surely found
His fortitude and life dissolv'd, even on his father's ground,
By Grecian valour if my Sire, infested with ill moods,
Did not so dote on these of Troy, too jelous of their bloods,   315
And ever an unjust repulse stands to my willing powres,
Little remembring what I did in all the desperate howres
Of his affected Hercules. I ever rescued him
In labours of Eurystheus, untoucht in life or lim,
When he (heaven knowes) with drowned eyes lookt up for   320
    helpe to heaven,
Which ever at command of Jove was by my suppliance given.
But had my wisdome reacht so farre to know of this event,
When to the solid-ported depths of hell his sonne was sent
To hale out hatefull Pluto's dog from darksome Erebus,
He had not scap't the streames of Styx, so deepe and dangerous.   325

Yet Jove hates me and shews his love in doing Thetis' will,
That kist his knees and strok't his chin, praid and importun'd
    still
That he would honour with his aid her cittie-razing sonne,
Displeasd Achilles: and for him our friends are thus undone.
But time shall come againe when he (to do his friends some aid) 330
Will call me his Glaucopides, his sweet and blew-eyd maid.
Then harnesse thou thy horse for me that his bright Pallace gates
I soone may enter, arming me, to order these debates:
And I will trie if Priam's sonne will still maintaine his cheare
When in the crimson paths of warre I dreadfully appeare—   335
For some prowd Troyans shall be sure to nourish dogs and foules
And pave the shore with fat and flesh, depriv'd of lives and
    soules.'
    Juno prepar'd her horse, whose manes Ribands of gold enlac't.

Pallas armes.   Pallas her partie-coloured robe on her bright shoulders cast,
Divinely wrought with her owne hands, in th' entrie of her Sire. 340
Then put she on her ample breast her under-arming tire,
And on it her celestiall armes. The chariot streight she takes,
With her huge heavie violent lance, with which she slaughter
    makes

Juno her   Of armies fatall to her wrath. Saturnia whipt her horse,
waggonnesse.   And heaven gates, guarded by the Howres, op't by their   345
    proper force,
Through which they flew. Whom when Jove saw (set neare
    th' Idalian springs)
Highly displeasd, he Iris cald, that hath the golden wings,

Jove to Iris.   And said: 'Flie, Iris, turne them backe; let them not come at me.
Our meetings (severally disposd) will nothing gracious be.
Beneath their o'rethrowne chariot I'le shiver their prowd steeds, 350
Hurle downe themselves, their wagon breake and, for their
    stubborne deeds,
In ten whole yeares they shall not heale the wounds I will
    impresse
With horrid thunder—that my maid may know when to addresse
Armes gainst her father. For my wife, she doth not so offend:
Tis but her use to interrupt what ever I intend.'   355

Iris to heaven.   Iris, with this, left Ida's hils and up t' Olympus flew,
Met (neare heaven gates) the Goddesses and thus their haste
    withdrew:
  'What course intend you? Why are you wrapt with your
    fancie's storme?
Jove likes not ye should aid the Greeks, but threats—and will
    performe—

[176]

To crush in peeces your swift horse beneath their glorious   360
     yokes,
Hurle downe your selves, your chariot breake, and those
     impoysoned strokes
His wounding thunder shall imprint in your celestiall parts,
In ten full Springs ye shall not cure—that she that tames
     proud hearts
(Thy selfe, Minerva) may be taught to know for what, and when,
Thou doest against thy father fight: for sometimes childeren   365
May with discretion plant themselves against their fathers' wils,
But not where humors onely rule in works beyond their skils.
For Juno, she offends him not, nor vexeth him so much,
For tis her use to crosse his will, her impudence is such.

Facile facit quod
semper facit.

The habite of offence in this she onely doth contract   370
And so grieves or incenseth lesse, though nere the lesse her fact.
But thou most griev'st him, dogged Dame, whom he rebukes
     in time,
Lest silence should pervert thy will and pride too highly clime
In thy bold bosome, desperate girle, if seriously thou dare
Lift thy unwieldie lance gainst Jove, as thy pretences are.'   375

Juno to Pallas.

    She left them, and Saturnia said: 'Ay me, thou seed of Jove,
By my advice we will no more unfit contention move
With Jupiter for mortall men; of whom, let this man die
And that man live, whoever he pursues with destinie.
And let him (plotting all events) dispose of either host   380
As he thinks fittest for them both and may become us most.'
    Thus turnd she backe, and to the Howres her rich-man'd
     horse resign'd,
Who them t' immortall mangers bound: the chariot they
     inclin'd
Beneath the Christall walls of heaven, and they in golden
     thrones
Consorted other Deities, repleate with passions.   385
Jove, in his bright-wheeld chariot, his firie horse now beats
Up to Olympus, and aspir'd the Gods' eternall seats.
Great Neptune loosd his horse, his Carre upon the Altar plac't
And heavenly-linnen Coverings did round about it cast.
The farre-seer usd his throne of gold: the vast Olympus shooke   390
Beneath his feete. His wife and maid apart their places tooke,
Nor any word afforded him. He knew their thoughts, and said:

Jove to Juno and
Pallas.
Scopticè.

'Why do you thus torment your selves? You need not sit dismaid
With the long labours you have usd in your victorious fight,
Destroying Troyans, gainst whose lives you heape such high   395
     despight.

[177]

Ye should have held your glorious course, for be assur'd, as farre
As all my powres (by all meanes urg'd) could have sustaind
    the warre,
Not all the host of Deities should have retir'd my hand
From vowd inflictions on the Greeks—much lesse, you two
    withstand.
But you before you saw the fight—much lesse the slaughter   400
    there—
Had all your goodly lineaments possest with shaking feare,
And never had your chariot borne their charge to heaven
    againe,
But thunder should have smit you both had you one Troyan
    slaine.'
    Both Goddesses let fall their chins upon their Ivorie breasts,
Set next to Jove, contriving still afflicted Troy's unrests.   405
Pallas for anger could not speake; Saturnia, contrarie,
Could not for anger hold her peace, but made this bold replie:

Juno to Jupiter.   'Not-to-be-suffred Jupiter, what needst thou still enforce
Thy matchlesse power? We know it well. But we must yeeld
    remorse
To them that yeeld us sacrifice—nor needst thou thus deride   410
Our kind obedience nor our griefes, but beare our powers
    applide
To just protection of the Greeks, that anger tombe not all
In Troy's foule gulfe of perjurie, and let them stand should fall.'

Jupiter to Juno.   'Greeve not,' said Jove, 'at all done yet: for if thy faire
    eyes please,
This next red morning they shall see the great Saturnides   415
Bring more destruction to the Greekes: and Hector shall not
    cease
Till he have rowsed from the Fleet swift-foot Æacides,
In that day when, before their ships, for his Patroclus slaine,
The Greekes in great distresse shall fight: for so the Fates
    ordaine.
I weigh not thy displeased spleene, though to th' extremest   420
    bounds
Of earth and seas it carrie thee, where endlesse night confounds
Japet and my dejected Sire, who sit so farre beneath
They never see the flying Sunne, nor heare the winds that breath
Neare to profoundest Tartarus—nor thither if thou went
Would I take pittie of thy moods, since none more impudent.'   425
    To this she nothing did replie. And now Sol's glorious light
Fell to the sea, and to the land drew up the drowsie night.

The Night.   The Troyans griev'd at Phœbus' fall, which all the Greeks
    desir'd,

[178]

And sable night (so often wisht) to earth's firme throne aspir'd.
  Hector (intending to consult) neare to the gulfie flood,   430
Farre from the Fleet, led to a place pure and exempt from blood
The Troyans' forces. From their horse all lighted and did heare
Th' Oration Jove-lov'd Hector made, who held a goodly speare
Eleven full cubits long: the head was brasse and did reflect
A wanton light before him still: it round about was deckt   435
With strong hoops of new-burnisht gold. On this he leand,
    and said:

Hector to his
friends.
  'Heare me, my worthie friends of Troy, and you our
    honord aid.
A little since I had conceipt we should have made retreate
By light of the inflamed fleet with all the Greeks' escheate.
But darknesse hath prevented us, and safte, with speciall grace,   440
These Achives and their shore-hal'd fleet. Let us then render
    place
To sacred Night, our suppers dresse, and from our chariot free
Our faire-man'd horse and meate them well: then let there
    convoid be
From forth the citie presently Oxen and well-fed sheepe,

Vina parant animos.
Sweet wine and bread; and fell much wood, that all night we   445
    may keepe
Plentie of fires, even till the light bring forth the lovely morne;
And let their brightnesse glase the skies, that night may
    not suborne
The Greeks' escape, if they for flight the seas' brode backe
    would take.
At least they may not part with ease, but, as retreit they make,
Each man may beare a wound with him to cure when he   450
    comes home,
Made with a shaft or sharpned speare; and others feare to come,
With charge of lamentable warre, gainst souldiers bred in Troy.
Then let our Heralds through the towne their offices imploy,
To warne the youth yet short of warre and time-white fathers,
    past,
That in our god-built towres they see strong courts of guard   455
    be plac't
About the wals: and let our Dames yet flourishing in yeares,
That (having beauties to keepe pure) are most inclin'd to feares
(Since darknesse in distressefull times more dreadfull is than
    light),
Make loftie fires in every house: and thus, the dangerous night
Held with strong watch, if th' enemie have ambuscadoes laid   460
Neare to our wals (and therefore seeme in flight the more
    dismaid,

[179]

Intending a surprise while we are all without the towne),
They every way shall be impugn'd, to every man's renowne.
Performe all this, brave Troyan friends: what now I have to say
Is all exprest: the chearfull morne shall other things display.   465
It is my glorie (putting trust in Jove and other Gods)
That I shall now expulse these dogs fates sent to our abodes:
Who bring ostents of destinie and blacke their threatning fleet.
But this night let us hold strong guards: tomorrow we will meet
(With fierce-made warre) before their ships, and I'le make   470
      knowne to all
If strong Tydides from their ships can drive me to their wall
Or I can pierce him with my sword and force his bloudy spoile.
The wished morne shall shew his powre, if he can shun his foile,
I running on him with my Lance. I thinke when day ascends
He shall lie wounded with the first and by him many friends.   475
O that I were as sure to live immortall and sustaine
No frailties with increasing yeares but evermore remaine
Ador'd like Pallas or the Sunne, as all doubts die in me
That heaven's next light shall be the last the Greekes shall
      ever see!'
   This speech all Troyans did applaud, who from their traces   480
      losde
Their sweating horse, which severally with headstals they reposde
And fastned by their chariots; when others brought from towne
Fat sheepe and oxen instantly, bread, wine, and hewed downe
Huge store of wood. The winds transferd into the friendly skie
Their supper's savour, to the which they sate delightfully   485

Ignes Troianorum And spent all night in open field. Fires round about them shinde.
astris similes. As when about the silver Moone, when aire is free from winde
And stars shine cleare, to whose sweete beames high
      prospects and the brows
Of all steepe hils and pinnacles thrust up themselves for showes
And even the lowly vallies joy to glitter in their sight,   490
When the unmeasur'd firmament bursts to disclose her light
And all the signes in heaven are seene that glad the shepheard's
      hart;
So many fires disclosde their beames, made by the Troyan part,
Before the face of Ilion and her bright turrets show'd.
A thousand courts of guard kept fires, and every guard allow'd   495
Fiftie stout men, by whom their horse eate oates and hard
      white corne,
And all did wishfully expect the silver-throned morne.

The End of the Eighth Booke

THE NINTH BOOKE

of

HOMER'S ILIADS

THE ARGUMENT

To Agamemnon (urging hopelesse flight)
Stand Diomed and Nestor opposite.
By Nestor's counsell, Legats are dismist
To Thetis' sonne, who still denies t' assist.

Another Argument

Iota sings the Ambassie,
And great Achilles' sterne replie.

So held the Troyans sleeplesse guard: the Greeks to flight were
    given.
The feeble consort of cold feare (strangely infusde from heaven),
Grief not to be endur'd did wound all Greeks of greatest worth.
And as two laterall-sited winds (the West wind and the North)
Meete at the Thracian sea's blacke breast, joyne in a sodaine   5
    blore,
Tumble together the darke waves and powre upon the shore
A mightie deale of froth and weed, with which men manure
    ground,
So Jove and Troy did drive the Greeks and all their minds
    confound.
But Agamemnon most of all was tortur'd at his heart,
Who to the voicefull Heralds went and bad them cite, apart,   10
Each Grecian leader severally, not openly proclaime.
In which he labourd with the first, and all together came.
They sadly sate. The king arose and pour'd out teares as fast
As from a loftie rocke a spring doth his blacke waters cast;

Agamemnon to the
Greeks.

And, deeply sighing, thus bespake the Achives: 'O my friends,   15
Princes and leaders of the Greeks, heaven's adverse king extends
His wrath, with too much detriment to my so just designe,
Since he hath often promist me, and bound it with the signe
Of his bent forehead, that this Troy our vengefull hands
    should race

[181]

And safe returne. Yet, now ingag'd, he plagues us with disgrace 20
When all our trust to him hath drawne so much bloud from
    our friends.
My glorie, nor my brother's wreake, were the proposed ends
For which he drew you to these toiles, but your whole
    countrie's shame,
Which had bene huge, to beare the rape of so divine a Dame
Made in despite of our revenge. And yet not that had mov'd 25
Our powres to these designes if Jove had not our drifts approv'd,
Which, since we see he did for bloud, tis desperate fight in us
To strive with him. Then let us flie: tis flight he urgeth thus.'
    Long time still silence held them all. At last did Diomed rise:

*Diomed to
Agamemnon, and
takes fit time to
answer his wrong
done by Agamemnon
in the fourth booke.*

'Atrides, I am first must crosse thy indiscreet advise, 30
As may become me, being a king, in this our martiall court.
Be not displeasd then, for thy selfe didst broadly misreport
In open field my fortitude, and cald me faint and weake.
Yet I was silent, knowing the time, loth any rites to breake
That appertaind thy publicke rule: yet all the Greekes knew well 35
(Of every age) thou didst me wrong. As thou then didst refell
My valour first of all the hoast, as of a man dismaid,
So now, with fit occasion given, I first blame thee afraid.
Inconstant Saturn's son hath given inconstant spirits to thee,
And, with a scepter over all, an eminent degree: 40
But with a scepter's soveraigne grace the chiefe powre, Fortitude,
(To bridle thee) he thought not best thy breast should be endude.
Unhappie king, think'st thou the Greeks are such a silly sort
And so excessive impotent as thy weake words import?
If thy mind move thee to be gone, the way is open: go. 45
Mycenian ships enow ride neare, that brought thee to this wo.
The rest of Greece will stay, nor stirre, till Troy be overcome
With full eversion—or, if not, but doters of their home,
Will put on wings to flie with thee, my selfe and Sthenelus
Will fight till (trusting favouring Jove) we bring home Troy 50
    with us.'
    This all applauded and admir'd the spirit of Diomed,
When Nestor (rising from the rest) his speech thus seconded:

*Nestor approves
Diomed's counsell
and goes further.*

'Tydides, thou art (questionlesse) our strongest Greeke in warre
And gravest in thy counsels too of all that equall are
In place with thee and stand on strength. Nor is there any one 55
Can blame or contradict thy speech. And yet thou hast not gone
So farre but we must further go. Th' art yong and well mightst be
My yongest sonne, though still I yeeld thy words had high degree
Of wisedome in them to our king, since well they did become
Their right in question and refute inglorious going home. 60

But I (well knowne thy senior far) will speake and handle all
Yet to propose—which none shall checke, no, not our Generall.
A hater of societie, unjust and wilde is he
That loves intestine warre, being stuft with manlesse crueltie,
And therefore in perswading peace and home-flight we the lesse 65
May blame our Generall, as one lothe to wrap in more distresse
His loved souldiers. But, because they bravely are resolv'd
To cast lives after toyles before they part in shame involv'd,
Provide we for our honourd stay: obey blacke night and fall
Now to our suppers, then appoint our guards without the wall 70
And in the bottome of the dike—which guards I wish may stand
Of our brave youth. And, Atreus' son, since thou art in command
Before our other Kings, be first in thy command's effect.
It well becomes thee, since tis both what all thy Peeres expect
And in the royall right of things is no impaire to thee. 75
Nor shall it stand with lesse than right that they invited be
To supper by thee: all thy tents are amply stor'd with wine

Vinum Thracium. Brought dayly in Greeke ships from Thrace, and to this grace
        of thine
All necessaries thou hast fit and store of men to wait.
And, many meeting there, thou maist heare every man's conceit 80
And take the best. It much concernes all Greekes to use advise
Of gravest nature, since so neare our ships our enemies
Have lighted such a sort of fires—with which, what man is joyd?
Looke how all beare themselves this night, so live or be destroyed.'
    All heard and followd his advice. There was appointed then 85
Seven Captaines of the watch, who forth did march with all
        their men.

Seven Captaines The first was famous Thrasymed, advicefull Nestor's sonne,
of the watch, and Ascalaphus and Ialmen and mightie Merion,
their names. Alphareus and Deipyrus and lovely Lycomed,
Old Creon's joy. These seven bold Lords an hundred souldiers 90
    led
In every severd company, and every man his pike,
Some placed on the rampire's top and some amidst the dike.
All fires made and their suppers tooke. Atrides to his tent
Invited all the Peeres of Greece, and food sufficient
Apposde before them, and the Peeres apposde their hands to it. 95
Hunger and thirst being quickly quencht, to counsell still they sit.
And first spake Nestor, who they thought of late advisde so well,
A father grave and rightly wise, who thus his tale did tell:

Nestor to   'Most high Atrides, since in thee I have intent to end,
Agamemnon. From thee will I begin my speech, to whom Jove doth commend 100
The Empire of so many men and puts into thy hand

[183]

A Scepter and establisht lawes, that thou mayst well command
And counsell all men under thee. It therefore doth behove
Thy selfe to speake most, since, of all, thy speeches most will
     move—
And yet to heare as well as speake, and then performe as well   105
A free just counsell: in thee still must sticke what others tell.
For me, what in my judgement stands the most convenient
I will advise, and am assur'd advice more competent
Shall not be given: the generall proofe that hath before
     bene made
Of what I speake confirmes me still, and now may well   110
     perswade,
Because I could not then, yet ought, when thou, most
     royall King,
Even from the tent Achilles' love didst violently bring
Against my counsell, urging thee by all meanes to relent.
But you, obeying your high mind, would venture the event,
Dishonoring our ablest Greeke, a man th' immortals grace.   115
Againe yet let's deliberate, to make him now embrace
Affection to our generall good and bring his force to field,
Both which kind words and pleasing gifts must make his
     vertues yeeld.'

Agamemnon to
Nestor.

     'O father,' answered the King, 'my wrongs thou tell'st me right.
Mine owne offence, mine owne tongue grants. One man must   120
     stand in fight
For our whole armie: him I wrongd, him Jove loves from
     his hart:
He shewes it in thus honoring him, who, living thus apart,
Proves us but number, for his want makes all our weaknesse
     seene.
Yet after my confest offence, soothing my humorous spleene,

Gifts offered to
Achilles.

I'le sweeten his affects againe with presents infinite,   125
Which (to approve my firme intent) I'le openly recite—
Seven sacred Tripods free from fire, ten talents of fine gold,
Twentie bright caldrons, twelve yong horse, well-shap't and
     well-controld,
And victors too, for they have wonne the price at many a race;
That man should not be poore that had but what their   130
     winged pace
Hath added to my treasury, nor feele sweet gold's defect.
Seven Lesbian Ladies he shall have that were the most select
And in their needles rarely skild, whom (when he tooke
     the towne
Of famous Lesbos) I did chuse, who wonne the chiefe renowne

For beautie from their whole faire sexe, amongst whom I'le   135
   resigne
Faire Brisis, and I deeply sweare (for any fact of mine
That may discourage her receit) she is untoucht and rests
As he resign'd her. To these gifts (if Jove to our requests
Vouchsafe performance and affoord the worke for which we
   waite
Of winning Troy) with brasse and gold he shall his navie freight 140
And (entring when we be at spoile) that princely hand of his
Shall chuse him twentie Troyan Dames, excepting Tyndaris,
The fairest Pergamus infolds; and, if we make retreat
To Argos (cald, of all the world, the Navill or chiefe seat)
He shall become my sonne in law, and I will honour him   145
Even as Orestes, my sole sonne, that doth in honours swim.
Three daughters in my wel-built court unmarried are and faire,
Laodice, Chrysothemis that hath the golden haire
And Iphianassa; of all three the worthiest let him take
All joynturelesse to Peleus' Court. I will her joynture make, 150
And that so great as never yet did any maide preferre—
Seven cities right magnificent I will bestow on her,
Enope and Cardamyle, Hira for herbes renownd,
The faire Æpeia, Pedasus that doth with grapes abound,
Anthæa girded with greene meades, Phera surnam'd Divine, 155
All whose bright turrets on the seas in sandie Pylos shine.
Th' inhabitants in flockes and heards are wondrous confluent,
Who like a God will honour him and him with gifts present,
And to his throne will contribute what tribute he will rate.
All this I gladly will performe to pacifie his hate.   160
Let him be milde and tractable: tis for the God of ghosts
To be unrul'd, implacable and seeke the bloud of hoasts,
Whom therefore men do much abhorre: then let him yeeld
   to me.
I am his greater, being a King and more in yeares than he.'
   'Brave King,' said Nestor, 'these rich gifts must needs   165
    make him relent.

Nestor makes
choice of
Ambassadors to
Achilles.

Chuse then fit legates instantly to greete him at his Tent—
But stay, admit my choice of them, and let them strait be gone:
Jove-loved Phœnix shall be chiefe, then Ajax Telamon
And Prince Ulysses, and on them let these two heralds wait,
Grave Odius and Eurybates. Come, Lords, take water strait, 170
Make pure your hands, and with sweet words appease
   Achilles' mind,
Which we will pray the king of Gods may gently make inclin'd.'
   All lik't his speech, and on their hands the Heralds water shed:

The youths crownd cups of sacred wine, to all distributed:
But, having sacrific'd and drunke to everie man's content   175
(With many notes by Nestor given), the Legats forwards went.
With courtship in fit gestures usd he did prepare them well,
But most Ulysses, for his grace did not so much excell.
Such rites beseeme Ambassadors, and Nestor urged these
That their most honours might reflect enrag'd Æacides.   180
They went along the shore and praid the God that earth
          doth bind
In brackish chaines they might not faile but bow his mightie
          mind.
     The quarter of the Myrmidons they reacht, and found him set

Achilles at his
Harpe.

Delighted with his solemne harpe, which curiously was fret,
With workes conceited, through the verge: the bawdricke   185
          that embrac't
His loftie necke was silver twist: this (when his hand laid waste
Eetion's citie) he did chuse as his especiall prise

Achilles' love of
Musicke. Himselfe
sings the deeds of
Heroes.

And (loving sacred musicke well) made it his exercise.
To it he sung the glorious deeds of great Heroes dead,
And his true mind, that practise faild, sweet contemplation fed. 190
With him, alone and opposite, all silent sat his friend
Attentive and beholding him, who now his song did end.
Th' Ambassadors did forwards preasse, renown'd Ulysses led,
And stood in view. Their sodaine sight his admiration bred,
Who with his harpe and all arose: so did Mencetius' sonne   195
When he beheld them. Their receipt Achilles thus begun:

Achilles' gentle
receit of Ulysses,
Ajax, &c.

     'Health to my Lords: right welcome men assure your selves
          you be,
Though some necessitie I know doth make you visite me,
Incenst with just cause gainst the Greeks.' This said, a severall
          seate
With purple cushions he set forth and did their ease intreate,   200
And said: 'Now, friend, our greatest bolle with wine unmixt
          and neate
Appose these Lords, and of the depth let everie man make proofe.
These are my best-esteemed friends, and underneath my roofe.'

Principes ipsi
servilia munera
obeunt, ut alibi.

     Patroclus did his deare friend's will: and he that did desire
To cheare the Lords (come faint from fight) set on a blasing fire 205
A great brasse pot and into it a chine of mutton put
And fat Goate's flesh. Automedon held while he peeces cut
To rost and boile right cunningly: then of a well-fed swine
A huge fat shoulder he cuts out and spits it wondrous fine.
His good friend made a goodly fire, of which the force   210
          once past,

[186]

He laid the spit low, neare the coales, to make it browne at last:
Then sprinkled it with sacred salt and tooke it from the rackes.
This rosted and on dresser set, his friend Patroclus takes
Bread in faire baskets, which set on, Achilles brought the meate
And to divinest Ithacus tooke his opposed seate   215
Upon the bench. Then did he will his friend to sacrifice,
Who cast sweet incense in the fire to all the Deities.

*Sacrifice before
meate.*

Thus fell they to their readie food. Hunger and thirst allaid,
Ajax to Phœnix made a signe as if too long they staid
Before they told their Legacie. Ulysses saw him winke   220
And (filling the great boule with wine) did to Achilles drinke:

Ulysses' oration.

    'Health to Achilles! But our plights stand not in need of meate,
Who late supt at Atrides' tent, though for thy love we eate
Of many things whereof a part would make a compleat feast.
Nor can we joy in these kind rites that have our hearts opprest,   225
O Prince, with feare of utter spoile: tis made a question now
If we can save our fleet or not, unlesse thy selfe endow
Thy powers with wonted fortitude. Now Troy and her consorts,
Bold of thy want, have pitcht their tents close to our fleet
        and forts,
And made a firmament of fires; and now no more they say   230
Will they be prison'd in their wals, but force their violent way
Even to our ships: and Jove himselfe hath with his lightnings
        showd
Their bold adventures happie signes, and Hector growes
        so prowd
Of his huge strength, borne out by Jove, that fearfully he raves,
Presuming neither men nor Gods can interrupt his braves.   235
Wilde rage invades him, and he prayes that soone the
        sacred morne
Would light his furie, boasting then our streamers shall be torne
And all our navall ornaments fall by his conquering stroke:
Our ships shall burne and we our selves lie stifl'd in the smoke.
And I am seriously affraid, heaven will performe his threats   240
And that tis fatall to us all, farre from our native seates,
To perish in victorious Troy. But rise, though it be late,
Deliver the afflicted Greeks from Troy's tumultuous hate.
It will hereafter be thy griefe, when no strength can suffise
To remedie th' effected threats of our calamities.   245
Consider these affaires in time, while thou maist use thy powre,
And have the grace to turne from Greece fate's unrecovered
        houre.
O friend! thou knowest thy royall Sire forewarnd what should
        be done,

[187]

That day he sent thee from his Court to honour Atreus' sonne.
"My sonne," said he, "the victory let Jove and Pallas use   250
At their high pleasures: but do thou no honor'd meanes refuse
That may advance her. In fit bounds containe thy mightie mind,
Nor let the knowledge of thy strength be factiously inclind,
Contriving mischiefes: be to fame and generall good profest:
The more will all sorts honour thee. Benignitie is best."   255
Thus charg'd thy sire, which thou forgetst. Yet now those
        thoughts appease
That torture thy great spirit with wrath: which if thou wilt
        surcease,
The King will merit it with gifts, and (if thou wilt give eare)
I'le tell how much he offers thee—yet thou sitst angrie here.
Seven Tripods that no fire must touch; twise ten pans fit   260
        for flame;
Ten talents of fine gold; twelve horse that ever overcame
And brought huge prises from the field with swiftnes of
        their feete.
That man should beare no poore account, nor want gold's
        quickning sweete,
That had but what he won with them. Seven worthiest
        Lesbian Dames
Renown'd for skill in houswifrie and beare the soveraigne fames   265
For beautie from their generall sexe; which at thy overthrow
Of wel-built Lesbos he did chuse; and these he will bestow,
And with these her he tooke from thee, whom (by his state)
        since then
He sweares he toucht not, as faire Dames use to be toucht
        by men.
All these are readie for thee now: and, if at length we take,   270
By helpes of Gods, this wealthie towne, thy ships shall burthen
        make
Of gold and brasse at thy desires, when we the spoile divide;
And twentie beautious Troyan Dames thou shalt select beside
(Next Helen) the most beautifull. And (when return'd we be
To Argos) be his sonne in law: for he will honour thee   275
Like his Orestes, his sole sonne, maintaind in height of blisse.
Three daughters beautifie his Court, the faire Chrysothemis,
Laodice and Iphianesse: of all, the fairest take
To Peleus' thy grave father's Court and never joynture make.
He will the joynture make himselfe—so great as never Sire   280
Gave to his daughter's nuptials: seven cities left entire,
Cardamyle and Enope and Hira full of flowers,
Anthæa for sweet meadowes praisd, and Phera deckt with towers,

The bright Æpeia, Pedasus that doth God Bacchus please,
All on the sandie Pylos' soyle are seated neare the seas: 285
Th' inhabitants in droves and flocks exceeding wealthie be,
Who like a God with worthie gifts will gladly honour thee
And tribute of especiall rate to thy high scepter pay.
All this he freely will performe thy anger to allay.
But if thy hate to him be more than his gifts may represse,   290
Yet pittie all the other Greeks in such extreme distresse,
Who with religion honour thee, and to their desperate ill
Thou shalt triumphant glorie bring and Hector thou maist kill
When pride makes him encounter thee, fild with a banefull
    sprite,
Who vaunts our whole fleet brought not one equall to him   295
    in fight.'

*Achilles answers
Ulysses' Oration.*

    Swift-foot Æacides replide: 'Divine Laertes' sonne,
Tis requisite I should be short and shew what place hath wonne
Thy serious speech, affirming nought but what you shall approve
Establisht in my settled heart, that in the rest I move
No murmure nor exception—for like hell mouth I loath   300
Who holds not in his words and thoughts one indistinguisht
    troth.
What fits the freenesse of my mind my speech shall make
    displaid:
Nor Atreus' sonne nor all the Greeks shall winne me to their aid.
Their suite is wretchedly enforc't, to free their owne despaires,
And my life never shall be hir'd with thanklesse desperate   305
    praires.
For never had I benefite, that ever foild the foe:
Even share hath he that keepes his tent and he to field doth go:
With equall honour cowards die and men most valiant,
The much performer and the man that can of nothing vant.
No overplus I ever found when, with my mind's most strife   310
To do them good, to dangerous fight I have exposd my life.
But even as to unfeatherd birds the carefull dam brings meate,
Which when she hath bestow'd, her selfe hath nothing left
    to eat:
So when my broken sleepes have drawne the nights
    t' extremest length
And ended many bloodie daies with still-employed strength,   315
To guard their weaknesse and preserve their wives'
    contents infract,
I have been robd before their eyes. Twelve cities I have sackt,
Assaild by sea, eleven by land, while this siege held at Troy,

[189]

And of all these, what was most deare and most might crowne
    the joy
Of Agamemnon, he enjoyd, who here behind remaind: 320
Which when he tooke, a few he gave and many things retaind;
Other to Optimates and Kings he gave, who hold them fast.
Yet mine he forceth: onely I sit with my losse disgrac't.
But so he gaine a lovely Dame to be his bed's delight,
It is enough. For what cause else do Greeks and Troyans fight? 325
Why brought he hither such an hoast? was it not for a Dame,
For faire-hair'd Helen? And doth love alone the hearts inflame
Of the Atrides to their wives, of all the men that move?
Every discreet and honest mind cares for his private love
As much as they—as I my selfe lov'd Brisis as my life,   330
Although my captive, and had will to take her for my wife:
Whom since he forc't, preventing me, in vaine he shall prolong
Hopes to appease me, that know well the deepnesse of my wrong.
But, good Ulysses, with thy selfe and all you other Kings,
Let him take stomacke to repell Troy's firie threatenings.   335
Much hath he done without my helpe—built him a goodly fort,
Cut a dike by it pitcht with pales, broad and of deepe import.
And cannot all these helpes represse this kil-man Hector's fright?
When I was arm'd amongst the Greekes, he would not offer fight
Without the shadow of his wals, but to the Scæan ports   340
Or to the holy Beech of Jove come backt with his consorts—
Where once he stood my charge alone and hardly made retreat:
And to make new proofe of our powers the doubt is not so great.
Tomorrow then with sacrifice, perform'd t' imperiall Jove
And all the Gods, I'le lanch my fleet and all my men remove, 345
Which (if thou wilt use so thy sight, or think'st it worth respect)
In forehead of the morne thine eyes shall see with sailes erect
Amidst the fishie Hellespont, helpt with laborious oares.
And if the sea-god send free saile, the fruitfull Phthian shores
Within three dayes we shall attaine—where I have store of prise, 350
Left when with prejudice I came to these indignities.
There have I gold as well as here and store of ruddie brasse,
Dames slender, elegantly girt, and steele as bright as glasse.
These will I take as I retire, as shares I firmly save,
Though Agamemnon be so base to take the gifts he gave.   355
Tell him all this, and openly, I on your honors charge,
That others may take shame to heare his lust's command so large.
And if there yet remaine a man he hopeth to deceive
(Being dide in endlesse impudence), that man may learne to leave
His trust and Empire. But, alas, though like a wolfe he be, 360
Shamelesse and rude, he durst not take my prise and looke on me.

[190]

I never will partake his works nor counsels as before:
He once deceiv'd and injur'd me, and he shall never more
Tie my affections with his words: enough is the increase
Of one successe in his deceits, which let him joy in peace   365
And beare it to a wretched end. Wise Jove hath reft his braine
To bring him plagues, and these his gifts I (as my foes) disdaine.
Even in the numnesse of calme death I will revengefull be,
Though ten or twentie times so much he would bestow on me—
All he hath here or any where, or Orchomen containes,   370
To which men bring their wealth for strength, or all the
    store remaines
In circuite of Ægyptian Thebes, where much hid treasure lies,
Whose wals containe an hundred ports of so admir'd a size
Two hundred souldiers may, afront, with horse and
    chariots passe.
Nor, would he amplifie all this like sand, or dust, or grasse,   375
Should he reclaime me till his wreake payd me for all the paines
That with his contumely burnd like poison in my veines.

*The free and most
ingenuous spirit of
Achilles.*

Nor shall his daughter be my wife, although she might contend
With golden Venus for her forme, or if she did transcend
Blew-eyd Minerva for her works: let him a Greeke select   380
Fit for her, and a greater King. For, if the Gods protect
My safetie to my father's court, he shall chuse me a wife.
Many faire Achive Princesses, of unimpeached life,
In Helle and in Phthia live whose Sires do cities hold,
Of whom I can have whom I will. And more an hundred fold   385
My true mind in my countrie likes to take a lawfull wife
Than in another nation, and there delight my life
With those goods that my father got much rather than die here.
Not all the wealth of wel-built Troy possest when peace
    was there,
All that Apollo's marble Fane in stonie Pythos holds,   390
I value equall with the life that my free breast infolds.
Sheepe, Oxen, Tripods, crest-deckt horse, though lost, may
    come againe,
But, when the white guard of our teeth no longer can containe
Our humane soule, away it flies; and, once gone, never more
To her fraile mansion any man can her lost powres restore.   395
And therefore since my mother-queene (fam'd for her silver feet)
Told me two fates about my death in my direction meet—
The one, that, if I here remaine t' assist our victorie,
My safe returne shall never live, my fame shall never die:
If my returne obtaine successe, much of my fame decayes   400
But death shall linger his approach and I live many dayes.

[191]

This being reveal'd, twere foolish pride t' abridge my life
    for praise.
Then with my selfe, I will advise others to hoise their saile,
For gainst the height of Ilion you never shall prevaile:
Jove with his hand protecteth it and makes the souldiers bold.   405
This tell the King in every part, for so grave Legates should,
That they may better counsels use to save their fleet and friends
By their owne valours, since this course, drown'd in my anger,
    ends.
Phœnix may in my tent repose and in the morne stere course
For Phthia, if he thinks it good; if not, I'le use no force.'   410
   All wondred at his sterne reply, and Phœnix, full of feares
His words would be more weake than just, supplide their
    wants with teares:

Phœnix' Oration
to Achilles.

   'If thy returne incline thee thus, Peleus' renowned joy,
And thou wilt let our ships be burnd with harmfull fire of Troy,
Since thou art angrie, O my sonne, how shall I after be   415
Alone in these extremes of death, relinquished by thee?
I, whom thy royall father sent as orderer of thy force
When to Atrides from his Court he left thee for this course,
Yet young, and when in skill of armes thou didst not so abound
Nor hadst the habite of discourse that makes men so renownd;   420
In all which I was set by him t' instruct thee as my sonne,
That thou mightst speake when speech was fit, and do when
    deeds were done,
Not sit as dumbe for want of words, idle for skill to move.
I would not then be left by thee, deare sonne, begot in love—
No, not if God would promise me to raze the prints of time   425
Carv'd in my bosome and my browes and grace me with
    the prime
Of manly youth as when at first I left sweet Helle's shore,
Deckt with faire Dames, and fled the grudge my angrie
    father bore;

Morem senum
observat, qui de
præteritis libenter
solent meminisse.

Who was the faire Amyntor cald, surnam'd Ormenides,
And for a faire-haird harlot's sake, that his affects could please,   430
Contemnd my mother his true wife, who ceaslesse urged me
To use his harlot Clytia, and still would claspe my knee
To do her will—that so my Sire might turne his love to hate
Of that lewde Dame, converting it to comfort her estate.
At last I was content to prove, to do my mother good   435
And reconcile my father's love; who straight suspitious stood,
Pursuing me with many a curse, and to the Furies praide
No Dame might love, nor bring me seed. The Deities obayd

That governe hell, infernall Jove and sterne Persephone.
Then durst I in no longer date with my sterne father be: 440
Yet did my friends and neare allies enclose me with desires
Not to depart, kild sheepe, bores, beeves, rost them at
  solemne fires,
And from my father's tuns we drunke exceeding store of wine.
Nine nights they guarded me by turns: their fires did
  ceaslesse shine,
One in the porch of his strong hall, and in the portall one 445
Before my chamber: but, when day beneath the tenth
  night shone,
I brake my chamber's thick-fram'd dores and through the hal's
  guard past,
Unseene of any man or maide. Through Greece, then, rich
  and vast,
I fled to Phthia, nurse of sheepe, and came to Peleus' Court,
Who entertaind me heartily and in as gracious sort 450
As any Sire his onely sonne, borne when his strength is spent
And blest with great possessions to leave to his descent.
He made me rich, and to my charge did much command
  commend.
I dwelt in th' utmost region rich Phthia doth extend
And governd the Dolopians and made thee what thou art, 455
O thou that like the Gods art fram'd. Since, dearest to my heart,
I usde thee so, thou lov'dst none else, nor any where wouldst eate
Till I had crownd my knee with thee and karv'd thee
  tenderst meate
And given thee wine so much, for love, that in thy infancie
(Which still discretion must protect and a continuall eye) 460
My bosome lovingly sustain'd the wine thine could not beare.
Then, now my strength needs thine as much, be mine to thee
  as deare.
Much have I sufferd for thy love, much labour'd, wished much,
Thinking, since I must have no heire (the Gods' decrees are such),
I would adopt thy selfe my heire: to thee my heart did give 465
What any Sire could give his sonne: in thee I hop't to live.
O mitigate thy mightie spirits! it fits not one that moves
The hearts of all to live unmov'd, and succour hates for loves.
The Gods themselves are flexible, whose vertues, honors, powers
Are more than thine; yet they will bend their breasts as we 470
  bend ours.
Perfumes, benigne devotions, savors of offrings burnd
And holy rites the engines are with which their hearts are turnd

Prayers, how necessary and helpful; if shund or neglected, how wreakefull. Jove's daughters, and cald Litæ.

By men that pray to them, whose faith their sinnes have
    falsified.
For prayers are daughters of great Jove, lame, wrinkled,
    ruddie-eyd
And ever following Injury, who (strong and sound of feet)   475
Flies through the world afflicting men. Beleeving prayers yet
(To all that love that seed of Jove) the certaine blessing get
To have Jove heare, and helpe them too; but, if he shall refuse
And stand inflexible to them, they flie to Jove and use
Their powres against him, that the wrongs he doth to them   480
    may fall
On his owne head and pay those paines whose cure he failes
    to call.
  Then, great Achilles, honour thou this sacred seed of Jove
And yeeld to them, since other men of greatest minds they move.
If Agamemnon would not give the selfe-same gifts he vowes
But offer other afterwards and in his stil-bent browes   485
Entombe his honour and his word, I would not thus exhort
(With wrath appeasde) thy aide to Greece, though plagu'd in
    heaviest sort.
But much he presently will give and after yeeld the rest,
T' assure which he hath sent to thee the men thou lovest best
And most renownd of all the hoast, that they might soften thee.   490
Then let not both their paines and prayers lost and despised be.
Before which, none could reprehend the tumult of thy heart,
But now to rest inexpiate were much too rude a part.
Of ancient worthies we have heard, when they were more
    displeasde,
(To their high fames) with gifts and prayers they have bene   495
    still appeasde.

Another narration, de bello Ætolico.

For instance, I remember well a fact perform'd of old,
Which to you all my friends I'le tell. The Curets warres did hold
With the well-fought Ætolians, where mutuall lives had end
About the citie Calydon. Th' Ætolians did defend
Their flourishing countrie, which to spoile the Curets did   500
    contend.
Diana with the golden throne with Œneus much incenc't,
Since with his plenteous land's first fruits she was not reverenc't,
Yet other Gods with Hecatombes had feasts, and she alone
(Great Jove's bright daughter) left unserv'd (or by oblivion
Or undue knowledge of her dues) much hurt in heart she swore.   505

Aper Calydonius.

And she, enrag'd, excited much, she sent a sylvan Bore
From their greene groves, with wounding tuskes, who usually
    did spoile

King Œneus' fields, his loftie woods layd prostrate on the soile,
Rent by the roots trees fresh, adornd with fragrant apple flow'rs;
Which Meleager, Œneus' sonne, slue with assembled pow'rs   510
Of hunters and of fiercest hounds from many cities brought.
For such he was that with few lives his death could not be
    bought;
Heapes of dead humanes by his rage the funerall piles applide,
Yet (slaine at last) the Goddesse stird about his head and hide
A wondrous tumult, and a warre betwixt the Curets wrought   515
And brave Ætolians. All the while fierce Meleager fought,
Ill far'd the Curets: neare the wals none durst advance his crest
Though they were many; but, when wrath inflam'd his
    hautie brest
(Which oft the firme mind of the wise with passion doth infest),
Since twixt his mother Queene and him arose a deadly strife,   520
He left the Court and privately liv'd with his lawfull wife,
Faire Cleopatra, femall birth of bright Marpessa's paine
And of Ideus, who of all terrestriall men did raigne
(At that time) king of fortitude, and for Marpessa's sake
Gainst wanton Phœbus, king of flames, his bow in hand   525
    did take,
Since he had ravisht her, his joy, whom her friends after gave
The surname of Alcyone, because they could not save
Their daughter from Alcyone's Fate. In Cleopatra's armes
Lay Meleager, feeding on his anger for the harmes
His mother praid might fall on him, who for her brother slaine   530
By Meleager griev'd and praid the Gods to wreake her paine
With all the horror could be pour'd upon her furious birth.
Still knockt she with her impious hands the many-feeding earth,
To urge sterne Pluto and his Queene t' incline their vengefull
    eares,
Fell on her knees and all her breast dewd with her fierie teares   535
To make them massacre her sonne, whose wrath enrag'd her thus.
Erinnys (wandring through the aire) heard, out of Erebus,
Pray'rs fit for her unpleased mind: yet Meleager lay
Obscurd in furie. Then the bruit of the tumultuous fray
Rung through the turrets as they scal'd: then came the Ætolian   540
    Peeres
To Meleager with low suits, to rise and free their feares:
Then sent they the chiefe Priests of Gods with offered gifts
    t' attone
His differing furie, bad him chuse in sweet-soild Calydon
Of the most fat and yeeldie soile what with an hundred steares

Might in a hundred dayes be plowde—halfe that rich   545
    vintage beares
And halfe of naked earth to plow. Yet yeelded not his ire.
Then to his loftie chamber dore ascends his royall Sire
With ruthfull plaints, shooke the strong barres: then came his
    sisters' cries:
His mother then, and all, intreate. Yet still more stiffe he lies.
His friends most reverend, most esteem'd—yet none   550
    impression tooke,
Till the high turrets where he lay and his strong chamber shooke
With the invading enemie, who now forc't dreadfull way
Along the cittie. Then his wife (in pittifull dismay)
Besought him, weeping, telling him the miseries sustaind
By all the citizens, whose towne the enemie had gaind,   555
Men slaughterd, children bondslaves made, sweet Ladies forc't
    with lust,
Fires climing towres and turning them to heapes of fruitlesse
    dust.
These dangers softned his steele heart: up the stout Prince arose,
Indude his bodie with rich armes and freed th' Ætolians' woes—
His smotherd anger giving aire, which gifts did not asswage   560
But his owne perill. And because he did not disingage
Their lives for gifts, their gifts he lost. But for my sake,
    deare friend,
Be not thou bent to see our plights to these extremes descend
Ere thou assist us: be not so by thy ill angell turnd
From thine owne honor: it were shame to see our navie burnd   565
And then come with thy timelesse aide. For offerd presents come
And all the Greeks will honour thee, as of celestiall roome:
But if without these gifts thou fight, forc't by thy private woe,
Thou wilt be nothing so renown'd, though thou repell the foe.'
    Achilles answerd the last part of this oration thus: 570

Achilles to
Phœnix.

'Phœnix, renown'd and reverend, the honors urgde on us
We need not: Jove doth honor me and to my safetie sees,
And will whiles I retaine a spirit or can command my knees.
Then do not thou, with teares and woes, impassion my affects,
Becoming gracious to my foe. Nor fits it the respects   575
Of thy vowd love to honor him that hath dishonord me,
Lest such loose kindnesse lose his heart that yet is firme to thee.
It were thy praise to hurt, with me, the hurter of my state,
Since halfe my honor and my Realme thou maist participate.
Let these Lords then returne th' event, and do thou here repose,   580
And when darke sleepe breakes with the day our counsels
    shall disclose

The course of our returne or stay.' This said, he with his eye
Made to his friend a covert signe to hasten instantly
A good soft bed, that the old Prince, soone as the Peeres
    were gone,
Might take his rest: when, souldier-like, brave Ajax Telamon   585
Spake to Ulysses, as with thought Achilles was not worth
The high direction of his speech, that stood so sternly forth,
Unmov'd with th' other Orators; and spake, not to appease
Pelides' wrath, but to depart. His arguments were these:

Ajax' souldier-
like speech and
fashion.

   'High-issued Laertiades! let us insist no more   590
On his perswasion. I perceive the world would end before
Our speeches end in this affaire. We must with utmost haste
Returne his answer, though but bad: the Peeres are
    else-where plac't
And will not rise till we returne. Great Thetis' sonne hath stor'd
Prowd wrath within him as his wealth, and will not be implor'd,   595
Rude that he is; nor his friends' love respects, do what they can,
Wherein past all we honourd him. O unremorsefull man!
Another for his brother slaine, another for his sonne,
Accepts of satisfaction; and he the deed hath done
Lives in belov'd societie long after his amends,   600
To which his foe's high heart, for gifts, with patience
    condescends.
But thee a wild and cruell spirit the Gods for plague have given,
And for one girle—of whose faire sexe we come to offer seaven
The most exempt for excellence and many a better prise.
Then put a sweet mind in thy breast, respect thy own allies,   605
Though others make thee not remisse. A multitude we are,
Sprung of thy royall familie, and our supremest care
Is to be most familiar and hold most love with thee
Of all the Greeks, how great an host soever here there be.'

Achilles to Ajax.

   He answerd: 'Noble Telamon, Prince of our souldiers here,   610
Out of thy heart I know thou speakst, and as thou holdst
    me deare:
But still, as often as I thinke how rudely I was usd
And like a stranger for all rites fit for our good refusd,
My heart doth swell against the man that durst be so profane
To violate his sacred place—not for my private bane,   615
But since wrackt vertue's generall lawes he shamelesse did
    infringe,
For whose sake I will loose the reines and give mine anger
    swinge
Without my wisedome's least impeach. He is a foole, and base,

That pitties vice-plagu'd minds, when paine, not love of right,
gives place.
And therefore tell your king, my Lords, my just wrath will   620
not care
For all his cares before my tents and navie charged are
By warlike Hector, making way through flockes of Grecian lives,
Enlightned by their navall fire: but when his rage arrives
About my tent and sable barke I doubt not but to shield
Them and my selfe, and make him flie the there-strong-bounded 625
field.'
   This said, each one but kist the cup and to the ships retir'd,
Ulysses first. Patroclus then the men and maids requir'd
To make grave Phœnix' bed with speed and see he nothing lacks.
They straite obeyd, and thereon laid the subtile fruite of flax
And warme sheep-fels for covering: and there the old man slept,   630
Attending till the golden Morne her usuall station kept.
Achilles lay in th' inner roome of his tent richly wrought,
And that faire Ladie by his side that he from Lesbos brought,
Bright Diomeda, Phorbas' seed. Patroclus did embrace
The beautious Iphis, given to him when his bold friend   635
did race
The loftie Scyrus, that was kept in Enyeius' hold.
   Now at the tent of Atreus' sonne, each man with cups of gold
Receiv'd th' Ambassadors returnd: all clusterd neare to know
What newes they brought, which first the king would have
Ulysses show:

*Agamemnon to
Ulysses.*

'Say, most praise-worthie Ithacus, the Grecians' great renowne,   640
Will he defend us? or not yet will his prowd stomacke downe?'

*Ulysses to
Agamemnon.*

   Ulysses made replie: 'Not yet will he appeased be,
But growes more wrathfull, prizing light thy offerd gifts and thee,
And wils thee to consult with us and take some other course
To save our armie and our fleete, and sayes, with all his force,   645
The morne shall light him on his way to Phthia's wished soile,
For never shall high-seated Troy be sackt with all our toile,
Jove holds his hand twixt us and it, the souldiers gather heart.
Thus he replies, which Ajax here can equally impart
And both these Heralds. Phœnix stayes, for so was his desire   650
To go with him, if he thought good; if not, he might retire.'
All wondred he should be so sterne: at last bold Diomed spake:

*Diomed to
Agamemnon.*

   'Would God, Atrides, thy request were yet to undertake,
And all thy gifts unofferd him! He's proud enough beside,
But this ambassage thou hast sent will make him burst   655
with pride.
But let us suffer him to stay or go at his desire,

Fight when his stomacke serves him best, or when Jove
    shall inspire.
Meane while, our watch being strongly held, let us a little rest
After our food: strength lives by both, and vertue is their guest.
Then, when the rosie-fingerd Morne holds out her silver light,   660
Bring forth thy host, encourage all, and be thou first in fight.'
   The kings admir'd the fortitude that so divinely mov'd
The skilfull horseman Diomed, and his advice approv'd.
Then, with their nightly sacrifice, each tooke his severall tent,
Where all receiv'd the soveraigne gifts soft Somnus did present.   665

The End of the Ninth Booke

THE TENTH BOOKE

of

HOMER'S ILIADS

THE ARGUMENT

Th' Atrides watching, wake the other Peeres,
And (in the Fort, consulting of their feares)
Two kings they send, most stout and honord most,
For royall skowts into the Troyan host:
Who, meeting Dolon (Hector's bribed Spie)　　　　5
Take him, and learne how all the Quarters lie.
He told them, in the Thracian regiment
Of rich king Rhesus, and his royall Tent—
Striving for safetie, but they end his strife
And rid poore Dolon of a dangerous life.　　　　10
Then, with digressive wyles, they use their force
On Rhesus' life and take his snowie horse.

Another Argument

Kappa *the Night exploits applies:*
Rhesus' and Dolon's tragedies.

Agamemnon's cares.
These are the
lightnings before
snow, &c. that
Scalliger's Criticus
so unworthily
taxeth, citing the
place falsly, as in
the 3 booke's
annotations, &c.

The other Princes at their ships soft-fingerd sleepe did bind,
But not the Generall: Somnus' silkes bound not his laboring mind,
That turnd and returnd many thoughts. And as quicke
　　　lightnings flie
From well-deckt Juno's soveraigne, out of the thickned skie,
Preparing some exceeding raine, or haile, the fruite of cold,　　5
Or downe-like Snow, that sodainly makes all the fields looke old,
Or opes the gulfie mouth of warre with his ensulphur'd hand,
In dazling flashes pour'd from clouds on any punisht land:
So from Atrides' troubled heart, through his darke sorowes, flew
Redoubled sighes: his intrailes shooke as often as his view　　10
Admir'd the multitude of fires that gilt the Phrygian shade
And heard the sounds of fifes and shawmes and tumults
　　　souldiers made.

But, when he saw his fleet and host kneele to his care and love,
He rent his haire up by the roots as sacrifice to Jove,
Burnt in his firie sighes, still breath'd out of his royall heart;   15
And first thought good to Nestor's care his sorowes to impart,
To trie if royall diligence, with his approv'd advise,
Might fashion counsels to prevent their threatned miseries.
    So up he rose, attir'd himselfe, and to his strong feet tide
Rich shoes, and cast upon his backe a ruddie Lion's hide,   20
So ample it his ankles reacht; then tooke his royall speare.

*Agamemnon's
habite, rising in
the night.
He wearing a
Lion's hide.*

    Like him was Menelaus pierc't with an industrious feare,
Nor sat sweet slumber on his eyes, lest bitter Fates should quite
The Greekes' high favours, that for him resolv'd such
        endlesse fight.

*Menelaus a
Leopard's.*

And first a freckled Panther's hide hid his brode backe athwart;   25
His head his brasen helme did arme, his able hand his dart.
Then made he all his haste to raise his brother's head as rare,
That he who most exceld in rule might helpe t' effect his care.
He found him at his ship's crookt sterne adorning him
        with armes,
Who joyd to see his brother's spirits awak't without alarmes,   30
Well weighing th' importance of the time. And first the
        yonger spake:

*Menelaus to
Agamemnon.*

'Why, brother, are ye arming thus? Is it to undertake
The sending of some ventrous Greeke t' explore the foe's intent?
Alas, I greatly feare not one will give that worke consent,
Exposd alone to all the feares that flow in gloomie night.   35
He that doth this must know death well, in which ends everie
        fright.'

*Agamemnon to
Menelaus.*

'Brother,' said he, 'in these affaires we both must use advice.
Jove is against us, and accepts great Hector's sacrifice.
For I have never seene nor heard in one day and by one
So many high attempts well urg'd as Hector's power hath done   40
Against the haplesse sons of Greece, being chiefly deare to Jove,
And without cause, being neither fruite of any Godesse' love
Nor helpfull God: and yet I feare the deepnesse of his hand,
Ere it be rac't out of our thoughts, will many yeares withstand.
But, brother, hie thee to thy ships and Idomen dis-ease   45
With warlike Ajax: I will haste to grave Neleides,
Exhorting him to rise and give the sacred watch command,
For they will specially embrace incitement at his hand,
And now his sonne their captaine is, and Idomen's good friend,
Bold Merion, to whose discharge we did that charge commend.'   50
    'Commandst thou then,' his brother askt, 'that I shall tarrie
        there

Attending thy resolv'd approach, or else the message beare
And quickly make returne to thee?' He answerd: 'Rather stay,
Lest otherwise we faile to meete; for many a different way
Lies through our labyrinthian host. Speake ever as you go;   55
Command strong watch; from Sire to sonne urge all t' observe
    the foe,
Familiarly, and with their praise, exciting everie eye,
Not with unseason'd violence of prowd authoritie.
We must our patience exercise and worke our selves with them,
Jove in our births combin'd such care to either's Diadem.'   60
    Thus he dismist him, knowing well his charge before: he went
Himselfe to Nestor, whom he found in bed within his tent.
By him his damaske curets hung, his shield, a paire of darts,
His shining caske, his arming waste: in these he led the hearts
Of his apt souldiers to sharpe warre, not yeelding to his yeares.   65
He quickly started from his bed when to his watchfull eares
Untimely feet told some approach: he tooke his lance in hand
And spake to him: 'Ho, what art thou that walk'st at midnight?
    Stand.
Is any wanting at the guards, or lack'st thou any Peere?
Speake: come not silent towards me: say what intendst thou   70
    here.'
    He answerd: 'O Neleides, grave honour of our host,
Tis Agamemnon thou maist know, whom Jove afflicteth most
Of all the wretched men that live, and will whilst any breath
Gives motion to my toiled lims and beares me up from death.
I walke the round thus since sweet sleepe cannot inclose mine   75
    eyes,
Nor shut those Organs care breaks ope for our calamities.
My feare is vehement for the Greeks: my heart (the fount of
    heate)
With his extreme affects made cold, without my breast
    doth beate;
And therefore are my sinewes strooke with trembling: everie part
Of what my friends may feele hath act in my dispersed heart.   80
But if thou thinkst of any course may to our good redound
(Since neither thou thy selfe canst sleepe) come, walke with me
    the round,
In way whereof we may confer and looke to everie guard,
Lest watching long and wearinesse, with labouring so hard,
Drowne their oppressed memories of what they have in charge.   85
The libertie we give the foe, alas, is over large:
Their campe is almost mixt with ours, and we have forth no
    spies

To learne their drifts, who may perchance this night intend
    surprise.'

    Grave Nestor answerd: 'Worthie king, let good hearts beare
    our ill.

Jove is not bound to perfect all this busie Hector's will: 90
But I am confidently given, his thoughts are much dismaid
With feare lest our distresse incite Achilles to our aide,
And therefore will not tempt his fate nor ours with further **pride**.
But I will gladly follow thee and stirre up more beside—
Tydides, famous for his lance, Ulysses, Telamon   95
And bold Phyleus' valiant heire. Or else, if any one
Would haste to call king Idomen and Ajax, since their saile
Lie so remov'd, with much good speed it might our haste availe.
But, (though he be our honord friend) thy brother I will blame,
Not fearing if I anger thee: it is his utter shame   100
He should commit all paines to thee that should himselfe
    imploy,
Past all our Princes, in the care and cure of our annoy,
And be so farre from needing spurres to these his due respects,
He should apply our spirits himselfe with pray'rs and urg'd
    affects.
Necessitie (a law to lawes, and not to be endur'd)   105
Makes proofe of all his faculties, not sound, if not inur'd.'

    'Good father,' said the king, 'sometimes you know I have
    desir'd
You would improve his negligence, too oft to ease retir'd;
Nor is it for defect of spirit or compasse of his braine,
But with observing my estate; he thinks he should abstaine   110
Till I commanded, knowing my place, unwilling to assume,
For being my brother, any thing might prove he did presume.
But now he rose before me farre and came, t' avoid delaies,
And I have sent him for the men your selfe desir'd to raise.
Come, we shall find them at the guards we plac't before the   115
    fort,
For thither my direction was they should with speed resort.'
    'Why now,' said Nestor, 'none will grudge, nor his just rule
    withstand.
Examples make excitements strong and sweeten a command.'
    Thus put he on his arming trusse, faire shoes upon his feet,
About him a mandilion, that did with buttons meet,   120
Of purple, large and full of folds, curld with a warmefull nap,
A garment that gainst cold in nights did souldiers use to wrap.
Then tooke he his strong lance in hand, made sharpe with
    proved steele,

And went along the Grecian fleet. First at Ulysses' keele
He cald, to breake the silken fumes that did his sences bind: 125
The voice through th' Organs of his eares straight rung about
    his mind.

Ulysses to
Agamemnon and Nestor
Nestor to Ulysses.

Forth came Ulysses, asking him: 'Why stirre ye thus so late?
Sustaine we such enforcive cause?' He answerd: 'Our estate
Doth force this perturbation: vouchsafe it, worthie friend,
And come, let us excite one more to counsell of some end   130
To our extremes, by fight or flight.' He backe and tooke his
    shield,
And both tooke course to Diomed. They found him laid in field

The manner of
Diomed's lodging.

Farre from his tent, his armour by; about him was dispread
A ring of souldiers, everie man his shield beneath his head,
His speare fixt by him as he slept, the great end in the ground;   135
The point, that bristled the darke earth, cast a reflection round
Like pallid lightnings throwne from Jove. Thus this Heroe lay,
And under him a big Oxe hide: his royall head had stay
On Arras hangings, rolled up, whereon he slept so fast

Nestor chideth
Diomed.

That Nestor stird him with his foote and chid to see him cast   140
In such deepe sleepe, in such deepe woes, and askt him why he
    spent
All night in sleepe or did not heare the Troyans neare
    his tent—
Their Campe drawne close upon their dike, small space twixt
    foes and foes.

Diomed to Nestor.

  He, starting up, said: 'Strange old man, that never tak'st
    repose,
Thou art too patient of our toile: have we not men more yong   145
To be imploid from king to king? Thine age hath too much
    wrong.'

Nestor to him.
Note the life of
these representations.

  'Said like a king,' replied the Sire, 'for I have sonnes
    renownd,
And there are many other men might go this toilesome round.
But you must see imperious Need hath all at her command.

ἐπὶ ξυροῦ
ἵσταται ἀκμῆς:
This went into a
Proverbe, used by
Theocritus in
Dioscaris out of
Homer.

Now on the eager razor's edge for life or death we stand.   150
Then go (thou art the yonger man) and, if thou love my ease,
Call swift-foot Ajax up thy selfe, and young Phyleides.'
  This said, he on his shoulders cast a yellow Lion's hide,
Big, and reacht earth; then tooke his speare and Nestor's will
    applide,
Raisd the Heroes, brought them both. All met, the round   155
    they went
And found not any captaine there asleepe or negligent,
But waking and in armes gave eare to everie lowest sound.

Simile.

And as keene dogs keepe sheepe in Cotes, or folds, of Hurdles
    bound,
And grin at everie breach of aire, envious of all that moves,
Still listning when the ravenous beast stalks through the hilly   160
    groves,
Then men and dogs stand on their guards and mightie
    tumults make,
Sleepe wanting weight to close one winke: so did the
    Captaines wake
That kept the watch the whole sad night, all with intentive
    eare
Converted to the enemies' tents, that they might timely heare
If they were stirring to surprise—which Nestor joyd to see.   165

*Nestor to the
Guards.*

   'Why so, deare sons, maintaine your watch: sleepe not a
    winke,' said he,
'Rather than make your fames the scorne of Troyan perjurie.'
   This said, he formost past the dike, the others seconded,
Even all the kings that had bene cald to counsell from the bed;
And with them went Meriones and Nestor's famous sonne,   170
For both were cald by all the kings to consultation.
Beyond the dike they chusde a place neare as they could from
    blood,
Where yet appear'd the fals of some and whence (the crimson
    flood
Of Grecian lives being pour'd on earth by Hector's furious
    chace)
He made retreate when night repour'd grim darknesse in   175
    his face.

*Nestor to the
Grecian Princes.*

There sate they downe, and Nestor spake: 'O friends, remaines
    not one
That will relie on his bold mind and view the campe alone
Of the prowd Troyans, to approve if any stragling mate
He can surprise neare th' utmost tents, or learne the briefe estate
Of their intentions for the time, and mixe like one of them   180
With their outguards, expiscating if the renown'd extreme
They force on us will serve their turnes with glorie to retire,
Or still encampe thus farre from Troy? This may he well enquire
And make a brave retreate untoucht, and this would win him
    fame
Of all men canapied with heaven, and everie man of name   185
In all this host shall honor him with an enriching meed—
A blacke Ewe and her sucking Lambe (rewards that now
    exceed
All other best possessions in all men's choice requests),

And still be bidden by our kings to kind and royall feasts.'
All reverenc't one another's worth and none would silence   190
    breake,
Lest worst should take best place of speech. At last did Diomed
    speake:

Diomed to Nestor.

'Nestor, thou ask'st if no man here have heart so well inclin'd
To worke this stratageme on Troy. Yes, I have such a mind.
Yet, if some other Prince would joyne, more probable will be
The strengthned hope of our exploite: two may together see   195
(One going before another still) slie danger everie way;
One spirit upon another workes, and takes with firmer stay
The benefit of all his powers—for, though one knew his course,
Yet might he well distrust himselfe, which th' other might
    enforce.'

This offer everie man assum'd; all would with Diomed go,   200
The two Ajaces, Merion and Menelaus too;
But Nestor's sonne enforc't it much, and hardie Ithacus,
Who had to everie ventrous deed a mind as venturous.

The grave counsell of Agamemnon to Diomed.

Amongst all these, thus spake the king: 'Tydides, most belov'd,
Chuse thy associate worthily, a man the most approv'd   205
For use and strength in these extremes. Many, thou seest,
    stand forth:
But chuse not thou by height of place, but by regard of worth,
Lest with thy nice respect of right to any man's degree
Thou wrongst thy venture, chusing one least fit to joyne
    with thee,
Although perhaps a greater king.' This spake he with suspect   210
That Diomed (for honor's sake) his brother would select.
Then said Tydides: 'Since thou giv'st my judgement leave
    to chuse,

Diomed's choice of Ulysses.

How can it so much truth forget, Ulysses to refuse—
That beares a mind so most exempt and vigorous in th' effect
Of all high labors, and a man Pallas doth most respect?   215
We shall returne through burning fire if I with him combine,
He sets strength in so true a course with counsels so divine.'

Ulysses' modestie in accepting.

Ulysses, loth to be esteemd a lover of his praise,
With such exceptions humbled him as did him higher raise
And said: 'Tydides, praise me not more than free truth will   220
    beare,
Nor yet empaire me: they are Greeks that give judiciall eare.
But come, the morning hasts; the stars are forward in their
    course;
Two parts of night are past, the third is left t' imploy our force.'

[206]

The Tenth Booke

Now borrowed they for haste some armes: bold Thrasymedes lent

The explorators armed.

Adventrous Diomed his sword (his owne was at his tent), 225
His shield and helme, tough and well-tann'd, without or plume or crest,
And cald a murrion: archers' heads it used to invest.
Meriones lent Ithacus his quiver and his bow,
His helmet fashiond of a hide: the workman did bestow
Much labour in it, quilting it with bowstrings, and, without, 230
With snowie tuskes of white-mouthd Bores twas armed round about
Right cunningly, and in the midst an arming cap was plac't
That with the fixt ends of the tuskes his head might not be rac't.
This, long since, by Autolycus was brought from Eleon
When he laid waste Amyntor's house, that was Ormenus' sonne. 235
In Scandia, to Cytherius, surnam'd Amphidamas,
Autolycus did give this helme: he, when he feasted was
By honord Molus, gave it him as present of a guest:
Molus to his sonne Merion did make it his bequest.
With this Ulysses arm'd his head; and thus they (both addrest) 240

Augurium ex cantu Ardeæ.

Tooke leave of all the other kings. To them a glad ostent
(As they were entring on their way) Minerva did present—
A Hernshaw consecrate to her, which they could ill discerne
Through sable night but by her clange they knew it was a Herne.

Ulysses invoketh Pallas.

Ulysses joy'd, and thus invok't: 'Heare me, great seed of Jove, 245
That ever dost my labors grace with presence of thy love
And all my motions dost attend, still love me, sacred Dame,
Especially in this exploit, and so protect our fame
We both may safely make retreate and thriftily imploy
Our boldnesse in some great affaire, banefull to them of Troy.' 250

Diomed to Pallas.

Then praid illustrate Diomed: 'Vouchsafe me likewise eare,
O thou unconquerd Queene of armes. Be with thy favors neare,
As to my royall father's steps thou wentst a bountious guide
When th' Achives and the Peeres of Thebes he would have pacifide,
Sent as the Greeks' Ambassador and left them at the flood 255
Of great Asopus, whose retreate thou mad'st to swim in blood
Of his enambush't enemies. And if thou so protect
My bold endevours, to thy name an Heiffer most select
That never yet was tam'd with yoke, brode-fronted, one yeare old,
I'le burne in zealous sacrifice and set the hornes in gold.' 260

[207]

The Goddesse heard, and both the kings their dreadlesse
    passage bore
Through slaughter, slaughterd carkasses, armes and discolord
    gore.

Hector to the
Troyans.

Nor Hector let his Princes sleepe, but all to counsell cald,
And askt: 'What one is here will vow, and keep it unappald,
To have a gift fit for his deed—a chariot and two horse   265
That passe for speed the rest of Greece? What one dares take
    this course
For his renowne (besides his gifts) to mixe amongst the foe
And learne if still they hold their guards, or with this overthrow
Determine flight, as being too weake to hold us longer warre?'

Dolon offers to be
explorator.

All silent stood: at last stood forth one Dolon that did dare   270
This dangerous worke, Eumedes' heire, a Herald much renownd.
This Dolon did in gold and brasse exceedingly abound
But in his forme was quite deform'd, yet passing swift to run.
Amongst five sisters he was left Eumedes' onely son.
And he told Hector his free heart would undertake t' explore   275
The Greeks' intentions: 'But,' said he, 'thou shalt be sworne
    before,
By this thy scepter, that the horse of great Æacides
And his strong chariot bound with brasse thou wilt (before
    all these)
Resigne me as my valour's prize; and so I rest unmov'd
To be thy spie and not returne before I have approv'd   280
(By venturing to Atrides' ship, where their consults are held)
If they resolve still to resist, or flie as quite expeld.'

Hector sweares to
Dolon.

He put his scepter in his hand and cald the thunder's God
(Saturnia's husband) to his oath those horse should not be rode
By any other man than he, but he for ever joy   285
(To his renowne) their services, for his good done to Troy.
Thus swore he, and forswore himselfe, yet made base Dolon
    bold,

Dolon armes.

Who on his shoulders hung his bow and did about him fold
A white wolve's hide and with a helme of weasels' skins
    did arme
His weasel's head; then tooke his dart; and never turnd to   290
    harme
The Greeks with their related drifts but, being past the troopes
Of horse and foote, he promptly runs and, as he runs, he stoopes
To undermine Achilles' horse. Ulysses straight did see

Ulysses to Diomed.

And said to Diomed: 'This man makes footing towards thee
Out of the tents. I know not well if he be usde as spie   295
Bent to our fleet or come to rob the slaughterd enemie.

But let us suffer him to come a little further on
And then pursue him. If it chance that we be overgone
By his more swiftnesse, urge him still to run upon our fleet
And (lest he scape us to the towne) still let thy Javeline meet   300
With all his offers of retreate.' Thus stept they from the plaine
Amongst the slaughterd carkasses. Dolon came on amaine,
Suspecting nothing; but once past as farre as Mules outdraw
Oxen at plough, being both put on, neither admitted law,
To plough a deepe-soild furrow forth, so farre was Dolon past;   305
Then they pursude—which he perceiv'd and staid his speedlesse
          hast,
Subtly supposing Hector sent to countermand his spie.
But in a Javelin's throw or lesse he knew them enemie.
Then laid he on his nimble knees, and they pursude like wind.

Simile.

As when a brace of greyhounds are laid in with Hare or Hind,   310
Close-mouth'd and skild to make the best of their industrious
          course,
Serve either's turne, and, set on hard, lose neither ground
          nor force:
So constantly did Tydeus' sonne and his towne-razing Peere
Pursue this spie, still turning him as he was winding neare
His covert, till he almost mixt with their out-courts of guard.   315

Diomed to Dolon.

     Then Pallas prompted Diomed, lest his due worth's reward
Should be empair'd if any man did vant he first did sheath
His sword in him and he be cald but second in his death.
Then spake he (threatning with his lance): 'Or stay, or this
          comes on,
And long thou canst not run before thou be by death   320
          out-gone.'
     This said, he threw his Javeline forth, which mist (as Diomed
          would);
Above his right arme making way, the pile stucke in the mould.
He staid and trembled, and his teeth did chatter in his head.

Dolon's surprise and offer.

They came in blowing, seisd him fast: he, weeping, offered
A wealthy ransome for his life, and told them he had brasse,   325
Much gold and iron that fit for use in many labours was;
From whose rich heapes his father would a wondrous portion
          give
If, at the great Achaian fleet, he heard his sonne did live.

Ulysses to Dolon.

     Ulysses bad him cheare his heart: 'Thinke not of death,'
          said he,
'But tell us true, why runst thou forth when others sleeping be?   330
Is it to spoile the carkasses? or art thou choicely sent

T' explore our drifts? or of thy selfe seek'st thou some wisht
    event?'

Dolon's answer.   He, trembling, answerd: 'Much reward did Hector's oth
    propose

And urg'd me much against my will t' indevour to disclose

If you determin'd still to stay, or bent your course for flight,   335

As all dismaid with your late foile and wearied with the fight:

For which exploite Pelides' horse and chariot he did sweare

I onely ever should enjoy.' Ulysses smil'd to heare

So base a swaine have any hope so high a prise t' aspire,

Ulysses to Dolon.   And said his labors did affect a great and precious hire,   340

And that the horse Pelides rein'd no mortall hand could use

But he himselfe, whose matchlesse life a Goddesse did produce:

'But tell us, and report but truth, where leftst thou Hector now?

Where are his armes? his famous horse? on whom doth he bestow

The watches' charge? where sleepe the Kings? intend they   345
    still to lie

Thus neare encampt? or turne suffisd with their late victorie?'

Dolon's relation.   'All this,' said he, 'I'le tell most true. At Ilus' monument

Hector with all our Princes sits t' advise of this event,

Who chuse that place remov'd to shun the rude confused
    sounds

The common souldiers throw about. But for our watch and   350
    rounds,

Whereof, brave Lord, thou mak'st demand, none orderly we
    keepe.

The Troyans that have roofes to save onely abandon sleepe

And privately, without command, each other they exhort

To make prevention of the worst; and in this slender sort

Is watch and guard maintaind with us. Th' auxiliarie bands   355

Sleepe soundly and commit their cares into the Troyans' hands,

For they have neither wives with them, nor children, to protect:

The lesse they need to care, the more they succour dull neglect.'

Ithacus.   'But tell me,' said wise Ithacus, 'are all these forreine powres

Appointed quarters by themselves, or else commixt with   360
    yours?'

Dolon.   'And this,' said Dolon, 'too, my Lords, I'le seriously unfold.

The Pæons with the crooked bowes, and Cares, quarters hold

Next to the sea, the Leleges and Caucons joyn'd with them,

And brave Pelasgians; Thymber's meade, remov'd more from
    the streame,

Is quarter to the Lycians, the loftie Mysian force,   365

The Phrygians and Mæonians, that fight with armed horse.

But what need these particulars? If ye intend surprise

Of any in our Troyan campe, the Thracian quarter lies
Utmost of all, and uncommixt with Troyan regiments
That keepe the voluntary watch: new pitcht are all their tents. 370
King Rhesus, Eioneus' son, commands them; who hath steeds

More white than snow, huge and well-shap't; their firie pace
    exceeds
The winds in swiftnesse. These I saw: his Chariot is with gold
And pallid silver richly fram'd and wondrous to behold.
His great and golden armour is not fit a man should weare 375
But for immortall shoulders fram'd. Come then, and quickly
    beare
Your happie prisoner to your fleet, or leave him here fast bound
Till your well-urg'd and rich returne prove my relation sound.'

Diomed's sterne
reply to Dolon.

    Tydides dreadfully replide: 'Thinke not of passage thus,
Though of right acceptable newes thou hast advertisde us. 380
Our hands are holds more strict than so, and should we set
    thee free
For offerd ransome, for this scape thou still wouldst scouting be
About our ships or do us scathe in plaine opposed armes;
But if I take thy life, no way can we repent thy harmes.'

Dolon's slaughter by
Diomed.

    With this, as Dolon reacht his hand to use a suppliant's part 385
And stroke the beard of Diomed, he strooke his necke athwart
With his forc't sword, and both the nerves he did in sunder
    wound,
And suddenly his head, deceiv'd, fell speaking on the ground.
His wesel's helme they tooke, his bow, his wolve's skin and his
    lance,
Which to Minerva Ithacus did zealously advance 390
With lifted arme into the aire, and to her thus he spake:

Ulysses proffers
Dolon's armes to
Pallas.

    'Goddesse, triumph in thine own spoiles: to thee we first
    will make
Our invocations, of all powers thron'd on th' Olympian hill.
Now to the Thracians and their horse and beds conduct us still.'
With this, he hung them up aloft upon a Tamricke bow 395
As eyefull Trophies, and the sprigs that did about it grow
He proined from the leavie armes, to make it easier viewd
When they should hastily retire and be perhaps pursude.
Forth went they through blacke bloud and armes, and presently
    aspir'd
The guardlesse Thracian regiment, fast bound with sleepe 400
    and tir'd.
Their armes lay by, and triple rankes they as they slept did
    keepe,

[211]

As they should watch and guard their king, who, in a fatall
    sleepe,
Lay in the midst; their charriot horse, as they coach fellowes
    were,
Fed by them, and the famous steeds that did their Generall beare
Stood next him, to the hinder part of his rich chariot tied.   405

Ulysses to Diomed.   Ulysses saw them first, and said: 'Tydides, I have spied
The horse that Dolon (whom we slue) assur'd us we should see.
Now use thy strength; now idle armes are most unfit for thee.
Prise thou the horse, or kill the guard and leave the horse to me.'
    Minerva with the Azure eyes breath'd strength into her   410
        King,
Who fild the tent with mixed death: the soules he set on wing
Issued in grones and made aire swell into her stormie floud.
Horror and slaughter had one power: the earth did blush
    with bloud.
As when a hungrie Lion flies, with purpose to devoure
On flocks unkept and on their lives doth freely use his power;   415
So Tydeus' sonne assaild the foe. Twelve soules before him flew.
Ulysses waited on his sword and ever as he slew
He drew them by their strengthlesse heeles out of the horses'
    sight,
That when he was to leade them forth they should not with
    affright
Bogle nor snore, in treading on the bloudie carkases—   420
For, being new come, they were unusde to such sterne sights
    as these.
Diomed slaughters   Through foure ranks now did Diomed the king himselfe
Rhesus, king of   attaine,
Thrace.   Who (snoring in his sweetest sleepe) was like his souldiers slaine.
An ill dreame, by Minerva sent, that night stood by his head,
Which was Œnides' royall sonne, unconquer'd Diomed.   425
    Meane while Ulysses loosd his horse, tooke all their raines
    in hand,
And led them forth; but Tydeus' sonne did in contention stand
With his great mind, to do some deed of more audacitie—
If he should take the chariot where his rich armes did lie
And draw it by the beame away, or beare it on his backe,   430
Or if of more dull Thracian lives he should their bosomes sacke.
Minerva to Diomed.   In this contention with himselfe, Minerva did suggest
And bad him thinke of his retreate, lest from their tempted rest
Some other God should stirre the foe and send him backe
    dismaid.

He knew the voice, tooke horse and fled. The Troyans'   435
    heavenly aid
(Apollo with the silver bow) stood no blind sentinell
To their secure and drowsie hoast, but did discover well
Minerva following Diomed; and, angrie with his act,
The mightie hoast of Ilion he entred and awak't
The cousen germane of the king, a counsellor of Thrace,   440
Hippocoon, who, when he rose and saw the desert place
Where Rhesus' horse did use to stand and th' other dismall
    harmes,
Men strugling with the pangs of death, he shriekt out thicke
    alarmes,

*Alarmes amongst
the Troyans.*

Cald: 'Rhesus! Rhesus!' but in vaine: then still 'Arme, arme!'
    he cride.
The noise and tumult was extreme on every startled side   445
Of Troy's huge hoast, from whence in throngs all gatherd and
    admir'd
Who could performe such harmfull facts and yet be safe retir'd.
  Now, comming where they slue the scout, Ulysses stayd
    the steeds.
Tydides lighted, and the spoiles (hung on the Tamricke reeds)
He tooke and gave to Ithacus, and up he got againe.   450
Then flew they joyfull to their fleet. Nestor did first attaine

*Nestor to the
Greeks.*

The sounds the horse hoofes strooke through aire, and said:
    'My royall Peeres,
Do I but dote? or say I true? Me thinkes about mine eares
The sounds of running horses beate. O would to God they were
Our friends thus soone returnd with spoiles! But I have   455
    heartie feare
Lest this high tumult of the foe doth their distresse intend.'
He scarce had spoke when they were come. Both did from horse
    descend.
All, with embraces and sweet words, to heaven their worth
    did raise.
Then Nestor spake: 'Great Ithacus, even heapt with Grecian
    praise,
How have you made these horse your prise? pierc't you the   460
    dangerous host,
Where such gemmes stand? or did some God your high attempts
    accost
And honord you with this reward? Why, they be like the Rayes
The Sunne effuseth. I have mixt with Troyans all my daies,
And now I hope you will not say I alwaies lye abord,
Though an old soldier, I confesse: yet did all Troy afford   465

[213]

Never the like to any sence that ever I possest.
But some good God, no doubt, hath met and your high valours
    blest—
For he that shadowes heaven with clouds loves both as his
    delights
And she that supples earth with blood can not forbeare your
    sights.'

Ulysses to Nestor.   Ulysses answerd: 'Honord Sire, the willing Gods can give   470
Horse much more worth than these men yeeld, since in more
    power they live.
These horse are of the Thracian breed: their King Tydides slue
And twelve of his most trusted guard; and of that meaner crew
A skowt for thirteenth man we kild, whom Hector sent to spie
The whole estate of our designes, if bent to fight or flie.'   475
    Thus (followed with whole troopes of friends) they with
      applauses past
The spacious dike, and in the tent of Diomed they plac't
The horse without contention, as his deservings' meed;
Which (with his other horse set up) on yellow wheat did feed.
Poore Dolon's spoiles Ulysses had, who shrin'd them on his   480
    sterne
As trophies vow'd to her that sent the good-aboding Herne.
    Then entred they the meere maine sea to cleanse their honord
      sweate
From off their feet, their thighes and neckes; and, when their
    vehement heate
Was calm'd and their swolne hearts refresht, more curious baths
    they usd,
Where odorous and dissolving Oyles they through their lims   485
    diffusde.
Then, taking breakfast, a big boule fild with the purest wine
They offerd to the maiden Queene that hath the azure eyne.

The End of the Tenth Booke

THE ELEVENTH BOOKE

of

HOMER'S ILIADS

THE ARGUMENT

Atrides and his other Peeres of name
Leade forth their men, whom Eris doth inflame.
Hector (by Iris' charge) takes deedlesse breath
While Agamemnon plies the worke of death,
Who with the first beares his imperiall head. 5
Himselfe, Ulysses and King Diomed,
Eurypylus and Æsculapius' sonne
(Enforc't with wounds) the furious skirmish shun.
Which martiall sight when great Achilles viewes,
A little his desire of fight renewes, 10
And forth he sends his friend to bring him word
From old Neleides what wounded Lord
He in his chariot from the skirmish brought:
Which was Machaon. Nestor then besought
He would perswade his friend to wreake their harmes, 15
Or come himselfe deckt in his dreadfull armes.

Another Argument

Lambda presents the Generall,
In fight the worthiest man of all.

Aurora out of restfull bed did from bright Tithon rise,
To bring each deathlesse essence light, and use to mortall eyes;
When Jove sent Eris to the Greekes, sustaining in her hand
Sterne signes of her designes for warre. She tooke her horrid
    stand
Upon Ulysses' huge blacke Barke, that did at anchor ride 5
Amidst the fleet; from whence her sounds might ring on every
    side,
Both to the tents of Telamon and th' authors of their smarts,
Who held, for fortitude and force, the navie's utmost parts.

[215]

The red-eyd Goddesse, seated there, thunderd th' Orthian
    song,
High and with horror, through the eares of all the Grecian   10
    throng.
Her verse with spirits invincible did all their breasts inspire,
Blew out all starknesse from their lims and set their hearts
    on fire.
And presently was bitter warre more sweet a thousand times
Than any choice in hollow keeles to greet their native climes.

    Atrides summon'd all to armes, to armes himselfe disposde.   15
First on his legs he put bright Greaves, with silver buttons closde,
Then with rich Curace arm'd his breast, which Cinyras bestow'd
To gratifie his royall guest; for even to Cyprus flow'd
Th' unbounded fame of those designes the Greeks proposde
    for Troy,
And therefore gave he him those armes and wisht his purpose   20
    joy.
Ten rowes of azure mixt with blacke, twelve golden like the
    Sunne,
Twise ten of tin, in beaten paths did through this armour runne.
Three serpents to the gorget crept, that like three rain-bowes
    shin'd,
Such as by Jove are fixt in clouds when wonders are divin'd.
About his shoulders hung his sword, whereof the hollow hilt   25
Was fashion'd all with shining barres exceeding richly gilt.
The scaberd was of silver plate with golden hangers grac't.
Then tooke he up his weightie shield, that round about him cast
Defensive shadowes. Ten bright zones of gold-affecting brasse
Were driven about it, and of tin (as full of glosse as glasse)   30
Sweld twentie bosses out of it: in center of them all
One of blacke mettall had engraven (full of extreme appall)
An ugly Gorgon, compassed with Terror and with Feare.
At it, a silver Bawdricke hung, with which he usde to beare
(Wound on his arme) his ample shield; and in it there was   35
    woven
An azure Dragon curl'd in folds, from whose one necke was
    cloven
Three heads contorted in an orbe. Then plac't he on his head
His foure-plum'd caske, and in his hands two darts he managed,
Arm'd with bright steele that blaz'd to heaven. Then Juno
    and the maide
That conquers Empires trumpets serv'd to summon out their   40
    aide
In honor of the Generall, and on a sable cloud

(To bring them furious to the field) sate thundring out aloud.
   Then all enjoyn'd their charioteers to ranke their chariot
     horse
Close to the dike; forth marcht the foot, whose front they did
   r'enforce
With some horse troupes. The battell then was all of   45
   Charioteers,
Lin'd with light horse. But Jupiter disturb'd this forme with
   feares,
And from aire's upper region did bloudie vapors raine
For sad ostent much noble life should ere their times be slaine.
The Troyan hoast, at Ilus' tombe, was in Battalia led
By Hector and Polydamas and old Anchises' seed,   50
Who God-like was esteem'd in Troy, by grave Antenor's race
Divine Agenor, Polybus, unmaried Acamas,
Proportion'd like the states of heaven. In front of all the field
Troy's great Priamides did beare his al-wayes-equall shield,

Simile.   Still plying th' ordering of his power. And as amids the skie   55
We sometimes see an ominous starre blaze cleare and dreadfully,
Then run his golden head in clouds and straight appeare againe:
So Hector otherwhiles did grace the vaunt-guard, shining plaine,
Then in the rere-guard hid himselfe and labour'd every where
To order and encourage all: his armor was so cleare   60
And he applide each place so fast that, like a lightning throwne
Out of the shield of Jupiter, in every eye he shone.

Another comparison.   And as upon a rich man's crop of barley or of wheate
(Opposde for swiftnesse at their worke) a sort of reapers sweate,
Beare downe the furrowes speedily, and thicke their handfuls 65
   fall:
So at the joyning of the hoasts ran Slaughter through them all.
None stoopt to any fainting thought of foule inglorious flight
But equall bore they up their heads and far'd like wolves in fight.
Sterne Eris, with such weeping sights, rejoyc't to feed her eies,
Who onely shew'd her selfe in field of all the Deities.   70
The other in Olympus' tops sate silent and repin'd
That Jove to do the Troyans grace should beare so fixt a mind.
He car'd not but (enthron'd apart) triumphant sat in sway

Jove's prospect.   Of his free power, and from his seate tooke pleasure to display
The citie so adorn'd with towres, the sea with vessels fild, 75
The splendor of refulgent armes, the killer and the kild.
As long as bright Aurora rul'd and sacred day increast,
So long their darts made mutuall wounds and neither had
    the best:

Periphrasis of
Noone.   But when in hill-environ'd vales the timber-feller takes

[217]

A sharpe-set stomacke to his meate and dinner ready makes,　80
His sinewes fainting and his spirits become surcharg'd and dull,
Time of accustom'd ease arriv'd, his hands with labour full,
Then by their valours Greeks brake through the Troyan rankes
　　and chear'd
Their generall Squadrons through the hoast. Then first of all
　　appear'd
The person of the King himselfe, and then the Troyans lost　85
Bianor by his royall charge, a leader in the host,

Agamemnon's
slaughters.

Who being slaine, his chariotere, Oileus, did alight
And stood in skirmish with the king. The king did deadly smite
His forehead with his eager lance and through his helme it
　　ranne,
Enforcing passage to his braine, quite through the hardned　90
　　pan;
His braine mixt with his clotterd bloud, his body strewd the
　　ground.
　　There left he them, and presently he other objects found,
Isus and Antiphus, two sonnes king Priam did beget,
One lawfull, th' other wantonly. Both in one chariot met
Their royall foe: the baser borne, Isus, was chariotere　95

Achilles.

And famous Antiphus did fight; both which king Peleus' heire
(Whilome in Ida keeping flocks) did deprehend and bind
With pliant Osiers and for prize them to their Sire resign'd.
Atrides with his well-aim'd lance smote Isus on the brest
Above the nipple, and his sword a mortall wound imprest　100
Beneath the eare of Antiphus: downe from their horse they fell.
The king had seene the youths before and now did know
　　them well,
Remembring them the prisoners of swift Æacides,
Who brought them to the sable fleet from Ida's foodie leas.

Simile.

　　And as a Lion having found the furrow of a Hind　105
Where she hath calv'd two little twins, at will and ease
　　doth grind
Their joynts snatcht in his sollide jawes and crusheth into mist
Their tender lives, their dam (though neare) not able to resist
But shooke with vehement feare her selfe, flies through the
　　Oaken chace
From that fell savage, drown'd in sweat, and seekes some covert　110
　　place:
So, when with most unmatched strength the Grecian Generall
　　bent
Gainst these two Princes, none durst ayd their native king's
　　descent

[218]

But fled themselves before the Greeks. And where these two
    were slaine,
Pisander and Hippolochus (not able to restraine
Their head-strong horse, the silken reines being from their   115
    hands let fall)
Were brought by their unruly guides before the Generall.
Antimachus begat them both, Antimachus that tooke
Rich guifts and gold of Helen's love and would by no meanes
    brooke
Just restitution should be made of Menelaus' wealth,

Paris.   Bereft him, with his ravisht Queene, by Alexander's stealth.   120
Atrides Lion-like did charge his sonnes, who on their knees
Fell from their chariot and besought regard to their degrees,
Who, being Antimachus his sonnes, their father would affoord
A worthie ransome for their lives, who in his house did hoord
Much hidden treasure, brasse and gold and steele wrought   125
    wondrous choise.
Thus wept they, using smoothing terms, and heard this rugged
    voice

Agamemnon to   Breath'd from the unrelenting king: 'If you be of the breed
Pisander and   Of stout Antimachus that staid the honorable deed
Hippolochus.   The other Peeres of Ilion in counsell had decreed
To render Helen and her wealth, and would have basely slaine   130
My brother and wise Ithacus, Ambassadors t' attaine
The most due motion, now receive wreake for his shamefull
    part.'
This said, in poore Pisander's breast he fixt his wreakfull dart,
Who upward spread th' oppressed earth. His brother croucht
    for dread,
And, as he lay, the angrie king cut off his armes and head   135
And let him like a football lie for everie man to spurne.
Then to th' extremest heate of fight he did his valour turne
And led a multitude of Greeks where foote did foote subdue,
Horse slaughterd horse, Need featherd flight, the batterd
    center flew
In clouds of dust about their eares, raisd from the horses'   140
    hooves,
That beat a thunder out of earth as horrible as Jove's.
The king (perswading speedie chace) gave his perswasions way
With his owne valour, slaughtring still. As in a stormie day
In thicke-set woods a ravenous fire wraps in his fierce repaire
The shaken trees, and by the rootes doth tosse them into aire: 145
Even so beneath Atrides' sword flew up Troy's flying heeles,

Their horse drew emptie chariots and sought their thundring
    wheeles
Some fresh directors through the field, where least the pursuite
    drives.
Thicke fell the Troyans, much more sweet to Vultures
    than their wives.
   Then Jove drew Hector from the darts, from dust,   150
    from death and blood
And from the tumult. Still the king firme to the pursuite stood
Till at old Ilus' monument, in midst of all the field,
They reacht the wild Figtree and long'd to make their towne
    their shield.
Yet there they rested not: the king still cride: 'Pursue, pursue,'
And all his unreproved hands did blood and dust embrue.   155
But when they came to Scæa's ports and to the Beech of Jove,
There made they stand; there everie eye, fixt on each other,
    strove
Who should outlooke his mate amaz'd: through all the field
    they fled.

Simile.

And as a Lion, when the night becomes most deafe and dead,
Invades Oxe heards, affrighting all, that he of one may wreake 160
His dreadfull hunger, and his necke he first of all doth breake,
Then laps his blood and entrailes up: so Agamemnon plide
The manage of the Troyan chace, and still the last man di'd,
The other fled, a number fell by his imperiall hand,
Some groveling downwards from their horse, some upwards   165
    strew'd the sand.
High was the furie of his lance; but, having beat them close
Beneath their walls, the both-world's Sire did now againe
    repose
On fountaine-flowing Ida's tops, being newly slid from heaven,
And held a lightning in his hand. From thence this charge was
    given

Jove to the
Rainbow.

To Iris with the golden wings: 'Thaumantia, flie,' said he,   170
'And tell Troy's Hector that as long as he enrag'd shall see
The souldier-loving Atreus' sonne amongst the formost fight,
Depopulating troopes of men, so long he must excite
Some other to resist the foe and he no armes advance:
But, when he wounded takes his horse, attain'd with shaft or 175
    lance,
Then will I fill his arme with death even till he reach the
    Fleet
And peacefull night treads busie day beneath her sacred feet.'
   The wind-foot-swift Thaumantia obeyd and usd her wings

To famous Ilion from the mount enchaste with silver springs,
And found in his bright chariot the hardie Troyan knight,   180
To whom she spake the words of Jove, and vanisht from his
    sight.
  He leapt upon the sounding earth and shooke his lengthfull
    dart
And everie where he breath'd exhorts and stird up everie heart.
A dreadfull fight he set on foote: his souldiers straight turnd
    head.
The Greekes stood firme: in both the hoasts the field was   185
    perfected.
But Agamemnon formost still did all his side exceed
And would not be the first in name unlesse the first in deed.
  Now sing, faire Presidents of verse that in the heavens
    embowre,
Who first encountred with the king of all the adverse powre.
Iphidamas, Antenor's sonne, ample and bigly set,   190
Brought up in pasture-springing Thrace that doth soft sheepe
    beget,
In grave Cisseus' noble house, that was his mother's Sire
(Faire Theano); and, when his breast was heightned with the
    fire
Of gaisome youth, his grandsire gave his daughter to his love,
Who straight his bridall chamber left. Fame with affection   195
    strove
And made him furnish twelve faire ships to lend faire Troy
    his hand.
His ships he in Percote left and came to Troy by land,
And now he tried the fame of Greece, encountring with the
    king,
Who threw his royall lance, and mist. Iphidamas did fling
And strooke him on the arming waste beneath his coate of   200
    brasse,
Which forc't him stay upon his arme, so violent it was;
Yet pierc't it not his wel-wrought zone, but when the lazie head
Tried hardnesse with his silver waste it turnd againe like lead.
He follow'd, grasping the ground end, but, with a Lion's wile
That wrests away a hunter's staffe, he caught it by the pile   205
And pluckt it from the caster's hand, whom with his sword he
    strooke

Iphidamas slain   Beneath the eare, and with his wound his timelesse death
by Agamemnon.   he tooke.
He fell and slept an iron sleepe: wretched young man, he dide
Farre from his newly-married wife, in aide of forreine pride,

[221]

And saw no pleasure of his love: yet was her joynture great— 210
An hundred Oxen gave he her, and vow'd in his retreate
Two thousand head of sheepe and Goates, of which he store
    did leave;
Much gave he of his love's first fruits and nothing did receive.
  When Coon (one that for his forme might feast an amorous
    eye,
And elder brother of the slaine) beheld this tragedie, 215
Deepe sorrow sate upon his eyes, and (standing laterally
And to the Generall undiscernd) his Javelin he let flie,
That twixt his elbow and his wrist transfixt his armelesse
    arme:
The bright head shin'd on th' other side. The unexpected
    harme
Imprest some horror in the king; yet so he ceast not fight, 220
But rusht on Coon with his lance, who made what haste he
    might
(Seising his slaughterd brother's foote) to draw him from the
    field
And cald the ablest to his aide, when under his round shield
The king's brasse Javelin, as he drew, did strike him helplesse
    dead,
Who made Iphidamas the blocke and cut off Coon's head. 225
  Thus under great Atrides' arme Antenor's issue thriv'd
And to suffise precisest fate to Pluto's mansion div'd.
He with his lance, sword, mightie stones, pour'd his Heroicke
    wreake
On other Squadrons of the foe, whiles yet warme blood did
    breake
Through his cleft veines: but, when the wound was quite 230
    exhaust and crude,
The eager anguish did approve his Princely fortitude.
As, when most sharpe and bitter pangs distract a labouring
    Dame,
Which the divine Ilithyæ that rule the painefull frame
Of humane child-birth poure on her—th' Ilithyæ that are
The daughters of Saturnia, with whose extreme repaire 235
The woman in her travell strives, to take the worst it gives,
With thought it must be, tis love's fruite, the end for which she
    lives,
The meane to make her selfe new-borne, what comforts will
    redound:
So Agamemnon did sustaine the torment of his wound.
Then tooke he chariot, and to Fleet bad haste his chariotere, 240

But first pour'd out his highest voice to purchase everie eare:

Agamemnon to the
Greeke Princes.

  'Princes and Leaders of the Greekes, brave friends, now from
    our fleet

Do you expell this boistrous sway. Jove will not let me meet
Illustrate Hector, nor give leave that I shall end the day
In fight against the Ilian power: my wound is in my way.'   245
  This said, his readie chariotere did scourge his spritefull
    horse,
That freely to the sable fleet performd their fierie course,
To beare their wounded Soveraigne apart the Martiall thrust,
Sprinkling their powerfull breasts with foame and snowing on
    the dust.
  When Hector heard of his retreate, thus he for fame   250
    contends:

Hector to the
Troyans.

'Troyans, Dardanians, Lycians, all my close-fighting friends,
Thinke what it is to be renownd: be souldiers all of name.
Our strongest enemie is gone: Jove vowes to do us fame.
Then in the Grecian faces drive your one-hov'd violent steeds
And farre above their best be best, and glorifie your deeds.'   255
  Thus as a dog-given Hunter sets upon a brace of Bores
His white-toothd hounds, pufs, showts, breaths terms and on
    his emprese pores
All his wild art to make them pinch: so Hector urg'd his host
To charge the Greeks, and he himselfe most bold and active
    most.
He brake into the heate of fight, as when a tempest raves,   260
Stoops from the clouds and all on heapes doth cuffe the purple
    waves.

Whom Hector slue.

  Who then was first and last he kild when Jove did grace his
    deed?
Asæus and Autonous, Opys and Clytus' seed,
Prince Dolops, and the honord Sire of sweet Euryalus,
Opheltes, Agelaus next and strong Hipponous,   265
Orus, Æsymnus, all of name. The common souldiers fell

Simile.

As when the hollow flood of aire in Zephyr's cheeks doth swell
And sparseth all the gatherd clouds white Notus' power did
    draw,
Wraps waves in waves, hurls up the froath beat with a
    vehement flaw:
So were the common souldiers wrackt in troops by Hector's   270
    hand.
Then ruine had enforc't such works as no Greeks could
    withstand:
Then in their fleete they had bene housd—had not Laertes'
    sonne

Stird up the spirit of Diomed with this impression:

Ulysses to Diomed.

    'Tydides, what do we sustaine, forgetting what we are?
Stand by me, dearest in my love: twere horrible impaire   275
For our two valours to endure a customarie flight,
To leave our navie still ingag'd and but by fits to fight.'

Diomed's answer to
Ulysses.

    He answerd: 'I am bent to stay and any thing sustaine:
But our delight to prove us men will prove but short and
    vaine,
For Jove makes Troyans instruments, and virtually then   280
Wields arms himselfe: our crosse affaires are not twixt men
    and men.'
    This said, Thymbræus with his lance he tumbled from his
    horse,
Neare his left nipple wounding him. Ulysses did enforce
Faire Molion, minion to this king that Diomed subdude.
Both sent they thence till they returnd, who now the king   285
    pursude
And furrowed through the thickned troopes. As when two
    chaced Bores
Turne head gainst kennels of bold hounds and race way through
    their gores,
So (turnd from flight) the forward kings shew'd Troyans
    backward death,
Nor fled the Greeks but by their wils, to get great Hector
    breath.

Ulysses' and
Diomed's slaughters.

    Then tooke they horse and chariot from two bold citie foes,   290
Merops Percosius' mightie sonnes: their father could disclose,
Beyond all men, hid Auguries and would not give consent
To their egression to these wars, yet wilfully they went,
For Fates that order sable death enforc't their tragedies.
Tydides slue them with his lance and made their armes his   295
    prise.
    Hypirochus and Hippodam, Ulysses reft of light,
But Jove, that out of Ida lookt, then equallisde the fight:
A Grecian for a Troyan then paide tribute to the Fates,
Yet royall Diomed slue one, even in those even debates,
That was of name more than the rest—Pæon's renowned sonne,   300
The Prince Agastrophus: his lance into his hip did run;
His Squire detain his horse apart, that hindred him to flie,
Which he repented at his heart; yet did his feet applie
His scape with all the speed they had alongst the formost
    bands,
And there his loved life dissolv'd. This Hector understands,   305
And rusht with clamor on the king, right soundly seconded

With troupes of Troyans; which perceiv'd by famous Diomed,
The deepe conceit of Jove's high will stifned his royall haire,

Who spake to neare-fought Ithacus: 'The fate of this affaire
Is bent to us: come, let us stand and bound his violence.'   310
Thus threw he his long Javelin forth, which smote his head's defence
Full on the top, yet pierc't no skin: brasse tooke repulse with brasse.
His helme (with three folds made, and sharpe) the gift of Phœbus was.
The blow made Hector take the troupe, sunke him upon his hand
And strooke him blind: the king pursude, before the formost band,   315
His dart's recoverie, which he found laid on the purple plaine:
By which time Hector was reviv'd and, taking horse againe,
Was farre commixt within his strength and fled his darksome grave.
He followd with his thirstie lance and this elusive Brave:

'Once more be thankfull to thy heeles, proud dog, for thy escape.   320
Mischiefe sate neare thy bosome now; and now another rape
Hath thy Apollo made of thee, to whom thou well maist pray
When through the singing of our darts thou findst such guarded way.
But I shall meet with thee at length and bring thy latest houre,
If with like favour any God be fautor of my powre.   325
Meane while, some other shall repay what I suspend in thee.'
This said, he set the wretched soule of Pæon's issue free,

Whom his late wound not fully slue. But Priam's amorous birth
Against Tydides bent his bow, hid with a hill of earth,
Part of the ruinated tombe for honor'd Ilus built,   330
And, as the Curace of the slaine (engraven and richly gilt)
Tydides from his breast had spoild and from his shoulders raft
His target and his solide helme, he shot; and his keene shaft
(That never flew from him in vaine) did naile unto the ground
The king's right foot. The spleenfull knight laught sweetly at the wound, 335

Crept from his covert and triumpht: 'Now art thou maimd,' said he,
'And would to God my happie hand had so much honor'd me

[225]

To have infixt it in thy breast as deepe as in thy foote,
Even to th' expulsure of thy soule: then blest had bene my
    shoote
Of all the Troyans, who had then breath'd from their long   340
    unrests,
Who feare thee as the braying Goates abhorre the king of
    beasts.'

Diomed's reply.
    Undanted Diomed replide: 'You Braver with your bow,
You slick-hair'd lover, you that hunt and fleere at wenches so,
Durst thou but stand in armes with me, thy silly archerie
Would give thee little cause to vaunt. As little suffer I   345
In this same tall exploit of thine, perform'd when thou wert
    hid,
As if a woman or a child, that knew not what it did,
Had toucht my foote. A coward's steele hath never any edge,
But mine (t' assure it sharpe) still layes dead carkasses in
    pledge.
Touch it: it renders livelesse straight: it strikes the fingers' ends   350
Of haplesse widowes in their cheeks, and children blind of
    friends:
The subject of it makes earth red and aire with sighes inflames,
And leaves lims more embrac't with birds than with enamour'd
    Dames.'
    Lance-fam'd Ulysses now came in and stept before the king,
Kneeld opposite, and drew the shaft. The eager paine   355
    did sting
Through all his bodie: straight he tooke his royall chariot there
And with direction to the fleete did charge his chariotere.
    Now was Ulysses desolate: feare made no friend remaine.

Ulysses to himselfe.
He thus spake to his mightie mind: 'What doth my
    state sustaine?
If I should flie this ods in feare, that thus comes clustring on,   360
Twere high dishonour: yet twere worse to be surprisd alone.
Tis Jove that drives the rest to flight; but that's a faint excuse.
Why do I tempt my mind so much? Pale cowards fight refuse:
He that affects renowne in warre must like a rocke be fixt,
Wound or be wounded: valour's truth puts no respect betwixt.'   365
    In this contention with himselfe, in flew the shadie bands
Of targateres, who sieg'd him round with mischiefe-filled hands.
As when a crew of gallants watch the wild muse of a Bore,
Their dogs put after in full crie, he rusheth on before,
Whets, with his lather-making jawes, his crooked tuskes for   370
    blood

[226]

And (holding firme his usuall haunts) breakes through the
    deepned wood,
They charging, though his hote approch be never so abhord:
So to assaile the Jove-lov'd Greeke, the Ilians did accord
And he made through them: first he hurt, upon his shoulder **blade**,
Deiops, a blamelesse man at armes, then sent to endlesse shade   375
Thoon and Ennomus, and strooke the strong Chersidamas,
As from his chariot he leapt downe, beneath his targe of brasse,
Who fell and crawld upon the earth with his sustaining palmes
And left the fight. Nor yet his lance left dealing Martiall almes,
But Socus' brother by both sides, yong Charops, did impresse.   380
Then Princely Socus to his aide made brotherly accesse
And (coming neare) spake in his charge: 'O great Laertes' sonne,
Insatiate in slie stratagems and labours never done,
This houre or thou shalt boast to kill the two Hippasides
And prize their armes, or fall thy selfe in my resolv'd accesse.'   385

Socus wounds Ulysses.   This said, he threw quite through his shield his fell and well-
    driven lance,
Which held way through his curaces and on his ribs did glance,
Plowing the flesh alongst his sides: but Pallas did repell
All inward passage to his life. Ulysses, knowing well
The wound undeadly, (setting backe his foote to forme his   390
    stand)
Thus spake to Socus: 'O thou wretch, thy death is in this hand,
That stay'st my victorie on Troy, and where thy charge was made
In doubtfull terms (or this or that) this shall thy life invade.'
    This frighted Socus to retreate, and in his faint reverse
The lance betwixt his shoulders fell and through his breast did   395
    perse.
Downe fell he sounding, and the king thus playd with his misease:

Ulysses' insultation.   'O Socus, you that make by birth the two Hippasides,
Now may your house and you perceive death can outflie the flier.
Ah wretch, thou canst not scape my vowes. Old Hippasus thy sire
Nor thy well-honord mother's hands, in both which lies thy   400
    worth,
Shall close thy wretched eyes in death, but Vultures dig them forth
And hide them with their darksome wings. But when Ulysses dies,
Divinest Greeks shall tombe my corse with all their obsequies.'
    Now from his bodie and his shield the violent lance he drew
That Princely Socus had infixt; which drawne, a crimson dew   405
Fell from his bosome on the earth: the wound did dare him sore.
And when the furious Troyans saw Ulysses' forced gore,
(Encouraging themselves in grosse) all his destruction vowd.
Then he retir'd and summond aide: thrise showted he allowd

[227]

(As did denote a man ingag'd): thrise Menelaus' eare   410
Observ'd his aid-suggesting voice and, Ajax being neare,
He told him of Ulysses' showts, as if he were enclosd
From all assistance, and advisd their aids might be disposd
Against the Ring that circled him—lest, charg'd with troopes alone,
(Though valiant) he might be opprest whom Greece so built   415
    upon.
    He led, and Ajax seconded: they found their Jove-lov'd king
Circled with foes. As when a den of bloodie Lucerns cling
About a goodly palmed Hart hurt with a hunter's bow,
Whose scape his nimble feet inforce, whilst his warme blood doth
    flow
And his light knees have power to move, but (maistred of his   420
    wound,
Embost within a shadie hill) the Lucerns charge him round
And teare his flesh, when instantly fortune sends in the powres
Of some sterne Lion, with whose sight they flie and he devours:
So charg'd the Ilians Ithacus, many and mightie men.

Ajax and Menelaus to the rescue of Ulysses.

But then made Menelaus in, and horrid Ajax then,   425
Bearing a target like a tower. Close was his violent stand,
And everie way the foe disperst, when, by the royall hand,
Kind Menelaus led away the hurt Laertes' sonne
Till his faire squire had brought his horse. Victorious Telamon
Still plied the foe and put to sword a young Priamides   430
Doryclus, Priam's bastard sonne. Then did his lance impresse
Pandocus and strong Pyrasus, Lysander and Pylartes.
As when a torrent from the hils, swolne with Saturnian showres,
Fals on the fields, beares blasted Oakes and witherd rosine
    flowres,
Loose weeds and all dispersed filth into the Ocean's force: 435
So matchlesse Ajax beat the field and slaughterd men and horse,
Yet had not Hector heard of this, who fought on the left wing
Of all the host, neare those sweet herbs Scamander's flood doth
    spring,
Where many foreheads trode the ground and where the skirmish
    burnd
Neare Nestor and king Idomen; where Hector overturnd   440
The Grecian squadrons, authoring high service with his lance
And skilfull manadge of his horse. Nor yet the discrepance
He made in death betwixt the hosts had made the Greeks retire
If faire-haird Helen's second spouse had not represt the fire
Of bold Machaon's fortitude, who with a three-forkt head   445
In his right shoulder wounded him: then had the Grecians dread

Lest, in his strength declin'd, the foe should slaughter their hurt
    friend.
Then Crete's king urg'd Neleides his chariot to ascend,
And, getting neare him, take him in and beare him to their
    tents:—
'A Surgeon is to be preferd, with physicke ornaments,   450
Before a multitude: his life gives hurt lives native bounds
With sweet inspersion of fit balmes and perfect search of wounds.'
    Thus spake the royall Idomen. Neleides obeyd
And to his chariot presently the wounded Greeke convaid,
The sonne of Æsculapius, the great Phisition.   455
To fleet they flew. Cebriones perceiv'd the slaughter done
By Ajax on the other troopes, and spake to Hector thus:
    'Whiles we encounter Grecians here, sterne Telamonius
Is yonder raging, turning up in heapes our horse and men.
I know him by his spacious shield. Let us turne chariot then   460
Where both of horse and foote the fight most hotely is proposde
In mutuall slaughters. Harke, their throats from cries are never
    closd.'
    This said, with his shrill scourge he strooke the horse, that
    fast ensude,
Stung with his lashes, tossing shields and carkasses imbrude.
The chariot-tree was drownd in blood and th' arches by the   465
    seate
Disperpled from the horses' hoves and from the wheele-bands'
    beate.
Great Hector long'd to breake the rankes and startle their close
    fight,
Who horribly amaz'd the Greeks and plyed their suddaine fright
With busie weapons, ever wingd—his lance, sword, weightie stones.
Yet charg'd he other Leaders' bands, not dreadfull Telamon's,   470
With whom he wisely shund foule blowes. But Jove (that weighs
    above
All humane pow'rs) to Ajax' breast divine repressions drove
And made him shun who shund himselfe: he ceast from fight
    amaz'd,
Cast on his backe his seaven-fold shield and round about him
    gaz'd
Like one turnd wilde, lookt on himselfe in his distract retreate: 475
Knee before knee did scarcely move. As when from heards of
    Neate
Whole threaves of Bores and mungrils chace a Lion skulking
    neare,
Loth he should taint the wel-prisd fat of any stall-fed steere,

Consuming all the night in watch; he (greedie of his prey)
Oft thrusting on is oft thrust off, so thicke the Javelins play   480
On his bold charges and so hote the burning firebrands shine,
Which he (though horrible) abhors about his glowing eyne
And early his great heart retires: so Ajax from the foe,
For feare their fleet should be inflam'd, gainst his swolne heart
    did go.

*Another simile
expressing the maner
of Ajax' retreate.*

    As when a dull mill Asse comes neare a goodly field of corne,   485
Kept from the birds by children's cries, the boyes are overborne
By his insensible approach and simply he will eate,
About whom many wands are broke, and still the children·beate,
And still the selfe-providing Asse doth with their weaknesse
    beare,
Not stirring till his panch be full, and scarcely then will stere: 490
So the huge sonne of Telamon amongst the Troyans far'd,
Bore showers of darts upon his shield, yet scornd to flie as skar'd;
And so kept softlie on his way, nor would he mend his pace
For all their violent pursuits, that still did arme the chace
With singing lances. But at last, when their Cur-like presumes,   495
More urg'd, the more forborne, his spirits did rarifie their fumes
And he revokt his active strength, turnd head and did repell
The horse troopes that were new made in; twixt whom the fight
    grew fell
And by degrees he stole retreate, yet with such puissant stay
That none could passe him to the fleet. In both the armies' sway   500
He stood and from strong hands receiv'd sharpe Javelins on his
    shield,
Where many stucke, throwne on before; many fell short in field
Ere the white bodie they could reach and stucke, as telling how
They purposd to have pierc't his flesh. His perill pierced now
The eyes of Prince Eurypylus, Euæmon's famous sonne,   505
Who came close on and with his dart strooke Duke Apisaon,
Whose surname was Phausiades, even to the concrete blood
That makes the liver: on the earth out gusht his vitall flood.
Eurypylus made in and easd his shoulders of his armes;
Which Paris seeing, he drew his bow and wreakt in part the   510
    harmes
Of his good friend Phausiades: his arrow he let flie
That smote Eurypylus and brake in his attainted thie.
Then tooke he troope to shun blacke death, and to the flyers
    cride:

*Eurypylus to the
Greekes.*

    'Princes, and Leaders of the Greeks, stand and repulse the tide
Of this our honour-wracking chace. Ajax is drownd in darts,   515

I feare past scape. Turne, honord friends, helpe out his ventrous
  parts.'
Thus spake the wounded Greeke: the sound cast on their backs
  their shields
And raisd their darts; to whose reliefe Ajax his person wields.
Then stood he firmely with his friends, retiring their retire.
And thus both hosts indifferent joynd; the fight grew hote as   520
  fire.
  Now had Neleides' sweating steeds brought him and his hurt
    friend
Amongst their Fleet. Æacides, that wishly did intend
(Standing asterne his tall-neckt ship) how deepe the skirmish
  drew
Amongst the Greeks and with what ruth the insecution grew,
Saw Nestor bring Machaon hurt, and from within did call   525
His friend Patroclus, who like Mars in forme celestiall
Came forth with first sound of his voice (first spring of his
  decay)

Achilles to Patroclus. And askt his Princely friend's desire. 'Deare friend,' said he,
  'this day
I doubt not will enforce the Greeks to swarme about my knees:
I see unsufferd Need imployd in their extremities.   530
Go, sweet Patroclus, and enquire of old Neleides
Whom he brought wounded from the fight: by his backe parts
    I guesse
It is Machaon, but his face I could not well descrie,
They past me in such earnest speed.' Patroclus presently
Obeyd his friend and ran to know. They now descended were   535
And Nestor's squire Eurymedon the horses did ungeare.
Themselves stood neare th' extremest shore, to let the gentle aire
Drie up their sweat; then to the tent, where Hecamed the faire
Set chaires and for the wounded Prince a potion did prepare.
  This Hecamed, by war's hard fate, fell to old Nestor's share 540
When Thetis' sonne sackt Tenedos. She was the Princely seed
Of worthie king Arsinous, and by the Greeks decreed
The prize of Nestor, since all men in counsell he surpast.
First, a faire table she apposd of which the feet were grac't
With blewish mettall mixt with blacke; and on the same   545
    she put
A brasse fruit dish, in which she serv'd a holsome Onion cut
For pittance to the potion, and honey newly wrought,
And bread, the fruite of sacred meale. Then to the boord
    she brought

[231]

A right faire cup, with gold studs driven, which Nestor did
     transfer
From Pylos; on whose swelling sides foure handles fixed were   550
And upon everie handle sate a paire of doves of gold,
Some billing and some pecking meate. Two gilt feet did uphold
The antique body, and withall, so weightie was the cup
That, being proposd brim full of wine, one scarse could lift
     it up:
Yet Nestor drunke in it with ease, spite of his yeares' respect.   555
In this the Goddesse-like faire Dame a potion did confect
With good old wine of Pramnius, and scrap't into the wine
Cheese made of Goate's milke, and on it sperst flow'r exceeding
    fine.
In this sort for the wounded Lord the potion she prepar'd
And bad him drinke: for companie, with him old Nestor   560
    shar'd.
    Thus physically quencht they thirst, and then their spirits
    reviv'd
With pleasant conference. And now Patroclus, being arriv'd,
Made stay at th' entrie of the tent. Old Nestor, seeing it,
Rose and receiv'd him by the hand and faine would have him sit.
He set that courtesie aside, excusing it with hast,   565
Since his much-to-be-reverenc't friend sent him to know who
    past
(Wounded with him in chariot) so swiftly through the shore—
'Whom now,' said he, 'I see and know, and now can stay no more.
You know, good father, our great friend is apt to take offence,
Whose fierie temper will inflame sometimes with innocence.'   570

Nestor to Patroclus.   He answerd: 'When will Peleus' sonne some royall pittie show
On his thus wounded contrimen? Ah, is he yet to know
How much affliction tires our host—how our especiall aide
(Tainted with lances) at their tents are miserably laide?
Ulysses, Diomed, our King, Eurypylus, Machaon   575
All hurt, and all our worthiest friends; yet no compassion
Can supple thy friend's friendlesse breast. Doth he reserve
    his eye
Till our fleet burne and we our selves one after other die?
Alas, my forces are not now as in my yonger life!
Oh would to God I had that strength I used in the strife   580
Betwixt us and the Elians, for Oxen to be driven,
When Itymoneus' loftie soule was by my valour given
As sacrifice to destinie, Hypirochus' strong sonne
That dwelt in Elis and fought first in our contention.
We forrag'd (as proclaimed foes) a wondrous wealthie boote   585

And he, in rescue of his Herds, fell breathlesse at my foote.
All the Dorpe Bores with terror fled: our prey was rich and great,
Twise five and twentie flocks of sheepe, as many herds of neate,
As many goates and nastie swine, a hundred fiftie mares
All sorrell, most with sucking foales; and these soone-monied   590
    wares
We drave into Neleius' towne, faire Pylos, all by night.
My father's heart was glad to see so much good fortune quite
The forward mind of his young sonne, that usde my youth in
    deeds
And would not smother it in moods. Now drew the Sun's bright
    steeds
Light from the hils: our heralds now accited all that were   595
Endamag'd by the Elians: our Princes did appeare:
Our boote was parted: many men th' Epeians much did owe,
That (being our neighbors) they did spoile: afflictions did so flow
On us poore Pylians, though but few. In brake great Hercules
To our sad confines of late yeares, and wholly did suppresse   600
Our haplesse Princes. Twice six sonnes renownd Neleius bred;
Onely my selfe am left of all, the rest subdude and dead.
And this was it that made so proud the base Epeian bands
On their neare neighbors, being opprest, to lay injurious hands.
A heard of Oxen for himselfe, a mightie flocke of sheepe,   605
My Syre selected, and made choice of shepheards for their keep;
And from the generall spoyle he culd three hundred of the best:
The Elians ought him infinite, most plagu'd of all the rest.
Foure wager-winning horse he lost and chariots intervented,
Being led to an appointed race. The prize that was presented   610
Was a religious threefoote urne. Augeas was the king
That did detaine them and dismist their keeper sorrowing
For his lov'd charge, lost with foule words. Then both for
    words and deeds
My Sire, being worthily incenst, thus justly he proceeds
To satisfaction, in first choice of all our wealthie prize;   615
And as he shar'd much, much he left his subjects to suffise,
That none might be opprest with power or want his portion due.
Thus for the publike good we shar'd. Then we to temples drue
Our complete citie, and to heaven we thankfull rights did burne
For our rich conquest. The third day ensuing our returne   620
The Elians flew on us in heapes: their generall Leaders were
The two Moliones, two boyes untrained in the feare
Of horrid warre or use of strength. A certaine citie shines
Upon a loftie Prominent and in th' extreme confines
Of sandie Pylos, seated where Alpheus' flood doth run   625

[233]

And cald Thryessa: this they sieg'd and gladly would have wun;
But (having past through all our fields) Minerva as our spie
Fell from Olympus in the night and arm'd us instantly.
Nor mustred she unwilling men nor unprepar'd for force.
My Sire yet would not let me arme, but hid away my horse,   630
Esteeming me no souldier yet: yet shin'd I nothing lesse
Amongst our Gallants, though on foote: Minerva's mightinesse
Led me to fight and made me beare a souldier's worthie name.
     There is a floud fals into sea and his crookt course doth frame
Close to Arena, and is cald bright Minyæus' streame.   635
There made we halt, and there the Sun cast many a glorious
          beame
On our bright armours: horse and foote insea'd together there;
Then marcht we on. By fierie noone we saw the sacred cleare
Of great Alpheus, where to Jove we did faire sacrifice,
And to the azure God that rules the under-liquid skies   640
We offerd up a solemne Bull, a bull t' Alpheus' name,
And to the blew-eyd maid we burnd a heifer never tame.
Now was it night: we supt and slept about the flood in armes.
The foe laide hard siege to our towne and shooke it with alarmes;
But for prevention of their splenes a mightie worke of warre   645
Appeard behind them. For, as soone as Phœbus' fierie Carre
Cast night's foule darknes from his wheeles, (invoking reverend
          Jove
And the unconquerd maide—his birth) we did th' event approve
And gave them battell. First of all, I slue (the armie saw)
The mightie souldier Mulius, Augeias' sonne in law,   650
And spoyld him of his one-hov'd horse: his eldest daughter was
Bright Agamede that for skill in simples did surpasse
And knew as many kind of drugs as earth's brode center bred.
Him charg'd I with my brasse-arm'd lance: the dust receiv'd
          him dead.
I (leaping to his chariot) amongst the formost prest,   655
And the great-hearted Elians fled frighted, seeing their best
And lofti'st souldier taken downe, the Generall of their horse.
I follow'd like a blacke whirlwind and did for prize enforce
Full fiftie chariots, everie one furnisht with two arm'd men,
Who eate the earth, slaine with my lance. And I had slaughterd   660
          then
The two young boyes, Moliones, if their world-circling Sire,
Great Neptune, had not saft their lives and covered their retire
With unpierc't clouds. Then Jove bestow'd a haughtie victorie
Upon us Pylians. For so long we did the chase apply,

[234]

Slaughtring and making spoile of armes, till sweet Buprasius'   665
   soile,
Alesius and Olenia were fam'd with our recoile.
For there Minerva turnd our power; and there the last I slew,
As when our battell joyn'd, the first: the Pylians then withdrew
To Pylos from Buprasius. Of all the Immortals then,
They most thankt Jove for victorie, Nestor the most of men.   670
Such was I ever, if I were employd with other Peeres,
And I had honour of my youth, which dies not in my yeares.
But Great Achilles onely joyes habilitie of act
In his brave Prime and doth not daine t' impart it where tis lackt.
No doubt he will extremely mourne, long after, that blacke   675
   howre
Wherein our ruine shall be wrought and rue his ruthlesse powre.
O friend, my memorie revives the charge Menœtius gave
Thy towardnesse when thou setst forth to keepe out of the grave
Our wounded honour. I my selfe and wise Ulysses were
Within the roome, where everie word then spoken we did   680
   heare;
For we were come to Peleus' Court as we did mustering passe
Through rich Achaia where thy Sire, renownd Menœtius, was,
Thy selfe and great Æacides—when Peleus the King
To thunder-loving Jove did burne an Oxe for offering
In his Court-yard: a cup of gold crownd with red wine he held   685
On th' holy Incensorie pour'd. You, when the Oxe was feld,
Were dressing his divided lims: we in the Portall stood.
Achilles seeing us come so neare, his honorable blood
Was strooke with a respective shame, rose, tooke us by the hands,
Brought us both in and made us sit and usde his kind   690
   commands
For seemely hospitable rights, which quickly were apposd.
Then (after needfulnesse of foode) I first of all disclosd
The royall cause of our repaire, mov'd you and your great
   friend
To consort our renown'd designes: both straight did condescend:
Your fathers knew it, gave consent and grave instruction   695
To both your valours. Peleus charg'd his most unequald sonne
To governe his victorious strength and shine past all the rest
In honour as in meere maine force. Then were thy partings blest
With deare advices from thy Sire. "My loved sonne," said he,
"Achilles by his grace of birth superiour is to thee   700
And for his force more excellent, yet thou more ripe in yeares.
Then with sound counsels (age's fruits) imploy his honord eares;
Command and overrule his moodes; his nature will obay

In any charge discreetly given that doth his good assay."
 Thus charg'd thy Sire, which thou forgetst. Yet now at last   705
 approve
(With forced reference of these) th' attraction of his love.
Who knowes if sacred influence may blesse thy good intent
And enter with thy gracious words even to his full consent?
The admonition of a friend is sweet and vehement.
If any Oracle he shun or if his mother Queene   710
Hath brought him some instinct from Jove that fortifies his
 spleene,
Let him resigne command to thee of all his Myrmidons
And yeeld by that meanes some repulse to our confusions,
Adorning thee in his bright armes, that his resembled forme
May haply make thee thought himselfe and calme this hostile   715
 storme—
That so a little we may ease our overcharged hands,
Draw some breath, not expire it all. The foe but faintly stands
Beneath his labours, and your charge, being fierce and freshly
 given,
They easly from our tents and fleet may to their walls be driven.'
 This mov'd the good Patroclus' mind, who made his utmost   720
 haste
T' informe his friend; and as the fleet of Ithacus he past
(At which their markets were disposd, counsels and martiall
 courts
And where to th' Altars of the Gods they made divine resorts)
He met renownd Eurypylus, Euæmon's noble sonne,
Halting, his thigh hurt with a shaft; the liquid sweate did run   725
Downe from his shoulders and his browes, and from his raging
 wound
Forth flow'd his melancholy blood, yet still his mind was sound.
His sight in kinde Patroclus' breast to sacred pittie turnd
And (nothing more immartiall for true ruth) thus he mournd:
'Ah wretched progenie of Greece, Princes, dejected kings,   730
Was it your fates to nourish beasts and serve the outcast wings
Of savage Vultures here in Troy? Tell me, Euæmon's fame,
Do yet the Greeks withstand his force whom yet no force can
 tame?
Or are they hopelesse throwne to death by his resistlesse lance?'
'Divine Patroclus,' he replide, 'no more can Greece advance   735
Defensive weapons, but to fleet they headlong must retire,
For those that to this howre have held our fleet from hostile fire
And are the bulwarks of our host lie wounded at their tents,
And Troy's unvanquishable powre still as it toiles augments.

[236]

But take me to thy blacke-sternd ship, save me, and from my   740
    thie
Cut out this arrow and the blood that is ingor'd and drie
Wash with warme water from the wound: then gentle salves
    apply,
Which thou knowest best—thy Princely friend hath taught thee
    surgerie,
Whom (of all Centaures the most just) Chiron did institute.
Thus to thy honorable hands my ease I prosecute,   745
Since our Physitians cannot helpe: Machaon at his tent
Needs a Physitian himselfe, being Leach and patient,
And Podalirius in the field the sharpe conflict sustaines.'
Strong Menœtiades replide: 'How shall I ease thy paines?
What shall we do, Eurypylus? I am to use all haste   750
To signifie to Thetis' sonne occurrents that have past,
At Nestor's honorable suite. But be that worke atchiev'd,
When this is done, I will not leave thy torments unreliev'd.'
   This said, athwart his backe he cast, beneath his breast,
    his arme
And nobly helpt him to his tent. His servants, seeing his harme,   755
Dispread Ox-hides upon the earth whereon Machaon lay.
Patroclus cut out the sharpe shaft and clearely washt away
With luke-warme water the blacke blood: then twixt his hands
    he brusde
A sharpe and mitigatorie roote, which, when he had infusde
Into the greene well-cleansed wound, the paines he felt before   760
Were well, and, instantly allaid, the wound did bleed no more.

The End of the Eleventh Booke

THE TWELFTH BOOKE

of

HOMER'S ILIADS

THE ARGUMENT

The Troyans at the trench their powres engage,
Though greeted by a bird of bad presage.
In five parts they divide their powre, to skale,
And Prince Sarpedon forceth downe the pale.
Great Hector, from the Ports, teares out a stone   5
And with so dead a strength he sets it gone
At those brode gates the Grecians made to guard
Their tents and ships that, broken and unbard,
They yeeld way to his powre; when all contend
To reach the ships, which all at last ascend.   10

Another Argument

My workes the Troyans all the grace
And doth the Grecian Fort deface.

Patroclus thus emploid in cure of hurt Eurypylus,
Both hosts are all for other wounds doubly contentious—
One all wayes labouring to expell, the other to invade.
Nor could the brode dike of the Greeks, nor that strong wall
    they made
To guard their fleete be long unrac't, because it was not raisd   5
By grave direction of the Gods, nor were their Deities praisd
(When they begun) with Hecatombes, that then they might
    be sure
(Their strength being season'd wel with heaven's) it should have
    force t' endure,
And so the safeguard of their fleete and all their treasure there
Infallibly had bene confirm'd; when now their bulwarks were   10
Not onely without powre of checke to their assaulting foe
(Even now, as soone as they were built) but apt to overthrow,

[238]

Such as in verie little time shall burie all their sight
And thought that ever they were made. As long as the despight
Of great Æacides held up and Hector went not downe   15
And that by those two meanes stood safe king Priam's sacred
    towne,
So long their rampire had some use (though now it gave
    some way),
But when Troy's best men sufferd Fate and many Greeks did pay
Deare for their sufferance, then the rest home to their
    countrie turnd
The tenth yeare of their warres at Troy, and Troy was sackt   20
    and burnd.
And then the Gods fell to their Fort, then they their powres
    imploy
To ruine their worke and left lesse of that than they of Troy.

*Neptune and Phœbus
overturne the Grecian
rampire.*

Neptune and Phœbus tumbl'd downe from the Idalian hils
An inundation of all floods that thence the brode sea fils
On their huge rampire: in one glut all these together rorde,   25
Rhesus, Heptaporus, Rhodius, Scamander the adorde,

*The names of the
rivers about Troy.*

Caresus, Simois, Grenicus, Æsepus: of them all
Apollo open'd the rough mouths and made their lustie fall
Ravish the dustie champian where many a helme and shield
And halfe-god race of men were strew'd. And that all these   30
    might yeeld
Full tribute to the heavenly worke, Neptune and Phœbus wun
Jove to unburthen the blacke wombes of clouds (fild by the Sun)
And poure them into all their streames, that quickly they
    might send
The huge wall swimming to the Sea. Nine dayes their lights
    did spend
To nights in tempests, and, when all their utmost depth   35
    had made,
Jove, Phœbus, Neptune all came downe and all in state
    did wade
To ruine of that impious fort. Great Neptune went before,
Wrought with his trident, and the stones, trunkes, rootes of trees
    he tore
Out of the rampire, tost them all into the Hellespont,
Even all the prowd toile of the Greeks with which they durst   40
    confront
The to-be-shunned Deities, and not a stone remaind
Of all their huge foundations; all with the earth were plaind.
Which done, againe the Gods turnd backe the silver-flowing
    floods

By that vast channell through whose vaults they pourd abrode
    their broods
And coverd all the ample shore againe with dustie sand.   45
And this the end was of that wall, where now so many a hand
Was emptied of stones and darts, contending to invade,
Where Clamor spent so high a throate, and where the fell
    blowes made
The new-built woodden turrets grone. And here the Greeks
    were pent,
Tam'd with the iron whip of Jove, that terrors vehement   50

Hector like a whirlwind and Lion.

Shooke over them by Hector's hand, who was (in everie thought)
The terror-maister of the field and like a whirlewind fought,
As fresh as in his morn's first charge. And as a savage Bore
Or Lion, hunted long, at last with hounds' and hunters' store
Is compast round; they charge him close and stand (as in a towre 55
They had inchac't him) pouring on of darts an iron showre;
His glorious heart yet, nought appald and forcing forth his way,
Here overthrowes a troope and there a running ring doth stay
His utter passage when againe that stay he overthrowes,
And then the whole field frees his rage: so Hector wearies   60
    blowes,
Runs out his charge upon the Fort, and all his force would force
To passe the dike: which being so deepe, they could not get
    their horse
To venter on, but trample, snore and, on the verie brinke,
To neigh with spirit, yet still stand off. Nor would a humane
    thinke
The passage safe, or, if it were, twas lesse safe for retreate,   65
The dike being everie where so deep and (where twas least
    deep) set
With stakes exceeding thicke, sharpe, strong, that horse could
    never passe,
Much lesse their chariots after them: yet for the foote there was
Some hopefull service, which they wisht. Polydamas then spake:

Polydamas' sound counsell to Hector.

   'Hector, and all our friends of Troy, we indiscreetly make   70
Offer of passage with our horse. Ye see the stakes, the wall,
Impossible for horse to take; nor can men fight at all,
The place being streight and much more apt to let us take
    our bane
Than give the enemie. And yet, if Jove decree the wane
Of Grecian glory utterly and so bereave their hearts   75
That we may freely charge them thus, and then will take
    our parts,

I would with all speed wish th' assault, that ugly shame
    might shed
(Thus farre from home) these Grecians' bloods. But, if they
    once turne head
And sallie on us from their fleet, when in so deepe a dike
We shall lie struggling, not a man of all our hoast is like   80
To live and carrie backe the newes. And, therefore, be it thus:
Here leave we horse, kept by our men, and all on foot let us
Hold close together and attend the grace of Hector's guide;
And then they shall not beare our charge, our conquest shall
    be dide
In their lives' purples.' This advice pleasd Hector, for   85
    twas sound,
Who first obeyd it and full-arm'd betooke him to the ground.
And then all left their chariots when he was seene to leade,
Rushing about him, and gave up each chariot and steed
To their directors to be kept in all procinct of warre,
There, and on that side of the dike. And thus the rest prepare   90
Their onset. In five regiments they all their powre divide,
Each regiment allow'd three Chiefes, of all which even the pride
Serv'd in great Hector's Regiment—for all were set on fire
(Their passage beaten through the wall) with hazardous desire
That they might once but fight at fleete. With Hector   95
    Captaines were
Polydamas and Cebriones, who was his chariotere,
But Hector found that place a worse. Chiefes of the second band
Were Paris and Alcathous, Agenor. The command
The third strong Phalanx had was given to th' Augure Helenus,
Deiphobus, that God-like man, and mightie Asius,   100
Even Asius Hyrtacides that from Arisbe rode
The huge bay horse and had his house where river Selleës flowde.
The fourth charge good Æneas led, and with him were combinde
Archelochus and Acamas (Antenor's dearest kinde
And excellent at everie fight). The fifth brave companie   105
Sarpedon had to charge, who chusde for his command's supply
Asteropæus great in armes, and Glaucus, for both these
Were best of all men but himselfe: but he was fellowlesse.
   Thus fitted with their well-wrought shields, downe the steepe
    dike they go,
And (thirstie of the wall's assault) beleeve in overthrow,   110
Not doubting but with headlong fals to tumble downe the
    Greeks
From their blacke navie. In which trust, all on, and no man seeks
To crosse Polydamas' advice with any other course

But Asīus Hyrtacides, who (prowd of his bay horse)

Would not forsake them nor his man that was their manager   115

(Foole that he was), but all to fleete, and little knew how neare

An ill death sat him, and a sure, and that he never more

Must looke on loftie Ilion; but lookes, and all, before

Put on th' all-covering mist of Fate that then did hang upon

Idomenætis.   The lance of great Deucalides: he fatally rusht on   120

The left hand way by which the Greeks with horse and chariot

Came usually from field to fleet. Close to the gates he got,

Which both unbard and ope he found, that so the easier might

An entrie be for any friend that was behind in flight;

Yet not much easier for a foe, because there was a guard   125

Maintaind upon it past his thought—who still put for it hard,

Eagerly showting, and with him were five more friends of name

That would not leave him, though none else would hunt that

    way for fame

(In their free choice) but he himselfe. Orestes, Iamenus,

And Adamas Asiades, Thoon, Œnomaus   130

Were those that followed Asius. Within the gates they found

Two eminently valorous, that from the race renownd

Of the right valiant Lapithes deriv'd their high descent.

Such maketh Virgil   Fierce Leonteus was the one, like Mars in detriment;

Pandarus and Bitias.   The other mightie Polypœt, the great Pirithous' sonne.   135

These stood within the loftie gates, and nothing more did shun

The charge of Asius and his friends than two high hill-bred Okes,

Well-rooted in the binding earth, obey the airie strokes

Of wind and weather, standing firme gainst everie season's spight.

Yet they poure on continued showts and beare their shields   140

    upright:

When in the meane space Polypœt and Leonteus cheard

Their souldiers to the fleet's defence. But when the rest had

    heard

The Troyans in attempt to skale, Clamor and flight did flow

Amongst the Grecians; and then (the rest dismaid) these two

Met Asius entring, thrust him backe and fought before their   145

    doores.

Nor far'd they then like Okes that stood, but as a brace of Bores,

Coucht in their owne bred hill, that heare a sort of hunters

    showt

And hounds in hote traile coming on, then from their dens

    breake out,

Traverse their force and suffer not, in wildnesse of their way,

About them any plant to stand, but thickets, offering stay,   150

Breake through and rend up by the roots, whet gnashes into aire,

Which Tumult fils with showts, hounds, horns and all the hote
    affaire
Beates at their bosomes: so their armes rung with assailing blowes,
And so they stird them in repulse, right well assur'd that those
Who were within and on the wall would adde their parts—   155
    who knew
They now fought for their tents, fleet, lives and fame, and
    therefore threw
Stones from the wals and towres as thicke as when a drift wind
    shakes
Blacke clouds in peeces and plucks snow in great and plumie
    flakes
From their soft bosomes, till the ground be wholly cloth'd
    in white.
So earth was hid with stones and darts—darts from the Troyan   160
    fight,
Stones from the Greeks, that on the helms and bossie Troyan
    shields
Kept such a rapping it amaz'd great Asius, who now yeelds
Sighes, beates his thighes and, in a rage, his fault to Jove applies:

'O Jove,' said he, 'now cleare thou shew'st thou art a friend
    to lies,
Pretending in the flight of Greece the making of it good   165
To all their ruines, which I thought could never be withstood.

Yet they, as yellow Waspes or Bees (that having made their nest
The gasping Cranny of a hill) when for a hunter's feast
Hunters come hote and hungrie in and dig for honny Comes,
They flie upon them, strike and sting, and from their hollow   170
    homes
Will not be beaten but defend their labour's fruite and brood.
No more will these be from their port but either lose their blood
(Although but two against all us) or be our prisoners made.'
All this, to do his action grace, could not firme Jove perswade,
Who for the generall counsell stood and (gainst his singular   175
    brave)
Bestow'd on Hector that daie's fame. Yet he and these behave
Themselves thus nobly at this port: but how at other ports
And all alongst the stony wall sole force, gainst force and forts,
Rag'd in contention twixt both hoasts it were no easie thing
(Had I the bosome of a God) to tune to life and sing.   180
The Troyans fought not of themselves: a fire from heaven was
    throwne
That ran amongst them, through the wall, meere added to their
    owne.

The Greeks held not their owne: weake griefe went with her
    witherd hand
And dipt it deepely in their spirits since they could not
    command
Their forces to abide the field, whom harsh Necessitie   185
(To save those ships should bring them home) and their good
    forts' supply
Drave to th' expulsive fight they made, and this might stoope
    them more
Than Need it selfe could elevate, for even Gods did deplore
Their dire estates and all the Gods that were their aids in war,
Who (though they could not cleare their plights) yet were their   190
    friends thus far
Still to uphold the better sort. For then did Polypœt passe
A lance at Damasus whose helme was made with cheekes of
    brasse
Yet had not proofe enough: the pyle drave through it and his
    skull:
His braine in blood drownd and the man, so late so spiritfull,
Fell now quite spirit-lesse to earth. So emptied he the veines   195
Of Pylon's and Ormenus' lives. And then Leonteus gaines
The life's end of Hippomachus, Antimachus his sonne:
His lance fell at his girdle stead and with his end begun
Another end. Leonteus left him and through the prease
(His keene sword drawne) ran desperatly upon Antiphates   200
And livelesse tumbled him to earth. Nor could all these lives
    quench
His fierie spirit that his flame in Menon's blood did drench,
And rag'd up even to Iamen's and yong Orestes' life.
All, heapt together, made their peace in that red field of strife,
Whose faire armes while the victors spoild, the youth of Ilion   205
(Of which there serv'd the most and best) still boldly built upon
The wisedome of Polydamas and Hector's matchlesse strength,
And follow'd, fild with wondrous spirit, with wish and hope at
    length
(The Greeks' wall wun) to fire their fleet. But (having past
    the dike
And willing now to passe the wall) this prodigie did strike   210
Their hearts with some deliberate stay. A high-flowne Eagle sorde
On their troope's left hand and sustaind a Dragon all engorde
In her strong seres, of wondrous sise and yet had no such checke
In life and spirit but still she fought and, turning backe her
    necke,
So stung the Eagle's gorge that downe she cast her fervent prey   215

Amongst the multitude and tooke upon the winds her way,
Crying with anguish. When they saw a branded Serpent sprawle
So full amongst them, from above and from Jove's fowle
    let fall,
They tooke it an ostent from him, stood frighted; and their cause

Polydamas to Hector. Polydamas thought just, and spake: 'Hector, you know   220
    applause
Of humour hath bene farre from me, nor fits it, or in warre
Or in affaires of Court, a man imploid in publicke care
To blanch things further than their truth, or flatter any powre:
And therefore, for that simple course, your strength hath oft
    bene sowre
To me in counsels. Yet againe what shewes in my thoughts best   225
I must discover. Let us ceasse and make their flight our rest
For this daye's honor, and not now attempt the Grecian fleet.
For this (I feare) will be th' event—the prodigie doth meet
So full with our affaire in hand. As this high-flying fowle
Upon the left wing of our host (implying our controwle)   230
Hoverd above us and did trusse within her golden seres
A Serpent so embrew'd and bigge, which yet (in all her feares)
Kept life and fervent spirit to fight, and wrought her owne
    release,
Nor did the Eagle's Airie feed: so, though we thus farre prease
Upon the Grecians and perhaps may overrune their wall,   235
Our high minds aiming at their fleet, and that we much appall
Their trussed spirits, yet are they so Serpent-like disposd
That they will fight, though in our seres, and will at length
    be losd
With all our outcries: and the life of many a Troyan breast
Shall with the Eagle flie before we carrie to our nest   240
Them or their navie.' Thus expounds the Augure this ostent,
Whose depth he knowes and these should feare. Hector, with
    countenance bent,

Hector to Polydamas. Thus answerd him: 'Polydamas, your depth in augurie
I like not, and know passing well thou dost not satisfie
Thy selfe in this opinion or, if thou think'st it true,   245
Thy thoughts the Gods blind, to advise and urge that as our due
That breakes our duties, and to Jove, whose vow and signe to me
Is past directly for our speed; yet light-wingd birds must be
(By thy advice) our Oracles, whose feathers little stay
My serious actions. What care I if this or th' other way   250
Their wild wings sway them—if the right, on which the Sunne
    doth rise,
Or to the left hand, where he sets? Tis Jove's high counsell flies

With those wings that shall beare up us—Jove's, that both earth
    and heaven,
Both men and Gods, sustaines and rules. One augurie is given
To order all men best of all—fight for thy countrie's right.   255
But why fearst thou our further charge? For though the
    dangerous fight
Strew all men here about the fleet, yet thou needst never feare
To beare their Fates; thy warie heart will never trust thee where
An enemie's looke is and yet fight: for, if thou dar'st abstaine
Or whisper into any eare an abstinence so vaine   260
As thou advisest, never feare that any foe shall take
Thy life from thee, for tis this lance.' This said, all forwards
    make,
Himselfe the first: yet before him exulting Clamor flew,
And thunder-loving Jupiter from loftie Ida blew
A storme that usherd their assault and made them charge like   265
    him.
It drave directly on the fleet a dust so fierce and dim
That it amaz'd the Grecians but was a grace divine
To Hector and his following troopes, who wholly did encline
To him, being now in grace with Jove, and so put boldly on
To raze the rampire, in whose height they fiercely set upon   270
The Parrapets and puld them downe, rac't every formost fight,
And all the Butteresses of stone that held their towers upright
They tore away with Crowes of Iron, and hop't to ruine all.
  The Greeks yet stood and still repaird the forefights of
    their wall
With hides of Oxen, and from thence they pourd downe   275
    stones in showres
Upon the underminers' heads. Within the formost towres
Both the Ajaces had command, who answer'd everie part
Th' assaulters and their souldiers represt and put in heart,
Repairing valour as their wall—spake some faire, some reprov'd,
Who ever made not good his place; and thus they all sorts   280
    mov'd:
  'O countrimen, now need in aid would have excesse be spent;
The excellent must be admir'd, the meanest excellent;
The worst do well; in changing warre all should not be alike,
Nor any idle. Which to know fits all, lest Hector strike
Your minds with frights, as eares with threats. Forward be all   285
    your hands:
Urge one another: this doubt downe that now betwixt us stands,
Jove will go with us to their wals.' To this effect alowd

Spake both the Princes, and as high (with this) th' expulsion
    flow'd.

Simile.

And as in winter time when Jove his cold-sharpe javelines
    throwes

Amongst us mortals and is mov'd to white earth with his   290
    snowes

(The winds asleepe) he freely poures, till highest Prominents,

Hill tops, low meddowes and the fields that crowne with most
    contents

The toiles of men, sea ports and shores are hid, and everie place

But floods (that snowe's faire tender flakes, as their owne brood,
    embrace):

So both sides coverd earth with stones, so both for life contend   295

To shew their sharpnesse. Through the wall, uprore stood up
    on end.

Nor had great Hector and his friends the rampire overrun

If heaven's great Counsellour, high Jove, had not inflam'd his
    sonne

Sarpedon (like the forrest's king when he on Oxen flies)

Against the Grecians: his round targe he to his arme applies,   300

Brasse-leav'd without and all within thicke Oxe-hides quilted
    hard,

The verge naild round with rods of gold; and with two darts
    prepard

He leades his people. As ye see a mountaine Lion fare,

Long kept from prey, in forcing which his high mind makes
    him dare

Assault upon the whole full fold, though guarded never so   305

With well-arm'd men and eager dogs—away he will not go

But venture on and either snatch a prey or be a prey:

So far'd divine Sarpedon's mind, resolv'd to force his way

Through all the fore-fights and the wall. Yet, since he did not see

Others as great as he in name, as great in mind as he,   310

He spake to Glaucus: 'Glaucus, say why are we honord more

*Sarpedon's speech to
Glaucus, never
equalled by any (in
this kind) of all that
have written.*

Than other men of Lycia in place—with greater store

Of meates and cups, with goodlier roofes, delightsome gardens,
    walks,

More lands and better, so much wealth that Court and countrie
    talks

Of us and our possessions and every way we go   315

Gaze on us as we were their Gods? This where we dwell is so:

The shores of Xanthus ring of this: and shall not we exceed

As much in merit as in noise? Come, be we great in deed

As well as looke, shine not in gold but in the flames of fight,

That so our neat-arm'd Lycians may say: "See, these are right   320
Our kings, our Rulers: these deserve to eate and drinke the best;
These governe not ingloriously; these thus exceed the rest,
Do more than they command to do." O friend, if keeping backe
Would keepe backe age from us, and death, and that we might
    not wracke
In this life's humane sea at all, but that deferring now   325
We shund death ever—nor would I halfe this vaine valour show,
Nor glorifie a folly so, to wish thee to advance:
But, since we must go though not here, and that, besides the
    chance
Proposd now, there are infinite fates of other sort in death
Which (neither to be fled nor scap't) a man must sinke   330
    beneath—
Come, trie we if this sort be ours and either render thus
Glorie to others or make them resigne the like to us.'

Sarpedon and Glaucus
charge together.

    This motion Glaucus shifted not but (without words) obeyd.
Fore-right went both: a mightie troope of Lycians followed.
Which by Menestheus observ'd, his haire stood up on end,   335
For at the towre where he had charge he saw Calamitie bend
Her horrid browes in their approch. He threw his looks about
The whole fights neare, to see what Chiefe might helpe the
    miserie out
Of his poore souldiers, and beheld where both th' Ajaces fought,
And Teucer, newly come from fleete, whom it would profit   340
    nought
To call, since Tumult on their helmes, shields and upon the
    ports
Laid such lowde claps; for everie way defences of all sorts
Were adding as Troy tooke away, and Clamor flew so high
Her wings strooke heaven and drownd all voice. The two Dukes
    yet so nigh
And at the offer of assault he to th' Ajaces sent   345

Thoos sent to the
Ajaces for aide by
Menestheus.

Thoos the herald with this charge: 'Run to the regiment
Of both th' Ajaces and call both, for both were better here
Since here will slaughter instantly be more enforc't than there.
The Lycian Captaines this way make, who in the fights of stand
Have often shew'd much excellence: yet if laborious hand   350
Be there more needfull than I hope, at least afford us some:
Let Ajax Telamonius and th' Archer Teucer come.'
    The Herald hasted and arriv'd, and both th' Ajaces told
That Peteus' noble sonne desir'd their little labour would
Employ it selfe in succouring him. Both their supplies were   355
    best

[248]

Since death assaild his quarter most, for on it fiercely prest
The well-prov'd mightie Lycian Chiefs. Yet if the service there
Allowd not both, he praid that one part of his charge would
    beare
And that was Ajax Telamon, with whom he wisht would come
The Archer Teucer. Telamon left instantly his roome   360
To strong Lycomedes and will'd Ajax Oiliades
With him to make up his supply and fill with courages
The Grecian hearts till his returne, which should be instantly
When he had well reliev'd his friend. With this, the companie
Of Teucer he tooke to his aide—Teucer that did descend   365
(As Ajax did) from Telamon: with these two did attend
Pandion that bore Teucer's bow. When to Menestheus' towre
They came alongst the wall, they found him and his heartned
    powre
Toyling in making strong their fort. The Lycian Princes set
Blacke-whirlwind-like, with both their powers, upon the   370
    Parapet.
Ajax, and all, resisted them. Clamor amongst them rose.
The slaughter Ajax led, who first the last deare sight did close
Of strong Epicles, that was friend to Jove's great Lycian sonne.
Amongst the high munition heape a mightie marble stone
Lay highest, neare the Pinnacle—a stone of such a paise   375
That one of this time's strongest men with both hands could not
    raise.
Yet this did Ajax rowse and throw, and all in sherds did drive
Epicles' foure-topt caske and skull, who (as ye see one dive
In some deepe river) left his height: life left his bones withall.

Glaucus wounded
by Teucer.

    Teucer shot Glaucus (rushing up yet higher on the wall)   380
Where naked he discernd his arme, and made him steale retreat
From that hote service, lest some Greeke, with an insulting threat,
(Beholding it) might fright the rest. Sarpedon much was griev'd

Sarpedon revengeth
Glaucus.

At Glaucus' parting, yet fought on, and his great heart reliev'd
A little with Alcmaon's blood, surnamed Thestorides,   385
Whose life he hurld out with his lance, which, following through
    the prease,
He drew from him. Downe from the towre Alcmaon dead it
    strooke,
His faire armes ringing out his death. Then fierce Sarpedon
    tooke
In his strong hand the battlement and downe he tore it quite,
The wall stript naked and brode way for entrie and full fight   390
He made the many. Against him Ajax and Teucer made.
Teucer the rich belt on his breast did with a shaft invade,

But Jupiter averted death, who would not see his sonne
Die at the tailes of th' Achive ships. Ajax did fetch his run
And (with his lance) strooke through the targe of that brave   395
    Lycian King,
Yet kept he it from further passe, nor did it any thing
Dismay his mind, although his men stood off from that high way
His valour made them, which he kept and hop'd that stormie day
Should ever make his glorie cleare. His men's fault thus he
    blam'd:

Sarpedon to his souldiers.

'O Lycians, why are your hote spirits so quickly disinflam'd?   400
Suppose me ablest of you all: tis hard for me alone
To ruine such a wall as this and make Confusion
Way to their Navie. Lend your hands. What many can dispatch
One cannot thinke: the noble worke of many hath no match.'

Πλεόνων
δέ τε
ἔϱγον
ἄμεινον.

    The wise king's just rebuke did strike a reverence to his will   405
Through all his souldiers: all stood in and gainst all th' Achives
    still
Made strong their Squadrons, insomuch that to the adverse side
The worke shewd mightie, and the wall, when twas within
    descride,
No easie service. Yet the Greeks could neither free their wall
Of these brave Lycians, that held firme the place they first   410
    did skale,
Nor could the Lycians from their fort the sturdie Grecians drive

Admiranda et penè inimitabilis comparatio, saith Spondanus, and yet in the explication of it he thinkes all superfluous but three words—
ὀλίγῳ ἐνὶ
χώϱῳ
exiguo in loco—*leaving out other words more expressive with his old rule,* uno pede &c.

Nor reach their fleet. But as two men about the limits strive
Of land that toucheth in a field, their measures in their hands,
They mete their parts out curiously and either stiffely stands
That so farre is his right in law, both hugely set on fire   415
About a passing little ground: so greedily aspire
Both these foes to their severall ends and all exhaust their most
About the verie battlements (for yet no more was lost).
    With sword and fire they vext for them, their targes hugely
    round,
With Oxehides lin'd, and bucklers light; and many a ghastly   420
    wound
The sterne steele gave for that one prise; whereof though some
    receiv'd
Their portions on their naked backs, yet others were bereav'd
Of brave lives, face-turnd, through their shields. Towres,
    bulwarks every where
Were freckled with the blood of men, nor yet the Greeks did
    beare
Base back-turnd faces, nor their foes would therefore be   425
    outfac't.

*A simile superior to
the other, in which,
comparing mightiest
things with meanest,
and the meanest
illustrating the
mightiest, both meeting
in one end of this
life's preservation
and credit, our Homer
is beyond comparison
and admiration.
Hector to the Troyans.*

But as a Spinster poore and just ye sometimes see straight-lac't
About the weighing of her web, who (carefull), having charge
For which she would provide some meanes, is loth to be too
    large
In giving or in taking weight, but ever with her hand
Is doing with the weights and wooll, till both in just paise   430
    stand:
So evenly stood it with these foes till Jove to Hector gave
The turning of the skoles, who first against the rampire drave
And spake so lowd that all might heare: 'O stand not at the
    pale,
Brave Troyan friends, but mend your hands! Up, and breake
    through the wall
And make a bonfire of their fleet.' All heard, and all in heapes   435
Got skaling ladders, and aloft. In meane space, Hector leapes
Upon the port, from whose out-part he tore a massie stone,
Thicke downwards, upward edg'd it was: it was so huge an one

δύ' ἀνέρε δήμου
duo viri plebei.

That two vast yoemen of most strength (such as these times beget)
Could not from earth lift to a Cart. Yet he did brandish it   440
Alone (Saturnius made it light) and, swinging it as nought,
He came before the plankie gates, that all for strength were
    wrought
And kept the Port: two-fold they were and with two rafters bard,
High and strong lockt. He raisd the stone, bent to the hurle
    so hard
And made it with so maine a strength that all the gates did   445
    cracke,
The rafters left them and the folds one from another brake,
The hinges peece-meale flew, and through the fervent little rocke
Thundred a passage. With his weight th' inwall his breast did
    knocke
And in rusht Hector, fierce and grimme as any stormie night:
His brasse armes round about his breast reflected terrible light.   450
Each arme held up held each a dart: his presence cald up all
The dreadfull spirits his Being held, that to the threatned wall
None but the Gods might checke his way: his eyes were furnaces.
And thus he look't backe, cald in all: all fir'd their courages
And in they flow'd. The Grecians fled—their fleet now and   455
    their freight
Askt all their rescue. Greece went downe: Tumult was at his
    height.

The End of the Twelfth Booke

THE THIRTEENTH BOOKE

of

HOMER'S ILIADS

THE ARGUMENT

Neptune (in pittie of the Greeks' hard plight),
Like Calchas, both th' Ajaces doth excite,
And others, to repell the charging foe.
Idomeneus bravely doth bestow
His kingly forces and doth sacrifice   5
Othryoneus to the Destinies,
With divers other. Faire Deiphobus
And his prophetique brother Helenus
Are wounded. But the great Priamides
(Gathering his forces) hartens their addresse   10
Against the enemie, and then the field
A mightie death on either side doth yeeld.

Another Argument

The Greeks, with Troy's bold powre dismaide,
Are chear'd by Neptune's secret aide.

Jove helping Hector and his host thus close to th' Achive fleet,
He let them then their own strengths try, and season there
    their sweet
With ceaslesse toils and grievances. For now he turnd his face,
Lookt downe and viewd the far-off land of welrode men in
    Thrace,
Of the renown'd milk-nourisht men, the Hippemolgians,   5
Long-liv'd, most just and innocent, and close-fought Mysians.
Nor turnd he any more to Troy his ever-shining eyes,
Because he thought not any one of all the Deities
(When his care left th' indifferent field) would aide on either
    side.
But this securitie in Jove the great Sea-Rector spide,   10

Neptune's prospect.

Who sate aloft on th' utmost top of shadie Samothrace
And viewd the fight. His chosen seate stood in so brave a place
That Priam's cittie, th' Achive ships, all Ida did appeare
To his full view, who from the sea was therefore seated there.
He tooke much ruth to see the Greeks by Troy sustaine such ill   15
And (mightily incenst with Jove) stoopt strait from that
    steepe hill,
That shooke as he flew off, so hard his parting prest the height.
The woods and all the great hils neare trembled beneath the
    weight
Of his immortall moving feet. Three steps he onely tooke
Before he far-off Ægas reacht, but with the fourth it shooke   20
With his drad entrie. In the depth of those seas he did hold
His bright and glorious pallace built of never-rusting gold:
And there arriv'd, he put in Coach his brazen-footed steeds.

The horse of Neptune.

All golden-man'd and pac't with wings; and all in golden weeds
He clothed himselfe. The golden scourge (most elegantly done)   25
He tooke and mounted to his seate, and then the God begun
To drive his chariot through the waves. From whirlepits every
    way
The whales exulted under him and knew their king: the Sea
For joy did open, and his horse so swift and lightly flew
The under-axeltree of brasse no drop of water drew.   30
And thus these deathlesse Coursers brought their king to
    th' Achive ships.

Chorographia.

    Twixt th' Imber Cliffs and Tenedos a certaine Caverne creepes
Into the deepe sea's gulphie breast, and there th' earth-shaker
    staid
His forward steeds, tooke them from coach and heavenly fodder
    laid
In reach before them. Their brasse hoves he girt with gives of   35
    gold,
Not to be broken nor dissolv'd, to make them firmely hold

Neptune goes to the
Greekes.

A fit attendance on their king—who went to th' Achive host
Which (like to tempests or wild flames) the clustring Troyans
    tost,
Insatiably valourous, in Hector's like command,
High sounding, and resounding, shouts, for Hope chear'd every   40
    hand
To make the Greek fleete now their prise and all the Greeks
    destroy.
But Neptune (circler of the earth) with fresh heart did employ
The Grecian hands. In strength of voice and body, he did take
Calchas' resemblance and (of all) th' Ajaces first bespake,

Neptune to the two Ajaces.

Who of themselves were free enough: 'Ajaces, you alone   45
Sustaine the common good of Greece, in ever putting on
The memorie of Fortitude and flying shamefull Flight.
Elsewhere, the desperate hands of Troy could give me no
    affright,
The brave Greeks have withstood their worst: but this our
    mightie wall
Being thus transcended by their powre, grave Feare doth much   50
    appall
My carefull spirits, lest we feele some fatall mischiefe here,
Where Hector, raging like a flame, doth in his charge appeare
And boasts himselfe the best God's sonne. Be you conceited so,
And fire so more than humane spirits, that God may seeme to do
In your deeds, and, with such thoughts chear'd, others to   55
    such exhort
And such resistance: these great minds will in as great a sort
Strengthen your bodies and force checke to all great Hector's
    charge,
Though nere so spirit-like, and though Jove still (past himselfe)
    enlarge
His sacred actions.' Thus he toucht with his forckt scepter's point
The brests of both, fild both their spirits and made up every   60
    joynt

Simile.

With powre responsive—when, hawk-like, swift and set sharpe
    to flie,
That fiercely stooping from a rocke inaccessible and hie
Cuts through a field and sets a fowle (not being of her kind)
Hard and gets ground still, Neptune so left these two, either's
    mind
Beyond themselves raisd. Of both which, Oileus first discern'd   65

Ajax Oileus to Ajax Telamonius.

The masking Deitie, and said: 'Ajax, some God hath warn'd
Our powres to fight and save our fleet. He put on him the hew
Of th' Augure Calchas: by his pace (in leaving us) I knew
(Without all question) twas a God: the Gods are easly knowne,
And in my tender brest I feele a greater spirit blowne   70
To execute affaires of fight: I find my hands so free
To all high motion and my feete seeme featherd under me.'

The two Ajaces to one another.

This Telamonius thus receiv'd: 'So to my thoughts my hands
Burne with desire to tosse my lance: each foote beneath me stands
Bare on bright fire to use his speed: my heart is raisd so hie   75
That to encounter Hector's selfe I long insatiately.'
    While these thus talkt, as over-joyd with studie for the fight
(Which God had stird up in their spirits) the same God did
    excite

[254]

The Greekes that were behind at fleet, refreshing their free hearts
And joynts, being even dissolv'd with toyle; and (seeing the   80
    desprate parts
Playd by the Troyans, past their wall) Griefe strooke them, and
    their eyes
Sweat teares from under their sad lids, their instant destinies
Never supposing they could scape. But Neptune, stepping in,
With ease stird up the able troopes, and did at first begin
With Teucer and Peneleus, th' Heroe Leitus,   85
Deipyrus, Meriones and yong Antilochus,

Neptune to the
Greekes.

All expert in the deeds of armes: 'O youths of Greece,' said he,
'What change is this? In your brave fight I onely lookt to see
Our fleet's whole safetie; and, if you neglect the harmefull field,
Now shines the day when Greece to Troy must all her honours   90
    yeeld.
O griefe! so great a miracle and horrible to sight
As now I see I never thought could have prophan'd the light.
The Troyans brave us at our ships, that have bene heretofore
Like faint and fearefull Deare in woods, distracted evermore
With everie sound, and yet scape not but prove the torne-up   95
    fare
Of Lynces, Wolves and Leopards, as never borne to warre:
Nor durst these Troyans at first siege in any least degree
Expect your strength or stand one shocke of Grecian Chivalrie.
Yet now farre from their walles they dare fight at our fleet
    maintaine,
All by our General's cowardise, that doth infect his men,   100
Who (still at ods with him) for that will needs themselves neglect
And suffer Slaughter in their ships. Suppose there was defect
(Beyond all question) in our king to wrong Æacides
And he for his particular wreake from all assistance cease;
We must not ceasse t' assist our selves. Forgive our Generall   105
    then,

Good-minded men
apt to forgive.

And quickly too: apt to forgive are all good-minded men.
Yet you (quite voide of their good minds) give good, in you
    quite lost,
For ill in others, though ye be the worthiest of your host.
As old as I am, I would scorne to fight with one that flies
Or leaves the fight, as you do now. The Generall slothfull lies,   110
And you (though sloughfull too) maintaine with him a fight
    of splene.
Out, out, I hate ye from my heart, ye rotten-minded men.
In this ye adde an ill that's worse than all your sloth's dislikes.
But, as I know to all your hearts my reprehension strikes,

So thither let just shame strike too, for, while you stand still   115
    here,
A mightie fight swarmes at your fleete, great Hector rageth there,
Hath burst the long barre and the gates.' Thus Neptune rowsd
    these men,
And round about th' Ajaces did their Phalanxes maintaine
Their station firme, whom Mars himselfe (had he amongst
    them gone)
Could not disparage, nor Jove's Maide that sets men fiercer on.   120
For now the best were chosen out, and they receiv'd th' advance
Of Hector and his men so full that lance was lin'd with lance,
Shields thickned with opposed shields, targets to targets nail'd,
Helmes stucke to helmes and man to man grew—they so close
    assail'd.
Plum'd caskes were hang'd in either's plumes, all joyn'd so   125
    close their stands,
Their lances stood thrust out so thicke by such all-daring hands.
All bent their firme brests to the point and made sad fight
    their joy.
Of both, Troy all in heapes strooke first, and Hector first of Troy.

Simile.   And as a round peece of a rocke, which with a winter's flood
Is from his top torne, when a showre, powr'd from a bursten   130
    cloud
Hath broke the naturall bond it held within the rough steepe
    rocke,
And, jumping, it flies downe the woods, resounding everie shocke,
And on, uncheckt, it headlong leapes till in a plaine it stay,
And then (though never so impeld) it stirs not any way:
So Hector hereto throated threats, to go to sea in blood   135
And reach the Grecian ships and tents without being once
    withstood,
But, when he fell into the strengths the Grecians did maintaine
And that they fought upon the square, he stood as fetterd then.
And so the adverse sons of Greece laid on with swords and darts
(Whose both ends hurt) that they repeld his worst, and he   140
    converts
His threats by all meanes to retreats; yet made as he retir'd
Onely t' encourage those behind, and thus those men inspir'd:

Hector to his friends.   'Troyans! Dardanians! Lycians! All warlike friends! Stand close.
The Greeks can never beare me long, though towre-like they
    oppose.
This lance (be sure) will be their spoile, if even the best of Gods, 145
High-thundring Juno's husband, stirres my spirite with true
    abodes.'

[256]

With this, all strengths and minds he mov'd, but yong
    Deiphobus,
Old Priam's sonne, amongst them all was chiefly vertuous.
He bore before him his round shield, tript lightly through
    the prease,
At all parts coverd with his shield. And him Meriones   150
Charg'd with a glittring dart that tooke his bul-hide orbie shield,
Yet pierc't it not but in the top it selfe did peecemeale yeeld.
    Deiphobus thrust forth his targe and fear'd the broken ends
Of strong Meriones his lance, who now turnd to his friends.
The great Heroe, scorning much by such a chance to part   155
With lance and conquest, forth he went to fetch another dart
Left at his tent. The rest fought on; the Clamor heightned there

Was most unmeasur'd. Teucer first did flesh the Massacre
And slue a goodly man at armes, the souldier Imbrius,
The sonne of Mentor, rich in horse: he dwelt at Pedasus   160
Before the sonnes of Greece sieg'd Troy, from whence he married
Medesicasté, one that sprung of Priam's bastard bed.
But when the Greeke ships (double-oar'd) arriv'd at Ilion,
To Ilion he returnd and prov'd beyond comparison
Amongst the Troyans: he was lodg'd with Priam, who   165
    held deare
His naturall sonnes no more than him. Yet him, beneath
    the eare,
The sonne of Telamon attain'd, and drew his lance. He fell

As when an Ash on some hil's top (it selfe topt wondrous well)
The steele hewes downe and he presents his young leaves to
    the soyle:
So fell he, and his faire armes gron'd—which Teucer long'd   170
    to spoyle,
And in he ranne; and Hector in, who sent a shining lance
At Teucer, who (beholding it) slipt by and gave it chance
On Actor's sonne Amphimachus, whose breast it strooke. And in
Flew Hector, at his sounding fall, with full intent to win
The tempting helmet from his head; but Ajax with a dart   175
Reacht Hector at his rushing in, yet toucht not any part
About his bodie: it was hid quite through with horrid brasse.
The bosse yet of his targe it tooke, whose firme stuffe staid
    the passe,
And he turnd safe from both the trunks, both which the
    Grecians bore
From off the field. Amphimachus, Menestheus did restore,   180
And Stichius, to th' Achaian strength. Th' Ajaces (that were
    pleasd

Still most with most hote services) on Troyan Imbrius seasd.
And as from sharply-bitten hounds a brace of Lions force
A new-slaine Goate, and through the woods beare in their jawes
the corse
Aloft, lift up into the aire: so up into the skies   185
Bore both th' Ajaces Imbrius, and made his armes their prise.
    Yet (not content) Oiliades, enrag'd to see there dead
His much-belov'd Amphimachus, he hewd off Imbrius' head
Which (swinging round) bowle-like he tost amongst the Troyan
prease,
And full at Hector's feete it fell. Amphimachus' decease   190
(Being nephew to the God of waves) much vext the Deitie's mind
And to the ships and tents he marcht, yet more to make inclinde
The Grecians to the Troyan bane. In hasting to which end,
Idomeneus met with him, returning from a friend
Whose hamme late hurt his men brought off, and, having given   195
command
To his Physitians for his cure (much fir'd to put his hand
To Troy's repulse) he left his tent. Him (like Andræmon's sonne,
Prince Thoas, that in Pleuron rulde, and loftie Calydon,
Th' Ætolian powres, and like a God was of his subjects lov'd)
Neptune encountred, and but thus his forward spirit mov'd: 200

    'Idomeneus, Prince of Crete, O whither now are fled
Those threats in thee which with the rest the Troyans menaced?'
    'O Thoas,' he replide, 'no one of all our host stands now
In any question of reproofe (as I am let to know)
And why is my intelligence false? We all know how to fight   205
And (Feare disanimating none) all do our knowledge right.
Nor can our harmes accuse our sloth: not one from worke we
misse.
The great God onely workes our ill, whose pleasure now it is
That, farre from home in hostile fields and with inglorious fate,
Some Greeks should perish. But do thou, O Thoas (that of late   210
Hast prov'd a souldier and was wont where thou hast Sloth
beheld
To chide it and exhort to paines) now hate to be repeld
And set on all men.' He replied: 'I would to heaven that he
Who ever this day doth abstaine from battell willinglie
May never turne his face from Troy, but here become the prey   215
And skorne of dogs! Come then, take armes, and let our kind
assay
Joyne both our forces: though but two, yet being both combinde
The worke of many single hands we may performe: we finde
That Vertue coaugmented thrives in men of little minde,

[258]

But we have, singly, matcht the great.' This said, the God again   220
(With all his conflicts) visited the ventrous fight of men.
The king turnd to his tent, rich armes put on his brest and tooke
Two darts in hand and forth he flew: his haste on made him
    looke
Much like a fierie Meteor with which Jove's sulphrie hand
Opes heaven and hurles about the aire, bright flashes showing   225
    aland
Abodes that ever run before tempest and plagues to men:
So, in his swift pace, shew'd his armes. He was encountred then
By his good friend Meriones, yet neare his tent, to whom
Thus spake the powre of Idomen: 'What reason makes thee
    come,
Thou sonne of Molus, my most lov'd, thus leaving fight alone?   230
Is't for some wound? The Javelin's head (still sticking in the
    bone)
Desir'st thou ease of? Bring'st thou newes? Or what is it that
    brings
Thy presence hither? Be assur'd, my spirite needs no stings
To this hote conflict. Of my selfe thou seest I come, and loth
For any tent's love to deserve the hatefull taint of Sloth.'   235
   He answerd, onely for a dart he that retreat did make
(Were any left him at his tent), for that he had he brake
On proud Deiphobus his shield. 'Is one dart all?' said he.
'Take one and twentie, if thou like, for in my tent they be:
They stand there shining by the walls: I tooke them as my prise   240
From those false Troyans I have slaine. And this is not the guise
Of one that loves his tent or fights afarre off with his foe,
But, since I love fight, therefore doth my martiall starre bestow
(Besides those darts) helmes, targets bost and corslets bright
    as day.'
   'So I,' said Merion, 'at my tent and sable barke may say   245
I many Troyan spoiles retaine; but now not neare they be
To serve me for my present use, and therefore aske I thee.
Not that I lacke a fortitude to store me with my owne,
For ever in the formost fights, that render men renowne,
I fight when any fight doth stirre—and this perhaps may well   250
Be hid to others, but thou know'st, and I to thee appeale.'
   'I know,' replide the king, 'how much thou weigh'st in everie
    worth:
What needst thou therefore utter this? If we should now chuse
    forth
The worthiest men for ambushes in all our fleet and host—
For ambushes are services that trie men's vertues most,   255

Since there the fearefull and the firme will as they are appeare,
The fearefull altering still his hue and rests not any where,
Nor is his spirit capable of th' ambush constancie
But riseth, changeth still his place and croucheth curiously
On his bent hanches, halfe his height scarce seene above the   260
    ground
For feare to be seene, yet must see, his heart with many a bound
Offring to leape out of his breast and (ever fearing death)
The coldnesse of it makes him gnash and halfe shakes out his
    teeth;
Where men of valour neither feare nor ever change their lookes
From lodging th' ambush till it rise, but, since there must be   265
    strokes,
Wish to be quickly in their midst—thy strength and hand in
    these
Who should reprove? For if, farre off or fighting in the prease,
Thou shouldst be wounded, I am sure the dart that gave the
    wound
Should not be drawne out of thy backe or make thy necke the
    ground,
But meete thy bellie or thy breast, in thrusting further yet   270
When thou art furthest till the first, and before him, thou get.
But on: like children, let not us stand bragging thus, but do,
Lest some heare and past measure chide that we stand still
    and wooe.
Go, chuse a better dart and make Mars yeeld a better chance.'
    This said, Mars-swift Meriones with haste a brazen lance   275
Tooke from his tent and overtooke (most carefull of the wars)
Idomeneus. And such two in field as harmfull Mars
And Terror, his beloved sonne, that without terror fights
And is of such strength that in warre the frighter he affrights,
When out of Thrace they both take armes against th' Ephyran   280
    bands
Or gainst the great-soul'd Phlegyans, nor favour their owne
    hands
But give the grace to others still—in such sort to the fight
Marcht these two managers of men in armours full of light.
    And first spake Merion: 'On which part, sonne of Deucalion,
Serves thy mind to invade the fight? Is't best to set upon   285
The Troyans, in our battel's aide, the right or left-hand wing,
For all parts I suppose employd?' To this the Cretan king
Thus answerd: 'In our navie's midst are others that assist—
The two Ajaces, Teucer too, with shafts the expertest
Of all the Grecians and, though small, is great in fights of stand.   290

And these (though huge he be of strength) will serve to fill
    the hand
Of Hector's selfe, that Priamist, that studier for blowes.
It shall be cald a deed of height for him (even suffring throwes
For knocks still) to out-labour them, and (bettring their tough
    hands)
Enflame our fleet. If Jove himselfe cast not his fier-brands   295
Amongst our navie, that affaire no man can bring to field.
Great Ajax Telamonius to none alive will yeeld
That yeelds to death and whose life takes Ceres' nutritions,
That can be cut with any iron or pasht with mightie stones.
Not to Æacides himselfe he yeelds for combats set,   300
Though cleare he must give place for pace and free swinge
    of his feete.
Since then the battell (being our place of most care) is made good
By his high valour, let our aid see all powres be withstood
That charge the left wing, and to that let us direct our course,
Where quickly feele we this hote foe or make him feele   305
    our force.'
    This orderd, swift Meriones went, and forewent, his king,
Till both arriv'd where one enjoynd. When in the Greeks'
    left wing
The Troyans saw the Cretan king, like fire in fortitude,
And his attendant, in bright armes so gloriously indude,
Both chearing the sinister troopes, all at the king addresst   310
And so the skirmish at their sternes on both parts was increast—

Simile.

That as from hollow bustling winds engenderd stormes arise
When dust doth chiefly clog the waies, which up into the skies
The wanton tempest ravisheth, begetting Night of Day,
So came together both the foes. Both lusted to assay   315
And worke with quicke steele either's death. Man's fierce
    corruptresse, Fight,
Set up her bristles in the field, with lances long and light,
Which thicke fell foule on either's face: the splendor of the
    steele,
In new-skowrd curets, radiant caskes and burnisht shields,
    did seele
Th' assailers' eyes up. He sustaind a huge spirit that was glad   320
To see that labour, or in soule that stood not stricken sad.
    Thus these two disagreeing Gods, old Saturn's mightie sonnes,
Afflicted these heroique men with huge oppressions.
Jove, honouring Æacides (to let the Greeks still trie
Their want without him), would bestow (yet still) the victorie   325
On Hector and the Troyan powre: yet for Æacides

[261]

And honor of his mother Queene, great Goddesse of the seas,
He would not let proude Ilion see the Grecians quite destroid,
And therefore, from the hoarie deepe, he sufferd so imploid
Great Neptune in the Grecian aid, who griev'd for them and   330
    storm'd
Extremely at his brother Jove. Yet both one Goddesse form'd

The Empire of Jove
exceeded Neptune's,
saith Plutarch upon
this place, because he
was more ancient and
excellent in knowledg
and wisedome. And
upon this verse, viz.
ἀλλὰ Ζεὺς
πρότερος
&c. sets downe this
his most worthy to be
noted opinion: viz.
'I thinke also that the
blessednesse of eternall
life which God enjoyes
is this—that by any
past time he forgets
not notions presently
apprehended: for
otherwise the
knowledge and
understanding of
things taken away,
Immortality shold
not be life but Time,
&c. Plutarch de Iside
et Osiride.

And one soile bred: but Jupiter precedence tooke in birth
And had more knowledge, for which cause the other came
    not forth
Of his wet kingdome but with care of not being seene t' excite
The Grecian host, and like a man appeard and made the fight.   335
So these Gods made men's valours great, but equald them with
    warre
As harmefull as their hearts were good, and stretcht those chaines
    as farre
On both sides as their lims could beare—in which they were
    involv'd
Past breach or loosing, that their knees might therefore be
    dissolv'd.
Then, though a halfe-gray man he were, Crete's soveraigne did   340
    excite
The Greeks to blowes and flew upon the Troyans even to flight.
For he, in sight of all the host, Othryoneus slew,
That from Cabesus with the fame of those warres thither drew
His new-come forces and requir'd, without respect of dowre,
Cassandra, fair'st of Priam's race, assuring with his powre   345
A mightie labour—to expell, in their despite, from Troy
The sons of Greece. The king did vow (that done) he should
    enjoy
His goodliest daughter. He (in trust of that faire purchase)
    fought,
And at him threw the Cretan king a lance that singl'd out
This great assumer, whom it strooke just in his navil's stead: 350
His brazen curets helping nought, resignd him to the dead.
Then did the conquerour exclaime, and thus insulted then:

Idomen's insultation
on Othryoneus.

    'Othryoneus, I will praise beyond all mortall men
Thy living vertues, if thou wilt now perfect the brave vow
Thou mad'st to Priam for the wife he promisd to bestow.   355
And where he should have kept his word there, we assure thee
    here
To give thee for thy Princely wife the fairest and most deare
Of our great General's femall race, which from his Argive hall
We all will waite upon to Troy, if with our aids and all

Thou wilt but race this well-built towne. Come, therefore,   360
    follow me,
That in our ships we may conclude this royall match with thee.
I'le be no jote worse than my word.' With that he tooke his feete,
And dragg'd him through the fervent fight: in which did Asius
    meete
The victor, to inflict revenge. He came on foote before
His horse, that on his shoulders breath'd, so closely evermore   365
His coachman led them to his Lord, who held a huge desire
To strike the King—but he strooke first, and underneath his chin

At his throat's height through th' other side his eager lance
    drave in,
And downe he busl'd, like an Oake, a Poplar or a Pine
Hewne downe for shipwood, and so lay. His fall did so decline   370
The spirit of his chariotere that, lest he should incense
The victor to empaire his spoile, he durst not drive from thence
His horse and chariot, and so pleasd with that respective part

Antilochus, that for his feare he reacht him with a dart
About his bellie's midst and downe his sad corse fell beneath   375
The richly-builded chariot, there labouring out his breath.
The horse Antilochus tooke off, when (griev'd for this event)

Deiphobus drew passing neare and at the victor sent
A shining Javelin, which he saw and shund with gathring round
His body in his all-round shield—at whose top, with a sound,   380
It overflew: yet, seising there, it did not idlely flie
From him that wing'd it: his strong hand still drave it mortally
On Prince Hypsenor. It did pierce his liver, underneath
The veines it passeth: his shrunke knees submitted him to death.
And then did loud Deiphobus miraculously vant: 385

'Now Asius lies not unreveng'd, nor doth his spirit want
The joy I wish it, though it be now entring the strong gate
Of mightie Pluto, since this hand hath sent him downe a mate.'
  This glorie in him griev'd the Greeks, and chiefly the great
    mind
Of martiall Antilochus, who (though to griefe inclind)   390
He left not yet his friend but ran and hid him with his shield,
And to him came two lovely friends that freed him from the
    field,
Mecisteus, sonne of Echius, and the right nobly borne
Alastor, bearing him to fleet, and did extremely mourne.
  Idomeneus suncke not yet, but held his nerves entire,   395
His mind, much lesse deficient, being fed with firme desire
To hide more Troyans in dim night, or sinke himselfe, in guard
Of his lov'd countrimen. And then Alcathous prepar'd

Worke for his valour, offring fate his owne destruction—
A great Heroe and had grace to be the loved sonne   400
Of Æsyetes, sonne in law to Prince Æneas' Sire,
Hippodamia marrying, who most enflam'd the fire
Of her deare parents' love and tooke precedence in her birth
Of all their daughters, and as much exceeded in her worth
(For beautie answerd with her mind and both with
    housewiferie)   405
All the faire beauty of young Dames that usde her companie;
And therefore (being the worthiest Dame) the worthiest man
    did wed
Of ample Troy. Him Neptune stoopt beneath the royall force
Of Idomen, his sparkling eyes deluding and the course
Of his illustrous lineaments so out of nature bound   410
That backe nor forward he could stirre, but (as he grew to
    ground)
Stood like a pillar or high tree and neither mov'd nor fear'd
When strait the royall Cretan's dart in his mid breast appear'd:
It brake the curets that were proofe to everie other dart,
Yet now they cleft and rung: the lance stucke shaking in his   415
    heart—
His heart with panting made it shake. But Mars did now remit
The greatnesse of it and the king, now quitting the bragge fit
Of glorie in Deiphobus, thus terribly exclam'd:

*Idomeneus to
Deiphobus.*

    'Deiphobus, now may we thinke that we are evenly fam'd,
That three for one have sent to Dis. But come, change blowes   420
    with me;
Thy vaunts for him thou slew'st were vaine. Come, wretch,
    that thou maist see
What issue Jove hath. Jove begot Minos, the strength of Crete;
Minos begot Deucalion; Deucalion did beget
Me, Idomen, now Creta's king, that here my ships have brought
To bring thy selfe, thy father, friends, all Ilion's pompe to   425
    nought.'
    Deiphobus at two wayes stood, in doubt to call some one
(With some retreat) to be his aide, or trie the chance alone.
At last, the first seem'd best to him, and backe he went to call
Anchises' sonne to friend, who stood in troope the last of all,

*Æneas angrie, being
ever disgraced by
Priam.*

Where still he serv'd—which made him still incense against   430
    the king,
That, being amongst his best their Peere, he grac't not anything
His wrong'd deserts. Deiphobus spake to him, standing neare:

To him Deiphobus.

    'Æneas, Prince of Troyans, if any touch appeare
Of glorie in thee, thou must now assist thy sister's Lord

And one that to thy tendrest youth did carefull guard afford,   435
Alcathous, whom Creta's king hath chiefly slaine to thee,
His right most challenging thy hand. Come, therefore; follow me.'
  This much excited his good mind and set his heart on fire
Against the Cretan, who, child-like dissolv'd not in his ire,

Simile.

But stood him firme. As when in hils a strength-relying Bore,   440
Alone and hearing hunters come (whom Tumult flies before),
Up-thrusts his bristles, whets his tusks, sets fire on his red eyes
And in his brave-prepar'd repulse both dogs and men despise:
So stood the famous-for-his-lance, nor shund the coming charge
That resolute Æneas brought: yet (since the ods was large)   445
He cald, with good right, to his aide war-skild Ascalaphus,
Aphareus, Meriones, the strong Deipyrus

Idomeneus cals his
friends to aid.

And Nestor's honorable sonne: 'Come neare, my friends,'
    said he,
'And adde your aids to me alone. Feare taints me worthilie,
Though firme I stand and shew it not. Æneas, great in fight,   450

Æneas yet a youth, as
Virgil makes him.

And one that beares youth in his flowre (that beares the
    greatest might)
Comes on with aime direct at me: had I his youthfull lim
To beare my mind, he should yeeld Fame or I would yeeld it
    him.'
  This said, all held in many soules one readie helpfull mind,
Clapt shields on shoulders and stood close. Æneas (not inclind   455
With more presumption than the king) cald aid as well as he—
Divine Agenor, Helen's love, who followd instantly
And all their forces following them, as after Bellwethers
The whole flocks follow to their drinke, which sight the
    shepheard cheres.
Nor was Æneas' joy lesse mov'd to see such troopes attend   460
His honord person, and all these fought close about his friend.

Æneas and Idomeneus
in conflict.

But two of them past all the rest had strong desire to shed
The blood of either—Idomen and Cytherea's seed.
Æneas first bestowd his lance, which th' other seeing shund,
And that (throwne from an idle hand) stucke trembling in the   465
    ground.
But Idomen's (discharg'd at him) had no such vaine successe,
Which Œnomaus' entrailes found, in which it did impresse
His sharpe pile to his fall: his palms tore his returning earth.
Idomeneus strait stept in and pluckt his Javelin forth
But could not spoile his goodly armes, they prest him so with   470
    darts.
And now the long toile of the fight had spent his vigorous parts
And made them lesse apt to avoid the foe that should advance,

Or (when himselfe advanc't againe) to run and fetch his lance.
And therefore in stiffe fights of stand he spent the cruell day,
When (coming softly from the slaine) Deiphobus gave way   475
To his bright Javelin at the king, whom he could never
    brooke.
But then he lost his envie too: his lance yet deadly tooke

Ascalaphus, the sonne of Mars, slaine by Deiphobus.

Ascalaphus, the sonne of Mars: quite through his shoulder
    flew
The violent head, and downe he fell. Nor yet by all meanes
    knew
Wide-throated Mars his sonne was falne, but in Olympus' top   480
Sat canapied with golden clouds. Jove's counsell had shut up
Both him and all the other Gods from that time's equall taske
Which now about Ascalaphus Strife set. His shining caske
Deiphobus had forc't from him, but instantly leapt in
Mars-swift Meriones and strooke, with his long Javelin,   485
The right arme of Deiphobus, which made his hand let fall

Deiphobus wounded by Meriones.

The sharp-topt helmet, the prest earth resounding therewithall.
When, Vulture-like, Meriones rusht in againe and drew
(From out the low part of his arme) his Javelin, and then flew
Backe to his friends. Deiphobus (faint with the blood's excesse   490
Falne from his wound) was carefully convaid out of the preasse
By his kind brother by both sides, Polites, till they gat
His horse and chariot, that were still set fit for his retreate,
And bore him now to Ilion. The rest fought fiercely on
And set a mightie fight on foote—when next Anchises' sonne   495
Aphareus Caletorides (that ran upon him) strooke
Just in the throate with his keene lance, and strait his head
    forsooke
His upright cariage, and his shield, his helme and all with him
Fell to the earth, where ruinous death made prise of everie lim.
    Antilochus (discovering well that Thoon's heart tooke   500
    checke)
Let flie and cut the hollow veine that runs up to his necke
Along his backe part quite in twaine: downe in the dust he fell
Upwards and, with extended hands, bad all the world farewell.
Antilochus rusht nimbly in and (looking round) made prise
Of his faire armes, in which affaire his round-set enemies   505
Let flie their lances, thundering, on his advanced targe,
But could not get his flesh. The God that shakes the earth
    tooke charge
Of Nestor's sonne and kept him safe, who never was away
But still amongst the thickest foes his busie lance did play,
Observing ever when he might far-off or neare offend.   510

And, watching Asius' sonne in prease, he spide him and did send
(Close coming on) a dart at him that smote in midst his shield,
In which the sharpe head of the lance the blew-hair'd God
    made yeeld,
Not pleasd to yeeld his pupil's life—in whose shield halfe
    the dart
Stucke like a trunchion burnd with fire, on earth lay th' other   51⸱
    part.
He, seeing no better end of all, retir'd, in feare of worse,
But him Meriones pursude, and his lance found full course
To th' other's life: it wounded him betwixt the privie parts
And navill, where (to wretched men that war's most violent
    smarts
Must undergo) wounds chiefly vexe. His dart Meriones   520
Pursude, and Adamas so striv'd with it and his misease,

Simile.   As doth a Bullocke puffe and storme, whom in disdained bands
The upland heardsmen strive to cast, so (falne beneath the hands
Of his sterne foe) Asiades did struggle, pant and rave—
But no long time: for when the lance was pluckt out up   525
    he gave
His tortur'd soule. Then Troy's turne came, when with a
    Thracian sword
The temples of Deipyrus did Helenus afford
So huge a blow it strooke all light out of his cloudie eyes
And cleft his helmet, which a Greeke (there fighting) made
    his prise
(It fell so full beneath his feet). Atrides griev'd to see   530
That sight, and (threatning) shooke a lance at Helenus, and he
A bow halfe drew at him: at once out flew both shaft and lance.
The shaft Atrides' curets strooke and farre away did glance:

Helenus wounded.   Atrides' dart, of Helenus the thrust-out bow-hand strooke,
And through the hand stucke in the bow. Agenor's hand did   535
    plucke
From forth the nailed prisoner the Javelin quickly out,
And fairely, with a little wooll enwrapping round about
The wounded hand, within a scarffe he bore it, which his Squire
Had readie for him: yet the wound would needs he should
    retire.
    Pisander, to revenge his hurt, right on the King ran he.   540
A bloodie fate suggested him to let him runne on thee,

Scopticè.   O Menelaus, that he might by thee in dangerous warre
Be done to death. Both coming on, Atrides' lance did erre.
Pisander strooke Atrides' shield, that brake at point, the dart
Not running through—yet he rejoyc't as playing a victor's part.   545

[267]

Atrides (drawing his faire sword) upon Pisander flew.
Pisander from beneath his shield his goodly weapon drew,
Two-edg'd, with right sharpe steele, and long, the handle
    Olive-tree
Well-polisht, and to blowes they go. Upon the top strooke he
Atrides' horse-hair'd-featherd helme. Atrides on his brow   550
(Above th' extreme part of his nose) laid such a heavie blow
That all the bones crasht under it and out his eyes did drop
Before his feete, in bloodie dust: he after, and shrunke up
His dying bodie, which the foote of his triumphing foe
Opened, and stood upon his breast, and off his armes did go,   555

Menelaus' most
ridiculous insultation.

This insultation usde the while: 'At length forsake our fleete
Thus, ye false Troyans, to whom warre never enough is sweet.
Nor want ye more impieties, with which ye have abusde
Me, ye bold dogs, that your chiefe friends so honourably usde.
Nor feare you hospitable Jove, that lets such thunders go.   560
But build upon't, he will unbuild your towres that clamber so,
For ravishing my goods and wife, in flowre of all her yeares,
And without cause—nay, when that faire and liberall hand
    of hers
Had usde you so most lovingly. And now againe ye would
Cast fire into our fleet and kill our Princes if ye could.   565
Go to, one day you will be curb'd (though never so ye thirst
Rude warre) by warre. O Father Jove, they say thou art the first
In wisedome of all Gods and men; yet all this comes from thee,
And still thou gratifiest these men, how lewd so ere they be,
Though never they be cloid with sinnes, nor can be satiate   570
(As good men should) with this vile warre. Satietie of state,
Satietie of sleepe and love, satietie of ease,
Of musicke, dancing, can find place, yet harsh warre still must
    please
Past all these pleasures, even past these. They will be cloyd
    with these
Before their warre joyes: never warre gives Troy satieties.'   575
  This said, the bloody armes were off and to his souldiers
    throwne,
He mixing in first fight againe. And then Harpalion,
Kind King Pylæmen's sonne, gave charge, who to those warres
    of Troy
His loved father followed, nor ever did enjoy
His countrie's sight againe. He strooke the targe of Atreus'   580
    sonne
Full in the midst: his javelin's steele yet had no powre to runne
The target through; nor had himselfe the heart to fetch his lance,

But tooke him to his strength and cast on every side a glance
Lest any his deare sides should dart. But Merion as he fled
Sent after him a brazen lance, that ranne his eager head   585
Through his right hippe and all along the bladder's region
Beneath the bone: it settl'd him and set his spirit gone
Amongst the hands of his best friends, and like a worme he lay
Stretcht on the earth, which his blacke blood embrewd and
      flow'd away.
His corse the Paphlagonians did sadly waite upon   590
(Reposd in his rich chariot) to sacred Ilion—
The king his father following, dissolv'd in kindly teares,
And no wreake sought for his slaine sonne. But at his slaughterers
Incensed Paris spent a lance (since he had bene a guest
To many Paphlagonians) and through the preasse it prest.   595
There was a certaine Augure's sonne, that did for wealth excell
And yet was honest: he was borne and did at Corinth dwell;
Who (though he knew his harmefull fate) would needs his ship
      ascend.
His father, Polyidus, oft would tell him that his end
Would either seise him at his house, upon a sharpe disease,   600
Or else amongst the Grecian ships, by Troyans slaine. Both these
Together he desir'd to shun, but the disease (at last,
And lingring death in it) he left and warre's quicke stroke
      embrac't.
The lance betwixt his eare and cheeke ran in, and drave the
      mind
Of both those bitter fortunes out. Night strooke his whole   605
      powres blind.
   Thus fought they like the spirit of fire, nor Jove-lov'd Hector
      knew
How in the fleet's left wing the Greekes his downe-put souldiers
      slew
Almost to victorie, the God that shakes the earth so well
Helpt with his owne strength and the Greeks so fiercely did
      impell.
Yet Hector made the first place good, where both the ports   610
      and wall
(The thicke rancke of the Greeke shields broke) he enterd and
      did skall
Where on the gray sea's shore were drawne (the wall being
      there but sleight)
Protesilaus' ships and those of Ajax, where the fight
Of men and horse were sharpest set. There the Bœotian bands,

By Iaons (for Ionians)
he intends the
Athenians.

Long-rob'd Iaones, Locrians and (brave men of their hands)   615
The Phthian and Epeian troopes did spritefully assaile
The God-like Hector rushing in, and yet could not prevaile
To his repulse, though choicest men of Athens there made head—

The names of the
Captaines at the fight
at the wall, and their
souldiers.

Amongst whom was Menestheus Chiefe, whom Phidias followed,
Stichius and Bias, huge in strength. Th' Epeian troopes   620
      were led
By Meges' and Phylides' cares, Amphion, Dracius.
Before the Phthians Medon marcht and Meneptolemus,
And these (with the Bœotian powres) bore up the fleet's defence.
Oileus by his brother's side stood close and would not thence

Simile, wherein the
two Ajaces are
compared to two
draught oxen.

For any moment of that time. But as through fallow fields   625
Blacke Oxen draw a well-joyn'd plough and either evenly yeelds
His thriftie labour, all heads coucht so close to earth they plow
The fallow with their hornes, till out the sweate begins to flow,
The stretcht yokes cracke, and yet at last the furrow forth is
      driven:
So toughly stood these to their taske and made their worke   630
      as even.
      But Ajax Telamonius had many helpfull men,
That, when sweate ran about his knees and labour flow'd,
      would then
Helpe beare his mightie seven-fold shield; when swift Oiliades
The Locrians left and would not make those murthrous fights
      of prease,

The Locrians which
Oileus Ajax led
were all Archers.

Because they wore no bright steele caskes nor bristl'd plumes   635
      for show,
Round shields nor darts of solid Ash, but with the trustie bow
And jackes well-quilted with soft wooll they came to Troy
      and were
(In their fit place) as confident as those that fought so neare,
And reacht their foes so thicke with shafts that these were they
      that brake
The Troyan orders first, and then the brave-arm'd men did   640
      make
Good worke with their close fights before. Behind whom, having
      shot,
The Locrians hid still, and their foes all thought of fight forgot
With shewes of those farre-striking shafts, their eyes were
      troubled so.
And then assur'dly from the ships and tents th' insulting foe
Had miserably fled to Troy had not Polydamas   645

Polydamas to Hector.

Thus spoke to Hector: 'Hector, still impossible tis to passe
Good counsell upon you. But say some God prefers thy deeds,

[270]

In counsels wouldst thou passe us too? In all things none exceeds:

*Polydamas' advice to
Hector.*

To some God gives the powre of warre, to some the sleight
    to dance,
To some the art of instruments, some doth for voice advance,   650
And that far-seeing God grants some the wisedome of the minde,
Which no man can keepe to himselfe, that (though but few
    can finde)
Doth profite many, that preserves the publique weale and state,
And that who hath he best can prise. But for me I'le relate
Onely my censure what's our best. The verie crowne of warre   655
Doth burne about thee, yet our men, when they have reacht thus
    farre,
Suppose their valours crownd, and ceasse. A few still stir their
    feet
And so a few with many fight, sperst thinly through the fleet.
Retire then, leave speech to the route and all thy Princes call,
That here, in counsels of most weight, we may resolve of all—   660
If, having likelihood to beleeve that God wil conquest give,
We shall charge through, or, with this grace, make our retreate
    and live.
For I must needs affirme I feare the debt of yesterday
(Since warre is such a God of change) the Grecians now will pay;
And, since th' insatiate man of warre remaines at fleet, if there   665
We tempt his safetie, no howre more his hote soule can forbeare.'
   This sound stuffe Hector lik't, approv'd, jumpt from his
    chariot
And said: 'Polydamas, make good this place and suffer not
One Prince to passe it. I my selfe will there go where you see
Those friends in skirmish and returne (when they have heard   670
    from me
Command that your advice obeys) with utmost speed.' This said,
With day-bright armes, white plume, white skarffe his goodly
    lims arraid,

*Hector for his goodly
forme compared to a
hill of snow.*

He parted from them, like a hill, removing, all of snow,
And to the Troyan Peres and Chiefes he flew, to let them know
The Counsell of Polydamas. All turnd and did rejoyce   675
To haste to Panthus' gentle sonne, being cald by Hector's
    voyce—
Who (through the forefights making way) lookt for Deiphobus,
King Helenus, Asiades, Hyrtasian Asius.
Of whom some were not to be found unhurt or undeceast,
Some onely hurt and gone from field. As further he addrest,   680
He found within the fight's left wing the faire-hair'd Helen's
    love

By all meanes moving men to blowes, which could by no
    meanes move
Hector's forbeareance, his friends' misse so put his powres in
    storme,

Hector chideth Paris.   But thus in wonted terms he chid: 'You with the finest forme,
Impostor, woman's man, where are (in your care markt) all   685
    these—
Deiphobus, king Helenus, Asius Hyrtacides,
Othryoneus, Adamas? Now haughtie Ilion
Shakes to his lowest groundworke, now just ruine fals upon
Thy head past rescue.' He replyed: 'Hector, why chid'st
    thou now
When I am guiltlesse? Other times there are for ease, I know,   690
Than these: for she that brought thee forth not utterly left me
Without some portion of thy spirit, to make me brother thee.
But, since thou first brought'st in thy force to this our navall
    fight,
I and my friends have ceaslesse fought to do thy service right.
But all those friends thou seek'st are slaine, excepting Helenus   695
(Who parted wounded in his hand) and so Deiphobus—
Jove yet averted death from them. And now leade thou as farre
As thy great heart affects: all we will second any warre
That thou endurest. And I hope my owne strength is not lost:
Though least, I'le fight it to his best—nor further fights the   700
    most.'
    This calm'd hote Hector's spleene, and both turnd where
    they saw the face
Of warre most fierce, and that was where their friends made
    good the place
About renowm'd Polydamas and God-like Polyphet,
Palmus, Ascanius, Morus that Hippotion did beget
And from Ascania's wealthie fields but even the day before   705
Arriv'd at Troy, that with their aide they kindly might restore
Some kindnesse they receiv'd from thence. And, in fierce fight,
    with these
Phalces and tall Orthæus stood and bold Cebriones.
And then the doubt that in advice Polydamas disclosd,
To fight or flie, Jove tooke away, and all to fight disposd.   710

Simile.   And as the floods of troubled aire to pitchie stormes increase,
That after thunder sweepes the fields and ravish up the seas,
Encountring with abhorred roares when the engrossed waves
Boile into foame; and endlesly one after other raves:

The Troyan host and   So rank't and guarded th' Ilians marcht; some now, more now,   715
Hector glorified.   and then

More upon more in shining steele; now Captaines, then
   their men.
And Hector, like man-killing Mars, advanc't before them all,
His huge round target before him, through thickn'd like a wall
With hides well-coucht with store of brasse; and on his temples
   shin'd
His bright helme, on which danc't his plume; and in this   720
   horrid kind
(All hid within his worldlike shield) he everie troope assaid
For entrie, that in his despite stood firme and undismaid.
Which when he saw, and kept more off, Ajax came stalking then,

And thus provokt him: 'O good man, why fright'st thou thus
   our men?
Come nearer. Not Art's want in warre makes us thus navie-   725
   bound,
But Jove's direct scourge; his arm'd hand makes our hands give
   you ground.
Yet thou hop'st (of thy selfe) our spoile. But we have likewise
   hands
To hold our owne as you to spoile; and, ere thy countermands
Stand good against our ransackt fleete, your hugely-peopl'd towne
Our hands shall take in, and her towres from all their heights   730
   pull downe.
And, I must tell thee, time drawes on when, flying, thou shalt
   crie
To Jove and all the Gods to make thy faire-man'd horses flie
More swift than Falkons, that their hoofes may rouse the dust
   and beare
Thy bodie, hid, to Ilion.' This said, his bold words were
Confirm'd as soone as spoke; Jove's bird, the high-flowne Eagle,   735
   tooke
The right hand of their host, whose wings high acclamations
   strooke
From foorth the glad breasts of the Greeks. Then Hector made
   replie:

'Vaine-spoken man and glorious, what hast thou said? Would I
As surely were the sonne of Jove, and of great Juno borne,
Adorn'd like Pallas and the God that lifts to earth the Morne,   740
As this day shall bring harmefull light to all your host; and thou
(If thou dar'st stand this lance) the earth before the ships shalt
   strow,
Thy bosome torne up, and the dogs, with all the fowle of Troy,
Be satiate with thy fat and flesh.' This said, with showting joy

[273]

His first troopes follow'd, and the last their showts with showts   745
    repeld.
Greece answerd all, nor could her spirits from all shew rest
    conceald.
And to so infinite a height all acclamations strove
They reacht the splendors stucke about the unreacht throne
    of Jove.

COMMENTARIUS

[5] Ἀγαυῶν Ἱππημολγῶν &t. illustrium Hippemolgorum:
Γλακτοφάγων Lacte Vescentium, &c. *Laurentius Valla and
Eobanus Hessus (who I thinke translated Homer into Hexameters
out of Valla's prose) take* ἀγαυῶν *the Epithete to* Ἱππημολγῶν
for a nation so called, and Ἱππημολγῶν, Γλακτοφάγων ἀβίων τε   5
translates utque sine ullis divitiis equino victitat lacte; *intending*
gens Agavorum, *which he takes for those just men of life likewise
which Homer commends; utterly mistaking* ἀγαυὸς *signifying*
præclarus *or* illustris, *whose genitive case plurall is used here,
and the word, Epithete to* Ἱππημολγῶν, *together signifying*   10
Illustrium Hippemolgorum, *and, they being bred and
continually fed with milke (which the next word* γλακτοφάγων
*signifies), Homer cals most just, long-lived and innocent, in the
words* ἀβίων τε δικαιοτάτων ἀνθρώπων—ἄβιος *signifying*
longævus, ab α epitatico, *and* βίος vita, but *of some*   15
inops, *being a compound ex* α privat. and βίος victus; *and from thence
had Valla his interpretation:* utque sine ullis divitiis; *but where is*
equino lacte? *But not to shew their errors, or that I understand how
others take this place different from my translation, I use this note
so much as to intimate what Homer would have noted and doth*   20
*teach—that men brought up with that gentle and soft-spirit-begetting
milk are long-lived and in nature most just and innocent. Which
kind of food, the most ingenious and grave Plutarch, in his oration*
De esu carnium, *seems to prefer before the foode of flesh, where
he saith: 'By this meanes also Tyrants laide the foundations of their* 25
*homicides: for (as amongst the Athenians) first they put to death
the most notorious or vilest Sycophant Epitedeius, so the second and
third; then being accustomed to blood, they slue good like bad, as
Niceratus, the Emperour Theramenes, Polemarchus the Philosopher,
&c. So, at the first, men killed some harmfull beast or other, then* 30
*some kind of fowle, some fish; till, taught by these and stirred up with
the lust of their pallats, they proceeded to slaughter of the laborious
Ox, the man-clothing or adorning sheepe, the house-guarding
cocke, &c. and, by little and little cloyed with these, warre, and
the foode of men, men fell to &c.'*   35

[118] Ἀμφὶ δ' ἄρ' Αἴαντας &c. Circum autem Ajaces, &c. *To
judgement of this place Spondanus calleth all sound judgements to*

[275]

condemnation of one Panædes, a Judge of games on Olympus, whose
brother Amphidamas being dead, Gamnictor his son celebrated his
funerals, calling all the most excellent to contention not onely for   40
strength and swiftnesse, but in learning likewise and force of
wisedome. To this generall contention came Homer and Hesiodus,
who casting downe verses on both parts and of all measures (Homer
by all consents questionlesse obtaining the garland) Panædes bade
both recite briefly their best; for which Hesiodus cited these verses,   45
which as well as I could, in haste, I have translated out of the
beginning of his second Booke of workes and dayes:

> When Atlas birth (the Pleiades) arise,
> Harvest begin; plow, when they leave the skies.
> Twise twentie nights and daies these hide their heads;   50
> The yeare then turning, leave againe their beds,
> And shew when first to whet the harvest steele.
> This likewise is the field's law, where men dwell
> Neare Neptune's Empire, and where, farre away,
> The winding vallies flie the flowing sea   55
> And men inhabite the fat region.
> There naked plow, sow naked, nak't cut downe,
> If Ceres' labours thou wilt timely use,
> That timely fruits and timely revenewes
> Serve thee at all parts, lest, at any, Need   60
> Send thee to others' grudging dores to feed, &c.

These verses (howsoever Spondanus stands for Homer's) in respect of
the peace and thrift they represent, are like enough to carrie it for
Hesiodus, even in these times' judgements. Homer's verses are these:

> ———— Thus Neptune rowsd these men,   65
> And round about th' Ajaces did their Phalanxes maintaine
> Their station firme, whom Mars himselfe (had he amongst them gone)
> Could not disparage, nor Jove's Maide that sets men fiercer on.
> For now the best were chosen out, and they receiv'd th' advance
> Of Hector and his men so full that lance was lin'd with lance,   70
> Shields thickned with opposed shields, targets to targets nail'd,
> Helmes stucke to helmes and man to man grew—they so close assail'd.
> Plum'd caskes were hang'd in either's plumes, all joyn'd so close
>   their stands,
> Their lances stood thrust home so thicke by such all-daring hands.
> All bent their firme breasts to the point and made sad fight their joy   75
> Of both, Troy all in heapes strooke first, and Hector first of Troy.
> And as a round peece of a rocke, &c.

Which martiall verses, though they are as high as may be for their

*place and end of our Homer, are yet infinitely short of his best in a
thousand other places. Nor thinke I the contention at any part true,* 80
*Homer being affirmed by good Authors to be a hundred yeares before
Hesiodus, and by al others much the older, Hesiodus being neare in
blood to him. And this, for some varietie in your delight, I thought
not amisse to insert here.*

[538] Σφενδόνη, *the Commentors translate in this place* funda, 85
*most untruly, there being no slings spoken of in all these
Iliads, nor any such service used in all these wars, which in my last
annotation in this booke will appeare more apparent. But here, and
in this place, to translate the word* funda *(though most commonly it
signifieth so much) is most ridiculous;* Σφενδόνη *likewise signifying* 90
ornamentum quoddam muliebre, *which therefore I translate a skarffe,
a fitter thing to hang his arme in than a sling, and likely that his
Squire carried about him, either as a favour of his owne mistresse, or
his maister's, or for either's ornament, skarffs being no unusuall
weare for souldiers.* 95

[556] Λείψετέ θην οὕτω *&c.* Relinquetis demum sic, *&c. 'At length
forsake our fleete,' &c. Now come we to the continuance (with cleare
notes) of Menelaus' ridiculous character. This verie beginning of his
insultation (in the maner of it) preparing it, and the simply uttered
upbraids of the Troyans following confirming it most ingeniously.* 100
*First, that the Troyans ravished his wife in the flowre of her yeares,
calling her* κουριδίην ἄλοχον, *which Spondanus translateth*
virginem uxorem, *being here to be translated* juvenilem uxorem,
κουρίδιος *signifying* juvenilis: *but they will have it* virginem,
because Homer must be taxed with ignorance of what the next age 105
*after Troy's siege revealed of the age before; in which Theseus is
remembred first to have ravisht Helen, and that by Theseus
Iphigenia was begotten of her: which being granted, maketh much
against Homer (if you marke at) for making Menelaus thinke yet he
maried her a virgin (if Spondanus' translation should passe.) First,* 110
*no man being so simple to thinke that the Poet thinketh alwaies
as he maketh others speake; and next, it being no verie strange or
rare credulitie in men to beleeve they marrie maids when they
do not. Much more such a man made for the purpose as Menelaus,
whose good husbandly imagination of his wive's maidenhead at* 115
*their mariage I hope answereth at full the most foolish taxation of
Homer's ignorance—in which a man may wonder at these learned
Criticks' overlearnednesse, and what ropes of sand they make with
their kinde of intelligencing knowledge—I meane in such as abuse
the name of Criticks, as many versers do of Poets; the rest for their* 120
industries I reverence. But all this time, I lose my collection of

Menelaus' sillie and ridiculous upbraids here given to the Troyans.
First (as above said) for ravishing his wife in the flowre of her yeares
—when should a man play such a part but then?—though in deed
poore Menelaus had the more wrong or losse in it, and yet Paris   125
the more reason. He addeth then, and without cause or injurie, a
most sharp one in Homer, and in Menelaus as much ridiculous:
as though lovers looked for more cause in their love-suits than the
beauties of their beloved, or that men were made cuckolds only for
spite, or revenge of some wrong precedent. But indeed Menelaus'   130
true simplicitie in this, to thinke harmes should not be done without
harmes foregoing (no, not in these unsmarting harmes) maketh him
well deserve his Epithete ἀγαθός. *Yet further, see how his pure*
imbecillitie prevaileth, and how by a thred Homer cutteth him out
here, ἐπεὶ φιλέεσθε παρ' αὐτῇ, postquam amicè tractati fuistis apud   135
ipsam, *after ye had bene kindly entertaind at her hands. I hope*
you will thinke nothing could encourage them more than that. See
how he speaketh against her in taking her part, and how ingeniously
Homer giveth him still some colour of reason for his senslesnesse,
which colour yet is enough to deceive our Commentors: they finde   140
not yet the tame figure of our horned. But they and all Translators
still force his speeches to the best part. Yet further then make we
our dissection. And now (saith our Simplician) you would againe
shew your iniquities, even to the casting of pernicious fire into our
fleete and killing our Princes if you could. Would any man thinke   145
this in an Enemie? And such an Enemie as the Troyans? Chide
Enemies in armes for offering to hurt their Enemies? Would you
have yet plainer this good King's simplicity? But his slaughters
sometimes, and wise words, are those mists our Homer casteth before
the eyes of his Readers, that hindereth their prospects to his more   150
constant and predominant softnesse and simplicitie. Which he doth,
imagining his understanding Reader's eyes more sharpe than not
to see pervially through them. And yet, would not have these great
ones themselves neede so subtle flatteries but that everie shadow
of their worth might remove all the substance of their worthlesnesse.   155
I am weary with beating this thin thicket for a woodcocke, and yet,
lest it prove still too thicke for our sanguine and gentle complexions
to shine through, in the next words of his lame reproofe, he crieth
out against Jupiter, saying ἦ τέ σε φασὶ περὶ φρένας ἔμμεναι ἄλλων.
Profectò te aiunt sapientia (vel circa mentem) superare cæteros   160
homines atque Deos: *wherein he affirmeth that men say so, building*
(poore man) even that unknowne secret to himselfe upon others,
and now, I hope, sheweth himselfe emptie enough. But, lest you
should say I strive to illustrate the Sun and make cleare a thing
plaine, heare how darke and perplext a riddle it sheweth yet to our   165

good *Spondanus, being an excellent scholler and Homer's Commentor—whose words upon this speech are these:* Facundiam Menelai cum acumine, antea prædicavit Homerus (*intending in Antenor's speech,* lib. 3. *unto which I pray you turne*) cuius hîc luculentum exemplum habes. Vehemens autem est eius hoc loco 170 oratio, ut qui iniuriarum sibi à Troianis in uxoris raptu illatarum recordetur, quas præsens eorumdem in Græcos impetus exacerbavit. Primùm itaque in Troianos invehitur, et eorum furorem tandem aliquando cohibitum iri comminatur. Deindè, per Apostrophem, ad Jovem conqueritur de inexplebili pugnandi ardore, quibus 175 Troiani vehementer inflammantur. *Would any man beleeve this serious blindnes in so great a scholler? Nor is he alone so taken in his eyes, but al the rest of our most prophaned and holy Homer's Traducers.*

[637] Καὶ ἐϋστρόφῳ οἰὸς ἀώτῳ *&c.* Et benè torta ovis lana (*or* 180 *rather,* benè torto ovis flore.) Definitio fundæ (*saith Spondanus*) vel potius periphrastica descriptio. *The definition, or rather paraphrasticall description, of a sling—a most unsufferable exposition, not a sling being to be heard of (as I before affirmed) in all the services exprest in these* Iliads. *It is therefore the true* 185 *periphrasis of a light kind of armor called a jacke, that all our archers used to serve in of old, and were ever quilted with wooll, and (because* εὖστροφος *signifieth as well* qui facili motu versatur et circumagitur, *as well as* benè vel pulchre tortus) *for their lightnesse and aptnesse to be worne, partaketh with the word in that* 190 *signification. Besides, note the words that follow, which are:*
τᾳρφέα βάλλοντες *and* ὄπισθεν* βάλλοντες *&c.* frequenter iacientes, *and* à tergo iacientes, *'shooting, striking or wounding so thicke, and at the backes of the armed men,' not 'hurling'; here being no talke of any stones, but onely* συνεχλόνεον γὰρ ὀϊστοὶ, 195
conturbabant enim sagittæ. *And when saw any man slings lined with wooll? To keepe their stones warme? Or to dull their deliverie? And I am sure they hurled not shafts out of them. The agreement of the Greekes with our English, as well in all other their greatest vertues, as this skill with their bowes, other places* 200 *of these Annotations shall clearely demonstrate, and give (in my conceipt) no little honour to our Countrie.*

* Metri causa usurpatur ὄπιθεν

The End of the Thirteenth Booke

THE FOURTEENTH BOOKE

of

HOMER'S ILIADS

THE ARGUMENT

Atrides, to behold the skirmish, brings
Old Nestor and the other wounded kings.
Juno (receiving of the Cyprian Dame
Her Ceston, whence her sweet enticements came)
Descends to Somnus, and gets him to bind   5
The powres of Jove with sleepe, to free her mind.
Neptune assists the Greeks, and of the foe
Slaughter inflicts a mightie overthrow.
Ajax so sore strikes Hector with a stone,
It makes him spit blood, and his sense sets gone.   10

Another Argument

In Ξ with sleepe, and bed, heaven's Queene
Even Jove himselfe makes overseene.

This first verse (after the first foure syllables) is to be read as one of our Tens.

Not wine, nor feasts, could lay their soft chaines on old
    Nestor's eare
To this high Clamor; who requir'd Machaon's thoughts to beare
His care in part about the cause: 'For me thinke still,' said he
'The crie increases. I must needs the watch towre mount to see
Which way the flood of warre doth drive. Still drinke thou   5
    wine, and eate
Till faire-hair'd Hecamed hath given a little water heate,
To cleanse the quitture from thy wound.' This said, the
    goodly shield
Of war-like Thrasymed, his sonne (who had his owne in field),
He tooke, snatcht up a mightie lance, and so stept forth to view
Cause of that Clamor. Instantly, th' unworthy cause he knew,   10
The Grecians wholly put in rout, the Troyans rowting still,

[280]

Close at the Greeks' backs, their wall rac't. The old man mournd
    this ill.

Simile. And as when, with unwieldie waves, the great Sea forefeeles winds
That both waies murmure, and no way her certaine current finds,
But pants and swels confusedly, here goes, and there will stay,   15
Till on it aire casts one firme winde, and then it rolles away:
So stood old Nestor in debate, two thoughts at once on wing
In his discourse—if first to take direct course to the King,
Or to the multitude in fight. At last he did conclude
To visit Agamemnon first. Meane time both hosts imbrewd   20
Their steele in one another's blood, nought wrought their
    healths but harmes,
Swords, huge stones, double-headed darts still thumping
    on their armes.
And now the Jove-kept Kings, whose wounds were yet in cure,
    did meet

Agamemnon, Ulysses, Old Nestor, Diomed, Ithacus, and Atreus' sonne, from fleet
and Diomed wounded, Bent for the fight, which was farre off, the ships being drawne   25
go towards the field.   to shore
On heapes at first, till all theire sterns a wall was raisd before;
Which (though not great) it yet suffisd to hide them, though
    their men
Were something streighted—for whose scope, in forme of
    battel then,
They drew them through the spacious shore one by another still,
Till all the bosome of the Strand their sable bulks did fill,   30
Even till they took up all the space twixt both the Promontories.
These kings (like Nestor), in desire to know for what those cries
Became so violent, came along (all leaning on their darts)
To see, though not of powre to fight, sad and suspicious hearts
Distempring them, and (meeting now Nestor) the king in feare   35

Agamemnon to Nestor. Cried out: 'O Nestor, our renowne, why shewes they presence
    here,
The harmefull fight abandoned? Now Hector will make good
The threatning vow he made (I feare) that till he had our blood,
And fir'd our fleet, he never more would turne to Ilion.
Nor is it long, I see, before his whole will will be done.   40
O Gods, I now see all the Greeks put on Achilles' ire
Against my honour—no meane left, to keepe our fleet from fire.'

Nestor to Agamemnon.   He answerd: 'Tis an evident truth, not Jove himselfe can now
(With all the thunder in his hands) prevent our overthrow.
The wall we thought invincible, and trusted more than Jove,   45
Is scal'd, rac't, enterd, and our powres (driven up), past
    breathing, prove

[281]

A most inevitable fight: both slaughters so commixt,
That for your life you cannot put your diligent'st thought
    betwixt
The Greeks and Troyans, and as close their throates cleave to
    the skie.
Consult we then (if that will serve). For fight, advise not I;   50
It fits not wounded men to fight.' Atrides answerd him:

*Agamemnon's replie
to Nestor, urging
flight.*

'If such a wall, as cost the Greeks so many a tired lim,
And such a dike be past and rac't, that (as your selfe said well)
We all esteemd invicible, and would past doubt repell
The world from both our fleete and us, it doth directly show,   55
That here Jove vowes our shames and deaths. I evermore
    did know
His hand from ours, when he helpt us: and now I see as cleare
That (like the blessed Gods) he holds our hated enemies deare,
Supports their armes, and pinnions ours. Conclude then, tis
    in vaine
To strive with him. Our ships drawne up, now let us lanch   60
    againe
And keepe at anchor, till calme Night; that then (perhaps)
    our foes
May calme their stormes, and in that time our scape we may
    dispose.
It is not any shame to flie from ill, although by night:
Knowne ill, he better does that flies than he it takes in fight.'

*Ulysses' bitter answer
to Agamemnon.*

Ulysses frown'd on him, and said: 'Accurst, why talk'st   65
    thou thus?
Would thou hadst led some barbarous host, and not
    commanded us
Whom Jove made souldiers from our youth, that age might
    scorne to flie
From any charge it undertakes, and every dazeled eye
The honord hand of warre might close. Thus wouldst thou
    leave this towne
For which our many miseries felt entitle it our owne?   70
Peace, lest some other Greeke give eare, and heare a sentence such
As no man's pallate should prophane—at least, that knew
    how much
His own right weigh'd, and being a Prince, and such a Prince
    as beares
Rule of so many Greeks as thou. This counsell lothes mine
    eares—
Let others toyle in fight and cries, and we so light of heeles   75
Upon their verie noise and grones to hoise away our keeles!

Thus we should fit the wish of Troy, that being something neare
The victorie we give it cleare. And we were sure to beare
A slaughter to the utmost man, for no man will sustaine
A stroke, the fleete gone, but at that looke still, and wish   80
    him slaine.
And therefore, Prince of men, be sure thy censure is unfit.'

Agamemnon to
Ulysses.

'O Ithacus,' replied the King, 'thy bitter termes have smit
My heart in sunder. At no hand, gainst any Prince's will
Do I command this. Would to God that any man of skill
To give a better counsell would, or old, or younger man: 85
My voice should gladly go with his.' Then Diomed began:

Diomed to Agamemnon
and the rest.

'The man not farre is, nor shall aske much labour to bring in,
That willingly would speake his thoughts, if, spoken, they
        might win
Fit eare, and suffer no empaire that I discover them,
Being yongest of you—since my Sire, that heir'd a Diadem,   90
May make my speech to Diadems decent enough, though he

Diomed's pedigree.

Lies in his sepulcher at Thebes. I bost this pedigree.
Portheus three famous sonnes begot, that in high Calydon
And Pleuron kept, with state of kings, their habitation.
Agrius, Melas and the third, the horseman Œneus,   95
My father's father, that exceld in actions generous
The other two. But these kept home, my father being driven
With wandring and adventrous spirits, for so the king of heaven
And th' other Gods set downe their willes, and he to Argos came,
Where he begun the world and dwelt, there marying a dame,   100
One of Adrastus' femall race. He kept a royall house,
For he had great demeanes, good land, and (being industrious)
He planted many orchard grounds about his house, and bred
Great store of sheepe. Besides all this, he was well qualited
And past all Argives for his speare. And these digressive things   105
Are such as you may well endure, since (being deriv'd
        from kings,
And kings not poore, nor vertulesse) you cannot hold me base,
Nor scorne my words, which oft (though true) in meane men
        meet disgrace.
How ever, they are these in short. Let us be seene at fight,
And yeeld to strong Necessitie, though wounded, that our sight   110
May set those men on that of late have to Achilles' spleene
Bene too indulgent, and left blowes: but be we onely seene,
Not come within the reach of darts, lest wound on wound
        we lay—
(Which reverend Nestor's speech implide) and so farre
        him obay.'

[283]

This counsell gladly all observ'd, went on, Atrides led. 115
Nor Neptune this advantage lost, but closely followed,

And like an aged man appear'd t' Atrides, whose right hand
He seisd, and said: 'Atrides, this doth passing fitly stand
With sterne Achilles' wreakfull spirit, that he can stand a sterne
His ship, and both in flight and death the Grecian bane 120
      discerne,
Since not in his breast glowes one sparke of any humane mind.

But be that his owne bane: let God by that losse make him find
How vile a thing he is. For know, the blest Gods have
      not given
Thee ever over; but perhaps the Troyans may from heaven
Receive that justice. Nay, tis sure, and thou shalt see their **fals,** 125
Your fleete soone freed, and for fights here they glad to take
      their wals.'
This said, he made knowne who he was, and parted with a crie
As if ten thousand men had joynd in battaile then, so hie
His throate flew through the host: and so this great
      earth-shaking God
Chear'd up the Greeke hearts that they wisht their paines 130
      no period.
      Saturnia from Olympus top saw her great brother there
And her great husband's brother too, exciting every where
The glorious spirits of the Greeks; which, as she joy'd to see,
So (on the fountfull Ida's top) Jove's sight did disagree
With her contentment, since she fear'd, that his hand would 135
      descend
And checke the sea-God's practises. And this she did contend
How to prevent, which thus seem'd best—to decke her curiously

And visite the Idalian hill, that so the Lightner's eye
She might enamour with her lookes and his high temples steepe
(Even to his wisedome) in the kind and golden juyce of sleepe. 140
So tooke she chamber, which her sonne, the God of ferrary,
With firme doores made, being joyned close and with a
      privie key,
That no God could command but Jove; where (enterd) she
      made fast
The shining gates, and then upon her lovely bodie cast
Ambrosia, that first made it cleare, and after laid on it 145

An odorous, rich and sacred oyle, that was so wondrous sweet
That, ever, when it was but toucht, it sweetn'd heaven
      and earth.
Her body being cleansd with this, her Tresses she let forth,

And comb'd (her combe dipt in the oyle), then wrapt them up
    in curles:
And thus (her deathlesse head adornd) a heavenly veile she   **150**
    hurles
On her white shoulders, wrought by her that rules in
    housewiferies,
Who wove it full of antique workes, of most divine device.
And this, with goodly clasps of gold, she fastn'd to her breast:
Then with a girdle (whose rich sphere a hunderd studs imprest)
She girt her small wast. In her eares (tenderly pierc't) she wore   **155**
Pearles, great and orient: on her head, a wreath not worne
    before
Cast beames out like the Sunne. At last, she to her feete did tie
Faire shoes, and thus, entire attir'd, she shin'd in open skie,
Cald the faire Paphian Queene apart from th' other Gods,
    and said:

Juno to Venus.   'Lov'd daughter, should I aske a grace, should I or be obeyd,   **160**
Or wouldst thou crosse me, being incenst, since I crosse thee
    and take

Venus to Juno.   The Greeks' part, thy hand helping Troy?' She answerd: 'That
    shall make
No difference in a different cause. Aske, ancient Deitie,
What most contents thee. My mind stands inclin'd as liberally
To grant it as thine owne to aske, provided that it be   **165**
A favour fit and in my powre.' She (given deceiptfully)
Thus said: 'Then give me those two powres with which both
    men and Gods
Thou vanquishest, Love and Desire. For now, the periods
Of all the many-feeding earth and the originall
Of all the gods, Oceanus, and Thetis, whom we call   **170**
Our mother, I am going to greet. They nurst me in their court
And brought me up, receiving me in most respectfull sort
From Rhea; when Jove under earth and the unfruitfull seas
Cast Saturne. These I go to see, intending to appease
Jarres growne betwixt them, having long abstaind from   **175**
    speech and bed—
Which jarres could I so reconcile that in their anger's stead
I could place love, and so renew their first societie,
I should their best lov'd be esteem'd and honord endlesly.'

Venus to Juno.   She answerd: ''Tis not fit nor just thy will should be denied,
Whom Jove in his embraces holds.' This spoken, she untied   **180**
And from her odorous bosome tooke her Ceston, in whose sphere
Were all enticements to delight, all Loves, all Longings were,

[285]

Kind conference, Faire speech, whose powre the wisest doth
    enflame.
This she resigning to her hands, thus urg'd her by her name:
    'Receive this bridle, thus faire wrought, and put it twixt   **185**
    thy brests,
Where all things to be done are done; and whatsoever rests
In thy desire, returne with it.' The great-eyd Juno smild
And put it twixt her brests. Love's Queene, thus cunningly
    beguild,
To Jove's court flew. Saturnia (straight stooping from heaven's
    height)
Pieria and Emathia (those countries of delight)   **190**
Soone reacht, and (to the snowy mounts where Thracian
    souldiers dwell
Approaching) past their tops untoucht. From Athos then she fell
Past all the brode sea and arriv'd in Lemnos, at the towres
Of god-like Thoas, where she met the Prince of all men's
    powres,

Juno to Somnus.   Death's brother, Sleepe, whose hand she tooke, and said: **195**
    'Thou king of men,
Prince of the Gods too, if before thou heardst my suites, againe
Give helpefull eare, and through all times I'le offer thanks
    to thee.
Lay slumber on Jove's fierie eyes that I may comfort me
With his embraces. For which grace, I'le grace thee with a throne
Incorruptible, all of gold, and elegantly done   **200**
By Mulciber, to which he forg'd a footestoole for the ease
Of thy soft feete, when wine and feasts thy golden humours
    please.'

Somnus to Juno.   Sweet Sleepe replyed: 'Saturnia, there lives not any god
(Besides Jove) but I would becalme—ay, if it were the flood
That fathers all the Deities, the great Oceanus.   **205**
But Jove we dare not come more neare than he commandeth us.
Now you command me, as you did when Jove's great-minded
    sonne
Alcides (having sackt the towne of stubborne Ilion)
Tooke saile from thence, when by your charge I pour'd about
    Jove's mind
A pleasing slumber, calming him till thou drav'st up the wind,   **210**
In all his cruelties, to sea, that set his sonne ashore
In Cous, farre from all his friends. Which (waking) vext so sore
The supreme godhead that he cast the gods about the skie
And me (above them all) he sought, whom he had utterly
Hurld from the sparkling firmament if all-gods-taming Night,   **215**

(Whom, flying, I besought for aid) had sufferd his despight
And not preserv'd me: but his wrath with my offence dispenc't,
For feare t' offend her, and so ceast, though never so incenst.
And now another such escape you wish I should prepare.'

Juno to Somnus.   She answerd: 'What hath thy deepe rest to do with his   220
            deepe care?
As though Jove's love to Ilion in all degrees were such
As twas to Hercules, his sonne, and so would storme as much
For their displeasure as for his? Away, I will remove
Thy feare with giving thee the dame that thou didst ever love,
One of the faire young Graces borne, divine Pasithae.'   225
     This started Somnus into joy, who answerd: 'Sweare to me,
By those inviolable springs that feed the Stygian lake,
With one hand touch the nourishing earth and in the other take
The marble sea, that all the gods of the infernall state
Which circle Saturne may to us be witnesses, and rate   230
What thou hast vow'd—that with all truth, thou wilt bestow
            on me
The dame (I grant) I ever lov'd, divine Pasithae.'

The oath of Juno   She swore, as he enjoyn'd, in all, and strengthend all his joyes,
to Somnus. By naming all th' infernall gods surnam'd the Titanois.
     The oath thus taken, both tooke way and made their   235
            quicke repaire
To Ida from the towne and Ile, all hid in liquid aire.
At Lecton first they left the sea, and there, the land they trod:
The fountfull nurse of savages with all her woods did nod
Beneath their feete: there Somnus staid, lest Jove's bright eye
            should see;

Somnus climes a   And yet (that he might see to Jove) he climb'd the   240
firre tree.   goodliest tree
That all th' Idalian mountaine bred, and crownd her progenie.
A firre it was, that shot past aire and kist the burning skie.
There sate he hid in his darke armes, and in the shape, withall,
Of that continuall prating bird whom all the Dieties call
Chalcis; but men Cymindis name. Saturnia tript apace   245
Up to the top of Gargarus, and shewd her heavenly face
To Jupiter, who saw, and lov'd, and with as hote a fire
(Being curious in her tempting view) as when with first desire
(The pleasure of it being stolne) they mixt in love and bed.

Jupiter to Juno. And (gazing on her still) he said: 'Saturnia, what hath bred   250
This haste in thee from our high court, and whither tends
            thy gate,
That voide of horse and chariot, fit for thy soveraigne state,

Thou lackiest here?' Her studied fraude replyed: 'My journey
now
Leaves state and labours to do good. And where in right I owe
All kindnesse to the Sire of gods and our good mother Queene,   255
That nurst and kept me curiously in court (since both have bene
Long time at discord) my desire is to attone their hearts.
And therefore go I now to see those earth's extremest parts,
For whose farre-seate I spar'd my horse the skaling of this hill,
And left them at the foote of it: for they must taste their fill   260
Of travaile with me, that must draw my coach through earth
and seas,
Whose farre-intended reach, respect and care not to displease
Thy graces made me not attempt without thy gracious leave.'
    The cloud-compelling god, her guile in this sort did receive;

'Juno, thou shalt have after leave, but, ere so farre thou stray,   265
Convert we our kind thoughts to love, that now doth every way
Circle with victorie my powers: nor yet with any dame
(Woman, or goddesse) did his fires my bosome so enflame
As now with thee. Not when it lov'd the parts so generous
Ixion's wife had, that brought foorth the wise Pirithous;   270
Nor when the lovely Danae, Acrisius' daughter, stird
My amorous powres, that Perseus bore, to all men else preferd;
Nor when the dame, that Phœnix got, surprisd me with
her sight,
Who the divine-soul'd Rhadamanth and Minos brought to light;
Nor Semele, that bore to me the joy of mortall men,   275
The sprightly Bacchus, nor the dame that Thebes renowned
then,
Alcmena, that bore Hercules; Latona, so renownd;
Queene Ceres, with the golden haire; nor thy faire eyes
did wound
My entrailes to such depth as now with thirst of amorous ease.'

    The cunning dame seem'd much incenst, and said: 'What   280
words are these,
Unsufferable Saturn's sonne? What? Here? In Ida's height?
Desir'st thou this? How fits it us? Or what if in the sight
Of any god thy will were pleasd, that he the rest might bring
To witnesse thy incontinence? T'were a dishonourd thing.
I would not shew my face in heaven, and rise from such a bed.   285
But, if love be so deare to thee, thou hast a chamber sted
Which Vulcan purposely contriv'd with all fit secrecie:

There sleepe at pleasure.' He replyed: 'I feare not if the eye
Of either god or man observe: so thicke a cloude of gold

[288]

I'le cast about us that the Sunne (who furthest can behold)   290
Shall never find us.' This resolv'd, into his kind embrace

The bed of Jupiter and Juno.

He tooke his wife. Beneath them both faire Tellus strewd
     the place
With fresh-sprung herbes, so soft and thicke that up aloft it bore
Their heavenly bodies: with his leaves did deawy Lotus store
Th' Elysian mountaine; Saffron flowres and Hyacinths   295
     helpt make
The sacred bed; and there they slept. When sodainly there brake
A golden vapour out of aire, whence shining dewes did fall,
In which they wrapt them close, and slept till Jove was
     tam'd withall.
     Meane space flew Somnus to the ships, found Neptune out,
     and said:

Somnus to Neptune.

'Now chearfully assist the Greeks and give them glorious head—   300
At least a little, while Jove sleepes, of whom through ever limme
I pour'd darke sleepe; Saturnia's love hath so illuded him.'
     This newes made Neptune more secure in giving Grecians
     heart,
And through the first fights thus he stird the men of most desert:

Neptune to the Greekes.

     'Yet, Grecians, shall we put our ships and conquest in   305
     the hands
Of Priam's Hector by our sloth? He thinks so, and commands
With pride according, all because Achilles keepes away.
Alas, as we were nought but him! We little need to stay
On his assistance, if we would our owne strengths call to field
And mutually maintaine repulse. Come on then, all men yeeld   310
To what I order; we that beare best armes in all our host,
Whose heads sustaine the brightest helms, whose hands are
     bristl'd most
With longest lances, let us on. But stay, I'le leade you all.
Nor thinke I but great Hector's spirits will suffer some apall,
Though they be never so inspir'd. The ablest of us then,   315
That on our shoulders worst shields beare, exchange with
     worser men
That fight with better.' This proposd, all heard it, and obeyd.
The kings (even those that sufferd wounds, Ulysses, Diomed
And Agamemnon) helpt t' instruct the complete army thus—
To good, gave good armes; worse, to worse, yet none were   320
     mutinous.

Neptune leades the Greekes.

     Thus (arm'd with order) forth they flew: the great
     Earth-shaker led,
A long sword in his sinowy hand, which when he brandished,

It lighten'd still: there was no law for him and it; poore men
Must quake before them. These thus man'd, illustrous
    Hector then
His hoast brought up. The blew-hair'd god and he stretcht   325
    through the prease
A greivous fight—when to the ships and tents of Greece the seas
Brake loose and rag'd. But when they joynd, the dreadfull
    Clamor rose
To such a height as not the sea, when up the North-spirit blowes
Her raging billowes, bellowes so against the beaten shore—
Nor such a rustling keeps a fire, driven with violent blore,   330
Through woods that grow against a hill—nor so the fervent
    strokes
Of almost-bursting winds resound against a grove of Okes:
As did the clamor of these hoasts, when both the battels closd.

Hector at Ajax.   Of all which, noble Hector first at Ajax' breast disposd
His javelin, since so right on him the great-soul'd souldier   335
    bore;
Nor mist it, but the bawdricks both that his brode bosome wore
To hang his shield and sword it strooke; both which his
    flesh preserv'd.
Hector (disdaining that his lance had thus as good as swerv'd)

Ajax at Hector.   Trode to his strength; but going off, great Ajax with a stone
(One of the many props for ships that there lay trampl'd on)   340
Strooke his brode breast above his shield, just underneath
    his throte,
And shooke him peecemeale—when the stone sprung backe
    againe and smote
Earth, like a whirlewind gathering dust with whirring
    fiercely round,
For fervour of his unspent strength, in setling on the ground.

Simile.   And, as when Jove's bolt by the rootes rends from the earth   345
    an Oke,
His sulphure casting with the blow a strong, unsavoury smoke,
And on the falne plant none dare looke but with amazed eyes,
(Jove's thunder being no laughing game), so bowd strong
    Hector's thyes,

Hector overthrowne.   And so with tost-up heeles he fell: away his lance he flung,
His round shield followd, then his helme, and out his   350
    armour rung.
    The Greeks then showted and ran in, and hop't to hale
    him off,
And therefore powr'd on darts in stormes, to keepe his aide
    aloofe.

Hector rescued.

But none could hurt the people's guide, nor stirre him from
    his ground.
Sarpedon, prince of Lycia, and Glaucus so renownd,
Divine Agenor, Venus' sonne, and wise Polydamas   355
Rusht to his rescue, and the rest; no one neglective was
Of Hector's safetie. All their shields they coucht about him close,
Raisd him from earth, and (giving him in their kind armes
    repose)
From off the labour caried him to his rich chariot,
And bore him mourning towards Troy. But when the flood   360
    they got
Of gulphy Xanthus, that was got by deathlesse Jupiter,
There tooke they him from chariot, and all besprinkled there
His temples with the streame. He breath'd, lookt up, assaid
    to rise,
And on his knees staid, spitting blood: againe then closd
    his eyes,
And backe againe his body fell; the maine blow had not done   365
Yet with his spirit. When the Greeks saw worthy Hector gone,
Then thought they of their worke, then charg'd with much
    more chere the foe,
And then (farre first) Oiliades began the overthrow.
He darted Satnius, Enops' sonne, whom famous Nais bore
(As she was keeping Enops' flocks) on Satnius' river's shore,   370
And strooke him in his bellie's rimme, who upwards fell
    and raisd
A mightie skirmish with his fall. And then Panthœdes seisd
Prothenor Areilycides with his revend'gfull speare
On his right shoulder, strooke it through, and laid him
    breathlesse there.

*Polydamas his
insultation.*

For which he insolently bragd, and cryed out: 'Not a dart   375
From great-soul'd Panthus' sonne, I thinke, shall ever
    vainlier part,
But some Greeke bosome it shall take, and make him give
    his ghost.'
This bragge the Grecians stomackt much, but Telamonius most,
Who stood most neare Prothenor's fall: and out he sent a lance,
Which Panthus' sonne (declining) scap't, yet tooke it to   380
    sad chance
Archelochus, Antenor's sonne, whom heaven did destinate
To that sterne end; twixt necke and head the javelin wrought
    his fate,
And ran in at the upper joint of all the back's long bone,
Cut both the nerves and such a lode of strength laid Ajax on

[291]

As, that small part he seisd outwaid all th' under lims, and strooke   385
His heeles up so that head and face the earth's possession tooke,
When all the low parts sprung in air. And thus did Ajax quit

Ajax insults in requitall of Polydamas.

Panthœdes' Brave: 'Now, Panthus' sonne, let thy prophetique wit
Consider and disclose a truth, if this man do not wey
Even with Prothenor. I conceive no one of you will say   390
That either he was base himselfe, or sprung of any base.
Antenor's brother, or his sonne, he should be by his face;
One of his race, past question, his likenesse shewes he is.'
    This spake he, knowing it well enough. The Troyans storm'd at this,
And then slue Acamas (to save his brother, yet ingag'd),   395
Bœotius, dragging him to spoile; and thus the Greeks enrag'd:
    'O Greeks, even borne to beare our darts, yet ever breathing threats,
Not alwayes under teares and toyles ye see our fortune sweats,
But sometimes you drop under death. See now your quicke among
Our dead, intranc't with my weake lance, to prove I have   400
    ere long
Reveng'd my brother. Tis the wish of every honest man
His brother slaine in Mars his field may rest wreakt in his Phane.'
    This stird fresh envie in the Greeks, but urg'd Peneleus most,
Who hurld his lance at Acamas; he scap't; nor yet it lost
The force he gave it, for it found the flocke-rich Phorbas'   405
    sonne,
Ilioneus, whose deare Sire (past all in Ilion)
Was lov'd of Hermes and enricht, and to him onely bore
His mother this now slaughterd man. The dart did undergore
His eye-lid, by his eye's deare rootes, and out the apple fell,
The eye pierc't through: nor could the nerve that staies the   410
    necke repell
His strong-wing'd lance, but necke and all gave way, and downe
    he dropt.
Peneleus then unsheath'd his sword, and from the shoulders
    chopt
His lucklesse head, which downe he threw, the helme still
    sticking on
And still the lance fixt in his eye; which not to see alone
Contented him, but up againe he snatcht and shewd it all   415
With this sterne Brave: 'Ilians, relate brave Ilioneus' fall

To his kind parents, that their roofes their teares may
    overrunne;
For so the house of Promachus, and Alegenor's sonne,
Must with his wive's eyes overflow, she never seeing more
Her deare Lord, though we tell his death when to our native   420
    shore
We bring from ruin'd Troy our fleete, and men so long forgone.'
This said, and seene, pale Feare possest all those of Ilion,
And ev'ry man cast round his eye to see where Death was not,
That he might flie him. Let not then his grac't hand be forgot
(O Muses you that dwell in heaven) that first embrude the field   425
With Troyan spoile, when Neptune thus had made their
    irons yeeld.
    First Ajax Telamonius the Mysian Captaine slew,
Great Hyrtius Gyrtiades. Antilochus o'rethrew
Phalces and Mermer, to their spoyle. Meriones gave end
To Morys and Hippotion. Teucer to Fate did send   430
Prothoon and Periphetes. Atrides' Javelin chac't
Duke Hyperenor, wounding him in that part that is plac't
Betwixt the short ribs and the bones that to the triple gut
Have pertinence. The Javelin's head did out his entrailes cut,
His forc't soule breaking through the wound: night's black   435
    hand closde his eies.

Ajax Oileus' vertue for   Then Ajax, great Oileus' sonne, had divers victories:
swiftnesse.   For when Saturnius sufferd flight, of all the Grecian race
Not one with swiftnesse of his feete could so enrich a chace.

COMMENTARIUS

[81] Ὄρχαμε λαῶν. Princeps populorum (*the end of Ulysses' speech in the beginning of this book*) *which ascription our Spondanus takes to be given in scorne and that all Ulysses' speech is* σκωπτική, *or scoffing; which is spoken altogether seriously and bitterly to this title at the end, which was spoken* ἤπιως, molliter *or* benigne, *of purpose*   5
to make Agamemnon beare the better the justice of his other austeritie.

[92] Καὶ ἐγὼ γένος εὔχομαι εἶναι et ego quoad genus glorior esse.
The long digression that followes this in the speech of Diomed (being next to Agamemnon's reply to Ulysses) bewrayes an affectation he had by all-any-thing-fit meanes to talke of his pedigree, and by reason   10
of that humor hath shewne his desire elsewhere to learne the pedigrees of others: as in the sixt booke, in his enquirie of Glaucus' pedigree. And herein is exprest part of his character.

[343] Στρόμβον δ' ὡς ἔσσευε βαλών, &c. *Overpassing, for speed, many things in this booke that crie out for the praise of our Homer,*   15
and note of that which in most readers I know will be lost, I must onely insist still on those parts that (in my poore understanding) could never yet find apprehension in any of our Commentors or translators: as in this simile againe of the whirlewind, to which the stone that Ajax hurled at Hector is resembled. Valla and Eobanus,   20
Salel in French, so understanding 'Hector turned about with the blow, like a whirlewind.' Valla's words are these (translating στρόμβον δ'ὡς ἔσσευε βαλών, περὶ δ'ἔδραμε πάντῃ, *which ad verbum saie thus much in every common translation:* Trochum autem sicut concussit feriens, rotatusque est undique): Quo ictu Hector velut turbo, quem   25
Strombum dicunt, rotato corpore, &c. *Eobanus converting it thus:*

——— Stetit ille tremens, ceu turbo rotatus.

Which though it harpe upon the other, makes yet much worse musicke, saying: 'Hector stood trembling, being wheeled about like a whirlwind. He stood, yet was turned about violently.' How grosse   30
both are, I thinke, the blindest see, and must needs acknowledge a monstrous unworthines in these men to touch our Homer, esteeming it an extreme losse to the world to have this and the like undiscovered. For (as I apprehend it) being exprest no better than in my silly conversion (and the stone, not Hector, likened to the whirlewind)   35

[294]

it is above the wit of a man to imitate our Homer's wit, for the most
fierie illustration both of Ajax' strength and Hector's: of Ajax for
giving such a force to it as could not spend it selfe upon Hector, but
turne after upon the earth in that whirlewind-like violence: of
Hector, for standing it so solidly, for without that consideration the 40
stone could never have recoild so fiercely. And here have we a ruled
case against our plaine and smug writers, that because their owne
unweildinesse will not let them rise themselves, would have every
man grovel like them, their fethers not passing the pitch of every
woman's capacity. And (indeed) where a man is understood, there 45
is ever a proportion betwixt the writer's wit and the writee's (that I
may speake with authority) according to my old lesson in Philosophy:
Intellectus in ipsa intelligibilia transit. But herein this case is ruled
against such men, that they affirme these hypertheticall or superlative
sort of expressions and illustrations are too bold and bumbasted; 50
and out of that word is spunne that which they call our Fustian, their
plaine writing being stuffe nothing so substantial but such grosse
sowtedge, or hairepatch, as every goose may eate oates through.
Against which, and all these plebeian opinions that a man is bound
to write to every vulgar reader's understanding, you see the great 55
master of all elocution hath written so darkly that almost three
thousand sunnes have not discovered him, no more in five hundred
other places than here—and yet all perviall enough (you may well say)
when such a one as I comprehend them. But the chiefe end why I
extend this annotation is onely to intreate your note here of Homer's 60
maner of writing, which (to utter his after-store of matter and
varietie) is so presse, and puts on with so strong a current, that it
farre over-runnes the most laborious pursuer, if he have not a
Poeticall foote and Poesie's quicke eye to guide it. The verse in
question, I referre you to before, which says, χερμάδιος, signifying 65
a stone of a handfull, or that with one hand may be raised and cast,
spoken of before, and (here being understood) shooke Hector at all
parts in striking him, and like a whirlwind wheeled or whirred about.
Wherein he speakes not of bounding to the earth again and raising
a dust with his violent turnings, in which the conceit and life of his 70
simile lies, but leaves it to his reader, and he leaves it to him.
Notwithstanding he utters enough to make a stone understand it,
how stupidly soever all his interpreters would have Hector (being
strooke into a trembling, and almost dead) turne about like a
whirlewind. I conclude then with this question: What fault is it in 75
me to furnish and adorne my verse (being his Translator) with
translating and adding the truth and fulnesse of his conceit, it being
as like to passe my reader as his, and therefore necessarie? If it be
no fault in me, but fit, then may I justly be said to better Homer? Or

[295]

not to have all my invention, matter and forme from him, though a   80
little I enlarge his forme? Virgil, in all places where he is compared
and preferred to Homer, doth nothing more. And therefore my
assertion in the second Booke is true, that Virgil hath in all places
wherein he is compared and preferred to Homer by Scaliger, &c.
both his invention, matter and forme from him.   85

[432] Οὗτα κατὰ λαπάρην, &c. vulneravit ad Ile, *it is translated, and*
is in the last verses of this Booke, where Menelaus is said to wound
Hyperenor. But λαπάρη, dicitur ea pars corporis quæ posita est
inter costas nothas, et ossa quæ ad Ilia pertinent, quòd inanis sit, et
desideat. Hip. in lib. περὶ ἀγμῶν; *and therefore I accordingly*   90
translate it. And note this beside, both out of this place
and many others, how excellent an Anatomist our
Homer was, whose skill in those times, me thinkes,
should be a secret.

The End of the Fourteenth Booke

THE FIFTEENTH BOOKE
of
HOMER'S ILIADS

THE ARGUMENT

Jove waking, and beholding Troy in flight,
Chides Juno and sends Iris to the fight,
To charge the sea-god to forsake the field,
And Phœbus to invade it with his shield,
Recovering Hector's broosde and crased powres.   5
To field he goes and makes new conquerours,
The Troyans giving now the Grecians chace
Even to their fleete. Then Ajax turnes his face
And feeds, with many Troyan lives, his ire;
Who then brought brands to set the fleete on fire.   10

Another Argument

Jove sees in O *his oversight,*
Chides Juno, Neptune cals from fight.

The Troyans (beate past pale and dike, and numbers prostrate
   laide)
All got to chariot, feare-driven all; and fear'd as men dismaide.
Then Jove, on Ida's top, awakt, rose from Saturnia's side,
Stood up, and lookt upon the warre; and all inverted spide,
Since he had seene it, th' Ilians now in rowt, the Greeks in fight;   5
King Neptune, with his long sword, Chiefe; great Hector put
   downe quite,
Laide flat in field, and with a crowne of Princes compassed,
So stopt up that he scarce could breath, his mind's sound habite
   fled
And he still spitting blood. Indeed, his hurt was not set on
By one that was the weakest Greeke. But him Jove lookt upon   10
With eyes of pittie, on his wife with horrible aspect,

[297]

Jupiter's wrath against Juno.

To whom he said: 'O thou in ill most cunning Architect,
All Arts and comments that exceedst! not onely to enforce
Hector from fight, but with his men to shew the Greeks a course.
I feare (as formerly so now) these ils have with thy hands   15
Their first fruits sowne, and therefore could lode all thy lims
     with bands.
Forgetst thou, when I hangd thee up, how to thy feete I tyed
Two Anvils, golden manacles on thy false wrists implied,
And let thee mercilesly hang from our refined heaven
Even to earth's vapors; all the gods in great Olympus given   20
To mutinies about thee, yet (though all stood staring on)
None durst dissolve thee; for these hands (had they but seisd
     upon
Thy friend) had headlong throwne him off from our star-bearing
     round
Till he had tumbl'd out his breath and peecemeale dasht the
     ground.
Nor was my angry spirit calm'd so soone for those foule seas   25
On which (inducing Northerne flawes) thou shipwrack'dst
     Hercules
And tost him to the Coan shore, that thou shouldst tempt againe
My wrath's importance, when thou seest (besides) how grosly
     vaine
My powres can make thy policies: for from their utmost force
I freed my sonne and set him safe in Argos, nurse of horse.   30
These I remember to thy thoughts, that thou mayst shun these
     sleights
And know how badly bed-sports thrive, procur'd by base deceits.'
     This frighted the offending Queene, who with this state
     excusde

Juno's oath in clearing her self to Jupiter.

Her kind unkindnesse: 'Witnesse earth and heaven, so farre
     diffusde,
Thou Flood whose silent-gliding waves the under ground doth   35
     beare,
(Which is the great'st and gravest oath that any god can sweare)
Thy sacred head, those secret joyes that our yong bed gave forth
(By which I never rashly swore), that he who shakes the earth
Not by my counsell did this wrong to Hector and his host;
But (pittying th' oppressed Greekes, their fleete being neerly   40
     lost)
Reliev'd their hard condition, yet utterly impeld
By his free mind. Which since I see is so offensive held
To thy high pleasure, I will now advise him not to tread
But where thy tempest-raising feete, O Jupiter, shall leade.'

iter's charge to
to and
onciliation.

Jove laught to heare her so submisse, and said: 'My faire-eyd   45
          love,
If still thus thou and I were one (in counsels held above),
Neptune would still in word and fact be ours, if not in heart.
If then thy tongue and heart agree, from hence to heaven depart
To call the excellent in bowes, the Raine-bow, and the Sunne,
That both may visite both the hosts—the Grecian armie, one,   50
And that is Iris, let her haste and make the sea-god cease
T' assist the Greekes and to his court retire from warre, in peace.
Let Phœbus (on the Troyan part) inspire with wonted powre
Great Hector's spirits, make his thoughts forget the late sterne
          houre
And all his anguish, setting on his whole recover'd man   55
To make good his late grace in fight, and hold in constant wane
The Grecian glories, till they fall in flight before the fleete
Of vext Achilles. Which extreme will prove the meane to greete
Thee with thy wish, for then the eyes of great Æacides
(Made witnesse of the generall ill that doth so neare him prease)   60
Will make his owne particular looke out and by degrees
Abate his wrath, that though himselfe for no extremities
Will seeme reflected, yet his friend may get of him the grace
To helpe his countrey in his Armes; and he shall make fit place
For his full presence with his death, which shall be well   65
          forerunne:
For I will first renowne his life with slaughter of my sonne,
Divine Sarpedon, and his death great Hector's powre shall
          wreake,
Ending his ends. Then, at once, out shall the furie breake
Of fierce Achilles, and with that the flight now felt shall turne,
And then last till in wrathfull flames the long-sieg'd Ilion burne.   70
Minerva's counsell shall become grave meane to this my will,
Which no god shall neglect before Achilles take his fill
Of slaughter for his slaughterd friend—even Hector's slaughter
          throwne
Under his anger—that these facts may then make fully knowne
My vowe's performance, made of late and with my bowed head   75
Confirm'd to Thetis, when her armes embrac't my knees and
          praid
That to her citie-racing sonne I would all honour shew.'
    This heard, his charge she seem'd t'intend and to Olympus
          flew.

ile.

But, as the mind of such a man that hath a great way gone
And, either knowing not his way, or then would let alone   80
His purposde journey, is distract and in his vexed mind

Resolves now not to go, now goes, still many wayes inclin'd:
So reverend Juno headlong flew, and gainst her stomacke striv'd.
For (being amongst th' immortall gods in high heaven soone
    arriv'd,
All rising, welcoming with cups her litle absence thence)   85
She all their courtships overpast with solemne negligence,
Save that which faire-cheekt Themis shewd, and her kind cup
    she tooke.

Themis to Juno.

For first, she ranne and met with her, and askt: What troubled
    looke
She brought to heaven? She thought (for truth) that Jove had
    terrified
Her spirits strangely, since she went. The faire-arm'd Queene   90
    replide:

Juno's reply.

  'That truth may easily be supposde: you, goddesse Themis,
    know
His old severitie and pride, but you bear't out with show,
And like the banquet's arbiter amongst th' Immortals fare,
Though well you heare amongst them all how bad his actions are.
Nor are all here, nor any where, mortals nor gods, (I feare)   95
Entirely pleasd with what he does, though thus ye banquet here.'
  Thus tooke she place displeasedly, the feast in generall
Bewraying privie splenes at Jove; and then (to colour all)
She laught, but meerly from her lips, for over her blacke browes
Her still-bent forehead was not cleer'd; yet this her passion's   100
    throwes
Brought forth in spight, being lately school'd: 'Alas, what fooles
    are we
That envie Jove, or that by act, word, thought can fantasie
Any resistance to his will. He sits farre off, nor cares,
Nor moves, but sayes he knowes his strength, to all degrees
    compares
His greatnesse past all other gods, and that in fortitude   105
And every other godlike powre he reignes past all indude.
For which great eminence all you Gods, what ever ill he does,

*Juno's speech of
purpose to incense
Mars* Scopticè.

Sustaine with patience. Here is Mars, I thinke, not free from
    woes,
And yet he beares them like himselfe. The great God had a sonne
Whom he himselfe yet justifies, one that from all men wonne   110
Just surname of their best belov'd, Ascalaphus; yet he
(By Jove's high grace to Troy) is slaine.' Mars started horribly
(As Juno knew he would) at this, beate with his hurld-out hands
His brawnie thighes, cried out, and said: 'O you that have
    commands

In these high temples, beare with me if I revenge the death   115
Of such a sonne. I'le to the fleete, and though I sinke beneath
The fate of being shot to hell by Jove's fell thunder stone
And lie all grim'd amongst the dead with dust and bloud,
          my sonne
Revenge shall honour.' Then he charg'd Feare and Dismay to
          joyne
His horse and chariot: he got armes, that over heaven did   120
          shine,
And then a wrath more great and grave in Jove had bene
          prepar'd
Against the gods than Juno causde, if Pallas had not car'd
More for the peace of heaven than Mars; who leapt out of her
          throne,
Rapt up her helmet, lance, and shield, and made her Phanes'
          porch grone
With her egression to his stay, and thus his rage defers: 125

Pallas to Mars.

'Furious and foolish, th' art undone! Hast thou for nought
          thine eares?
Heard'st thou not Juno, being arriv'd from heaven's great king
          but now?
Or wouldst thou he himselfe should rise (forc't with thy rage)
          to show
The dreadfull powre she urg'd in him, so justly being stird?
Know (thou most impudent and mad) thy wrath had not inferd   130
Mischiefe to thee, but to us all: his spirit had instantly
Left both the hosts and turn'd his hands to uprores in the skie.
Guiltie and guiltlesse both to wracke in his high rage had gone.
And therefore (as thou lovest thy selfe) ceasse furie for thy sonne.
Another, farre exceeding him in heart and strength of hand,   135
Or is, or will be shortly slaine. It were a worke would stand
Jove in much trouble to free all from death that would not die.'
    This threat even nail'd him to his throne, when heaven's
          chiefe Majestie
Cald bright Apollo from his Phane and Iris that had place
Of Internunciesse from the Gods; to whom she did the grace   140
Of Jupiter to this effect: 'It is Saturnius' will

*Juno to Apollo
and Iris.*

That both, with utmost speed, should stoope to the Idalian hill
To know his further pleasure there. And this let me advise,
When you arrive and are in reach of his refulgent eyes,
His pleasure heard, performe it all, of whatsoever kind.'   145
    Thus mov'd she backe, and usde her throne. Those two
          outstript the wind,
And Ida (all enchac't with springs) they soone attaind and found

Where farre-discerning Jupiter, in his repose, had crown'd
The browes of Gargarus and wrapt an odoriferous cloud
About his bosome. Coming neare, they stood, nor now he   150
    show'd
His angry countenance since so soone he saw they made
    th' accesse
That his lov'd wife enjoyn'd. But first, the faire Ambassadresse

Jove to Iris.   He thus commanded: 'Iris, go to Neptune, and relate
Our pleasure truly and at large; command him from the Fate
Of humane warre, and either greete the gods' societie   155
Or the divine sea make his seate. If proudly he denie,
Let better counsels be his guides than such as bid me warre
And tempt my charge, though he be strong; for I am stronger
    farre
And elder borne: nor let him dare to boast even state with me,
Whom all Gods else preferre in feare.' This said, downe   160
    hasted she
From Ida's top to Ilion. And like a mightie snow
Or gelide haile that from the clouds the Northerne spirit
    doth blow,
So fell the windie-footed Dame, and found with quicke repaire

Iris to Neptune.   The watrie God, to whom she said: 'God with the sable haire,
I come from Ægis-bearing Jove to bid thee ceasse from fight   165
And visite heaven or th' ample seas; which, if in his despight
Or disobedience, thou deniest, he threatens thee to come
(In opposite fight) to field himselfe—and therefore warnes
    thee home,
His hånds eschewing, since his powre is farre superiour,
His birth before thee, and affirmes thy lov'd heart should   170
    abhorre
To vaunt equalitie with him, whom every deitie feares.'

Neptune to Iris being   He answerd: 'O unworthy thing! though he be great, he beares
incenst with Jupiter. His tongue too proudly, that our selfe, borne to an equall share
Of state and freedome, he would force. Three brothers borne
    we are

The rule proper to   To Saturne; Rhea brought us forth—this Jupiter and I   175
Jupiter, Neptune and And Pluto, god of under-grounds. The world indifferently
Pluto, being three   Disposde betwixt us; every one his kingdome; I, the seas;
brothers.   Pluto, the blacke lot; Jupiter, the principalities
Of broad heaven, all the skie and clouds, was sorted out:
    the earth
And high Olympus common are and due to either's birth.   180
Why then should I be aw'd by him? Content he his great heart
With his third portion and not thinke to amplifie his part

With terrors of his stronger hands on me, as if I were
The most ignoble of us all. Let him containe in feare
His daughters and his sonnes, begot by his owne person: this   185
Holds more convenience: they must heare these violent threats
    of his.'

Iris to Neptune.   'Shall I,' said Iris, 'beare from thee an answer so austere?
Or wilt thou change it? Changing minds all noble natures beare:
And well thou know'st these greatest borne the Furies follow
    still.'

Neptune againe to Iris.   He answerd: 'Iris, thy reply keepes time, and shewes   190
    thy skill.
O tis a most praise-worthy thing when messengers can tell
(Besides their messages) such things as fit th' occasion well.
But this much grieves my heart and soule, that being in powre
    and state
All wayes his equall and so fixt by one decree in fate,
He should to me, as under him, ill language give and chide.   195
Yet now (though still incenst) I yeeld, affirming this beside—
And I enforce it with a threat—that if without consent
Of me, Minerva, Mercurie, the Queene of regiment,
And Vulcan, he will either spare high Ilion or not race
Her turrets to the lowest stone, and (with both these) not grace   200
The Greekes as victors absolute, informe him this from me,
His pride and my contempt shall live at endlesse enmitie.'
    This said, he left the Greeks and rusht into his watrie throne,
Much mist of all th' heroicke host. When Jove discern'd
    him gone,

Jupiter to Apollo.   Apollo's service he employd, and said: 'Lov'd Phœbus, go   205
To Hector: now th' earth-shaking god hath taken sea and so
Shrunke from the horrors I denounc't, which standing, he and all
The under-seated deities that circle Saturne's fall
Had heard of me in such a fight as had gone hard for them.
But both for them and me tis best that thus they flie   210
    th' extreme
That had not past us without sweate. Now then, in thy hands take
My Adder-fring'd affrighting shield, which with such terror shake
That Feare may shake the Greekes to flight: besides this, adde
    thy care
(O Phœbus, farre-off-shooting god) that this so sickly fare
Of famous Hector be recur'd, and quickly so excite   215
His amplest powres that all the Greeks may grace him with their
    flight
Even to their ships and Hellespont; and then will I devise
All words and facts againe for Greece, that largely may suffice

To breathe them from their instant toiles.' Thus from th' Idæan height

(Like ayre's swift pigeon-killer) stoupt the far-shot God of light,   220

Apollo visits Hector.   And found great Hector sitting up, not stretcht upon his bed,

Not wheasing with a stopt-up spirit, not in cold sweates, but fed

With fresh and comfortable veines, but his mind all his owne,

But round about him all his friends as well as ever knowne.

And this was with the mind of Jove, that flew to him before   225

Apollo came, who (as he saw no signe of any sore)

Askt (like a chearfull visitant): 'Why in this sickly kind,

Great Hector, sitst thou so apart? Can any griefe of mind

Hector to Apollo.   Invade thy fortitude?' He spake, but with a feeble voice:

'O thou, the best of deities! Why (since I thus rejoyce   230

By thy so serious benefite) demandst thou (as in mirth,

And to my face) if I were ill? For (more than what thy worth

Must needs take note of) doth not Fame from all mouthes fill thine eares,

That (as my hand at th' Achive fleete was making massacres

Of men whom valiant Ajax led) his strength strooke with a stone   235

All powre of more hurt from my brest? My very soule was gone,

And once to day I thought to see the house of Dis and Death.'

Apollo to Hector.   'Be strong,' said he, 'for such a spirit now sends the god of breath

From airie Ida as shall runne through all Greeke spirits in thee.

Apollo with the golden sword, the cleare farre-seer, see,   240

Him who betwixt death and thy life, twixt ruine and those towres,

Ere this day oft hath held his shield. Come then, be all thy powres

In wonted vigour: let thy knights, with all their horse assay

The Grecian fleete; my selfe will leade and scoure so cleare the way

That Flight shall leave no Greeke a Rub.' Thus instantly inspir'd   245

Were all his nerves with matchlesse strength, and then his friends he fir'd

Against their foes, when (to his eyes) his eares confirm'd the god.

Simile.   Then, as a goodly-headed Hart, or Goate, bred in the wood,

A rout of country huntsmen chase with all their hounds in crie,

The beast yet or the shadie woods or rocks excessive hie   250

Keepe safe, or our unwieldie fates (that even in hunters sway)

Barre them the poore beast's pulling downe, when straight the
    clamorous fray
Cals out a Lion hugely man'd, and his abhorred view
Turnes headlong in unturning flight (though ventrous) all
    the crew:
So hitherto the chasing Greeks their slaughter dealt by troupes,   255
But, after Hector was beheld, range here and there. Then stoupes
The boldest courage, then their heeles tooke in their dropping
    harts,
And then spake Andræmonides, a man of farre-best parts
Of all th' Ætolians, skild in darts, strenuous in fights of stand,
And one of whom few of the Greekes could get the better hand   260
(For Rhetorique) which they fought with words; with all which
    being wise,

Andræmonides to the
Greekes.

Thus spake he to his Grecian friends: 'O mischiefe! Now mine
    eyes
Discerne no litle miracle—Hector escapt from death
And all recoverd, when all thought his soule had sunke beneath
The hands of Ajax. But some God hath sav'd and freed againe   265
Him that but now dissolv'd the knees of many a Grecian
And now I feare will weaken more; for not without the hand
Of him that thunders can his powres thus still the forefights
    stand,
Thus still triumphant. Heare me then: our troupes in quicke
    retreate
Let's draw up to our fleete, and we that boast our selves the   270
    Great
Stand firme and trie if these that raise so high their charging darts
May be resisted. I beleeve even this great heart of harts
Will feare himselfe to be too bold in charging thorow us.'
   They easely heard him, and obeyd; when all the generous
They cald t' encounter Hector's charge and turn'd the   275
    common men
Backe to the fleete. And these were they that bravely furnisht
    then
The fierce forefight—th' Ajaces both, the worthy Cretan king,
The Mars-like Meges, Merion, and Teucer. Up then bring
The Troyan chiefes their men in heapes, before whom
    (amply pac't)
Marcht Hector, and in front of him Apollo, who had cast   280
About his bright aspect a cloud and did before him beare
Jove's huge and each-where shaggie shield, which (to containe
    in feare
Offending men) the god-smith gave to Jove: with this he led

The Troyan forces. The Greeks stood. A fervent clamor spred
The aire on both sides as they joyn'd; out flew the shafts   285
     and darts,
Some falling short, but othersome found buts in brests and harts.

Apollo's sight discomfits the Grecians.

As long as Phœbus held but out his horrid shield, so long
The darts flew raging either way, and death grew both
     wayes strong.
But when the Greeks had seene his face and who it was
     that shooke
The bristled targe knew by his voice, then all their strengths   290
     forsooke

Simile.

Their nerves and minds. And then looke how a goodly herd
     of Neate,
Or wealthy flocke of sheepe, being close and dreadlesse at
     their meate,
In some blacke midnight sodainly (and not a keeper neere)
A brace of horrid Beares rush in, and then flie here and there
The poore affrighted flocks or herds; so every way disperst   295
The heartlesse Grecians, so the Sunne their headstrong
     chace reverst
To headlong flight, and that day raisde, with all grace,
     Hector's head.
     Arcesilaus then he slue, and Stichius; Stichius led
Bœotia's brazen-coted men; the other was the friend
Of mightie-soul'd Menestheus. Æneas brought to end   300
Medon and Jasus; Medon was the brother (though but base)
Of swift Oiliades, and dwelt farre from his breeding place
In Phylace; the other led th' Athenian bands, his Sire
Was Sphelus, Bucolus his sonne, Mecisteus did expire
Beneath Polydamas his hand. Polites, Echius slew   305
Just at the joyning of the hosts. Agenor overthrew
Clonius. Bold Deiochus felt Alexander's lance;
It strooke his shoulder's upper part and did his head advance
Quite through his brest, as from the fight he turn'd him
     for retreat.
     While these stood spoiling of the slaine, the Greeks found   310
     time to get
Beyond the dike and th' undik't pales: all scapes they gladly
     gain'd
Till all had past the utmost wall: Necessitie so raign'd.

Hector to his souldiers.

     Then Hector cried out: 'Take no spoile, but rush on to
     the fleete,
From whose assault (for spoile or flight) if any man I meete,
He meets his death: nor in the fire of holy funerall   315

His brother's or his sister's hands shall cast (within our wall)
His lothed body, but, without, the throtes of dogs shall grave
His manlesse lims.' This said, the scourge his forward
    horses drave
Through every order, and with him all whipt their chariots on,
All threatningly out thundering shouts as earth were   320
    overthrowne.

Apollo leades the
Troyans.

    Before them marcht Apollo still, and, as he marcht, digd
    downe
(Without all labour) with his feete the dike, till with his owne
He fild it to the top and made way both for man and horse
As broade and long as with a lance (cast out to trie one's force)
A man could measure. Into this they powr'd whole troupes   325
    as fast
As numerous, Phœbus still before, for all their hast,
Still shaking Jove's unvalewed shield, and held it up to all.
And then as he had chok't their dike he tumbl'd downe
    their wall.

A simile, from how
low things it may be
taken, to expresse the
highest.

And looke how easely any boy upon the sea-ebd shore
Makes with a litle sand a toy and cares for it no more,   330
But as he raisd it childishly, so in his wanton vaine
Both with his hands and feete he puls and spurnes it
    downe againe:
So sleight, O Phœbus, thy hands made of that huge Grecian toile
And their late stand, so well resolv'd, as easely mad'st recoile.
    Thus stood they driven up at their fleete, where each heard   335
    other's thought
Exhorted, passing humbly prayd, all, all the gods besought
(With hands held up to heaven) for helpe. Mongst all the good
    old man,
Grave Nestor (for his counsels cald the Argives' guardian),
Fell on his aged knees and prayd, and to the starrie host
Stretcht out his hands for ayd to theirs, of all thus   340
    moving most:

Nestor's prayer to
Jupiter.

'O father Jove, if ever man of all our host did burne
Fat thighes of oxen or of sheepe (for grace of safe returne)
In fruitfull Argos, and obtaind the bowing of thy head
For promise of his humble prayers, O now remember him,
Thou meerly heavenly, and cleare up the foule browes of this   345
    dim
And cruell day; do not destroy our zeale for Troyan pride.'
He prayd, and heaven's great Counsellor with store of
    thunder tride

[307]

His former grace good, and so heard the old man's heartie
   prayres.
The Troyans tooke Jove's signe for them, and powr'd out
   their affaires
In much more violence on the Greeks and thought on nought   350
   but fight.

Simile.   And as a huge wave of a sea, swolne to his rudest height,
         Breakes over both sides of a ship, being all urg'd by the wind,
Intending they were   For that's it makes the wave so proud in such a borne-up kind,
puft up by Apollo.   The Troyans overgat the wall and, getting in their horse,
         Fought close at fleete, which now the Greeks ascended for   355
            their force.
         Then from their chariots they with darts, the Greeks with
            bead-hooks fought
         (Kept still aboord for navall fights), their heads with iron
            wrought
         In hookes and pikes. Achilles' friend still while he saw the wall
         That stood without their fleete affoord employment for them all
         Was never absent from the tent of that man-loving Greeke,   360
         Late-hurt Eurypylus, but sate and every way did seeke
         To spend the sharpe time of his wound with all the ease he could
         In medicines and in kind discourse: but when he might behold
         The Troyans past the wall, the Greekes flight driven and all
            in cries,
         Then cride he out, cast downe his hands and beate with griefe   365
            his thighes:
Patroclus to   Then, 'O Eurypylus,' he cride, 'now all thy need of me
Eurypylus.   Must beare my absence: now a worke of more necessitie
         Cals hence, and I must hast to call Achilles to the field.
         Who knowes but (God assisting me) my words may make him
            yeeld?
         The motion of a friend is strong.' His feete thus tooke him   370
            thence.
         The rest yet stood their enemies firme, but all their violence
         (Though Troy fought there with fewer men) lackt vigor to repell
         Those fewer from their Navie's charge, and so that charge as well
A divine simile.   Lackt force to spoile their fleete or tents. And as a shipwright's
            line
         (Disposde by such a hand as learn'd from th' Artizan divine   375
         The perfect practise of his Art) directs or guards so well
         The navall timber then in frame that all the layd-on steele
         Can hew no further than may serve to give the timber th' end
         Fore-purposde by the skilfull wright: so both hosts did contend

With such a line or law applide to what their steele would   380
  gaine.
  At other ships fought other men, but Hector did maintaine
His quarrell firme at Ajax' ship, and so did both employ
About one vessell all their toyle: nor could the one destroy
The ship with fire nor force the man, nor that man yet get gone
The other from so neare his ship; for God had brought him on.   385
  But now did Ajax with a dart wound deadly in the brest

Ajax slaughters   Caletor, sonne of Clytius, as he with fire addrest
Caletor.   To burne the vessell; as he fell, the brand fell from his hand.
  When Hector saw his sister's sonne lie slaughterd in the sand,
He cald to all his friends and prayd they would not in that   390
  streight
Forsake his nephew but maintaine about his corse the fight

Hector at Ajax.   And save it from the spoile of Greece. Then sent he out a lance
At Ajax in his nephewe's wreake, which mist but made the
  chance

Hector missing Ajax,   On Lycophron Mastorides, that was the houshold friend
slayes his friend.   Of Ajax, borne in Cythera, whom Ajax did defend   395
(Being fled to his protection) for killing of a man
Amongst the god-like Cytherans. The vengefull Javelin ran
Quite through his head above his eare as he was standing by
His Fautor, then asterne his ship, from whence his soule did flie
And to the earth his body fell. The haire stood up an end   400
On Ajax, who to Teucer cald (his brother) saying: 'Friend,
Our loved consort, whom we brought from Cythera and grac't
So like our father, Hector's hand hath made him breathe
  his last.
Where then are all thy death-borne shafts and that unvallewed
  bow
Apollo gave thee?' Teucer strait his brother's thoughts did   405
  know,
Stood neare him and dispatcht a shaft amongst the Troyan fight.
It strooke Pisenor's goodly sonne, yong Cleitus, the delight
Of the renowm'd Polydamas, the bridle in his hand,
As he was labouring his horse to please the high command
Of Hector and his Troyan friends and bring him where the   410
  fight
Made greatest tumult. But his strife for honour in their sight
Wrought not what sight or wishes helpt; for, turning backe
  his looke,
The hollow of his necke the shaft came singing on, and strooke,
And downe he fell; his horses backe and hurried through
  the field

[309]

The emptie chariot. Panthus' sonne made all haste and   415
    withheld
Their loose carier, disposing them to Protiaon's sonne,
Astynous, with speciall charge to keepe them ever on
And in his sight: so he againe amongst the foremost went.

Teucer at Hector.   At Hector then another shaft incensed Teucer sent,
Which, had it hit him, sure had hurt and, had it hurt him,   420
    slaine—
And had it slaine him, it had driven all those to Troy againe.
    But Jove's mind was not sleeping now; it wak't to Hector's
    fame

Jove breakes Teucer's And Teucer's infamie, himselfe (in Teucer's deadly aime)
bow.   His well-wrought string dissevering that serv'd his bravest bow:
His shaft flew quite another way, his bow the earth did strow.   425
At all which, Teucer stood amaz'd and to his brother cride:

Teucer to Ajax.   'O prodigie! Without all doubt our Angell doth deride
The counsels of our fight; he brake a string my hands put on
This morning and was newly made and well might have set gone
A hundred arrowes; and beside, he strooke out of my hand   430

Ajax to Teucer.   The bow Apollo gave.' He sayd: 'Then, good friend,
    do not stand
More on thy archerie, since God (preventer of all grace
Desir'd by Grecians) sleights it so. Take therefore in the place
A good large lance, and on thy necke a target cast as bright;
With which, come fight thy selfe with some and othersome   435
    excite,
That without labour at the least (though we prove worser men)
Troy may not brag it tooke our ships: come, mind our businesse
    then.'

Teucer changeth his   This said, he hasted to his tent, left there his shafts and bow,
armes.   And then his double, double shield, did on his shoulders throw,
Upon his honor'd head he plac't his helmet, thickly plum'd,   440
And then his strong and well-pilde lance in his faire hand
    assum'd,
Return'd, and boldly tooke his place by his great brother's side.

Hector's admiration of   When Hector saw his arrowes broke, out to his friends
Jove's breaking   he cride:
Teucer's bow.
'O friends, be yet more comforted! I saw the hands of Jove
Breake the great Grecian archer's shafts. 'Tis easie to approve   445
That Jove's powre is direct with men, as well in those set hie
Upon the sodaine as in those deprest as sodainly,
And those not put in state at all—as now he takes away
Strength from the Greeks and gives it us. Then use it, and assay
With joyn'd hands this approched fleete. If any bravely buy   450

His fame or fate with wounds or death, in Jove's name let him
    die.
Who for his country suffers death sustaines no shamefull thing:
His wife in honour shall survive, his progenie shall spring
In endlesse summers and their roofes with patrimonie swell;
And all this, though, with all their freight, the Greeke ships   455
    we repell.'
    His friends thus cheer'd, on th' other part strong Ajax stird
    his friends:

Ajax to the Greekes.   'O Greeks,' said he, 'what shame is this that no man more defends
His fame and safetie than to live, and thus be forc't to shrinke!
Now either save your fleet, or die—unlesse ye vainly thinke
That you can live and they destroyd? Perceives not every eare   460
How Hector hartens up his men and hath his firebrands here
Now ready to enflame our fleet? He doth not bid them dance,
That you may take your ease and see, but to the fight advance.
No counsell can serve us but this—to mixe both hands and harts
And beare up close; tis better much t' expose our utmost parts   465
To one daie's certaine life or death than languish in a warre
So base as this, beate to our ships by our inferiours farre.'
    Thus rowsd he up their spirits and strengths. To work then
    both sides went,
When Hector, the Phocensian Duke, to fields of darknesse sent
Fierce Schedius, Perimedes' sonne; which Ajax did requite   470
With slaughter of Laodamas, that led the foote to fight
And was Antenor's famous sonne. Polydamas did end
Otus, surnam'd Cyllenius, whom Phyleus made his friend,
Being chiefe of the Epeians' Bands: whose fall, when Meges
    viewd,
He let flie at his feller's life, who (shrinking-in) eschew'd   475
The wel-aym'd lance. Apollo's will denied that Panthus' sonne
Should fall amongst the foremost fights; the dart the mid-brest
    wonne
Of Crœsmus; Meges wonne his armes. At Meges, Dolops then
Bestow'd his lance; he was the sonne of Lampus, best of men,
And Lampus, of Laomedon, well-skild in strength of mind.   480
He strooke Phylides' shield quite through, whose curets,
    better lin'd
And hollow'd fitly, sav'd his life. Phyleus left him them,
Who from Epirus brought them home, on that part where the
    streme
Of famous Seléés doth runne; Euphetes did bestow
(Being guest with him) those wel-prov'd armes to weare against   485
    the foe,

And now they sav'd his sonne from death. At Dolops, Meges
    threw
A speare well-pilde, that strooke his caske full in the height;
    off flew
His purple feather, newly made, and in the dust it fell.
    While these thus striv'd for victorie and either's hope
    serv'd well,
Atrides came to Meges' aide, and (hidden with his side)   490
Let loose a javelin at his foe that through his backe implied
His lustie head, even past his breast; the ground receiv'd his
    weight.
    While these made-in to spoyle his armes, great Hector
    did excite
All his allies to quicke revenge; and first he wrought upon
Strong Melanippus (that was sonne to great Hicetaon)   495
With some reproofe. Before these warres, he in Percote fed
Cloven-footed Oxen, but did since returne where he was bred,
Exceld amongst the Ilians, was much of Priam lov'd,
And in his court kept as his sonne. Him Hector thus reprov'd:

    'Thus, Melanippus, shall our blood accuse us of neglect?   500
Nor moves it thy lov'd heart (thus urg'd) thy kinsman to protect?
Seest thou not how they seeke his spoyle? Come, follow;
    now no more
Our fight must stand at length, but close: nor leave the close
    before
We close the latest eye of them—or they the lowest stone
Teare up and sacke the citizens of loftie Ilion.'   505
He led; he followd like a god. And then must Ajax needs
(As well as Hector) cheare his men, and thus their spirits
    he feeds:

'Good friends, bring but your selves to feele the noble stings
    of shame
For what ye suffer, and be men: respect each other's fame,
For which who strives in shame's fit feare and puts on ne'er   510
    so farre
Comes oftner off than sticke engag'd: these fugitives of warre
Save neither life, nor get renowne, nor beare more minds
    than sheepe.'
    This short speech fir'd them in his aide, his spirit toucht them
    deepe
And turn'd them all before the fleet into a wall of brasse:
To whose assault Jove stird their foes, and young Atrides was   515
Jove's instrument, who thus set on the yong Antilochus:

'Antilochus, in all our host there is not one of us
More yong than thou, more swift of foote, nor (with both those)
   so strong.
O would thou wouldst then (for thou canst) one of this lustie
   throng
That thus comes skipping out before (whoever, any where)   520
Make sticke (for my sake) twixt both hosts, and leave his bold
   blood there.'
   He said no sooner and retir'd, but forth he rusht before
The foremost fighters, yet his eye did every way explore
For doubt of ods; out flew his lance: the Troyans did abstaine
While he was darting, yet his dart he cast not off in vaine,   525

For Melanippus, that rare sonne of great Hicetaon
(As bravely he put foorth to fight) it fiercely flew upon,
And at the nipple of his breast, his breast and life did part.

And then, much like an eager hound cast off at some yong Hart
Hurt by the hunter, that had left his covert then but new,   530
The great-in-warre Antilochus (O Melanippus) flew
On thy torne bosome for thy spoyle. But thy death could not lie
Hid to great Hector, who all haste made to thee and made flie
Antilochus, although in warre he were at all parts skild.

But as some wild beast, having done some shrewd turne (either   535
   kild
The heardsman, or the heardsman's dogge,) and skulks away
   before
The gatherd multitude makes in: so Nestor's sonne forbore,
But after him with horrid cryes both Hector and the rest
Showres of teare-thirstie lances powr'd, who, having arm'd
   his brest
With all his friends, he turn'd it then. Then on the ships   540
   all Troy,
Like raw-flesh-nourisht Lions, rusht, and knew they did imploy
Their powres to perfect Jove's high will, who still their spirits
   enflam'd
And quencht the Grecians; one, renownd; the other, often
   sham'd.
For Hector's glorie still he stood, and ever went about
To make him cast the fleet such fire as never should go out,   545
Heard Thetis' foule petition, and wisht, in any wise,
The splendor of the burning ships might satiate his eyes.
From him yet the repulse was then to be on Troy conferd
The honor of it given the Greeks, which (thinking on) he stird
(With such addition of his spirit) the spirit Hector bore   550
To burne the fleet, that of it selfe was hote enough before.

But now he far'd like Mars himselfe, so brandishing his lance
As through the deepe shades of a wood a raging fire should
    glance,

Held up to all eyes by a hill; about his lips a fome
Stood, as when th' Ocean is enrag'd; his eyes were overcome   555
With fervour and resembl'd flames, set off by his darke browes;
And from his temples his bright helme abhorred lightnings
    throwes.
For Jove, from foorth the sphere of starres, to his state put
    his owne
And all the blaze of both the hosts confin'd in him alone.
And all this was, since after this he had not long to live;   560
This lightning flew before his death, which Pallas was to give
(A small time thence, and now prepar'd) beneath the violence
Of great Pelides. In meane time, his present eminence
Thought all things under it: and he, still where he saw the stands
Of greatest strength and bravest arm'd, there he would prove   565
    his hands
Or no where, offering to breake through. But that past all
    his powre,
Although his will were past all theirs; they stood him like a
    towre
Conjoynd so firme that as a rocke, exceeding high and great
And standing neare the hoarie sea, beares many a boisterous
    threate
Of high-voic't winds and billowes huge belcht on it by the   570
    stormes;
So stood the Greeks great Hector's charge, nor stird their
    battellous formes.
    He (guirt in fire, borne for the fleet) still rusht at every troope,

And fell upon it like a wave high raisd that then doth stoope
Out from the clouds, grows as it stoops with stormes, then downe
    doth come
And cuffe a ship, when all her sides are hid in brackish fome,   575
Strong gales still raging in her sailes, her sailers' minds dismaid,
Death being but little from their lives: so Jove-like Hector fraid
And plyde the Greeks, who knew not what would chance for all
    their guards.

    And as the banefull king of beasts, leapt in to Oxen heards
Fed in the meddowes of a fenne exceeding great, the beasts   580
In number infinite, mongst whom (their heardsmen wanting
    breasts
To fight with Lions for the price of a blacke Oxe's life)
He here and there jumps, first and last in his bloodthirstie strife

[314]

Chac't and assaulted, and at length downe in the midst goes one,
And all the rest sperst through the fenne: so now, all Greece   585
   was gone—
So Hector (in a flight from heaven upon the Grecians cast)
Turnd all their backs; yet onely one his deadly lance laid fast,
Brave Mycenæus Periphes, Copreus dearest sonne,
Who of the heaven's-Queene-lov'd-king (great Eurystheus)
   wonne
The grace to greet in Ambassie the strength of Hercules,   590
Was farre superiour to his sire in feete, fight, noblenes
Of all the vertues, and all those did such a wisedome guide
As all Mycena could not match: and this man dignified
(Stil making greater his renowne) the state of Priam's sonne.
For his unhappie hastie foote, as he addrest to runne,   595
Stucke in th' extreme ring of his shield that to his ankles reacht,
And downe he upwards fell; his fall up from the center fetcht
A huge sound with his head and helme; which Hector quickly
   spide,
Ranne in, and in his worthy breast his lance's head did hide
And slue about him all his friends, who could not give him   600
   aide:
They griev'd, and of his god-like foe fled so extreme afraid.
   And now amongst the nearest ships that first were drawne
   to shore
The Greeks were driven, beneath whose sides, behind them
   and before
And into them, they powr'd themselves, and thence were driven
   againe
Up to their tents, and there they stood—not daring to   605
   maintaine
Their guards more outward, but betwixt the bounds of Feare
   and Shame
Chear'd still each other; when th' old man that of the Grecian
   name
Was cald the pillar every man thus by his parents praid:

Nestor to the Greekes.   'O friends, be men, and in your minds let others' shames
   be weigh'd.
Know you have friends besides your selves, possessions, parents,   610
   wives,
As well those that are dead to you as those ye love with lives—
All sharing still their good, or bad, with yours. By these I pray
That are not present (and the more should therefore
   make ye wey
Their misse of you, as yours of them), that you will bravely stand

[315]

And this forc't flight you have sustain'd at length yet   615
    countermand.'
    Supplies of good words thus supplide the deeds and spirits
    of all

Minerva cleares the darknes Jove powred on the Grecian armie.

And so at last Minerva clear'd the cloud that Jove let fall
Before their eyes: a mightie light flew beaming every way,
As well about their ships as where their darts did hotest play.
Then saw they Hector great in armes and his associates,   620
As well all those that then abstaind as those that helpt the fates,
And all their owne fight at the fleete. Nor did it now content
Ajax to keepe downe like the rest; he up the hatches went,
Stalkt here and there, and in his hand a huge great beadhooke
    held,

A simile of Ajax managing the fight at the fleet.

Twelve cubits long and full of Iron. And as a man well skild   625
In horse made to the martiall race, when (of a number more)
He chuseth foure and brings them foorth to runne them all
    before
Swarmes of admiring citizens amids their towne's high-way,
And (in their full carier) he leapes from one to one, no stay
Enforc't on any, nor failes he in either seate or leape: 630
So Ajax with his beadhooke leapt nimbly from ship to ship
As actively, commanding all—them in their men as well
As men in them most terribly exhorting to repell,
To save their navie and their tents. But Hector nothing needs
To stand on exhortations now at home; he strives for deeds.   635

Simile of Hector.

And looke how Jove's great Queene of birds (sharpe set) lookes
    out for prey,
Knowes floods that nourish wild-wing'd fowles and (from her
    airie way)
Beholds where Cranes, Swans, Cormorands have made their
    foody fall,
Darkens the river with her wings and stoopes amongst them all:
So Hector flew amongst the Greekes, directing his command   640
(In chiefe) against one opposite ship, Jove with a mightie hand
Still backing him and all his men. And then againe there grew
A bitter conflict at the fleet; you would have said none drew
A wearie breath, nor ever would, they layd so freshly on.
And this was it that fir'd them both: the Greeks did build upon   645
No hope but what the field would yeeld, flight an impossible
    course;
The Troyans all hope entertaind that sword and fire should force
Both ships and lives of all the Greekes; and thus unlike affects
Bred like strenuitie in both. Great Hector still directs

His powres against the first neare ship. Twas that faire   650
    barke that brought
Protesilaus to those warres, and now her selfe to nought
With many Greeke and Troyan lives, all spoyld about her spoyle.
One slue another desperately, and close the deadly toyle
Was pitcht on both parts. Not a shaft nor farre-off striking dart
Was usde through all: one fight fell out of one despitefull hart.   655
Sharpe axes, twibils, two-hand swords and speares with two heads
    borne
Were then the weapons, faire short swords, with sanguine hilts
    still worne,
Had use in like sort; of which last ye might have numbers view'd
Drop with dissolv'd armes from their hands, as many downright
    hew'd
From off their shoulders as they fought, their bawdricks cut in   660
    twaine.
And thus the blacke blood flow'd on earth from souldiers hurt
    and slaine.
    When Hector once had seisd the ship, he clapt his faire
    brode hand

*Hector seising
Protesilaus' ship, to
the Troyans.*

Fast on the sterne and held it there; and there gave this
    command:
    'Bring fire, and altogether showt. Now Jove hath drawne
    the veile
From such a day as makes amends for all his stormes of haile;   665
By whose blest light we take those ships that, in despite of
    heaven,
Tooke sea and brought us worlds of woe—all since our Peeres
    were given
To such a lasinesse and feare they would not let me end
Our lingring banes and charge thus home, but keepe home
    and defend.
And so they rul'd the men I led. But though Jove then   670
    withheld
My naturall spirit, now by Jove tis freed, and thus impeld.'

*Ajax forced to
withdraw himselfe
from the fight.*

    This more inflam'd them; in so much that Ajax now no more
Kept up, he was so drownd in darts; a little he forbore
The hatches to a seate beneath, of seven foote long, but thought
It was impossible to scape; he sate yet where he fought   675
And hurld out lances thicke as haile at all men that assaid
To fire the ship—with whom he found his hands so overlaid
That on his souldiers thus he cryed: 'O friends, fight I alone?
Expect ye more wals at your backes? Townes rampir'd here
    are none—

[317]

No citizens to take ye in, no helpe in any kind.   680
We are, I tell you, in Troy's fields, have nought but seas behind
And foes before, farre, farre, from Greece. For shame, obey
    commands;
There is no mercie in the warres; your healthes lie in your
    hands.'
   Thus rag'd he, and powr'd out his darts: who ever he espied
Come neare the vessell arm'd with fire, on his fierce dart   685
    he died.
All that pleasd Hector made him mad, all, that his thanks
    would erne—
Of which twelve men, his most resolv'd, lay dead before
    his sterne.

COMMENTARIUS

[83] *I must here be enforced, for your easier examination of a simile*
before, to cite the originall words of it; which of all Homer's
translators and commentors have bene most grosly mistaken, his
whole intent and sence in it utterly falsified. The simile illustrates the
manner of Juno's parting from Jove, being commanded by him to a   5
businesse so abhorring from her will, is this:

ὡς δ᾽ ὅτ᾽ ἂν ἀΐξῃ νόος ἀνέρος, ὅς τ᾽ ἐπὶ πολλὴν
γαῖαν ἐληλουθὼς φρεσὶ πευκαλίμῃσι νοήσῃ,
ἔνθ᾽ εἴην, ἢ ἔνθα, μενοινήῃσί τε πολλά,
ὡς κραιπνῶς μεμαυῖα διέπτατο πότνια Ἥρη·   10

Which is thus converted ad verbum *by Spondanus:*

Sicut autem quando discurrit mens viri, qui per multam
Terram profectus, mentibus prudentibus considerarit,
Huc iveram vel illuc, cogitaritque multa;
Sic citò properans pervolavit veneranda Iuno.   15

Which Lauren. Valla in prose thus translates:

Subvolavit Iuno in cœlum, eadem festinatione ac celeritate, quâ
mens prudentis hominis, et qui multum terrarum peragravit,
recursat, cum multa sibi agenda instant, huc se conferat an illuc.

Eobanus Hessus in verse thus: 20

Tam subitò, quàm sana viri mens plura scientis,
Quique peragrarit vastæ loca plurima terræ,
Multa movens animo, nunc huc nunc avolat illuc.

To this purpose likewise the Italian and French copies have it. All
understanding Homer's intent was (as by the speedinesse of a man's   25
thought or mind) to illustrate Juno's swiftnesse in hasting about
the commandement of Jupiter, which was utterly otherwise: viz. *to*
shew the distraction of Juno's mind in going against her will and
in her despite about Jove's commandment, which all the history
before, in her inveterate and inflexible grudge to do any thing   30
for the good of the Troyans, confirmeth without question. Besides,
her morositie and solemne apparance amongst the gods and goddesses
(which Themis notes in her lookes) shewes, if she went willingly,
much lesse swiftly, about that busines. Nor can the illustration of
swiftnes be Homer's end in this simile, because he makes the man's   35
mind, to which he resembles her going, stagger, inclining him to go

*this way and that, not resolved which way to go: which very poorely
expresseth swiftnesse and as properly agrees with the propertie of a
wise man, when he hath undertaken and gone farre in a journey,
not to know whether he should go forward or backeward. Let us
therefore examine the originall words:*   40

ὡς δ' ὅτ' ἂν ἀΐξῃ νόος ἀνέρος, ὅς τ' ἐπὶ πολλὴν
γαῖαν ἐληλουθὼς &c.

                                                    Sicut verò quando discurrit
vel prorumpit; vel cum impetu exurgit mens viri, ἀναΐσσω   45
signifying ruo, prorumpo, *vel cum impetu exurgo: as having
travelled farre on an yrkesome journey (as Juno had done for the
Greekes, faining to Jove and Venus she was going to visite*
πολυφόρβου πείρατα γαίης multa nutrientes fines terræ) *and then
knowes not whether he should go backeward or forward, sustaines*   50
*a vehement discourse with himselfe on what course to resolve, and
vext in mind (which the words,* φρεσὶ πευκαλίμῃσι *expresse, being
to be understood* mentibus amaris, vexatis, *or* distractis:*with a
spitefull, sorrowfull, vext, or distracted mind: not* mentibus
prudentibus, *as all most unwisely in this place convert it, though in*   55
*other places it intimates so much. But here the other holds
congruence with the rest of the simile, from which in the wise sence
it abhorres:* πευκάλιμος *signifying* amarus *more properly than*
prudens, *being translated* prudens *meerely metaphorically according
to the second deduction; where here it is used more properly*   60
according to the first deduction, which is taken from πευκὴ
*the Larcher tree, whose gumme is exceeding bitter; and because
things irkesome and bitter (as afflictions, crosses, &c.) are meanes
to make men wise and take heede by others' harmes, therefore
according to the second deduction* πευκάλιμος *is taken for*   65
cautus *or* prudens. *But now that the* ἀπόδοσις *or application
seemes to make with their sence of swiftnesse, the words*
ὣς κραιπνῶς μεμαυῖα, *being translated by them* sic citò properans,
it is thus to be turned in this place, sic rapidè et impetu pulsa, *so
snatchingly or headlongly driven flew Juno. As we often see with a*   70
*clap of thunder Doves or other fowles driven headlong from their
seates, not in direct flight but as they would breake their neckes
with a kind of reeling:* μαιμαυῖα *being derived of* μαίω *or* μαιμάω
signifying impetu ferri, *vel* furibundo impetu ferri—*all which most
aptly agreeth with Juno's enforced and wrathfull parting from Jove*   75
*and doing his charge distractedly. This for me; if another can give
better, let him shew it and take it. But in infinite other places is this
divine Poet thus prophaned, which for the extreme labour I cannot
yet touch at.*

[136] 'Αϱγαλέον &c., Difficile est, *it is a hard thing (saith Minerva*   80
to Mars, when she answers his anger for the slaughter of his sonne
Ascalaphus) for Jove to deliver the generation and birth of all men
from death; which Commentors thus understand—There were some
men that never died, as Tithon the husband of Aurora, Chiron,
Glaucus made a sea god, &c. and in holy Writ (as Spondanus   85
pleaseth to mixe them) Enoch and Elias: but because these few were
freed from death, Mars must not looke that all others were. But
this interpretation (I thinke) will appeare to all men at first sight
both ridiculous and prophane—Homer making Minerva onely jest
at Mars here (as she doth in other places) bidding him not storme   90
that his sonne should be slaine more than better borne, stronger
and worthier men; for Jove should have enough to do (or it
were hard for Jove) to free all men from Death that are
unwilling to die. This mine, with the rest: the other
others; accept which you please.

The End of the Fifteenth Booke

THE SIXTEENTH BOOKE

of

HOMER'S ILIADS

THE ARGUMENT

Achilles, at Patroclus' suite, doth yeeld
His armes and Myrmidons; which brought to field,
The Troyans flie. Patroclus hath the grace
Of great Sarpedon's death, sprong of the race
Of Jupiter, he having slaine the horse   5
Of Thetis' sonne (fierce Pedasus); the force
Of Hector doth revenge the much-ru'd end
Of most renown'd Sarpedon on the friend
Of Thetides, first by Euphorbus harm'd
And by Apollo's personall powre disarm'd.   10

Another Argument

In Πι *Patroclus beares the chance*
Of death, imposd by Hector's lance.

Thus fighting for this well-built ship, Patroclus all that space
Stood by his friend, preparing words to win the Greeks his grace
With powre of uncontained teares: and (like a fountaine pour'd
In blacke streams, from a lofty rocke) the Greeks so plagu'd
    deplor'd.

Achilles chides   Achilles (ruthfull for his teares) said: 'Wherefore weepes   5
Patroclus for his   my friend
teares.   So like a girle, who, though she sees her mother cannot tend
Her childish humours, hangs on her and would be taken up,
Stil viewing her with teare-drownd eyes when she hath made her
    stoope.
To nothing liker I can shape thy so unseemely teares.
What causeth them? Hath any ill sollicited thine eares,   10
Befalne my Myrmidons? Or newes from loved Phthia brought,
Told onely thee lest I should grieve, and therefore thus hath
    wrought

On thy kind spirit? Actor's sonne, the good Menœtius
(Thy father) lives and Peleus (mine), great sonne of Æacus,
Amongst his Myrmidons, whose deaths, in dutie we should   15
    mourne.
Or is it what the Greeks sustaine that doth thy stomacke turne,
On whom (for their injustice sake) plagues are so justly laide?
Speake, man, let both know either's heart.' Patroclus (sighing)
    said:

Patroclus' answer to Achilles.

  'O Peleus' sonne (thou strongest Greeke, by all degrees,
    that lives)
Still be not angrie; our sad state such cause of pittie gives.   20
Our greatest Greeks lie at their ships sore wounded—Ithacus,
King Agamemnon, Diomed, and good Eurypylus.
But these much-medcine-knowing men (Physitions) can recure,
Thou yet unmedcinable still though thy wound all endure.
Heaven blesse my bosome from such wrath as thou sooth'st   25
    as thy blisse
(Unprofitably vertuous). How shall our progenies,
Borne in thine age, enjoy thine aide, when these friends
    in thy flowre
Thou leav'st to such unworthy death? O idle, cruell powre!
Great Peleus never did beget, nor Thetis bring foorth thee;
Thou from the blew sea and her rockes deriv'st thy pedegree.   30
What so declines thee? If thy mind shuns any augurie
Related by thy mother Queene from heaven's foreseeing eye,
And therefore thou forsak'st thy friends, let me go ease their
    mones
With those brave reliques of our host, thy mightie Myrmidons,
That I may bring to field more light to Conquest than hath   35
    bene.
To which end grace me with thine armes, since any shadow seene
Of thy resemblance, all the powre of perjur'd Troy will flie
And our so tired friends will breathe: our fresh-set-on supplie
Will easily drive their wearied off.' Thus (foolish man) he su'd
For his sure death; of all whose speech Achilles first renu'd   40

Achilles to Patroclus.

The last part, thus: 'O worthy friend, what have thy speeches
    bene?
I shun the fight for Oracles, or what my mother Queene
Hath told from Jove? I take no care nor note of one such thing.
But this fit anger stings me still, that the insulting king
Should from his equall take his right, since he exceeds in powre.   45
This (still his wrong) is still my griefe; he tooke my Paramour
That all men gave and whom I wonne by vertue of my speare,
That (for her) overturn'd a Towne. This rape he made of her

[323]

And usde me like a fugitive, an Inmate in a towne
That is no citie libertine, nor capable of their gowne.   50
But beare we this as out of date; tis past, nor must we still
Feed anger in our noblest parts; yet thus I have my will
As well as our great king of men, for I did ever vow
Never to cast off my disdaine till (as it fals out now)
Their misse of me knockt at my fleet and told me in their cries   55
I was reveng'd and had my wish of all my enemies.
And so of this repeate enough. Take thou my fame-blaz'd armes
And my fight-thirstie Myrmidons leade to these hote alarmes.
Whole clouds of Troyans circle us with hatefull eminence,
The Greeks shut in a little shore, a sort of citizens   60
Skipping upon them—all because their prowd eyes do not see
The radiance of my helmet there, whose beames had instantly
Thrust backe and all these ditches fild with carrion of their flesh,
If Agamemnon had bene kind: where now they fight as fresh
As thus farre they had put at ease, and at our tents contend—   65
And may, for the repulsive hand of Diomed doth not spend
His raging darts there that their Death could fright out of
        our fleet:
Nor from that head of enmitie can my poore hearers meet
The voice of great Atrides now. Now Hector's onely voyce
Breakes all the aire about both hosts, and with the very noise,   70
Bred by his lowd encouragements, his forces fill the field
And fight the poore Achaians downe. But on, put thou my shield
Betwixt the fire-plague and our fleet: rush bravely on and turne
Warre's tide as headlong on their throtes. No more let
        them ajourne
Our sweet home-turning. But observe the charge I lay on thee   75
To each least point, that thy rul'd hand may highly honour me
And get such glorie from the Greeks that they may send againe
My most sweet wench and gifts to boote, when thou hast cast
        a raine
On these so head-strong citizens and forc't them from our fleet.

*Jupiter called the god
of sounds for the chiefe
sound his thunder.*
With which grace, if the gods of sounds thy kind egression greet, 80
Retire and be not tempted on (with pride to see thy hand
Raine slaughterd carkasses on earth) to runne forth thy command
As farre as Ilion, lest the gods that favour Troy come forth
To thy encounter—for the Sunne much loves it—and my worth
(In what thou suffer'st) will be wrong'd, that I would let   85
        my friend
Assume an action of such weight without me and transcend
His friend's prescription. Do not then affect a further fight

Than I may strengthen: let the rest (when thou hast done
  this right)
Performe the rest. O would to Jove, thou Pallas, and thou Sunne,
That not a man housd underneath those towres of Ilion,   90
Nor any one of all the Greeks (how infinite a summe
Soever altogether make) might live unovercome,
But onely we two (scaping death) might have the thundring
  downe
Of every stone stucke in the wals of this so sacred towne.'
    Thus spake they onely twixt themselves. And now the foe   95
    no more
Could Ajax stand, being so opprest with all the iron store
The Troyans powr'd on, with whose darts, and with Jove's
  will beside,
His powres were cloyd, and his bright helme did deafning
  blowes abide;
His plume and all head-ornaments could never hang in rest.
His arme yet laboured up his shield, and, having done their   100
  best,
They could not stirre him from his stand, although he wrought
  it out
With short respirings and with sweate that ceaslesse flow'd about
His reeking lims—no least time given to take in any breath.
Ill strengthned ill; when one was up, another was beneath.
    Now, Muses, you that dwell in heaven, the dreadfull meane   105
    inspire
That first enforc't the Grecian fleete to take in Troyan fire.
First Hector with his huge brode sword cut off, at setting on,
The head of Ajax' Ashen lance; which Ajax seeing gone,
And that he shooke a headlesse speare (a little while unware)
His warie spirits told him straight the hand of heaven was   110
  there,
And trembld'd under his conceipt, which was that twas
  Jove's deed,
Who, as he pold off his darts' heads, so sure he had decreed
That all the counsels of their warre he would polle off like it
And give the Troyans victorie. So, trusted he his wit,
And left his darts. And then the ship was heapt with horrid   115
  brands
Of kindling fire, which instantly was seene through all the
  strands
In unextinguishible flames that all the ship embrac't.
And then Achilles beate his thighes, cryed out: 'Patroclus, haste,
Make way with horse; I see at fleet a fire of fearfull rage.

[325]

Arme, arme, lest all our fleet it fire and all our powre engage. 120
Arme quickly, I'le bring up the troopes.' To these so dreadfull
    warres
Patroclus, in Achilles' armes (enlightned all with starres
And richly ameld), all haste made: he wore his sword, his shield,
His huge-plum'd helme and two such speares as he could
    nimbly wield.
But the most fam'd Achilles' speare, big, solid, full of weight, 125
He onely left of all his armes, for that farre past the might
Of any Greeke to shake but his. Achilles' onely ire
Shooke that huge weapon, that was given by Chiron to his sire,
Cut from the top of Pelion to be Heroes' deaths.

Automedon friend to
Patroclus and manager
of Achilles' horses.

His steeds Automedon straight joyn'd, like whom no man 130
    that breaths
(Next Peleus' sonne) Patroclus lov'd, for like him none so great
He found, in faith, at every fight, nor to out-looke a threat.
Automedon did therefore guide (for him) Achilles' steeds,
Xanthus and Balius, swift as wind, begotten by the seeds
Of Zephyr and the Harpie-borne Pordarge in a meade 135
Close to the Wavie Ocean, where that fierce Harpye feade.
Automedon joyn'd these before and with the hindmost geres
He fastn'd famous Pedasus, whom from the massakers
Made by Achilles when he tooke Eetion's wealthie towne
He brought, and (though of mortall race) yet gave him the 140
    renowne
To follow his immortall horse. And now before his tents
Himselfe had seene his Myrmidons in all habiliments

A simile most lively
expressive.

Of dreadfull warre. And when ye see (upon a mountaine bred)
A den of Wolves (about whose hearts unmeasur'd strengths
    are fed)
New come from currie of a Stagge, their jawes all 145
    blood-besmeard,
And when from some blacke water-fount they altogether herd,
There having plentifully lapt with thin and thrust-out tongs
The top and clearest of the spring, go belching from their lungs
The clotterd gore, looke dreadfully and entertaine no dread,
Their bellies gaunt, all taken up with being so rawly fed: 150
Then say that such in strength and looke were great Achilles'
    men
Now orderd for the dreadfull fight: and so with all them then
Their Princes and their Chiefes did show about their
    General's friend—
His friend and all about himselfe, who chiefly did intend

*The powers Achilles
brought to Troy.*

Th' embattelling of horse and foote. To that siege, held so long,   155
Twise five and twenty saile he brought; twise five and twentie strong
Of able men was every saile; five Colonels he made
Of all those forces—trustie men, and all of powre to leade,
But he of powre beyond them all. Menesthius was one,
That ever wore discolour'd armes; he was a river's sonne   160
That fell from heaven, and good to drinke was his delightfull streame—
His name, unwearied Sperchius; he lov'd the lovely dame
Faire Polydora, Peleus' seed and deare in Borus' sight,
And she to that celestiall flood gave this Menesthius light—
A woman mixing with a god. Yet Borus bore the name   165
Of father to Menesthius, he marrying the dame
And giving her a mightie dowre; he was the kind descent
Of Perieres. The next man renown'd with regiment
Was strong Eudorus, brought to life by one supposd a maide,
Bright Polymela (Phylas' seed) but had the wanton plaid   170
With Argus-killing Mercurie, who (fir'd with her faire eyes
As she was singing in the quire of her that makes the cries
In clamorous hunting and doth beare the crooked bow of gold)
Stole to her bed in that chaste roome that Phœbe chast did hold
And gave her that swift warrelike sonne Eudorus, brought to light   175

*Eudorus borne as
Polymela his mother
was dancing.*

As she was dancing: but as soone as she that rules the plight
Of labouring women easd her throwes and shew'd her sonne the Sunne,
Strong Echeclæus, Actor's heire, woo'd earnestly and wonne
Her second favour, feeing her with gifts of infinite prise,
And after brought her to his house, where in his grandsire's eyes   180
(Old Phylas) Polymela's sonne obtaind exceeding grace
And found as carefull bringing up as of his naturall race

*Mæmalides the third
Collonell.*

He had descended. The third chiefe was faire Mæmalides
Pisandrus, who in skill of darts obtaind supremest praise
Of all the Myrmidons except their Lord's companion.   185

*Phœnix the fourth.
Alcimedon the fifth.*

The fourth charge aged Phœnix had. The fifth, Alcimedon,
Sonne of Laerces, and much fam'd. All these digested thus
In fit place by the mightie sonne of royall Peleus,

*Achilles to his
Myrmidons.*

This sterne remembrance he gave all: 'You Myrmidons,' said he,
'Lest any of you should forget his threatnings usde to me   190
In this place, and through all the time that my just anger raign'd
Attempting me with bitter words for being so restrain'd

[327]

(For my hote humour) from the fight, remember them as these:
"Thou cruell sonne of Peleus, whom she that rules the seas
Did onely nourish with her gall, thou dost ungently hold   195
Our hands against our wills from fight; we will not be controld
But take our ships and saile for home before we loyter here
And feed thy furie." These high words exceeding often were
The threates that, in your mutinous troopes, ye usde to me
    for wrath
To be detaind so from the field: now then, your splenes may   200
    bath
In sweate of those great works ye wisht; now he that can employ
A generous heart, go fight and fright these bragging sonnes of
    Troy.'
    This set their minds and strengths on fire, the speech
    enforcing well,
Being usde in time; but being their king's, it much more did
    impell

Simile.

And closer rusht-in all the troopes. And, as for buildings hie   205
The Mazon layes his stones more thicke against th' extremitie
Of wind and weather, and even then, if any storme arise,
He thickens them the more for that, the present act so plies
His honest mind to make sure worke: so, for the high estate
This worke was brought to, these men's minds (according   210
    to the rate)
Were raisd and all their bodies joyn'd: but their well-spoken
    king
With his so timely-thought-on speech more sharpe made valour's
    sting
And thickn'd so their targets bost, so all their helmets then,
That shields propt shields, helmes helmets knockt and men
    encourag'd men.

Patroclus and
Automedon arme
together.

    Patroclus and Automedon did arme before them all   215
Two bodies with one mind inform'd; and then the Generall
Betooke him to his private Tent, where (from a coffer wrought
Most rich and curiously, and given by Thetis to be brought
In his owne ship, top-fild with vests, warme robes to checke
    cold wind
And tapistries all golden-fring'd and curl'd with thrumbs   220
    behind)

Achilles' sacrifice for
his friend's safe
returne.

He tooke a most unvalewed boule, in which none dranke but he,
Nor he but to the deities, nor any deitie
But Jove himselfe was serv'd with that. And that he first did
    clense
With sulphure, then with fluences of sweetest water rense.

[328]

Then washt his hands and drew himselfe a mightie boule of   225
   wine,
Which (standing midst the place enclosde for services divine
And looking up to heaven and Jove, who saw him well)
   he pour'd
Upon the place of sacrifice, and humbly thus implor'd:

Achilles' invocation.
   'Great Dodonæus, President of cold Dodona's towres,
Divine Pelasgicus that dwell'st farre hence, about whose bowres   230
Th' austere prophetique Selli dwell that still sleepe on the
   ground,
Go bare and never clense their feete—as I before have found
Grace to my vowes and hurt to Greece, so now my prayres intend.
I still stay in the gatherd fleete, but have dismist my friend
Amongst my many Myrmidons to danger of the dart.   235
O grant his valour my renowne; arme with my mind his hart,
That Hector's selfe may know my friend can worke in single
   warre
And not then onely shew his hands so hote and singular
When my kind presence seconds him. But fight he nere so well,
No further let him trust his fight but, when he shall repell   240
Clamor and Danger from our fleete, vouchsafe a safe retreate
To him and all his companies, with fames and armes compleate.'
   He prayd, and heaven's great Counsellor gave satisfying eare
To one part of his orisons, but left the other there:
He let him free the fleete of foes but safe retreate denide.   245
Achilles left that utter part where he his zeale applide
And turn'd into his inner tent, made fast his cup and then
Stood forth and with his mind beheld the foe's fight and his men
That follow'd his great-minded friend embattail'd till they brake

Simile.
With gallant spirit upon the foe. And as fell waspes that make   250
Their dwellings in the broade high way, which foolish children
   use
(Their cottages being neare their nests) to anger and abuse
With ever vexing them and breed (to sooth their childish warre)
A common ill to many men, since if a traveller
(That would his journey's end apply and passe them unassayd)   255
Come neare and vexe them, upon him the children's faults
   are layd,
For on they flie as he were such and still defend their owne:
So far'd it with the fervent mind of every Myrmidon,
Who pour'd themselves out of their fleete upon their wanton foes,
That needs would stirre them, thrust so neare, and cause the   260
   overthrowes
Of many others that had else bene never toucht by them

Nor would have toucht. Patroclus then put his wind to the
    streame,

Patroclus to the
Myrmidons.

And thus exhorted: 'Now my friends, remember you expresse
Your late-urg'd vertue, and renowme our great Æacides,
That, he being strongst of all the Greeks, his eminence may   265
    dimme
All others likewise in our strengths that farre off imitate him.
And Agamemnon now may see his fault as generall
As his place high, dishonoring him that so much honors all.'
    Thus made he sparkle their fresh fire, and on they rusht;
       the fleete
Fild full her hollow sides with sounds that terribly did greete   270
Th' amazed Troyans, and their eyes did second their amaze

The terror of Patroclus
to the Troyans.

When great Menœtius' sonne they saw and his friend's armor
    blaze.
All troupes stood troubl'd with conceit that Peleus' sonne
    was there,
His anger cast off at the ships, and each lookt every where
For some authoritie to leade the then prepared flight.   275
Patroclus greeted with a lance the region where the fight
Made strongest tumult, neare the ship Protesilaus brought,
And strooke Pyræchmen, who before the faire-helmd Pæons
    fought,
Led from Amydon, neare whose wals the broad-stream'd Axius
    flowes.

Pyræchmen slain by
Patroclus, and the ships
rescued.

Through his right shoulder flew the dart, whose blow strooke   280
    all the blowes
In his powre from his powrelesse arme, and downe he groning
    fell—
His men all flying (their Leader fled). This one dart did repell
The whole guard plac't about the ship, whose fire extinct
    halfe burn'd
The Pæons left her, and full crie to clamorous flight return'd.
Then spread the Greeks about their ships; triumphant tumult   285
    flow'd.

Simile.

And as from top of some steepe hill the lightner strips a clowd
And lets a great skie out from heaven, in whose delightsome
    light
All prominent foreheads, forrests, towres and temples cheare
    the sight:
So chear'd these Greeks this Troyan cloud, and at their ships
    and tents
Obtain'd a litle time to breathe, but found no present vents   290
To their inclusions; nor did Troy (though these Pæonians fled)

Lose any ground, but from this ship they needfully turn'd head.
  Then every man a man subdude. Patroclus in the thigh
Strooke Areilycus; his dart the bone did breake and flie
Quite through, and sunke him to the earth. Good Menelaus   295
    slew
Accomplisht Thoas, in whose breast (being nak'd) his lance
    he threw
Above his shield, and freed his soule. Phylides (taking note
That bold Amphiclus bent at him) prevented him, and smote
His thighe's extreme part where (of man) his fattest muscle lies,
The nerves torne with his lance's pile, and darknesse closde   300
    his eyes.
Antilochus Atymnius seizd, his steele lance did impresse
His first three guts and loosd his life. At yong Nestorides,
Maris, Atymnius' brother flew, and at him Thrasymed
(The brother to Antilochus); his eager Javelin's head
The muscles of his arme cut out and shiver'd all the bone;   305
Night closde his eyes; his livelesse corse his brother fell upon.
And so by two kind brothers' hands did two kind brothers
    bleed—
Both being divine Sarpedon's friends, and were the darting seed
Of Amisodarus, that kept the bane of many men,
Abhord Chimæra—and such bane now caught his childeren.   310
Ajax Oiliades did take Cleobulus alive,
Invading him (staid by the prease) and at him then let drive
With his short sword, that cut his necke; whose bloud warm'd
    all the steele,
And cold Death with a violent fate his sable eyes did seele.
Peneleus and Lycon cast together off their darts;   315
Both mist, and both together then went with their swords;
    in parts
The blade and hilt went, laying on upon the helmet's height.
Peneleus' sword caught Lycon's necke and cut it thorough quite.
His head hung by the very skin. The swift Meriones,
Pursuing flying Acamas, just as he got accesse   320
To horse and chariot overtooke, and tooke him such a blow
On his right shoulder that he left his chariot, and did strow
The dustie earth; life left his lims and night his eyes possest.
  Idomeneus his sterne dart at Erymas addrest,
As (like to Acamas) he fled; it cut the sundry bones   325
Beneath his braine betwixt his necke and foreparts, and so runs
(Shaking his teeth out) through his mouth, his eyes all drown'd
    in blood:
So through his nostrils and his mouth (that now dart-open stood)

He breath'd his spirit. Thus had death from every Grecian Chiefe

A Chiefe of Troy. For as to Kids, or Lambes, their cruelst   330
    thiefe

(The Wolfe) steales in, and when he sees that, by the shepheard's
    sloth,

The dams are sperst about the hils, then serves his ravenous
    tooth

With ease, because his prey is weake: so serv'd the Greeks
    their foes,

Discerning well how shrieking flight did all their spirits dispose,

Their biding vertues quite forgot. And now the naturall   335
    splene

That Ajax bore to Hector still by all meanes would have bene

Within his bosome with a dart: but he, that knew the warre,

(Well cover'd in a well-lin'd shield) did well perceive how farre

The arrowes and the javelins reacht, by being within their
    sounds

And ominous singings, and observ'd the there-inclining bounds   340

Of Conquest in her aide of him, and so obeyd her change,

Tooke safest course for him and his, and stood to her as strange.

And as when Jove intends a storme, he lets out of the starres

From steepe Olympus a blacke cloud, that all heaven's splendor
    barres

From men on earth: so from the hearts of all the Troyan host   345

All comfort lately found from Jove in flight and cries was lost.

Nor made they any faire retreat; Hector's unruly horse

Would needs retire him, and he left engag'd his Troyan force,

Forc't by the steepnesse of the dike that in ill place they tooke

And kept them that would faine have gone. Their horses   350
    quite forsooke

A number of the Troyan kings and left them in the dike,

Their chariots in their foreteames broke. Patroclus then
    did strike

While steele was hote and chear'd his friends; nor meant his
    enemies good,

Who, when they once began to flie, each way receiv'd a flood

And chok't themselves with drifts of dust. And now were   355
    clouds begot

Beneath the clouds with flight and noise; the horse neglected not

Their home intendments, and where rout was busiest, there
    pour'd on

Patroclus' most exhorts and threats. And then lay overthrowne

Numbers beneath their axle-trees, who (lying in flight's streame)

Made th' after chariots jot and jumpe in driving over them.   360

Th' immortall horse Patroclus rode did passe the dike
    with ease
And wisht the depth and danger more: and Menœtiades
As great a spirit had to reach retiring Hector's hast,
But his fleete horse had too much law and fetcht him off too fast.

Simile.

And as in Autumne the blacke earth is loden with the stormes   365
That Jove in gluts of raine poures downe, being angry with
    the formes
Of judgement in authorisde men that in their courts maintaine
(With violent office) wrested lawes and (fearing gods nor men)
Exile all justice, for whose faults, whole fields are overflowne
And many valleys cut away with torrents headlong throwne   370
From neighbour mountaines, till the sea receive them, roring in—
And judg'd men's labours then are vaine, plagu'd for their
    Judge's sin:
So now the foule defaults of some all Troy were laid upon,
So like those torrents roar'd they backe to windie Ilion,
And so like tempests blew the horse with ravishing backe   375
    againe
Those hote assailants, all their workes at fleete now rendred
    vaine.

    Patroclus (when he had disperst the formost Phalanxes)
Cald backe his forces to the fleete and would not let them prease
(As they desir'd) too neare the towne; but twixt the ships
    and floud
And their steepe rampire his hand steept Revenge in seas   380
    of bloud.

    Then Pronous was first that fell beneath his fierie lance,
Which strooke his bare brest neare his shield. The second,
    Thestor's chance
(Old Enops' sonne) did make himselfe, who, shrinking and
    set close
In his faire seate (even with th' approch Patroclus made),
    did lose
All manly courage, insomuch that from his hands his raines   385
Fell flowing downe, and his right jaw Patroclus' lance attaines,
Strooke through his teeth; and there it stucke, and by it to him
    drew
Dead Thestor to his chariot. It shewd as when you view

Simile.

An Angler from some prominent rocke draw with his line
    and hooke
A mightie fish out of the sea: for so the Greeke did plucke   390
The Troyan gaping from his seate, his jawes op't with the dart—
Which when Patroclus drew, he fell; his life and brest did part.

Homer's Iliads

Then rusht he on Euryalus, at whom he hurl'd a stone
Which strake his head so in the midst that two was made of one;
Two wayes it fell, cleft through his caske. And then   395
    Tlepolemus,
Epaltes, Damastorides, Evippus, Echius,
Ipheus, bold Amphoterus and valiant Erymas,
And Polymelus (by his sire surnam'd Argeadas)
He heapt upon the much-fed earth. When Jove's most
    worthy sonne
(Divine Sarpedon) saw these friends thus stayd and others   400
    runne:

Sarpedon to the   'O shame! why flie ye?' then he cride, 'Now shew ye feete
Lycians.   enow.

On, keepe your way; my selfe will meete the man that startles you,
To make me understand his name, that flants in conquest thus
And hath so many able knees so soon dissolv'd to us.'
    Downe jumpt he from his chariot; downe leapt his foe   405
    as light.

Simile.   And as on some farre-looking rocke a cast of Vultures fight,
Flie on each other, strike and trusse, part, meete, and then
    sticke by,
Tug both with crooked beakes and seres, crie, fight, and fight
    and cry:
So fiercely fought these angry kings and shew'd as bitter gals.

Jove to Juno about the   Jove (turning eyes to this sterne fight) his wife and sister cals,   410
fate of Sarpedon. And (much mov'd for the Lycian Prince) said: 'O that to
    my sonne
Fate, by this day and man, should cut a thread so nobly spunne!
Two minds distract me—if I should now ravish him from fight
And set him safe in Lycia, or give the Fates their right.'

Juno to Jove.   'Austere Saturnius,' she replide, 'what unjust words are   415
    theise?
A mortall long since markt by Fate wouldst thou immortalise?
Do; but by no god be approv'd. Free him, and numbers more
(Sonnes of immortals) will live free, that death must taste before
These gates of Ilion; every god will have his sonne a god
Or storme extremely. Give him then an honest period   420
In brave fight by Patroclus' sword, if he be deare to thee
And grieves thee for his danger'd life: of which, when he is free,
Let Death and Somnus beare him hence, till Lycia's naturall
    wombe
Receive him from his brother's hands, and citizens a Tombe
And columne raise to him; this is the honor of the dead.'   425

She said, and her speech rul'd his powre: but in his
　　safetie's stead,
For sad ostent of his neare death, he steept his living name
In drops of blood; heaven swet for him, which earth drunke
　　to his fame.
And now, as this high combat grew to this too humble end,
Sarpedon's death had this state more; twas usherd by his friend　430
And chariotere, brave Thrasymed, whom in his bellie's rim
Patroclus wounded with his lance, and endlesse ended him.
And then another act of name foreranne his princely fate;

Sarpedon kils Pedasus,　His first lance missing, he let flie a second that gave date
one of Achilles' horse.　Of violent death to Pedasus, who (as he joy'd to die　　435
By his so honorable hand) did (even in dying) ney.
His ruine startl'd th' other steeds; the geres crackt and
　　the raines
Strappl'd his fellowes, whose mis-rule Automedon restraines
By cutting the intangling geres and so dissundering quite
The brave-slaine Beast, when both the rest obeyd and went　440
　　foreright.

The last encounter of　And then the royall combattants fought for the finall stroke,
Sarpedon and　When Lycia's Generall mist againe; his high-raisde Javelin
Patroclus.　　tooke
Above his shoulder emptie way. But no such speedlesse flight
Patroclus let his speare performe, that on the breast did light
Of his brave foe where life's strings close about the solid hart,　445
Impressing a recurelesse wound; his knees then left their part
And let him fall, when, like an Oke, a Poplar or a Pine
New feld by arts-men on the hils, he stretcht his forme divine

Simile.　Before his horse and chariot. And as a Lion leapes
Upon a goodly yellow Bull, drives all the herd in heapes,　　450
And under his unconquerd jawes the brave beast sighing dies:
So sigh'd Sarpedon underneath this prince of enemies,

Sarpedon, dying, to　Cald Glaucus to him (his deare friend) and said: 'Now, friend,
Glaucus his friend.　　thy hands
Much dutie owe to fight and armes; now, for my love, it stands
Thy heart in much hand to approve that warre is harmefull;　455
　　now
How active all thy forces are this one houre's act must show.
First call our Lycian Captaines up, looke round and bring up all,
And all exhort to stand like friends about Sarpedon's fall.
And spend thy selfe thy steele for me: for be assur'd, no day
Of all thy life to thy last houre can cleare thy blacke dismay　460
In woe and infamie for me if I be taken hence
Spoil'd of mine armes and thy renowme despoil'd of my defence.

[335]

Stand firme then, and confirme thy men.' This said, the
    bounds of death
Concluded all sight to his eyes and to his nosthrils breath.
  Patroclus (though his guard was strong) forc't way through   465
    every doubt,
Climb'd his high bosome with his foote and pluckt his
    javelin out,
And with it drew the filme and strings of his yet-panting hart—
And last, together with the pile, his princely soule did part.
  His horse (spoil'd both of guide and king, thicke snoring
    and amaz'd,
And apt to flight) the Myrmidons made nimbly to and seaz'd.   470
  Glaucus, to heare his friend aske aide of him past all the rest

The sorrow of Glaucus (Though well he knew his wound uncur'd) Confusion fild
for Sarpedon, and   his brest—
praier to Phœbus. Not to have good in any powre, and yet so much good will.

And (laying his hand upon his wound, that pain'd him sharply
    still,
And was by Teucer's hand set on from their assail'd steepe   475
    wall,
In keeping hurt from other men) he did on Phœbus call
(The god of Medcines) for his cure: 'Thou king of cures,'
    said he,
'That art perhaps in Lycia with her rich progenie,
Or here in Troy, but any where, since thou hast powre to heare—
O give a hurt and wofull man (as I am now) thine eare.   480
This arme sustaines a cruell wound whose paines shoot
    every way,
Afflict this shoulder and this hand, and nothing long can stay,
A fluxe of blood still issuing; nor therefore can I stand
With any enemie in fight, nor hardly make my hand
Support my lance. And here lies dead the worthiest of men,   485
Sarpedon, worthy sonne to Jove (whose power could yet abstaine
From all aide in this deadly need). Give thou then aide to me
(O king of all aide to men hurt), asswage th' extremitie
Of this arme's anguish, give it strength that by my president
I may excite my men to blowes, and this dead corse prevent   490
Of further violence.' He praid, and kind Apollo heard,
Allayd his anguish and his wound of all the blacke bloud clear'd
That vext it so, infusde fresh powres into his weakened mind
And all his spirits flow'd with joy that Phœbus stood inclin'd
(In such quicke bountie) to his prayres. Then, as Sarpedon   495
    wild,
He cast about his greedie eye, and first of all instild

To all his Captaines all the stings that could inflame their fight
For good Sarpedon. And from them he stretcht his speedie pace
T' Agenor, Hector, Venus' sonne and wise Polydamas,

Glaucus, being cured,
to Hector.

And (onely naming Hector) said: 'Hector, you now forget   500
Your poore auxiliarie friends that in your toiles have swet
Their friendlesse soules out farre from home. Sarpedon,
    that sustain'd
With Justice and his vertues all broade Lycia, hath not gain'd
The like guard for his person here, for yonder dead he lies
Beneath the great Patroclus' lance. But come, let your supplies,   505
Good friends, stand neare him. O disdaine to see his corse defil'd
With Grecian furie and his armes by their oppressions spoil'd.
The Myrmidons are come enrag'd that such a mightie boote
Of Greekes Troy's darts have made at fleete.' This said,
    from head to foote
Griefe strooke their powres past patience and not to be   510
    restrain'd
To heare newes of Sarpedon's death, who, though he appertain'd
To other cities, yet to theirs he was the very Fort
And led a mightie people there, of all whose better sort
Himselfe was best. This made them runne in flames upon
    the foe—
The first man, Hector, to whose heart Sarpedon's death did go.   515

Patroclus to the
Grecians, and
particularly to both the
Ajaces.

    Patroclus stird the Grecian spirits, and first th' Ajaces, thus:
'Now, brothers, be it deare to you to fight and succour us,
As ever heretofore ye did, with men first excellent.
The man lies slaine that first did scale and raze the battlement
That crown'd our wall, the Lycian Prince. But if we now   520
    shall adde
Force to his corse and spoile his armes, a prise may more be had
Of many great ones that for him will put on to the death.'
    To this worke these were prompt enough; and each side
    ordereth
Those Phalanxes that most had rate of resolutions—
The Troyans and the Lycian powres, the Greeks and   525
    Myrmidons.
These ranne together for the corse and closde with horrid cries,
Their armours thundering with the claps laid on about the prise.
And Jove about th' impetuous broile pernicious night powr'd out
As long as for his loved sonne pernicious Labour fought.
    The first of Troy the first Greekes foil'd, when not the last   530
    indeed
Amongst the Myrmidons was slaine—the great Agacleus' seed,
Divine Epigeus, that before had exercisde command

In faire Budeius; but because he laid a bloudie hand
On his owne sister's valiant sonne, to Peleus and his Queene
He came for pardon and obtain'd—his slaughter being the   535
    meane
He came to Troy, and so to this. He ventur'd even to touch
The princely carkasse, when a stone did more to him by much;
(Sent out of able Hector's hand) it cut his skull in twaine
And strooke him dead. Patroclus (griev'd to see his friend
    so slaine)

Simile.   Before the foremost thrust himselfe. And as a Faulcon frayes 540
A flocke of Stares or Caddesses, such feare brought his assayes
Amongst the Troyans and their friends; and (angry at the hart
As well as griev'd for him so slaine) another stonie dart,
As good as Hector's he let flie, that dusted in the necke
Of Sthenelaus, thrust his head to earth first, and did breake   545
The nerves in sunder with his fall. Off fell the Troyans too,
Even Hector's selfe, and all as farre as any man can throw
(Provokt for games, or in the warres to shed an enemie's soule)
A light, long dart. The first that turn'd was he that did controule
The Targatiers of Lycia, Prince Glaucus, who to hell   550
Sent Bathycleus, Chalcon's sonne; he did in Hellas dwell
And shin'd, for wealth and happinesse, amongst the Myrmidons.
His bosome's midst the Javelin strooke, his fall gat earth
    with grones.
The Greeks griev'd and the Troyans joy'd for so renowm'd a man,
About whom stood the Grecians firme. And then the death   555
    began
On Troy's side by Meriones; he slue one great in warre,
Laogonus, Onetor's sonne, the Priest of Jupiter
Created in th' Idæan hill. Betwixt his jaw and eare
The dart stucke fast and loosde his soule, sad mists of
    Hate and Feare
Invading him. Anchises' sonne dispatcht a brazen lance   560
At bold Meriones, and hop't to make an equall chance
On him with bold Laogonus, though under his broade shield
He lay so close. But he discern'd and made his bodie yeeld
So low that over him it flew and, trembling, tooke the ground,
With which Mars made it quench his thirst; and, since   565
    the head could wound
No better bodie and yet throwne from nere the worse a hand,
It turnd from earth and lookt awrie. Æneas let it stand,

Æneas jests at   Much angrie at the vaine event, and told Meriones
Meriones.   He scap't but hardly, nor had cause to hope for such successe
Another time, though well he knew his dancing facultie   570

By whose agilitie he scap't—for, had his dart gone by
With any least touch, instantly he had bene ever slaine.

Meriones to Æneas.

He answerd: 'Though thy strength be good, it cannot render
    vaine
The strength of others with thy jests; nor art thou so divine,
But when my lance shall touch at thee with equall speed   575
    to thine,
Death will share with it thy life's powres. Thy confidence
    can shun
No more than mine what his right claimes.' Menœtius' noble
    sonne
Rebuk't Meriones, and said: 'What needst thou use this speech?
Nor thy strength is approv'd with words, good friend, nor can
    we reach
The bodie nor make th' enemie yeeld with these our   580
    counterbraves.
We must enforce the binding earth to hold them in her graves.
If you will warre, fight. Will you speake? Give counsell.
    Counsell, blowes
Are th' ends of warres and words. Talke here the time in vaine
    bestowes.'
He said, and led; and nothing lesse for any thing he said
(His speech being season'd with such right) the Worthy   585
    seconded.

Simile.

And then, as in a sounding vale (neare neighbour to a hill)
Wood-fellers make a farre-heard noise, with chopping,
    chopping still,
And laying on on blocks and trees: so they on men laid lode,
And beate like noises into aire both as they strooke and trod.
But (past their noise) so full of bloud, of dust, of darts,   590
    lay smit
Divine Sarpedon that a man must have an excellent wit
That could but know him; and might faile—so from his utmost
    head
Even to the low plants of his feete his forme was altered.
All thrusting neare it every way, as thicke as flies in spring
That in a sheepe-cote (when new milke assembles them)   595
    make wing
And buzze about the top-full pailes. Nor ever was the eye
Of Jove averted from the fight; he viewd, thought ceaslesly
And diversly upon the death of great Achilles' friend—
If Hector there (to wreake his sonne) should with his javelin end
His life and force away his armes, or still augment the field.   600

He then concluded that the flight of much more soule
    should yeeld
Achilles' good friend more renowne, and that even to their gates
He should drive Hector and his host: and so disanimates
The mind of Hector that he mounts his chariot and takes Flight
Up with him, tempting all to her—affirming his insight   605
Knew evidently that the beame of Jove's all-ordering scoles
Was then in sinking on their side, surcharg'd with flockes of
    soules.
    Then not the noble Lycians staid, but left their slaughterd
    Lord
Amongst the corses' common heape—for many more were pour'd
About and on him while Jove's hand held out the bitter broile. 610
And now they spoil'd Sarpedon's armes, and to the ships
    the spoile
Was sent by Menœtiades. Then Jove thus charg'd the Sunne:

Jove to Phœbus.   'Haste, honor'd Phœbus, let no more Greeke violence be done
To my Sarpedon but his corse, of all the sable bloud
And javelins purg'd, then carry him farre hence to some   615
    cleare floud,
With whose waves wash, and then embalme, each
    thorough-cleansed lim
With our Ambrosia; which perform'd, divine weeds put on him,
And then to those swift mates and twins, sweete Sleepe and
    Death, commit
His princely person, that with speed they both may carrie it
To wealthy Lycia, where his friends and brothers will embrace 620
And tombe it in some monument as fits a Prince's place.'

Apollo sends   Then flew Apollo to the fight from the Idalian hill,
Sarpedon's body by At all parts putting into act his great Commander's will—
Sleep and Death to Drew all the darts, washt, balm'd the corse, which (deckt
Lycia.   with ornament,
By Sleepe and Death, those featherd twins) he into Lycia sent. 625
    Patroclus then Automedon commands to give his steeds
Large raines, and all way to the chace: so madly he exceeds
The strict commission of his friend—which had he kept had kept
A blacke death from him. But Jove's mind hath evermore
    outstept
The mind of man, who both affrights and takes the victorie 630
From any hardiest hand with ease; which he can justifie,
Though he himselfe commands him fight—as now he put
    this chace
In Menœtiades his mind. How much then weighs the grace,

Patroclus, that Jove gives thee now, in scoles put with thy
    death,
Of all these great and famous men the honorable breath?   635
    Of which, Adrestus first he slue, and next Autonous,
Epistora, and Perimus, Pylartes, Elasus,
Swift Melanippus, Molius—all these were overthrowne

*Patroclus scaling the
wals of Troy, resisted
by Phœbus.*

By him, and all else put in rout. And then proud Ilion
Had stoopt beneath his glorious hand, he rag'd so with his   640
    lance,
If Phœbus had not kept the towre and helpt the Ilians,
Sustaining ill thoughts gainst the Prince. Thrice to the
    prominence
Of Troy's steepe wall he bravely leapt: thrice Phœbus thrust
    him thence,
Objecting his all-dazeling shield with his resistlesse hand.
But fourthly, when (like one of heaven) he would have   645
    stird his stand,

*Apollo threatens
Patroclus.*

Apollo threatned him, and said: 'Ceasse, it exceeds thy fate,
Forward Patroclus, to expugne with thy bold lance this state;
Nor under great Achilles' powres (to thine superiour farre)
Lies Troy's grave ruine.' When he spake, Patroclus left that
    warre,
Leapt farre backe, and his anger shund. Hector detain'd his   650
    horse
Within the Scæan ports, in doubt to put his personall force
Amongst the rout and turne their heads, or shun in Troy
    the storme.
    Apollo, seeing his suspence, assum'd the goodly forme

*Apollo in shape of
Asius to Hector.*

Of Hector's unkle, Asius, the Phrygian Dymas' sonne,
Who neare the deepe Sangarius had habitation,   655
Being brother to the Troyan Queene. His shape Apollo tooke,
And askt of Hector why his spirit so cleare the fight forsooke—
Affirming twas unfit for him, and wisht his forces were
As much above his as they mov'd in an inferiour sphere.
He should (with shame to him) be gone; and so bad, drive away   660
Against Patroclus, to approve, if he that gave them day,
Would give the glorie of his death to his preferred lance.
So left he him, and to the fight did his bright head advance,
Mixt with the multitude, and stird foule Tumult for the foe.
Then Hector bad Cebriones put on; himselfe let go   665
All other Greeks within his reach and onely gave command
To front Patroclus. He at him jumpt downe. His strong left hand
A Javelin held, his right, a stone—a marble sharpe and such

[341]

As his large hand had powre to gripe, and gave it strength
    as much
As he could lie to. Nor stood long in feare of that huge man   670
That made against him, but full on with his huge stone he ran,
Discharg'd and drave it twixt the browes of bold Cebriones.
Nor could the thicke bone there prepar'd extenuate so
    th' accesse
But out it drave his broken eyes, which in the dust fell downe,
And he div'd after—which conceit of diving tooke the sonne   675
Of old Menœtius, who thus plaid upon the other's bane:

    'O heavens! For truth, this Troyan was a passing active man!
With what exceeding ease he dives, as if at worke he were
Within the fishie seas! This man alone would furnish cheare
For twentie men, though twere a storme, to leape out of a saile   680
And gather oisters for them all; he does it here as well.
And there are many such in Troy.' Thus jested he so neare
His owne grave death, and then made in to spoile the Chariotere,
With such a Lion's force and fate as (often ruining
Stals of fat oxen) gets at length a mortall wound to sting   685
His soule out of that ravenous breast that was so insolent,
And so his life's blisse proves his bane: so deadly confident
Wert thou, Patroclus, in pursuite of good Cebriones,

To whose defence now Hector leapt. The opposite addresse
These masters of the crie in warre now made was of the kind   690
Of two fierce kings of beasts, opposd in strife about a Hind
Slaine on the forehead of a hill, both sharpe and hungry set,
And to the Currie never came but like two Deaths they met.
Nor these two entertain'd lesse mind of mutuall prejudice
About the bodie, close to which, when each had prest for prise,   695
Hector the head laid hand upon, which, once gript, never could
Be forc't from him; Patroclus then upon the feete got hold
And he pincht with as sure a naile. So both stood tugging there,
While all the rest made eager fight and grappl'd every where.

And as the East and South wind strive to make a loftie wood   700
Bow to their greatnesse, barkie Elmes, wild Ashes, Beeches bowd
Even with the earth, in whose thicke armes the mightie vapors lie
And tosse by turnes all either way; their leaves at randon flie,
Boughs murmure and their bodies cracke; and with
    perpetuall din
The Sylvans falter, and the stormes are never to begin: 705
So rag'd the fight, and all from Flight pluckt her forgotten wings,
While some still stucke; still new-wingd shafts flew dancing
    from their strings,
Huge stones sent after that did shake the shields about the corse,

Who now (in dust's soft forehead stretcht) forgat his guiding
    horse.
  As long as Phœbus turn'd his wheeles about the midst of   710
    heaven,
So long the touch of either's darts the fals of both made even:
But when his waine drew neare the West, the Greeks past
    measure were
The abler souldiers, and so swept the Troyan tumult cleare
From off the bodie, out of which they drew the hurl'd-in darts
And from his shoulders stript his armes. And then to more   715
    such parts
Patroclus turn'd his striving thoughts to do the Troyans ill.
Thrice, like the god of warre he charg'd, his voice as horrible:
And thrice nine those three charges slue. But in the fourth assay,
O then, Patroclus, shew'd thy last. The dreadfull Sunne
    made way
Against that on-set, yet the Prince discern'd no deitie—   720
He kept the prease so, and besides obscur'd his glorious eye
With such felt darknesse. At his backe he made a sodaine stand,
And twixt his necke and shoulders laid downe-right with
    either hand
A blow so weightie that his eyes a giddie darknesse tooke,
And from his head his three-plum'd helme the bounding   725
    violence shooke,
That rung beneath his horses hooves and, like a water-spout,
Was crusht together with the fall—the plumes that set it out
All spatterd with blacke bloud and dust, when ever heretofore
It was a capitall offence to have or dust or gore
Defile the triple-feather'd helme, but on the head divine   730
And youthfull temples of their Prince it usde untoucht
    to shine.
Yet now Jove gave it Hector's hands; the other's death was
    neare—
Besides whose lost and filed helme, his huge long weightie
    speare,
Well bound with iron, in his hand was shiverd and his shield
Fell from his shoulders to his feete, the bawdricke strewing   735
    the field.
His Curets left him like the rest, and all this onely done
By great Apollo. Then his mind tooke in confusion;
The vigorous knittings of his joynts dissolv'd; and
    (thus dismaid)
A Dardan (one of Panthus' sons, and one that overlaid

[343]

All Troyans of his place with darts, swift footing, skill, and   740
    force
In noble horsmanship, and one that tumbl'd from their horse,
One after other, twentie men, and when he did but learne
The art of warre—nay when he first did in the field discerne
A horse and chariot of his guide) this man with all these parts
(His name Euphorbus) comes behind and twixt the   745
    shoulders darts
Forlorne Patroclus, who yet liv'd, and th' other (getting forth
His Javelin) tooke him to his strength. Nor durst he stand the
    worth
Of thee, Patroclus, though disarmd, who yet (discomfited
By Phœbus' and Euphorbus' wound) the red heape of the dead
He now too late shund, and retir'd. When Hector saw   750
    him yeeld
And knew he yeelded with a wound, he scour'd the armed field,
Came close up to him and both sides strooke quite through
    with his lance.
He fell, and his most weightie fall gave fit tune to his chance—

Simile.   For which all Greece extremely mourn'd. And as a
    mightie strife
About a litle fount begins and riseth to the life   755
Of some fell Bore resolv'd to drinke, when likewise to
    the spring
A Lion comes alike disposde; the Bore thirsts, and his King,
Both proud and both will first be serv'd; and then the
    Lion takes
Advantage of his soveraigne strength, and th' other
    (fainting) makes
Resigne his thirst up with his bloud: Patroclus (so enforc't   760
When he had forc't so much brave life) was from his
    owne divorc't.

Hector's insultation   And thus his great Divorcer brav'd: 'Patroclus, thy conceit
over Patroclus, being   Gave thee th' eversion of our Troy, and to thy fleete a freight
wounded under him.   Of Troyan Ladies, their free lives put all in bands by thee:
But (too much priser of thy selfe) all these are propt by me.   765
For these have my horse stretcht their hoofes to this so long a
    warre,
And I (farre best of Troy in armes) keepe off from Troy as
    farre—
Even to the last beame of my life—their necessary day.
And here (in place of us and ours) on thee shall Vultures prey,
Poore wretch. Nor shall thy mightie Friend affoord thee any   770
    aid,

[344]

That gave thy parting much deepe charge. And this
    perhaps he said:
"Martiall Patroclus, turne not face nor see my fleete before
The curets from great Hector's breast, all guilded with his gore,
Thou hew'st in peeces." If thus vaine were his far-stretcht
    commands,
As vaine was thy heart to beleeve his words lay in thy hands.'   775

   He, languishing, replide: 'This proves thy glory worse than
    vaine,
That when two gods have given thy hands what their
    powres did obtaine
(They conquering, and they spoiling me both of my armes and
    mind,
It being a worke of ease for them) thy soule should be so blind
To oversee their evident deeds and take their powres to thee—   780
When, if the powres of twentie such had dar'd t' encounter me,
My lance had strew'd earth with them all. Thou onely doest
    obtaine
A third place in my death, whom first a harmfull fate hath
    slaine
Effected by Latona's sonne; second, and first of men,
Euphorbus. And this one thing more concernes thee; note   785
    it then:
Thou shalt not long survive thy selfe; nay, now Death cals for
    thee,
And violent fate. Achilles' lance shall make this good for me.'
   Thus death joyn'd to his words his end; his soule tooke
    instant wing,
And to the house that hath no lights descended, sorrowing
For his sad fate, to leave him yong and in his ablest age.   790
He dead, yet Hector askt him why, in that prophetique rage,
He so forespake him, when none knew but great Achilles
    might
Prevent his death and on his lance receive his latest light?
Thus, setting on his side his foote, he drew out of his wound
His brazen lance, and upwards cast the body on the ground—   795

*Hector charges on
Automedon for
Achilles' horses.*

When quickly, while the dart was hote, he charg'd Automedon
(Divine guide of Achilles' steeds) in great contention
To seise him too: but his so swift and deathlesse horse, that
    fetch
Their gift to Peleus from the gods, soone rap't him from
    his reach.

*Patroclus, languishing,
to Hector.*

COMMENTARIUS

[89] Aἳ γάϱ, Zεῦ τε πάτεϱ &c. *These last verses in the originall by many austere ancients have suffered expunction, as being unworthy the mouth of an Heroe, because he seems to make such a wish in them: which is as poorely conceipted of the expungers as the rest* 5 *of the places in Homer that have groned or laughed under their castigations—Achilles not out of his heart (which any true eye may see) wishing it, but out of a frolicke and delightsome humour, being merry with his friend in private, which the verse following in part expresseth:*

Ὣς οἱ μὲν τοιαῦτα πϱὸς ἀλλήλους ἀγόϱευον:　　10

Sic hi quidem talia inter se loquebantur—Inter se *intimating the meaning aforesaid. But our divine Maister's most ingenious imitating the life of things (which is the soule of a Poeme) is never respected nor perceived by his Interpreters, onely standing pedantically on the Grammar and words, utterly ignorant of the* 15 *sence and grace of him.*

[111] γνῶ δ'Αἴας κατὰ θυμὸν &c. ἔϱγα θεῶν &c. Agnovit autem Ajax in animo inculpato opera deorum; ῥίγησέν τε: exhorruitque. *Another most ingenious and spritefull imitation of the life and ridiculous humor of Ajax I must needs note here, because it flies* 20 *all his Translators and Interpreters, who take it meerely for serious, when it is apparently scopticall and ridiculous, with which our author would delite his understanding Reader and mixe mirth with matter. He saith that Hector cut off the head of Ajax' lance, which he seeing, would needs affect a kind of prophetique wisedome (with* 25 *which he is never charged in Homer) and imagined strongly the cutting off his lance's head cast a figure thus deepe—that as Hector cut off that, Jove would utterly cut off the heads of their counsels to that fight, and give the Troyans victory: which to take seriously and gravely is most dull (and as I may say) Ajanticall: the voyce* 30 κεῖϱε *(which they expound* præcidebat, *and indeed is* tondebat, κείϱω *signifying most properly* tondeo) *helping well to decipher the Ironie. But to understand gravely that the cutting off his lance's head argued Jove's intent to cut off their counsels, and to allow the wit of Ajax for his so farre-fetcht apprehension, I suppose no* 35 *man can make lesse than idle and witlesse. A plaine continuance therefore it is of Ajax' humor, whom in divers other places he playes*

[346]

upon, as in likening him in the eleventh booke to a mill Asse, *and else where to be noted hereafter.*

[625] Ὕπνῳ καὶ Θανάτῳ διδυμάοσιν —by Sleepe and Death (which 40
he ingeniously calleth Twins) was the body of Jove's sonne Sarpedon
taken from the fight and borne to Lycia. On which place, Eustathius
doubts whether truly and indeed it was transferd to Lycia, and he
makes the cause of his doubt this: That Death and Sleepe are
inania quædam, *things empty and voide;* οὐ στερέμνια πρόσωπα 45
not solid or firme persons, ἀλλ' ἀνυπόστατα πάθη *but* quæ nihil ferre
possunt. *And therefore he thought there was* κενήριον quoddam,
*that is, some voyde or emptie sepulcher or monument prepared for
that Heroe in Lycia, &c. or else makes another strange translation
of it, by wonder—which Spondanus thinkes to have happened truly—* 50
*but rather would interprete it merely and nakedly a poeticall fiction.
His reason I will forbeare to utter because it is unworthy of him.
But would not a man wonder that our great and grave Eustathius
would doubt whether Sleepe and Death carried Sarpedon's person
personally to Lycia, or not rather make no question of the contrary?* 55
*—Homer nor any Poet's end in such poeticall relations being to
affirme the truth of things personally done, but to please with the
truth of their matchlesse wits and some worthy doctrine conveyed
in it. Nor would Homer have any one beleeve the personall
transportance of Sarpedon by Sleepe and Death, but onely varieth* 60
*and graceth his Poeme with these Prosopopeias, and delivers us this
most ingenious and grave doctrine in it—that the Heroe's body, for
which both those mightie Hosts so mightily contended, Sleepe and
Death (those same* quædam inania) *tooke from all their personall
and solid forces. Wherein he would further note to us that, from* 65
*all the bitterest and deadliest conflicts and tyrannies of the world,
Sleepe and Death, when their worst is done, delivers and transfers
men—a little mocking withall the vehement and greedy prosecutions
of tyrants and souldiers against, or for that, which two such deedlesse
poore things takes from all their Emperie. And yet against* 70
*Eustathius' manner of sleighting their powers, what is there of all
things belonging to man so powerfull over him as Death and Sleep?
And why may not our Homer (whose words I hold with Spondanus
ought to be an undisputable deed and authoritie with us) as well
personate Sleepe and Death as all men besides personate Love,* 75
*Anger, Sloth, &c.? Thus onely where the sence and soule of my most
worthily reverenced Author is abused, or not seene, I still
insist, and gleane these few poore corne eares after all other
men's harvests.*

The End of the Sixteenth Booke

THE SEVENTEENTH BOOKE

of

HOMER'S ILIADS

THE ARGUMENT

A dreadfull fight about Patroclus' corse;
Euphorbus slaine by Menelaus' force;
Hector in th' armour of Æacides;
Antilochus relating the decease
Of slaine Patroclus to faire Thetis' sonne;   5
The body from the striving Troyans wonne;
Th' Ajaces making good the after field—
Make all the subject that this booke doth yeeld.

Another Argument

In Rho, *the ventrous hosts maintaine*
A slaughterous conflict for the slaine.

Nor could his slaughter rest conceald from Menelaus' eare,
Who flew amongst the formost fights, and with his targe and
    speare
Circled the body, as much griev'd and with as tender heed
To keepe it theirs as any damme about her first-borne seed,
Not proving what the paine of birth, would make the
    love before.   5

Euphorbus to   Nor to pursue his first attaint Euphorbus' spirit forebore;
Menelaus. This   But, seeing Menelaus chiefe in rescue of the dead,
Euphorbus was he   Assaid him thus: 'Atrides, ceasse, and leave the slaughtered
that, in Ovid,   With his embrew'd spoyle to the man that first of all our state
Pythagoras saith he   And famous succours, in faire fight, made passage to his fate. 10
was in the wars of   And therefore suffer me to weare the good name I have wonne
Troy.   Amongst the Troyans, lest thy life repay what his hath done.'

Menelaus to   'O Jupiter,' said he, incenst, 'Thou art no honest man
Euphorbus.   To boast so past thy powre to do. Not any Lion can,

Nor spotted Leopard, nor Bore (whose mind is mightiest   15
In powring furie from his strength) advance so prowd a crest
As Panthus' fighting progenie. But Hyperenor's pride
That joy'd so little time his youth, when he so vilifide
My force in armes and cald me worst of all our chevalrie
And stood my worst, might teach ye all to shun this surcuidrie: 20
I thinke he came not safely home to tell his wife his acts.
Nor lesse right of thy insolence my equall fate exacts
And will obtaine me, if thou stay'st. Retire then, take advise:
A foole sees nought before tis done, and still too late is wise.'
    This mov'd not him but to the worse, since it renew'd the   25
        sting
That his slaine brother shot in him, rememberd by the king—
To whom he answer'd: 'Thou shalt pay for all the
        paines endur'd
By that slaine brother, all the wounds sustaind for
        him recur'd
With one made in thy heart by me. Tis true, thou mad'st his
        wife
A heavie widow when her joyes of wedlocke scarce had life,   30
And hurt'st our parents with his griefe—all which thou
        gloriest in,
Forespeaking so thy death, that now their griefe's end shall
        begin.
To Panthus and the snowy hand of Phrontes I will bring
Those armes and that proud head of thine. And this
        laborious thing
Shall aske no long time to performe: nor be my words alone,   35
But their performance; Strength, and Fight, and Terror thus
        sets on.'
    This said, he strooke his all-round shield, nor shrunke
        that, but his lance
That turn'd head in it. Then the king assaid the
        second chance,

Euphorbus slain by   First praying to the king of gods, and his dart entrie got
Menelaus.   (The force much driving backe his foe) in low part of his   40
        throte
And ranne his necke through. Then fell pride, and he, and
        all with gore
His locks, that like the Graces were and which he ever wore
In gold and silver ribands wrapt, were piteously wet.

Simile.   And when alone in some choice place a husband-man hath
        set
The young plant of an Olive tree, whose roote being ever fed   45

With plentie of delicious springs, his branches bravely spred
And all his fresh and lovely head growne curld with snowy
flowres
That dance and florish with the winds that are of gentlest
powres;
But when a whirlewind (got aloft) stoopes with a sodaine gale,
Teares from his head his tender curles, and tosseth therewithall   50
His fixt roote from his hollow mines: it well presents the force
Of Sparta's king, and so the Plant, Euphorbus, and his Corse.
    He slaine, the king stript off his armes, and with their
        worthy prise
(All fearing him) had clearely past if heaven's faire eye of eyes
Had not (in envy of his acts) to his encounter stird   55
The Mars-like Hector, to whose powres the rescue he preferd
Of those faire armes, and tooke the shape of Mentes (Colonell
Of all the Cicones that neare the Thracian Hebrus dwell):
Like him, he thus put forth his voice: 'Hector, thou
        scowr'st the field
In headstrong pursuite of those horse that hardly are compeld   60
To take the draught of chariots by any mortal's hand.

Achilles.
The great grand child of Æacus hath onely their command,
Whom an immortall mother bore. While thou attendst on
        these,

Patroclus, so called,
of Menœtius his
father.
The young Atrides, in defence of Menœtiades,
Hath slaine Euphorbus.' Thus the god tooke troope with   65
        men againe,
And Hector (heartily perplext) lookt round and saw the slaine,
Still shedding rivers from his wound; and then tooke
        envious view
Of brave Atrides with his spoyle, in way to whom he flew
Like one of Vulcan's quenchlesse flames. Atrides heard the crie

Note the manly and
wise discourse of
Menelaus with
himselfe, seeing Hector
advancing towards him.
That ever usherd him, and sigh'd, and said: 'O me, if I   70
Should leave these goodly armes and him that here lies dead
        for me,
I feare I should offend the Greeks. If I should stay and be
Alone with Hector and his men, I may be compast in;
Some sleight or other they may use. Many may quickly win
Their wils of one, and all Troy comes ever where   75
        Hector leades.
But why, deare mind, dost thou thus talke? When men dare
        set their heads
Against the gods (as sure they do that fight with men they
        love),
Straight one or other plague ensues. It cannot therefore move

The grudge of any Greeke that sees I yeeld to Hector, he
Still fighting with a spirit from heaven. And yet if I could see   80
Brave Ajax, he and I would stand, though gainst a god; and
    sure
Tis best I seeke him, and then see if we two can procure
This Corse's freedome through all these. A little then let rest
The body, and my mind be still. Of two bads chuse the best.'
    In this discourse, the troopes of Troy were in with him, and he   85

Simile.

Made such a Lionlike retreate, as when the herdsmen see
The royall savage and come on with men, dogs, cries and
    speares
To cleare their horned stall, and then the kingly heart he beares
(With all his high disdaine) fals off: so from this ods of aide
The golden-haird Atrides fled and in his strength displaid   90
Upon his left hand him he wisht, extremely busied
About encouraging his men, to whom an extreme dread
Apollo had infusde. The king reacht Ajax instantly,

Menelaus to Ajax.

And said: 'Come, friend, let us two haste, and from the tyranny
Of Hector free Patroclus' corse.' He strait and gladly went.   95
And then was Hector haling off the body, with intent
To spoile the shoulders of the head and give the dogs the rest
(His armes he having prisde before)—when Ajax brought
    his brest
To barre all further spoyle. With that he had sure,
    Hector thought
Twas best to satisfie his splene, which temper Ajax wrought   100
With his mere sight, and Hector fled. The armes he
    sent to Troy
To make his citizens admire and pray Jove send him joy.
    Then Ajax gatherd to the corse and hid it with his targe,
There setting downe as sure a foote as (in the tender charge

Simile.

Of his lov'd whelps) a Lion doth; two hundred hunters neare   105
To give him onset, their more force makes him the
    more austere,
Drownes all their clamors in his rores, darts, dogs, doth all
    despise,
And lets his rough browes downe so low they cover all his
    eyes:
So Ajax lookt, and stood, and stayd for great Priamides.
    When Glaucus Hippolochides saw Ajax thus depresse   110

*Glaucus upbraids
Hector.*

The spirit of Hector, thus he chid: 'O goodly man at armes,
In fight a Paris, why should Fame make thee fort gainst our
    harmes,
Being such a fugitive? Now marke how well thy boasts defend

Thy citie onely with her owne. Be sure, it shall descend
To that proofe wholly. Not a man of any Lycian ranke   115
Shall strike one stroke more for thy towne: for no man gets a
    thanke
Should he eternally fight here, nor any guard of thee.
How wilt thou (worthlesse that thou art) keepe off an enemie
From our poore shoulders, when their Prince, Sarpedon, guest
    and friend
To thee (and most deservedly) thou flew'st from in his end   120
And left'st to all the lust of Greece? O gods, a man that was
(In life) so huge a good to Troy, and to thee such a grace,
(In death) not kept by thee from dogs? If my friends will
    do well,
We'le take our shoulders from your walls and let all sinke to
    hell—
As all will, were our faces turn'd. Did such a spirit breath   125
In all you Troyans as becomes all men that fight beneath
Their countrie's standerd, you would see that such as prop
    your cause
With like exposure of their lives have all the honour'd lawes
Of such a deare confederacie kept to them to a thred—
As now ye might reprise the armes Sarpedon forfeited   130
By forfeit of your rights to him, would you but lend your
    hands
And force Patroclus to your Troy. Ye know how deare he
    stands
In his love that of all the Greeks is (for himselfe) farre best
And leades the best, neare-fighting men: and therefore would
    (at least)
Redeeme Sarpedon's armes—nay him, whom you have likewise 135
    lost.
This body drawne to Ilion would after draw and cost
A greater ransome, if you pleasd. But Ajax startles you.
Tis his breast barres this right to us. His lookes are darts enow
To mixe great Hector with his men. And not to blame ye are
You chuse foes underneath your strengths; Ajax exceeds   140
    ye farre.'
Hector to Glaucus.   Hector lookt passing sowre at this, and answerd: 'Why
    dar'st thou
(So under) talke above me so? O friend, I thought till now
Thy wisdome was superiour to all th' inhabitants
Of gleby Lycia, but now impute apparent wants
To that discretion thy words shew, to say I lost my ground   145
For Ajax' greatnesse. Nor feare I the field in combats drownd,

Nor force of chariots: but I feare a powre much better seene,
In right of all warre, than all we—that god that holds betweene
Our victorie and us his shield, lets conquest come and go
At his free pleasure, and with feare converts her changes so   150
Upon the strongest: men must fight when his just spirit impels,
Not their vaine glories. But come on, make thy steps
    parallels
To these of mine, and then be judge how deepe the worke will
    draw—
If then I spend the day in shifts, or thou canst give such law
To thy detractive speeches then, or if the Grecian host   155
Holds any that in pride of strength holds up his spirit most
Whom (for the cariage of this Prince that thou enforcest so)
I make not stoope in his defence. You, friends, ye heare and
    know
How much it fits ye to make good this Grecian I have slaine
For ransome of Jove's sonne, our friend. Play then the   160
    worthy men
Till I endue Achilles' armes.' This said, he left the fight
And cald backe those that bore the armes, not yet without his
    sight
In convoy of them towards Troy. For them, he chang'd his
    owne,
Remov'd from where it rained teares, and sent them backe to
    towne.
    Then put he on th' eternall armes that the celestiall states   165
Gave Peleus; Peleus, being old, their use appropriates
To his Achilles, that (like him) forsooke them not for age.
When he whose Empire is in clouds saw Hector bent to wage
Warre in divine Achilles' armes, he shooke his head, and said:

Jove's discourse with   'Poore wretch, thy thoughts are farre from death, though he   170
himselfe of Hector in   so neare hath laid
the armes of Achilles.   His ambush for thee. Thou putst on those armes as
    braving him
Whom others feare, hast slaine his friend and from his
    youthfull lim
Torne rudely off his heavenly armes, himselfe being
    gentle, kind
And valiant. Equall measure then thy life in youth must find.
Yet since the justice is so strickt that not Andromache   175
(In thy denied returne from fight) must ever take of thee
Those armes in glory of thy acts, thou shalt have that fraile
    blaze

[353]

Of excellence that neighbours death—a strength even to
    amaze.'
  To this his sable browes did bow, and he made fit his lim
To those great armes, to fill which up the Warre god entred   180
    him,
Austere and terrible: his joynts and every part extends
With strength and fortitude; and thus to his admiring friends
High Clamor brought him. He so shin'd that all could
    thinke no lesse
But he resembl'd every way great-soul'd Æacides.
Then every way he scowr'd the field, his Captaines calling on— 185
Asteropæus, Ennomus (that foresaw all things done),
Glaucus and Medon, Deisenor and strong Thersilochus,

Phorcys and Mesthles, Chromius and great Hippothous:
To all these and their populous troopes, these his
    excitements were:
  'Heare us, innumerable friends; neare-bordering nations,   190
    heare.
We have not cald you from our townes to fill our idle eye
With number of so many men (no such vaine Emperie
Did ever joy us) but to fight, and of our Troyan wives
With all their children manfully to save the innocent lives.
In whose cares we draw all our townes of aiding souldiers drie 195

With gifts, guards, victuall, all things fit, and hearten their
    supplie
With all like rights; and therefore now let all sides set downe
    this,
Or live, or perish: this of warre the speciall secret is.
In which most resolute designe, who ever beares to towne
Patroclus (laid dead to his hand) by winning the renowne   200

Of Ajax' slaughter, the halfe spoyle we wholly will impart
To his free use, and to our selfe the other halfe convert.
And so the glory shall be shar'd; our selfe will have no more
Than he shall shine in.' This drew all to bring abrode their
    store
Before the body: every man had hope it would be his   205
And forc't from Ajax. Silly fooles, Ajax prevented this
By raising rampiers to his friend with halfe their carkasses.
And yet his humour was to rore and feare—and now, no lesse

To startle Sparta's king, to whom he cried out: 'O my friend!
O Menelaus! Now no hope to get off; here's the end   210
Of all our labours. Not so much I feare to lose the Corse
(For that's sure gone, the fowles of Troy and dogs will
    quickly force

That peece-meale) as I feare my head, and thine, O Atreus' sonne,
Hector a cloud brings will hide all; instant destruction
Grievous and heavie comes. O call, our Peeres to aid us; flie.'   215
    He hasted and usde all his voice, sent farre and nere his crie:
'O Princes, chiefe lights of the Greeks, and you that publickly
Eate with our Generall and me—all men of charge, O know
Jove gives both grace and dignitie to any that will show
Good minds for onely good it selfe, though presently the eye   220
Of him that rules discerne him not. Tis hard for me t' espie
(Through all this smoke of burning fight) each Captaine in
        his place
And call assistance to our need. Be then each other's grace
And freely follow each his next; disdaine to let the joy
Of great Æacides be forc't to feed the beasts of Troy.'   225
    His voyce was first heard and obeyd by swift Oiliades.
Idomeneus and his mate (renown'd Meriones)
Were seconds to Oileus' sonne: but of the rest, whose mind
Can lay upon his voice the names that after these combind
In setting up this fight on end? The Troyans first gave on.   230

Simile.

And as into the sea's vast mouth, when mightie rivers run,
Their billowes and the sea resound, and all the utter shore
Rebellowes (in her angry shocks) the sea's repulsive rore:
With such sounds gave the Troyans charge; so was their charge
        represt.
One mind fild all Greeks, good brasse shields close coucht to   235
        every brest.
And on their bright helmes Jove powr'd downe a mightie
        deale of night
To hide Patroclus—whom alive, and when he was the knight
Of that grand child of Æacus, Saturnius did not hate,
Nor, dead, would see him dealt to dogs and so did instigate
His fellowes to his worthy guard. At first the Troyans drave   240
The blacke-ey'd Grecians from the Corse; but not a blow they
        gave
That came at death. A while they hung about the bodie's
        heeles,
The Greekes quite gone. But all that while did Ajax whet the
        steeles
Of all his forces, that cut backe way to the Corse againe.
Brave Ajax (that for forme and fact past all that did maintaine   245
The Grecian fame, next Thetis' sonne) now flew before the
        first.

Simile.

And as a sort of dogs and youths are by a Bore disperst
About a mountaine: so fled these from mightie Ajax, all

[355]

That stood in conflict for the Corse—who thought no chance
    could fall
Betwixt them and the prise at Troy. For bold Hippothous   250
(Lethus' Pelasgus' famous sonne) was so adventurous
That he would stand to bore the Corse about the ankle bone,
Where all the nervie fibers meete and ligaments in one,
That make the motion of those parts; through which he did
    convay
The thong or bawdricke of his shield, and so was drawing   255
    away
All thanks from Hector and his friends; but in their steed he
    drew
An ill that no man could avert. For Telamonius threw
A lance that strooke quite through his helme; his braine came
    leaping out;
Downe fell Letheides, and with him the bodie's hoisted foote.
Farre from Larissa's soyle he fell, a little time allow'd   260
To his industrious spirits to quit the benefits bestow'd
By his kind parents. But his wreake Priamides assaid,
And threw at Ajax; but his dart (discovered) past, and staid
At Schedius, sonne of Iphitus, a man of ablest hand
Of all the strong Phocensians, and liv'd with great command   265
In Panopeus. The fell dart fell through his channell bone,
Pierc't through his shoulder's upper part, and set his spirit gone.
When (after his) another flew, the same hand giving wing
To martiall Phorcys' startled soule, that was the after spring
Of Phænops' seed: the javelin strooke his curets through and   270
    tore
The bowels from the bellie's midst. His fall made those before
Give backe a little, Hector's selfe enforc't to turne his face.
And then the Greeks bestow'd their showts, took vantage of
    the chace,
Drew off, and spoild Hippothous and Phorcys of their armes.
And then ascended Ilion had shaken with alarmes   275
(Discovering th' impotence of Troy) even past the will of Jove
And by the proper force of Greece, had Phœbus faild to move
Æneas, in similitude of Periphas (the sonne
Of grave Epytus) king at armes, and had good service done
To old Anchises, being wise and even with him in yeares.   280
Apollo disguised like   But (like this man) the farre-seene god to Venus' sonne
Periphas to Æneas.   appeares,
And askt him how he would maintaine steepe Ilion in her
    height,
In spite of gods (as he presum'd), when men approv'd so sleight

[356]

All his presumptions, and all theirs that puft him with that
    pride,
Beleeving in their proper strengths, and generally supplied   285
With such unfrighted multitudes? But he well knew that Jove
(Besides their selfe conceipts) sustaind their forces with more
    love
Than theirs of Greece, and yet all that lackt power to hearten
    them.

Æneas to the Troyans.   Æneas knew the god, and said: It was a shame extreme
That those of Greece should beate them so, and by their   290
    cowardise,
Not want of man's aide. nor the gods; and this (before his eyes)
A deitie stood even now and voucht, affirming Jove their aide—
And so bad Hector and the rest (to whom all this he said)
Turne head, and not in that quicke ease part with the corse to
    Greece.

    This said, before them all he flew; and all (as of a peece)   295
Against the Greeks flew. Venus' sonne Leocritus did end,
Sonne of Arisbas, and had place of Lycomedes' friend;
Whose fall he friendly pittied, and in revenge bestow'd
A lance that Apisaon strooke so sore that straite he strow'd
The dustie center; it did sticke in that congealed blood   300
That formes the liver. Second man he was of all that stood
In name for armes amongst the troope that from Pæonia came,
Asteropæus being the first; who was in ruth the same
That Lycomedes was, like whom he put forth for the wreake
Of his slaine friend, but wrought it not because he could not   305
    breake
That bulwarke made of Grecian shields and bristl'd wood of
    speares
Combin'd about the body slaine. Amongst whom Ajax beares
The greatest labour, every way exhorting to abide
And no man flie the corse a foote, nor breake their rankes in
    pride
Of any foremost daring spirit, but each foote hold his stand   310
And use the closest fight they could. And this was the command
Ajax his souldierly Of mightie Ajax: which observ'd, they steept the earth in blood.
command. The Troyans and their friends fell thicke. Nor all the Grecians
    stood
(Though farre the fewer suffred fate) for ever they had care
To shun confusion and the toyle that still oppresseth there.   315
    So set they all the field on fire, with which you would have
    thought

The Sunne and Moone had bene put out, in such a smoke they
    fought
About the person of the Prince. But all the field beside
Fought underneath a lightsome heaven: the Sun was in his
    pride,
And such expansure of his beames he thrust out of his throne   320
That not a vapour durst appeare in all that region—
No, not upon the highest hill. There fought they still and
    breathd,
Shund danger, cast their darts aloofe, and not a sword unsheathd.
The other plyde it, and the warre and Night plyde them
    as well,
The cruell steele afflicting all; the strongest did not dwell   325
Unhurt within their iron roofes. Two men of speciall name,
Antilochus and Thrasymed were yet unserv'd by Fame
With notice of Patroclus' death: they thought him still alive
In foremost tumult—and might well, for (seeing their
    fellowes thrive
In no more comfortable sort than Fight and Death would yeeld) 330
They fought apart; for so their Sire, old Nestor, strictly wild,
Enjoyning fight more from the fleet. Warre here increast
    his heate
The whole day long, continually the labour and the sweate
The knees, calves, feete, hands, faces smear'd of men that
    Mars applide

An inimitable Simile.   About the good Achilles' friend. And as a huge Oxe hide   335
A Currier gives amongst his men to supple and extend
With oyle, till it be drunke withall; they tug, stretch out,
    and spend
Their oyle and licour liberally, and chafe the leather so
That out they make a vapour breathe, and in their oyle
    doth go;
A number of them set on worke, and in an Orbe they pull   340
That all waies all parts of the hide they may extend at full:
So here and there did both parts hale the Corse in little place,
And wrought it al waies with their sweate; the Troyans hop't
    for grace
To make it reach to Ilion, the Grecians to their fleet.
A cruell tumult they stird up, and such as should Mars see't   345
(That horrid hurrier of men) or she that betters him,
Minerva, never so incenst, they could not disesteeme.
So banefull a Contention did Jove that day extend
Of men and horse about the slaine. Of whom his god-like
    friend

Had no instruction—so farre off, and underneath the wall   350
Of Troy, that conflict was maintaind which was not thought
    at all
By great Achilles, since he charg'd that, having set his foote
Upon the Ports, he would retire, well knowing Troy no boote
For his assaults without himselfe, since not by him, as well
He knew, it was to be subdu'd. His mother oft would tell   355
The mind of mightie Jove therein, oft hearing it in heaven;
But of that great ill to his friend was no instruction given
By carefull Thetis. By degrees must ill events be knowne.
    The foes cleft one to other still about the overthrowne.
His death with death infected both. Even private Greekes   360
    would say
Either to other: 'Twere a shame for us to go our way
And let the Troyans beare to Troy the praise of such a prise:
Which let the blacke earth gaspe and drinke our blood for
    sacrifise
Before we suffer: tis an act much lesse infortunate.'

The common souldiers'
resolutions.
And then would those of Troy resolve: 'Though certainly our   365
    fate
Will fell us altogether here, of all not turne a face.'
Thus either side his fellowe's strength excited past his place,
And thus through all th' unfruitfull aire an iron sound
    ascended
Up to the golden firmament—when strange affects contended
In these immortall heaven-bred horse of great Æacides,   370
Whom (once remov'd from forth the fight) a sodaine sense
    did seise
Of good Patroclus' death, whose hands they oft had undergone,
And bitterly they wept for him. Nor could Automedon
With any manage make them stirre; oft use the scourge to them,
Oft use his fairest speech, as oft threats never so extreme,   375
They neither to the Hellespont would beare him, nor the fight.

Simile.
But still as any tombe-stone layes his never-stirred weight
On some good man or woman's grave for rites of funerall:
So unremoved stood these steeds, their heads to earth let fall
And warme teares gushing from their eyes with passionate desire 380
Of their kind manager; their manes, that florisht with the fire
Of endlesse youth allotted them, fell through the yokie sphere
Ruthfully rufl'd and defilde. Jove saw their heavy cheare,
And (pittying them) spake to his mind: 'Poore wretched
    beasts,' said he,
'Why gave we you t' a mortall king, when immortalitie   385
And incapacitie of age so dignifies your states?

Jove's discourse with
himselfe of the
wretched state of
humanitie.

Was it to tast the miseries pour'd out on humane fates?
Of all the miserabl'st things that breathe and creepe on earth
No one more wretched is than man. And for your deathlesse
    birth,
Hector must faile to make you prise. Is't not enough he weares   390
And glories vainly in those armes? Your chariots, and rich
    geares
(Besides you) are too much for him. Your knees and spirits
    againe
My care of you shall fill with strength, that so ye may
    sustaine
Automedon and beare him off. To Troy I still will give
The grace of slaughter, till at fleet their bloody feete arrive,   395
Till Phoebus drinke the Westerne sea and sacred darknesse
    throwes
Her sable mantle twixt their points.' Thus in the steeds he
    blowes
Excessive spirit, and through the Greeks and Ilians they rapt
The whirring chariot, shaking off the crumbl'd center, wrapt
Amongst their tresses. And with them Automedon let flie   400
Amongst the Troyans, making way through all as frightfully

Simile.

As through a jangling flocke of Geese a lordly Vulture beats,
Given way with shrikes by every Goose that comes but neare
    his threats:
With such state fled he through the preasse, pursuing as he
    fled—
But made no slaughter; nor he could, alone being carried   405
Upon the sacred chariot. How could he both works do,
Direct his javelin and command his fiery horses too?
   At length, he came where he beheld his friend Alcimedon,
That was the good Laercius', the sonne of Hæmon's sonne,

Alcimedon to
Automedon.

Who close came to his chariot side, and askt: 'What god is he   410
That hath so robd thee of thy soule, to runne thus frantickly
Amongst these forefights, being alone, thy fighter being slaine
And Hector glorying in his armes?' He gave these words againe:

Automedon to
Alcimedon.

   'Alcimedon, what man is he, of all the Argive race,
So able as thy selfe to keepe in use of preasse and pace   415
These deathlesse horse—himselfe being gone that like the
    gods had th' art
Of their high manage? Therefore take to thy command his part
And ease me of the double charge, which thou hast blam'd
    with right.'
   He tooke the scourge and reines in hand, Automedon the
    fight.

Which Hector seeing, instantly (Æneas standing neare)   420

Hector to Æneas.

He told him he discern'd the horse that mere immortall were
Addrest to fight with coward guides, and therefore hop't to
    make
A rich prise of them if his mind would helpe to undertake—
For those two could not stand their charge. He granted, and
    both cast
Drie solid hides upon their neckes, exceeding soundly brast;   425
And forth they went, associate with two more god-like men,
Aretus and bold Chromius; nor made they question then
To prise the goodly-crested horse and safely send to hell
The soules of both their guardians. O fooles, that could
    not tell
They could not worke out their returne from fierce Automedon   430
Without the liberall cost of blood; who first made Orizon
To father Jove and then was fild with fortitude and strength;
When (counselling Alcimedon to keepe at no great length
The horse from him, but let them breathe upon his backe,
    because
He saw th' advance that Hector made, whose furie had no lawes   435
Proposd to it but both their lives and those horse made his
    prise—
Or his life theirs—he cald to friend these well-approv'd supplies,

*Automedon cals for aid
to the Ajaces and
Menelaus.*

Th' Ajaces and the Spartan king, and said: 'Come, Princes,
    leave
A sure guard with the corse, and then to your kind care
    receive
Our threatned safeties. I discerne the two chief props of Troy   440
Prepar'd against us. But herein what best men can enjoy

*In the Greeke alwayes
this phrase is used, not
in the hands, but ἐν
γούνασι κεῖται,
in the knees of the gods
lies our helps, &c.*

Lies in the free knees of the gods. My dart shall leade
    ye all;
The sequell to the care of Jove I leave, what ever fall.'
    All this spake good Automedon; then, brandishing his lance,
He threw and strooke Aretus' shield, that gave it enterance   445
Through all the steele and (by his belt) his bellie's inmost
    part
It pierc't, and all his trembling lims gave life up to his dart.
Then Hector at Automedon a blazing lance let flie,
Whose flight he saw and, falling flat, the compasse was too hie
And made it sticke beyond in earth; th' extreme part burst,   450
    and there
Mars buried all his violence. The sword then for the speare
Had chang'd the conflict, had not haste sent both th'
    Ajaces in

(Both serving close their fellowe's call), who where they did
    begin
There drew the end. Priamides, Æneas, Chromius
(In doubt of what such aid might worke) left broken-hearted   455
    thus
Aretus to Automedon, who spoild his armes, and said:

Automedon insults.   'A little this revives my life for him so lately dead
(Though by this nothing countervail'd).' And with this little
    vent
Of inward griefe he tooke the spoile; with which he made
    ascent
Up to his Chariot, hands and feete of bloudie staines so full   460
That Lion-like he lookt, new turn'd from tearing up a Bull.
    And now another bitter fight about Patroclus grew,
Teare-thirstie, and of toile enough; which Pallas did renew,
Descending from the cope of starres, dismist by sharp-eyd Jove
To animate the Greeks; for now inconstant change did move   465

Simile.   His mind from what he held of late. And as the purple bow
Jove bends at mortals when of warre he will the signall show,
Or make it a presage of cold in such tempestuous sort
That men are of their labours easde, but labouring cattell
    hurt:
So Pallas in a purple cloud involv'd her selfe, and went   470
Amongst the Grecians, stird up all, but first encouragement
She breath'd in Atreus' yonger sonne, and (for disguise) made
    choise
Of aged Phœnix' shape, and spake with his unwearied voice:

Pallas like Phœnix   'O Menelaus, much defame and equall heavinesse
to Menelaus.   Will touch at thee, if this true friend of great Æacides   475
Dogs teare beneath the Troyan wals; and therefore beare thee
    well,
Toile through the host, and every man with all thy spirit
    impell.'

Menelaus to Pallas   He answerd: 'O thou long-since borne, O Phœnix, that
supposed Phœnix.   hast wonne
The honor'd foster-father's name of Thetis' god-like sonne,
I would Minerva would but give strength to me and but keepe   480
These busie darts off; I would then make in indeed and steepe
My income in their bloods, in aide of good Patroclus. Much
His death afflicts me, much; but yet this Hector's grace is such
With Jove, and such a fierie strength and spirit he has, that still
His steele is killing, killing still.' The king's so royall will   485
Minerva joy'd to heare, since she did all the gods outgo
In his remembrance. For which grace she kindly did bestow

Strength on his shoulders and did fill his knees as liberally
With swiftnesse, breathing in his breast the courage of a flie
Which loves to bite so and doth beare man's bloud so much   490
    good will
That still (though beaten from a man) she flies upon him still:
With such a courage Pallas fild the blacke parts neare his hart.
And then he hasted to the slaine, cast off a shining dart,
And tooke one Podes, that was heire to old Eetion,
A rich man and a strenuous and by the people done   495
Much honour, and by Hector too, being consort and his guest.
And him the yellow-headed king laid hold on at his waste
In offering flight; his iron pile strooke through him; downe
    he fell,
And up Atrides drew his corse. Then Phœbus did impell

Phœbus like Asiades   The spirit of Hector, Phænops like, surnam'd Asiades,   500
to Hector.   Whom Hector usde (of all his guests) with greatest
    friendlinesse,
And in Abydus stood his house; in whose forme thus he spake:
  'Hector! What man of all the Greeks will any terror make
Of meeting thy strength any more, when thou art terrified
By Menelaus, who, before he slue thy friend, was tried   505
A passing easie souldier, where now (besides his end
Imposde by him) he drawes him off (and not a man to friend)
From all the Troyans? This friend is Podes, Eetion's sonne.'
  This hid him in a cloud of griefe and set him formost on.
And then Jove tooke his Snake-fring'd shield, and Ida cover'd   510
    all
With sulphurie clouds, from whence he let abhorred
    lightnings fall
And thunderd till the mountaine shooke: and with this
    dreadfull state
He usherd victorie to Troy, to Argos flight and fate.
Peneleus Bœotius was he that formost fled,
Being wounded in his shoulder's height, but there the lance's   515
    head
Strooke lightly, glancing to his mouth, because it strooke him
    neare,
Throwne from Polydamas. Leitus next left the fight in feare
(Being hurt by Hector in his hand) because he doubted sore
His hand, in wished fight with Troy, would hold his lance
    no more.

Idomeneus at Hector.   Idomeneus sent a dart at Hector (rushing in   520
And following Leitus) that strooke his bosome neare his chin
And brake at top; the Ilians for his escape did shout.

When Hector at Deucalides another lance sent out
As in his chariot he stood; it mist him narrowly,
For (as it fell) Cœranus drave his speedie chariot by   525
And tooke the Troyan lance himselfe; he was the Chariotere
Of sterne Meriones and first on foote did service there,
Which well he left to governe horse, for saving now his king
With driving twixt him and his death, though thence his
      owne did spring—
Which kept a mightie victorie from Troy in keeping death   530
From his great Soveraigne. The fierce dart did enter him
      beneath
His eare, betwixt his jaw and it, drave downe, cut through
      his tongue
And strooke his teeth out; from his hands the horses' raines
      he flung,
Which now Meriones receiv'd as they bestrew'd the field
And bad his Soveraigne scourge away; he saw that day would   535
      yeeld
No hope of victorie for them. He fear'd the same and fled.
  Nor from the mightie-minded sonne of Telamon lay hid
(For all his clouds) high Jove himselfe, nor from the
      Spartan king.
They saw him in the victorie he still was varying
For Troy. For which sight Ajax said: 'O heavens, what foole is   540
      he
That sees not Jove's hand in the grace now done our enemie?
Not any dart they touch but takes, from whom soever throwne,
Valiant or coward. What he wants, Jove addes; not any one
Wants his direction to strike sure—nor ours, to misse as sure.

Ajax' good counsell.   But come, let us be sure of this, to put the best in ure   545
That lies in us; which two-fold is—both to fetch off our friend
And so to fetch him off as we may likeliest contend
To fetch our selves off—that our friends surviving may have right
In joy of our secure retreat, as he that fell in fight
Being kept as sure from further wrong. Of which perhaps   550
      they doubt,
And, looking this way, grieve for us, not able to worke out
Our passe from this man-slaughterer, great Hector, and
      his hands
That are too hote for men to touch, but that these thirstie sands
Before our fleete will be enforc't to drinke our headlong death.
Which to prevent by all fit meanes, I would the parted breath   555
Of good Patroclus to his friend with speed imparted were
By some he loves: for I beleeve no heavie messenger

Hath yet inform'd him. But, alas, I see no man to send;
Both men and horse are hid in mists that every way descend.
O father Jupiter, do thou the sonnes of Greece release   560
Of this felt darknesse; grace this day with fit transparences
And give the eyes thou giv'st, their use; destroy us in the light
And worke thy will with us, since needs thou wilt against us
    fight.'
    This spake he weeping, and his teares Saturnius pitie show'd,
Disperst the darknesse instantly and drew away the clowd   565
From whence it fell: the Sunne shin'd out and all the host
    appear'd.
And then spake Ajax, whose heard prayre his spirits highly
    chear'd:

Ajax to Menelaus.
'Brave Menelaus, looke about, and, if thou canst descrie
Nestor's Antilochus alive, incite him instantly
To tell Achilles that his friend most deare to him is dead.'   570
    He said; nor Menelaus stucke at any thing he said
(As loth to do it) but he went. As from a Grasier's stall

Simile.
A Lion goes when overlaid (with men, dogs, darts, and all
Not easely losing a fat Oxe, but strong watch all night held),
His teeth yet watering; oft he comes, and is as oft repeld,   575
The adverse darts so thicke are pour'd before his brow-hid eyes,
And burning firebrands; which, for all his great heart's heate,
    he flies
And (grumbling) goes his way betimes: so from Patroclus went
Atrides much against his mind, his doubts being vehement
Lest (he gone from his guard) the rest would leave (for   580
    very feare)

*Another direct scoffe
at Menelaus.*
The person to the spoile of Troy. And yet his guardians were
Th' Ajaces and Meriones, whom much his care did presse

*Menelaus to the
Ajaces, like himself.*
And thus exhort: 'Ajaces both, and you Meriones,
Now let some true friend call to mind the gentle and sweete
    nature
Of poore Patroclus; let him thinke how kind to every creature   585
His heart was, living, though now dead.' Thus urg'd the
    faire-hair'd king,
And parted, casting round his eye. As when upon her wing

Simile.
An Eagle is, whom men affirme to have the sharpest sight
Of all aire's region of fowles, and, though of mightie height,
Sees yet within her leavie forme of humble shrubs, close laid,   590
A light-foote Hare, which straight she stoupes, trusses and strikes
    her dead:
So dead thou strook'st thy charge, O king, through all warre's
    thickets so

Thou look'dst and swiftly found'st thy man, exhorting gainst
    the foe
And heartning his plied men to blowes, usde in the warre's
    left wing.
To whom thou saidst: 'Thou god-lov'd man, come here, and   595
    heare a thing
Which I wish never were to heare. I thinke even thy eye sees
What a destruction God hath laid upon the sonnes of Greece,
And what a conquest he gives Troy; in which the best of men,
Patroclus, lies exanimate, whose person passing faine
The Greeks would rescue and beare home; and therefore   600
    give thy speed
To his great friend, to prove if he will do so good a deed
To fetch the naked person off, for Hector's shoulders weare

Antilochus' grief for   His prised armes.' Antilochus was highly griev'd to heare
Patroclus.   This heavie newes, and stood surprisde with stupid silence long,
His faire eyes standing full of teares; his voice, so sweete   605
    and strong,
Stucke in his bosome; yet all this wrought in him no neglect
Of what Atrides gave in charge, but for that quicke effect
He gave Laodocus his armes (his friend that had the guide
Of his swift horse), and then his knees were speedily applide
In his sad message, which his eyes told all the way in teares.   610

Another notable Ironie,   Nor would thy generous heart assist his sore-charg'd souldiers,
expressing what Homer   O Menelaus, in meane time, though left in much distresse.
made of Menelaus.   Thou sentst them god-like Thrasymed, and mad'st thy kind
    regresse
Backe to Patroclus, where arriv'd, halfe breathlesse thou didst say
To both th' Ajaces: 'I have sent this messenger away   615
To swift Achilles, who, I feare, will hardly helpe us now
(Though mad with Hector); without armes he cannot fight,
    ye know.
Let us then thinke of some best meane, both how we may
    remove
The bodie and get off our selves from this vociferous drove
And fate of Troyans.' 'Bravely spoke at all parts,' Ajax said,   620
'O glorious sonne of Atreus. Take thou then straite the dead,
And thou Meriones. We two, of one mind as one name,
Will backe ye soundly and on us receive the wild-fire flame
That Hector's rage breathes after you, before it come at you.'

Menelaus and Meriones   This said, they tooke into their armes the bodie—all the show   625
beare off the body of   That might be made to those of Troy, at arme's end bearing it.
Patroclus.   Out shriekt the Troyans when they saw the bodie borne to fleete,
Simile.   And rusht on. As at any Bore, gasht with the hunters' wounds,

[366]

A kennell of the sharpest set and sorest bitten hounds
Before their youthfull huntsmen haste, and eagerly a while   630
Pursue as if they were assur'd of their affected spoile;
But when the Savage (in his strength as confident as they)
Turnes head amongst them, backe they flie, and every one
    his way:
So troope-meale Troy pursu'd a while, laying on with swords
    and darts,
But when th' Ajaces turn'd on them and made their stand,   635
    their harts
Drunke from their faces all their blouds, and not a man sustain'd
The forechace nor the after fight. And thus Greece nobly gain'd
The person towards home: but thus the changing warre was rackt
Out to a passing bloudie length. For as, once put in act,

Simile.
A fire invading citie roofes is sodainly engrost   640
And made a wondrous mightie flame, in which is quickly lost
A house long building, all the while a boisterous gust of wind
Lumbring amongst it: so the Greekes (in bearing of their friend)
More and more foes drew, at their heeles a tumult thundering
    still

Simile.
Of horse and foote. Yet as when Mules, in haling from a hill   645
A beame or mast through foule deepe way, well clapt and
    heartned, close
Lie to their labour, tug and sweate, and passing hard it goes
(Urg'd by their drivers to all hast): so dragg'd they on the corse,
Still both th' Ajaces at their backs, who backe still turn'd
    the force,

Simile, illustrating the valour of both the Ajaces.
Though after it grew still the more. Yet as a sylvane hill   650
Thrusts backe a torrent that hath kept a narrow channell still,
Till at his Oken breast it beates, but there a checke it takes
That sends it over all the vale with all the stirre it makes,
Nor can with all the confluence breake through his rootie sides:
In no lesse firme and brave repulse th' Ajaces curb'd the prides   655
Of all the Troyans: yet all held the pursuite in his strength
Their chiefes being Hector and the sonne of Venus, who
    at length
Put all the youth of Greece besides in most amazefull rout—
Forgetting all their fortitudes, distraught and shrieking out,
A number of their rich armes lost, falne from them   660
    here and there
About and in the dike. And yet, the warre concludes not here.

COMMENTARIUS

[335] ὡς δ'ὅτ' ἀνὴρ ταύροιο βοὸς μεγάλοιο βοείην
λαοῖσιν δώῃ τανύειν, μεθύουσαν ἀλοιφῇ·
δεξάμενοι δ'ἄρα τοί γε διαστάντες τανύουσι
κυκλόσ', ἄφαρ δέ τε ἰκμὰς ἔβη, δύνει τ'ἀλοιφὴ
πολλῶν ἑλκόντων, τάνυται δέ τε πᾶσα διαπρό: 5
ὡς οἵ γ'ἔνθα καὶ ἔνθα νέκυν ὀλίγῃ ἐνὶ χώρῃ
εἵλκεον ἀμφότεροι·

Thus translated ad verbum *by Spondanus:*

> Sicut autem quando vir tauri bovis magni pellem
> Populis dederit distendendam temulentam pinguedine,   10
> Accipientes autem utique hi dispositi extendunt
> In orbem, statim autem humor exiit, penetratque adeps,
> Multis trahentibus: tenditur autem tota undique;
> Sic hi huc et illuc cadaver parvo in spatio
> Trahebant utrique.   15

Laurent. Valla thus in prose:

> Et quemadmodum si quis pinguem Tauri pellem à pluribus extendi
> juberet; inter extendendum et humor et pingue desudat. Sic
> illi huc parvo in spatio distrahebant.

Eobanus thus in verse: 20

> ————Ac si quis distendere pellem
> Taurinam jubeat, crassam pinguedine multa,
> Multorum manibus, terræ desudet omasum
> Et liquor omnis humi. Sic ipsum tempore parvo
> Patroclum in diversa, manus numerosa trahebat, &c.   25

*To answer a hote objection made to me by a great scholler for not
translating Homer word for word and letter for letter (as out of his
heate he strained it) I am enforced to cite this admirable Simile
(like the other before in my annotations at the end of the fifteenth
Booke) and referre it to my judiciall reader's examination whether*   30
*such a translation becomes Homer or not, by noting so much as needs
to be by one example; whether the two last above-said translators,
in being so short with our everlasting master, do him so much right
as my poore conversion, expressing him by necessary exposition and
illustration of his words and meaning with more words or not.*   35
The reason of his Simile is to illustrate the strife of both the

armies for the body of Patroclus, which it doth performe most
inimitably, their toile and sweate about it being considered (which
I must pray you to turne to before). The Simile it selfe yet I thought
not unfit to insert here, to come up the closer to them with whom I 40
am to be compared. My paines and understanding converting it thus:

    ————And as a huge oxe hide
A Currier gives amongst his men to supple and extend
With oile, till it be drunke withall; they tug, stretch out,
  and spend
Their oile and licour liberally, and chafe the leather so   45
They make it breathe a vapour out, and in their licours go;
A number of them set a worke, and in an orbe they pull
That all wayes all parts of the hide they may extend at full:
So here and there did both hosts hale the corse in litle place,
And wrought it all wayes with their sweate, &c.   50

In which last words of the application considered lies the life of this
illustration. Our Homer's divine invention wherein I see not in
any of their shorter translations toucht at. But what could expresse
more the toile about this body, forcing it this way and that, as the
opposite advantage served on both sides? An Oxe's hide, after the 55
tanning, asking so much labour and oile to supple and extend it——
ταννειν, μεθύουσαν ἀλοιφῇ, *distendendam,* temulentam pinguedine;
to be stretcht out, being drunke with tallow, oile or licour: the word
μεθύουσαν, *which signifies* temulentam, *of* μεθύω, *signifying* ebrius sum
(being a metaphor) and used by Homer, I thought fit to expresse so, 60
both because it is Homer's and doth much more illustrate than crassam
pinguedine multa, *as Eobanus turnes it. But Valla leaves it clearely*
out, and with his briefenesse utterly maimes the Simile; which (to my
understanding being so excellent) I could not but with thus much
repetition and labour inculcate the sence of it, since I see not that 65
any translator hath ever thought of it. And therefore (against the
objector that would have no more words than Homer used in his
translator) I hope those few words I use more, being necessarie to
expresse such a sence as I understand in Homer, will be at least borne
withall; without which, and other such needfull explanations, the 70
most ingenious invention and sence of so matchlesse a writer might
passe endlesly obscured and unthought on. My manner of translation
being partly built on this learned and judicious authoritie:
Est sciti interpretis, non verborum numerum et ordinem sectari, sed
res ipsas et sententias attentè perpendere, easque verbis et formulis 75
orationis vestire idoneis et aptis ei linguæ in quam convertitur.

[480] —εἰ γὰρ 'Aθήνη *&c. Minerva appearing to Menelaus*

like Phœnix, and encouraging him (as you may reade before) to
fight, he speakes as to Phœnix and wishes Minerva would but put
away the force or violence of the darts, and he would aid and fight   80
bravely: which is a continuance of his character, being exprest for
the most part by Homer ridiculous and simple. The originall words
yet (because neither Eobanus nor Valla understood the character)
they utterly pervert, as, if you please to examine them, you may see.
The words are these, βελέων δ'ἀπερύκοι ἐρωήν, which Spondanus   85
truly interprets telorum verò depulerit impetum; ἀπερύκω being a
compound of ἐρύκω, signifying arceo, repello, propulso, abigo;
and yet they translate the words, et telis vim afferret, as if Menelaus
wisht that Pallas would give force to his darts; which Eobanus
followes, saying, et tela valentia præstet, most ignorantly and   90
unsufferably converting it, supposing them to be his owne darts he
spake of and would have blest with Minerva's addition of vertue
and power; where Homer's are plaine; he spake of the enemie's darts,
whose force if she would avert, he would fight for Patroclus.

[489] καί οἱ μυίης θάρσος ἐνὶ στήθεσσιν ἐνῆκεν, &c. Et ei Muscæ   95
audaciam in pectoribus immisit. Minerva inspired him with the
courage of a flie; which all his interpreters very ridiculously laugh at
in Homer, as if he heartily intended to praise Menelaus by it, not
understanding his Ironie here, agreeing with all the other sillinesse
noted in his character. Eobanus Hessus, in pitie of Homer, leaves it   100
utterly out, and Valla comes over him with a little salve for the sore
disgrace he hath by his ignorant readers' laughters, and expounds
the words abovesaid thus: Lene namque eius ingenium prudenti
audacia implevit, laying his medicine nothing neare the place.
Spondanus (disliking Homer with the rest in this Simile) would not   105
have Lucian forgotten in his merry Encomium of a Flie, and
therefore cites him upon this place, playing upon Homer; which,
because it is already answered in the Ironie to be understood in
Homer (he laughing at all men so ridiculous), I forbeare to repeate,
and cite onely Eustathius, that would salve it with altering the word   110
θάρσος, which signifies confidentia or audacia (per Metathesin literæ
ϱ for θράσος which is temeritas); of which I see not the end, and
yet cite all, to shew how such great Clerks are perplext and abuse
Homer as not being satis compotes mentis Poeticæ; for want of which
(which all their reading and language cannot supply) they are thus   115
often graveld and mistaken.

[588] ὥς αἰετός, &c. Veluti Aquila. The sport Homer makes with
Menelaus is here likewise confirmed and amplified in another Simile,
resembling him intentionally to a harefinder, though for colour's
sake he useth the word Eagle; as in all other places where he   120

The Seventeenth Booke, Commentarius

presents him (being so eminent a person) he hides his simplicity
with some shadow of glory or other. The circumstances making it
cleare, being here and in divers other places made a messenger from
Ajax and others, to call such and such to their aid—which was unfit
for a man of his place, if he had bene in magnanimitie and valour   125
equall, or any thing neare it. But to confirme his imperfection
therein in divers other places, he is called μαλθακὸς αἰχμητὴς, mollis
bellator; and therefore was fittest to be employed to cal up those
that were hardier and abler. In going about which businesse,
Homer shewes how he looks about, leering like a hare-finder: for to   130
make it simply a Simile illustrating the state of his address in that
base affaire had neither wit nor decorum. Both which being at their
height in the other sence (because our Homer was their great
master to all accomplishment) let none detract so miserably
from him as to take this otherwise than a continuance   135
of his Ironie.

The End of the Seventeenth Booke

THE EIGHTEENTH BOOKE

of

HOMER'S ILIADS

THE ARGUMENT

Achilles mournes, told of Patroclus' end;
When Thetis doth from forth the sea ascend
And comfort him, advising to abstaine
From any fight till her request could gaine
Fit armes of Vulcan. Juno yet commands   5
To shew himselfe. And at the dike he stands
In sight of th' enemie, who with his sight
Flies, and a number perish in the flight.
Patroclus' person (safe brought from the warres)
His souldiers wash. Vulcan the armes prepares.   10

Another Argument

Sigma continues the alarmes,
And fashions the renowmed armes.

They fought still like the rage of fire. And now Antilochus
Came to Æacides, whose mind was much solicitous
For that which (as he fear'd) was falne. He found him neer
    the fleet
With upright saile-yeards, uttering this to his heroike conceit:

'Ay me, why see the Greeks themselves thus beaten from the field   5
And routed headlong to their fleet? O let not heaven yeeld
Effect to what my sad soule feares, that (as I was foretold)
The strongest Myrmidon (next me), when I should still behold
The Sunne's faire light, must part with it. Past doubt Menœtius'
    sonne
Is he on whom that fate is wrought. O wretch, to leave undone   10
What I commanded, that the fleete once freed of hostile fire
(Not meeting Hector) instantly he should his powres retire.'
    As thus his troubl'd mind discourst, Antilochus appear'd,

[372]

Antilochus relates Patroclus' death.

And told with teares the sad newes thus: 'My Lord, that must be heard

Which would to heaven I might not tell; Menœtius' sonne lies dead,　　　　　　　　　　15

And for his naked corse (his armes alreadie forfeited

And worne by Hector) the debate is now most vehement.'

　　This said, Griefe darkned all his powres. With both his hands he rent

Achilles his rage.
The blacke mould from the forced earth and pour'd it on his head,

Smear'd all his lovely face, his weeds (divinely fashioned)　　20

All filde and mangl'd, and himselfe he threw upon the shore,

Lay as laid out for funerall, then tumbl'd round, and tore

His gracious curles. His Ecstacie he did so farre extend

That all the Ladies wonne by him and his now slaughterd friend

(Afflicted strangely for his plight) came shrieking from the tents　25

And fell about him, beate their breasts, their tender lineaments

Dissolv'd with sorrow. And with them wept Nestor's warlike sonne,

Fell by him, holding his faire hands in feare he would have done

His person violence; his heart (extremely streightned) burn'd,

Beate, sweld and sighd, as it would burst. So terribly he mourn'd　30

That Thetis, sitting in the deepes of her old father's seas,

Heard and lamented. To her plaints the bright Nereides

Flockt all, how many those darke gulfes soever comprehend.

There Glauce and Cymodoce and Spio did attend,

Nesæa and Cymothoe and calme Amphithoe,　　　　　　35

Thalia, Thoe, Panope and swift Dynamene,

Actæa and Limnoria and Halia the faire,

Fam'd for the beautie of her eyes, Amathia for her haire,

Iæra, Proto, Clymene and curl'd Dexamene,

Pherusa, Doris, and with these the smooth Amphinome,　　40

Chast Galatea so renowm'd and Callianira came

With Doto and Orithia, to cheare the mournfull Dame;

Apseudes likewise visited, and Callianassa gave

Her kind attendance, and with her Agave grac't the Cave;

Nemertes, Mæra followed, Melita, Ianesse,　　　　　45

With Ianira and the rest of those Nereides

That in the deepe seas make abode; all which together beate

Their dewie bosomes, and to all thus Thetis did repeate

Thetis to the Nereides.
Her cause of mourning: 'Sisters, heare how much the sorrowes wey,

Whose cries now cald ye. Haplesse I brought forth unhappily　50

The best of all the sonnes of men; who (like a well-set plant

In best soiles) grew and flourished; and when his spirit did want
Employment for his youth and strength, I sent him with a fleete
To fight at Ilion, from whence his fate-confined feete
Passe all my deitie to retire. The court of his high birth,　　　　55
The glorious court of Peleus, must entertaine his worth
Never hereafter. All the life he hath to live with me
Must wast in sorrowes. And this sonne I now am bent to see,
Being now afflicted with some griefe not usually grave,
Whose knowledge and recure I seeke.' This said, she left her　　60
　　cave,
Which all left with her; swimming forth, the greene waves, as
　　they swom,
Cleft with their bosomes, curld, and gave quicke way to Troy.
　　Being come,
They all ascended, two and two, and trod the honor'd shore,
Till where the fleete of Myrmidons (drawne up in heapes)
　　it bore.
Thetis to Achilles.　　There stayd they at Achilles' ship, and there did Thetis lay　　65
Her faire hand on her sonne's curl'd head, sigh'd, wept, and
　　bad him say
What griefe drew from his eyes those teares. 'Conceale it not,'
　　said she,
'Till this houre thy uplifted hands have all things granted thee.
The Greeks (all thrust up at their sternes) have pour'd out
　　teares enow,
And in them seene how much they misse remission of thy vow.'　　70
Achilles to Thetis.　　He said: ''Tis true, Olympius hath done me all that grace:
But what joy have I of it all, when thus thrusts in the place
Losse of my whole selfe in my friend? Whom, when his foe
　　had slaine,
He spoil'd of those prophaned armes that Peleus did obtaine
From heaven's high powres, solemnizing thy sacred nuptiall　　75
　　bands
As th' onely present of them all, and fitted well their hands,
Being lovely, radiant, marvellous. O would to heaven thy throne,
With these faire deities of the sea, thou still hadst sate upon,
And Peleus had a mortall wife; since by his meanes is done
So much wrong to thy grieved mind, my death being set　　80
　　so soone,
And never suffering my returne to grace of Peleus' court;
Nor do I wish it, nor to live in any man's resort,
But onely that the crying bloud for vengeance of my friend,
Mangl'd by Hector, may be stild, his foe's death paying his end.'

Thetis to Achilles.

She weeping, said: 'That houre is neare, and thy death's   85
    houre then nie,
Which in thy wish serv'd of thy foe succeedeth instantly.'

Achilles to Thetis.

    'And instantly it shall succeed,' he answerd, 'since my fate
Allow'd not to my will a powre to rescue (ere the date
Of his late slaughter) my true friend. Farre from his friends
    he died,
Whose wrong therein my eyes had light and right to see denied.   90
Yet now I neither light my selfe, nor have so spent my light,
That either this friend or the rest (in numbers infinite
Slaughterd by Hector) I can helpe, nor grace with wisht repaire
To our deare country, but breathe here unprofitable aire,
And onely live a lode to earth with all my strength, though none   95
Of all the Grecians equall it. In counsell many a one
Is my superiour; what I have, no grace gets; what I want,
Disgraceth all. How then too soone can hastiest death supplant
My fate-curst life?—her instrument, to my indignitie,
Being that blacke fiend Contention, whom would to God   100
    might die
To gods and men, and Anger too, that kindles tyrannie
In men most wise, being much more sweete than liquid hony is
To men of powre to satiate their watchfull enmities.
And like a pliant fume it spreds through all their breasts, as late
It stole sterne passage thorough mine, which he did instigate   105
That is our Generall. But the fact so long past, the effect
Must vanish with it, though both griev'd; nor must we still
    respect
Our soothed humours; Need now takes the rule of either's mind.
And when the loser of my friend his death in me shall find,
Let death take all. Send him, ye gods; I'le give him my   110
    embrace.
Not Hercules himselfe shund death, though dearest in the grace
Of Jupiter; even him Fate stoopt, and Juno's crueltie;
And if such Fate expect my life, where death strikes I will lie.
Meane time I wish a good renowme, that these deepe-brested
    Dames
Of Ilion and Dardania may, for th' extinguisht flames   115
Of their friends' lives, with both their hands wipe miserable teares
From their so curiously-kept cheekes, and be the officers
To execute my sighs on Troy—when (seeing my long retreate
But gatherd strength, and gives my charge an answerable heate)
They well may know twas I lay still, and that my being away   120
Presented all their happinesse. But any further stay,
(Which your much love perhaps may wish) assay not to perswade.

All vowes are kept, all prayres heard; now free way for fight
   is made.'

The silver-footed Dame replide: 'It fits thee well, my sonne,
To keepe destruction from thy friends, but those faire armes   125
   are wonne
And worne by Hector, that should keepe thy selfe in keeping
   them,
Though their fruition be but short, a long death being neare him
Whose cruell glorie they are yet. By all meanes then forbeare
To tread the massacres of warre till I againe appeare
From Mulciber with fit new armes; which, when thy eye   130
   shall see
The Sunne next rise, shall enter here with his first beames
   and me.'
   Thus to her sisters of the sea she turn'd, and bad them ope
The doores and deepes of Nereus; she in Olympus top
Must visite Vulcan for new armes to serve her wreakfull sonne,
And bad informe her father so, with all things further done.   135

This said, they underwent the sea, her selfe flew up to heaven.
In meane space, to the Hellespont and ships the Greeks were
   driven
In shamefull rout; nor could they yet from rage of Priam's sonne
Secure the dead of new assaults, both horse and men made on
With such impression. Thrice the feete the hands of Hector   140
   seasd,
And thrice th' Ajaces thumpt him off. With whose repulse
   displeasd,
He wreakt his wrath upon the troupes, then to the corse againe
Made horrid turnings, crying out of his repulsed men,
And would not quit him quite for death. A Lion almost sterv'd
Is not by upland herdsmen driven from urging to be serv'd   145
With more contention that his strength by those two of a name;
And had perhaps his much-praisd will, if th' airie-footed dame
(Swift Iris) had not stoopt in hast, Ambassadresse from heaven,

To Peleus' sonne to bid him arme; her message being given
By Juno, kept from all the gods, she thus excited him: 150
'Rise, thou most terrible of men, and save the precious lim
Of thy belov'd, in whose behalfe the conflict now runnes hie
Before the fleete; the either host fels other mutually,
These to retaine, those to obtaine; amongst whom most of all
Is Hector prompt; hee's apt to drag thy friend home; he   155
   your pall
Will make his shoulders, his head forc't; hee'l be most famous;
   rise,

No more lie idle; set the foe a much more costly prise
Of thy friend's value than let dogs make him a monument,
Where thy name will be graven.' He askt: 'What deitie hath sent
Thy presence hither?' She repli'd: 'Saturnia, she alone,   160
Not high Jove knowing, nor one god that doth inhabite on
Snowie Olympus.' He againe: 'How shall I set upon
The worke of slaughter when mine armes are worne by
     Priam's son?
How will my goddesse mother grieve, that bad I should not arme
Till she brought armes from Mulciber? But should I do such   165
     harme
To her and dutie, who is he (but Ajax) that can vant
The fitting my brest with his armes? And he is conversant
Amongst the first in use of his, and rampiers of the foe
(Slaine neare Patroclus) builds to him.' 'All this,' said she,
     'we know,
And wish thou onely wouldst but show thy person to the eyes   170
Of these hote Ilians, that (afraid of further enterprise)
The Greeks may gaine some litle breath.' She woo'd, and he
     was won,
And straite Minerva honor'd him, who Jove's shield clapt upon
His mightie shoulders, and his head girt with a cloud of gold,
That cast beames round about his browes. And as when armes   175
     enfold

Simile.

A citie in an Ile, from thence a fume at first appeares
(Being in the day), but when the Even her cloudie forehead
     reares,
Thicke show the fires, and up they cast their splendor, that
     men nie,
Seeing their distresse, perhaps may set ships out to their supply:
So (to shew such aid) from his head a light rose, scaling heaven. 180
And forth the wall he stept and stood, nor brake the precept
     given
By his great mother (mixt in fight), but sent abroad his voice,
Which Pallas farre off ecchoed—who did betwixt them hoise
Shrill Tumult to a toplesse height. And as a voice is heard
Simile.   With emulous affection, when any towne is spher'd   185
With siege of such a foe as kils men's minds, and for the towne
Makes sound his trumpet: so the voice from Thetis' issue
     throwne
Won emulously th' eares of all. His brazen voice once heard,
The minds of all were startl'd so, they yeelded; and so feard
The faire-man'd horses that they flew backe and their chariots   190
     turn'd,

Presaging in their augurous hearts the labours that they mourn'd
A litle after; and their guides a repercussive dread
Tooke from the horrid radiance of his refulgent head,
Which Pallas set on fire with grace. Thrice great Achilles spake,
And thrice (in heate of all the charge) the Troyans started   195
    backe.
Twelve men, of greatest strength in Troy, left with their lives
    exhald
Their chariots and their darts to death with his three
    summons cald.
And then the Grecians spritefully drew from the darts the corse
And hearst it, bearing it to fleete, his friends with all remorse
Marching about it. His great friend, dissolving then in teares   200
To see his truly-lov'd return'd so horst upon an herse,
Whom with such horse and chariot he set out safe and whole—
Now wounded with unpittying steele, now sent without a soule,
Never againe to be restor'd, never receiv'd but so—
He follow'd mourning bitterly. The Sunne (yet farre to go)   205

*Juno commands the
Sunne to go downe
before his time.*

Juno commanded to go downe, who in his powre's despight
Sunke to the Ocean, over earth dispersing sodaine Night.
And then the Greeks and Troyans both gave up their horse
    and darts.
The Troyans all to counsell call'd ere they refresht their hearts
With any supper, nor would sit, they grew so stiffe with feare   210
To see (so long from heavie fight) Æacides appeare.
    Polydamas began to speake, who onely could discerne
Things future by things past, and was vow'd friend to Hector,
    borne

*Polydamas to Hector
and the Troyans.*

In one night both; he thus advisde: 'Consider well, my friends,
In this so great and sodaine change that now it selfe extends,   215
What change is best for us t' oppose. To this stands my command;
Make now the towne our strength, not here abide light's
    rosie hand,
Our wall being farre off, and our foe (much greater) still as nere.
Till this foe came, I well was pleasde to keepe our watches here;
My fit hope of the fleete's surprise enclin'd me so. But now   220
Tis stronglier guarded, and (their strength increast) we must
    allow
Our owne proportionate amends. I doubt exceedingly
That this indifferencie of fight twixt us and th' enemie,
And these bounds we prefixe to them, will nothing so confine
Th' uncurb'd mind of Æacides. The height of his designe   225
Aimes at our citie and our wives, and all barres in his way

(Being backt with lesse than wals) his powre will scorne to
    make his stay,
And overrunne, as overseene, and not his object. Then
Let Troy be freely our retreate, lest, being enforc't, our men
Twixt this and that be taken up by Vultures; who by night   230
May safe come off, it being a time untimely for his might
To spend at randome. That being sure, if next light shew
    us here
To his assaults, each man will wish that Troy his refuge were,
And then feele what he heares not now. I would to heaven
    mine eare
Were free even now of those complaints that you must after   235
    heare,
If ye remove not. If ye yeeld (though wearied with a fight)
So late and long, we shall have strength in counsell and the
    night.
And (where we here have no more force than Need will force
    us to,
And which must rise out of our nerves) high ports, towres,
    walls will do
What wants in us. And in the morne, all arm'd upon our   240
    towres,
We all will stand out to our foe. Twill trouble all his powres
To come from fleet and give us charge, when his high-crested
    horse
His rage shall satiate with the toyle of this and that waye's course,
Vaine entrie seeking underneath our well-defended wals,
And he be glad to turne to fleet about his funerals.   245
For of his entrie here at home, what mind will serve his thirst,
Or ever feed him with sackt Troy? The dogs shall eate him first.'

Hector's angry reply to
Polydamas.
    At this speech, Hector bent his browes, and said: 'This makes
    not great
Your grace with me, Polydamas, that argue for retreate
To Troy's old prison. Have we not enough of those towres yet? 250
And is not Troy yet charg'd enough with impositions set
Upon her citizens, to keepe our men from spoyle without,
But still we must impose within? That houses with our rout,
As well as purses, may be plagu'd? Before time, Priam's towne
Traffickt with divers-languag'd men, and all gave the renowne 255
Of rich Troy to it, brasse and gold abounding: but her store
Is now from every house exhaust, possessions evermore
Are sold out into Phrygia and lovely Mæonie,
And have bene ever since Jove's wrath. And now his clemencie
Gives me the meane to quit our want with glorie, and conclude 260

The Greeks in sea-bords and our seas. To slacke it, and extrude
His offerd bountie by our flight, foole that thou art, bewray
This counsell to no common eare, for no man shall obay.
If any will, I'le checke his will. But what our selfe command
Let all observe: take suppers all, keepe watch of every hand.   265
If any Troyan have some spoyle that takes his too much care,
Make him dispose it publickly; tis better any fare
The better for him than the Greeks. When light then deckes
      the skies,
Let all arme for a fierce assault. If great Achilles rise
And will enforce our greater toyle, it may rise so to him;   270
On my backe he shall find no wings; my spirit shall force my lim
To stand his worst, and give or take. Mars is our common Lord,
And the desirous sword-man's life he ever puts to sword.'
      This counsell gat applause of all, so much were all unwise.
Minerva robd them of their braines, to like the ill advice   275
The great man gave, and leave the good, since by the meaner
      given.
All tooke their suppers; but the Greeks spent all the heavy Even
About Patroclus' mournfull rites, Pelides leading all
In all the formes of heavinesse: he by his side did fall,
And his man-slaughtering hands imposd into his oft-kist brest;   280

Simile.

Sighes blew up sighes: and Lion-like, grac't with a goodly crest,
That in his absence being robd by hunters of his whelps,
Returnes to his so desolate den, and (for his wanted helps)
Beholding his unlookt-for wants, flies roring backe againe,
Hunts the slie hunter, many a vale resounding his disdaine: 285
So mourn'd Pelides his late losse, so weightie were his mones,
Which (for their dumbe sounds now gave words to all his
      Myrmidons:

*Achilles to his
Myrmidons.*

'O gods,' said he, 'how vaine a vow I made (to cheare the mind)
Of sad Menœtius, when his sonne his hand to mine resign'd,
That high-towr'd Opus he should see, and leave rac't Ilion   290
With spoyle and honor, even with me? But Jove vouchsafes
      to none
Wisht passages to all his vowes; we both were destinate
To bloody one earth here in Troy; nor any more estate
In my returne hath Peleus or Thetis. But because
I last must undergo the ground, I'le keepe no funerall lawes,   295

*Achilles to Patroclus'
body.*

O my Patroclus, for thy Corse before I hither bring
The armes of Hector, and his head, to thee for offering.
Twelve youths, the most renown'd of Troy, I'le sacrifise beside
Before thy heape of funerall, to thee unpacifide.

[380]

In meane time, by our crooked sternes lye drawing teares   300
    from me;
And round about thy honour'd Corse these dames of Dardanie
And Ilion with the ample breasts (whom our long speares,
    and powres,
And labours purchast from the rich and by-us-ruind towres
And cities strong and populous, with divers-languag'd men)
Shall kneele, and neither day nor night be licenst to abstaine   305
From solemne watches, their toil'd eyes held ope with endlesse
    teares.'
    This passion past, he gave command to his neare souldiers
To put a Tripod to the fire, to cleanse the festred gore
From off the person. They obeyd, and presently did powre
Fresh water in it, kindl'd wood, and with an instant flame   310
The belly of the Tripod girt till fire's hote qualitie came
Up to the water. Then they washt and fild the mortall wound
With wealthy oyle of nine yeares old, then wrapt the body round
In largenesse of a fine white sheete, and put it then in bed,
When all watcht all night with their Lord, and spent sighes   315
    on the dead.

Jove to Juno.   Then Jove askt Juno, if at length she had suffisde her splene,
Achilles being wonne to armes? Or if she had not bene
The naturall mother of the Greeks, she did so still preferre
Juno to Jove.   Their quarrell? She, incenst, askt why he still was tanting her
For doing good to those she lov'd?—since man to man might   320
    show
Kind offices, though thrall to death, and though they did not
    know
Halfe such deepe counsels as disclosd beneath her farre-seeing
    state,
She reigning Queene of goddesses; and being ingenerate
Of one stocke with himselfe, besides the state of being his wife.
And must her wrath and ill to Troy continue such a strife   325
From time to time twixt him and her? This private speech
    they had.
Thetis enters the Court   And now the silver-footed Queene had her ascension made,
of Vulcan.   To that incorruptible house, that starry golden court
Of fiery Vulcan, beautifull amongst th' immortall sort,
Which yet the lame god built himselfe. She found him in a   330
    sweate
About his bellowes, and in haste had twentie Tripods beate,
To set for stooles about the sides of his well-builded hall.
To whose feete little wheeles of gold he put, to go withall
And enter his rich dining roome—alone, their motion free,

[381]

And backe againe go out alone, miraculous to see.   335
And thus much he had done of them, yet handles were to adde,
For which he now was making studs. And while their fashion had
Employment of his skilfull hand, bright Thetis was come neare,
Whom first faire well-haird Charis saw, that was the nuptiall
    fere

*Charis, the wife of
Vulcan, to Thetis.*

Of famous Vulcan, who the hand of Thetis tooke, and said: 340
  'Why, faire-train'd, lov'd and honour'd Dame, are we
    thus visited
By your kind presence? You, I thinke, were never here before.
Come neare, that I may banquet you and make you visite more.'
  She led her in, and in a chaire of silver (being the fruite
Of Vulcan's hand) she made her sit, a footstoole, of a suite,   345
Apposing to her Cristall feete; and cald the god of fire—
For Thetis was arriv'd, she said, and entertain'd desire

Vulcan to Charis.

Of some grace that his art might grant. 'Thetis to me,' said he,
'Is mightie, and most reverend, as one that nourisht me
When Griefe consum'd me, being cast from heaven by want   350
  of shame
In my proud mother, who because she brought me forth so lame
Would have me made away. And then had I bene much distrest
Had Thetis and Eurynome in either's silver breast
Not rescu'd me—Eurynome, that to her father had
Reciprocall Oceanus. Nine yeares with them I made   355
A number of well-arted things, round bracelets, buttons brave,
Whistles, and Carquenets. My forge stood in a hollow Cave,
About which (murmuring with fome) th' unmeasur'd Ocean
Was ever beating, my abode knowne nor to god nor man
But Thetis and Eurymone, and they would see me still: 360
They were my loving guardians. Now then the starry hill,
And our particular roofe, thus grac't with bright-hair'd Thetis
  here,
It fits me alwaies to repay a recompence as deare
To her thoughts as my life to me. Haste, Charis, and appose
Some daintie guest-rites to our friend, while I my bellowes lose   365
From fire and lay up all my tooles.' Then from an anvile rose
Th' unweildy Monster, halted downe, and all awry he went.
He tooke his bellowes from the fire, and every instrument
Lockt safe up in a silver chest. Then with a sponge he drest
His face all over, necke and hands, and all his hairie breast,   370
Put on his Cote, his Scepter tooke, and then went halting forth,

Vulcan's attendants.

Handmaids of gold attending him—resembling in all worth
Living yong damzels, fild with minds and wisedome, and
    were train'd

In all immortall ministrie, virtue and voice contain'd,
And mov'd with voluntarie powres. And these still waited on   375
Their fierie Soveraigne, who (not apt to walke) sate neare
    the throne
Of faire-hair'd Thetis, tooke her hand, and thus he courted her:

Vulcan to Thetis.   'For what affaire, O faire-train'd Queene, reverend to me and
    deare,
Is our Court honord with thy state, that hast not heretofore
Perform'd this kindnesse? Speake thy thoughts; thy suite can   380
    be no more
Than my mind gives me charge to grant. Can my powre get it
    wrought?
Or that it have not onely powre of onely act in thought?'

Thetis to Vulcan.   She thus: 'O Vulcan, is there one, of all that are of heaven,
That in her never-quiet mind Saturnius hath given
So much affliction as to me?—whom onely he subjects   385
(Of all the Sea-Nymphs) to a man, and makes me beare th' affects
Of his fraile bed, and all against the freedome of my will,
And he worne to his roote with age. From him another ill
Ariseth to me. Jupiter, you know, hath given a sonne
(The excellentst of men) to me, whose education,   390
On my part, well hath answered his owne worth, having growne,
As in a fruitfull soyle a tree that puts not up alone
His body to a naked height but joyntly gives his growth
A thousand branches. Yet to him so short a life I brought
That never I shall see him more return'd to Peleus' Court.   395
And all that short life he hath spent in most unhappy sort.
For first he wonne a worthy Dame, and had her by the hands
Of all the Grecians; yet this Dame Atrides countermands:
For which in much disdaine he mourn'd, and almost pin'd away.
And yet for this wrong he receiv'd some honor, I must say,   400
The Greeks being shut up at their ships, not sufferd to advance
A head out of their batterd sternes, and mightie suppliance
By all their grave men hath bene made, gifts, honors, all proposde
For his reflection; yet he still kept close, and saw enclosde
Their whole host in this generall plague. But now his friend   405
    put on
His armes, being sent by him to field and many a Myrmidon
In conduct of him. All the day they fought before the gates
Of Scæa; and most certainly that day had seene the dates
Of all Troy's honors in her dust, if Phœbus (having done
Much mischiefe more) the envyed life of good Menœtius' sonne   410
Had not with partiall hands enforc't, and all the honor given
To Hector, who hath prisd his armes. And therefore I am driven

[383]

T' embrace thy knees for new defence to my lov'd sonne. Ahlas,
His life prefixt so short a date had need spend that with grace.
A shield then for him, and a helme, faire greaves, and curets   415
    such
As may renowne thy workmanship and honor him as much,

Vulcan to Thetis.

I sue for at thy famous hands.' 'Be confident,' said he,
'Let these wants breed thy thoughts no care. I would it lay in me
To hide him from his heavy death when Fate shall seeke for him,
As well as with renowned armes to fit his goodly limme—   420
Which thy hands shall convey to him, and all eyes shall admire.
See, and desire againe to see, thy satisfied desire.'

*Vulcan begins to forge
armes for Achilles.*

    This said, he left her there, and forth did to his bellows go,
Apposde them to the fire againe, commanding them to blow.
Through twenty holes made to his harth at once blew twenty   425
    paire,
That fir'd his coles, sometimes with soft, sometimes with
    vehement ayre,
As he will'd and his worke requir'd. Amids the flame he cast
Tin, Silver, precious Gold and Brasse, and in the stocke he plac't
A mightie anvile; his right hand a weightie hammer held,
His left his tongs. And first he forg'd a strong and spacious shield 430
Adornd with twenty severall hewes: about whose verge he beate
A ring, three-fold and radiant, and on the backe he set
A silver handle; five-fold were the equall lines he drew
About the whole circumference, in which his hand did shew
(Directed with a knowing mind) a rare varietie.   435
For in it he presented earth, in it, the sea and skie,
In it, the never-wearied Sunne, the Moone exactly round
And all those starres with which the browes of ample heaven
    are crownd—
Orion, all the Pleiades, and those seven Atlas got,
The close-beam'd Hyades, the Beare, surnam'd the Chariot,   440
That turnes about heaven's axeltree, holds ope a constant eye
Upon Orion; and, of all the Cressets in the skie,
His golden forehead never bowes to th' Ocean Emperie.

*Two cities forged in
Achilles' armes.*

    Two cities in the spacious shield he built with goodly state
Of diverse-languag'd men. The one did nuptials celebrate,   445
Observing at them solemne feasts; the Brides from foorth their
    bowres
With torches usherd through the streets, a world of Paramours
Excited by them; youths and maides in lovely circles danc't,
To whom the merrie Pipe and Harpe their spritely sounds
    advanc't,
The matrones standing in their dores admiring. Otherwhere   450

[384]

A solemne Court of law was kept, where throngs of people were.
The case in question was a fine imposde on one that slue
The friend of him that follow'd it and for the fine did sue,
Which th' other pleaded he had paide. The adverse part denied,
And openly affirm'd he had no penny satisfied.   455
Both put it to arbiterment. The people cryed twas best
For both parts, and th' Assistants too gave their doomes like
    the rest.
The Heralds made the people peace. The Seniors then did beare
The voicefull Heralds' scepters, sate within a sacred sphere
On polisht stones, and gave by turnes their sentence. In   460
    the Court
Two talents gold were cast for him that judg'd in justest sort.
    The other citie other warres employ'd as busily.
Two armies glittering in armes, of one confederacie,
Besieg'd it, and a parle had with those within the towne.
Two wayes they stood resolv'd—to see the citie overthrowne,   465
Or that the citizens should heape in two parts all their wealth
And give them halfe. They neither lik't, but arm'd themselves
    by stealth,
Left all their old men, wives and boyes behind to man their wals,
And stole out to their enemie's towne. The Queene of martials
And Mars himselfe conducted them, both which, being forg'd   470
    of gold,
Must needs have golden furniture, and men might so behold
They were presented deities. The people Vulcan forg'd
Of meaner mettall. When they came where that was to be urg'd
For which they went, within a vale close to a flood, whose streame
Usde to give all their cattell drinke, they there enambusht them, 475
And sent two scouts out to descrie when th' enemie's heards
    and sheepe
Were setting out. They strait came forth, with two that usde to
    keepe
Their passage alwayes; both which pip't and went on merrily,
Nor dream'd of Ambuscados there. The Ambush then let flie,
Slue all their white fleec't sheepe and neate, and by them laid   480
    their guard.
When those in siege before the towne so strange an uprore heard
Behind, amongst their flocks and heards (being then in
    counsell set)
They then start up, tooke horse, and soone their subtle enemie
    met,
Fought with them on the river's shore, where both gave
    mutuall blowes

*The martiall citie in
the shield of Achilles.*

[385]

With well-pil'd darts. Amongst them all perverse Contention   485
    rose,
Amongst them Tumult was enrag'd, amongst them ruinous Fate
Had her red finger; some they tooke in an unhurt estate,
Some hurt yet living, some quite slaine—and those they tug'd
    to them
By both the feete, strip't off and tooke their weeds, with all
    the streame
Of blood upon them that their steeles had manfully let out.   490
They far'd as men alive indeed, drew dead indeed about.
    To these the fierie Artizan did adde a new-ear'd field,

A new-eared field in
the shield.

Large and thrice plowd, the soyle being soft and of a wealthy
    yeeld;
And many men at plow he made that drave earth here and there
And turnd up stitches orderly; at whose end when they were,   495
A fellow ever gave their hands full cups of luscious wine,
Which emptied, for another stitch the earth they undermine,
And long till th' utmost bound be reacht of all the ample Close.
The soyle turnd up behind the plow, all blacke like earth arose,
Though forg'd of nothing else but gold, and lay in show as light 500
As if it had bene plowd indeed, miraculous to sight.
    There grew by this a field of corne, high, ripe, where reapers
    wrought,

A field of corne.

And let thicke handfuls fall to earth, for which some other
    brought
Bands, and made sheaves. Three binders stood and tooke the
    handfuls reapt
From boyes that gatherd quickly up, and by them armefuls   505
    heapt.
Amongst these at a furrowe's end the king stood pleasd at heart,
Said no word, but his scepter shewd. And from him, much apart,
His harvest Bailiffes underneath an Oke a feast prepar'd,
And, having kild a mightie Oxe, stood there to see him shar'd,
Which women for their harvest folks (then come to sup) had 510
    drest,
And many white wheate-cakes bestow'd, to make it up a feast.
    He set neare this a vine of gold that crackt beneath the weight

A vine of gold.

Of bunches blacke with being ripe; to keepe which, at the height,
A silver raile ranne all along, and round about it flow'd
An azure mote, and to this guard a quick-set was bestow'd   515
Of Tin, one onely path to all, by which the pressemen came
In time of vintage: youths and maids, that bore not yet the flame
Of manly Hymen, baskets bore of grapes and mellow fruite.
A lad that sweetly toucht a harpe, to which his voice did suite,

[386]

Centerd the circles of that youth, all whose skill could not do   520
The wanton's pleasure to their minds, that danc't, sung,
      whistl'd too.

A heard of oxen.   A herd of Oxen then he carv'd with high-raisd heads, forg'd all
Of Gold and Tin (for colour mixt), and bellowing from their stall
Rusht to their pastures at a flood, that eccho'd all their throtes,
Exceeding swift and full of reeds. And all in yellow cotes,   525
Foure heardsmen follow'd; after whom nine Mastives went.
      In head
Of all the heard, upon a Bull, that deadly bellowed,
Two horrid Lions rampt, and seisd, and tugg'd off bellowing still.
Both men and dogs came, yet they tore the hide and lapt their fill
Of blacke blood, and the entrailes eate. In vaine the men assayd   530
To set their dogs on: none durst pinch, but curre-like stood
      and bayd
In both the faces of their kings, and all their onsets fled.

Flocks of sheepe.   Then in a passing pleasant vale the famous Artsman fed
(Upon a goodly pasture ground) rich flocks of white-fleec't sheepe,
Built stables, cottages and cotes, that did the sheapheards keepe   535
A labyrinth.   From winde and weather. Next to these he cut a dancing place
All full of turnings, that was like the admirable maze
For faire-hair'd Ariadne made by cunning Dædalus;
And in it youths and virgins danc't, all yong and beautious,
And glewed in another's palmes. Weeds that the winde did tosse   540
The virgines wore, the youths, woven cotes that cast a faint
      dimme glosse,
Like that of oyle. Fresh garlands too the virgines' temples crownd;
The youths guilt swords wore at their thighs, with silver
      bawdricks bound.
Sometimes all wound close in a ring, to which as fast they spunne
As any wheele a Turner makes, being tried how it will runne   545
While he is set; and out againe, as full of speed, they wound,
Not one left fast or breaking hands. A multitude stood round,
Delighted with their nimble sport: to end which, two begun
(Mids all) a song, and, turning, sung the sport's conclusion.
All this he circl'd in the shield, with pouring round about   550
(In all his rage) the Ocean, that it might never out.

      This shield thus done, he forg'd for him such curets as outshin'd
The blaze of fire. A helmet then (through which no steele
      could find
Forc't passage) he composde, whose hue a hundred colours tooke;
And in the crest a plume of gold, that each breath stirr'd,   555
      he stucke.

[387]

All done, he all to Thetis brought, and held all up to her.
She tooke them all, and like t' the hawke (surnam'd the
    Osspringer),
From Vulcan to her mightie sonne, with that so glorious show,
Stoopt from the steepe Olympian hill, hid in eternall snow.

COMMENTARIUS

[184] ὡς δ'ὅτ ἀριζήλη φωνή, ὅτε τ'ἴαχε σάλπιγξ
ἄστυ περιπλομένων δηΐων ὕπο θυμοραϊστέων,
ὡς τότ' ἀριζήλη φωνὴ γένετ' Αἰακίδαο.
οἱ δ' ὡς οὖν ἄϊον ὄπα χάλκεον Αἰακίδαο
πᾶσιν ὀρίνθη θυμός·   5

Thus turned by Spondanus ad verbum:

Ut autem cum cognitu facilis vox est, cum clangit tuba
Urbem obsidentes hostes propter perniciosos:
Sic tunc clara vox fuit Æacidæ,
Hi autem postquam igitur audiverunt vocem ferream Æacidæ,   10
Omnibus commotus est animus.

Valla thus:

Sicut enim cum obsidentibus sævis urbem hostibus, vel clarior
vox, vel classicum perstrepit; ita nunc Achilles magna voce
inclamavit—quam cum audirent Troiani, perturbati sunt animis. 15

Eobanus Hessus thus:

————Nam sicut ab urbe
Obsessa increpuere tubæ, vel classica cantu
Ferrea; sic Troas vox perturbabat Achillis.

Mine owne harsh conversion (which I will be bold to repeate after   20
these thus closely for your easier examination) is this, as before:

————And as a voice is heard
With emulous attention, when any towne is spher'd
With siege of such a foe as kils men's minds, and for the towne
Makes sound his trumpet: so the voice from Thetis' issue throwne   25
Wonne emulously th' eares of all. His brazen voice once heard,
The minds of all were startl'd so, they yeelded.

In conference of all our translations, I would gladly learne of my more
learned Reader if the two last conversions do any thing neare expresse
the conceipt of Homer, or if they beare any grace worth the   30
signification of his words and the sence of his illustration—whose
intent was not to expresse the clearenesse or shrilnesse of his voice
in it self, but the envious terror it wrought in the Troyans—
ἀριζήλη φωνὴ *not signifying in this place* clara, *or* cognitu facilis,
vox, *but* emulanda vox, ἀρίζηλος *signifying* quem valde æmulamur,   35

[389]

aut valde æmulandus, *though these interpreters would rather receive
it here for* ἀρίδηλος, *verso* δ *in* ζ, ut sit clarus, illustris, &c. *But
how silly a curiositie is it to alter the word upon ignorance of the
signification it hath in his place—the word* ἀρίζηλος *being a compound
of* ἀρι, *which signifieth* valde, *and* ζῆλος, *which is* æmulatio,   40
or of ζηλόω *which signifies* æmulor. *To this effect then (saith Homer
in this Simile)—As a voice that workes a terror, carrying an envy
with it, sounds to a citie besieged when the trumpet of a dreadfull and
mind-destroying enemie summons it (for so* δηΐων θυμοραϊστέων
signifies, θυμοραϊστὴς *signifying* animum destruens, *being a*   45
compound of ῥαίω *, which signifies* destruo, *and* θυμὸς *which is*
animum—*that is, when the parle comes, after the trumpets
sound, uttering the resolution of the dreadfull enemie
before it. The further application of this simile
is left out by mischance.*

The End of the Eighteenth Booke

THE NINETEENTH BOOKE

of

HOMER'S ILIADS

THE ARGUMENT

Thetis, presenting armour to her sonne,
He cals a Court, with full reflection
Of all his wrath; takes of the king of men
Free-offerd gifts. All take their breakefast then;
He onely fasting, armes, and brings abrode   5
The Grecian host. And (hearing the abode
Of his neare death by Xanthus prophecied)
The horse, for his so bold presage, doth chide.

Another Argument

Ταυ gives the anger period,
And great Achilles comes abrode.

The Morne arose and from the Ocean, in her saffron robe,
Gave light to all, as well to gods as men of th' under globe.

Thetis appeares to Achilles.
Thetis stoopt home, and found the prostrate person of her sonne
About his friend, still pouring out himselfe in passion,
A number more being heavy consorts to him in his cares.   5
Amongst them all Thetis appear'd, and, sacred comforters,
Made these short words: 'Though we must grieve, yet beare it
    thus, my son:
It was no man that prostrated in this sad fashion
Thy dearest friend; it was a god that first laid on his hand,
Whose will is law: the gods' decrees no humane must withstand.   10
Do thou embrace this Fabricke of a god, whose hand before
Nere forg'd the like, and such as yet no humane shoulder wore.'
    Thus (setting downe) the precious mettall of the armes was such
That all the roome rung with the weight of every slendrest touch.

[391]

Cold tremblings tooke the Myrmidons; none durst sustaine,   15
    all fear'd
T' oppose their eyes. Achilles, yet, as soone as they appear'd,
Sterne Anger enterd. From his eyes (as if the day-starre rose)
A radiance terrifying men did all the state enclose.

Achilles' rapture at the   At length he tooke into his hands the rich gift of the god,
sight of his armes.   And (much pleasd to behold the art that in the shield he show'd) 20
He brake forth into this applause: 'O mother, these right well
Shew an immortall finger's touch; man's hand must never deale
With armes againe. Now I will arme, yet (that no honour make
My friend forgotten) I much feare lest with the blowes of flies
His brasse-inflicted wounds are filde; life gone, his person lies 25
All apt to putrifaction.' She bad him doubt no harme
Of those offences: she would care to keepe the petulant swarme
Of flies (that usually taint the bodies of the slaine)
From his friend's person: though a yeare the earth's top should
    sustaine
His slaughterd body, it should still rest sound, and rather hold 30
A better state than worse since time that death first made him cold.
And so bad call a Councell to dispose of new alarmes,
Where (to the king, that was the Pastor of that flocke in armes)
He should depose all anger and put on a fortitude
Fit for his armes. All this his powres with dreadfull strength 35
    indude.
She with her faire hand still'd into the nostrils of his friend
Red Nectar and Ambrosia, with which she did defend
The Corse from putrifaction. He trod along the shore

Achilles summons all   And summon'd all th' Heroique Greekes, with all that spent
the Greeks to Counsell.   before
The time in exercise with him, the Maisters, Pilots too, 40
Victlers, and all. All, when they saw Achilles summon so,
Swarm'd to the Councell, having long left the laborious wars.
To all these came two halting kings, true servitors of Mars,
Tydides and wise Ithacus, both leaning on their speares,
Their wounds still painefull, and both these sat first of all the 45
    Peeres.
    The last come was the king of men, sore wounded with the lance
Of Coon Antenorides. All set, the first in utterance

Achilles first speaker in   Was Thetis' sonne, who rose and said: 'Atrides, had not this
the Councell.   Conferd most profite to us both, when both our enmities
Consum'd us so, and for a wench, whom, when I chusde for 50
    prise
(In laying Lyrnessus' ruin'd walls amongst our victories),
I would to heaven (as first she set her daintie foote abord)

Diana's hand had tumbl'd off and with a javelin gor'd?
For then th' unmeasurable earth had not so thick bene gnawne
(In death's convulsions) by our friends, since my affects were   55
    drawne
To such distemper. To our foe and to our foe's chiefe friend
Our jarre brought profite, but the Greeks will never give an end
To thought of what it prejudic't them. Past things yet past
    our aide;
Fit griefe for what wrath rulde in them must make th' amends
    repaid
With that necessitie of love that now forbids our ire—   60
Which I with free affects obey. Tis for the senslesse fire
Still to be burning, having stuffe, but men must curbe rage still,
Being fram'd with voluntarie powres, as well to checke the will
As gives it raines. Give you then charge that for our instant fight
The Greeks may follow me to field, to trie if still the Night   65
Will beare out Troyans at our ships. I hope there is some one,
Amongst their chiefe encouragers, will thanke me to be gone,
And bring his heart downe to his knees in that submission.'
    The Greeks rejoyc't to heare the heart of Peleus' mightie sonne
So quallified. And then the king (not rising from his throne,   70
For his late hurt), to get good eare, thus orderd his replie:

Agamemnon to the
Princes of Greece.

    'Princes of Greece, your states shall suffer no indignitie,
If (being farre off) ye stand and heare, nor fits it such as stand
At greater distance to disturbe the counsell now in hand
By uprore, in their too much care of hearing. Some, of force,   75
Must lose some words: for hard it is, in such a great concourse,
(Though hearers' eares be nere so sharpe) to touch at all things
    spoke.
And, in assemblies of such thrust, how can a man provoke
Fit powre to heare, or leave to speake? Best auditors may there
Lose fittest words, and the most vocall Orator fit eare.   80
My maine end, then, to satisfie Pelides with replie,
My words shall prosecute. To him my speech especially
Shall beare direction. Yet I wish the court in generall
Would give fit eare; my speech shall need attention of all.
    Oft have our Peeres of Greece much blam'd my forcing of   85
        the prise
Due to Achilles; of which act not I, but destinies
And Jove himselfe and blacke Erinys (that casts false mists still
Betwixt us and our actions done, both by her powre and will)
Are authors. What could I do then? The very day and howre
Of our debate that furie stole, in that act, on my powre.   90

[393]

And more:—all things are done by strife; that ancient **seed**
    of Jove,

Ate, that hurts all, perfects all. Her feete are soft and move
Not on the earth; they beare her still aloft men's heads, and **there**
She harmefull hurts them. Nor was I alone her prisoner:
Jove (best of men and gods) hath bene. Not he himselfe hath gone 95
Beyond her fetters: no, she made a woman put them on.
For when Alcmena was to vent the force of Hercules
In well-wall'd Thebes, thus Jove triumpht: "Heare, gods
    and goddesses,
The words my joyes urg'd. In this day, Lucina (bringing paine
To labouring women) shall produce into the light of men   100
A man that all his neighbour kings shall in his Empire hold,
And vant that more than manly race whose honor'd veines enfold
My eminent blood." Saturnia conceiv'd a present sleight,
And urg'd confirmation of his vant, t' infringe it; her conceipt
In this sort urg'd: "Thou wilt not hold thy word with this rare   105
    man:
Or if thou wilt, confirme it with the oath Olympian,
That whosoever fals this day betwixt a woman's knees
Of those men's stockes that from thy blood derive their pedigrees
Shall all his neighbour townes command." Jove (ignorant
    of fraude)

Tooke that great oth, which his great ill gave little cause   110
    t'applaude.
Downe from Olympus top she stoopt, and quickly reacht
    the place
In Argos where the famous wife of Sthenelus (whose **race**
He fetch'd from Jove by Perseus) dwelt. She was but **seven**
    months gone
With issue, yet she brought it forth; Alcmena's matchlesse sonne
Delaide from light, Saturnia represt the teeming throwes   115
Of his great mother. Up to heaven she mounts againe, and showes
(In glorie) her deceipt to Jove. "Bright-lightning Jove," said she,

"Now th' Argives have an Emperour; a sonne deriv'd from thee
Is borne to Persean Sthenelus, Eurystheus his name,
Noble and worthy of the rule thou swor'st to him." This came   120
Close to the heart of Jupiter, and Ate, that had wrought
This anger by Saturnia, by her bright haire he caught,
Held downe her head, and over her made this infallible vow:
That never to the cope of starres should reascend that brow,
Being so infortunate to all. Thus, swinging her about,   125
He cast her from the fierie heaven, who ever since thrust out
Her forkt sting in th' affaires of men. Jove ever since did grieve,

Since his deare issue Hercules did by his vow atchieve
Th' unjust toyles of Eurystheus. Thus fares it now with me,
Since under Hector's violence the Grecian progenie   130
Fell so unfitly by my splene, whose fals will ever sticke
In my griev'd thoughts. My weaknesse yet (Saturnius making sicke
The state my mind held) now recur'd, th' amends shall make
    even weight
With my offence: and therefore rouse thy spirits to the fight
With all thy forces. All the gifts proposde thee at thy tent   135
(Last day) by royall Ithacus, my officers shall present;
And (if it like thee) strike no stroke (though never so on thornes
Thy mind stands to thy friend's revenge) till my command adornes
Thy tents and cofers with such gifts as well may let thee know

Achilles his noble   How much I wish thee satisfied.' He answerd: 'Let thy vow,   140
answer of Agamemnon.   Renown'd Atrides, at thy will be kept (as justice would),
Or keepe thy gifts; tis all in thee. The counsell now we hold
Is for repairing our maine field with all our fortitude.
My faire shew made brookes no retreat; nor must delaies delude
Our deed's expectance. Yet undone the great worke is; all eyes   145
Must see Achilles in first fight, depeopling enemies—
As well as counsell it in court—that every man set on
May chuse his man, to imitate my exercise upon.'

Ulysses to Achilles.   Ulysses answerd: 'Do not yet (thou man made like the gods)
Take fasting men to field. Suppose that whatsoever ods   150
It brings against them, with full men, thy boundlesse eminence
Can amplie answer, yet refraine to tempt a violence.
The conflict wearing out our men was late, and held as long,
Wherein, though most Jove stood for Troy, he yet made our
    part strong
To beare that most. But twas to beare, and that breeds little   155
    heart.
Let wine and bread then adde to it: they helpe the twofold part,
The soule and body in a man, both force and fortitude.
All day men cannot fight and fast, though never so indude
With minds to fight, for, that supposde, there lurks yet secretly
Thirst, hunger, in th' oppressed joynts, which no mind can   160
    supply.
They take away a marcher's knees. Men's bodyes throughly fed,
Their minds share with them in their strength, and (all day
    combatted)
One stirres not till you call off all. Dismisse them then to meate,
And let Atrides tender here, in sight of all this seate,
The gifts he promist. Let him sweare before us all, and rise   165
To that oath—that he never toucht in any wanton wise

[395]

The Ladie he enforc't. Besides, that he remaines in mind
As chastly satisfied, not toucht or privily enclind
With future vantages. And last, tis fit he should approve
All these rites at a solemne feast in honour of your love,   170
That so you take no mangl'd law for merites absolute.
And thus the honours you receive, resolving the pursuite
Of your friend's quarrell, well will quit your sorrow for your
    friend.
And thou, Atrides, in the tast of so severe an end,
Hereafter may on others hold a juster government.   175
Nor will it ought empaire a king to give a sound content

Agamemnon to Ulysses. To any subject, soundly wrong'd.' 'I joy,' replide the king,
'O Laertiades, to heare thy liberall counselling.
In which is all decorum kept; nor any point lackes touch
That might be thought on, to conclude a reconcilement such   180
As fits example, and us two. My mind yet makes me sweare,
Not your impulsion. And that mind shall rest so kind and cleare
That I will not forsweare to God. Let then Achilles stay
(Though never so inflam'd for fight), and all men here I pray
To stay till from my tents these gifts be brought here, and the   185
    truce
At all parts finisht before all. And thou, of all I chuse,
Divine Ulysses, and command, to chuse of all your host
Youths of most honour, to present to him we honour most
The gifts we late vow'd, and the Dames. Meane space, about
    our tents
Talthybius shall provide a Bore, to crowne these kind events   190
With thankfull sacrifice to Jove and to the God of light.'

Achilles to Ulysses.   Achilles answerd: 'These affaires will shew more requisite,
Great king of men, some other time, when our more free estates
Yeeld fit cessation from the warre, and when my splene abates.
But now (to all our shames besides) our friends by Hector slaine   195
(And Jove to friend) lie unfetch'd off. Haste then, and meate
    your men—
Though I must still say, my command would leade them fasting
    forth,
And all together feast at night. Meate will be something worth,
When stomacks first have made it way with venting infamie
(And other sorrowes late sustain'd) with long'd-for wreakes,   200
    that lie
Heavie upon them for right's sake. Before which lode be got
From off my stomacke, meate nor drinke, I vow, shall downe
    my throte,

My friend being dead, who, digd with wounds, and bor'd
    through both his feet,
Lies in the entrie of my tent, and in the teares doth fleete
Of his associates. Meate and drinke have litle merit then   205
To comfort me, but bloud and death and deadly grones of men.'

Ulysses his reply.   The great in counsels yet made good his former counsels thus:
'O Peleus' sonne, of all the Greeks by much most valorous;
Better and mightier than my selfe, no little, with thy lance
I yeeld thy worth. In wisedome yet no lesse I dare advance   210
My right above thee, since above in yeares, and knowing more.
Let then thy mind rest in my words: we quickly shall have store
And all satietie of fight, whose steele heapes store of straw
And little corne upon a floore, when Jove (that doth withdraw
And joyne all battels) once begins t' encline his ballances   215
In which he weighs the lives of men. The Greeks you must not
    presse
To mourning with the belly; death hath nought to do with that
In healthfull men that mourne for friends. His steele we
    stumble at
And fall at every day, you see, sufficient store and fast.
What houre is it that any breathes? We must not use more hast   220
Than speed holds fit for our revenge, nor should we mourne
    too much.
Who dead is, must be buried; men's patience should be such
That one daye's mone should serve one man: the dead must end
    with Death,
And life last with what strengthens life. All those that held
    their breath
From death in fight the more should eate, that so they may   225
    supply
Their fellowes that have stucke in field, and fight incessantly.
Let none expect reply to this nor stay; for this shall stand
Or fall with some offence to him that lookes for new command,
Who ever in dislike holds backe. All joyne then, all things fit
Allow'd for all; set on a charge, at all parts answering it.'   230

The names of those   This said, he chusde (for noblest youths, to beare the
that caried the presents   presents) these—
to Achilles.   The sonnes of Nestor, and with them renowm'd Meriones,
Phylides, Thoas, Lycomed and Meges, all which went
(And Melanippus following Ulysses) to the tent
Of Agamemnon. He but spake, and with the word the deed   235
Had joynt effect: the fitnesse well was answerd in the speed.

The presents.   The presents, added to the Dame the Generall did enforce,

Were twentie Caldrons, Tripods seven, twelve yong and goodly
    horse,
Seven Ladies excellently seene in all Minerva's skill,
The eighth Briseis, who had powre to ravish every will,   240
Twelve talents of the finest gold. All which Ulysses weyd
And caried first, and after him the other youths conveyd
The other presents, tenderd all in face of all the Court.
Up rose the King. Talthybius (whose voice had a report
Like to a god) cald to the rites. There, having brought the Bore, 245
Atrides with his knife tooke sey upon the part before,

Agamemnon's
attestation.

And lifting up his sacred hands to Jove to make his vowes.
Grave Silence strooke the compleate Court, when (casting his
    high browes
Up to the broad heaven) thus he spake: 'Now witnesse, Jupiter
(First, highest, and thou best of gods), thou Earth that all   250
    doest beare,
Thou Sunne, ye Furies under earth that every soule torment
Whom impious perjury distaines—that nought incontinent
In bed, or any other act, to any slendrest touch
Of my light vowes hath wrong'd the Dame; and let my plagues
    be such
As are inflicted by the gods in all extremitie   255
On whomsoever perjur'd men, if godlesse perjurie
In least degree dishonor me.' This said, the bristl'd throte
Of the submitted sacrifice with ruthlesse steele he cut.
Which straight into the horie sea Talthybius cast, to feed
The sea-borne nation. Then stood up the halfe-celestiall seed 260
Of faire-hair'd Thetis, strengthning thus Atrides' innocence:

Achilles to Jupiter.

   'O father Jupiter, from thee descends the confluence
Of all man's ill; for now I see the mightie king of men
At no hand forc't away my prise, nor first inflam'd my splene
With any set ill in himselfe, but thou, the king of gods,   265
(Incenst with Greece) made that the meane to all their periods.
Which now amend we as we may, and give all suffrages
To what wise Ithacus advisde. Take breakfasts, and addresse
For instant conflict.' Thus he raisd the Court, and all tooke way
To severall ships. The Myrmidons the presents did convay 270
T' Achilles' fleete and in his tents disposde them, doing grace
Of seate and all rites to the Dames—the horses put in place
With others of Æacides. When (like Love's golden Queene)
Briseis (all in ghastly wounds) had dead Patroclus seene,
She fell about him, shrieking out, and with her white hands tore 275
Her haire, breasts, radiant cheekes, and, drown'd in warme
    teares, did deplore

His cruell destinie. At length she gat powre to expresse
Her violent passion, and thus spake this like-the-goddesses:

Briseis' complaint over
the body of Patroclus.

'O good Patroclus, to my life the dearest grace it had,
I (wretched dame) departing hence enforc't, and dying sad,   280
Left thee alive when thou hadst chear'd my poore captivitie,
And, now return'd, I find thee dead, misery on miserie
Ever increasing with my steps. The Lord to whom my Sire
And dearest mother gave my life in nuptials, his life's fire
I saw before our citie gates extinguisht, and his fate   285
Three of my worthy brothers' lives in one wombe generate,
Felt all in that blake day of death. And when Achilles' hand
Had slaine all these and rac't the towne Mynetes did command,
(All cause of never-ending griefes presented) thou took'st all
On thy endevour to convert to joy as Generall,   290
Affirming he that hurt should heale, and thou wouldst make
      thy friend
(Brave Captaine that thou wert) supply my vowed husband's end,
And in rich Phthia celebrate, amongst his Myrmidons,
Our nuptiall banquets—for which grace, with these most worthy
      mones
I never shall be satiate, thou ever being kind,   295
Ever delightsome, one sweete grace fed still with one sweete
      mind.'
      Thus spake she weeping, and with her did th' other Ladies
      mone,
Patroclus' fortunes in pretext, but in sad truth their owne.
      About Æacides himselfe the kings of Greece were plac't,
Entreating him to food; and he entreated them as fast   300
(Still intermixing words and sighes), if any friend were there
Of all his dearest, they would ceasse and offer him no cheare
But his due sorrowes, for before the Sunne had left that skie
He would not eate, but of that day sustaine th' extremitie.
      Thus all the kings (in resolute griefe and fasting) he dismist; 305

Nestor.

But both th' Atrides, Ithacus and warre's old Martialist,
Idomeneus and his friend, and Phœnix, these remain'd
Endevoring comfort, but no thought of his vow'd woe restrain'd—
Nor could, till that daye's bloudie fight had calm'd his bloud;
      he still
Rememberd something of his friend, whose good was all his ill.   310
Their urging meate the diligent fashion of his friend renew'd
In that excitement: 'Thou,' said he, 'when this speed was pursu'd
Against the Troyans, evermore apposedst in my tent
A pleasing breakfast; being so free and sweetly diligent,

[399]

Thou mad'st all meate sweete. Then the warre was tearefull   315
    to our foe,
But now to me, thy wounds so wound me and thy overthrow.
For which my readie food I flie and on thy longings feed.
Nothing could more afflict me: Fame, relating the foule deed
Of my deare father's slaughter, bloud drawne from my sole
    sonne's heart,
No more could wound me. Cursed man, that in this forrein part 320
(For hatefull Helen), my true love, my countrey, Sire and son,
I thus should part with. Scyros now gives education,
O Neoptolemus, to thee (if living yet): from whence
I hop't, deare friend, thy longer life (safely return'd from hence
And my life quitting thine) had powre to ship him home, and   325
    show
His yong eyes Phthia, subjects, court—my father being now
Dead, or most short-liv'd, troublous age oppressing him and feare
Still of my death's newes.' These sad words he blew into the eare
Of every visitant with sighs, all eccho'd by the Peeres,
Remembring who they left at home. All whose so humane teares 330
Jove pitied: and, since they all would in the good of one
Be much reviv'd, he thus bespake Minerva: 'Thetis' sonne
Now, daughter, thou hast quite forgot. O, is Achilles' care
Extinguisht in thee? Prostrated in most extreme ill fare,
He lies before his high-sail'd fleet for his dead friend; the rest   335
Are strengthning them with meate, but he lies desperatly
    opprest
With heartlesse fasting. Go thy wayes, and to his brest instill
Red Nectar and Ambrosia, that Fast procure no ill
To his neare enterprise.' This spurre he added to the free;
And like a Harpye (with a voice that shriekes so dreadfully,   340
And feathers that like needles pricke) she stoopt through all
    the starres
Amongst the Grecians, all whose tents were now fill'd for the
    warres.
Her seres strooke through Achilles' tent, and closely she instill'd
Heaven's most-to-be-desired feast to his great breast, and fill'd
His sinewes with that sweete supply, for feare unsavorie Fast   345
Should creepe into his knees. Her selfe the skies againe enchac't.
    The host set forth, and pour'd his steele waves farre out of
    the fleete
And as from aire the frostie Northwind blowes a cold thicke sleete
That dazels eyes, flakes after flakes incessantly descending:
So thicke helmes, curets, ashen darts and round shields, never   350
    ending,

Scyros was an Ile in the sea Ægeum, where Achilles himself was brought up as well as his son.

Jove to Minerva.

The show of the army, setting forth under Achilles' conduct.

Flow'd from the navie's hollow wombe: their splendors gave
    heaven's eye
His beames againe; Earth laught to see her face so like the skie—
Armes shin'd so hote, and she such clouds made with the dust
    she cast,
She thunderd, feete of men and horse importun'd her so fast.
In midst of all divine Achilles his faire person arm'd;   355
His teeth gnasht as he stood, his eyes so full of fire they warm'd,
Unsufferd griefe and anger at the Troyans so combin'd.
His greaves first usde, his goodly curets on his bosome shin'd,
His sword, his shield, that cast a brightnesse from it like the
    Moone.
And as from sea sailers discerne a harmfull fire, let runne   360
By herdsmen's faults, till all their stall flies up in wrastling flame;
Which being on hils is seene farre off, but being alone, none
    came
To give it quench, at shore no neighbours, and at sea their
    friends
Driven off with tempests: such a fire from his bright shield
    extends
His ominous radiance, and in heaven imprest his fervent blaze.   365
His crested helmet, grave and high, had next triumphant place
On his curl'd head: and like a starre it cast a spurrie ray,
About which a bright thickned bush of golden haire did play,
Which Vulcan forg'd him for his plume. Thus compleate arm'd,
    he tride
How fit they were, and if his motion could with ease abide   370
Their brave instruction; and so farre they were from hindring it
That to it they were nimble wings, and made so light his spirit
That from the earth the princely Captaine they tooke up to aire.
    Then from his armoury he drew his lance, his father's speare,
Huge, weightie, firme, that not a Greeke but he himselfe alone   375
Knew how to shake; it grew upon the mountaine Pelion,
From whose height Chiron hew'd it for his Sire, and fatall twas
To great-soul'd men, of Pelion surnamed Pelias.
    Then from the stable their bright horse Automedon withdrawes
And Alcimus, put Poitrils on and cast upon their jawes   380
Their bridles, hurling backe the raines, and hung them
    on the seate.
The faire scourge then Automedon takes up, and up doth get
To guide the horse. The fight's seate last Achilles tooke behind,
Who lookt so arm'd as if the Sunne, there falne from heaven,
    had shin'd—

Achilles to his horses.   And terribly thus charg'd his steeds: 'Xanthus and Balius,   385

Seed of the Harpye, in the charge ye undertake of us,
Discharge it not as when Patroclus ye left dead in field.
But when with bloud, for this daye's fast observ'd, Revenge
    shall yeeld
Our heart satietie, bring us off.' Thus since Achilles spake
As if his aw'd steeds understood, twas Juno's will to make   390
Vocall the pallat of the one, who, shaking his faire head
(Which in his mane (let fall to earth) he almost buried),

Xanthus, the horse of
Achilles, to Achilles.

Thus Xanthus spake: 'Ablest Achilles, now (at least) our care
Shall bring thee off; but not farre hence the fatall minutes are
Of thy grave ruine. Nor shall we be then to be reprov'd,   395
But mightiest Fate and the great God. Nor was thy best belov'd
Spoil'd so of armes by our slow pace or courage's empaire.
The best of gods, Latona's sonne that weares the golden haire,
Gave him his death's wound through the grace he gave to Hector's
    hand.
We, like the spirit of the West that all spirits can command   400
For powre of wing, could runne him off. But thou thy selfe
    must go;
So Fate ordaines; God and a man must give thee overthrow.'
    This said, the Furies stopt his voice. Achilles, farre in rage,

Achilles' reply to
Xanthus.

Thus answerd him: 'It fits not thee thus proudly to presage
My overthrow. I know my selfe it is my fate to fall   405
Thus farre from Phthia; yet that Fate shall faile to vent her gall
Till mine vent thousands.' These words usde, he fell to horrid
    deeds,
Gave dreadfull signall, and forthright made flie his one-hov'd
    steeds.

COMMENTARIUS

[191] κάπρον ἐτοιμασάτω &c. Aprum præparet mactandum Iovique
Solique: *He shall prepare a Bore for sacrifice to Jove and the Sunne.*
It is the end of Agamemnon's speech in this booke before to Ulysses,
and promiseth that sacrifice to Jove and the Sun at the reconciliation
of himselfe and Achilles. Our Commentors (Eustathius and   5
Spondanus, &c.) will by no meanes allow the word κάπρος *here for*
Homer's, but an unskilfulnesse in the divulger, and will needs have it
ὗς *or* ὗς, *which Spondanus sayes is altogether here to be understood as*
Eustathius' words teach—for to offer so fierce a beast to Jove as a Bore
he sayes is absurd, and cites Natalis lib.I. cap. 17. *where he sayes*   10
Homer in this place makes a tame Sow sacrificed to Jove, who was as
tamely and simply deceived as the rest. Eustathius' reason for it is,
that sus *is* animal salax; *and since the oath Agamemnon takes at this*
sacrifice to satisfie Achilles (that he hath not toucht Briseis) is
concerning a woman, very fitly is a Sow here sacrificed. But this seemes 15
to Spondanus something ridiculous (as I hope you will easily judge it).
And, as I conceive, so is his owne opinion to have the originall word
κάπρον *altered, and expounded* suem. *His reason for it he makes nice*
to utter, saying he knowes what is set downe amongst the learned
touching the sacrifice of a Sow. But because it is, he sayes, ἀπροσδιόνυσον, 20
nihil ad rem *(though, as they expound it, tis too much* ad rem*), he is*
willing to keepe his opinion in silence, unlesse you will take it for a
splayed or gelded Sow; as if Agamemnon would innuate that, as this
Sow (being splayed) is free from Venus, so had he never attempted
the dishonour of Briseis. And peradventure, sayes Spondanus, you   25
cannot think of a better exposition: when a worse cannot be
conjectured, unlesse that of Eustathius, as I hope you will cleerly
grant me when you heare but mine. Which is this: The sacrifice is
not made by Agamemnon for any resemblance or reference it hath to
the Lady now to be restored (which since these Clerkes will needs   30
have it a Sow, in behalfe of Ladies, I disdaine), but onely to the
reconciliation of Agamemnon and Achilles; for a sacred signe whereof,
and that their wraths were now absolutely appeased, Agamemnon
thought fit a Bore (being the most wrathfull of all beasts) should be
sacrificed to Jove, intimating that in that Bore they sacrificed their   35
wraths to Jupiter and became friends. And thus is the originall word
preserved, which (together with the sacred sence of our Homer) in a
thousand other places, suffers most ignorant and barbarous violence.
But here (being weary both with finding faults and my labour) till a

refreshing come, I wil end my poore Comment—holding it not   40
altogether unfit with this ridiculous contention of our Commentors a
litle to quicken you, and make it something probable that their
oversight in this trifle is accompanied with a thousand other errors
in matter of our divine Homer's depth and gravitie. Which
will not open it selfe to the curious austeritie of   45
belabouring art, but onely to the naturall
and most ingenuous soule of our
thrice-sacred Poesie.

The End of the Nineteenth Booke

THE TWENTIETH BOOKE

of

HOMER'S ILIADS

THE ARGUMENT

By Jove's permission, all the gods descend
To aide on both parts. For the Greekes contend
Juno, Minerva, Neptune, Mulciber
And Mercurie. The deities that prefer
The Troyan part are Phœbus, Cyprides,   5
Phœbe, Latona and the foe to Peace,
With bright Scamander. Neptune in a mist
Preserves Æneas (daring to resist
Achilles), by whose hand much skath is done;
Besides the slaughter of old Priam's sonne   10
(Yong Polydor) whose rescue Hector makes;
Him (flying) Phœbus to his rescue takes.
The rest (all shunning their importun'd fates)
Achilles beates even to the Ilian gates.

Mars.

Another Argument

In Upsilon *Strife stirres in heaven.*
The daye's grace to the Greekes is given.

The Greeks thus arm'd, and made insatiate with desire of fight,
About thee, Peleus' sonne, the foe, in ground of greatest height,
Stood opposite, rang'd. Then Jove charg'd Themis from
    Olympus' top
To call a court; she every way disperst, and summon'd up

Jove summons all the   All deities. Not any floud (besides Oceanus)   5
deities to counsell.   But made apparance, not a Nymph (that arbours odorous,
The heads of flouds, and flowrie medowes make their sweete
    abodes)
Was absent there; but all at his court that is king of gods

[405]

Assembl'd, and in lightsome seates of admirable frame
(Perform'd for Jove by Vulcan) sate. Even angry Neptune came,　10
Nor heard the goddesse with unwilling eare; but with the rest
Made free ascension from the sea, and did his state invest
In midst of all, begun the counsell, and inquir'd of Jove
His reason for that session, and on what point did move
His high intention for the foes; he thought the heate of warre　15
Was then neare breaking out in flames. To him the Thunderer:
'Thou know'st this counsell by the rest of those forepurposes
That still inclin'd me; my cares still must succour the distresse
Of Troy, though in the mouth of Fate; yet vow I not to stirre
One step from off this top of heaven, but all th' affaire referre　20
To any one. Here I'le hold state and freely take the joy
Of either's fate. Helpe whom ye please, for tis assur'd that Troy
Not one daye's conflict can sustaine against Æacides
If heaven oppose not. His meere lookes threw darts enow
　　t' impresse
Their powres with trembling, but when blowes sent from his　25
　　fiery hand
(Thrice heat by slaughter of his friend) shall come and
　　countermand
Their former glories, we have feare that, though Fate keepe
　　their wall,
Hee'l overturne it. Then descend, and ceasse not till ye all
Adde all your aides; mixe earth and heaven together with the
　　fight
Achilles urgeth.' These his words did such a warre excite　30
As no man's powre could wrastle downe; the gods with
　　parted harts
Departed heaven, and made earth warre. To guide the Grecian
　　darts,

The names of the gods Juno and Pallas, with the god that doth the earth embrace,
partakers with either And most-for-man's-use Mercurie (whom good wise inwards grace)
part. Were partially and all emploid; and with them halted downe　35
(Proud of his strength) lame Mulciber, his walkers quite
　　misgrowne,
But made him tread exceeding sure. To aide the Ilian side
The changeable-in-armes went (Mars), and him accompanied
Diana, that delights in shafts, and Phœbus, never shorne,
And Aphrodite, laughter-pleasde, and she of whom was borne　40
Still-yong Apollo, and the floud that runnes on golden sands,
Bright Xanthus. All these aided Troy; and till these lent
　　their hands,
The Grecians triumpht in the aide Æacides did adde,

[406]

The Troyans trembling with his sight, so gloriously clad:
He overshin'd the field; and, Mars no harmfuller than he,   45
He bore the iron streame on cleare. But when Jove's high decree
Let fall the gods amongst their troupes, the field sweld and the
    fight

Pallas.

Grew fierce and horrible. The Dame that armies doth excite
Thunderd with Clamor, sometimes set at dike without the wall,
And sometimes on the bellowing shore. On th' other side, the   50
    Call
Of Mars to fight was terrible; he cried out like a storme,
Set on the citie's pinnacles, and there he would informe
Sometimes his heartnings, other times where Simois
    powres on
His silver currant, at the foote of high Callicolon.
And thus the blest gods both sides urg'd; they all stood   55
    in the mids

*The state of the
preparation to the
fight, when the gods
were to encounter.*

And brake Contention to the hosts. And over all their heads
The god's king, in abhorred claps, his thunder rattl'd out.
Beneath them Neptune tost the earth; the mountaines
    round about
Bow'd with affright and shooke their heads; Jove's hill
    the earth-quake felt
(Steepe Ida), trembling at her rootes, and all her fountaines   60
    spilt,
Their browes all crannied. Troy did nod; the Grecian
    navie plaid
(As on the sea); th' infernall king, that all things frayes,
    was fraid,
And leapt affrighted from his throne, cried out, lest over him
Neptune should rend in two the earth, and so his house
    so dim,
So lothsome, filthy and abhord of all the gods beside,   65
Should open both to gods and men. Thus all things shooke
    and cri'd,
When this blacke battell of the gods was joyning,
    thus arraied.
  Gainst Neptune, Phœbus, with wing'd shafts; gainst Mars,
    the blew-eyd maid;
Gainst Juno, Phœbe, whose white hands bore singing darts
    of gold,
Her side arm'd with a sheafe of shafts, and (by the birth   70
    twofold
Of bright Latona) sister twin to him that shootes so farre.

Against Latona, Hermes stood (grave guard, in peace and
    warre,
Of human beings); gainst the god whose Empire is in fire,
The watry godhead, that great flood, to shew whose powre
    entire
In spoile as th' other, all his streame on lurking whirlepits   75
    trod—
Xanthus by gods, by men Scamander cald. Thus god
    gainst god
Enterd the field. Æacides sustain'd a fervent mind
To cope with Hector; past all these his spirit stood enclin'd
To glut Mars with the bloud of him. And at Æacides,
Apollo set Anchises' sonne. But first he did impresse   80

Apollo instigates Æneas A more than naturall strength in him, and made him feele
to the encounter of   th' excesse
Achilles, in shape of Infusde from heaven. Lycaon's shape gave show to his
Lycaon.   addresse

Æneas to Apollo. (Old Priam's sonne), and thus he spake: 'Thou counseller
    of Troy,
Where now flie out those threats that late put all our
    Peeres in joy
Of thy fight with Æacides? Thy tongue once (steept   85
    in wine)
Durst vant as much.' He answerd him: 'But why wouldst
    thou incline
My powres gainst that proud enemie and gainst my present
    heate?
I meane not now to bid him blowes; that feare sounds my
    retreate
That heretofore discourag'd me when, after he had rac't
Lyrnessus and strong Pedasus, his still-breath'd furie chac't   90
Our oxen from th' Idæan hill, and set on me; but Jove
Gave strength and knees, and bore me off, that had not walkt
    above
This center now but propt by him. Minerva's hand (that held
A light to this her favorite, whose beames shew'd and impeld
His powres to spoile) had ruin'd me. For these eares heard   95
    her crie:
"Kill, kill the seed of Ilion; kill th' Asian Lelegi."
Meere man then must not fight with him, that still hath gods
    to friend,
Averting death on others' darts, and giving his no end
But with the ends of men. If God like Fortune in the fight

Would give my forces, not with ease wing'd Victorie should   100
    light
On his proud shoulders, nor he scape, though all of brasse
    he bosts
His plight consisteth.' He replide: 'Pray thou those gods
    of hosts
Whom he implores, as well as he; and his chance may
    be thine.
Thou cam'st of gods like him: the Queene that reignes
    in Salamine
Fame sounds thy mother—he deriv'd of lower deitie,   105
Old Nereus' daughter bearing him. Beare then thy heart
    as hie
And thy unwearied steele as right; not utterly be beate
With onely crueltie of words, not proofe against a threat.'
    This strengthned him, and forth he rusht; nor could his
      strengthening flie
White-wristed Juno, nor his drifts. She every deitie   110

Juno to the gods of Of th' Achive faction cald to her, and said: 'Ye must have care,
Greece. Neptune and Pallas, for the frame of this important warre
Ye undertake here. Venus' sonne (by Phœbus being impeld)
Runnes on Achilles. Turne him backe, or see our friend
    upheld
By one of us. Let not the spirit of Æacides   115
Be over-dar'd, but make him know the mightiest deities
Stand kind to him, and that the gods, protectors of these
    towres
That fight against Greece and were here before our
    eminent powres,
Beare no importance. And, besides, that all we stoope
    from heaven
To curbe this fight, that no empaire be to his person given   120
By any Troyans nor their aides, while this day beares the
    Sunne.
Hereafter, all things that are wrapt in his birth-threed
    and spunne
By Parcas (in that point of time his mother gave him aire)
He must sustaine. But if Report performe not the repaire
Of all this to him by the Voice of some immortall state,   125
He may be fearfull (if some god should set on him)
    that Fate
Makes him her minister. The gods, when they appeare
    to men
And manifest their proper formes, are passing dreadfull then.'

Neptune to Juno.

Neptune replide: 'Saturnia, at no time let your Care
Exceed your Reason; tis not fit. Where onely humanes are,   130
We must not mixe the hands of gods; our ods is too extreme.
Sit we by in some place of height, where we may see to them,
And leave the warres of men to men. But if we see from
    thence
Or Mars or Phœbus enter fight or offer least offence
To Thetis' sonne, not giving free way to his conquering rage,   135
Then comes the conflict to our cares. We soone shall dis-engage
Achilles, and send them to heaven to settle their abode
With Equals, flying under-strifes.' This said, the
    blacke-hair'd god
Led to the towre of Hercules, built circular and hie
By Pallas and the Ilians for fit securitie   140

Hercules. To Jove's divine sonne gainst the Whale that drave him
    from the shore
To th' ample field. There Neptune sate and all the gods
    that bore
The Greekes good meaning, casting all thicke mantles
    made of clouds
On their bright shoulders. Th' oppos'd gods sate hid in
    other shrouds
On top of steepe Callicolon, about thy golden sides,   145
O Phœbus, brandisher of darts, and thine whose rage abides
No peace in cities. In this state these gods in counsell sate,
All lingring purposde fight, to trie who first would elevate

Jove sets on the other
gods to fight.

His heavenly weapon. High-thron'd Jove cried out to set
    them on,
Said, all the field was full of men and that the earth did grone   150
With feete of proud encounterers, burn'd with the armes
    of men
And barbed horse. Two champions for both the armies then
Met in their midst, prepar'd for blowes—divine Æacides
And Venus' sonne. Æneas first stept threatning forth the
    preasse,
His high helme nodding, and his breast bard with a shadie   155
    shield,
And shooke his javelin. Thetis' sonne did his part to the field,

Simile.

As when the harmfull king of beasts (sore threatn'd to
    be slaine
By all the countrie up in armes) at first makes coy Disdaine
Prepare resistance, but at last, when any one hath led
Bold charge upon him with his dart, he then turnes yawning   160
    head;

[410]

Fell Anger lathers in his jawes, his great heart swels,
    his sterne
Lasheth his strength up, sides and thighes wadl'd with
    stripes to learne
Their owne powre, his eyes glow, he rores, and in he leapes
    to kill,
Secure of killing: so his powre then rowsde up to his will
Matchlesse Achilles, coming on to meete Anchises' sonne.   165

Achilles to Æneas.   Both neare, Achilles thus enquir'd: 'Why standst thou thus
    alone,
Thou sonne of Venus? Cals thy heart to change of blowes
    with me?
Sure Troy's whole kingdome is proposde; some one hath
    promist thee
The throne of Priam for my life; but Priam's selfe is wise,
And (for my slaughter) not so mad to make his throne thy   170
    prise.
Priam hath sonnes to second him. Is't then some peece
    of land,
Past others fit to set and sow, that thy victorious hand
The Ilians offer for my head? I hope that prise will prove
No easie conquest: once, I thinke, my busie javelin drove
(With terror) those thoughts from your spleene. Retain'st thou   175
    not the time
When, single on th' Idæan hill, I tooke thee with the crime
Of Run-away, thy Oxen left, and when thou hadst no face
That I could see, thy knees bereft it, and Lyrnessus was
The maske for that. Then that maske, too, I opened to
    the aire
(By Jove and Pallas' helpe) and tooke the free light from the   180
    faire,
Your Ladies bearing prisoners. But Jove and th' other gods
Then saft thee; yet againe I hope they will not adde
    their ods
To save thy wants, as thou presum'st; retire then, aime not at
Troy's throne by me; flie ere thy soule flies; fooles are wise
    too late.'

Æneas to Achilles.   He answerd him: 'Hope not that words can child-like terrifie   185
My stroke-proofe breast. I well could speake in this
    indecencie,
And use tart termes; but we know well what stocke us both
    put out—
Too gentle to beare fruites so rude. Our parents ring about

[411]

The world's round bosome, and by fame their dignities
    are blowne
To both our knowledges, by sight, neither to either knowne—   190
Thine, to mine eyes, nor mine to thine. Fame sounds
    thy worthinesse
From famous Peleus, the sea Nymph that hath the lovely
    tresse
(Thetis) thy mother; I my selfe affirme my Sire to be
Great-soul'd Anchises, she that holds the Paphian deitie
My mother. And of these, this light is now t' exhale the   195
    teares
For their lov'd issue, thee or me; childish, unworthy dares
Are not enough to part our powres. For if thy spirits want
Due excitation (by distrust of that desert I vant)
To set up all rests for my life, I'le lineally prove

Æneas' pedigree.   (Which many will confirme) my race. First, cloud-commanding   200
    Jove
Was sire to Dardanus, that built Dardania; for the wals
Of sacred Ilion spred not yet these fields, those faire-built hals
Of divers-languag'd men not raisd; all then made populous
The foote of Ida's fountfull hill. This Jove-got Dardanus
Begot king Erichthonius, for wealth past all compares   205
Of living mortals; in his fens he fed three thousand mares,
All neighing by their tender foles; of which twice sixe
    were bred
By loftie Boreas, their dams lov'd by him as they fed;
He tooke the brave forme of a horse that shooke an azure mane,
And slept with them. These twice sixe colts had pace so swift   210
    they ranne
Upon the top-ayles of corne-eares, nor bent them any whit.
And when the brode backe of the sea their pleasure was
    to sit,
The superficies of his waves they slid upon, their hoves
Not dipt in danke sweate of his browes. Of Erichthonius' loves
Sprang Tros, the king of Troyans; Tros three yong princes   215
    bred,
Ilus, renowm'd Assaracus and heavenly Ganymed,
The fairest youth of all that breath'd, whom (for his
    beautie's love)
The gods did ravish to their state to beare the cup to Jove.
Ilus begot Laomedon; god-like Laomedon
Got Tithon, Priam, Clytius, Mars-like Hicetaon   220
And Lampus, Great Assaracus, Capys begot, and he
Anchises, Prince Anchises, me, King Priam, Hector. We

Sprang both of one high family. Thus fortunate men give
    birth,
But Jove gives vertue; he augments and he empaires the
    worth
Of all men, and his will, their Rule; he, strong'st, all strength   225
    affoords.
Why then paint we (like dames) the face of Conflict with
    our words?
Both may give language that a ship, driven with a hundred
    ores,
Would over-burthen: a man's tongue is voluble and poures
Words out of all sorts every way; such as you speake,
    you heare.
What then need we vie calumnies, like women that will weare   230
Their tongues out, being once incenst, and strive for strife
    to part
(Being on their way) they travell so? From words, words
    may avert—
From vertue, not. It is your steele, divine Æacides,
Must prove my proofe, as mine shall yours.' Thus amply did
    he ease

Æneas chargeth
Achilles.

His great heart of his pedigree, and sharply sent away   235
A dart, that caught Achilles' shield, and rung so, it did fray
The sonne of Thetis, his faire hand farre-thrusting out his
    shield,
For feare the long lance had driven through. O foole, to
    thinke twould yeeld,
And not to know the gods' firme gifts want want to yeeld
    so soone
To men's poore powres. The eager lance had onely conquest   240
    wonne
Of two plates, and the shield had five—two forg'd of tin,
    two brasse,
One (that was center-plate) of gold, and that forbad the passe

Achilles at Æneas.

Of Anchisiades his lance. Then sent Achilles forth
His lance, that through the first fold strooke, where brasse of
    litle worth
And no great proofe of hides was laid; through all which   245
    Pelias ranne
His iron head, and after it his ashen body wanne
Passe to the earth, and there it stucke his top on th' other
    side,
And hung the shield up; which hard downe Æneas pluckt
    to hide

[413]

His breast from sword blowes, shrunke up round, and in his
    heavie eye
Was much griefe shadowed, much afraid that Pelias stucke so   250
    nie.
Then prompt Achilles, rushing in, his sword drew, and
    the field
Rung with his voice. Æneas now left and let hang his shield,
And (all distracted) up he snatcht a two-men's strength
    of stone
And either at his shield or caske he set it rudely gone,
Nor car'd where, so it strooke a place that put on armes for   255
    death.
But he (Achilles came so close) had doubtlesse sunke
    beneath
His owne death, had not Neptune seene and interposde
    the ods
Of his divine powre, uttering this to the Achaian gods:

*Neptune to the other
gods of Greece.*

'I grieve for this great-hearted man; he will be sent to hell
Even instantly by Peleus' sonne, being onely mov'd to deale   260
By Phœbus' words. What foole is he! Phœbus did never
    meane
To adde to his great words his guard against the ruine then
Summon'd against him. And what cause hath he to head
    him on
To others' miseries, he being cleare of any trespasse done
Against the Grecians? Thankfull gifts he oft hath given to us;   265
Let us then quit him, and withdraw this combat; for if thus
Achilles end him, Jove will rage—since his escape in fate

*Homer's prophecy of
Æneas, to propagate
the Troyan race.*

Is purposde, lest the progenie of Dardanus take date,
Whom Jove past all his issue lov'd, begot of mortall dames.
All Priam's race he hates, and this must propagate the names   270
Of Troyans, and their sonnes' sonnes rule to all posteritie.'

Juno to Neptune.

    Saturnia said: 'Make free your pleasure; save, or let him die.
Pallas and I have taken many and most publique oathes
That th' ill day never shall avert her eye (red with our wroths)
From hated Troy. No, not when all in studied fire she   275
    flames
The Greeke rage, blowing her last coale.' This nothing
    turn'd his aimes
From present rescue, but through all the whizzing speares
    he past,
And came where both were combatting; when instantly
    he cast
A mist before Achilles' eyes, drew from the earth and shield

His lance, and laid it at his feete; and then tooke up and   280
    held
Aloft the light Anchises' sonne, who past (with Neptune's
    force)
Whole orders of Heroes' heads and many a troope of horse
Leapt over, till the bounds he reacht of all the fervent
    broyle,
Where all the Caucons' quarters lay. Thus (farre freed from
    the toyle)

Neptune to Æneas.   Neptune had time to use these words: 'Æneas, who was he   285
Of all the gods that did so much neglect thy good, and thee,
To urge thy fight with Thetis' sonne—who in immortall rates
Is better and more deare than thee? Hereafter, lest (past
    fates)
Hell be thy headlong home, retire; make bold stand
    never neare
Where he advanceth; but, his fate once satisfied, then beare   290
A free, and full sayle: no Greeke else shall end thee.' This
    reveald,
He left him, and disperst the cloud that all this act conceald
From vext Achilles, who againe had cleare light from the
    skies,

Achilles admires the   And (much disdaining the escape) said: 'O ye gods, mine eyes
scape of Æneas.   Discover miracles: my lance submitted, and he gone   295
At whom I sent it with desire of his confusion!
Æneas sure was lov'd of heaven; I thought his vant from
    thence
Had flow'd from glorie. Let him go; no more experience
Will his mind long for of my hands, he flies them now so
    cleare.
Cheare then the Greeks and others trie.' Thus rang'd he every   300
    where
The Grecian orders; every man (of which the most lookt on
To see their fresh Lord shake his lance) he thus put
    charge upon:
  'Divine Greeks, stand not thus at gaze, but man to man
    apply
Your severall valours: tis a taske laide too unequally
On me—left to so many men, one man opposde to all.   305
Not Mars, immortall and a god, nor warre's She-Generall,
A field of so much fight could chace and worke it out
    with blowes.
But what a man may execute, that all lims will expose,

And all their strength to th' utmost nerve (though now I
    lost some play
By some strange miracle) no more shall burne in vaine the day   310
To any least beame. All this host I'le ransacke, and have hope
Of all not one (againe) will scape, whoever gives such scope
To his adventure, and so neare dares tempt my angry lance.'
    Thus he excited. Hector then as much strives to advance
The hearts of his men, adding threates, affirming he would   315
    stand

Hector to his Ilians.   In combat with Æacides. 'Give Feare,' said he, 'no hand
Of your great hearts, brave Ilians, for Peleus' talking Sonne.
I'le fight with any god with words; but when their speares
    put on,
The worke runs high, their strength exceeds mortalitie so farre
And they may make works crowne their words, which holds   320
    not in the warre
Achilles makes; his hands have bounds; this word he shall
    make good
And leave another to the field: his worst shall be withstood
With sole objection of my selfe. Though in his hands he
    beare
A rage like fire, though fire it selfe his raging fingers were
And burning steele flew in his strength.' Thus he incited his,   325
And they raisd lances, and to worke with mixed courages.
And up flew Clamor, but the heate in Hector Phœbus gave

Phœbus to Hector.   This temper: 'Do not meet,' said he, 'in any single brave
The man thou threatn'st, but in preasse and in thy strength
    impeach
His violence; for farre off or neare his sword or dart will   330
    reach.'
    The god's voice made a difference in Hector's owne conceipt
Betwixt his and Achilles' words, and gave such overweight
As weigh'd him backe into his strength and curb'd his flying
    out.
At all threw fierce Æacides, and gave a horrid shout.

Iphition slaine by   The first of all he put to dart was fierce Iphition,   335
Achilles.   Surnam'd Otryntides, whom Nais, the water Nymph, made
    sonne
To towne-destroyer Otrynteus. Beneath the snowy hill
Of Tmolus, in the wealthie towne of Hyde, at his will,
Were many able men at armes. He, rushing in, tooke full
Pelides' lance in his head's midst, that cleft in two his skull.   340
Achilles knew him one much fam'd, and thus insulted then:
    'Th' art dead, Otryntides, though cald the terriblest of men.

Thy race runs at Gygæus' lake, there thy inheritance lay,
Neare fishy Hyllus and the gulfs of Hermus; but this day
Removes it to the fields of Troy.' Thus left he Night to sease   345
His closed eyes, his body laid in course of all the prease,
Which Grecian horse broke with the strakes naild to their
        chariot wheels.

Demoleon slaine by
Achilles.

Next (through the temples) the burst eyes his deadly javelin
        seeles
Of great-in-Troy Antenor's sonne, renown'd Demoleon,
A mightie turner of a field. His overthrow set gone   350
Hippodamas, who leapt from horse and, as he fled before
Æacides, his turned backe he made fell Pelias gore,

Simile.

And forth he puft his flying soule. And as a tortur'd Bull
(To Neptune brought for sacrifice) a troope of yongsters pull
Downe to the earth, and dragge him round about the hallowed   355
        shore
To please the watry deitie, with forcing him to rore,
And forth he powres his utmost throte: so bellow'd this
        slaine friend
Of flying Ilion, with the breath that gave his being end.
    Then rusht he on, and in his eye had heavenly Polydore,
Old Priam's sonne, whom last of all his fruitfull Princesse bore, 360
And for his youth (being deare to him) the king forbad to
        fight.
Yet (hote of unexperienc't blood, to shew how exquisite
He was of foote, for which of all the fiftie sonnes he held
The speciall name) he flew before the first heate of the field,
Even till he flew out breath and soule—which, through the   365
        backe, the lance

Polydore slaine by
Achilles.

Of swift Achilles put in ayre, and did his head advance
Out at his navill. On his knees the poore Prince crying fell,
And gatherd with his tender hands his entrailes, that did swell
Quite through the wide wound, till a cloud as blacke as
        death conceald
Their sight and all the world from him. When Hector had   370
        beheld
His brother tumbl'd so to earth (his entrailes still in hand),
Darke sorrow overcast his eyes, nor farre off could he stand
A minute longer, but like fire he brake out of the throng,
Shooke his long lance at Thetis' sonne; and then came he along

Achilles' passion at the
sight of Hector.

To feed th' encounter: 'O,' said he, 'here comes the man that   375
        most
Of all the world destroyes my minde, the man by whom I lost
My deare Patroclus. Now not long the crooked paths of warre

Can yeeld us any privie scapes. Come, keepe not off so farre,'
He cryed to Hector, 'make the paine of thy sure death
    as short

Hector to Achilles.

As one so desperate of his life hath reason.' In no sort   380
This frighted Hector, who bore close, and said: 'Æacides,
Leave threates for children. I have powre to thunder
    calumnies
As well as others, and well know thy strength superiour farre
To that my nerves hold. But the gods (not nerves)
    determine warre.
And yet (for nerves) there will be found a strength of powre in 385
    mine
To drive a lance home to thy life; my lance as well as thine
Hath point and sharpenesse, and tis this.' Thus brandishing
    his speare,

Pallas breathes backe
Hector's lance throwne
at Achilles.

He set it flying, which a breath of Pallas backe did beare
From Thetis' sonne to Hector's selfe, and at his feet it fell.
Achilles usde no dart but close flew in, and thought to deale   390
With no strokes but of sure dispatch; but what with all
    his blood
He labor'd Phœbus clear'd with ease, as being a god, and stood
For Hector's guard, as Pallas did, Æacides, for thine.

Apollo rescues Hector.

He rapt him from him, and a cloud of much Night cast
    betweene
His person and the point opposde. Achilles then exclaim'd: 395
'O see, yet more gods are at worke; Apollo's hand hath
    fram'd,
Dog that thou art, thy rescue now—to whom go pay the vowes
Thy safetie owes him. I shall vent, in time, those fatall
    blowes
That yet beate in my heart on thine, if any god remaine
My equall fautor. In meane time, my anger must maintaine   400
His fire on other Ilians.' Then laid he at his feet
Great Demuchus, Philetor's sonne, and Dryope did greet
With like encounter. Dardanus, and strong Laogonus
(Wise Bias' sonnes) he hurld from horse, of one victorious
With his close sword, the other's life he conquerd with his   405
    lance.
   Then Tros, Alastor's sonne, made in, and sought to scape
    their chance
With free submission. Downe he fell, and praid about his
    knees
He would not kill him, but take ruth, as one that Destinies

Made to that purpose, being a man borne in the selfe
    same yeare
That he himselfe was. O poore foole, to sue to him to beare   410
A ruthfull mind; he well might know he could not fashion him
In Ruth's soft mould; he had no spirit to brooke that interim
In his hote furie, he was none of these remorsefull men,
Gentle and affable, but fierce at all times, and mad then.
  He gladly would have made a prayre, and still so hugg'd his   415
    knee
He could not quit him: till at last his sword was faine to free
His fetterd knees, that made a vent for his white liver's
    blood
That causd such pittifull affects: of which it pour'd a flood
About his bosome, which it fild even till it drownd his eyes
And all sense faild him. Forth then flew this Prince of   420
    tragedies,
Who next stoopt Mulius even to death with his insatiate speare;
One eare it enterd and made good his passe to th' other eare.
  Echeclus then (Agenor's sonne) he strooke betwixt the
    browes,
Whose blood set fire upon his sword that coold it till the
    throwes
Of his then labouring braine let out his soule to fixed fate,   425
And gave cold entrie to blacke death. Deucalion then had
    state
In these men's beings; where the nerves about the elbow knit
Downe to his hand his speare's steele pierc't, and brought
    such paine to it
As led Death joyntly, whom he saw before his fainting eyes
And in his necke felt, with a stroke laid on so that off flies   430
His head; one of the twise twelve bones that all the backe
    bone make
Let out his marrow—when the head he, helme and all,
    did take
And hurl'd amongst the Ilians, the body stretcht on earth.
  Rhigmus of fruitfull Thrace next fell; he was the famous
    birth
Of Pireus. His bellie's midst the lance tooke, whose sterne   435
    force
Quite tumbl'd him from chariot. In turning backe the horse,
Their guider Areithous receiv'd another lance
That threw him to his Lord. No end was put to the mischance
Simile.   Achilles enterd. But as fire falne in a flash from heaven,

[419]

Inflames the high-woods of drie hils, and with a storme is   440
    driven
Through all the Sylvane deepes, and raves, till downe goes
    every where
The smotherd hill: so every way Achilles and his speare
Consum'd the Champaine, the blacke earth flow'd with the
    veines he tore.

Simile.

And looke how Oxen (yok't and driven about the circular
    floore
Of some faire barne) treade sodainly the thicke sheaves thin   445
    of corne,
And all the corne consum'd with chaffe; so mixt and
    overborne
Beneath Achilles' one-hov'd horse shields, speares and men
    lay trod,
His axel--tree and chariot wheeles all spatterd with the
    blood
Hurl'd from the steeds' hoves and the strakes. Thus to be
    magnified,
His most inaccessible hands in humane blood he died.

The End of the Twentieth Booke

THE TWENTY-FIRST BOOKE

of

HOMER'S ILIADS

THE ARGUMENT

In two parts Troy's host parted; Thetis' sonne
One to Scamander, one to Ilion
Pursues. Twelve Lords he takes alive, to end
In sacrifice for vengeance to his friend.
Asteropæus dies by his fierce hand,   5
And Priam's sonne Lycaon. Over land
The flood breakes, where, Achilles being engag'd,
Vulcan preserves him, and with spirit enrag'd
Sets all the Champaine and the Flood on fire.
Contention then doth all the gods inspire.   10
Apollo, in Agenor's shape, doth stay
Achilles' furie, and by giving way,
Makes him pursue, till the deceipt gives leave
That Troy in safetie might her freinds receive.

Another Argument

Phy, at the flood's shore doth expresse
The labours of Æacides.

And now they reacht the goodly swelling channell of the
    flood,
Gulfe-eating Xanthus, whom Jove mixt with his immortall
    brood.
And there Achilles cleft the host of Ilion: one side fell
On Xanthus, th' other on the towne: and that did he impell
The same way that the last daie's rage put all the Greeks in rout,   5
When Hector's furie reign'd. These now Achilles powr'd about
The scatterd field. To stay the flight, Saturnia cast before
Their hastie feete a standing fogge, and then Flight's violence
    bore

The other halfe full on the flood. The silver-gulphed deepe
Receiv'd them with a mightie crie, the billowes vast and steepe   10
Ror'd at their armours, which the shores did round about
    resound.
This way and that they swum, and shriekt as in the gulphs they
    drownd.

Simile.

And as in fir'd fields Locusts rise, as the unwearied blaze
Plies still their rising, till in swarmes all rush as in amaze
(For scape) into some neighbour flood: so th' Achilleian stroke   15
Here drave the foe. The gulfie flood with men and horse
    did choke.
   Then on the shore the Worthy hid and left his horrid lance
Amids the Tamriskes, and spritelike did with his sword
    advance
Up to the river. Ill affaires tooke up his furious braine
For Troy's engagements: every way he doubl'd slaine on slaine.   20
A most unmanly noise was made with those he put to sword,
Of grones and outcries; the flood blusht to be so much
    engor'd

Simile.

With such base soules. And as small fish the swift-finn'd
    Dolphin flie,
Filling the deepe pits in the ports, on whose close strength
    they lie,
And there he swallowes them in sholes: so here, to rockes and   25
    holes
About the flood the Troyans fled, and there most lost their
    soules,
Even till he tir'd his slaughterous arme. Twelve faire yong
    Princes then
He chusde of all to take alive, to have them freshly slaine
On that most solemne day of wreake resolv'd on for his
    friend.
These led he trembling forth the flood, as fearefull of their end   30
As any Hinde calves: all their hands he pinnioned behind
With their owne girdles worne upon their rich weeds, and
    resign'd
Their persons to his Myrmidons to beare to fleete—and he
Plung'd in the streame againe to take more worke of Tragedie.

*Achilles his strange
encounter of Lycaon.*

He met, then issuing the flood with all intent of flight,   35
Lycaon (Dardan Priam's sonne) whom lately in the night
He had surprisde, as in a wood of Priam's he had cut
The greene armes of a wild figge tree, to make him spokes
    to put
In Naves of his new chariot. An ill then, all unthought,

Stole on him in Achilles' shape, who tooke him thence and   40
    brought
To well-built Lemnos, selling him to famous Jason's sonne,
From whom a guest then in his house (Imbrius Eetion)
Redeem'd at high rate and sent home t' Arisbe; whence
    he fled
And saw againe his father's court; eleven daies banquetted
Amongst his friends, the twelfth, god thrust his haplesse head   45
    againe
In th' hands of sterne Æacides, who now must send him slaine
To Pluto's Court, and gainst his will. Him, when Achilles knew,
Naked of helmet, shield, sword, lance (all which for ease he
    threw
To earth, being overcome with sweate, and labour wearying
His flying knees) he storm'd, and said: 'O heaven, a wondrous   50
    thing
Invades mine eyes! Those Ilians that heretofore I slue
Rise from the darke dead, quicke againe. This man fate makes
    eschew
Her owne steele fingers: he was sold in Lemnos, and the deepe
Of all Seas twixt this Troy and that (that many a man doth
    keepe
From his lov'd countrie) barres not him. Come then; he now shall   55
    tast
The head of Pelias, and trie if steele will downe as fast
As other fortunes, or kind earth can any surer seise
On his slie person, whose strong armes have held downe
    Hercules.'

Lycaon's feare to be
seene of Achilles.
    His thoughts thus mov'd, while he stood firme to see if he
    he spide
Would offer flight (which first he thought), but, when he had   60
    descride
He was descried and flight was vaine, fearefull, he made more
    nie,
With purpose to embrace his knees, and now long'd much
    to flie
His blacke fate and abhorred death by coming in. His foe
Observ'd all this, and up he raisd his lance as he would throw.
And then Lycaon close ran in, fell on his breast and tooke   65
Achilles' knees, whose lance (on earth now staid) did overlooke
His still-turn'd backe, with thirst to glut his sharpe point with
    the blood
That lay so readie. But that thirst Lycaon's thirst withstood.
To save his blood, Achilles' knee in his one hand he knit,

[423]

His other held the long lance hard and would not part with it,   70
*Lycaon's ruthfull
intercession to Achilles
for his life.*
But thus besought: 'I kisse thy knees, divine Æacides.
Respect me, and my fortunes rue. I now present th' accesse
Of a poore suppliant for thy ruth: and I am one that is
Worthy thy ruth, O Jove's belov'd. First houre my miseries
Fell into any hand, twas thine. I tasted all my bread   75
By thy gift since—O since that houre that thy surprisall led
From forth the faire wood my sad feete, farre from my
        lov'd allies,
To famous Lemnos, where I found an hundred Oxen's prise
To make my ransome: for which now I thrise the worth will
        raise.
This day makes twelve since I arriv'd in Ilion, many daies   80
Being spent before in sufferance; and now a cruell fate
Thrusts me againe into thy hands. I should hant Jove with
        hate,
That with such set malignitie gives thee my life againe.
There were but two of us for whom Laothoe sufferd paine,
(Laothoe, old Altes' seed—Altes, whose pallace stood   85
In height of upper Pedasus, neare Satnius' silver flood,
And rulde the warre-like Lelegi). Whose seed (as many more)
King Priam married, and begot the godlike Polydor
And me acurst. Thou slaughterdst him, and now thy hand on
        me
Will prove as mortall. I did thinke, when here I met with thee,   90
I could not scape thee; yet give eare and adde thy mind to it.
I told my birth to intimate, though one sire did beget
Yet one wombe brought not into light Hector (that slue thy
        friend)
And me. O do not kill me then, but let the wretched end
Of Polydor excuse my life. For halfe our being bred   95
Brothers to Hector he (halfe) paid; no more is forfeited.'
    Thus su'd he humbly, but he heard with this austere replie:
'Foole, urge not ruth nor price to me, til that solemnitie
Resolv'd on for Patroclus' death pay all his rites to fate.
Till his death, I did grace to Troy, and many lives did rate   100
At price of ransome: but none now of all the brood of Troy
(Who ever Jove throwes to my hands) shall any breath enjoy
That death can beate out—specially that touch at Priam's race.
Die, die, my friend. What teares are these? What sad lookes
        spoile thy face?
Patroclus died, that farre past thee. Nay, seest thou not beside,   105
My selfe, even I, a faire yong man and rarely magnifide,
And (to my father, being a king) a mother have that sits

[424]

In ranke with goddesses; and yet, when thou hast spent thy
    spirits,
Death and as violent a fate must overtake even me—
By twilight, morne-light, day, high noone, when ever Destinie   110
Sets on her man to hurle a lance or knit out of his string
An arrow that must reach my life.' This said, alanguishing,
Lycaon's heart bent like his knees, yet left him strength
    t' advance
Both hands for mercie as he kneeld. His foe yet leaves his
    lance
And forth his sword flies, which he hid in furrow of a wound   115
Driven through the joynture of his necke; flat fell he on the
    ground,
Stretcht with death's pangs, and all the earth embrew'd with
    timelesse blood.
Then gript Æacides his heele and to the loftie flood
Flung (swinging) his unpitied corse, to see it swim and tosse
Up on the rough waves, and said: 'Go, feed fat the fish with   120
    losse
Of thy left blood: they cleane will sucke thy greene wounds,
    and this saves
Thy mother teares upon thy bed. Deepe Xanthus on his waves
Shall hoyse thee bravely to a tombe that in her burly breast
The sea shall open, where great fish may keepe thy funerall
    feast
With thy white fat, and on the waves dance at thy wedding   125
    fate,
Clad in blacke horror, keeping close inaccessible state.
So perish Ilians, till we plucke the browes of Ilion
Downe to her feete, you flying still, I flying still upon

The word is
κεραΐζων
which they translate
cædens, *but properly*
signifies dissipans, ut
boves infestis cornibus.

Thus in the rere, and (as my browes were forckt with rabid
    hornes)
Tosse ye together. This brave flood, that strengthens and   130
    adornes
Your citie with his silver gulfes, to whom so many buls
Your zeale hath offerd, which blind zeale his sacred current guls
With casting chariots and horse quicke to his prayd-for aide,
Shall nothing profite. Perish then, till cruell'st Death hath laide
All at the red feet of Revenge for my slaine friend, and all   135
With whom the absence of my hands made yours a festivall.'
    This speech great Xanthus more enrag'd, and made his
    spirit contend
For meanes to shut up the o'pt vaine against him, and defend

The Troyans in it from his plague. In meane time Peleus'
    sonne
(And now with that long lance he hid) for more blood set upon   140
Asteropæus, the descent of Pelegon, and he
Of brode-stream'd Axius and the dame (of first nativitie
To all the daughters that renown'd Acessamenus' seed),
Bright Peribœa, whom the flood (arm'd thicke with loftie reed)
Comprest. At her grandchild now went Thetis' great sonne,   145
    whose foe
Stood arm'd with two darts, being set on by Xanthus, angerd so
For those youths' blood shed in his streame by vengefull
    Thetis' sonne
Without all mercie. (Both being neare) great Thetides begunne

Achilles to Asteropæus. With this high question: 'Of what race art thou that dar'st
    oppose
Thy powre to mine thus? Cursed wombs they ever did disclose   150

Asteropæus to Achilles. That stood my anger.' He reply'd: 'What makes thy furie's
    heate
Talke and seeke Pedigrees? Farre hence lies my innative seate
In rich Pæonia. My race from brode-stream'd Axius runs—
Axius that gives earth purest drinke of all the watrie sons
Of great Oceanus, and got the famous-for-his-speare   155
Pelegonus, that fatherd me; and these Pæonians here,
Arm'd with long lances, here I leade; and here th' eleventh
    faire light
Shines on us since we enterd Troy. Come now, brave man, let's
    fight.'
    Thus spake he, threatning; and to him Pelides made replie

Asteropæus with two With shaken Pelias. But his foe with two at once let flie   160
darts at once at (For both his hands were dexterous): one javelin strooke the
Achilles.   shield
Of Thetis' sonne but strooke not through (the gold, god's gift,
    repeld
The eager point); the other lance fell lightly on the part
Of his faire right hand's cubit. Forth the blacke blood spunne;
    the dart
Glanc't over, fastening on the earth, and there his splene was   165
    spent
That wisht the body. With which wish, Achilles his lance sent,
That quite mist and infixt it selfe fast in the steepe-up shore.
Even to the midst it enterd it. Himselfe then fiercely bore
Upon his enemie with his sword. His foe was tugging hard
To get his lance out: thrise he pluckt, and thrise sure   170
    Pelias bard

His wisht evulsion. The fourth plucke, he bow'd and meant to
    breake

The Ashen plant, but (ere that act) Achilles' sword did checke

His bent powre, and brake out his soule. Full in the navill stead

He ript his belly up, and out his entrailes fell, and dead

His breathlesse body. Whence his armes Achilles drew, and   175
    said:

  'Lie there, and prove it dangerous to lift up adverse head

Against Jove's sonnes, although a flood were Ancestor to thee.

Thy vants urg'd him; but I may vant a higher pedigree—

From Jove himselfe. King Peleus was sonne to Æacus;

Infernall Æacus, to Jove; and I, to Peleus.   180

Thunder-voic't Jove farre passeth floods, that onely murmures
    raise

With earth and water, as they runne with tribute to the seas.

And his seede theirs exceeds as farre. A flood, a mightie flood,

Rag'd nere thee now, but with no aide. Jove must not be
    withstood.

King Achelous yeelds to him, and great Oceanus,   185

Whence all floods, all the sea, all founts, wells, all deepes
    humorous,

Fetch their beginnings; yet even he feares Jove's flash and the
    cracke

The racke, or motion of
the clouds, for the
clouds.

His thunder gives, when out of heaven it teares atwo his racke.'

  Thus pluckt he from the shore his lance, and left the waves to
    wash

The wave-sprung entrailes, about which Fausens and other fish   190

Did shole, to nibble at the fat which his sweet kidneyes hid.

This for himselfe; now to his men (the well-rode Pæons) did

His rage contend. All which cold Feare shooke into flight, to
    see

Their Captaine slaine; at whose mazde flight (as much
    enrag'd) flew he.

And then fell all these: Thrasius, Mydon, Astypylus,   195

Great Ophelestes, Ænius, Mnesus, Thersilochus.

And on these many more had falne, unlesse the angry flood

Had tooke the figure of a man and in a whirlepit stood,

Thus speaking to Æacides: 'Past all, powre feeds thy will,

Thou great grandchild of Æacus, and past all, th' art in ill—   200

And gods themselves, confederates, and Jove (the best of gods)

All deaths gives thee, all places, not. Make my shore's periods

To all shore service. In the field let thy field acts run hie,

Not in my waters. My sweet streames choake with mortalitie

Of men slaine by thee. Carkasses so glut me that I faile   205

To powre into the sacred sea my waves. Yet still assaile
Thy cruell forces. Ceasse; amaze affects me with thy rage,

Achilles to Xanthus.

Prince of the people.' He reply'd: 'Shall thy command asswage,
Gulfe-fed Scamander, my free wrath? I'le never leave pursude
Prowd Ilion's slaughters till this hand in her fild walls conclude 210
Her flying forces, and hath tried in single fight the chance
Of warre with Hector; whose event with starke death shall
    advance
One of our conquests.' Thus againe he like a Furie flew
Upon the Troyans; when the flood his sad plaint did pursue

*Xanthus complains
to Apollo.*

To bright Apollo, telling him he was too negligent 215
Of Jove's high charge, importuning by all meanes vehement
His helpe of Troy till latest Even should her blacke shadowes
    poure
On earth's brode breast. In all his worst, Achilles yet from
    shore
Leapt to his middest. Then sweld his waves, then rag'd, then
    boyld againe
Against Achilles. Up flew all, and all the bodies slaine 220
In all his deeps (of which the heapes made bridges to his waves)
He belcht out, roring like a Bull. The unslaine yet he saves
In his blacke whirlepits, vast and deepe. A horrid billow stood
About Achilles. On his shield the violence of the flood
Beate so, it drave him backe and tooke his feet up, his faire 225
    palme
Enforc't to catch into his stay a brode and loftie Elme,

*Note the continued
height and admired
expression of Achilles'
glorie.*

Whose roots he tost up with his hold, and tore up all the
    shore.
With this then he repeld the waves, and those thicke armes it
    bore
He made a bridge to beare him off (for all fell in), when he
Forth from the channell threw himselfe. The rage did terrifie 230
Even his great spirit and made him adde wings to his swiftest
    feet,
And treade the land. And yet not there the flood left his
    retreate,
But thrust his billowes after him, and blackt them all at top,
To make him feare and flie his charge, and set the brode field
    ope
For Troy to scape in. He sprong out a dart's cast, but came on 235
Againe with a redoubl'd force. As when the swiftest flowne
And strong'st of all fowles, Jove's blacke Hawke, the
    huntresse, stoopes upon

A much lov'd Quarrie: so charg'd he. His armes with
    horror rung
Against the blacke waves: yet againe he was so urg'd, he flung
His body from the flood, and fled. And after him againe   240

Simile.

The waves flew roring. As a man that finds a water vaine,
And from some blacke fount is to bring his streames through
    plants and groves,
Goes with his Mattocke, and all checks set to his course
    removes,
When that runnes freely; under it the pibbles all give way
And, where it finds a fall, runnes swift; nor can the leader stay   245
His current then; before himselfe, full pac't, it murmures on:
So, of Achilles evermore the strong flood vantage wonne.
Though most deliver, gods are still above the powres of men.
   As oft as th' able godlike man endevour'd to maintaine
His charge on them that kept the flood (and charg'd as he   250
    would trie
If all the gods inhabiting the brode unreached skie
Could dant his spirit), so oft still the rude waves charg'd
    him round,
Rampt on his shoulders, from whose depth his strength and
    spirit would bound
Up to the free aire vext in soule. And now the vehement flood
Made faint his knees: so overthwart his waves were, they   255
    withstood
All the denyed dust which he wisht; and now was faine to crie,
Casting his eyes to that brode heaven that late he long'd to trie,

Achilles' complaint to
the gods in his
extremitie.

And said: 'O Jove, how am I left? No god vouchsafes to free
Me, miserable man. Helpe now, and after torture me
With any outrage. Would to heaven, Hector (the mightiest   260
Bred in this region) had imbrew'd his javelin in my breast,
That strong might fall by strong. Where now weake water's
    luxurie
Must make my death blush: one heaven-borne shall like a
    hog-herd die,
Drown'd in a durtie torrent's rage. Yet none of you in heaven
I blame for this: but she alone by whom this life was given,   265
That now must die thus. She would still delude me with her
    tales,
Affirming Phœbus' shafts should end within the Troyan walls
My curst beginning.' In this straight, Neptune and Pallas flew
To fetch him off. In men's shapes, both close to his danger
    drew,

And, taking both, both hands, thus spake the shaker of the   270
    world:

Neptune to Achilles,   'Pelides, do not stirre a foot, nor these waves, prowdly curld
Pallas and he rescuing   Against thy bold breast, feare a jote, thou hast us two thy
him.   friends
(Neptune and Pallas), Jove himselfe approving th' aide we
    lend.
Tis nothing as thou fearst with fate; she will not see thee
    drown'd.
This height shall soone downe; thine owne eyes shall see it   275
    set aground.
Be rulde then, weele advise thee well; take not thy hand away
From putting all indifferently to all that it can lay
Upon the Troyans, till the walles of haughtie Ilion
Conclude all in a desperate flight. And when thou hast set gone
The soule of Hector, turne to fleet: our hands shall plant a   280
    wreath
Of endlesse glorie on thy browes.' Thus to the free from death
Both made retreate. He (much impeld by charge the
    godheads gave)
The field, that now was overcome with many a boundlesse wave,
He overcame: on their wild breasts they tost the carkasses
And armes of many a slaughterd man. And now the   285
    winged knees
Of this great Captaine bore aloft; against the flood he flies
With full assault, nor could that god make shrinke
    his rescu'd thies.
Nor shrunke the flood, but, as his foe grew powrefull,
    he grew mad,
Thrust up a billow to the skie and cristall Simois bad

Xanthus to Simois.   To his assistance: 'Simois, hoe, brother,' out he cried,   290
'Come, adde thy current and resist this man halfe deified,
Or Ilion he will pul downe straite; the Troyans cannot stand
A minute longer. Come, assist; and instantly command
All fountaines in thy rule to rise, all torrents to make in
And stuffe thy billowes; with whose height engender   295
    such a din
(With trees torne up and justling stones) as so immane a man
May shrinke beneath us; whose powre thrives, do my powre
    all it can—
He dares things fitter for a god. But nor his forme, nor force,
Nor glorious armes shall profit him: all which, and his
    dead corse,
I vow to rowle up in my sands—nay, burie in my mud—   300

[430]

Nay, in the very sincks of Troy: that, pour'd into my flood,
Shall make him drowning worke enough, and, being drown'd,
    I'le set
A fort of such strong filth on him that Greece shall never get
His bones from it. There, there shall stand Achilles' sepulcher,
And save a buriall for his friends.' This Furie did transferre   305
His high-ridg'd billowes on the Prince, roring with blood
    and fome
And carkasses. The crimson streame did snatch into her wombe
Surprisd Achilles, and her height stood, held up by the hand
Of Jove himselfe. Then Juno cried, and cald (to countermand
This watry Deitie) the god that holds command in fire,   310
Affraid lest that gulf-stomackt flood would satiate his desire

Juno to Vulcan.

On great Achilles: 'Mulciber! my best-lov'd sonne!' she cried,
'Rouse thee: for all the gods conceive this flood thus amplified
Is raisd at thee, and shewes as if his waves would drowne the skie
And put out all the sphere of fire. Haste, helpe thy Emperie.   315
Light flames deepe as his pits. Our selfe the West wind
    and the South
Will call out of the sea, and breathe in either's full-charg'd
    mouth
A storme t' enrage thy fires gainst Troy, which shall
    (in one exhal'd)
Blow flames of sweate about their browes and make their
    armors skald.
Go thou then, and (gainst these winds rise) make worke on   320
    Xanthus' shore
With setting all his trees on fire, and in his owne breast poure
A fervor that shall make it burne. Nor let faire words or threats
Avert thy furie till I speake; and then subdue the heates
Of all thy Blazes.' Mulciber prepar'd a mightie fire,
First in the field usde, burning up the bodies that the ire   325
Of great Achilles reft of soules; the quite-drown'd field it dried

Simile.

And shrunke the flood up. And as fields that have bene
    long time cloide
With catching wether, when their corne lies on the gavill heape,
Are with a constant North wind dried, with which for
    comfort leape
Their hearts that sow'd them: so this field was dride, the   330
    bodies burn'd,
And even the flood into a fire as bright as day was turn'd.
Elmes, willowes, tamrisks were enflam'd; the lote trees,
    sea-grasse reeds

And rushes, with the galingale rootes (of which abundance
  breeds
About the sweet flood) all were fir'd: the gliding fishes flew
Upwards in flames; the groveling Eeles crept upright—   335
  all which slew
Wise Vulcan's unresisted spirit. The flood out of a flame

*Xanthus out of a
flaming whirlepit to
Vulcan.*

Cried to him: 'Ceasse, O Mulciber. No deitie can tame
Thy matchlesse virtue, nor would I (since thou art thus hote)
  strive.
Ceasse then thy strife, let Thetis' sonne with all thy wisht
  hast drive
Even to their gates these Ilians. What toucheth me their aide,   340
Or this Contention?' Thus, in flames, the burning river prayde.

Simile.

And as a Caldron, underput with store of fire, and wrought
With boyling of a well-fed Brawne, up leapes his wave aloft,
Bavins of sere wood urging it and spending flames apace,
Till all the Caldron be engirt with a consuming blaze: 345
So round this flood burn'd, and so sod his sweete and
  tortur'd streames—
Nor could flow forth, bound in the fumes of Vulcan's fierie
  beames.
Who (then not mov'd) his mother's ruth by all his meanes
  he craves,
And askt, why Vulcan should invade and so torment his waves
Past other floods, when his offence rose not to such degree   350
As that of other gods for Troy; and that himselfe would free
Her wrath to it if she were pleasde; and prayd her that
  her sonne
Might be reflected; adding this, that he would nere be wonne
To helpe keepe off the ruinous day in which all Troy
  should burne,
Fir'd by the Grecians. This vow heard, she charg'd her sonne   355
  to turne
His fierie spirits to their homes, and said it was not fit
A god should suffer so for men. Then Vulcan did remit
His so unmeasur'd violence, and backe the pleasant flood
Ranne to his channell. Thus these gods she made friends;
  th' other stood
At weightie difference; both sides ranne together with a sound   360
That Earth resounded, and great heaven about did surrebound.
  Jove heard it, sitting on his hill, and laught to see the gods
Buckle to armes like angry men; and (he pleasde with their ods)
They laid it freely. Of them all thump-buckler Mars began,

Mars against Minerva. And at Minerva with a lance of brasse he headlong ran,   365

These vile words ushering his blowes: 'Thou, dog-flie,
    what's the cause
Thou mak'st gods fight thus? Thy huge heart breakes all
    our peacefull lawes
With thy insatiate shamelesnesse. Rememberst thou the houre
When Diomed charg'd me, and by thee, and thou with all
    thy powre
Took'st lance thy selfe and in all sights rusht on me   370
    with a wound?
Now vengeance fals on thee for all.' This said, the shield
    fring'd round
With fighting Adders, borne by Jove, that not to thunder yeelds,
He clapt his lance on; and this god, that with the bloud
    of fields
Pollutes his godhead, that shield pierst and hurt the
    armed Maid.
But backe she leapt, and with her strong hand rapt   375
    a huge stone, laid
Above the Champaine, blacke and sharpe, that did in old time
    breake
Partitions to men's lands. And that she dusted in the necke
Of that impetuous challenger. Downe to the earth he swayd
And overlaid seven Acres land; his haire was all berayd
With dust and bloud mixt, and his armes rung out.   380
    Minerva laught,

Minerva insults over   And thus insulted: 'O thou foole, yet hast thou not bene taught
Mars.   To know mine eminence? Thy strength opposest thou to mine?
So pay thy mother's furies then, who for these aides of thine
(Ever affoorded perjur'd Troy, Greece ever left) takes spleene
And vowes thee mischiefe.' Thus she turn'd her blew eyes,   385
    when Love's Queen
The hand of Mars tooke, and from earth raisd him with
    thick-drawne breath,
His spirits not yet got up againe. But from the prease of death
Venus.   Kind Aphrodite was his guide. Which Juno seeing, exclam'd:
'Pallas, see, Mars is helpt from field! Dog-flie, his rude tongue
    nam'd
Thy selfe even now; but that his love, that dog-flie, will not   390
    leave
Her old consort. Upon her. Flie.' Minerva did receave
This excitation joyfully and at the Cyprian flew,
Mars and Venus   Strooke with her hard hand her soft breast a blow that overthrew
overthrowne by Pallas.   Both her and Mars, and there both lay together in broad field—
When thus she triumpht: 'So lie all that any succours yeeld   395

To these false Troyans gainst the Greeks—so bold and patient
As Venus (shunning charge of me), and no lesse impotent
Be all their aides than hers to Mars: so short worke would
    be made
In our depopulating Troy (this hardiest to invade
Of all earth's cities).' At this wish white-wristed Juno smil'd.   400
Next Neptune and Apollo stood upon the point of field,
And thus spake Neptune: 'Phœbus! Come, why at the
    lance's end
Stand we two thus? Twill be a shame for us to re-ascend
Jove's golden house, being thus in field and not to fight. Begin,
For tis no gracefull worke for me: thou hast the yonger chin,   405
I older and know more. O foole! what a forgetfull heart
Thou bear'st about thee, to stand here, prest to take
    th' Ilian part
And fight with me! Forgetst thou then what we two, we alone
(Of all the gods), have sufferd here, when proud Laomedon
Enjoyd our service a whole yeare for our agreed reward?   410
Jove in his sway would have it so, and in that yeare I rear'd
This broad brave wall about this towne, that (being a worke
    of mine)
It might be inexpugnable. This service then was thine—
In Ida (that so many hils and curld-head forrests crowne)
To feed his oxen, crooked-shankt and headed like the Moone.   415
But when the much-joy-bringing houres brought terme for
    our reward,
The terrible Laomedon dismist us both and scard
Our high deservings—not alone to hold our promist fee,
But give us threats too. Hands and feete he swore to fetter thee
And sell thee as a slave, dismist farre hence to forreine Iles—   420
Nay more, he would have both our eares. His vowe's breach
    and reviles
Made us part angry with him then. And doest thou gratulate now
Such a king's subjects, or with us not their destruction vow,

Apollo to Neptune.   Even to their chast wives and their babes?' He answerd, he
    might hold
His wisedome litle, if with him (a god) for men he would   425
Maintaine contention—wretched men, that flourish for a time
Like leaves, eate some of that Earth yeelds, and give Earth, in their
    prime,
Their whole selves for it: 'Quickly then let us flie fight for them,
Nor shew it offerd: let themselves beare out their owne extreme.'
    Thus he retir'd, and fear'd to change blowes with his   430
    unkle's hands.

His sister therefore chid him much (the goddesse that commands

In games of hunting) and thus spake: 'Fliest thou, and leav'st
    the field
To Neptune's glorie? And no blowes? O foole! why doest thou
    wield
Thy idle bow? No more my eares shall heare thee vant in skies
Dares to meete Neptune, but I'le tell thy coward's tongue it lies.'   435
    He answerd nothing, yet Jove's wife could put on no such
    raines,

But spake thus loosly: 'How dar'st thou, dog, whom no feares
    containes,
Encounter me? Twill prove a match of hard condition,
Though the great Ladie of the bow and Jove hath set thee downe
For Lion of thy sexe, with gift to slaughter any Dame   440
Thy proud will envies. Yet some Dames will prove th' hadst
    better tame
Wilde Lions upon hils than them. But if this question rests
Yet under judgement in thy thoughts, and that thy mind contests,
I'le make thee know it.' Sodainly, with her left hand she catcht
Both Cynthia's palmes, lockt fingers fast, and with her right   445
    she snatcht
From her faire shoulders her guilt bow, and (laughing) laid it on
About her eares; and every way her turnings seisd upon,
Till all her arrowes scatterd out, her quiver emptied quite.

And as a Dove, that (flying a Hauke) takes to some rocke
    her flight
And in his hollow breasts sits safe, her fate not yet to die: 450
So fled she mourning, and her bow left there. Then Mercurie
His opposite thus undertooke: 'Latona, at no hand
Will I bide combat; tis a worke right dangerous to stand
At difference with the wives of Jove. Go therefore, freely vant
Amongst the deities th' hast subdu'd and made thy combattant   455
Yeeld with plaine powre.' She answer'd not, but gather'd up
    the bow
And shafts falne from her daughter's side, retiring. Up did go
Diana to Jove's starrie hall, her incorrupted vaile
Trembling about her, so she shooke. Phœbus (lest Troy should
    faile
Before her Fate) flew to her wals; the other deities flew   460
Up to Olympus, some enrag'd, some glad. Achilles slew

Both men and horse of Ilion. And as a citie, fir'd,
Casts up a heate that purples heaven, Clamors and shriekes
    expir'd
In every corner, toile to all, to many, miserie,

Which fire th' incensed gods let fall; Achilles so let flie   465
Rage on the Troyans, toiles and shriekes as much by him imposde.
Old Priam in his sacred towre stood, and the flight disclosde
Of his forc't people, all in rout, and not a stroke return'd
By fled Resistance. His eyes saw in what a furie burnd

Priam's amaze at
Achilles.

The sonne of Peleus, and downe went weeping from the towre   470
To all the port-guards, and their Chiefes told of his flying powre,
Commanding th' opening of the ports, but not to let their hands
Stirre from them, for Æacides would poure in with his bands.
'Destruction comes. O shut them straight, when we are in,'
    he praid,
'For not our walls, I feare, will checke this violent man.'   475
    This said,
Off lifted they the barres, the ports hal'd open, and they gave
Safetie her entrie with the host; which yet they could not save
Had not Apollo sallied out and strooke Destruction
(Brought by Achilles in their neckes) backe; when they right upon
The ports bore all, drie, dustie, spent; and on their   480
    shoulders rode
Rabide Achilles with his lance, still Glorie being the gode
That prickt his Furie. Then the Greeks high-ported Ilion
Had seiz'd, had not Apollo stird Antenor's famous sonne,

Agenor spirited by
Apollo.

Divine Agenor, and cast in an undertaking spirit
To his bold bosome, and himselfe stood by to strengthen it   485
And keepe the heavie hand of death from breaking in. The god
Stood by him, leaning on a beach, and cover'd his abode
With night-like darknesse; yet for all the spirit he inspir'd,
When that great citie-racer's force his thoughts strooke, he retir'd,
Stood, and went on, a world of doubts still falling in his way—   490

Agenor's discourse with
himselfe.

When (angry with himselfe) he said: 'Why suffer I this stay
In this so strong need to go on? If, like the rest, I flie,
Tis his best weapon to give chace, being swift, and I should die
Like to a coward. If I stand, I fall too. These two wayes
Please not my purpose; I would live. What if I suffer these   495
Still to be routed, and (my feete affoording further length)
Passe all these fields of Ilion till Ida's sylvane strength
And steepe heights shroud me, and at Even refresh me in
    the flood
And turne to Ilion? O my soule, why drown'st thou in the blood
Of these discourses? If this course that talkes of further flight   500
I give my feete, his feete, more swift, have more ods. Get he sight
Of that passe, I passe least; for pace, and length of pace, his thies
Will stand out all men. Meete him then; my steele hath faculties

Of powre to pierce him; his great breast but one soule holds,
    and that
Death claimes his right in (all men say). But he holds speciall   505
    state

Jove's bountie serves   In Jove's high bountie: that's past man, that every way will hold,
all men all wayes.   And that serves all men every way.' This last heart made
    him bold
To stand Achilles, and stird up a mightie mind to blowes.

Simile.   And as a Panther (having heard the hounds' traile) doth disclose
Her freckl'd forhead, and stares forth from out some   510
    deepe-growne wood
To trie what strength dares her abroad; and, when her
    fierie blood
The hounds have kindl'd, no quench serves of love to live or
    feare;
Though strooke, though wounded, though quite through she
    feels the mortal speare,
But till the man's close strength she tries, or strowes earth with
    his dart,
She puts her strength out: so it far'd with brave Agenor's hart;   515
And till Achilles he had prov'd, no thoughts, no deeds, once stird
His fixed foote. To his broad breast his round shield he preferd,
And up his arme went with his aime, his voice out, with this crie:

Agenor to Achilles.   'Thy hope is too great, Peleus' sonne, this day to shew thine eye
Troy's Ilion at thy foote. O foole! the Greeks with much   520
    more woes,
More than are sufferd yet, must buy great Ilion's overthrowes.
We are within her many strong, that for our parents' sakes,
Our wives and children, will save Troy, and thou (though he
    that makes
Thy name so terrible) shalt make a sacrifice to her
With thine owne ruines.' Thus he threw, nor did his   525
    javelin erre,
But strooke his foe's leg neare his knee; the fervent steele did ring
Against his tin greaves and leapt backe. The fire's strong-handed
    king
Gave vertue of repulse; and then Æacides assail'd
Divine Agenor, but in vaine; Apollo's powre prevail'd,
And rapt Agenor from his reach, whom quietly he plac't   530
Without the skirmish, casting mists to save from being chac't
His tenderd person, and (he gone), to give his souldiers scape,
The deitie turn'd Achilles still by putting on the shape
Of him he thirsted; evermore he fed his eye, and fled,
And he with all his knees pursu'd. So cunningly he led   535

[437]

That still he would be neare his reach to draw his rage with hope,
Farre from the conflict, to the flood, maintaining still the scope
Of his attraction. In meane time, the other frighted powres
Came to the citie, comforted, when Troy and all her towres
Strooted with fillers; none would stand to see who staid without,   540
Who scapt, and who came short. The ports cleft to receive
      the rout
That pour'd it selfe in. Every man was for himselfe—most fleete,
Most fortunate. Who ever scapt, his head might thanke his feete.

The End of the One and Twentieth Booke

THE TWENTY-SECOND BOOKE

of

HOMER'S ILIADS

THE ARGUMENT

All Troyans housd but Hector, onely he,
Keepes field and undergoes th' extremitie.
Æacides assaulting, Hector flies.
Minerva stayes him, he resists, and dies.
Achilles to his chariot doth enforce   5
And to the navall station drags his corse.

Another Argument

Hector (in Chi*) to death is done,*
By powre of Peleus' angry sonne.

Thus (chac't like Hinds) the Ilians tooke time to drinke
    and eate
And to refresh them, getting off the mingl'd dust and sweate,
And good strong rampires on in stead. The Greeks then cast
    their shields
Aloft their shoulders; and now Fate their neare invasion yeelds
Of those tough wals, her deadly hand compelling Hector's stay   5
Before Troy at the Scæan ports. Achilles still made way

Apollo to Achilles.   At Phœbus, who his bright head turn'd, and askt: 'Why,
    Peleus' sonne,
Pursu'st thou (being a man) a god? Thy rage hath never done.
Acknowledge not thine eyes my state? Esteemes thy mind
    no more
Thy honor in the chase of Troy, but puts my chace before   10
Their utter conquest? They are all now housde in Ilion,
While thou hunt'st me. What wishest thou? My bloud will
    never runne

Achilles to Apollo.   On thy proud javelin.' 'It is thou,' repli'd Æacides,

'That putst dishonor thus on me, thou worst of deities.
Thou turndst me from the walls, whose ports had never 15
    entertaind
Numbers now enter'd, over whom thy saving hand hath raign'd
And robd my honor. And all is, since all thy actions stand
Past feare of reckoning. But held I the measure in my hand,
It should affoord thee deare-bought scapes.' Thus with elated
    spirits
(Steed-like, that at Olympus' games weares garlands for his 20
    merits
And rattles home his chariot, extending all his pride)
Achilles so parts with the god. When aged Priam spide
The great Greek come, sphear'd round with beames, and
    show'ng as if the star
Surnam'd Orion's hound, that springs in Autumne and sends
    farre
His radiance through a world of starres, of all whose beames 25
    his owne
Cast greatest splendor, the midnight that renders them most
    showne
Then being their foile, and on their points cure-passing
    Fevers then
Come shaking downe into the joynts of miserable men—
As this were falne to earth, and shot along the field his raies,

Priam's fright at the sight of Achilles.

Now towards Priam (when he saw in great Æacides) 30
Out flew his tender voice in shriekes, and with raisde hands
    he smit
His reverend head, then up to heaven he cast them, shewing it
What plagues it sent him, downe againe then threw them
    to his sonne,
To make him shun them. He now stood without steepe Ilion,
Thirsting the combat, and to him thus miserably cride 35

Priam to Hector.

The kind old king: 'O Hector! flie this man, this homicide,
That strait will stroy thee. Hee's too strong, and would to heaven
    he were
As strong in heaven's love as in mine! Vultures and dogs
    should teare
His prostrate carkasse, all my woes quencht with his bloudy
    spirits.
He has robd me of many sonnes and worthy, and their merits 40
Sold to farre Ilands. Two of them (aye me) I misse but now;
They are not enterd, nor stay here. Laothoe, O twas thou,
O Queene of women, from whose wombe they breath'd. O did
    the tents

Detaine them onely, brasse and gold would purchase safe events
To their sad durance: tis within. Old Altes (yong in fame)   45
Gave plentie for his daughter's dowre. But if they fed the flame
Of this man's furie, woe is me, woe to my wretched Queene.
But in our state's woe their two deaths will nought at all be seene,
So thy life quit them. Take the towne; retire, deare sonne,
     and save
Troy's husbands and her wives, nor give thine owne life   50
     to the grave
For this man's glorie. Pitie me—me, wretch, so long alive,
Whom in the doore of Age Jove keepes, that so he may deprive
My being in Fortune's utmost curse, to see the blackest thred
Of this life's miseries—my sonnes slaine, my daughters ravished,
Their resting chambers sackt, their babes torne from them,   55
     on their knees
Pleading for mercie, themselves dragd to Grecian slaveries
(And all this drawne through my red eyes.) Then last of all
     kneele I,
Alone, all helplesse, at my gates before my enemie,
That (ruthlesse) gives me to my dogs—all the deformitie
Of age discover'd. And all this thy death (sought wilfully)   60
Will poure on me. A faire yong man at all parts it beseemes
(Being bravely slaine) to lie all gasht and weare the worst
     extremes
Of warre's most crueltie; no wound, of whatsoever ruth,
But is his ornament. But I, a man so farre from youth,
White head, white-bearded, wrinkl'd, pin'd, all shames must   65
     shew the eye.
Live; prevent this then, this most shame of all man's miserie.'
     Thus wept the old king, and tore off his white haire;
     yet all these
Retir'd not Hector. Hecuba then fell upon her knees,
Stript nak't her bosome, shew'd her breasts and bad him
     reverence them
And pitie her—if ever she had quieted his exclaime,   70
He would ceasse hers and take the towne, not tempting the
     rude field
When all had left it: 'Thinke,' said she, 'I gave thee life to yeeld
My life recomfort; thy rich wife shall have no rites of thee,
Nor do thee rites: our teares shall pay thy corse no obsequie,
Being ravisht from us, Grecian dogs nourisht with what I nurst.'   75
     Thus wept both these, and to his ruth proposde the utmost
     worst

[441]

Of what could chance them; yet he staid. And now drew deadly
    neare
Mightie Achilles; yet he still kept deadly station there.

*A Simile expressing
how Hector stood
Achilles.*

Looke how a Dragon, when she sees a traveller bent upon
Her breeding den, her bosome fed with fell contagion,   80
Gathers her forces, sits him firme, and at his nearest pace
Wraps all her Caverne in her folds, and thrusts a horrid face
Out at his entrie: Hector so, with unextinguisht spirit,
Stood great Achilles, stird no foote, but at the prominent turret
Bent to his bright shield, and resolv'd to beare falne heaven   85
    on it.
Yet all this resolute abode did not so truly fit
His free election, but he felt a much more galling spurre
To the performance with conceit of what he should incurre
Entring, like others, for this cause; to which, he thus gave way:

Hector's discourse.

   'O me, if I shall take the towne, Polydamas will lay   90
This flight and all this death on me, who counseld me to leade
My powres to Troy this last blacke night, when so I saw
    make head
Incenst Achilles. I yet staid, though (past all doubt) that course
Had much more profited than mine—which (being by so much
    worse
As comes to all our flight and death) my folly now I feare   95
Hath bred this scandall. All our towne now burnes my ominous
    eare
With whispering: Hector's selfe conceit hath cast away his host.
And (this true) this extremitie that I relie on most
Is best for me; stay and retire with this man's life, or die
Here for our citie with renowme, since all else fled but I.   100
And yet one way cuts both these wayes. What if I hang my shield,
My helme and lance here on these wals, and meete in humble
    field
Renowm'd Achilles, offering him Helen and all the wealth
What ever in his hollow keeles bore Alexander's stealth
For both th' Atrides? For the rest, what ever is possest   105
In all this citie, knowne or hid, by oath shall be confest
Of all our citizens, of which one halfe the Greeks shall have,
One halfe themselves. But why, lov'd soule, would these
    suggestions save
Thy state still in me? I'le not sue, nor would he grant, but I
(Mine armes cast off) should be assur'd a woman's death to die.   110
To men of oke and rocke, no words; virgins and youths
    talke thus—

Virgins and youths that love and wooe. There's other warre
  with us.
What blowes and conflicts urge, we crie hates and defiances,
And with the garlands these trees beare trie which hand Jove
  will blesse.'

*Achilles' dreadfull
approch to Hector.*

These thoughts emploid his stay; and now Achilles comes;   115
  now neare
His Mars-like presence terribly came brandishing his speare.
His right arme shooke it; his bright armes like day came
  glittering on,
Like fire-light, or the light of heaven shot from the rising Sun.
This sight outwrought discourse; cold Feare shooke Hector from
  his stand.
No more stay now; all ports were left; he fled in feare the hand   120
Of that Feare-master, who, hauk-like, aire's swiftest passenger,
That holds a timorous Dove in chace, and with command doth
  beare
His fierie onset; the Dove hasts; the Hauke comes whizzing on;
This way and that he turnes and winds and cuffes the Pigeon,
And till he trusse it his great spirit layes hote charge on his   125
  wing:
So urg'd Achilles Hector's flight; so still Feare's point did sting
His troubl'd spirit. His knees wrought hard; along the wall
  he flew
In that faire chariot way that runnes beneath the towre of view

*The pleasing
description of two
springs under the walls
of Troy.*

And Troy's wilde fig-tree, till they reacht where those two
  mother springs
Of deepe Scamander pour'd abroad their silver murmurings—   130
One warme and casts out fumes as fire, the other, cold as snow
Or haile dissolv'd. And when the Sunne made ardent sommer
  glow,
There water's concrete cristall shin'd, neare which were cisternes
  made
All pav'd and cleare, where Troyan wives and their faire
  daughters had
Landrie for their fine linnen weeds, in times of cleanly Peace   135
Before the Grecians brought their siege. These Captaines noted
  these,

*Hector's flight from
Achilles, and his chace
of Hector.*

One flying, th' other in pursuite; a strong man flew before,
A stronger follow'd him by farre, and close up to him bore.
Both did their best, for neither now ranne for a sacrifice,
Or for the sacrificer's hide (our runners' usuall prise).   140
These ranne for tame-horse Hector's soule. And as two running
  Steeds

Backt in some set race for a game, that tries their swiftest speeds
(A tripod or a woman given for some man's funerals):

Up and downe the wals,
it is to be understood. Such speed made these men, and on foote ranne thrice about
    the wals.

The gods beheld them, all much mov'd; and Jove said: 145
  'O ill sight!

A man I love much I see forc't in most unworthy flight

Jove's griefe for Hector. About great Ilion. My heart grieves; he paid so many vowes
With thighes of sacrificed beeves, both on the loftie browes
Of Ida and in Ilion's height. Consult we; shall we free
His life from death, or give it now t' Achilles' victorie?'   150

Pallas against Hector's   Minerva answer'd: 'Alter Fate? One long since markt for death
preservation. Now take from death? Do thou; but know he still shall runne
    beneath

Our other censures.' 'Be it then,' replide the Thunderer,
'My lov'd Tritonia, at thy will; in this I will preferre
Thy free intention; worke it all.' Then stoopt she from the skie 155
To this great combat. Peleus' sonne pursu'd incessantly

Simile. Still-flying Hector. As a Hound that, having rouz'd a Hart,
Although he tappish ne're so oft and every shrubbie part
Attempts for strength and trembles in, the Hound doth still
    pursue
So close that not a foote he failes, but hunts it still at view: 160
So plied Achilles Hector's steps. As oft as he assail'd
The Dardan ports and towres for strength (to fetch from thence
    some aid
With winged shafts), so oft forc't he amends of pace, and stept
Twixt him and all his hopes, and still upon the field he kept

A most ingenious His utmost turnings to the towne. And yet, as in a dreame, 165
Simile, used (as all our One thinkes he gives another chace, when such a fain'd extreame
Homer besides) by Possesseth both that he in chace the chacer cannot flie,
Virgil, but this as a Nor can the chacer get to hand his flying enemie:
translator meerly. So nor Achilles' chace could reach the flight of Hector's pace,
Nor Hector's flight enlarge it selfe of swift Achilles' chace. 170
  But how chanc't this? How, all this time, could Hector beare
    the knees
Of fierce Achilles with his owne, and keepe off Destinies,
If Phœbus (for his last and best) through all that course had
    fail'd
To adde his succours to his nerves, and (as his foe assail'd)
Neare and within him fed his scape? Achilles yet well knew 175
His knees would fetch him, and gave signes to some friends
    (making shew
Of shooting at him) to forbeare, lest they detracted so

[444]

From his full glorie in first wounds, and in the overthrow
Make his hand last. But when they reacht the fourth time the
　　two founts,
Then Jove his golden skoles weigh'd up, and tooke the last　　180
　　accounts
Of Fate for Hector, putting in for him and Peleus' sonne
Two fates of bitter death—of which high heaven receiv'd the one,
The other hell: so low declin'd the light of Hector's life.
Then Phœbus left him, when warre's Queene came to resolve
　　the strife

Pallas to Achilles.　　In th' other's knowledge: 'Now,' said she, 'Jove-lov'd Æacides,　　185
I hope at last to make Renowme performe a brave accesse
To all the Grecians; we shall now lay low this champion's height,
Though never so insatiate was his great heart of fight.
Nor must he scape our pursuite still, though at the feete of Jove
Apollo bowes into a sphere, soliciting more love　　190
To his most favour'd. Breath thee then, stand firme; my selfe
　　will hast
And hearten Hector to change blowes.' She went, and he stood
　　fast,
Lean'd on his lance, and much was joy'd that single strokes
　　should trie
This fadging conflict. Then came close the changed deitie
To Hector, like Deiphobus in shape and voice, and said:　　195

Pallas like Deiphobus　　'O brother, thou art too much urg'd to be thus combatted
to Hector.　　About our owne wals; let us stand and force to a retreat
Th' insulting Chaser.' Hector joy'd at this so kind deceit,

Hector to Pallas for　　And said: 'O good Deiphobus, thy love was most before
Deiphobus.　　(Of all my brothers) deare to me; but now exceeding more　　200
It costs me honor, that, thus urg'd, thou com'st to part the
　　charge
Of my last fortunes; other friends keepe towne and leave
　　at large
My rackt endevours.' She replide: 'Good brother, tis most true;
One after other, King and Queene and all our friends did sue
(Even on their knees) to stay me there, such tremblings shake　　205
　　them all
With this man's terror: but my mind so griev'd to see our wall
Girt with thy chases that to death I long'd to urge thy stay.
Come, fight we, thirstie of his bloud; no more let's feare to lay
Cost on our lances, but approve if, bloudied with our spoiles,
He can beare glorie to their fleete, or shut up all their toiles　　210
In his one sufferance on thy lance.' With this deceit, she led,

[445]

Hector to Achilles.

And (both come neare) thus Hector spake: 'Thrice I have compassed
This great towne, Peleus' sonne, in flight, with aversation
That out of Fate put off my steps; but now all flight is flowne,
The short course set up—death or life. Our resolutions yet   215
Must shun all rudenesse, and the gods before our valour set
For use of victorie; and, they being worthiest witnesses
Of all vowes, since they keepe vowes best, before their deities
Let vowes of fit respect passe both, when Conquest hath bestow'd
Her wreath on either. Here I vow no furie shall be show'd   220
That is not manly on thy corse, but, having spoil'd thy armes,
Resigne thy person—which sweare thou.' These faire and temperate termes
Farre fled Achilles; his browes bent, and out flew this reply:

*Achilles' sterne reply
to Hector.*

'Hector, thou onely pestilence in all mortalitie
To my sere spirits, never set the point twixt thee and me   225
Any conditions; but as farre as men and Lions flie
All termes of covenant, lambes and wolves, in so farre opposite state
(Impossible for love t' attone) stand we, till our soules satiate
The god of souldiers. Do not dreame that our disjunction can
Endure condition. Therefore now all worth that fits a man   230
Call to thee, all particular parts that fit a souldier;
And they all this include (besides the skill and spirit of warre)
Hunger for slaughter, and a hate that eates thy heart to eate
Thy foe's heart. This stirs, this supplies in death the killing heate;
And all this needst thou. No more flight. Pallas Athenia   235
Will quickly cast thee to my lance. Now, now together draw
All griefes for vengeance, both in me and all my friends late dead

*Achilles' first encounter
with Hector.*

That bled thee, raging with thy lance.' This said, he brandished
His long lance, and away it sung; which Hector, giving view,
Stoupt low, stood firme (foreseeing it best) and quite it overflew, 240

Pallas.

Fastening on earth. Athenia drew it and gave her friend,
Unseene of Hector. Hector then thus spake: 'Thou want'st thy end,
God-like Achilles; now I see thou hast not learn'd my fate
Of Jove at all, as thy high words would bravely intimate.
Much tongue affects thee; cunning words well serve thee to   245
prepare
Thy blowes with threats, that mine might faint with want of spirit to dare.
But my backe never turnes with breath; it was not borne to beare

Burthens of wounds; strike home before; drive at my breast
    thy speare
As mine at thine shall, and trie then if heavens will favor thee
With scape of my lance. O would Jove would take it after me,   250
And make thy bosome take it all, an easie end would crowne
Our difficult warres were thy soule fled, thou most bane of
    our towne.'

Hector at Achilles.   Thus flew his dart, toucht at the midst of his vast shield, and
    flew
A huge way from it; but his heart wrath enterd with the view
Of that hard scape, and heavie thoughts strooke through him   255
    when he spide
His brother vanisht, and no lance beside left. Out he cride:

Hector's amaze with   'Deiphobus! another lance.' Lance nor Deiphobus
the deceit of Pallas.   Stood neare his call. And then his mind saw all things ominous,
And thus suggested: 'Woe is me! The gods have cald, and I
Must meete Death here. Deiphobus I well hop't had bene by   260
With his white shield; but our strong wals shield him, and
    this deceit
Flowes from Minerva. Now, O now, ill death comes; no more
    flight,
No more recoverie. O Jove, this hath bene otherwise;
Thy bright sonne and thy selfe have set the Greeks a greater prise
Of Hector's bloud than now, of which (even jealous) you had   265
    care.
But Fate now conquers; I am hers. And yet not she shall share
In my renowme; that life is left to every noble spirit,
And that some great deed shall beget that all lives shall inherit.'

The last encounter of   Thus forth his sword flew, sharpe and broad, and bore a
Achilles and Hector.   deadly weight,
With which he rusht in. And looke how an Eagle from her   270
    height
Stoopes to the rapture of a Lambe, or cuffes a timorous Hare:
So fell in Hector, and at him Achilles; his mind's fare
Was fierce and mightie; his shield cast a Sun-like radiance,
Helme nodded, and his foure plumes shooke; and, when he
    raisde his lance,
Up Hesperus rose mongst th' evening starres. His bright and   275
    sparkling eies
Lookt through the body of his foe, and sought through all
    that prise
The next way to his thirsted life. Of all wayes only one
Appear'd to him; and that was where th' unequall winding bone

[447]

That joynes the shoulders and the necke had place, and where there lay

The speeding way to death; and there his quicke eye could display   280

The place it sought, even through those armes his friend Patroclus wore,

When Hector slue him. There he aim'd, and there his javelin tore

Sterne passage quite through Hector's necke, yet mist it so his throte,

Hector wounded to death. Achilles' insultation. It gave him powre to change some words; but downe to earth it got

His fainting bodie. Then triumpht divine Æacides: 285

'Hector,' said he, 'thy heart supposde that in my friend's deceasse

Thy life was safe, my absent arme not car'd for. Foole! he left

One at the fleete that better'd him, and he it is that reft

Thy strong knees thus. And now the dogs and fowles in foulest use

Shall teare thee up, thy corse exposde to all the Greeks' abuse.'   290

Hector's dying request to Achilles. He, fainting, said: 'Let me implore, even by thy knees and soule

And thy great parents; do not see a crueltie so foule

Inflicted on me. Brasse and gold receive at any rate

And quit my person, that the Peeres and Ladies of our state

May tombe it, and to sacred fire turne thy prophane decrees.'   295

Achilles' inflexibilitie. 'Dog,' he replied, 'urge not my ruth by parents, soule, nor knees.

I would to God that any rage would let me eate thee raw,

Slic't into peeces, so beyond the right of any law

I tast thy merits. And beleeve it flies the force of man

To rescue thy head from the dogs. Give all the gold they can,   300

If ten or twentie times so much as friends would rate thy price

Were tenderd here, with vowes of more, to buy the cruelties

I here have vow'd, and, after that, thy father with his gold

Would free thy selfe—all that should faile to let thy mother hold

Solemnities of death with thee and do thee such a grace   305

To mourne thy whole corse on a bed—which peecemeale I'le deface

With fowles and dogs.' He (dying) said: 'I (knowing thee well) foresaw

Thy now tried tyrannie, nor hop't for any other law,

Of nature, or of nations: and that feare forc't much more

Than death my flight, which never toucht at Hector's foote before.   310

*Hector's prophecy of
Achilles' death.*

A soule of iron informes thee. Marke, what vengeance th' equall
  fates
Will give me of thee for this rage, when in the Scæan gates
Phœbus and Paris meete with thee.' Thus death's hand closde
  his eyes,
His soule flying his faire lims to hell, mourning his destinies
To part so with his youth and strength. Thus dead, thus   315
  Thetis' sonne
His prophecie answer'd: 'Die thou now; when my short thred
  is spunne,
I'le beare it as the will of Jove.' This said, his brazen speare
He drew and stucke by: then his armes (that all embrewed were)
He spoil'd his shoulders off. Then all the Greeks ran in to him

*The Greeks'
admiration of Hector's
person being slaine.*

To see his person, and admir'd his terror-stirring lim.   320
Yet none stood by that gave no wound to his so goodly forme,
When each to other said: 'O Jove, he is not in the storme
He came to fleete in with his fire; he handles now more soft.'

*Achilles to the
Grecians.*

  'O friends,' said sterne Æacides, 'now that the gods have
  brought
This man thus downe, I'le freely say he brought more bane to   325
  Greece
Than all his aiders. Trie we then (thus arm'd at every peece,
And girding all Troy with our host) if now their hearts will
  leave
Their citie cleare, her cleare stay slaine, and all their lives
  receave,
Or hold yet, Hector being no more. But why use I a word
Of any act but what concernes my friend? Dead, undeplor'd,   330
Unsepulcherd, he lies at fleete, unthought on; never houre
Shall make his dead state while the quicke enjoyes me and
  this powre
To move these movers. Though in hell men say that such as die
Oblivion seiseth, yet in hell in me shall Memorie
Hold all her formes still of my friend. Now, youths of Greece,   335
  to fleete
Beare we this body, Pæans sing, and all our navie greete
With endlesse honor. We have slaine Hector, the period

*Achilles' tyranny to
Hector's person, which
we lay on his fury and
love to his slaine
friend, for whom
himselfe living
sufferd so much.*

Of all Troy's glorie, to whose worth all vow'd as to a god.'
  This said, a worke not worthy him he set to. Of both feete
He bor'd the nerves through from the heele to th' ankle, and   340
  then knit
Both to his chariot with a thong of whitleather, his head
Trailing the center. Up he got to chariot, where he laid

The armes repurchac't, and scourg'd on his horse, that freely
    flew.
A whirlewind made of startl'd dust drave with them as they drew;
With which were all his black-browne curls knotted in heapes   345
    and fil'd.
And there lay Troy's late Gracious, by Jupiter exil'd
To all disgrace, in his owne land and by his parents seene.
   When (like her sonne's head) all with dust Troy's miserable
      Queene
Distain'd her temples, plucking off her honor'd haire, and tore

*Priam and Hecuba's
miserable plight for
Hector.*

Her royall garments, shrieking out. In like kind, Priam bore   350
His sacred person, like a wretch that never saw good day,
Broken with outcries. About both the people prostrate lay,
Held downe with Clamor, all the towne vail'd with a cloud of
    teares.
Ilion with all his tops on fire and all the massacres
Left for the Greeks could put on lookes of no more overthrow   355
Than now fraid life. And yet the king did all their lookes
    outshow.
The wretched people could not beare his soveraigne
    wretchednesse,
Plaguing himselfe so, thrusting out and praying all the
    preasse
To open him the Dardan ports, that he alone might fetch
His dearest sonne in. And (all fil'd with trembling) did   360
    beseech

Priam to his friends.

Each man by name, thus: 'Loved friends, be you content; let me
(Though much ye grieve) be that poore meane to our sad
    remedie
Now in our wishes. I will go and pray this impious man
(Author of horrors), making proofe if age's reverence can
Excite his pitie. His owne sire is old like me, and he   365
That got him to our griefes perhaps may (for my likenesse) be
Meane for our ruth to him. Ahlas, you have no cause of cares
Compar'd with me—I many sonnes grac't with their freshest
    yeares
Have lost by him, and all their deaths in slaughter of this one
(Afflicted man) are doubl'd: this will bitterly set gone   370
My soule to hell. O would to heaven I could but hold him dead
In these pin'd armes: then teares on teares might fall till all
    were shed
In common fortune. Now amaze their naturall course doth stop
And pricks a mad veine.' Thus he mourn'd, and with him all
    brake ope

[450]

Their store of sorrowes. The poore Queene amongst the women   375
  wept,

 Turn'd into anguish: 'O my sonne,' she cried out, 'why still kept
 Patient of horrors is my life, when thine is vanished?
My dayes thou glorifiedst, my nights rung of some honour'd deed
Done by the virtues—joy to me, profite to all our care.
All made a god of thee, and thou mad'st them all that they   380
  are—
Now under fate, now dead.' These two thus vented as they
  could
Their sorrowe's furnace, Hector's wife not having yet bene told
So much as of his stay without. She in her chamber close
Sate at her Loome: a peece of worke, grac't with a both sides
  glosse,
Strew'd curiously with varied flowres, her pleasure was; her care   385
To heate a Caldron for her Lord to bath him, turn'd from warre—
Of which she chiefe charge gave her maides. Poore Dame,
  she little knew
How much her cares lackt of his case. But now the Clamor flew
Up to her turret: then she shooke; her worke fell from her
  hand,
And up she started, cald her maides, she needs must understand   390
That ominous outcrie. 'Come,' said she, 'I heare through all
  this crie
My mother's voyce shrieke; to my throte my heart bounds.
  Ecstasie
Utterly alters me: some fate is neare the haplesse sonnes
Of fading Priam. Would to god my words' suspicions
No eare had heard yet! O I feare, and that most heartily,   395
That with some stratageme the sonne of Peleus hath put by
The wall of Ilion my Lord, and (trusty of his feet)
Obtaind the chase of him alone, and now the curious heate
Of his still desperate spirit is cool'd. It let him never keep
In guard of others; before all his violent foote must step,   400
Or his place forfeited he held.' Thus furie-like she went,
Two women (as she will'd) at hand, and made her quicke ascent
Up to the towre and preasse of men, her spirit in uprore. Round
She cast her greedy eye, and saw her Hector slaine and bound
T' Achilles' chariot, manlesly dragg'd to the Grecian fleet.   405
Blacke night strooke through her, under her Trance tooke away
  her feet,
And backe she shrunke with such a sway that off her head-tire
  flew,
Her Coronet, Call, Ribands, Vaile that golden Venus threw

On her white shoulders that high day when warre-like Hector
    wonne
Her hand in nuptials in the Court of king Eetion,   410
And that great dowre then given with her. About her on their
    knees
Her husband's sisters, brothers' wives, fell round, and by
    degrees
Recoverd her. Then, when againe her respirations found
Free passe (her mind and spirit met), these thoughts her words
    did sound:

Andromache's   'O Hector, O me cursed dame, both borne beneath one fate,   415
complaint for Hector. Thou here, I in Cilician Thebes, where Placus doth elate
                  His shadie forehead, in the Court where king Eetion
                  (Haplesse) begot unhappy me—which would he had not done
                  To live past thee. Thou now art div'd to Pluto's gloomie
                    throne,
Sunke through the coverts of the earth, I in a hell of mone   420
Left here thy widdow—one poore babe borne to unhappy both
Who thou leav'st helplesse, as he thee, he borne to all the
    wroth
Of woe and labour. Lands left him will others seise upon:
The Orphan day of all friends' helps robs every mother's son.
An Orphan all men suffer sad; his eyes stand still with teares;   425
Need tries his father's friends, and failes. Of all his favourers
If one the cup gives, tis not long; the wine he finds in it
Scarce moists his palate: if he chance to gaine the grace to sit,
Surviving father's sonnes repine, use contumelies, strike,
Bid: 'Leave us; where's thy father's place?' He (weeping with   430
    dislike)
Retires to me. To me, ahlas, Astyanax is he
Borne to these miseries—he that late fed on his father's knee,
To whom all knees bow'd, daintiest fare apposde him, and, when
    Sleepe
Lay on his temples, his cries still'd (his heart even laid in steepe
Of all things precious), a soft bed, a carefull nurse's armes   435
Tooke him to guardiance. But now as huge a world of harmes
Lies on his suffrance. Now thou wantst thy father's hand to
    friend,
O my Astyanax—O my Lord, thy hand that did defend
These gates of Ilion, these long walls by thy arme measur'd still,
Amply and onely. Yet at fleete thy naked corse must fill   440
Vile wormes when dogs are satiate, farre from thy parents' care,
Farre from those funerall ornaments that thy mind would
    prepare

(So sodaine being the chance of armes), ever expecting death.

Which taske (though my heart would not serve t' employ
   my hands beneath)

Andromache wrought
many funerall
ornaments for Hector
before his death.

I made my women yet performe. Many and much in price   445
Were those integuments they wrought t' adorne thy Exequies;
Which, since they flie thy use, thy Corse not laid in their
   attire,
Thy sacrifice they shall be made; these hands in mischievous fire
Shall vent their vanities. And yet (being consecrate to thee)
They shall be kept for citizens and their faire wives to see.'   450
   Thus spake shee weeping; all the dames, endevouring to
   cheare
Her desert state (fearing their owne), wept with her teare for
   teare.

The End of the Two and Twentieth Booke

THE TWENTY-THIRD BOOKE

of

HOMER'S ILIADS

THE ARGUMENT

Achilles orders Justs of exequies
For his Patroclus, and doth sacrifise
Twelve Troyan Princes, most lov'd hounds and horse,
And other offerings to the honour'd Corse.
He institutes, besides, a funerall game,   5
Where Diomed, for horse-race, wins the fame,
For foote, Ulysses; others otherwise
Strive and obtaine, and end the exequies.

Another Argument

Psi sings the rites of the decease
Ordaind by great Æacides.

Thus mourn'd all Troy: but when at fleet and Hellespontus'
    shore
The Greeks arriv'd each to his ship, onely the Conqueror

Achilles to his
Myrmidons.
Kept undisperst his Myrmidons, and said: 'Lov'd countrimen,
Disjoyne not we chariots and horse, but (bearing hard our reine)
With state of both march soft and close, and mourne about the   5
    corse.
Tis proper honour to the dead. Then take we out our horse,
When with our friend's kind woe our hearts have felt delight to
    do
A virtuous soule right, and then sup.' This said, all full of woe
Circl'd the Corse. Achilles led, and thrise about him close
All bore their goodly-coted horse. Amongst all, Thetis rose   10
And stirr'd up a delight in griefe, till all their armes with teares
And all the sands were wet—so much they lov'd that Lord of
    Feares.

Then to the center fell the Prince, and (putting in the breast
Of his slaine friend his slaughtring hands) began to all the rest

*Achilles to the person
of Patroclus.*

Words to their teares: 'Rejoyce,' said he, 'O my Patroclus, thou   15
Courted by Dis now, now I pay to thy late overthrow
All my revenges vow'd before. Hector lies slaughterd here
Dragd at my chariot, and our dogs shall all in peeces teare
His hated lims. Twelve Troyan youths, borne of their noblest
    straines,
I tooke alive, and (yet enrag'd) will emptie all their vaines   20
Of vitall spirits, sacrifisde before thy heape of fire.'
   This said, a worke unworthy him he put upon his ire,
And trampl'd Hector under foote at his friend's feet. The rest
Disarm'd, tooke horse from chariot, and all to sleepe addrest
At his blacke vessell. Infinite were those that rested there.   25
   Himselfe yet sleepes not; now his spirits were wrought about
    the chere
Fit for so high a funerall. About the steele usde then
Oxen in heapes lay bellowing, preparing food for men.
Bleating of sheepe and goates fild aire; numbers of white-tooth'd
    swine
(Swimming in fat) lay sindging there: the person of the slaine   30
Was girt with slaughter. All this done, all the Greeke kings
    convaid
Achilles to the king of men, his rage not yet allaid
For his Patroclus. Being arriv'd at Agamemnon's tent,
Himselfe bad Heralds put to fire a Caldron and present
The service of it to the Prince, to trie if they could win   35
His pleasure to admit their paines to cleanse the blood sok't in
About his conquering hands and browes. 'Not, by the king of
    heaven!'

*Achilles' overhearing
used this abruption.*

He swore. 'The lawes of friendship damne this false-heart licence
    given
To men that lose friends: not a drop shall touch me till I put
Patroclus in the funerall pile, before these curles be cut,   40
His tombe erected. Tis the last of all care I shall take,
While I consort the carefull. Yet, for your entreaties' sake
(And though I lothe food) I will eate. But early in the morne,
Atrides, use your strict command that lodes of wood be borne
To our design'd place, all that fits to light home such a one   45
As is to passe the shades of Death—that fire enough set gone
His person quickly from our eyes, and our diverted men
May plie their businesse.' This all eares did freely entertaine
And found observance. Then they supt with all things fit,
    and all

Repair'd to tents and rest. The friend the shores maritimall 50
Sought for his bed, and found a place, faire, and upon which
    plaide
The murmuring billowes. There his lims to rest, not sleepe, he
    laid,
Heavily sighing. Round about (silent, and not too neare)
Stood all his Myrmidons, when straite (so over-labour'd were
His goodly lineaments with chace of Hector that beyond 55
His resolution not to sleepe) Sleepe cast his sodaine bond
Over his sense and losde his care. Then of his wretched friend
The soule appear'd; at every part the forme did comprehend
His likenesse; his faire eyes, his voice, his stature, every weed
His person wore it fantased, and stood above his head, 60
This sad speech uttering: 'Dost thou sleepe? Æacides, am I
Forgotten of thee? Being alive, I found thy memorie
Ever respectfull, but now, dead, thy dying love abates.
Interre me quickly; enter me in Pluto's iron gates;
For now the soules (the shades) of men fled from this being 65
    beate
My spirit from rest and stay my much desir'd receipt
Amongst soules plac't beyond the flood. Now every way I erre
About this brode-dor'd house of Dis. O helpe then to preferre
My soule yet further; here I mourne, but had the funerall fire
Consum'd my bodie, never more my spirit should retire 70
From hel's low region: from thence soules never are retriv'd
To talke with friends here, nor shall I. A hatefull fate depriv'd
My being here, that at my birth was fixt; and to such fate
Even thou, O god-like man, art markt; the deadly Ilian gate
Must entertaine thy death. O then, I charge thee now take care 75
That our bones part not, but, as life combinde in equall fare,
Our loving beings, so let Death. When from Opunta's towres
My father brought me to your roofes (since (gainst my will) my
    powres,
Incenst and indiscreet at dice, slue faire Amphidamas),
Then Peleus entertaind me well; then in thy charge I was 80
By his injunction and thy love: and therein let me still
Receive protection. Both our bones provide, in thy last Will,
That one Urne may containe, and make that vessell all of gold
That Thetis gave thee—that rich Urne.' This said, Sleepe ceast
    to hold
Achilles' temples, and the shade thus he receiv'd: 'O friend, 85
What needed these commands? My care, before, meant to
    commend
My bones to thine, and in that Urne. Be sure thy will is done.

Achilles' retreate from company to the sea's shore.

Patroclus appeares to Achilles sleeping.

Achilles, waking, to the shade of Patroclus.

A little stay yet, let's delight, with some full passion
Of woe enough, either's affects; embrace we.' Opening thus
His greedie armes, he felt no friend: like matter vaporous   90
The spirit vanisht under earth and murmur'd in his stoope.
Achilles started; both his hands he clapt and lifted up,

*Achilles his discourse
with himselfe about the
apparition of Patroclus'
shade.*

In this sort wondring: 'O ye gods, I see we have a soule
In th' underdwellings, and a kind of man-resembling idole:
The soule's seate yet, all matter left, staies with the carkasse   95
    here.
O friends, haplesse Patroclus' soule did all this night appeare,
Weeping and making mone to me, commanding every thing
That I intended towards him, so truly figuring
Himselfe at all parts as was strange.' This accident did turne
To much more sorrow, and begat a greedinesse to mourne   100
In all that heard. When, mourning thus, the rosie morne arose

*The morning.
Agamemnon sends out
companies to fetch
fewell for the funerall
heape, of which
company Meriones was
Captaine.*

And Agamemnon through the tents wak't all, and did dispose
Both men and Mules for cariage of matter for the fire—
Of all which worke Meriones (the Cretan soveraign's squire)
Was Captaine, and abrode they went. Wood-cutting tooles   105
    they bore
Of all hands, and well-twisted cords. The Mules marcht all
    before,
Up hill and downe hill, overthwarts, and breake-necke clifts
    they past.
But when the fountfull Ida's tops they scal'd, with utmost haste
All fell upon the high-hair'd Okes, and downe their curled
    browes
Fell busling to the earth, and up went all the boles and bowes   110
Bound to the Mules; and backe againe they parted the harsh way
Amongst them through the tangling shrubs—and long they
    thought the day
Till in the plaine field all arriv'd, for all the woodmen bore
Logs on their neckes—Meriones would have it so. The shore
At last they reacht yet, and then downe their cariages they cast   115
And sat upon them, where the sonne of Peleus had plac't
The ground for his great sepulcher, and for his friend's, in one.
    They raisd a huge pile, and to armes went every Myrmidon,
Charg'd by Achilles. Chariots and horse were harnessed;
Fighters and charioters got up, and they the sad march led,   120
A cloude of infinite foote behind. In midst of all was borne
Patroclus' person by his Peeres: on him were all heads shorne,
Even till they cover'd him with curles. Next to him marcht
    his friend
Embracing his cold necke, all sad since now he was to send

[457]

His dearest to his endlesse home. Arriv'd all where the wood   125
Was heapt for funerall, they set downe. Apart Achilles stood,

Achilles cuts his haire
over his friend's body.

And, when enough wood was heapt on, he cut his golden haire,
Long kept for Sperchius, the flood, in hope of safe repaire
To Phthia by that river's powre; but now, left hopelesse thus,
(Enrag'd, and looking on the sea) he cried out: 'Sperchius,   130
In vaine my father's pietie vow'd (at my implor'd returne
To my lov'd countrie) that these curls should on thy shores
      be shorne—
Besides a sacred Hecatombe, and sacrifice beside
Of fiftie Weathers, at those founts where men have edifide
A loftie temple and perfum'd an altar to thy name.   135
There vow'd he all these offerings; but fate prevents thy fame,
His hopes not suffering satisfied. And since I never more
Shall see my lov'd soyle, my friend's hands shall to the Stygian
      shore
Convey these Tresses.' Thus he put in his friend's hands the
      haire.
And this bred fresh desire of mone; and in that sad affaire   140
The Sunne had set amongst them all, had Thetis' sonne
      not spoke

Achilles to
Agamemnon.

Thus to Atrides: 'King of men, thy aide I still invoke,
Since thy Command all men still heare. Dismisse thy souldiers
      now
And let them victle; they have mourn'd sufficient; tis we owe
The dead this honour, and with us let all the Captaines stay.'   145
   This heard, Atrides instantly the souldiers sent away.
The funerall officers remain'd and heapt on matter still,
Till of an hundred foote about they made the funerall pile,
In whose hote height they cast the Corse; and then they pour'd
      on teares.
Numbers of fat sheepe, and like store of crooked-going steres,   150
They slue before the solemne fire, stript off their hides and drest.
Of which Achilles tooke the fat, and cover'd the deceast
From head to foote, and round about he made the officers pile
The beasts' nak't bodyes, vessels full of honey and of oyle
Pour'd in them laide upon a bere, and cast into the fire.   155
Foure goodly horse, and of nine hounds two most in the desire
Of that great Prince and trencher-fed, all fed that hungry flame.

Twelve Princes
sacrifised on the
funerall pile of
Patroclus.

   Twelve Troyan Princes last stood foorth, yong and of toward
      fame—
All which (set on with wicked spirits) there strooke he,
      there he slew.
And to the iron strength of fire their noble lims he threw.   160

Then breath'd his last sighes, and these words: 'Againe rejoyce,
   my friend,
Even in the joylesse depth of hell: now give I complete end
To all my vowes. Alone thy life sustain'd not violence;
Twelve Troyan Princes waite on thee and labour to incense
Thy glorious heape of funerall. Great Hector I'le excuse;   165
The dogs shall eate him.' These high threates perform'd not
   their abuse;
Jove's daughter, Venus, tooke the guard of noble Hector's Corse
And kept the dogs off, night and day applying soveraigne force
Of rosie balmes that to the dogs were horrible in tast,
And with which she the body fild. Renowm'd Apollo cast   170
A cloude from heaven, lest with the Sunne the nerves and
   lineaments
Might drie and putrifie. And now some powres denide consents
To this solemnitie: the fire (for all the oyly fewell
It had injected) would not burne; and then the loving Cruell
Studied for helpe and, standing off, invokt the two faire winds   175
(Zephyr and Boreas) to affoord the rage of both their kinds
To aid his outrage. Precious gifts his earnest zeale did vow,
Powr'd from a golden bowle much wine, and prayde them both
   to blow,
That quickly his friend's Corse might burne and that heape's
   sturdy breast
Embrace Consumption. Iris heard. The winds were at a feast,   180
All in the Court of Zephyrus (that boisterous blowing aire)

Iris to the winds.   Gather'd together. She that weares the thousand-colourd haire
Flew thither, standing in the porch. They (seeing her) all arose,
Cald to her; every one desir'd she would a while repose
And eate with them. She answerd: 'No, no place of seate is   185
   here;
Retreate cals to the Ocean and Æthiopia where
A Hecatombe is offering now to heaven; and there must I
Partake the feast of sacrifise. I come to signifie
That Thetis' sonne implores your aides, Princes of North
   and West,
With vowes of much faire sacrifise if each will set his breast   190
Against his heape of funerall and make it quickly burne.
Patroclus lies there, whose deceasse all the Achaians mourne.'

The North and West   She said, and parted; and out rusht with an unmeasur'd rore
wind flie to incense the   Those two winds, tumbling clouds in heapes, ushers to either's
funerall pile.   blore.
And instantly they reacht the sea. Up flew the waves; the gale   195
Was strong, reacht fruitfull Troy, and full upon the fire they fall.

The huge heape thunderd. All night long from his chok't breast
        they blew
A liberall flame up; and all night swift-foote Achilles threw
Wine from a golden bowle on earth, and steept the soyle in wine,
Still calling on Patroclus' soule. No father could incline   200
More to a sonne most deare, nor more mourne at his burned
        bones,
Than did the great Prince to his friend at his combustions—
Still creeping neare and neare the heape, still sighing, weeping
        still.

The morning. But when the day-starre look't abrode and promist from his hill
Light, which the saffron morne made good and sprinkl'd on   205
        the seas,
Then languisht the great pile, then sunke the flames, and then
        calme Peace
Turn'd backe the rough winds to their homes; the Thracian
        billow rings
Their high retreate, rufl'd with cuffes of their triumphant wings.
    Pelides then forsooke the pile and to his tired limme
Chusd place of rest, where laide, sweete sleepe fell to his   210
        wish on him—
When all the king's guard (waiting then, perceiving will to rise
In that great Session) hurried in, and op't againe his eyes
With tumult of their troope and haste. A little then he rear'd
His troubled person, sitting up, and this affaire referd

Achilles to Agamemnon To wisht commandment of the kings: 'Atrides, and the rest   215
and the other kings. Of our Commanders generall, vouchsafe me this request
Before your parting. Give in charge the quenching with blacke
        wine
Of this heape's reliques, every brand the yellow fire made shine.
And then let search Patroclus' bones, distinguishing them well;
As well ye may, they kept the midst, the rest at randome fell   220
About th' extreme part of the pile—men's bones, and horses' mixt.
Being found, I'le finde an urne of gold t' enclose them, and
        betwixt
The aire and them two kels of fat lay on them, and to Rest
Commit them till mine owne bones seale our love, my soule
        deceast.
The sepulcher I have not charg'd to make of too much state,   225
But of a modell something meane, that you of yonger Fate
(When I am gone) may amplifie with such a bredth and height
As fits your judgements and our worths.' This charge receiv'd
        his weight
In all observance. First they quencht with sable wine the heape,

As farre as it had fed the flame. The ash fell wondrous deepe, 230
In which his consorts, that his life religiously lov'd,
Searcht weeping for his bones; which found, they consciionably
    prov'd
His will made to Æacides, and what his love did adde.
A golden vessell, double fat, contain them—all which (clad
In vailes of linnen, pure and rich) were solemnly convaid 235
T' Achilles' tent. The platforme then about the pile they laid
Of his fit sepulcher, and raisd a heape of earth, and then
Offerd departure. But the Prince retaind there still his men,
Employing them to fetch from fleete rich Tripods for his games,
Caldrons, Horse, Mules, brode-headed Beeves, bright steele 240
    and brighter dames.

*The games for
Patroclus' funerall.*

    The best at horse race he ordain'd a Lady for his prise,
Generally praisefull, faire and yong, and skild in housewiferies
Of all kinds fitting, and withall, a Trivet that enclosde
Twentie two measures roome, with eares. The next prise he
    proposde
Was (that which then had high respect) a mare of six yeares 245
    old,
Unhandl'd, horsed with a mule, and readie to have foald.
The third game was a Caldron, new, faire, bright, and could
    for sise
Containe two measures. For the fourth two talents' quantities
Of finest gold. The fift game was a great new standing cup
To set downe both waies. These brought in, Achilles then 250
    stood up,

*Achilles to the Grecian
kings.*

And said: 'Atrides, and my Lords, chiefe horsemen of our host,
These games expect ye. If my selfe should interpose my most
For our horse race, I make no doubt but I should take againe
These gifts proposde. Ye all know well of how divine a straine
My horse are, and how eminent. Of Neptune's gift they are 255
To Peleus, and of his to me. My selfe then will not share
In gifts given others, nor my steeds breathe any spirit to shake
Their airie pasterns, so they mourne for their kind guider's sake,
Late lost, that usde with humorous oyle to slick their loftie manes,
Cleare water having cleansd them first; and (his bane being 260
    their banes)
Those loftie manes now strew the earth, their heads held shaken
    downe.
You then that trust in chariots and hope with horse to crowne
Your conquering temples, gird your selves; now fame and prise
    stretch for
All that have spirits.' This fir'd all. The first competitor

[461]

Was king Eumelus, whom the Art of horsemanship did grace,   265
Sonne to Admetus. Next to him rose Diomed to the race,
That under reines rul'd Troyan horse, of late forc't from the
      sonne
Of Lord Anchises, himselfe freed of neare confusion
By Phœbus. Next to him set foorth the yellow-headed king
Of Lacedæmon, Jove's high seed, and in his managing   270
Podargus and swift Æthe trod, steeds to the king of men—
Æthe given by Echepolus, the Anchisiaden,
As bribe to free him from the warre resolv'd for Ilion,
So Delicacie feasted him whom Jove bestow'd upon
A mightie wealth; his dwelling was in brode Sicyone.   275
Old Nestor's sonne, Antilochus, was fourth for chivalrie
In this Contention; his faire horse were of the Pylian breed,
And his old father (coming neare) inform'd him (for good speed)
With good Race notes, in which himselfe could good instruction
      give:

*Nestor to his son
Antilochus gives
instructions for the
race with chariots.*

'Antilochus, though yong thou art, yet thy grave virtues live   280
Belov'd of Neptune and of Jove: their spirits have taught thee all
The art of horsemanship, for which the lesse thy merits fall
In need of doctrine. Well thy skill can wield a chariot
In all fit turnings; yet thy horse their slow feet handle not
As fits thy manage, which makes me cast doubts of thy successe.   285
I well know all these are not seene in art of this addresse
More than thy selfe: their horses yet superior are to thine
For their parts; thine want speed to make discharge of a designe
To please an Artist. But go on, shew but thy art and hart
At all points, and set them against their horses, heart and art;   290
Good Judges will not see thee lose. A Carpenter's desert
Stands more in cunning than in powre. A Pylote doth avert
His vessell from the rocke and wracke, tost with the churlish
      winds,
By skill, not strength. So sorts it here. One chariotere that finds
Want of another's powre in horse must in his owne skill set   295
An overplus of that to that; and so the proofe will get
Skill, that still rests within a man, more grace than powre without.
He that in horse and chariots trusts is often hurl'd about
This way and that unhandsomely, all heaven wide of his end.
He better skild, that rules worse horse, will all observance bend   300
Right on the scope still of a Race, beare neare, know ever when
      to reine,
When give reine, as his foe before (well noted in his veine
Of manage and his steeds' estate) presents occasion.
I'le give thee instance now, as plaine as if thou saw'st it done.

Here stands a drie stub of some tree, a cubite from the ground   305
(Suppose the stub of Oake or Larch, for either are so sound

A Comment might well
be bestowed upon this
speech of Nestor.

That neither rots with wet) two stones, white (marke you)
        white for view,
Parted on either side the stub; and these lay where they drew
The way into a streight, the Race betwixt both lying cleare.
Imagine them some monument of one long since tomb'd there,   310
Or that they had bene lists of race for men of former yeares—
As now the lists Achilles sets may serve for charioteres
Many yeares hence. When neare to these the race growes,
        then as right
Drive on them as thy eye can judge; then lay thy bridle's weight
Most of thy left side, thy right horse then switching; all thy   315
        throte
(Spent in encouragments) give him, and all the reine let flote
About his shoulders. Thy neare horse will yet be he that gave
Thy skill the prise, and him reine so his head may touch the Nave
Of thy left wheele—but then take care thou runst not on the
        stone
(With wracke of horse and chariot) which so thou bear'st upon.   320
Shipwracke within the haven avoide by all meanes; that will
        breed
Others' delight, and thee a shame. Be wise then and take heed
(My lov'd sonne) get but to be first at turning in the course;
He lives not that can cote thee then, not if he backt the horse
The gods bred and Adrastus ow'd. Divine Arion's speed   325
Could not outpace thee, or the horse Laomedon did breed,

*Nestor's aged love of
speech was here briefly
noted.*

Whose race is famous and fed here.' Thus sat Neleides,
When all that could be said was said. And then Meriones
Set fiftly forth his faire-man'd horse. All leapt to chariot,
And every man then for the start cast in his proper lot.   330
Achilles drew. Antilochus the lot set foremost foorth,
Eumelus next, Atrides third, Meriones the fourth;
The fifth and last was Diomed, farre first in excellence.
All stood in order, and the lists Achilles fixt farre thence
In plaine field, and a seate ordain'd fast by, in which he set   335

*Phœnix chiefe judge of
the best deservers in
the race.*

Renowmed Phœnix, that in grace of Peleus was so great,
To see the race and give a truth of all their passages.
All start together, scourg'd, and cried, and gave their businesse
Study and order. Through the field they held a winged pace.
Beneath the bosome of their steeds a dust so dim'd the race   340
It stood above their heads in clowds, or like to stormes amaz'd.
Manes flew like ensignes with the wind; the chariots sometime
        graz'd

And sometimes jumpt up to the aire, yet still sat fast the men
Their spirits even panting in their breasts with fervour to
    obtaine.
But when they turn'd to fleet againe, then all men's skils   345
    were tride,
Then stretcht the pasternes of their steeds. Eumelus' horse
    in pride
Still bore their Soveraigne. After them came Diomed's coursers
    close,
Still apt to leape their chariot and ready to repose
Upon the shoulders of their king their heads. His backe even
    burn'd
With fire that from their nostrils flew. And then their Lord   350
    had turn'd
The race for him, or given it doubt, if Phœbus had not smit
The scourge out of his hands, and teares of helplesse wrath
    with it
From forth his eyes to see his horse for want of scourge made
    slow,
And th' others (by Apollo's helpe) with much more swiftnesse go.
    Apollo's spite Pallas discern'd and flew to Tydeus' sonne,   355
His scourge reacht, and his horse made fresh. Then tooke her
    angry runne
At king Eumelus, brake his geres, his mares on both sides flew,
His draught tree fell to earth, and him the tost-up chariot threw
Downe to the earth, his elbowes torne, his forehead, all his face
Strooke at the center, his speech lost. And then the turned race   360
Fell to Tydides; before all his conquering horse he drave,
And first he glitter'd in the race; divine Athenia gave
Strength to his horse, and fame to him. Next him drave Sparta's
    king.
Antilochus his father's horse then urg'd with all his sting

Antilochus to his
steeds.
Of scourge and voice. 'Runne low,' said he, 'stretch out your   365
    lims and flie.
With Diomed's horse I bid not strive, nor with himselfe strive I.
Athenia wings his horse and him renowmes. Atrides' steeds
Are they ye must not faile but reach—and soone, lest soone
    succeeds
The blot of all your fames, to yeeld in swiftnesse to a mare,
To femall Æthe. What's the cause (ye best that ever were)   370
That thus ye faile us? Be assur'd that Nestor's love ye lose
For ever if ye faile his sonne; through both your both sides goes
His hote steele if ye suffer me to bring the last prise home.
Haste, overtake them instantly; we needs must overcome.

This harsh way next us, this my mind will take, this I despise   375
For perill, this I'le creepe through. Hard the way to honor lies,
And that take I, and that shall yeeld.' His horse by all this knew
He was not pleasde and fear'd his voice, and for a while they
    flew.
But straite more cleare appear'd the streight Antilochus foresaw:
It was a gaspe the earth gave, forc't by humours cold and raw   380
Pour'd out of Winter's watrie breast, met there and cleaving
    deepe
All that neare passage to the lists. This Nestor's sonne would
    keepe
And left the rode-way, being about. Atrides fear'd, and cride:

Menelaus in feare to   'Antilochus! thy course is mad; containe thy horse; we ride
follow Antilochus, who   A way most dangerous; turne head, betime take larger field,   385
ye may see playd upon   We shall be splitted.' Nestor's sonne with much more scourge
him.   impeld
His horse for this, as if not heard; and got as farre before
As any youth can cast a quoyte. Atrides would no more;
He backe againe, for feare himselfe, his goodly chariot
And horse together strew'd the dust, in being so dustie hote   390
Of thirsted conquest. But he chid at parting, passing sore:

Menelaus chides   'Antilochus,' said he, 'a worse than thee earth never bore.
Antilochus.   Farewell; we never thought thee wise, that were wise; but not so
Without othes shall the wreath (be sure) crowne thy mad temples.
    Go.'
    Yet he bethought him and went too, thus stirring up his   395
    steeds:
'Leave me not last thus, nor stand vext. Let these faile in the
    speeds
Of feet and knees, not you. Shall these, these old jades (past
    the flowre
Of youth that you have) passe you?' This the horse fear'd and
    more powre
Put to their knees, straite getting ground. Both flew, and
    so the rest;
All came in smokes, like spirits; the Greeks (set to see who   400
    did best,
Without the race, aloft) now made a new discoverie
Other than that they made at first. Idomeneus' eye
Distinguisht all; he knew the voice of Diomed, seeing a horse
Of speciall marke, of colour bay and was the first in course,
His forehead putting forth a starre round like the Moone and   405
    white.

Idomeneus the king of Crete first discovers the runners.
Up stood the Cretan, uttering this: 'Is it alone my sight,
Princes and Captaines, that discernes another leade the race
With other horse than led of late? Eumelus made most pace
With his fleete mares, and he began the flexure, as we thought.
Now all the field I search and find no where his view.   410
      Hath nought
Befalne amisse to him? Perhaps he hath not with successe
Perform'd his flexure, his reines lost or seate, or with the tresse
His chariot faild him, and his mares have outraid with affright:
Stand up, trie you your eyes, for mine hold with the second sight.
This seemes to me th' Ætolian king, the Tydean Diomed.'   415

Ajax Oileus angry with Idomeneus.
      'To you it seemes so,' rustickly Ajax Oileus said,
'Your words are suited to your eyes. Those mares leade still
      that led;
Eumelus owes them, and he still holds reines and place that did,
Not falne as you hop't. You must prate before us all, though last
In judgement of all: y' are too old, your tongue goes still   420
      too fast;
You must not talke so. Here are those that better thee and looke
For first place in the censure.' This Idomeneus tooke

Idomeneus to Ajax.
In much disdaine, and thus replide: 'Thou best in speeches worst,
Barbarous languag'd, others here might have reprov'd me first,
Not thou, unfitst of all. I hold a Tripode with thee here,   425
Or Caldron, and our Generall make our equall arbiter,
Whose horse are first—that when thou paist, thou then maist
      know.' This fir'd
Oiliades more; and more than words this quarell had inspir'd,
Had not Achilles rose and usde this pacifying speech:

Achilles pacifies Idomeneus and Ajax.
      'No more. Away with words in warre. It toucheth both   430
      with breach
Of that which fits ye. Your deserts should others reprehend
That give such foule termes. Sit ye still—the men themselves
      will end
The strife betwixt you instantly, and either's owne lode beare
On his owne shoulders. Then to both the first horse will appeare,
And which is second.' These words usde, Tydides was at hand.   435
His horse ranne high, glanc't on the way, and up they tost
      the sand
Thicke on their Coachman; on their pace their chariot deckt
      with gold
Swiftly attended, no wheele seene, nor wheele's print in the
      mould
Imprest behind them. These horse flew a flight, not ranne a race.

The runners arrive at
the race's end.

Arriv'd, amids the lists they stood, sweate trickling downe   440
    apace
Their high manes and their prominent breasts; and downe jumpt
    Diomed,
Laid up his scorge aloft the seate, and straite his prise was led
Home to his tent: rough Sthenelus laid quicke hand on the dame
And handled Trivet, and sent both home by his men. Next came
Antilochus, that wonne with wiles, not swiftnesse of his horse,   445
Precedence of the gold-lockt king, who yet maintaind the course
So close that not the king's owne horse gat more before the wheele
Of his rich chariot than might still the insecution feele
With the extreme haires of his taile (and that sufficient close
Held to his leader, no great space it let him interpose   450
Considerd in so great a field). Then Nestor's wilie sonne
Gate of the king now at his heeles, though at the breach he wonne
A quoyte's cast of him, which the king againe at th' instant gaind.
Æthe Agamemnonides, that was so richly maind,
Gat strength still as she spent; which words her worth had   455
    prov'd with deeds
Had more ground bene allow'd the race, and coted farre his
    steeds,
No question leaving for the prise. And now Meriones
A dart's cast came behind the king, his horse of speed much lesse,
Himselfe lesse skild t' importune them and give a chariot wing.
Admetus' sonne was last, whose plight Achilles pittying,   460

Achilles' sentence.

Thus spake: 'Best man comes last, yet Right must see his prise
    not least;
The second his deserts must beare, and Diomed the best.'
    He said, and all allow'd; and sure the mare had bene his owne
Had not Antilochus stood forth, and in his answer showne

Antilochus to Achilles.

Good reason for his interest. 'Achilles,' he replied,   465
'I should be angry with you much to see this ratified.
Ought you to take from me my right, because his horse had
    wrong,
Himselfe being good? He should have usde (as good men do)
    his tongue
In prayre to their powres that blesse good (not trusting to
    his owne)
Not to have bene in this good, last. His chariot overthrowne   470
O'rethrew not me. Who's last? Who's first? Men's goodnesse
    without these
Is not our question. If his good you pitie yet and please
Princely to grace it, your tents hold a goodly deale of gold,

[467]

Brasse, horse, sheepe, women; out of these your bountie may
    be bold
To take a much more worthy prise than my poore merit seekes,   475
And give it here before my face and all these, that the Greekes
May glorifie your liberall hands. This prise I will not yeeld.
Who beares this (whatsoever man) he beares a tried field.
His hand and mine must change some blowes.' Achilles laught,
    and said:
    'If thy will be, Antilochus, I'le see Eumelus paid   480
Out of my tents; I'le give him th' armes which late I conquerd in
Asteropæus, forg'd of brasse and wav'd about with tin;
Twill be a present worthy him.' This said, Automedon
He sent for them. He went, and brought; and to Admetus' sonne
Achilles gave them. He, well pleasde, receiv'd them. Then arose   485
Wrong'd Menelaus, much incenst with yong Antilochus.
He bent to speake, a herald tooke his Scepter and gave charge
Of silence to the other Greeks; then did the king enlarge

Note Menelaus'
ridiculous speech for
conclusion of his
character.

The spleene he prisoned, uttering this: 'Antilochus, till now
We grant thee wise, but in this act what wisedome utter'st   490
    thou?
Thou hast disgrac't my vertue, wrong'd my horse, preferring
    thine,
Much their inferiors. But go to, Princes, nor his nor mine
Judge of with favour, him nor me, lest any Grecian use
This scandall: "Menelaus wonne with Nestor's sonne's abuse
The prise in question; his horse worst, himselfe yet wanne   495
    the best
By powre and greatnesse." Yet because I would not thus contest
To make parts taking, I'le be judge; and I suppose none here
Will blame my judgement. I'le do right. Antilochus, come neare.
Come, noble gentleman, tis your place; sweare by
    th' earth-circling god
(Standing before your chariot and horse, and that selfe rod   500
With which you scourg'd them in your hand) if both with
    will and wile
You did not crosse my chariot.' He thus did reconcile
Grace with his disgrace, and with wit restor'd him to his wit:

Antilochus his ironicall
reply.

'Now crave I patience. O king, what ever was unfit,
Ascribe to much more youth in me than you. You more in age   505
And more in excellence, know well the outraies that engage
All yong men's actions; sharper wits but duller wisedomes still
From us flow than from you; for which, curbe, with your
    wisedome, will.

The prise I thought mine, I yeeld yours; and (if you please)
a prise
Of greater value to my tent I'le send for, and suffise   510
Your will at full and instantly. For in this point of time
I rather wish to be enjoyn'd your favor's top to clime

Ironicè.

Than to be falling all my time from height of such a grace,
O Jove-lov'd king, and of the gods receive a curse in place.'
     This said, he fetcht the prise to him; and it rejoyc't him so   515

This Simile likewise is
meerly Ironicall.
Menelaus to
Antilochus.

That, as corne-eares shine with the dew, yet having time to grow
When fields set all their bristles up, in such a ruffe wert thou,
O Menelaus, answering thus: 'Antilochus, I now
(Though I were angry) yeeld to thee because I see th' hadst wit,
When I thought not; thy youth hath got the mastery of thy   520
spirit.
And yet for all this, tis more safe not to abuse at all
Great men than (ventring) trust to wit to take up what may fall.
For no man in our host beside had easely calm'd my spleene,
Stird with like tempest. But thy selfe hast a sustainer bene
Of much affliction in my cause; so thy good father too,   525
And so thy brother, at thy suite. I therefore let all go;
Give thee the game here, though mine owne—that all these may
discerne
King Menelaus beares a mind at no part proud or sterne.'
     The king thus calm'd, Antilochus receiv'd and gave the steed
To lov'd Noemon to leade thence, and then receiv'd beside   530
The caldron. Next Meriones, for fourth game, was to have

Achilles his gift to
Nestor.

Two talents gold. The fift (unwonne) renowm'd Achilles gave
To reverend Nestor, being a boule to set on either end,
Which through the preasse he caried him: 'Receive,' said he,
'old friend,
This gift as funerall monument of my deare friend deceast,   535
Whom never you must see againe. I make it his bequest
To you as, without any strife, obtaining it from all.
Your shoulders must not undergo the churlish whoorlbat's fall;
Wrastling is past you, strife in darts, the foote's celeritie;
Harsh age in his yeares fetters you, and honor sets you free.'   540
     Thus gave he it; he tooke and joyd, but, ere he thankt, he said:

Nestor's glorie in the
gift of Achilles.

'Now sure, my honorable sonne, in all points thou hast plaid
The comely Orator; no more must I contend with nerves;
Feete faile, and hands; armes want that strength that this and that
swinge serves
Under your shoulders. Would to heaven I were so yong-chind   545
now
And strength threw such a many of bones to celebrate this show

As when the Epians brought to fire (actively honoring thus)
King Amarynces' funerals in faire Buprasius.
His sonnes put prises downe for him, where not a man matcht me
Of all the Epians, or the sonnes of great-soul'd Ætolie—   550
No, nor the Pylians themselves, my countrimen. I beate
Great Clytomedeus, Enops' sonne, at buffets; at the feate
Of wrastling I laid under me one that against me rose,
Ancæus, cald Pleuronius. I made Iphiclus lose
The foot-game to me. At the speare I conquer'd Polydore   555
And strong Phyleus. Actor's sonnes (of all men) onely bore
The palme at horse race, conquering with lashing on more horse—
And envying my victorie, because (before their course)
All the best games were gone with me. These men were twins;
    one was
A most sure guide, a most sure guide. The other gave the passe   560
With rod and mettle. This was then. But now yong men must
    wage
These workes, and my joynts undergo the sad defects of age.

His desire of praise
pants still.

Though then I was another man—at that time I exceld
Amongst th' heroes. But forth now, let th' other rites be held
For thy deceast friend: this thy gift in all kind part I take,   565
And much it joyes my heart that still, for my true kindnesse sake,
You give me memorie. You perceive in what fit grace I stand
Amongst the Grecians, and to theirs you set your gracefull hand.

Another note of
Nestor's humor, not
so much being to be
plainly observed in all
these Iliads as in this
booke.

The gods give ample recompence of grace againe to thee
For this and all thy favors.' Thus backe through the thrust   570
    drave he,
When he had staid out all the praise of old Neleides.
   And now for buffets (that rough game) he orderd passages,
Proposing a laborious Mule of six yeares old, untam'd
And fierce in handling, brought and bound in that place where
    they gam'd;
And to the conquerd, a round cup. Both which he thus   575
    proclames:

Achilles proposes the
game for buffets.

   'Atrides, and all friends of Greece, two men for these two games
I bid stand forth; who best can strike with high contracted fists
(Apollo giving him the wreath), know all about these lists,
Shall winne a Mule patient of toyle—the vanquisht, this round
    cup.'
   This utterd, Panopeus' sonne, Epeus, straight stood up,   580

Note the sharpnes of
wit in our Homer, if
where you looke not
for it, you can find it.

A tall huge man that to the naile knew that rude sport of hand,
And (seising the tough mule) thus spake: 'Now let some other
    stand
Forth for the cup; this Mule is mine; at cuffes I bost me best.

Is't not enough I am no souldier? Who is worthiest
At all workes? None; not possible. At this yet, this I say   585
And will performe this; who stands forth, I'le burst him; I will
    bray
His bones as in a mortar. Fetch surgeons enow to take
His corse from under me.' This speech did all men silent make.
At last stood forth Euryalus, a man god-like, and sonne
To king Mecisteus, the grand child of honor'd Talaon.   590
He was so strong that (coming once to Thebes, when Œdipus
Had like rites solemniz'd for him) he went victorious
From all the Thebanes. This rare man Tydides would prepare,
Put on his girdle, oxehide cords faire wrought, and spent
    much care
That he might conquer, heartned him, and taught him trickes.   595
    Both drest
Fit for th' affaire; both forth were brought; then, breast opposde
    to breast,
Fists against fists rose, and they joynd. Ratling of jawes was there,
Gnashing of teeth, and heavie blowes dasht bloud out every
    where.
At length Epeus spide cleare way, rusht in, and such a blow
Drave underneath the other's eare that his neate lims did strow   600
The knockt earth; no more legs had he. But as a huge fish laid
Neare to the cold-weed-gathering shore is with a North flaw fraid,
Shootes backe and in the blacke deepe hides: so sent against the
    ground
Was foyl'd Euryalus, his strength so hid in more profound
Deepes of Epeus, who tooke up th' intranc't Competitor—   605
About whom rusht a crowd of friends that through the clusters
    bore
His faltring knees, he spitting up thicke clods of bloud, his head
Totterd of one side, his sence gone. When (to a by-place led)

Achilles puts downe
prise for wrastlers.

Thither they brought him the round cup. Pelides then set forth
Prise for a wrastling; to the best, a trivet that was worth   610
Twelve oxen, great and fit for fire; the conquer'd was t' obtaine
A woman excellent in workes, her beautie and her gaine
Prisde at foure oxen. Up he stood, and thus proclaim'd: 'Arise,
You wrastlers that will prove for these.' Out stept the ample sise

Ulysses and Ajax
wrastle.

Of mightie Ajax, huge in strength, to him Laertes' sonne,   615
That craftie one, as huge in sleight. Their ceremonie done
Of making readie, forth they stept, catch elbowes with strong
    hands.

Simile.

And as the beames of some high house cracke with a storme,
    yet stands

[471]

The house, being built by well-skild men: so crackt their
    backebones wrincht
With horrid twitches. In their sides, armes, shoulders (all   620
    bepincht)
Ran thicke the wals, red with the bloud ready to start out. Both
Long'd for the conquest and the prise, yet shewd no play,
    being loth
To lose both; nor could Ithacus stirre Ajax, nor could he
Hale downe Ulysses—being more strong than with mere strength
    to be
Hurl'd from all vantage of his sleight. Tir'd then with tugging   625
    play,

Ajax to Ulysses. Great Ajax Telamonius said: 'Thou wisest man, or lay
My face up or let me lay thine; let Jove take care for these.'
This said, he hoist him up to aire, when Laertiades
His wiles forgat not; Ajax' thigh he strooke behind, and flat
He on his backe fell, on his breast Ulysses. Wonderd at   630
Was this of all; all stood amaz'd. Then the much-suffering man
(Divine Ulysses) at next close the Telamonian
A litle raisde from earth, not quite, but with his knee implide
Lockt legs; and downe fell both on earth close by each other's
    side,
Both fil'd with dust. But, starting up, the third close they had   635
    made
Had not Achilles selfe stood up, restraining them, and bad:

Achilles parts Ulysses 'No more tug one another thus, nor moyle your selves; receive
and Ajax. Prise equall; conquest crownes ye both; the lists to others leave.'
    They heard and yeelded willingly, brusht off the dust, and on

Prises for runners. Put other vests. Pelides then to those that swiftest runne   640
Proposde another prise—a boule beyond comparison
(Both for the sise and workmanship) past all the boules of earth;
It held sixe measures, silver all, but had his speciall worth
For workmanship, receiving forme from those ingenious men
Of Sidon. The Phœnicians made choise and brought it then   645
Along the greene sea, giving it to Thoas; by degrees
It came t' Euneus, Jason's sonne, who yong Priamides
(Lycaon) of Achilles' friend bought with it. And this, here,
Achilles made best game for him that best his feete could beare.
For second, he proposde an Oxe, a huge one and a fat;   650
And halfe a talent gold for last. These thus he set them at:

Ulysses, Ajax Oileus   'Rise, you that will assay for these.' Forth stept Oiliades;
and Antilochus for the Ulysses answerd; and the third was one esteem'd past these
Foot-race. For footmanship, Antilochus. All rankt, Achilles show'd
The race-scope. From the start they glid; Oiliades bestow'd   655

His feete the swiftest; close to him flew god-like Ithacus.

Simile.

And as a Ladie at her loome, being yong and beauteous,
Her silke-shittle close to her breast (with grace that doth inflame,
And her white hand) lifts quicke and oft in drawing from her
    frame
Her gentle thred, which she unwinds, with ever at her brest   660
Gracing her faire hand: so close still, and with such interest
In all men's likings, Ithacus unwound and spent the race
By him before; tooke out his steps, with putting in their place
Promptly and gracefully his owne; sprinkl'd the dust before,
And clouded with his breath his head. So facilie he bore   665
His royall person that he strooke shoutes from the Greekes
    with thirst
That he should conquer. Though he flew, yet—'Come, come,
    O come first'—
Ever they cried to him; and this even his wise breast did move
To more desire of victorie. It made him pray and prove

*Ulysses prayes to
Minerva for speed.*

Minerva's aide (his fautresse still): 'O goddesse, heare,' said he,   670
'And to my feete stoope with thy helpe; now happie Fautresse be.'
    She was, and light made all his lims; and now (both neare
    their crowne)
Minerva tript up Ajax' heeles, and headlong he fell downe
Amids the ordure of the beasts there negligently left
Since they were slaine there; and by this, Minerva's friend   675
    bereft
Oiliades of that rich bowle, and left his lips, nose, eyes,
Ruthfully smer'd. The fat oxe yet he seisd for second prise,
Held by the horne, spit out the taile, and thus spake, all
    besmear'd:

*Ajax Oileus jests out
his fall to the Greekes.*

'O villanous chance! This Ithacus so highly is indear'd
To his Minerva that her hand is ever in his deeds.   680
She like his mother nestles him—for from her it proceeds
(I know) that I am usde thus.' This all in light laughter cast,
Amongst whom quicke Antilochus laught out his coming last

*Antilochus likewise
helpes out his coming
last.*

Thus wittily: 'Know, all my friends, that all times past, and now,
The gods most honour most-liv'd men; Oiliades ye know   685
More old than I, but Ithacus is of the formost race,
First generation of men. Give the old man his grace;
They count him of the greene-hair'd eld; they may, or in his
    flowre—
For not our greatest flourisher can equall him in powre
Of foote-strife but Æacides.' Thus sooth'd he Thetis' sonne,   690

Achilles to Antilochus.

Who thus accepted it: 'Well, youth, your praises shall not runne
With unrewarded feete on mine. Your halfe a talent's prise

I'le make a whole one: take you, sir.' He tooke, and joy'd.
    Then flies
Another game forth. Thetis' sonne set in the lists a lance,
A shield and helmet, being th' armes Sarpedon did advance   695
Against Patroclus, and he prisde. And thus he nam'd th' addresse:

    'Stand forth, two the most excellent, arm'd; and before all
       these
Give mutuall onset to the touch and wound of either's flesh;
Who first shall wound through other's armes, his blood appearing
    fresh,
Shall win this sword, silverd and hatcht; the blade is right   700
    of Thrace;
Asteropæus yeelded it. These armes shall part their grace
With either's valour, and the men I'le liberally feast
At my pavilion.' To this game the first man that addrest

Diomed and Ajax combat.

Was Ajax Telamonius; to him, king Diomed.
Both, in opposde parts of the preasse, full arm'd; both entered   705
The lists amids the multitude, put lookes on so austere,
And joyn'd so roughly, that amaze surprisde the Greeks in feare
Of either's mischiefe. Thrice they threw their fierce darts,
    and closde thrice.
Then Ajax strooke through Diomed's shield but did no prejudice;
His curets saft him. Diomed's dart still over shoulders flew,   710
Still mounting with the spirit it bore. And now rough Ajax grew
So violent that the Greeks cried: 'Hold; no more; let them
    no more—
Give equall prise to either.' Yet the sword, proposde before

Achilles proposes a game for hurling of the stone or boule.

For him did best, Achilles gave to Diomed. Then a stone,
(In fashion of a sphere) he show'd, of no invention,   715
But naturall, onely melted through with iron. Twas the boule
That king Eetion usde to hurle; but he, bereft of soule
By great Achilles, to the fleete with store of other prise
He brought it, and proposde it now, both for the exercise
And prise it selfe. He stood, and said: 'Rise, you that will   720
    approve
Your arme's strengths now in this brave strife. His vigor
    that can move
This furthest needs no game but this; for, reach he nere so farre
With large fields of his owne in Greece (and so needs for his
    Carre,
His Plow or other tooles of thrift much iron) I'le able this

Ironicè.

For five revolved yeares; no need shall use his messages   725
To any towne to furnish him; this onely boule shall yeeld
Iron enough for all affaires.' This said, to trie this field

[474]

First Polypœtes issued; next Leonteus; third
Great Ajax; huge Epeus fourth. Yet he was first that stird
That myne of iron. Up it went, and up he tost it so   730
That laughter tooke up all the field. The next man that did throw
Was Leonteus; Ajax third, who gave it such a hand
That farre past both their markes it flew. But now twas to be
    mann'd
By Polypœtes: and as farre as at an Oxe that strayes
A herdsman can swing out his goade, so farre did he outraise   735
The stone past all men; all the field rose in a shout to see't.
About him flockt his friends, and bore the royall game to fleete.

Another game.
    For Archerie he then set forth ten axes, edg'd two waies,
And ten of one edge. On the shore, farre off, he causd to raise
A ship-mast, to whose top they tied a fearfull Dove by th' foote, 740
At which all shot—the game put thus: He that the Dove
    could shoote,
Nor touch the string that fastn'd her, the two-edg'd tooles should
    beare
All to the fleete. Who toucht the string and mist the Dove
    should share
The one-edg'd axes. This proposde, king Teucer's force arose,
And with him rose Meriones; and now lots must dispose   745
Their shooting first. Both which let fall into a helme of brasse,
First Teucer's came, and first he shot; and his crosse fortune was
To shoote the string, the Dove untoucht. Apollo did envie
His skill, since not to him he vow'd (being god of archerie)
A first-falne Lambe. The bitter shaft yet cut in two the cord,   750
That downe fell, and the Dove aloft up to the Welkin soar'd.
The Greeks gave shouts. Meriones first made a heartie vow
To sacrifice a first-falne Lambe to him that rules the Bow,
And then fell to his aime, his shaft being ready nockt before.
He spide her in the clouds, that here, there, every where   755
    did soare,
Yet at her height he reacht her side, strooke her quite through,
    and downe
The shaft fell at his feete; the Dove the mast againe did crowne.
There hung the head, and all her plumes were ruffl'd, she starke
    dead;
And there (farre off from him) she fell. The people wondered
And stood astonisht, th' Archer pleasd. Æacides then shewes   760
A long lance and a caldron, new, engrail'd with twentie hewes,
Prisde at an Oxe. These games were shew'd for men at darts.
    And then
Up rose the Generall of all, up rose the king of men,

Up rose late-crown'd Meriones. Achilles (seeing the king
Do him this grace), prevents more deed, his royall offering   765
Thus interrupting: 'King of men, we well conceive how farre
Thy worth superiour is to all, how much most singular
Thy powre is, and thy skill in darts. Accept then this poore prise
Without contention, and (your will pleasde with what I advise)
Affoord Meriones the lance.' The king was nothing slow   770
To that fit grace; Achilles then the brasse lance did bestow
On good Meriones. The king his present would not save,
But to renowm'd Talthybius the goodly Caldron gave.

The End of the Three and Twentieth Booke

THE TWENTY-FOURTH BOOKE

of

HOMER'S ILIADS

THE ARGUMENT

Jove, entertaining care of Hector's corse,
Sends Thetis to her sonne for his remorse
And fit dismission of it. Iris then
He sends to Priam, willing him to gaine
His sonne for ransome. He, by Hermes led,   5
Gets through Achilles' guards, sleepes deepe and dead
Cast on them by his guide. When, with accesse
And humble sute made to Æacides,
He gaines the bodie, which to Troy he beares
And buries it with feasts, buried in teares.   10

Another Argument

Omega *sings the exequies,*
And Hector's redemptorie prise.

The games perform'd, the souldiers wholly disperst to fleete,
Supper and sleepe their onely care. Constant Achilles yet
Wept for his friend; nor sleepe it selfe, that all things doth
     subdue,
Could touch at him. This way and that he turn'd, and did renue
His friend's deare memorie—his grace in managing his strength,   5
And his strength's greatnesse—how life rackt into their utmost
     length
Griefes, battels, and the wraths of seas in their joynt sufferance.
Each thought of which turn'd to a teare. Sometimes he would
     advance
(In tumbling on the shore) his side, sometimes his face, then turne
Flat on his bosome, start upright. Although he saw the morne   10
Shew sea and shore his extasie he left not, till at last

Rage varied his distraction. Horse, chariot, in hast
He cald for, and (those joyn'd) the corse was to his chariot tide,
And thrice about the sepulcher he made his Furie ride,
Dragging the person. All this past, in his pavilion   15
Rest seisd him; but with Hector's corse his rage had never done,
Still suffering it t' oppresse the dust. Apollo yet, even dead,
Pitied the Prince, and would not see inhumane tyrannie fed
With more pollution of his lims; and therefore coverd round
His person with his golden shield, that rude dogs might not   20
    wound
His manly lineaments (which threat Achilles cruelly
Had usde in furie). But now heaven let fall a generall eye
Of pitie on him; the blest gods perswaded Mercurie
(Their good observer) to his stealth, and every deitie
Stood pleasd with it, Juno except, greene Neptune and the   25
    Maide
Grac't with the blew eyes. All their hearts stood hatefully appaid
Long since, and held it as at first to Priam, Ilion
And all his subjects for the rape of his licentious sonne,
Proud Paris, that despisde these dames in their divine accesse
Made to his cottage, and praisd her that his sad wantonnesse   30
So costly nourisht. The twelfth morne now shin'd on the delay
Of Hector's rescue, and then spake the deitie of the day
*Apollo to the other
gods.* Thus to th' immortals: 'Shamelesse gods, authors of ill ye are
To suffer ill. Hath Hector's life at all times show'd his care
Of all your rights, in burning thighs of Beeves and Goates   35
    to you,
And are your cares no more of him? Vouchsafe ye not even now
(Even dead) to keepe him—that his wife, his mother and his sonne,
Father and subjects may be mov'd to those deeds he hath done,
See'ng you preserve him that serv'd you, and sending to their
    hands
His person for the rites of fire? Achilles, that withstands   40
All helpe to others, you can helpe—one that hath neither hart
Nor soule within him that will move or yeeld to any part
That fits a man; but Lion-like, uplandish and meere wilde,
Slave to his pride, and, all his nerves being naturally compil'd
Of eminent strength, stalkes out and preyes upon a silly sheepe— 45
*Shame a quality that
hurts and helpes men
exceedingly.* And so fares this man. That fit ruth that now should draw
    so deepe
In all the world being lost in him, and Shame (a qualitie
Of so much weight that both it helpes and hurts excessively
Men in their manners) is not knowne, nor hath the powre to be
In this man's being. Other men a greater losse than he   50

Have undergone—a sonne, suppose, or brother of one wombe;
Yet, after dues of woes and teares, they bury in his tombe
All their deplorings. Fates have given to all that are true men
True manly patience, but this man so soothes his bloudy veine
That no bloud serves it; he must have divine-soul'd Hector   55
    bound
To his proud chariot, and danc't in a most barbarous round
About his lov'd friend's sepulcher, when he is slaine. Tis vile,
And drawes no profit after it. But let him now awhile
Marke but our angers; his is spent; let all his strength take heed
It tempts not our wraths; he begets, in this outragious deed,   60
The dull earth with his furie's hate.' White-wristed Juno said
(Being much incenst): 'This doome is one that thou wouldst
    have obaid,
Thou bearer of the silver bow—that we in equall care
And honour should hold Hector's worth with him that claimes
    a share
In our deservings? Hector suckt a mortall woman's brest,   65
Æacides a goddesse's. Our selfe had interest
Both in her infant nourishment and bringing up with state,
And to the humane Peleus we gave his bridall mate,
Because he had th' immortals' love. To celebrate the feast
Of their high nuptials every god was glad to be a guest,   70
And thou fedst of his father's cates, touching thy harpe in grace
Of that beginning of our friend—whom thy perfidious face
(In his perfection) blusheth not to match with Priam's sonne.
O thou, that to betray and shame art still companion.'

Jove to Juno.   Jove thus receiv'd her: 'Never give these brode termes to   75
    a god.
Those two men shall not be compar'd; and yet, of all that trod
The well-pav'd Ilion, none so deare to all the deities
As Hector was, at least to me. For offrings most of prise
His hands would never pretermit. Our altars ever stood
Furnisht with banquets fitting us; odors, and every good,   80
Smokt in our temples. And for this (foreseeing it) his fate
We markt with honour, which must stand: but to give stealth
    estate
In his deliverance, shun we that; nor must we favour one
To shame another. Privily, with wrong to Thetis' sonne,
We must not worke out Hector's right. There is a ransome due   85
And open course by lawes of armes, in which must humbly sue
The friends of Hector. Which just meane, if any god would stay
And use the other, twould not serve, for Thetis, night and day,
Is guardian to him. But would one call Iris hither, I

Would give directions, that for gifts the Troyan king should **buy**   90
His Hector's body, which the sonne of Thetis shall resigne.'
  This said, his will was done; the Dame that doth in vapours
    shine,
Dewie and thin, footed with stormes, jumpt to the sable seas
Twixt Samos and sharpe Imber's cliffes; the lake gron'd
    with the presse
Of her rough feete, and (plummet-like, put in an oxe's horne   95
That beares death to the raw-fed fish) she div'd, and found
    forlorne
Thetis, lamenting her sonne's fate, who was in Troy to have
(Farre from his countrey) his death serv'd. Close to her Iris stood,

And said: 'Rise, Thetis: prudent Jove (whose counsels thirst
    not blood)
Cals for thee.' Thetis answerd her with asking: 'What's the   100
    cause
The great god cals? My sad powres fear'd to breake th' immortall
    lawes
In going, fil'd with griefes, to heaven. But he sets snares for none
With colourd counsels; not a word of him but shall be done.'
  She said, and tooke a sable vaile, a blacker never wore
A heavenly shoulder, and gave way. Swift Iris swum before;   105
About both rowld the brackish waves. They tooke their banks
    and flew
Up to Olympus, where they found Saturnius (farre-of-view)
Spher'd with heaven's everbeing states. Minerva rose and gave
Her place to Thetis neare to Jove, and Juno did receive
Her entry with a cup of gold, in which she dranke to her,   110
Grac't her with comfort, and the cup to her hand did referre.
She dranke, resigning it. And then the sire of men and gods
Thus entertain'd her: 'Com'st thou up to these our blest abodes,
Faire goddesse Thetis, yet art sad, and that in so high kind
As passeth suffrance? This I know, and try'd thee, and now find   115
Thy will by mine rulde, which is rule to all worlds' government.
Besides this triall yet, this cause sent downe for thy ascent.
Nine dayes' Contention hath bene held amongst th' immortals
    here
For Hector's person and thy sonne; and some advices were
To have our good spie Mercurie steale from thy sonne the   120
    Corse:
But that reproch I kept farre off, to keepe in future force
Thy former love and reverence. Haste then, and tell thy sonne
The gods are angrie, and my selfe take that wrong he hath done
To Hector in worst part of all—the rather, since he still

Detaines his person. Charge him then, if he respect my will   125
For any reason, to resigne slaine Hector. I will send
Iris to Priam to redeeme his sonne, and recommend
Fit ransome to Achilles' grace; in which right he may joy,
And end his vaine griefe.' To this charge bright Thetis did
    employ
Instant endevour. From heaven's tops she reacht Achilles' tent,   130
Found him still sighing, and some friends with all their
    complements
Soothing his humour, othersome with all contention
Dressing his dinner, all their paines and skils consum'd upon
A huge wooll-bearer slaughterd there. His reverend mother then

Thetis to Achilles.   Came neare, tooke kindly his faire hand, and askt him: 135
    'Deare sonne, when
Will sorrow leave thee? How long time wilt thou thus eate
    thy heart,
Fed with no other food, nor rest? Twere good thou wouldst
    divert
Thy friend's love to some Ladie; cheare thy spirits with such
    kind parts
As she can quit thy grace withall. The joy of thy deserts
I shall not long have; death is neare and thy all-conquering   140
    fate,
Whose haste thou must not haste with griefe, but understand
    the state
Of things belonging to thy life, which quickly order. I
Am sent from Jove t' advertise thee that every deitie
Is angry with thee, himselfe most, that rage thus reigns in thee
Still to keepe Hector. Quit him then, and for fit ransome free   145
His injur'd person.' He replied: 'Let him come that shall give
The ransome, and the person take. Jove's pleasure must deprive
Men of all pleasures.' This good speech, and many more,
    the sonne
And mother usde in eare of all the navall Station.

Jove sends Iris to   And now to holy Ilion Saturnius Iris sent: 150
Priam.   'Go, swiftfoote Iris, bid Troy's king beare fit gifts, and content
Achilles for his sonne's release; but let him greet alone
The Grecian navie, not a man, excepting such a one
As may his horse and chariot guide, a herald, or one old,
Attending him; and let him take his Hector. Be he bold,   155
Discourag'd nor with death nor feare; wise Mercurie shall guide
His passage till the Prince be neare. And (he gone) let him ride
Resolv'd even in Achilles' tent. He shall not touch the state
Of his high person, nor admit the deadliest desperate

[481]

Of all about him. For (though fierce) he is not yet unwise,   160
Nor inconsiderate, nor a man past awe of deities,
But passing free and curious to do a suppliant grace.'
   This said, the Rainbow to her feet tied whirlewinds, and the
     place
Reacht instantly. The heavie Court Clamor and Mourning fill'd,
The sonnes all set about the sire; and there stood Griefe   165
     and still'd
Teares on their garments. In the midst the old king sate, his weed
All wrinkl'd, head and necke dust fil'd, the Princesses, his seed,
The Princesses, his sonnes' faire wives, all mourning by;
     the thought
Of friends so many, and so good (being turn'd so soone to
     nought
By Grecian hands) consum'd their youth, rain'd beautie from   170
     their eyes.
   Iris came neare the king; her sight shooke all his faculties,

Iris to Priam.   And therefore spake she soft, and said: 'Be glad, Dardanides.
Of good occurrents, and none ill, am I Ambassadresse.
Jove greets thee, who, in care (as much as he is distant) daines
Eye to thy sorrowes, pitying thee. My ambassie containes   175
This charge to thee from him; he wills thou shouldst redeeme
     thy sonne;
Beare gifts t' Achilles, cheare him so, but visite him alone;
None but some herald let attend, thy mules and chariot
To manage for thee. Feare nor death let dant thee; Jove
     hath got
Hermes to guide thee, who as neare to Thetis' sonne as needs   180
Shall guard thee: and, being once with him, nor his nor others'
     deeds

Jove's witnesse of   Stand toucht with; he will all containe. Nor is he mad, nor vaine,
Achilles.   Nor impious, but with all his nerves studious to entertaine
One that submits with all fit grace.' Thus vanisht she like wind.
   He mules and chariot cals, his sonnes bids see them joynd   185
     and bind
A trunke behind it; he himselfe downe to his wardrobe goes,
Built all of Cedar, highly rooft and odoriferous,
That much stuffe worth the sight containd. To him he cald his
     Queene,

Priam to Hecuba.   Thus greeting her: 'Come, haplesse dame, an Angell I have
     seene
Sent downe from Jove, that bad me free our deare sonne from   190
     the fleet

With ransome pleasing to our foe. What holds thy judgement
    meet?
My strength and spirit layes high charge on all my being to beare
The Greeks' worst, ventring through their host.' The Queene
    cried out to heare

Hecuba to Priam.
His ventrous purpose, and replyed: 'O whither now is fled
The late discretion that renown'd thy grave and knowing head   195
In forreine and thine owne rulde realmes, that thus thou dar'st
    assay
Sight of that man, in whose browes sticks the horrible decay
Of sonnes so many and so strong? Thy heart is iron I thinke.
If this sterne man (whose thirst of blood makes crueltie his
    drinke)
Take or but see thee, thou art dead. He nothing pities woe,   200
Nor honours age. Without his sight, we have enough to do
To mourne with thought of him: keepe we our Pallace, weepe
    we here;
Our sonne is past our helpes. Those throwes that my deliverers
    were
Of his unhappy lineaments told me they should be torne
With blacke-foote dogs. Almightie fate that blacke howre   205
    he was borne
Spunne in his springing thred that end, farre from his parents
    reach—
This bloodie fellow then ordain'd to be their meane—this wretch
Whose stony liver would to heaven I might devoure, my teeth
My sonnes' Revengers made. Curst Greeke, he gave him not
    his death
Doing an ill worke; he alone fought for his countrie; he   210
Fled not nor fear'd, but stood his worst, and cursed policie
Was his undoing.' He replied: 'What ever was his end
Is not our question; we must now use all meanes to defend
His end from scandall, from which act disswade not my just will,
Nor let me nourish in my house a bird presaging ill   215
To my good actions: tis in vaine. Had any earthly spirit
Given this suggestion, if our Priests or Soothsayers, challenging
    merit
Of Prophets, I might hold it false, and be the rather mov'd
To keepe my Pallace; but these eares and these selfe eyes
    approv'd
It was a goddesse. I will go; for not a word she spake   220
I know was idle. If it were, and that my fate will make
Quicke riddance of me at the fleet, kill me, Achilles. Come,
When, getting to thee, I shall find a happy dying roome

[483]

On Hector's bosome, when enough thirst of my teares finds there
Quench to his fervour.' This resolv'd, the works most faire   225
   and deare
Of his rich screenes he brought abrode; twelve veiles wrought
   curiously,
Twelve plaine gownes and as many suits of wealthy tapistry,
As many mantles, horsemen's coates, ten talents of fine gold,
Two Tripods, Caldrons foure, a bowle whose value he did hold
Beyond all price, presented by th' Ambassadors of Thrace.   230
The old king nothing held too deare to rescue from disgrace
His gracious Hector. Forth he came. At entry of his Court

Priam enraged against his citizens.

The Troyan citizens so prest that this opprobrious sort
Of checke he usde: 'Hence, cast-awayes; away ye impious crew!
Are not your griefes enough at home? What come ye here   235
   to view?
Care ye for my griefes? Would ye see how miserable I am?
Is't not enough, imagine ye? Ye might know ere ye came
What such a sonne's losse weigh'd with me. But know this
   for your paines,
Your houses have the weaker doores: the Greeks will find
   their gaines
The easier for his losse, be sure: but, O Troy, ere I see   240
Thy ruine, let the doores of hell receive and ruine me.'
   Thus with his scepter set he on, the crowding citizens,
Who gave backe, seeing him so urge. And now he entertaines
His sonnes as roughly—Helenus, Paris, Hippothous,
Pammon, divine Agathones, renowm'd Deiphobus,   245
Agavus and Antiphonus, and last, not least in armes,
The strong Polites. These nine sonnes the violence of his harmes

Priam enraged against his sons.

Helpt him to vent in these sharpe termes: 'Haste, you infamous
   brood,
And get my chariot. Would to heaven that all the abject blood
In all your veines had Hector scusde. O me, accursed man,   250
All my good sonnes are gone; my light the shades Cimmerian
Have swallow'd from me. I have lost Mestor, surnam'd the faire;
Troilus, that readie knight at armes that made his field repaire
Ever so prompt and joyfully; and Hector, amongst men
Esteem'd a god; not from a mortal's seed but of th' eternall   255
   straine
He seem'd to all eyes. These are gone; you that survive are base,
Liers and common free-booters, all faultie, not a grace
But in your heeles in all your parts; dancing companions,
Ye all are excellent. Hence, ye brats! Love ye to heare my mones?
Will ye not get my chariot? Command it quickly; flie,   260

[484]

That I may perfect this deare worke.' This all did terrifie,
And straite his mule-drawne chariot came, to which they fast
    did bind
The trunke with gifts. And then came forth, with an afflicted
    mind,
Old Hecuba. In her right hand a bowle of gold she bore
With sweet wine crown'd, stood neare, and said: 'Receive this,   265
    and implore
(With sacrificing it to Jove) thy safe returne. I see
Thy mind likes still to go, though mine dislikes it utterly.
Pray to the blacke-cloud-gathering god (Idæan Jove) that viewes
All Troy and all her miseries, that he will deine to use
His most lov'd bird to ratifie thy hopes, that, her brode wing   270
Spred on thy right hand, thou maist know thy zealous offering
Accepted and thy safe returne confirm'd; but if he faile,
Faile thy intent, though never so it labours to prevaile.'
    'This I refuse not,' he replide, 'for no faith is so great
In Jove's high favour, but it must with held-up hands intreate.'   275
    This said, the chamber-maid that held the Ewre and Basin by,
He bad powre water on his hands, when, looking to the skie,

Priam's prayer to Jove.   He tooke the bowle, did sacrifice, and thus implor'd: 'O Jove,
From Ida using thy commands, in all deserts above
All other gods, vouchsafe me safe, and pitie in the sight   280
Of great Achilles: and for trust to that wisht grace, excite
Thy swift-wing'd messenger, most strong, most of aire's region
    lov'd,
To sore on my right hand, which sight may firmely see approv'd
Thy former summons and my speed.' He prayd, and heaven's
    king heard,
And instantly cast from his fist aire's all-commanding bird,   285
The blacke-wing'd huntresse, perfectest of all fowles, which gods
    call
Percnos, the Eagle. And how brode the chamber nuptiall
Of any mightie man hath dores, such breadth cast either wing;
Which now she usde and spred them wide on right hand of
    the king.
All saw it, and rejoyc't; and up to chariot he arose,   290
Drave foorth, the Portall and the Porch resounding as he goes.
His friends all follow'd him, and mourn'd as if he went to die,
And, bringing him past towne to field, all left him, and the eye
Of Jupiter was then his guard—who pittied him, and usde

Jove to Mercury.   These words to Hermes: 'Mercurie, thy helpe hath bene   295
    profusde
Ever with most grace in consorts of travailers distrest.

Now consort Priam to the fleet, but so that not the least
Suspicion of him be attaind till at Achilles' tent
Thy convoy hath arriv'd him safe.' This charge incontient
He put in practise. To his feete his featherd shoes he tide,   300
Immortall and made all of gold, with which he usde to ride
The rough sea and th' unmeasur'd earth, and equald in his pace
The pufts of wind. Then tooke he up his rod, that hath the grace
To shut what eyes he lists with sleep and open them againe
In strongest trances. This he held, flew forth, and did attaine   305
To Troy and Hellespontus straite. Then, like a faire yong Prince
First-downe-chinn'd, and of such a grace as makes his lookes
    convince
Contending eyes to view him, forth he went to meete the king.
He, having past the mightie tombe of Ilus, watering
His Mules in Xanthus, the darke Even fell on the earth;   310
    and then
Idæus (guider of the Mules) discern'd this Grace of men,
And spake affraide to Priamus: 'Beware, Dardanides,
Our states aske counsell: I discerne the dangerous accesse
Of some man neare us. Now I feare we perish. Is it best
To flie, or kisse his knees and aske his ruth of men distrest?'   315
    Confusion strooke the king; cold Feare extremely quencht
        his vaines;
Upright upon his languishing head his haire stood; and the
    chaines
Priam's amaze.   Of strong Amaze bound all his powres. To both which then
    came neare
The Prince-turn'd Deitie, tooke his hand, and thus bespake
    the Peere:
Mercurie appeares
to him.   'To what place, father, driv'st thou out through solitarie   320
                Night
When others sleepe? Give not the Greeks sufficient cause of fright
To these late travailes, being so neare, and such vow'd enemies?
Of all which, if with all this lode any should cast his eyes
On thy adventures, what would then thy minde esteeme thy state,
Thy selfe old and thy follower old? Resistance could not rate   325
At any value. As for me, be sure I mind no harme
To thy grave person, but against the hurt of others' arme.
Mine owne lov'd father did not get a greater love in me
Priam to Mercurie.   To his good than thou dost to thine.' He answerd: 'The degree
Of danger in my course, faire sonne, is nothing lesse than that   330
Thou urgest; but some god's faire hand puts in for my safe state
That sends so sweete a Guardian in this so sterne a Time
Of night and danger as thy selfe, that all grace in his prime

[486]

Of body and of beautie shew'st, all answerd with a mind
So knowing that it cannot be but of some blessed kind   335
Thou art descended.' 'Not untrue,' said Hermes, 'thy conceipt
In all this holds; but further truth relate, if of such weight
As I conceive thy cariage be, and that thy care convaies
Thy goods of most price to more guard? Or go ye all your waies
Frighted from holy Ilion, so excellent a sonne   340
As thou had'st (being your speciall strength) falne to Destruction,
Whom no Greeke betterd for his fight?' 'O what art thou,' said he,
'Most worthy youth, of what race borne, that thus recountst to me
My wretched sonne's death with such truth?' 'Now, father,'
      he replide,
'You tempt me farre, in wondering how the death was signifide   345
Of your divine sonne to a man so mere a stranger here
As you hold me: but I am one that oft have seene him beare
His person like a god in field; and, when in heapes he slew
The Greeks, all routed to their fleet, his so victorious view
Made me admire, not feele his hand; because Æacides   350
(Incenst) admitted not our fight, my selfe being of accesse
To his high person, serving him, and both to Ilion
In one ship saild. Besides, by birth I breathe a Myrmidon,
Polyctor (cald the rich) my sire, declin'd with age like you.
Sixe sonnes he hath, and me a seventh; and all those sixe   355
      live now
In Phthia, since, all casting lots, my chance did onely fall
To follow hither. Now for walke I left my Generall.
Tomorrow all the Sunne-burn'd Greeks will circle Troy with
      armes;
The Princes rage to be withheld so idlely, your alarmes
Not given halfe hote enough they thinke, and can containe   360
      no more.'
He answerd: 'If you serve the Prince, let me be bold t' implore
This grace of thee, and tell me true, lies Hector here at fleet,

Mercurie to Priam.   Or have the dogs his flesh?' He said: 'Nor dogs nor fowle have yet
Toucht at his person: still he lies at fleet and in the tent
Of our great Captaine, who indeed is much too negligent   365
Of his fit usage: but, though now twelve dayes have spent
      their heate
On his cold body, neither wormes with any taint have eate,
Nor putrifaction perisht it. Yet ever when the Morne
Lifts her divine light from the sea, unmercifully borne
About Patroclus' sepulcher it beares his friend's disdaine,   370
Bound to his chariot. But no Fits of further outrage raigne
In his distemper: you would muse to see how deepe a dew

[487]

Even steepes the body, all the blood washt off, no slenderst shew
Of gore or quitture, but his wounds all closde, though many were
Opened about him. Such a love the blest immortals beare   375
Even dead to thy deare sonne, because his life shew'd love
     to them.'

Priam to Mercurie.
     He joyfull answerd: 'O my sonne, it is a grace supreme
In any man to serve the gods. And I must needs say this:
For no cause (having season fit) my Hector's hands would misse
Advancement to the gods with gifts, and therefore do not they   380
Misse his remembrance after death. Now let an old man pray
Thy graces to receive this cup and keepe it for my love;
Nor leave me till the gods and thee have made my prayres
     approve
Achilles' pitie, by thy guide brought to his Princely tent.'

*Hermes againe to
Priam.*
     Hermes replide: 'You tempt me now, old king, to a consent   385
Farre from me, though youth aptly erres. I secretly receive
Gifts that I cannot brodely vouch? take graces that will give
My Lord dishonour? or what he knowes not? or will esteeme
Perhaps unfit? Such briberies perhaps at first may seeme
Sweet and secure, but futurely they still prove sowre and breed 390
Both feare and danger. I could wish thy grave affaires did need
My guide to Argos, either shipt, or lackying by thy side;
And would be studious in thy guard, so nothing could be tride
But care in me to keepe thee safe, for that I could excuse
And vouch to all men.' These words past, he put the deeds   395
     in use
For which Jove sent him. Up he leapt to Priam's chariot,
Tooke scourge and reines, and blew in strength to his free
     steeds, and got
The navall towres and deepe dike strait. The guards were all
     at meat;
Those he enslumberd, op't the ports, and in he safely let
Old Priam with his wealthy prise. Forthwith they reacht   400
     the Tent
Of great Achilles. Large and high, and in his most ascent
A shaggie roofe of seedy reeds mowne from the meades, a hall
Of state they made their king in it, and strengthned it withall,
Thicke with firre rafters; whose approch was let in by a dore
That had but one barre, but so bigge that three men evermore   405
Raisd it to shut, three fresh take downe—which yet Æacides
Would shut and ope himselfe. And this with farre more ease
Hermes set ope, entring the king, then leapt from horse, and said:
     'Now know, old king, that Mercurie (a god) hath given this aid
To thy endevour, sent by Jove; and now, away must I,   410

[488]

For men would envy thy estate to see a Deitie
Affect a man thus. Enter thou, embrace Achilles' knee,
And by his sire, sonne, mother, pray his ruth and grace to thee.'
   This said, he high Olympus reacht. The king then left his
      coach
To grave Idæus, and went on, made his resolv'd approach   415

Priam enters Achilles' tent.

And enterd in a goodly roome, where with his Princes sate
Jove-lov'd Achilles at their feast; two onely kept the state
Of his attendance, Alcimus and Lord Automedon.
At Priam's entrie a great time Achilles gaz'd upon
His wonderd-at approch, nor eate: the rest did nothing see   420
While close he came up, with his hands fast holding the bent knee
Of Hector's conqueror, and kist that large man-slaughtring hand

Simile.

That much blood from his sonnes had drawne. And as in some
      strange land
And great man's house, a man is driven (with that abhorr'd
      dismay
That followes wilfull bloodshed still, his fortune being to slay   425
One whose blood cries alowde for his) to pleade protection
In such a miserable plight as frights the lookers on:
In such a stupefied estate Achilles sate to see,
So unexpected, so in night, and so incrediblie,
Old Priam's entrie. All his friends one on another star'd   430
To see his strange lookes, seeing no cause. Thus Priam then
      prepar'd

Priam to Achilles.

His sonne's redemption: 'See in me, O godlike Thetis' sonne,
Thy aged father, and perhaps even now being outrunne
With some of my woes, neighbour foes (thou absent) taking time
To do him mischiefe, no meane left to terrifie the crime   435
Of his oppression; yet he heares thy graces still survive
And joyes to heare it, hoping still to see thee safe arrive
From ruin'd Troy. But I (curst man) of all my race shall live
To see none living. Fiftie sonnes the Deities did give
My hopes to live in—all alive when neare our trembling shore   440
The Greeke ships harbor'd—and one wombe nineteene of those
      sons bore.
Now Mars a number of their knees hath strengthlesse left, and he
That was (of all) my onely joy and Troy's sole guard, by thee
(Late fighting for his countrey) slaine, whose tenderd person now
I come to ransome. Infinite is that I offer you,   445
My selfe conferring it, exposde alone to all your oddes,
Onely imploring right of armes. Achilles, feare the gods,
Pitie an old man like thy sire—different in onely this,
That I am wretcheder, and beare that weight of miseries

That never man did, my curst lips enforc't to kisse that hand   450
That slue my children.' This mov'd teares; his father's name
    did stand
(Mention'd by Priam) in much helpe to his compassion,
And mov'd Æacides so much he could not looke upon
The weeping father. With his hand, he gently put away
His grave face; calme remission now did mutually display   455
Her powre in either's heavinesse. Old Priam, to record
His sonne's death and his deathsman see, his teares and bosome
    pour'd
Before Achilles. At his feete he laid his reverend head.
Achilles' thoughts now with his sire, now with his friend,
    were fed.
Betwixt both Sorrow fild the tent. But now Æacides   460
Achilles' remorse of   (Satiate at all parts with the ruth of their calamities)
Priam.   Start up, and up he raisd the king. His milke-white head and
    beard
With pittie he beheld, and said: 'Poore man, thy mind is scar'd
With much affliction. How durst thy person thus alone
Venture on his sight that hath slaine so many a worthy sonne,   465
And so deare to thee? Thy old heart is made of iron. Sit
And settle we our woes, though huge, for nothing profits it.
Cold mourning wastes but our lives' heates. The gods have
    destinate
That wretched mortals must live sad. Tis the immortall state
Of Deitie that lives secure. Two Tunnes of gifts there lie   470
In Jove's gate, one of good, one ill, that our mortalitie
Maintaine, spoile, order; which when Jove doth mixe to any man,
One while he frolicks, one while mourns. If of his mournfull Kan
A man drinks onely, onely wrongs he doth expose him to.
Sad hunger in th' abundant earth doth tosse him to and froe,   475
Respected nor of gods nor men. The mixt cup Peleus dranke;
Even from his birth heaven blest his life; he liv'd not that could
    thanke
The gods for such rare benefits as set foorth his estate.
He reign'd among his Myrmidons most rich, most fortunate,
And (though a mortall) had his bed deckt with a deathlesse   480
    Dame.
And yet withall this good, one ill god mixt, that takes all name
From all that goodnesse—his Name now (whose preservation here
Men count the crowne of their most good) not blest with powre
    to beare
One blossome but my selfe, and I shaken as soone as blowne.
Nor shall I live to cheare his age and give nutrition   485

[490]

To him that nourisht me. Farre off my rest is set in Troy,
To leave thee restlesse and thy seed. Thy selfe, that did enjoy
(As we have heard) a happie life—what Lesbos doth containe
(In times past being a blest man's seate), what the unmeasur'd
    maine
Of Hellespontus, Phrygia, holds, are all said to adorne   490
Thy Empire, wealth and sonnes enow—but, when the gods did
    turne
Thy blest state to partake with bane, warre and the bloods of
    men
Circl'd thy citie, never cleare. Sit downe and suffer then.
Mourne not inevitable things; thy teares can spring no deeds
To helpe thee, nor recall thy sonne: impacience ever breeds   495
Ill upon ill, makes worst things worse. And therefore sit.' He said:

Priam to Achilles. 'Give me no seate, great seed of Jove, when yet unransomed
Hector lies ritelesse in thy tents: but daigne with utmost speed
His resignation, that these eyes may see his person freed,
And thy grace satisfied with gifts. Accept what I have brought,   500
And turne to Phthia; tis enough thy conquering hand hath fought
Till Hector faltred under it, and Hector's father stood

Achilles angry with With free humanitie safe.' He frown'd, and said: 'Give not my
Priam.   blood
Fresh cause of furie. I know well I must resigne thy sonne—
Jove by my mother utterd it; and what besides is done,   505
I know as amply, and thy selfe, old Priam, I know too.
Some god hath brought thee, for no man durst use a thought to go
On such a service; I have guards, and I have gates to stay
Easie accesses. Do not then presume thy will can sway
Like Jove's will, and incense againe my quencht blood, lest   510
    nor thou
Nor Jove gets the command of me.' This made the old king bow,
And downe he sate in feare; the Prince leapt like a Lion forth,
Automedon and Alcimus attending; all the worth
Brought for the body they tooke downe and brought in, and
    with it
Idæus, herald to the king; a cote embroderd yet,   515
And two rich cloakes, they left to hide the person. Thetis' sonne
Cald out his women to annoint and quickly overrunne
The Corse with water, lifting it in private to the coach
Lest Priam saw and his cold blood embrac't a fierie touch
Of anger at the turpitude prophaning it and blew   520
Againe his wrath's fire to his death. This done, his women threw
The cote and cloake on; but the Corse Achilles' owne hand laide
Upon a bed, and, with his friends, to chariot it convaide.

For which forc't grace (abhorring so from his free mind) he wept,
Cried out for anger, and thus praide: 'O friend, do not except   525
Against this favour to our foe (if in the deepe thou heare)
And that I give him to his Sire; he gave faire ransome; deare
In my observance is Jove's will, and whatsoever part
Of all these gifts by any meane I fitly may convert
To thy renowne here and will there, it shall be pour'd upon   530
Thy honour'd sepulcher.' This said, he went, and what was done
Told Priam, saying: 'Father, now thy wil's fit rites are paide,
Thy sonne is given up; in the morne thine eyes shall see him laid
Deckt in thy chariot on his bed; in meane space, let us eate.
The rich-hair'd Niobe found thoughts that made her take   535
    her meate,
Though twelve deare children she saw slaine—six daughters,
    six yong sons.
The sonnes incenst Apollo slue; the maides' confusions
Diana wrought, since Niobe her merits durst compare
With great Latona's, arguing that she did onely beare
Two children and her selfe had twelve. For which those onely   540
    two
Slue all her twelve; nine dayes they lay steept in their blood;
    her woe
Found no friend to afford them fire; Saturnius had turnd
Humanes to stones. The tenth day yet the good celestials burnd
The trunkes themselves, and Niobe, when she was tyr'd with
    teares,
Fell to her foode; and now with rockes and wilde hils mixt   545
    she beares
(In Sipylus) the gods' wraths still—in that place where, tis said,
The Goddesse Fairies use to dance about the funerall bed
Of Achelous; where (though turn'd with cold griefe to a stone)
Heaven gives her heate enough to feele what plague comparison
With his powers (made by earth) deserves. Affect not then   550
    too farre
With griefe, like a god, being a man; but for a man's life care,
And take fit foode. Thou shalt have time, beside, to mourne
    thy sonne;
He shall be tearefull, thou being full; not here but Ilion
Shall finde thee weeping roomes enow.' He said, and so arose,
And causd a silver-fleec't sheepe kill'd; his friends' skils did   555
    dispose
The fleaing, cutting of it up, and cookely spitted it,
Rosted, and drew it artfully. Automedon as fit

[492]

Was for the reverend Sewer's place, and all the browne joynts serv'd
On wicker vessell to the boord; Achilles' owne hands kerv'd;
And close they fell too. Hunger stancht, talke and observing time   560

Their mutuall observation of either's fashion at the table.

Was usde of all hands. Priam sate, amaz'd to see the prime
Of Thetis' sonne, accomplisht so with stature, lookes and grace—
In which the fashion of a god he thought had chang'd his place.
Achilles fell to him as fast, admir'd as much his yeares
(Told in his grave and good aspect); his speech even charm'd his eares,   565
So orderd, so materiall. With this food feasted too,

Priam to Achilles.

Old Priam spake thus: 'Now, Jove's seed, command that I may go,
And adde to this feast grace of rest: these lids nere closde mine eyes
Since under thy hands fled the soule of my deare sonne; sighes, cries
And woes all use from food and sleepe have taken; the base courts   570
Of my sad Pallace made my beds, where all the abject sorts
Of sorrow I have varied, tumbl'd in dust and hid,
No bit, no drop, of sustenance toucht.' Then did Achilles bid
His men and women see his bed laid downe and covered
With purple Blankets, and on them an Arras Coverlid,   575
Wast costs of silke plush laying by. The women straite tooke lights
And two beds made with utmost speed, and all the other rites
Their Lord nam'd usde; who pleasantly the king in hand thus bore:

Achilles to Priam.

'Good father, you must sleepe without, lest any Counsellor
Make his accesse in depth of night—as oft their industrie   580
Brings them t' impart our warre-affaires—of whom should any eye
Discerne your presence, his next steps to Agamemnon flie,
And then shall I lose all these gifts. But go to, signifie
(And that with truth) how many daies you meane to keepe the state
Of Hector's funerals; because so long would I rebate   585
Mine owne edge set to sacke your towne, and all our host containe
From interruption of your rites.' He answerd: 'If you meane
To suffer such rites to my sonne, you shall performe a part
Of most grace to me. But you know with how dismaid a heart
Our host tooke Troy, and how much Feare will therefore apprehend   590
Their spirits to make out againe so farre as we must send

[493]

For wood to raise our heape of death—unlesse I may assure
That this your high grace will stand good and make their passe
    secure;
Which if you seriously confirme, nine daies I meane to mourne,
The tenth keepe funerall and feast, th' eleventh raise and   595
    adorne
My sonne's fit Sepulcher. The twelfth (if we must needs) weele
    fight.'
    'Be it,' replyed Æacides, 'do Hector all this right.
I'le hold warre backe those whole twelve daies—of which,
    to free all feare,
Take this my right hand.' This confirm'd, the old king rested
    there.
His Herald lodg'd by him; and both in forepart of the tent;   600
Achilles in an inmost roome of wondrous ornament,
Whose side bright-cheekt Briseis warm'd. Soft Sleepe tam'd
    gods and men—
All but most usefull Mercurie. Sleepe could not lay one chaine
On his quicke temples, taking care for getting off againe
Engaged Priam undiscern'd of those that did maintaine   605
The sacred watch. Above his head he stood with this demand:

*Mercurie appeares to
Priam in his sleepe.*

    'O father, sleep'st thou so secure, still lying in the hand
Of so much ill, and being dismist by great Æacides?
Tis true, thou hast redeem'd the dead, but for thy life's release
(Should Agamemnon heare thee here) three times the price now 610
    paide
Thy sonnes' hands must repay for thee.' This said, the king
    (affraid)
Start from his sleepe, Idæus cald; and (for both) Mercurie
The horse and mules (before losde) joyn'd, so soft and curiously
That no eare heard, and through the host he drave; but when
    they drew
To gulphy Xanthus' bright-wav'd streame up to Olympus flew 615
Industrious Mercurie. And now the saffron morning rose,
Spreading her white robe over all the world—when (full of woes)
They scourg'd on with the Corse to Troy, from whence no eye
    had seene
(Before Cassandra) their returne. She (like love's golden Queene,
Ascending Pergamus) discern'd her father's person nie,   620
His Herald, and her brother's Corse; and then she cast this crie

*Cassandra to the
Troyans.*

Round about Troy: 'O Troyans, if ever ye did greet
Hector return'd from fight alive, now looke ye out and meet
His ransom'd person. Then his worth was all your citie's joy;
Now do it honour.' Out all rusht; woman nor man in Troy 625

Was left; a most unmeasur'd crie tooke up their voices. Close
To Scæa's Ports they met the Corse, and to it headlong goes
The reverend mother, the deare wife, upon it strowe their haire
And lie entranced. Round about, the people broke the aire
In lamentations, and all day had staid the people there,   630
If Priam had not cryed: 'Give way, give me but leave to beare
The body home, and mourne your fils.' Then cleft the preasse
    and gave
Way to the chariot. To the Court Herald Idæus drave,
Where on a rich bed they bestow'd the honor'd person; round
Girt it with Singers, that the woe with skillfull voices crownd. 635
A wofull Elegie they sung, wept singing, and the dames
Sigh'd as they sung. Andromache the downeright prose exclames
Began to all; she on the necke of slaughterd Hector fell

*Andromache's
lamentation for her
husband.*

And cried out: 'O my husband! thou in youth badst youth
    farewell,
Left'st me a widdow, thy sole sonne an infant; our selves curst 640
In our birth made him right our child, for all my care, that nurst
His infancie, will never give life to his youth. Ere that,
Troy from her top will be destroy'd. Thou guardian of our state,
Thou even of all her strength the strength, thou that in care
    wert past
Her carefull mothers of their babes, being gone, how can she 645
    last?
Soone will the swolne fleete fill her wombe with all their
    servitude,
My selfe with them and thou with me, deare sonne, in labours
    rude
Shalt be emploid, sternely survaid by cruell **Conquerors**;
Or, rage not suffering life so long, some one whose hate abhorres
Thy presence (putting him in mind of his sire slaine by thine, 650
His brother, sonne or friend) shall worke thy ruine before mine,

*Andromache's
lamentation for Hector.*

Tost from some towre—for many Greeks have eate earth from
    the hand
Of thy strong father. In sad fight his spirit was too much mann'd,
And therefore mourne his people; we, thy Parents, my deare
    Lord,
For that thou mak'st endure a woe blacke and to be abhorr'd. 655
Of all yet thou hast left me worst, not dying in thy bed
And reaching me thy last-raisd hand; in nothing counselled,
Nothing commanded by that powre thou hadst of me, to do
Some deed for thy sake. O for these never will end my woe,
Never my teares ceasse.' Thus wept she, and all the Ladies 660
    closde

Her passion with a generall shrieke. Then Hecuba disposde

Her thoughts in like words: 'O my sonne, of all mine much
   most deare,
Deare while thou liv'dst too even to gods, and after death
   they were
Carefull to save thee. Being best, thou most wer't envied.
My other sonnes Achilles sold, but thee he left not dead.   665
Imber and Samos, the false Ports of Lemnos entertain'd
Their persons, thine, no Port but death; nor there in rest
   remain'd
Thy violated Corse; the Tombe of his great friend was spher'd
With thy dragg'd person; yet from death he was not therefore
   rer'd,
But (all his rage usde) so the gods have tenderd thy dead state   670
Thou liest as living, sweete and fresh, as he that felt the Fate
Of Phœbus' holy shafts.' These words the Queene usde for her
   mone,
And next her Helen held that state of speech and passion:

'O Hector, all my brothers more were not so lov'd of me
As thy most vertues. Not my Lord I held so deare as thee,   675
That brought me hither; before which I would I had bene
   brought
To ruine; for what breeds that wish (which is the mischiefe
   wrought
By my accesse) yet never found one harsh taunt, one word's ill
From thy sweet cariage. Twenty yeares do now their circles fill
Since my arrivall, all which time thou didst not onely beare   680
Thy selfe without checke, but all else that my Lord's brothers
   were,
Their sisters' Lords, sisters themselves, the Queen my mother
   in law
(The king being never but most milde), when thy man's spirits
   saw
Sowre and reprochfull, it would still reprove their bitternesse
With sweet words, and thy gentle soule. And therefore thy   685
   deceasse
I truly mourne for, and my selfe curse as the wretched cause,
All brode Troy yeelding me not one that any humane lawes
Of pitie or forgivenesse mov'd t' entreate me humanely,
But onely thee; all else abhorr'd me for my destinie.'

These words made even the commons mourn; to whom the   690
   king said: 'Friends,
Now fetch wood for our funerall fire, nor feare the foe intends
Ambush or any violence. Achilles gave his word

[496]

At my dismission that twelve dayes he would keepe sheath'd
    his sword
And all men's else.' Thus oxen, mules, in chariots straite they put,
Went forth, and an unmeasur'd pile of Sylvane matter cut;   695
Nine daies emploide in cariage; but, when the tenth morne
    shinde
On wretched mortals, then they brought the fit-to-be-divin'd
Forth to be burn'd. Troy swum in teares. Upon the pile's most
    height
They laid the person, and gave fire; all day it burn'd, all night—
But, when th' eleventh morne let on earth her rosie fingers   700
    shine,
The people flockt about the pile, and first with blackish wine
Quencht all the flames. His brothers then and friends the
    snowy bones
Gatherd into an urne of gold, still powring on their mones.
Then wrapt they in soft purple veiles the rich urne, digg'd a pit,
Grav'd it, ramb'd up the grave with stones, and quickly built   705
    to it
A sepulcher. But while that worke and all the funerall rites
Were in performance, guards were held at all parts, dayes and
    nights,
For feare of false surprise before they had imposde the crowne
To these solemnities. The tombe advanc't once, all the towne
In Jove-nurst Priam's Court partooke a passing sumptuous   710
    feast.
And so horse-taming Hector's rites gave up his soule to Rest.

Thus farre the Ilian Ruines I have laid
Open to English eyes. In which (repaid
With thine owne value) go, unvalu'd Booke,
Live and be lov'd. If any envious looke
Hurt thy cleare fame, learne that no state more hie
Attends on vertue than pin'd Envie's eye.
Would thou wert worth it, that the best doth wound
Which this Age feedes, and which the last shall bound.

*Thus, with labour enough (though with more comfort in the merits
of my divine Author) I have brought my translation of his* Iliads *to
an end. If either therein, or in the harsh utterance, or matter of my
Comment before, I have, for haste, scatterd with my burthen (lesse
than fifteene weekes being the whole time that the last twelve bookes'* 5
*translation stood me in), I desire my present will and (I doubt not)
hability (if God give life) to reforme and perfect all heareafter may
be ingenuously accepted for the absolute worke—the rather,
considering the most learned (with all their helpes and time) have
bene so often, and unanswerably, miserably taken halting. In the* 10
*meane time, that most assistfull and unspeakeable spirit by whose
thrice-sacred conduct and inspiration I have finished this labour,
diffuse the fruitfull horne of his blessings through these goodnesse-
thirsting watchings; without which, utterly dry and bloodlesse is
whatsoever Mortality soweth.* 15
*But where our most diligent Spondanus ends his worke with a
prayer to be taken out of these Mæanders and Euripian rivers (as he
termes them) of Ethnicke and prophane writers (being quite contrarie
to himselfe at the beginning), I thrice humbly beseech the most deare
and divine mercie (ever most incomparably preferring the great light* 20
*of his truth in his direct and infallible Scriptures) I may ever be
enabled, by resting wondring in his right comfortable shadowes in
these, to magnifie the clearenesse of his almighty apparance in the
other.*
And with this salutation of Poesie given by our Spondanus in his 25
Preface *to these* Iliads—'*All haile, Saint-sacred Poesie, that under so
much gall of fiction, such abundance of honey doctrine, hast hidden,
not revealing them to the unworthy worldly, wouldst thou but so much
make me that amongst thy Novices I might be numbred, no time
should ever come neare my life that could make me forsake thee'—* 30
*I will conclude with this my daily and nightly prayer, learn'd of the
most learned Simplicius:*

[498]

Supplico tibi, Domine, Pater et Dux rationis nostræ, ut nostræ
nobilitatis recordemur qua tu nos ornasti; et ut tu nobis præstò
sis ut iis qui per sese moventur; ut et à corporis contagio   35
brutorumque affectuum repurgemur, eosque superemus et regamus,
et, sicut decet, pro instrumentis iis utamur. Deinde ut nobis
adiumento sis, ad accuratam rationis nostræ correctionem, et
coniunctionem cum iis qui verè sunt per lucem veritatis.

Et tertium, Salvatori supplex oro, ut ab oculis animorum   40
nostrorum caliginem prorsus abstergas, ut (quod apud Homerum est)
norimus bene qui Deus, aut mortalis, habendus.

Amen.

F I N I S

Seaven Bookes

of

The Iliades

1 5 9 8

TO THE MOST HONORED

now living Instance of the Achilleian vertues
eternized by divine HOMERE, the Earle
of ESSEXE, Earle Marshall &c.

How irrationall and brutish an impietie so ever it be, not only to
increase the curse of humanity in making the scum of the body the
Crown of the soule, but to murther and burie her in it, none needs
to be benumd with admiration, since her intellectual blood is shed
with such auctoritie, preferment and profession—and to be a perfect   5
villanizer of her faculties is to seate Custome and Imputation (like
Justice and Wisdome) on both sides of his Chaire, crowning him with
honor. And this even of a plaguy necessitie must come to passe, since
all the meanes we have to make her excellencie knowne to us and to
forge out of that holie knowledge darts to enamour us with her   10
unpainted bewties are held, with too true experience of their effects,
the only Parasites to entangle our estates in miseries and massacres.
Her substance yet being too pure and illustrate to be discernd with
ignorant and barbarous sence, and the matter whereon she works too
passive and drossie to propagate her earthlie residence to eternitie,   15
shee hath devisde (in despight of that worm-eaten Idoll) another
fruitles, dead and despised receptacle to reserve her apparance with
unspeakable profit, comfort and life to al posterities—and that is this
poor scribling, this toy, this too living a preservative for the deathful
toombs of nobility, being accounted in our most gentle and   20
complementall use of it onlie the droppings of an idle humor, farre
unworthie the serious expence of an exact Gentleman's tyme. So is
poore Learning the inseparable Genius of this Homericall writing
I intend; wherein notwithstanding the soules of al the recorded
worthies that ever liv'de become eternally embodyed even upon   25
earth and, our understanding parts making transition in that we
understand, the lyves of worthilie-termed Poets are their earthlie
Elisummes; wherein we walke with survivall of all the deceased
worthies we reade of, everie conceipt, sentence, figure and word
being a most bewtifull lyneament of their soules' infinite bodies, and, 30

could a beautie be objected to sence, composde of as many divine
members, and that wee had sences responsible for their full
apprehension, they should impresse no more pleasure to such a bodie
than is sweetly enjoyde in this true manner of communication and
combination of soules. But as it is not possible such a beauty and   35
such organs of apprehension should be compact, no more can any
sensuall delight compare with the Felicitie of the Minde. And ought
not this to be so, where the incomprehensible figure of God is diffusde
in sacred and everlasting Beames, where wee have in earth societie
with Eternitie? Al this walkes upon the bosome of Death in the   40
worthiest writing—and shall a man vayle to a painted Begger on
horseback and goe sawcilie by such a godlike resplendence with
a wall eye and an horned countenance? For, as Number, Sound and
Ryme can challenge no inclusion of the soule without divine
invention, judgement and disposition, no more can the soule expect   45
Eternitie on earth without such eternall writing. And to cast this
with our vanities at our backs is to beare the lives of beasts in our
bosomes, in which base portage is ever borne contempt of fame,
honor and love of the best, which never hath accompanied any
humaine or lesse than barbarous condition.   50

   To you then, most abundant President of true Noblesse, in whose
manifest actions all these sacred objects are divinely pursude, I most
humblie and affectionatlie consecrate this President of all learning,
vertue, valour, honor and societie, who (with his owne soule) hath
eternizde Armies of Kings and Princes, whose imperiall Muse, the   55
great Monarch of the world would say effected more of his Conquests
than his universall power. And therefore at Achilles' toombe (with
most holy impression of fame and the zeale of eternitie) pronouncst
him most happie to have so firme an Eternizer as Homere.

   Most true Achilles (whom by sacred prophecie Homere did but   60
prefigure in his admirable object and in whose unmatched vertues
shyne the dignities of the soule and the whole excellence of royall
humanitie), let not the Pessant-common polities of the world, that
count all things servile and simple that pamper not their own private
sensualities, burying quick in their filthie sepulchres of earth the   65
whole bodies and soules of honor, vertue and pietie, stirre your
divine temper from perseverance in godlike pursute of Eternitie.

   We must assure our selves that the soule hath use, comfort and
benifite in her dissolution and second being of the fame, love and
example shee proposed here, since shee hath generall combination   70
with blessed Eternitie, and fame, love and example being all eternall.

   Now, if eternity be so victorious and triumphant a Goddesse that
with her adamantine foote shee treades uppon scepters, riches, sences,
sensualities and all the safron-guilded pompe of ignorant braveries,

onely knowledge having the assentfull spirite to treade upon that   75
foote and be lifted to the height and sweetenes of her bosome, what
place with the greatest doth an eternizer merite? The foote and the
backe parts? How to be accounted? According to his unfashionable
habite of povertie that, like the poisoned mists of thawing mucpits,
smokes from the horded treasure of soulelesse goldwormes? If the   80
crowne of humanitie be the soule, and the soule an intellectual beam
of God, the essence of her substance being intellection and
intellection or understanding the strength and eminence of her
faculties, the differencing of men in excellencie must be directed
onelie by their proportions of true knowledge. Homericall writing,   85
then, being the native deduction, image and true heire of true
knowledge, must needes in desert inherite his father's dignitie.

Helpe then, renown'de Achilles, to preferre and defend your grave
and blamelesse Prophet of Phœbus from the doting and vitious furie
of the two Atrides—Arrogancie and Detraction. Be dreadlesse   90
bulwarkes to bashfull and fainting vertue against all those whose
faces Barbarisme and Fortune have congealde with standing Lakes
of impudencie, who, being damd up with their muddie ignorance,
retaine no feeling of that to which al their sences are dutifully
consecrate, against our five-witted censors, through whose braines all   95
thinges exact and refinde run to the earth in heapes—when nothing
remaines but stones and unserviceable rubbish. And gratulate in
English extraction, with free and honorable encouragement, this
poore assaye of Poesie's Greeke Nectar—which I durst not more
liberally powre out for feare of vulgar prophanation, if that divine   100
sweetenes and nourishment it hath wrought in divinest tempers
should for want of pallat and constitution in others want his due
attribution. My hope of excuse, therefore, may be worthilie
grounded, since this penurie being effected with such store of labor
and so much quintessence to be drawne from so little a project, it   105
will ask as much judgement to peruse worthily as whole volumes
of more perviall inventions.

Besides, this enforced breach of the commandement—to live
without care of tomorrow (which ever carries his confounded
punishment with it, distracts invention necessarie even in translation) 110
—interrupts the industry of conceipt and the discourse of the soule—
and then the too true consideration that whatsoever is laborde in
this kinde is esteemde but idlenes and vanitie, though of such sacred
importance that all wholesome lawes and constitutions have
heretofore beene exhalde, and the conceipte, direction and highest   115
wing of most grave soules have taken strength and inspiration from
it. This I say, most excellent Earle, could not as yet admit more
English to this most excellent Poet and Philosopher, the flood and

variety of my native language, as it were, with dumbnes fettered in my
unhappie bosome, and every comfort that might dissolve and   120
encourage it utterlie bereft me. Your honord countenance yet and
vouchsafte reacknowledgement of one so unworthy as my selfe (being
the great objects of al my labors in their first dedication) shal draw
on the rest.

 And thus wishing for the worthy expence of my future life to   125
follow by al opportunitie your honord attempts and admirde
disposition, I doubt not my zeale to the truth of your rare vertues
will enable me (inferior to none) to turne my paper to Christall,
from whence no time shall race the engraven figures of your graces.
In the meane time, if your Lordship descend to acceptation of these   130
few disordred Iliades, I shall recompence their defects in their next
edition. Nor can it be reputed an unworthy incitement to propose
the true image of all vertues and humaine governement (even in
the hart of this tumultuous season) to your other serious affaires,
especially since it contaynes the true portraite of ancient stratagems 135
and diciplines of war, wherein it wilbe worthie little lesse than
admiration of your apprehensive judgement to note in many thinges
the affinitie they have with your present complementes of field—
the orations, counsailes, attempts and exploits not to be exceeded
by the freshest brains of this hote-spirited time, the horror of arms   140
endlesly thundering, piety, justice, valour and royaltie eternally
shining in his soule-infused verse. To which (honorably pardoning
this tedious induction) turne and heare your divine Homer
(according to Spondanus' attraction) *magnificè canentem.*

> By him that first and ever freely   145
> consecrates his whole faculties to the
> honor of your princelie vertues.
>
> GEORGE CHAPMAN

TO THE READER

I suppose you to be no meare reader since you intend to reade
Homer, and therefore wish I may walke free from their common
objections that can onelie reade. When my disorder is seene—that
fower bookes are skipped (as a man would say) and yet the Poem
continued according to the Greeke alphabet: viz. that for Gamma   5
which is Eta, *and that for* Delta *which is* Theta *&c.—then comes my*
knowne condemnation more greevously than charitie would wish,
especially with those that, having no eyes to peruse and judge of the
translation and whatsoever the maine matter deserves, will be glad
to shew thay see something in finding fault with that forme and   10
peradventure finde their queasie stomackes turnde at whatsoever is
merited in the much laborde worke.

   But to him that is more than a reader I write, and so consequentlie
to him that will disdaine those easie objections which every speller
may put together. The worth of a skilfull and worthy translator   15
is to observe the sentences, figures and formes of speech proposed
in his author, his true sence and height, and to adorne them with
figures and formes of oration fitted to the originall in the same tongue
to which they are translated: and these things I would gladlie have
made the questions of whatsoever my labors have deserved—not   20
slighted with the slight disorder of some bookes, which if I can put
in as fit place hereafter without checke to your due understanding
and course of the Poet, then is their easie objection answerde that I
expect wilbe drounde in the fome of their eager and emptie spleanes.
For likelyhood of which habilitie I have good authoritie that the   25
bookes were not set together by Homer *himselfe,* Lycurgus *first*
bringing them out of Ionia *in* Greece *as an entire Poeme, before*
whose time his verses were sung dissevered into many workes—one
calde the battaile fought at the fleete, another Doloniades, another
Agamemnon's *fortitude, another the Catalogue of ships, another*   30
Patroclus' *death, another* Hector's *redemption, another the funerall*
games, &c. All which are the titles of severall Iliades: and, if those
were ordred by others, why may not I chalenge as much authority,
reserving the right of my president? But to omit what I can say
further for reason to my present alteration, in the next edition when   35
they come out by the dosen I will reserve the ancient and common
received forme. In the meane time do me the encouragement to
confer that which I have translated with the same in Homer and

*according to the worth of that let this first edition passe. So shall you
do me but lawfull favor and make me take paines to give you this* 40
*Emperor of all wisedome (for so Plato will allow him) in your owne
language, which will more honor it (if my part bee worthily
discharged) than any thing else can be translated. In the meane time
peruse the pamphlet of errors in the impression and helpe to point
the rest with your judgement—wherein, and in purchase of the* 45
*whole seaven, if you be quicke and acceptive, you shall in the next
edition have the life of Homer, a table, a prettie comment, true
printing, the due praise of your mother tongue above all others for
Poesie and such demonstrative proofe of our English wits above
beyond-sea muses (if we would use them) that a proficient* 50
wit should be the better to heare it.

THE FIRST BOOKE

of

HOMER'S ILIADES

THE ARGUMENT

Apollo's Priest to th' Argive Fleete doth bring
Gifts for his daughter, prisoner to the King.
For which her tendred freedome he intreates:
But, being dismist with contumelious threates,
At Phœbus' hands by vengefull prayer he seekes   5
To have a plague inflicted on the Greekes.
Which done, Achilles doth a Counsell cite
And forceth Calchas in the King's despite
To tell the trueth why they were punishte so,
From whence their fierce and deadlie strife doth grow— 10
In which Achilles so extreamelie raves
That Goddesse Thetis from her Throne of waves
(Ascending Heaven) of Jove assistance wonn
T'afflict the Greekes by absence of her Sonne
And make the Gennerall himselfe repent   15
To wrong so much his Armie's Ornament.
This found by Juno, shee with Jove contends
Till Vulcan with Heaven's cuppe the quarrell ends.

Another Argument

Alpha the prayer of Chryses sings,
The Armie's plague, th' incensed Kings.

Achilles' banefull wrath resound, great Goddesse of my verse,
That through th'afflicted host of Greece did worlds of woes
    disperse
And timelesse sent by troopes to hell the glorie-thirsting soules
Of great Heroes, but their lims left foode for beasts and foules.
So Jove's high counsell tooke event, from whence that Jarr begun 5
Twixte Agamemnon, King of men, and Thetis' Godlike sonn.
What God did give them up to strife? Jove's and Latona's seede

Who, angrie with the King for wrongs against his Priest decreede,
Excited sicknes through the host, which much life put to flight.
His Priest came to the Greekes' swift Fleete with ransome   10
    infinite,
The golden Scepter and the Crowne far-shooting Phœbus wore,
To free his daughter—which in hand he did propose before
The Peeres of Greece, whome he besought, but both th'Atrides
    most,
Who were most mightie in the rule of all th'imperiall Host:
    'Atrides and the wel-greavde Greekes, Gods that in heavenlie   15
    hals
Make blest abodes, renowme your swords with Priam's razed wals
And grant you safe retreat to Greece. Meane tyme accept of mee
This holie ransome and returne my dearest daughter free,
Approving your religious mindes to him from Jove descends,
Divine Apollo, that his darts through all the earth extends.'   20
The gennerall presence well allowd the Priest and his demands
And thought the shyning presents fitte to free his daughter's
    bands:
But Agamemnon was displeasde and did his gifts refuse,
Dismist him with unfitte repulse, and this hard charge did use:
    'Hence, doating Priest, nor let me find thy stay protracted now   25
In circuite of our hollow Fleete, or once hereafter know
Of thy returne: for, if I doe, the Crowne thou doest sustaine
And golden scepter of thy God thou shalt present in vaine.
Thy daughter I will not dissolve till age deflower her hed,
Till in my Royall Argive court her bewties strow my bed   30
And shee her twisting spindle turnes farre from her native shore,
To which if thou wilt safe returne, tempte our contempte
    no more.'
    This answere strooke the Priest with feare, who servd his
    sterne command,
In silence shunning his abode, and walkt along the strand
Of Neptune's high-resounding rule. When from the Fleete   35
    farre gone,
Thus prayde he to the King of Flames, faire-hayrd Latona's sonne:
'Heare thou that bearest the silver Bow, that dost on Chrysa shine,
That stronglie governst Tenedos and Cylla most divine!
O Sminthius! if ever I thy thankfull Temple crownde,
Or with fatte thighes of Buls and Goats hath made thy fires   40
    abound,
Give full effect to my desires, and for these teares I shed
Let Greekes pay paines and with thy shafts in troopes be striken
    deade.'
    Thus prayd he, and Apollo heard, who, at the heart offended,

Downe from the toples browes of heaven into the hoast
    descended.
His bowe and Quiver coverd rounde his golden shoulders wore; 45
His angry arrowes (as he movde) did thunder on the Shore.
So, like the lowring night, he walkt and tooke his wreakfull
    stande
Athwart the Fleete. His silver Bowe with his hard-losing hande
A dreadfull sound did make, and first the mules and dogges
    he wounds
And after with the brests of men his mortall shafts confounds. 50
The funerall pyles did ever burne with heapes of men he slew.
Nine dayes together through the host his poysoned arrowes flew;
The tenth a counsell through the Camp Æacides designde,
Which Juno with the silver Armes did put into his minde,
Who stoode remorsefull of the Greekes, to see them everie where 55
Employ the greedy fires of death. And now convented were
The chiefe commanders of the camp, who altogether plaste,
From sacred Thetis' swifte-foote sonne this supposition paste:
  'Atrides, some new error now procures this plague, I feare,
To drive us hence, if with our lives we may th'impulsions beare 60
Of this our double pestilence—th'infection and our warre.
But let us some grave Prophet aske, or Priest that sees from
    farre,
Or some interpretor of dreames (for dreames proceede from Jove),
Who may report what sinne doth thus the Delphian Archer move
To punish us—if Hecatombs or fumes of offered sheepe, 65
Or soundest Goates, or vowes unkept which now our zeales may
    keepe,
That his sharpe arrowes in our breasts he may refraine to steepe.'
  Achilles, having said, sat downe; when Calchas, Thestor's
    sonne,
(The best of Augures, that was skilde in all things present done,
Deedes past and everie act to come, and did direct the course 70
Of th'Argive Fleete to Ilion, for his prophetique force
Given by Apollo) next stoode up, and thus did silence breake:
  'Jove-lovd Achilles, if thou wish and wilt command me speake
My knowledge of Apollo's wrath, covenant and sweare to mee
That readie with thy hand and sword thou will assistant bee 75
Both now and in affaires to come. For him that most doth sway
The soveragne Empire of the hoste, whome all the Greekes obay,
I feare my sentence will offend; and if a mightie state
Against a much inferiour man conceive a lordlie hate,
Though he depresse it for the time, yet he reserves it still 80
Till best advauntage of his power have perfected his will.
Say then if thou wilt warrant me against the worst event.'

Achilles answerd: 'All thou knowest, speake, and be confident.
For by the deere-belovd of Jove, the daye's Eternall King,
From whome, O Calchas, to the Greekes thou Oracles dost sing,   85
Not one of all the Peeres shall lay offensive hands on thee
While my truth-shielding forces last or that in earth I see—
No, not if Agamemnon's frowne be object of thy feares,
Who to be soveraigne of us all the glorious title beares.'
      Then tooke the blamelesse prophet hart and saide: 'They   90
      were not vowes
Yet unperformd, nor Hecatombes, but love that Phœbus showes
In honor of his prieste disgrast by Agamemnon's will,
That skornd his ransome and reserves his dearest daughter still;
For this Apollo sends this plague and yet will send us more,
Nor will containe from our distresse his heavie hand before   95
The blacke-eyde virgin be releast unbought and ransomlesse
And convoyed hence with Hecatombes, till her chaste foot
      do presse
The flowrie Chrysa's holie shoore. And so, if we shall please
Th'offended God, perhaps he may recure this keene disease.'
    He sat. The great Heroe rose, the far-commanding king   100
Atrides, full of frowarde griefe, excessive anger's sting
Sperst blacke fumes round about his brest; his eyes like burning
      fire
Sparcled beneath his bended browes, as lightnings of his ire,
And, looking sternelie on the priest, 'Prophet of ill,' said he,
'That never didst presage my good, but tookest delight to be   105
Offensive in thy Auguries, not one good worde proceedes
From thy rude lips, nor is performd in anie future deedes!
And now thou frowardlie dost preach, in midst of al the Greekes,
That heaven's farre-shooter in this plague the restitution seekes
Of my faire prisoner, who, retaind, is cause of our annoy—   110
And all because thou knowest in her I take such speciall joy
And wish to bring her to my Court, since I esteeme her more
Than Clytemnestra that to me the nuptiall contract swore
When shee was yet a maide and young, nor doth she merite lesse
Both for her bodie's comelie forme, her native towardenesse,   115
Her wisedome and her huswiferie. Yet will I render her,
If it be best: for to my good my Souldiers' I preferre.
But in her place some other pryse see quickelie you prepare,
That I alone of all the Greekes loose not my honor's share—
Which needes must bee confest unfit: but thus, my friendes,   120
      you see
That what by all your mindes is myne another takes from mee.'
    To him the excellentest of foot, divine Achilles, said:
'Ambitious and most covetous man, what prise can be repaid

By these our noble-minded friendes for thy desirde supply?
All know how scantlie we have storde our common treasury.   125
For what the spoiled Citties gave, ech souldier for his paine
Hath duelie shard by our consentes, which to exact againe
Were base and ignominious. But to the God resigne
Thy pleasure for our common good, and, if the most divine
So grace us that this well-walled towne we leavill with the   130
     plaine,
We fourefold will repay the losse thy fortunes now sustaine.'
    The king replide: 'Be not deceyved, nor thinke though thou
     art strong
And godlike framde, thou canst perswade my patience to my
     wrong,
Or that thy feet into thy breath can transmigrated bee
To passe me with thy sleightes as well as in outrunning mee.   135
Wouldst thou thy selfe injoy thy prise, and I sit dispossest?
Then let the Greekes apply themselves as much to my request
And with some other fit amendes my satisfaction make.
If not, I'le make mine owne amendes, and come my selfe,
     and take
Thyne, Ajax' or Ulysses' prise (men of most excellence   140
And most admitted to thy love) and let him take offence
On whome I shall performe my vow: but touching this designe
We will hereafter or elsewhere decide what shall be mine.
Now let us lanch the sable barke into the holy seas,
Shippe chosen rowers in her bankes and Hecatombes to ease   145
Our instant plague; and wee wil cause bright Chryseis to ascend,
Whose charge to some Greeke prince in chiefe tis fit we should
     commend—
Or to the royal Idomen, or Ajax Telamon,
Or to the prudent counsaylor, divine Laertes' sonne,
Or to the terriblest of men, thy selfe, Æacides,   150
That offrings made by thy strong hands Apollo may appease.'
    Æacides, observing well the urgte authoritie
Of his proud foe with browes contract, returnd this sharp reply:
'O thou possest with Impudence, that in command of men
Affectst the brute mind of a Fox, for so thou fill thy denne   155
With forced or betrayed spoiles thou feelest no sence of shame!
What souldier can take any spirite to put on (for thy fame)
Contempt of violence and death, or in the open field
Or secret ambush, when the heyre his hie desert should yeeld
Is beforehand condemnd to glut thy gulfe of avarice?   160
For me, I have no cause t'account these Ilians enemies;
Nor of my Oxen nor my horse have they made hostile spoile,
Nor hurt the comfortable fruites of Phthia's populous soyle,

For manie shadie distances, hils and resounding Seas
Are interposde: but our kinde armes are lifted to release   165
(Thou sencelesse of all Royaltie) thyne and thy brother's fame,
Imprisond in disgracefull Troy, which nothing doth inflame
Thy dogged nature to requite with favour or renowne.
Our ceaslesse and important toiles—for which what is myne own,
Given by the generall hands of Greece yet by the valure got   170
Of my free labours, thy rude lust will wrest into thy lot.
In distribution of all townes wun from our Troyan foes,
Still more than mine to thy heapt store th'uneven proportion
          rose,
But in proportion of the fight the heaviest part did rise
To my discharge, for which I find much praise and little prise.   175
But I'le endure this ods no more; tis better to retire
And to my countrie take my fleet, not feeding thy desire
Both with the wracke of my renowne and of my wealth beside,
Exhausted by the barbarous thirst of thy degenerat pride.'
     'Affectst thow flight,' replyed the king, 'be gon and let not me 180
Nor anie good of mine be cause to stay the fleete or thee.
There are enow besides will stay and do my state renowne,
But chiefely prudent Jupiter. Of all his hand doth crowne
Thou still art bittrest to my rule; contention and sterne fight
To thee are unitie and peace; if thou exceed in might,   185
God gave it thee; and tis absurde to glorie as our owne
In that we have not of our selves but is from others growne.
Home with thy fleet and Myrmidons: there let thy rule be seene.
I loath so much to feare thy rage or glorifie thy spleene
That to thy face I threaten thee; and, since th'offended Sunne   190
Takes Chryseis from me, whome by right of all consents I wun,
Yet I with mine owne shippe and men must send her to her Syre,
My selfe will to thy tent repayre and take thy hart's desire,
Even bright-cheekt Briseis, from thine arms—that then thy pride
          may sweare
Atrides is thy better far, and all the rest may feare   195
To vaunt equallitie with mee or take ambitious hart
To stand with insolence comparde in any adverse part.'
     This set Pelides' soule on fire, and in his brisled brest
His rationall and angrie parts a doutfull strife possest,
If he should draw his wreakefull sword and, forcing way   200
          through all,
Make Agamemnon's braverie fit for bloudie funerall
Or else restraine his forward mind and calme his anger's heat.
Whilst in his thus devided selfe these agitations beate
And he his mightie sword unsheathde, wise Pallas was in place
Foresent by great Saturnia that makes the white embrace,   205

[514]

Who of the two late enimies had wondrous love and care.
She stood behind Æacides, and by the goulden hayre
She puld him to her, and to him she onelie did appeare—
Who, turning to her heavenlie sight, was stroke with reverend
    feare
But by her dreadefull sparkling eyes her godhead straight   210
    he knew
And said: 'Why comes Jove's daughter here? The arrogance
    to view
Of Atreus' sonne? Twere fitter death his barbarous pride should
    bowe,
Whose Author I have vowd to be and wil performe my vow.'
    She answered: 'Tis not best for thee; and I am come t'appease
Thy violent furie, if thou wilt for my perswasions cease,   215
Sent by the ivorie-fingerd Queene, that tenders both your lives.
Forbeare then thy adviseles sword and rule that part that strives,
Reprooving him with words more safe. And here I promise thee
What shalbe perfectlie performd: thou shalt presented bee
With giftes of threefold eminence to thy receyved wrong.   220
And therefore serve our deities, and onely use thy tong.'
    'Tis fit,' Pelides did replie, 'Your godheades shold be pleasd,
Though at my soule I bee incenst. Who is for heaven appeasd
Heaven will appease his wrongs for him.' This said, his ample
    hand,
Closd in his silver hilt, forbore and did the Dame's command.   225
So to the heavenlie house she flew of Ægis-bearing Jove,
To keep her state with other Queenes that sway the thrones
    above.
She gone, Pelides did renew breach of his temper's peace
And gave the king dispightful words, nor yet his wrath wold
    cease:
'Thou great in wine with dogged lookes and hart but of a Hart,   230
That never with the formost troups in fight darst shake thy dart,
Nor in darke ambush arme thy selfe—these seeme too ful of death
For thy cold spirite: tis more safe, with contumelious breath,
To show thy manhood gainst a man that contradicts thy lust
And with thy covetous valour take his spoiles with force   235
    unjust,
Because thou knowest a man of fame will take wrong ere he be
A generall mischiefe, nor shamst thou though all the armie see.
Thou souldier-eating king, it is on beasts thou rule hast won,
Or else this wrong had beene the last thou ever shouldst
    have done.
But I protest and sweare to thee a great and sacred oath,   240
Even by this scepter which with kings lawes and religion both

Was wont to institute, and held a symbole of the right
By partles justice ministred, and stil bewrayes the might
Of princes carried in their hands, protecting all the lawes
We all receive from Jupiter—which gives sufficient cause   245
To make thee thinke I meane t'observe what I so deepelie
    sweare—
That as it never since it grew did leaves or branches beare,
Cut from the hils, and can no more produce delightsome shade,
So, since thy most inhumaine wrongs have such a slaughter made
Of my affections borne to thee, they never shall renew   250
Those sweet and comfortable flowers with which of late they
    grew,
But when the universall hoast shall faint with strong desire
Of wrongd Achilles, though thou pyne thou never shalt aspyre
Helpe to their miseries from me, when underneath the hand
Of bloody Hector cold as death their bodies spred the sand   255
And thou with inwarde hands of griefe shalt teare thy desperate
    minde
That to the most kinde-worthie Greeke thou wert so most
    unkind.'
    This said, he threw against the ground the scepter he susteind,
Through which in bright transfixed droppes a shower of gould
    was raynd.
    So sate the king and he inragde, when up old Nestor stood,   260
The thundering Pylean Orator whose tong powrde forth a floud
Of hony-sweeting eloquence: two ages he had liv'de
Of sundrie-languagde men, all which were dead yet he survivde
And now amongst the third he raignd. He thus bespake the
    peeres:
    'O Gods! what mightie woes wil pierce through all true   265
    Achive eares,
And how will Priam and his sonnes, with all the Ilian seed,
Even at their harts rejoyce to heare these haynous discordes
    breed
Twixt you who in the skill of fight and counsels so excell
All other Greekes! Let my advise this bitternes expell:
You are not both so old as I, who livde with men that were   270
Your betters far yet ever held my exhortations deare—
I never saw nor ever shall behold the like of them
Of whome my counsels were esteemd—the godlike Polyphem,
Exadius, and Perithous, and Dryas great in power,
And Theseus wedded to renowne with an immortall dower,   275
And Cæneus a right worthie man, all which the strongest were
Of all the earth then nourished, the strongest past compare,

And with the strongest Centaures fought that ever mountaine
    bred
And bravelie slew them; and with these my Lycians forth I led
Far from the land of Apia. Themselves did call me forth   280
And to my outmost strength I fought, and these were men
    whose worth
No men that now live durst withstand, yet these would gladlie
    heare
My counsels and obey them too. Then do not both you beare
Greater conceipts than greater men, but, as they did, obey.
Obedience better is than rule, where rule erres in his sway.   285
Let not the king officiously by force the damsell take
But yeeld her whome the Greekes at first Pelides' prise did make.
Nor let a king's heire against a king with such contempt repine,
Since never scepter-state attain an honour so divine,
And rightfully, by Jove's high gift—though better borne   290
    thou bee
Because a goddesse brought thee foorth, yet better man is he
Since his command exceedes so much. Then let the king subdue
His spirite's greatnesse, and my selfe to Thetis' sonne will sue
That he depose his furie's heat, who is the mightiest barre
Betwixt the Grecians' safe estate and power of impious warre.'   295
    'With good decorum, reverend Syre,' Atrides did replie,
'Thou givest us counsell, but this man above us all will flie,
All in his power he will conclude and over all men raigne,
Commanding al—all which I thinke his thoughtes attempt in
    vaine.
What if the ever-being state to him such strength affordes?   300
Is it to rende up men's renownes with contumelious wordes?'
Achilles interrupted him: 'Thou mightst esteeme me base
And cowardlie to let thee use thy will in my disgrace;
To beare such burthens never were my strength and spirites
    combinde,
But to reforme their insolence, and that thy soule should finde   305
Were it not hurt of common good more than mine owne delight.
But I, not soothing Nestor's sute, for right's sake reverence right,
Which thou dost servilely commend but violate it quite.
And this even in thy intrayles print—I'le not prophane my hand
With battell in my lust's defence: a gyrle cannot command   310
My honour and my force like thine, who yet commandes our
    hoast.
Slave live he to the world that lives slave to his lusts engrost.
But feed it, come, and take the dame; safe go thy violent feete,
But whatsoever else thou findst aborde my sable fleete

Dare not to touch without my leave, for feele my life   315
    mischance
If then thy blacke and lust-burnt bloud flow not upon my
    Lance.'
  Contending thus in wordes apposde, they rose. The counsaile
    brake.
Pelides to his tents and ships, his friend and men did take.
Atrides lancht the swift-sayld shippe into the brackish seas
And put therein the Hecatombe that should the God appease;   320
Twise ten selected rowers then; then Chryseis foorth he brings,
Made her ascend the sacred shippe. With her the grace of kings,
Wise Ithacus, ascended too. All shipt together then,
Neptune's moist wildernes they plow. The king chargde all
    his men
Should hallowed Lustrations use, which done, into the floud   325
They threw the offall and the barke purgde from polluted blood.
Thus sweet and due solemnities they to Apollo keepe
Of Buls and Goates, neere to the shore of the unfruitefull deep.
The savor wrapt in cloudes of smoake ascended to the skies;
And thus they sanctified the Campe with generall sacrifice.   330
Yet Agamemnon's froward thoughts did not from discord cease,
But cald to him Talthybius and grave Eurybates,
Herralds and carefull ministers of all his high commandes,
And this injurious Ambasie committed to their hands:
'Goe to Achilles' tent and take the bright-cheekt Briseis   335
    thence.
If he denie, tell him my selfe with more extreame offence
Will come and force her from his armes with unresisted bandes.'
The Herralds all unwilling went along the barren sands.
The tentes and fleet of Myrmidons they reatcht and found the
    king
In his blacke shippe and tent, his lookes markt with his   340
    anger's sting,
Greeting their entrie—which amazde and made them reverend
    stand,
Not daring to salute his moode nor what they sought demande.
He, seeing them loath th'injurious cause of his offence to be,
'Welcome, ye Herraldes, messengers of gods and men!' said he.
'Come neare. I blame not you, but him that gainst your wils   345
    doth send
To have the lovelie Briseis brought. Patroclus, princelie frend,
Bring foorth the dame and render her. Pleasd be their soveraign
    then.
But here before the blessed gods, before the eyes of men,
Before your ignominious king, be faithfull witnesses

Of what I beare. If ever worke in future bitternes   350
Of anie plague to be remoovde from your unhappy host
Be needeful of my friendlie hand, wrong hath your refuge lost.
Your king not present harmes conceives, much lesse succeeding
    woes,
But, led by envious counsell, raves and knowes not what he does,
Nor how to winne his name renowne, being carefull to foretell   355
How with lest death his men might fight and have them bulwarkt
    well.'
    This said, Patroclus well allow'd the patience of his frend,
Brought Briseis forth, and to her guides her comforts did
    commend
With utmost kindenesse, which his frend could not for anguish
    use.
Shee wept and lookt upon her love; he sigh't and did refuse.   360
O how his wisdome with his power did mightilie contend—
His love incouraging his power and spirite, that durst descend
As far as Hercules for her, yet wisedome all subdude,
Wherein a high exploite he showd, and sacred fortitude.
Briseis without her soule did move and went to th'Achive   365
    tents:
Achilles, severd from his frendes, melts anger in lamentes
Upon the shore of th'aged deepe; vewing the purple seas
And lifting his broade hands to heaven, he did with utterance
    ease
His manlie bosome, and his wrongs to Thetis thus relate:
    'O mother, since you brought me forth to breath so short   370
    a date,
Th'Olympian thunderer might commix some boone with my
    short breath,
That what my mind's power, wanting time, contracts in timeles
    death,
Short life wel-gract might amplifie—which Jupiter denies,
As if his gifts, being given in vaine, men justlie might despise,
Admitting Atreus' sonne to vaunt th'enforcement of my prise.'   375
His mother (seated in the deepes of Neptune's softned skye
With old Oceanus) forsakes the gray seas like a clowde
And presentlie before him sate, whome ruthfull sorrowes bowde.
She myniond him with her soft hand and said: 'Why mourns
    my sonne?
What bold woes dare invade thy breast? Conceale not what is   380
    done,
But tell that we may both partake one mournefull injury.'

He, sighing, said: 'Why should I tell? Thou knowest as well
    as I.
We went and ransackt sacred Thebes, Eetion's wealthie towne,
Brought thence the spoyle and parted it; each man possest
    his owne.
Th'Atrides bewteous Chryseis chusde, whose libertie was sought   385
By her grave Father, Phœbus' Priest, that to the Navie brought
A precious ransome, even the Crowne and Scepter of his God;
Which Atreus' impious sonne despisde and threatned his abode,
Dismissing him with all disgrace; for which his vengefull prayer
Attaind of Phœbus such a plague as poysoned all the Ayer,   390
In which his shafts flew through our Campe and manie soldiers
    died.
We had an Augure that our cause of mischief prophesied:
I urgde th'appeasure of the Gods, which vext Atrides so
He threatned his amends on me, which with disgracefull woe
He hath performd: his heralds now fetcht Briseis from my tent,   395
Whose bewtie was my valour's prise by everie Greek's consent.
If then thou canst assist thy sonne, ascend Olympus' top;
Pray Jove, if ever his estate thy godhead helpt to prop,
By ministrie of words or works he will assistance grant,
Since often in my father's Court mine eares have heard thee   400
    vant
(As women love to tell their worth) thou didst avert, alone
Of all th'immortals, cruell skath from that clowde-maker's
    throne,
When Juno, Neptune and the dame he shooke out of his braine
Offerd to binde him: thy repaire their furies did restraine
And brought the hundred-handed power to high Olympus'   405
    Hall,
Whome Gods doe Briareus name but men Ægæon call,
Whose strength redoubled his strong Syre's. He fraied the
    immortall states
And drave them from the impious chains should execute their
    hates:
For which in Jove's owne throne he joyd. Let this remembred
    bee:
Sit ever praying at his foote, never forsake his knee,   410
Till (if by any meanes he meane to helpe Troy) now he daine
To fight for Ilion and expell the Greekes to sea againe,
Or, slaughterd at their Fleete, their lives may wreake their king's
    offence
And he in his acknowledgde harmes confesse my Eminence.'
Thetis powrd out replie in teares: 'Ay me, my Sonne,'   415
    said shee,

'Why, bearing thee to such hard fate, did my breasts nourish
    thee?
O would thou wouldst conteyne thy self at Fleete from wrongs
    and teares
Since fates allow thee little life, and that too swiftlie weares.
Soone must thou die, and yet the date is hastned with such woes
As none indures: and therefore sad and haples were my throes   420
That brought thee forth. But Jupiter, that doth in thunder joy,
I will importune as thou wilst and all my powers imploy,
Skaling Olympus' snowie browes to order, if I may,
An honorable wreake for thee. Meane time unmoved stay
Hid in thy tent, and skorne the Greekes: thought of their ayde   425
    abstaine.
Jove by Oceanus yesterday with all th'immortall traine
Went to the holy Æthiops' feast, which thrise fower dayes will
    end:
Then will he turne to heaven againe, and then will I ascend
His Pyramis, whose base is brasse, where round about his knee
I will sollicite thy revenge and hope to bring it thee.'   430
    Thus left shee her deare sonne, with wrath for his lost love
        still fed,
Whome wilfull force, against his will, tooke from his mournfull
    bed.
Ulysses with the Hecatombe arivde on Chrysa's shore,
And when into the haven's deepe mouth they came to use
    the Ore,
They straite strooke saile, they rowld them up and them on   435
    th'hatches threw,
The topmaste by the kelsine laide with Cables downe they drew.
The ship then into harbor brought with Ores, they Anker cast
And gainst the violent sway of stormes make her for drifting fast.
All come ashore, they all exposde the sacred Hecatome
To angrie Phœbus, and withall faire Chryseis forth doth come,   440
Who wise Ulysses to her Syre, that did at th'Altar stand,
For honor leade, and with these words resignde her to his hand:
    'Chryses, the mightie King of men, great Agamemnon, sends
Thy loved daughter safe to thee, and to thy god commends
This holy Hecatombe, to cease the plague he doth extend   445
Amongst the sighe-expiring Greekes and make his power their
    friend.'
    Thus he resignde her to her Syre, who tooke her full of joy.
The honord offring to the god they orderlie imploy
About the Altar, wash their hands and take their salted cakes,
When Chryses with erected hands this prayer to Phœbus makes: 450
'O thou that bearst the silver bow, that Chrysa dost dispose,

[521]

Celestiall Cylla and with power commandst in Tenedos,
O heare thy Priest, and, as thine eares gave honour to my prayers
In shooting sicknes mongst the Greekes, now harten their affayres
With health renewed and quite exhall th'infection from their   455
    breasts.'
   He prayd, and gracious Phœbus heard both his allowd
    requeasts.
All after prayer cast on salt heapes, draw backe, kill, flea the
    beeves,
Cut off their thighes dubd with the fatte, drest fayre in doubled
    leaves,
And pricke the sweetebreads thereupon in cleft perfumed woode.
The grave old Priest did sacrifice, and red wyne as they stoode   460
He gave to everie one to taste. The young men held to him
Fivefoulded Grydyrons, on the which he laid each choysest lim,
Which broyld and with the inwards eate: the rest, in gygots slitt,
They fix on spits till, rosted well, they draw and fall to it.
The Mariners (their labors past) have foode for them preparde,   465
Which eaten, not a man was left but competentlie farde.
Their hunger and their thirst thus quencht, the youths crown
    cups with wine,
Begin and distribute to all. That day was held divine,
Consumde in Pæans to the Sunne, who heard with pleased eare,
And when his Chariot tooke the sea and twylight hid the cleare   470
All soundlie on their cables slept even till the night was worne;
And when the Ladie of the light, the roysie-fingerd morne,
Rose from the hils, they freshlie rose and to the campe retyrde.
Apollo with a prosperous wind their swelling Bark inspyrde;
The top maste hoysted, milke-white sayles upon the same they   475
    put;
The misens then were fild with wind; the ship her course did cut
So swiftlie that the parted waves about her sides did rore,
Which comming to the campe, they drew upon the sandie shore,
Where (layd on stocks) each solder kept his quarter as before.
   But Peleus' sonne at his blacke fleete sat gyrt in Anger's flame,   480
Nor to Consults that make men wise, nor forth to battaill came,
But did consume his mightie heart in desolate desires
Of mortall shrieks and massacres made in the Greekes' retires.
And now the day-starre had appeard twelve times in furthest East,
When all the Gods returnd to heaven from th'Æthiopian feast   485
And Jupiter before them all. Then Thetis cald to mind
Her mournfull issue, and above the sea's greene billowes shinde.
The great Heaven earlie shee ascends and doth the King behould,
Set from the rest in heaven's bright toppe, adornd with pearle
    and gould.

[522]

By him shee fals; her left hand holdes his knee, her right his   490
    chynne;
And thus her sonne's desire of Jove by prayer she seekes to
    winne:
'Celestiall Jove, if ever I amongst th'immortals stood
Thy trustie aide in word or act, doe my desires this good:
Honour my sonne above the rest, since past the rest his life
Hath so short date. Yet Atreus' sonne in a disgracefull strife   495
His labor's recompence hath forst. But thou, most prudent Jove,
That with just will rewards desires, with glorie grace the love
Of my sad sonne, so shew his strength with adding strength to
    Troy
Now he is absent, that the Greekes may let him clearelie joy
Gaine of his honour in their losse, and so augment his fame   500
By that disgrace they let him beare to their eternall shame.'
   Jove answerd not a word to this, but silent sate so long
Till shee, still hanging on his knee insisting on her wrong,
Intreated promise at his hands by his resistles becke
Or flat rebuke. 'I know,' said she, 'the servile feare of checke   505
Is far from him may checke all powers. Then, if thy power denie,
I well may see my selfe least grac't of everie deitie.'
   Jove thundred out a sigh and said: 'Thou urgest workes of
    death
And strife betwixt my Queene and me, who with opprobrious
    breath
Still stirs the tempest of my wrath, though vainelie shee contend,   510
And chargeth my respectfull hand to be the Troyans' frend.
But covertlie do thou descend lest her eye sease on thee.
Care of thy will I will assume, which shall effected be—
Whereof to make thee sure, my head shal to my bosome bow,
Which with the gods is greatest signe of anie fact I vow,   515
Not by my selfe to be revokte, nor spic'te with anie guile,
Nor can it ever to my brest without effect recuile.'
Now bowde the sable browes of Jove; the thicke Ambrosian
    hayre
Flowd on his most immortall hed; heaven shooke beneath his
    chaire.
Their conference dissolude, shee slid to th'Ocean from the skies,   520
Jove to his house—when all the Gods did from their thrones arise
To meete their Syre; none durst sustaine to save that reverence
    done
Till he came neere; all met with him, attending to his throne.
Nor Juno ignorantlie sate, but, when her ielous view
Saw Thetis with the silver feet, shee confidentlie knew   525

[523]

Shee brought some plots to heaven with her, and thus began to
    chide:
  'What goddesse' counsailes yet againe deceitefull dost thou*
    hide?
Stil thou takest joy to be from me, and siftst in corners still
Secrets that I must never know, nor ever with thy will
Thou canst endure a word to me of all thy actions' scope.'   530
  The Sire of men and gods replide: 'Saturnia, do not hope
That all my counsels thou shalt know: they are too deepe
    for thee,
Although my wife; but for thy eare what decent I shall see
Not anie God nor man shall know before thy selfe pertake.
Yet what I list to understand and no God partner make   535
Enquire not their particulers, nor urge them at my hand.'
Then Juno with the ox-faire eyes: 'On what nice termes you
    stand,
As if I did so much affect or urge to know thy mind,
Froward Saturnides, till now! But wondrous close you bind
Your loose indevoures, and my hart susteines exceeding feare 540
The aged sea-god's daughter breathde seducements in thine eare.
Shee kneeld so earelie at thy feet, and tooke thee by the knee,
For whome thy chinne against thy brest my minde suggesteth mee
Thou erst didst knocke and promise her some honor for her
    sonne,
Though for his moode the Greekes in heapes do on their ruines 545
    run.'
  'Wretch!' answerde Jove. 'Still thy suspects into my bosome*
    dive,
Yet canst thou hinder me in nought, but thou dost ever strive
To bee ungratious in my thoughts—which humor, if I please,
I can make horrible to thee. Obey me then, and cease,
Lest all the Gods Olympus houldes suffice not for thy aide   550
If my inaccessible hands upon thy lims be laid.'
The reverend faire-eyde Juno sate with this high threat afraide;
Nor anie word shee answerd him, her hart had such a fall.
The rest of gods with murmur fild the high Saturnian hall.
The famouse fyery Artisan, the white-armd goddesse' Son,   555
Lame Vulcan, stood betwixt them both, and with kind wordes
    begun
To ease his loved mother's hart. He said: 'This strife will breede
Intollerable plaguy acts, if you of heavenlie seede
For paltrie mortals thus contend. Amongst the Gods yee make
A tumult here and all the mirth from our sweet banquet take, 560
Because the worse the better hath. But, mother, I advise
(Although I neede not counsell you, because I know you wise)

Give good respect to my good Syre, lest once againe he chide
And make our banquet bitterer yet—for he is magnified
With power to throw us from our thrones, th'Olympian   565
    lightner is.
With gentle wordes then supple him; it wil not be amisse
To make benevolent and calme that thundring hart of his.'
With this, the doble-eared bowle put in his mother's hand,
Upon his admonition still the crookt-legd God did stand:
'Beare, mother, and forbeare,' said he, 'though it be paine to   570
    you,
Lest I that hold you deare behold stripes make your stomacke
    bow,
And cannot helpe you if I would, although it cost me teares.
It is not easie to repugne the king of all our spheres.
How servde he mee, though seeking helpe I wish it otherwise?
Hee tooke me by the helples foote and threw me from the skies.   575
The whole day long I hedlong fell, even till the Sunne and I
Did set together—he at ease, I in extremitie,
He on the sea, and I by land. In Lemnos I did fall,
And there the Sintii tooke me up, halfe dead with my apall.'
The ivorie-fingerd goddesse laught and did that laughter make   580
An Eccho with a counter laugh, and then the bowle did take
Of her kind Sonne, who now began carowse to all the Gods
Of heaven's sweet wine, from his right hand, round in despight
    of ods,
Which unextinguisht laughter stird in everie blessed breast,
To see him halt about the house and fill to all the feast.   585
So all that day they banquetted till sun-set raisd the night,
And wanted nought that with content might crowne the appetite.
There did the God of musicke touch his harp's stone-quickning
    strings,
To which ech sacred muse consortes and most divinelie sings.
But when the comfortable Sunne left to enlighten aire,   590
To severall houses all the Gods with sleepie browes repaire.
The famouse both-foot-halter wrought their roomes with
    wondrous art.
With them the heavenlie-wild fire-god did to his rest depart
Where Somnus usde to close his eyes, and to his side ascends
Faire Juno with the golden throne: and there their quarrel   595
    ends.

The End of the First Booke
of Homer's Iliades

THE SECOND BOOKE

of

HOMER'S ILIADES

THE ARGUMENT

Jove cals a vision up from Somnus' den,
To will Atrides muster up his men.
The king to Greekes dissembling his desire
Perswades them to their Countrie to retire.
By Pallas' will, Ulysses stayes their flight,   5
And prudent Nestor hartens them to fight.
They take repast: which done, to armes they goe
And marche in good aray against the foe;
So those of Troy, when Iris from the skie
Of frendlie Jove performes the Ambasie.   10

Another Argument

Beta, the dreame and synod cites
And Catalogues the Navale knights.

The other Gods and Knights at armes slept all the humorous
    night,
But Jove lay waking, and his thoughts kept in discursive fight
How he might honor Thetis' Sonne with slaughtering at their
    tents
Whole troupes of Greekes. This counsell then seemd best for
    these events:
He instantlie would send a dreame to Atreus' eldest sonne,   5
That with darke vowes might draw his powers to their confusion.
  And, calling him, he wingd these wordes: 'Flie to the Grecian
    fleet,
Pernicious vision, and the king at our high summons greet,
Uttering the truth of all I charge. Give him command to arme
His universall faire-hayrd host. This is the last Alarme: 10
He shall enthunder gainst proud Troy and take her ayrie towers,
For now no more remaine disjoinde the heavenlie-housed powers.
Saturnia with successive prayers hath drawne in one right line
Their generall forces: instant ylles shall Ilion's pompe decline.'

This heard, the dreame with utmost hast the Greekes' swift   15
    fleet attaind,
Where, entring Agamemnon's tent, he found him fast enchaind
In sleepe divine. Aloft his head he tooke impressive place
Informde like Nestor, whom the king past all old men did grace:
And thus he spoke: 'Sleeps Atreus' sonne, whose brave
        horse-taming Syre
Was so exceeding politique? A man that guards the fire   20
Of state and counsell must not drowne the compleat night in
        sleepe,
Since such a multitude of lives are tenderd him to keepe
And cares in such abundance swarme about his laboring minde.
Then wake, and give mee instant eare, sent from the most
        devinde,
Who (though farre hence) is neere in care. He gives the charge   25
        to arme
Thy universall faire-hayrd host. This is the last alarme.
Thou shalt enthunder gainst proude Troy and take her ayrie
        towers,
For now no more remaine disjoinde the heavenly-housed powers.
Saturnia with successive prayers hath drawne in one right line
Their generall forces: instant ylles shall Ilion's pompe decline.   30
This Jove assures, which well observe, nor let oblivion sease
Thy loosse affections, carelesly dissolvde in sleepe and ease.'
Thus left he him, who in his minde with deepe contention tost
These wisht events—farre short of date, yet he supposde his host
Should raze in that next day the towne, so indiscreete he was,   35
Not knowing what repugnant works did Jove's designements
        passe,
Who platted miseries and sighes to smoke from either's syde
In skathfull battaill long before Troy's generall spoyle was tryde.
    He rose from heaven-infused sleepe: the dreame's celestiall
        sounds
Still rung about his pleased eares, sweetned with cause of   40
        wounds.
He deckt him with his silken weed, right beautifull and new,
On which he cast his plenteous robe: then on his feete he drew
Faire shooes, and on his shoulders girt his silver-stooded sword:
The never-tainted scepter then his birthright did afforde,
He tooke, and went amongst the fleete. Aurora now arose,   45
Clymbd steepe Olympus and sweete light did to al Gods disclose,
When he the voicefull heralds chargde in counsell to convent
The curled Greekes. They summond all, and all with one consent
Together came. The court in chiefe the Generall did decree
At Nestor's ship, the Pylian king, should all of princes bee   50

And men of counsell: all which met, Atrides thus did frame
The consultation: 'Princelie friends, a sacred vision came
In this Night's depth and in my sleepe, like Nestor greeting me
For stature, habite, forme of face and head as white as he,
He stood above my head and said: "Sleep'st thou, wise Atreus' 55
sonne?
A Counsailler's state-charged thoughts through broken sleepes
should run,
To whom so many cares and lives are in commission given:
Then give me audience instantly, th'Ambassadour of heaven,
Whose soveragne, though so farre remov'de, vows his exceeding
care
And easefull pittie of thy toyles: he biddes thee straight prepare 60
Thy faire-hayrd compleat host for fight, for now thy royall hand
Shall take Troy's ample-streeted towne. No more at difference
stand
The great immortals: Juno's suite hath cleare enclinde them all
To smoother Ilion's fatall pride in ashie funerall.
This Jove affirmes, which let thy thoughts be sure to memorise." 65
Then tooke he wings, and golden sleepe flew with him from
mine eyes.
Resolve then; let us prove to arme our powers to this designe,
Whom to make eager of exployt I will in shew encline
To sayle and flight, as farre as may with their incitements stand,
Which will be much the fiercer made if you shall countermand 70
With words of honorable stay, assuring them the prise
By their firme valures: soldiers' spirits are firde by contraries.'
    This said, he usde his royall throne; and up did Nestor rise,
Grave king of Pylos' sandie soyle, who thus gave his advise:
'Ye friends, commanders of the Greekes, ye princes of estate, 75
If, save our Generall, any Greeke his vision should relate
We might esteeme it fabulous, or rather flat reject
The strange narration; but because his soveraigne intellect
(With which and with the like, high soules, Jove and the powers
divine
Have proprest mixture) had the grace to have this glory shine 80
In his immortall faculties, serve we their high contract,
Admitting utmost power to give this excitation act.'
To this affayre he first went forth. The other scepter-states
Rose and obayde the Generall, and helpt t'effect the fates
Jove platted by the banefull dreame, endevoring to attone 85
Their compleat host to their attempte in publique Session—
To which in troopes the soldiers ran, as when black swarms of
Bees
Breake ceaseles from a crannied rock, and none th'exhausture sees

Of their sweete vault, they fill it so and furnish the supplie
Of their fresh issue still with flocks that every way doe flie 90
To pray upon the flowrie spring: so from the ships and tents
The Soldiers multiplied the shore in endles regiments,
And Fame, th'ambassadour of Jove, amongst them all did shine,
Enflamming their desires to heare th'intent of this designe;
Whose utterance much disturbance found, so thicke they did 95
    appeare
And th'earth did crack beneath the weight of such as sate to heare.
Rude tumult sprung out of the thrust: nyne heralds cryde
    for peace
And audience of the Jove-kept king, and straite they sit and cease.
Divine Atrides stoode aloft, and in his hand he closde
Th'elaborate scepter Vulcan wrought and to heaven's king 100
    disposde:
Jove gave it to his messinger that slew Saturnia's spie,
Hermes to Pelops rendred it, renoumde for chevalrie,
Pelops to Chieftaine Atreus, and Atreus at his death
Gave it Thyestes, rich in herds; Thyestes did bequeath
The high successive use thereof to Agamemnon's hands 105
To rule great Argos and the powers of many sea-siegde lands.
He, leaning on this scepter, said: 'Princes of Greece and friends,
The houshold and the guard of Mars, cruell Saturnius ends
Our actions in extreame disgrace, who promisde my desire
And bound it with his moved brow, to honor our retire 110
With wel-wald Troy's eversion; but now th'event approoves
His plaine deceate, since gloryles he urgeth our removoes,
Commanding our retreate to Greece with losse of so much blood
Of our deare countrimen and friends, who must not be withstood,
That hath in desolation drownde the free commerciall steapes 115
Of many citties and of more will make subverted heapes,
His power is so surpassing great. But it will loath the eare
Of all posteritie that we, who such a number were
And so renownd, with men so few should wage successles warre,
Of whose drifts yet no end appeares. That we exceed them 120
    farre—
If we should strike firme truce and try, by numbring either syde,
Take all the towne's inhabitants and into tennes devide
Our Achive power, and let each ten at banquet chuse them one
Of Troy to minister them wine, and Troy should harber none
To fill the cuppe to manie tennes; so much, I say, transcends 125
Our powers th'inhabitants of Troy. But their assistent friends,
From manie citties drawne, are they that stay this cittie's spoyle
In spight of our affected wreake. Nyne yeares have past our toyle,
And now the substance of our ships corrupts, our tacklings fayle,

Our wives and seed sit in their doores expecting our resayle,   130
When that we sought is yet unfound. But come, hoyse sayle and
    home—
For never shall Troy's spatious towne by us be overcome.'
    This mov'de to flight in every minde th'inglorious multitude,
Who heard not what in private court the counsell did conclude.
Th'assembly grew most turbulent, as billowes rude and vast   135
Rowsde in the rough Icarian seas when East and Southerne blasts
Breake fiercelie from the clouds of Jove, or as when Zephyr flies
Upon a wealthie fielde of Corne, makes all his forces rise,
And all the field bows her faire heads beneath his violence:
So did the common soldiers yeeld t'Atrides' forst pretence;   140
All to the ships with showting ran. Earth smoakd beneath
    their feete
And mutually they made exhort to haile the crased Fleete
Into the seas, pumpt and made cleane and drew the stockes away,
Offering to lanch. The other Peeres could not be heard for stay:
A noyse confusde alongst the shore did smite the golden stars   145
From souldiers' throates, whose harts did long to leave such
    irksome wars.
Then glorilesse the Greekes had fled, past al presage of fate,
Had not Saturnia thus advisde Jove's tardg-supporting state:
'Out on this shame, O Jove's fayre seede, thou conquering deitie!
Shall thus upon the sea's brode backe th'infamous Argives flie,   150
Admitting Priam and his Peeres a glorie so dispisde
As Helen's rapture in despight and have so dearelie prisde
Their long-sworne honor of revenge, with Greekes so manie
    slaine
Far from their countrie? But descend to Argos' brasse-armd traine
And with perswasive gentle speech will everie man to stay—   155
Not suffring anie go aborde nor hale their ships away,
Which now are everie where preparde to flie out of the bay.'
    So said shee, nor the gray-eyde maide stoode adverse to her will,
But left the undiscerned browes of Jove's Olympian hill
And quickelie reacht the Grecian fleet, where, standing still,   160
    shee found
Th'advicefull king of Ithaca, like Jove in counsailes sound,
Who yet had not so much as toucht his blacke wel-transomde
    barke
But, vexed in his hart and soule, the armie's shame did marke.
    To him said Pallas, comming neare: 'Great Laertiades,
Most wise Ulysses, make ye flight thus headlong to the seas   165
In your well-furnisht men of warre, and long so much for home?
What honor to the king of Troy and his consortes will come
In leaving Argive Helen here, the price of so much bloud

Suckt from the woful brests of Greece, robde of her dearest broud?
But run, and interpose no stay, through every Grecian band　　170
And with thy sweet perswasive tong let none depart the land
Nor draw the ore-enforced fleete from off the Troyan strand.'
　So Pallas chargde, whose heavenlie voice prudent Ulysses knew.
Then foorth he ran, and for more speede his cloake on earth
　　he threw,
Which diligent Eurybates, a Herald of renowne　　175
Who came from Ithaca with him to siedge of Priam's towne,
Tooke up. Ulysses met the king, from whome he was so bold
To take the scepter never-staind held in his line of old,
With which he went amongst the troupes to stay them from the
　　fleete,
And with what prince or gentleman his royall steps did meete　　180
In these faire termes he willed him pretended flight forbeare:
'Sir, tis not fit for such as you to flye, as checkt with feare,
But rather stay and with bold wordes make others so enclinde,
For you as yet not rightlie know king Agamemnon's minde.
He makes but tryall of such spirites as he may most renowne　　185
And hee wil quicklie punish such as flying humors drowne.
All we in counsel heard not all comprisde in his command
Nor durst wee prease too neare for feare of his offended hand.
The anger of a king is death, his honor springs from Jove,
His person is in spight of hate protected in his love.'　　190
But if he saw the vulgar sorte, or if in crie hee tooke
A souldier with exclaimes for flight, him with his mace hee
　　stroke
And usde these speeches of reproofe: 'Wretch! keepe thy place
　　and heare
Others besides thy Generall that place above thee beare.
Thou art unfit to rule, and base, without a name in war　　195
Or state of counsaile. Nor must Greekes be so irregular—
To live as every man may take the scepter from the king.
The rule of many is absurd: one Lord must leade the ring
Of far-resounding government—one king whome Saturn's sonne
Hath given a scepter and sound lawes to beare dominion.'　　200
Thus ruling, governd hee the host. Againe to counsayle then
From ships and tents in tumults swarmde these base disordred
　　men,
With such a blustring as against the Ponticke shore reboundes
A storme-driven billow with whose rage the sea itselfe resoundes.
All sate and sylent usde their seates, Thersites sole except,　　205
A man of tongue whose ravenlike voice a tuneles jarring kept,
Who in his ranke minde coppy had of unregarded wordes
That rashly and beyond al rule usde to oppugne the Lords,

But what soever came from him was laught at mightilie.
The filthiest Greeke that came to Troy, he had a goggle eye;　　210
Starcke-lame he was of eyther foote; his shoulders were contract
Into his brest and crookt withall; his head was sharpe compact
And here and there it had a hayre. To mighty Thetides
And wise Ulysses he retaind much anger and disease,
For still he chid them eagerlie; and then against the state　　215
Of Agamemnon he would rayle. The Greekes in vehement hate
And high disdaine conceipted him, yet he with violent throate
Would needes upbraide the General, and thus himselfe forgot:
　　'*Atrides, why complainst thou now? What dost thou covet*
　　　more?
Thy thriftie tents are full of coine and thou hast women store,　　220
Faire and well-favorde, which we Greekes, at every towne
　　we take,
Resigne to thee. Thinkst thou, thou wantst some treasure thou
　　mightst make
To bee deduc't thee out of Troy, by one that comes to seeke
His sonne for ransome, who my selfe or any other Greeke
Should bring thee captive? Or a wench fild with her sweets　　225
　　of youth,
Which thou maist love and private keepe for thy insaciate tooth?
But it becomes not kings to tempt, by wicked president,
Their subjects to dishonestie. O mindes most impotent!
Not Achives but Achaian gyrles, come, fall aborde and home!
Let him concoct his pray alone, alone Troy overcome,　　230
To make him know if our free eares his proud commandes
　　would heare
In any thing, or not disdaine his longer yoke to beare,
Who hath with contumely wrongd a better man than hee—
Achilles, from whose armes, in spight that all the world might see,
He tooke a prise wun with his sword. But now it plaine　　235
　　appeares
Achilles hath no splene in him but most remislie beares
A femall stomacke, else be sure the robberie of his meede,
O Agamemnon, would have prov'd thy last injurious deede.'
Thus did Thersites chide the king to whome al Greece did bow,
When wise Ulysses straite stood up and, with contracted brow　　240
Beholding him, usde this rebuke: 'Prating Thersites, cease,
Though thou canst raile so cunninglie, nor dare to tempt the
　　peace
Of sacred kings—for well thou knowest I know well what thou art.
A baser wretch came not to Troy to take the Grecians' part.
Prophane not kings then with thy lips, examining our retreate,　　245
Whereof our selves are ignorant, nor are our states so greate

That we dare urge upon the king what he will onelie know.
Sit, then, and cease thy barbarous tauntes to him whome all
    wee owe
So much observance, though from thee these insolent poisons
    flow.
But I protest, and will performe, if I shall deprehend   250
Such phrensie in thy pride againe as now doth all offend,
Then let Ulysses loose his head and cease inglorious
To be the native father cald of yong Telemachus,
If from thee to thy nakednes thy garments be not stript
And from the counsayle to the fleete thou be not soundlie   255
    whipt.'
    This said, his backe and shoulder blades he with his scepter
    smit,
Who then shrunke round, and downe his cheekes the servile
    teares did flit.
The golden scepter in his flesh a bloody print did raise,
With which he, trembling, tooke his seat and, looking twentie
    waies
Illfavoredlie, he wipte the teares from his selfe-pittying eyes.   260
And then, though all the host were sad, they laught to heare his
    cries,
When thus flew speeches intermixt: 'O Gods! what endles good
Ulysses still bestowes on us—that to the field of bloud
Instructs us, and in counsaile doth for chiefe director serve!
Yet never action past his hands that did more praise deserve   265
Than to disgrace this rayling foole in all the armie's sight,
Whose rudenes henceforth will take heed how he doth princes
    bite.'
    This all the multitude affirmd, when now againe did rise
The racer of repugnant townes, Ulysses bold and wise,
With scepter of the Generall and prudent Pallas by   270
That did a Heralde's forme assume and for still silence crie,
That through the host the souldierye might understand th'intent
The counsaile urgde, and thus their flight his wisedome did
    prevent:
'Atrides, if in these faint driftes the Greekes have licence given,
Thou will be most opprobrious of all men under heaven,   275
Since they infringde their vowes to thee at our designes for Troy,
From horse-race Argos, to persist till Ilion they destroy.
But like young babes amongst themselves, or widdowes, they
    lament
And would goe home. And, I confesse, a tedious discontent
May stirre some humor to returne—for, if a man remaine   280

But twyise two sevenights from his wife, much moode he doth
    sustaine
Within his many-seated ship, which winter's stormes enfoulde
And fierce commotion of the sea, where thrise three heavens
    have roulde
About the circle of the yeare since this our ankerd stay.
I can not then reproove such Greekes as greeve at this delay: 285
Yet were it shame to stay so long and emptie-handed flie.
Sustaine a little, then, my friendes, that we the trueth may trie
Of reverend Calchas' prophesy—for we remember well,
And you in hart are witnesses whom death-armde fates from hell
The third day past and yesterday have held in soveraigne   290
    guarde,
That, when in Aulis' long-ring gulf we Grecian ships preparde
To ruine Priam and his friends, on holie Altars made
About a fountaine and within a goodlie Platane shade,
We perfect hecatombs did burne to all the Gods divine,
Where straite appearde to all our eyes a most prodigious   295
    signe—
A Dragon with a bloodie backe most horrible to sight,
Which great Olympius himselfe did send into the light:
This, tumbling from the Altar's foote, did to the Platane creepe,
Where, nestling in an utter Bow and under shade, did sleepe
The russet sparrowe's little young, which eight in number   300
    were,
The dam the ninth that brought them forth, with which the
    beast did smere
His ruthles jawes and crasht their bones: the mother round about
Flew mourning her beloved birth, who by her wing stretcht out
The dragon caught and, crying, eate as he her young had done.
This openly Olympius wrought, and turnd into a stone   305
The purple serpent, which effect we, standing by, admirde
That such a terrible portent should answere offrings firde.
A little after, Calchas said: 'Why stand ye wonder-driven,
Ye men of Greece? This miracle Almighty Jove hath given
Thus late to shew the late event whose fame shall never dy: 310
For, as these eight young birds he eate and she that mourned by
Did make the ninth, so we nine yeares should here firme battaill
    wage
And in the tenth yeare take the towne. Thus Calchas did presage:
All which is almost now fulfild. Then stay, renowmed Greekes,
Till every man possesse the spoile he honorably seekes.'   315
Ulysses having spoken thus, his words so liked were
That of his praise the ships, the tents, the shore did witnes beare,

Resounding with the people's noice, who gave his speech
　the prise.
Th'applawse once ceast, from seate to speake old Nestor doth
　arise:
'Fy, Greekes, what infamie is this? Ye play at children's game, 　320
Your warlike actions thus farre brought, now to neglect their
　fame!
O whether from our lips prophane shal othes and compacts fly?
The counsailes and the cares of men now in the fire shall die
With those our sacred offringes made by pure unmixed wine,
And our right hands, with which our faiths we freely did 　325
　combine.
The cause is, since amongst our selves we use discursive words
And goe not manlike to the field to manage it with swords,
Nor with the finenes of our wits by stratagems devise
In all this while against a world to worke our enterprise.
But, great Atrides, as at first, thy counsell being sound, 　330
Command to field and be not led corruptly from the ground
Of our endevors by the moodes of one or two that use
Counsails apart. They shall not goe to Greece till Jove refuse
To ratifie his promise made, or we may surely know
If those ostents were true or false that he from heaven did 　335
　show.
But I am sure (to cheare our hopes) his beck the Heavens did
　shake
That day of choise when towards Troy our fleete first sayle
　did make,
Conferring on our conquering sterns the powers of death and
　fate,
His lightning right hand shewing us presages fortunate.
And therefore not a man shall doe himself that wrong to fly 　340
Before with Phrygian maids and wives he at his pleasure ly,
That Helen's rape and all our sighes may be revengde thereby.
But if some be so mutinous, whom nothing may restraine,
Let him but touch his black-armde Bark that he may first be
　slaine.
Then, great Atrides, be advisde and other reasons see: 　345
It shall not prove an abject speech that I will utter thee.
In tribes and nations let thy men be presentlie arraide,
That still the tribes may second tribes, and nations nations aide.
Of everie chiefe and soldier thus the proofe shall rest in sight,
For both will thirst their countries' fame and prease for single 　350
　fight.
What soldier, when he is allowde his countryman for guide,
Will not more closely sticke to him than to a stranger's side?

Thus shalt thou know if Gods detaine thy hand from Ilion's
    harmes
Or else the faintnes of thy men and ignorance in armes.'
    Thus to autentique Nestor's speech Atrides' answer was: 355
'All Grecian birth, thryse reverend King, thy counsails farre
    surpasse.
O would King Jove, Tritonea and he that guides the Sunne
Would grant me ten such counsellers, then should our toyles
    be done.
Then Priam's high-topt towers should stoope, outfacing us
    no more,
But fall beneath our conquering hands, dispoylde of all her   360
    store.
But Jove hath storde my life with woes that no good houre
    can spend
And throwne me in the midst of strifes that never thinke of end,
Since with Achilles for a Gyrle in humorous termes I strove
And I the Author of the strife. But if intreated love
Make us, with reunited mindes, consult in one againe,   365
Troy shall not in the least delay her lothed pride sustaine.
But now to foode: that to the fight ye may your valours yielde.
Well let each soldier sharpe his lance and well addresse his
    shielde:
Well let each horse-man meate his horse, to breake the bristled
    fielde:
Well let each Cocheman view his wheeles and chariot-furniture,   370
And arme them so that all the day we soundly may endure.
For faint conceipts must be expeld, that pyne at labour lest
Till night take strength from both our hosts and force us to
    our rest.
The bosomes of our Targatiers must all be steept in sweate;
The Lancer's arme must fall dissolvde; our chariot horse with   375
    heate
Must seeme to melt; and if I find one soldier byde the chace
Pursude by any enemie, or fight not in his face,
Or els be found a shipboord hid, not all the world shall save
His hatefull lyms, but foules and beasts be his abhorred grave.'
This speech applausive murmure stird, as when upon the shore   380
The waves run high, driven with South gales, and gainst a rock
    doe rore,
Plyde with a divers flood of ayre at one self time so fast
That their hoarse rages never cease, such lasting murmures past
The pleased Greekes. They rose disperst; all hast to shipward
    make,

Where all made fires within their tents and did their suppers   385
     take.
And every man to some of heaven did sacrifice and pray
To scape the furie of the fight in that important day.
Atrides to the king of Gods a well-fed Oxe first kild
Of five yeares grought, and al the host to waite on him were wil'd.
Wise Nestor first, then Idomen of Creete the kinglie name,   390
Then both th'Ajaces in consort with Diomedes came,
Antient Laertes' sonne was sixt, whose counsaile bore the sway,
And, uninvited, last of all came sweet-voic't Menelay,
Acknowledging his brother's cares and toyles in his respect.
King Agamemnon in the midst did pray to this effect: 395
   'Most happie and almightie Jove, great thickner of the skie,
Descend on our long-toyled host with thy remorcefull eye.
Let not the lightsome Sun be set, nor set the night on wing,
Before old Priam's high-raisd towers to levill earth I bring,
Before his brode-leav'd ports enflamde may far off be descride,   400
Before my sword on Hector's brest his Curace may devide
And his chiefe frendes falne dead in dust may spread his carcase
     round
And in fell deathe's convulsions eate the many-feeding ground.'
   At this Jove bended not his head, but did more labors guise
For him and his associates, yet tooke his sacrifice.   405
Then, after prayer, salt lumps of dow cast on the altar's sides,
They strike the offrings downe, then strike and strip them of
     their hydes,
Then quarter them and all the thighes with thriftie fat they
     spred,
Put one in other, and to them the little fragments shred.
All these with sere and leaveles woode they consequentlie   410
     burne
And all the inwardes put to spit before the fire they turne;
The thighes burnd up, th'entrayles rost they eate, and peecemeale
     slice
In little gobbits all the rest reservde for sacrifice.
They roste it wondrous cunninglie and draw it from the spit,
And, when their labors were performde and all their suppers   415
     fit,
They usde their stomackes, wanting nought that appertaind
     a feast;
When, thirst and hunger being alaid, thus spake the Pylian
     guest:
   'Great Agamemnon, king of men, effect thy wordes with
     handes,
Nor more defer the worke high Jove so instantlie commandes,

But give the Heraldes charge t'accite all souldiers to the fleete,   420
And let our selves assist their paines to set Mars on his feet,
With expedition more exact.' The king was pleasde and wil'd
The Heraldes cite the curld-head Greekes, who with quicke
    concourse filde
The smotherd shore, and all the kings enrankt themselves about
The great Atrides, and, with them, Jove's gray-eyde maide   425
    went out.
She bore the Tardge her Father made of Amalthæa's hyde,
Not to be pierst nor worne with time, but all eternefied:
A hundred serpents fringde it round, quick strugling, al of golde,
And at a hundred Oxens' price ech serpent might be sold.
Shee through the Achive armie ran, enforcing utmost hast,   430
And every stomake fild with thirst to lay proud Ilion wast,
Enabling all their faculties to fierce and ceaselesse fight,
And made Troy's irkesome warre more wisht than their deare
    countrie's sight.
Then as a hungry fire enflames a mightie wood that growes
Upon the high tops of a hill and far his splendor throwes,   435
So from the Grecians' burnisht arms an admirable light
Flew through the aire with golden wings and did the Gods
    affright.
Or as whole flockes of geese, or cranes, or swans with neckes
    so tall,
Flie cloud-like over Asian meedes to faire Caister's fall,
Who, proud of their supportfull wings, as they take streame   440
    or ground
Make all the river-bordering lawnes their melody resound:
So the thicke troupes from ships and tents throngd to Scamander's
    plaine
And under sway of foote and horse the earth did grone againe.
They stood in that enflowred meade as infinite as leaves
Or flowers the spring doth amplifie, or as the cloudie threaves   445
Of busie flies that sheepe-coates fill when summer's golden vailes
Enrich the fieldes and nourishing milke bedewes the sprinkled
    pailes:
So many faire-haird Grecians stoode upon that equal ground,
The Troyan rankes with deadlie charge desirous to confound.
And as good goate-heardes, when their goates at foode in   450
    herdes abide,
Though they be never so commixt can easily them devide,
So did the leaders well digest their bandes for fight applide—
Mongst whome the mightie king of men, with browes and eyes
    like Jove,
Like Mars in wast, in brest like him that most doth waters love.

And as a Bull amidst the hearde most proudly far doth goe   455
(For he, with well-brancht Oxen fed, makes most illustrious
        show):
So Jupiter made Atreus' sonne in that death-threatning day
The bravest object of all Greekes that held supremest sway.
Sing then, faire muses, ye that hold celestiall pallaces
(For you are Goddesses, know all and fil the farthest places,   460
We knowing nought but onelie heare th'uncertaine voice
        of fame)
What Grecian princes and their peeres to haples Phrygia came.
The common souldiers by their names I not assay to sing,
Although ten tongues and ten big throates I could to utterance
        bring,
Though I sustaind a brazen hart and breathd a voice infract—   465
For onely you, the seed of Jove, can tell the troupes exact
That under Ilion's lofty wals imploid revengefull fight.
The princes, therefore, of the fleete, and fleet it selfe, I cite.

[*Note:* The Catalogue of the Ships follows, but this was not substan-
tially revised for the edition of 1609 and is therefore omitted here.]

Achilles' Shield

1598

TO THE MOST HONORED EARLE,
EARLE MARSHALL

Spondanus, one of the most desertfull Commentars of Homer, cals
all sorts of all men learned to be judicial beholders of this more than
Artificiall and no lesse than Divine Rapture, than which nothing can
be imagined more full of soule and humaine extraction: for what is
here prefigurde by our miraculous Artist but the universall world,   5
which being so spatious and almost unmeasurable, one circlet of a
Shield representes and imbraceth? In it heaven turnes, the starres
shine, the earth is enflowred, the sea swelles and rageth, Citties are
built—one in the happinesse and sweetnesse of peace, the other in
open warre and the terrors of ambush &c. And all these so lively   10
proposde as not without reason many in times past have believed that
all these thinges have in them a kind of voluntarie motion, even as
those Tripods of Vulcan and that Dædalian Venus αὐτοκινητέος *: nor*
can I be resolv'd that their opinions be sufficiently refuted by
Aristonicus, for so are all things here described by our divinest Poet,   15
as if they consisted not of hard and solid mettals but of a truely living
and moving soule. The ground of his invention he shews out of
Eustathius, intending by the Orbiguitie of the Shield the roundnesse
of the world; by the foure mettalles, the foure elementes, viz. by gold,
fire, by brasse, earth for the hardnes, by Tinne, water for the softnes   20
and inclination to fluxure, by silver, Aire for the grosnes and
obscuritie of the mettal before it be refind. That which he cals ἄντυγα
τρίπλακα μαρμαρέην *he understands the Zodiack, which is said to be*
triple for the latitude it contains and shining by reason of the
perpetual course of the Sun made in that circle, by ἀργύρεον τελαμῶνα   25
the Axletree, about which heaven hath his motion &c. Nor do I deny,
saith Spondanus, Æneas' arms to be forged with an exceeding height
of wit by Virgil, but comparde with these of Homer they are nothing.
And this is it, most honorde, that maketh me thus sodainely translate
this Shield of Achilles, for since my publication of the other seven   30
bookes comparison hath beene made betweene Virgill and Homer,
who can be comparde in nothing with more decysall and cutting
of all argument than in these two Shieldes; and whosoever shall reade
Homer throughly and worthily will know the question comes from a
superficiall and too unripe a reader, for Homer's Poems were writ   35
from a free furie, an absolute and full soule—Virgil's out of a courtly,
laborious and altogether imitatorie spirit. Not a Simile hee hath
but is Homer's, not an invention, person or disposition but is

wholly or originally built upon Homericall foundations, and in
many places hath the verie wordes Homer useth. Besides, where   40
Virgill hath had no more plentifull and liberall a wit than to frame
twelve imperfect bookes of the troubles and travailes of Æneas,
Homer hath of as little subject finisht eight and fortie perfect;
and that the triviall objection may be answerd that not the number
of bookes but the nature and excellence of the worke commends it,   45
all Homer's bookes are such as have been presidents ever since of all
sortes of Poems, imitating none, nor ever worthily imitated of any.
Yet would I not be thought so ill created as to bee a malicious
detracter of so admired a Poet as Virgill, but a true justifier of
Homer, who must not bee read for a few lynes with leaves turned   50
over caprichiously in dismembred fractions, but throughout—the
whole drift, weight and height of his workes set before the
apprehensive eyes of his judge. The majestie he enthrones and the
spirit he infuseth into the scope of his worke so farre outshining
Virgill that his skirmishes are but meere scramblings of boyes to   55
Homer's, the silken body of Virgil's muse curiously drest in guilt
and embrodered silver, but Homer's in plaine, massie and unvalued
gold, not onely all learning, government and wisedome being deduc't
as from a bottomlesse fountaine from him, but all wit, elegancie,
disposition and judgement. Ὅμηρος πρῶτος διδάσκαλος καὶ ἡγεμών   60
&c: Homer, saith Plato, was the Prince and maister of all prayses
and vertues, the Emperour of wise men—an host of men against any
depraver in any principle he held. All the ancient and lately learned
have had him in equall estimation. And for anie to be now
contrarilie affected, it must needes proceed from a meere   65
wantonnesse of witte, an idle unthriftie spirit, wilfull because they
may choose whether they will think otherwise or not, and have
power and fortune enough to live like true men without truth,
or els they must presume of puritanicall inspiration to have that
with delicacie and squemishnes which others, with as good means,   70
ten times more time and ten thousand times more labour, could
never conceive. But some will convey their imperfections under his
Greeke Shield, and from thence bestowe bitter arrowes against the
traduction, affirming their want of admiration grows from defect
of our language, not able to expresse the coppie and elegancie   75
of the originall; but this easie and traditionall pretext hides them
not enough, for, how full of height and roundnesse soever Greeke
be above English, yet is there no depth of conceipt triumphing in it
but, as in a meere admirer it may bee imagined, so in a sufficient
translator it may be exprest. And Homer, that hath his chiefe   80
holinesse of estimation for matter and instruction, would scorne
to have his supreame worthinesse glosing in his courtshippe and
priviledge of tongue. And if Italian, French and Spanish have not

made it daintie, nor thought it any presumption, to turne him into
their languages, but a fit and honorable labour and (in respect   85
of their countrie's profit and their poesie's credit) almost necessarie,
what curious, proud and poore shamefastnesse should let an English
muse to traduce him, when the language she workes withall is more
conformable, fluent and expressive, which I would your Lordship
would commaunde mee to prove against all our whippers of their   90
owne complement in their countrie's dialect.

    O what peevish ingratitude and most unreasonable scorne of our
selves we commit, to bee so extravagent and forreignely witted to
honour and imitate that in a strange tongue which wee condemne
and contemne in our native! For, if the substance of the Poet's will   95
be exprest and his sentence and sence rendred with truth and
elocution, hee that takes judiciall pleasure in him in Greeke cannot
beare so rough a browe to him in English to entombe his
acceptance in austeritie!

    But thou, soule-blind Scalliger, that never hadst any thing but   100
place, time and termes to paint thy proficiencie in learning, nor
ever writest any thing of thine owne impotent braine but thy onely
impalsied diminution of Homer (which I may sweare was the
absolute inspiration of thine owne ridiculous Genius) never didst
thou more palpably damn thy drossy spirit in al thy all-countries-   105
exploded filcheries, which are so grossely illiterate that no man will
vouchsafe their refutation, than in thy sencelesse reprehensions of
Homer, whose spirit flew as much above thy groveling capacitie
as heaven moves above Barathrum: but as none will vouchsafe
repetition nor answere of thy other unmanly fooleries, no more   110
will I of these, my Epistle being too tedious to your Lordship
besides, and no man's judgement serving better (if your high
affaires could admit their diligent perusall) than your Lordship
to refute and reject him. But alas! Homer is not now to bee lift
up by my weake arme more than he is now deprest by more   115
feeble oppositions, if any feele not their conceiptes so ravisht with
the eminent beauties of his ascentiall muse as the greatest men of
all sorts and of all ages have beene. Their most modest course is
(unlesse they will be powerfully insolent) to ascribe the defect to
their apprehension, because they read him but sleightly, not in his   120
surmised frugalitie of object, that really and most feastfully powres
out himselfe in right divine occasion. But the chiefe and
unanswerable meane to his generall and just acceptance must be
your Lordship's high and of all men expected president, without
which hee must, like a poore snayle, pull in his English hornes,   125
that out of all other languages (in regard of the countrie's affection
and royaltie of his Patrones) hath appeard like an Angell from a

*clowde or the world out of Chaos. When no language can make
comparison of him with ours if he be worthily converted, wherein
before he should have beene borne so lame and defective as the*   130
*French midwife hath brought him forth, he had never made
question how your Lordship would accept him; and yet have two
of their Kings embraced him as a wealthy ornament to their studies
and the main battayle of their armies.*

If then your bountie would do me but the grace to conferre my   135
*unhappie labours with theirs so successefull and commended (your
judgement serving you much better than your leysure and yet your
leisure in thinges honourable being to bee inforced by your
judgement) no malitious and dishonorable whisperer, that comes
armed with an army of authority and state against harmeles and*   140
*armeles vertue, could wrest your wonted impression so much from
it self to reject (with imitation of tiranous contempt) any affection
so zealous and able in this kind to honor your estate as mine. Onely
kings and princes have been Homer's Patrones, amongst whom
Ptolomie would say, he that had sleight handes to entertayne*   145
*Homer had as sleight braines to rule his common wealth. And an
usuall severitie he used, but a most rationall (how precise and
ridiculous soever it may seeme to men made of ridiculous matter),
that, in reverence of the pietie and perfect humanitie he taught,
whosoever writ or committed any proud detraction against Homer*   150
*(as even so much a man wanted not his malitious depravers) hee
put him with torments to extreamest death. O high and magically
raysed prospect, from whence a true eye may see meanes to the
absolute redresse or much to be wished extenuation of all the
unmanly degeneracies now tyranysing amongst us, for, if that*   155
*which teacheth happinesse and hath unpainefull corosives in it
(being entertayned and observed) to eate out the hart of that raging
ulcer, which like a Lernean Fen of corruption furnaceth the
universall sighes and complaintes of this transposed world, were
seriously and as with armed garrisons defended and hartned, that*   160
*which engenders and disperseth that wilfull pestilence would bee
purged and extirpate; but that which teacheth being overturned,
that which is taught is consequently subject to eversion; and if the
honour, happinesse and preservation of true humanitie consist in
observing the lawes fit for man's dignitie, and that the elaborate*   165
*prescription of those lawes must of necessitie be authorised, favoured
and defended before any observation can succeed, is it unreasonable
to punish the contempt of that moving prescription with one man's
death, when at the heeles of it followes common neglect of
observation and, in the necke of it, an universall ruine? This, my*   170
Lord, I enforce only to interrupt in others that may reade this

unsavorie stuffe the too open-mouthd damnation of royall and
vertuous Ptolomie's severitie. For to digest, transforme and sweat a
man's soule into rules and attractions to societie, such as are
fashiond and temperd with her exact and long-laborde contention 175
of studie, in which she tosseth with her impertiall discourse before
her all cause of fantasticall objections and reproofes, and without
which she were as wise as the greatest number of detractors that
shall presume to censure her, and yet by their flash and insolent
castigations to bee sleighted and turnde over their miserably vaine 180
tongues in an instant, is an injurie worthy no lesse penaltie than
Ptolomie inflicted. To take away the heeles of which running
prophanation, I hope your Lordship's honourable countenance
will be as the Unicorn's horne, to leade the way to English Homer's
yet poysoned fountaine, for, till that favour be vouchsafed, the 185
herde will never drinke, since the venemous galles of some of their
fellowes have infected it—whom, alas! I pittie. Thus confidently
affirming your name and dignities shall never bee more honored in a
poore booke than in English Homer, I cease to afflict your
Lordshippe with my tedious dedicatories, and to still sacred 190
Homer's spirit through a language so fitte and so favourles, humbly
presenting your Achilleian vertues with Achilles' Shield, wishing, as
it is much more admirable and divine, so it were as many times
more rich than the Shield the Cardinall pawnd at Antwerp.

By him that wisheth all the degrees of
judgement and honour to attend
your deserts to the highest,
GEORGE CHAPMAN.

TO THE UNDERSTANDER

You are not every bodie: to you (as to one of my very few
friends) I may be bold to utter my minde—nor is it more empaire
to an honest and absolute man's sufficiencie to have few friendes
than to an Homericall Poeme to have few commenders, for neyther
doe common dispositions keepe fitte or plausible consort with 5
judiciall and simple honestie, nor are idle capacities comprehensible
of an elaborate Poeme. My Epistle dedicatorie before my seven
bookes is accounted darke and too much laboured: for the darkenes
there is nothing good or bad, hard or softe, darke or perspicuous
but in respect, and in respect of men's light, sleight or envious 10
perusalles (to whose loose capacities any worke worthily composde
is knit with a riddle) and that the stile is materiall flowing and not
ranke, it may perhaps seeme darke to ranke riders or readers that
have no more soules than burbolts: but to your comprehension and
in it selfe I knew it is not. For the affected labour bestowed in it, 15
I protest two morninges both ended it and the Reader's Epistle:
but the truth is, my desire and strange disposition in all things
I write is to set downe uncommon and most profitable coherents
for the time, yet further removed from abhorde affectation than
from the most popular and cold digestion. And I ever imagine 20
that as Italian and French Poems to our studious linguistes win
much of their discountryed affection as well because the
understanding of forreigne tongues is sweete to their apprehension
as that the matter and invention is pleasing, so my farre-fetcht
and, as it were, beyond-sea manner of writing, if they would take 25
as much paines for their poore countrimen as for a proud stranger,
when they once understand it, should be much more gracious to
their choice conceiptes than a discourse that fals naked before
them and hath nothing but what mixeth it selfe with ordinarie
table talke. For my varietie of new wordes, I have none Inckepot, 30
I am sure you know, but such as I give pasport with such authoritie,
so significant and not ill-sounding that if my countrey language
were an usurer, or a man of this age speaking it, hee would thanke
mee for enriching him. Why alas! will my young mayster the reader
affect nothing common and yet like nothing extraordinarie? 35
Swaggering is a new worde amongst them and rounde-headed custome
gives it priviledge with much imitation, being created, as it were,
by a naturall Prosopopeia without etimologie or derivation: and

why may not an elegancie authentically derived and, as I may say,
of the upper house bee entertayned as well in their lower 40
consultation with authoritie of Arte as their owne forgeries lickt
up by nature? All tongues have inricht themselves from their
originall (onely the Hebrew and Greeke, which are not spoken
amongst us) with good neighbourly borrowing and as with infusion
of fresh ayre and nourishment of newe blood in their still growing 45
bodies: and why may not ours? Chaucer (by whom we will needes
authorise our true English) had more newe wordes for his time than
any man needes to devise now. And therefore for currant wits to
crie from standing braines, like a broode of Frogs from a ditch,
to have the ceaselesse flowing river of our tongue turnde into their 50
Frogpoole is a song farre from their arrogation of sweetnes, and a
sin wold soone bring the plague of barbarisme amongst us—which
in faith needes not bee hastned with defences of his ignorant
furtherers, since it comes with meale-mouth'd toleration too savagely
upon us. To be short: since I had the reward of my labours in their 55
consummation and the chiefe pleasure of them in mine owne profit,
no young prejudicate or castigatorie braine hath reason to thinke
I stande trembling under the ayry stroke of his feverie censure,
or that I did ever expect any flowing applause from his drie fingers;
but the satisfaction and delight that might probably redound to 60
everie true lover of vertue I set in the seat of mine owne profit and
contentment; and, if there be any one in whome this successe is
enflowred, a few sprigges of it shall bee my garland. Since, then, this
never-equald Poet is to bee understood, and so full of government
and direction to all estates, sterne anger and the affrights of warre 65
bearing the mayne face of his subject, soldiers shall never spende
their idle howres more profitablie than with his studious and
industrious perusall, in whose honors his deserts are infinite:
Counsellors have never better oracles than his lines: fathers have
no morales so profitable for their children as his counsailes, nor 70
shal they ever give them more honord injunctions than to learne
Homer without book that, being continually conversant in him,
his height may descend to their capacities, and his substance prove
their worthiest riches. Husbands, wives, lovers, friends and allies
having in him mirrors for all their duties, all sortes of which 75
concourse and societie in other more happy ages have in steed of
sonnets and lascivious ballades sung his Iliades. Let the length of
the verse never discourage your endevours, for, talke our
quidditicall Italianistes of what proportion soever their strooting
lips affect, unlesse it be in these coopplets into which I have hastely 80
translated this Shield they shall never doe Homer so much right

[549]

in any octaves, canzons, canzonets or with whatsoever fustian
Epigraphes they shall entitle their measures. Onely the extreame
false printing troubles my conscience, for feare of your deserved
discouragement in the empaire of our Poet's sweetnes,   85
              whose generall divinitie of spirit, clad in
                    my willing labours (envious of none
                    nor detracting any) I commit to
                          your good nature and
                                solid capacitie.   90

ACHILLES' SHIELD

Bright-footed Thetis did the Spheare aspire
(Amongst th'Immortals) of the God of fire,
Starrie, incorruptible and had frame
Of ruddie brasse, right shaped by the lame.
She found him at his swelling bellowes sweating   5
And twenty Tripods seriously beating,
To stand and beautifie his royall hall
For chaires of honour round about the wall:
And to the feet he fixt of everie one
Wheeles of man-making gold to runne alone   10
To the Gods' Temples—to the which they were
Religious ornaments, when, standing there
Till sacrifice were done, they would retyre
To Vulcan's house, which all eyes did admire.
Yet the Dædalean handles to hold by   15
Were unimposde, which straite he did apply.
These while he fashiond with miraculous Art,
The fayre white-footed dame appearde apart
To Charis with the rich-attyred head,
Whose heavenly beauties strowd the nuptiall bed   20
Of that illustrate Smith. She tooke her hand
And entertaind her with this kind demand:
    'What makes the Goddesse with the ample traine,
Reverend and friendly Thetis, entertaine
Conceipt to honour us with her repaire,   25
That never yet was kind in that affaire?
But enter further, that so wisht a guest
May be receiv'd with hospitable feast.'
    Thus led she Thetis to a chaire of state,
Rich and exceedingly elaborate,   30
And set a footstoole at her silver feet.
Then cald her famous Smith: 'Vulcan my sweet,
Thetis in some use needes thy fierie hand.'
He answerd: 'Thetis hath a strong command
Of all my powers, who gave my life defence,   35
Cast by my mother's wilfull impudence
Out of Olympus, who would have obscur'd
My native lamenes: then had I endurde
Unhelped griefes if on her shining brest
Hospitious Thetis had not let me rest,   40

And bright Eurynome, my Guardian,
Faire daughter of the labouring Ocean,
With whom nine yeares I wrought up divers thinges—
Buttons and bracelets, whistles, chaines and rings—
In concluse of a Cave; and over us 45
The swelling waves of old Oceanus
With fomie murmure flowd, and not a God
Nor any mortall knew my close abode
But Thetis and divine Eurynome
Who succord me. And now from gulphy sea 50
To our steepe house hath Thetis made ascent,
To whom requitall more than competent
It fits me much my safetie should repay.
Charis, do thou some sumptuous feast purvay
Whiles I my ayrie bellowes may lay by 55
And all my tooles of heavenly ferrarie.'
 Thus from his anvile the huge monster rose
And with distorted knees he limping goes
To a bright chest of silver Ore composde,
Where all his wonder-working tooles were closde, 60
And tooke his sighing bellows from the fire.
Then with a spunge his breast with hayres like wire,
His brawned necke, his hard handes and his face
He clensde, put on his robe, assumde his mace
And halted forth; and on his steps attended 65
Handmaides of gold that with stronge paces wended
Like dames in flowre of life, in whom were mindes
Furnisht with wisedome, knowing all the kinds
Of the God's powers, from whom did voyces flie,
In whom were strengthes and motions voluntary. 70
 These at his elbow ever ministred.
And these (drawing after him his legges) he led
To Thetis seated in a shining throne,
Whose hand he shooke and askt this question:
 'What wisht occasion brings the sea's bright Queen 75
To Vulcan's house, that ever yet hath beene
So great a stranger? Shew thy reverend will
Which mine of choyce commands me to fulfill,
If in the reach of all mine Arte it lie
Or it be possible to satisfie.' 80
 Thetis powrd out this sad reply in teares:
'O Vulcan, is there any Goddesse beares
(Of all the deities that decke the skie)
So much of mortall wretchednes as I,
Whom Jove past all deprives of heavenly peace? 85

My selfe of all the blew Nereides
He hath subjected to a mortal's bed,
Which I against my will have suffered
To Peleus, surnamed Æacides,
Who in his court lies slaine with the disease   90
Of wofull age; and now with new infortunes
He all my joyes to discontents importunes
In giving me a sonne, chiefe in renowne
Of all Heroes, who hath palme-like growne
Set in a fruitfull soyle; and, when my care   95
Had nurst him to a forme so singulare,
I sent him in the Grecians' crooke-sternd fleete
To Ilion, with the swiftnes of his feete
And dreadfull strength that his choyce lims indude
To fight against the Troyan fortitude;   100
And him I never shall receyve, retirde
To Peleus' court, but while he lives inspirde
With humaine breath and sees the Sun's cleare light
He must live sad and moodie as the night.
Nor can I cheer him, since his valure's prise,   105
Resignde by all the Grecian's compromise,
Atrides forst into his fortune's part,
For which Consumption tires uppon his hart.
Yet, since the Troyans all the Greekes conclude
Within theyr forte, the Peeres of Greece have sude   110
With worthynes of gifts and humble prayers
To winne his hand to harten their affayres,
Which he denyde; but to appease theyr harmes
He deckt his dear Patroclus in his armes
And sent him with his bandes to those debates.   115
All daye they fought before the Scæan gates
And well might have expugnde, by that blacke light,
The Ilian Cittie, if Apollo's spight,
Thirsting the blood of good Menœtius' sonne,
Had not in face of all the fight foredone   120
His faultlesse life and authord the renowne
On Hector's prowesse, making th'act his owne.
Since, therefore, to revenge the timelesse death
Of his true friend my sonne determineth
T'embrue the field, for want whereof he lies   125
Buried in dust and drownde in miseries,
Here at thy knees I sue, that the short date
Prefixt his life by power of envious fate
Thou wilt with heavenly armes grace and maintaine,
Since his are lost with his Patroclus slaine.'   130

He answerd: 'Be assurde, nor let the care
Of these desires thy firmest hopes empaire.
Would God as farre from lamentable death,
When heavie fates shall see it with his breath,
I could reserve him, as unequald armes   135
Shal be found neere t'avert all instant harmes—
Such armes as all worlds shall for art admire,
That by their eyes their excellence aspire.'
    This said, the smith did to his bellowes goe,
Set them to fire and made his Cyclops blow.   140
Full twentie paire breathd through his furnace holes
All sorts of blastes t'enflame his temperd coles,
Now blusterd hard and now did contrarise
As Vulcan would, and, as his exercise
Might with perfection serve the dame's desire,   145
Hard brasse and tinne he cast into the fire,
High-prised gold and silver, and did set
Within the stocke an anvile bright and great.
His massie hammer then his right hand held,
His other hand his gasping tonges compeld.   150
    And first he forgde a huge and solid Shield
Which every way did variant artship yeeld,
Through which he three ambitious circles cast,
Round and refulgent; and, without, he plac't
A silver handle. Fivefold proofe it was,   155
And in it many thinges with speciall grace
And passing arteficiall pompe were graven.
In it was earthe's greene globe, the sea and heaven,
Th'unwearied Sunne, the Moone exactly round
And all the starres with which the skie is crownd,   160
The Pleiades, the Hyads and the force
Of great Orion, and the Beare, whose course
Turnes her about his Sphere observing him
Surnam'de the Chariot, and doth never swimme
Upon the unmeasur'de Ocean's marble face   165
Of all the flames that heaven's blew vayle enchace.
    In it two beautious Citties he did build
Of divers-languag'd men. The one was fild
With sacred nuptialles and with solemne feastes
And through the streetes the faire officious guests   170
Lead from their brydall chambers their faire brides
With golden torches burning by their sides.
Hymen's sweet triumphes were abundant there
Of youthes and damzels dauncing in a Sphere,
Amongst whom masking flutes and harps were heard.   175

And all the matrones in their dores appearde
Admiring their enamored braveries.
Amongst the rest busie contention flies
About a slaughter, and to solemne Court
The Cittizens were drawne in thicke resort,   180
Where two contended for a penaltie:
The one due satisfaction did deny
At th'other's hands for slaughter of his friend;
The other did the contrarie defend.
At last by arbitration both desirde   185
To have their long and costly suit expirde.
The friends cast sounds confusde on eyther side,
Whose tumult straight the Herraldes pacifide.
   In holy circle and on polisht stones
The reverend Judges made their sessions,   190
The voycefull Herralds awfull scepters holding,
And their grave doomes on eyther side unfolding.
   In middest two golden talents were proposde
For his rich fee by whom should be disclosde
The most applausive sentence. Th'other towne   195
Two hosts besiegde to have it overthrown
Or in two parts to share the wealthy spoyle,
And this must all the Cittizens assoyle.
They yeeld to neyther, but with close alarme
To sallies and to ambuscados arme.   200
Their wives and children on their walles did stand,
With whom and with the old men they were mand.
The other issude: Mars and Pallas went,
Propitious Captaines to their brave intent.
Both golden did in golden garments shine   205
Ample and faire, and seemde indeede divine.
The soldiers were in humbler habites deckt.
When they had found a valley most select
To couch their ambush (at a river's brinke
Where all their heards had usuall place to drinke)   210
There (clad in shining steele) they close did lie
And set farre off two sentinels to spie
When all their flocks and crooke-hancht heards came neere—
Which soone succeeded, and they followed were
By two poore heardsmen that on bagpipes plaid,   215
Doubtlesse of any ambuscados laid.
The sentinels gave word, and in they flew,
Tooke heards and flockes and both their keepers slew.
The enemie, hearing such a strange uprore
About their cattell, being set before   220

In solemne counsell, instantly tooke horse,
Pursude and, at the flood, with mutuall force
The conflict joynd: betwixt them flew debate,
Disorderd Tumult and exitial Fate.
Here was one taken with wounds bleeding greene   225
And here one pale and yeelding, no wound seene:
Another slaine, drawne by the strengthles heeles
From the red slaughter of the ruthles steeles,
And he that slew him on his shoulders wearing
His bloodie weedes as trophies of his daring.   230
Like men alive they did converse in fight
And tyrde on death with mutuall appetite.
   He carvde besides a soft and fruitfull field,
Brode and thrice new tild in that heavenly shield,
Where many plowmen turnd up here and there   235
The earth in furrowes, and their soveraigne neere
They striv'd to worke: and, every furrow ended,
A bowle of sweetest wine hee still extended
To him that first had done; then turnde they hand,
Desirous to dispatch that peece of land,   240
Deep and new earde; black grew the plough with mould,
Which lookt like blackish earth, though forgd of gold,
And this he did with miracle adorne.
Then made he grow a field of high-sprung corne,
In which did reapers sharpned sickles plie: 245
Others their handfulles, falne confusedly,
Laid on the ridge together: others bound
Their gatherd handfulles to sheaves hard and round.
Three binders were appointed for the place
And at their heeles did children gleane apace   250
Whole armefulles, to the binders ministring.
Amongst all these, all silent stood their king
Upon a balke, his Scepter in his hand,
Glad at his heart to see his yeeldie land.
The herraldes then the harvest feast prepare   255
Beneath an Oke far off, and for their fare
A mightie Oxe was slaine, and women drest
Store of white cakes and mixt the labourers' feast.
In it, besides, a vine yee might behold
Loded with grapes; the leaves were all of gold;   260
The bunches blacke and thicke did through it growe
And silver props sustainde them from below.
About the vine an azure dike was wrought
And about it a hedge of tinne he brought.
One path went through it, through the which did passe   265

The vintagers, when ripe their vintage was.
The virgines then and youthes (childishly wise)
For the sweet fruit did painted cuppes devise
And in a circle bore them dauncing round,
In midst whereof a boy did sweetly sound   270
His silver harpe and with a piercing voyce
Sung a sweete song, when each youth with his choice,
Triumphing over earth, quicke daunces treades.
   A heard of Oxen, thrusting out their heades
And bellowing, from their stalles rushing to feed   275
Neere a swift flood, raging and crownd with reed,
In gold and tinne he carved next the vine,
Foure golden heardsemen following, heard-dogs nine
Waiting on them: in head of all the heard
Two Lyons shooke a Bull, that, bellowing, rerde   280
In desperate horror and was dragde away:
The dogs and youthes pursude, but their slaine pray
The Lions rent out of his spacious hide
And in their entrailes did his flesh divide,
Lapping his sable blood: the men to fight   285
Set on their dogges in vaine, that durst not byte
But barckt and backewards flew. He forgde beside,
In a faire vale, a pasture sweete and wide
Of white-fleest sheepe, in which he did impresse
Sheepecotes, sheepfolds and coverd cottages.   290
   In this rare Shield the famous Vulcan cast
A dauncing maze, like that in ages past
Which in brode Cnossus Dædalus did dresse
For Ariadne with the golden tresse.
    There youthes and maids with beauties past compare   295
Daunc't with commixed palms: the maids did weare
Light silken robes, the youthes in coats were deckt
Embroyderd faire, whose colours did reflect
Glosses like oyle: the maides faire cronets wore,
The youthes guilt swords in silver hangers bore: 300
And these sometimes would in a circle meet
Exceeding nimblie and with skilfull feet,
Turning as round as doth a wheele new done,
The wheelewright sitting trying how t'will runne.
Then would they breake the ring and take their places   305
As at the first; when troupes, pleasde with their graces,
Stood looking on, two youthes then with a song
Daunc't in the midst to please th'admiring throng.
About this living shielde's circumference
He wrought the Ocean's curled violence,   310

Arming his worke as with a christall wall.
The Targe, thus firme and huge, now finisht all,
He Curace made that did for light out shine
The blaze of fire, impierceable, divine,
A helme fit for his browes, whose loftie crest   315
Was with a waving Plume of gold imprest.
Then shining Greaves he made of brightest brasse,
And, when this smith of heaven brought to full passe
This ful of wonder and unmatcht affaire,
To goddesse Thetis he addrest repaire   320
And laid it sounding at her Christall feete,
Which with refreshed mind and countenance sweete
She tooke and, like a Haulke, stoopt from the browes
Of steepe Olympus: and the wreakefull vowes
Of her enraged Sonne shee helpt to pay   325
With Vulcan's armes wrought for eternall day.

GLOSSARY

GLOSSARY

[In view of Chapman's characteristically cavalier treatment of English, a glossary to any of his works might well be made to occupy more space than the original text. There is hardly a word or a phrase that he does not twist and wrest to suit his individual purposes, and his approach towards grammatical construction is ruthless.

Here, no more is attempted than a list of such elements in his vocabulary as might cause difficulty to a reader. At the same time, since part of the interest of Chapman's style depends on his innovations, asterisks are used to indicate any words, or meanings of words, which have been noted for the first time in the *Iliads* and for many of which Chapman probably was responsible. In some instances, Chapman's priority in use has already been recorded in the *NED*, but there are numerous entries in the following glossary of words which the *NED* omits or else quotes from much later sources. It is to be observed also that, in general, the *NED* classifies its Chapman quotations under the one date, 1611, whereas numerous interesting words were first used by him either in the 1598 text or in that of 1609. I have here sought to provide indications of date by bracketed references to the *A, B, C* and *D* texts (1598 for *A* and *B,* 1609 for *C* and 1611 for *D*). In this connection, note should be taken of the fact that only a few of the many compound words in the *Iliads* have been listed here; for these reference may be made to G. G. Loane, 'Chapman's Compounds in N.E.D.' (*Notes and Queries,* clxxxi, Sept. 6, 1941, 130–1). It should also be observed that normally the words presented in this glossary are listed in modern spellings; only those original forms which might cause difficulty have been included.

A complete study of Chapman's vocabulary would, of course, necessarily demand constant reference to the Latin text in Spondanus' edition (from which came many of his borrowings) and also to his own earlier works. No attempt has been made in this glossary to discuss either of these; the following list of words is to be regarded as a guide to the perusal of the *Iliads,* not as an analysis of Chapman's use of words in general.]

abate	diminish
abhor	shrink back in horror from; hence move away from
abhorred	filled with horror or fear
abide	remain, remain on
abject	* useless, i.e. thrown away as useless (*D*)
able	make one able to do; make capable

abless	* skill, ability, power (C)
aboard, lie	* remain on board ship (A)
abode	1) place of dwelling
	* 2) premonition, omen (D)
aboord	aboard (q.v.)
about, being	* a little at one side (A)
abrode	abroad
absolute	complete, perfect
accept	* receive (in sense of interpret) (C)
acceptable	welcome, pleasing
acceptive	* receptive (A; as in 'acceptive darts'—darts receptive of the darts offered by Hector)
access	approach
accite	summon
accomplished	completed, fully carried out
accord	agree, join in company (as in 'did accord to attack')
accost	* address, greet (A)
Achilleian	* resembling Achilles, noble (A)
addiction	inclination
address	1) make ready, prepare
	2) accoutre, array
	3) direct one's course; advance
	4) turn or apply to
address	* preparation, advance (D)
addressed	1) directed, dispatched
	2) made ready
addression	* entry, approach, advance, direction of one's course (C)
addrest	addressed (q.v.)
admirable	wonderful
admire	wonder, wonder at
admit	permit, consent
advance	set up, establish. (This sense differs slightly from any in the NED)
adverse	opposed, standing opposed to
advertise	give news of; notify
adviceful	* wise, experienced in giving advice (A)
adviseless	* unwise, unconsidered (A)
Æacides	Achilles
Æthiopian	* Ethiopian (A)
affair	business, endeavour ('with his best affair' is 'to the best of his ability')
affect	passion, emotion, mood
affect	1) aim at, aspire to

	2) make an ostentatious show of (Chapman's 'much tongue affects thee,' meaning 'you use your tongue a great deal; you are always apt to be talking,' does not seem covered by any of the *NED* definitions)
affected	1) sought after
	* 2) beloved (*C*)
	* 3) supposed, assumed (*B*)
affection	passion, emotion, desire
affray	make afraid
after	following after, succeeding
agent	a person who carries out work for another (In *A* there seems an unrecorded sense as 'active participator')
aid	1) assistance
	2) assistant, ally
aider	assistant, ally
airie	eyry, eagle's nest
airy	unsubstantial
Ajantical	* resembling Ajax, foolish (*D*)
ajourn	adjourn, put off, defer
al	all
alaid	allayed
aland	on land
all-countries-exploded	* (*A;* this seems to have the sense of 'rejected by all countries,' or 'already out of fashion in all countries')
allow	1) approve
	2) grant, provide with
allowance	approval
allowed	approved, welcomed
alongst	along the length of
amaze	amazement
ambasie	embassy, message given to an ambassador
ambassadress	female ambassador
ambitious	* circular (*B*)
ambrosian	* divine (*A*)
ambuscade	ambush
ameld	amelled, enamelled
amends	1) retribution
	2) reward, award
	* 3) change of plan, i.e. a device compensating for a change in conditions (*D*)
amendsful	* making amends or giving satisfaction (*C*)
amplify	augment, increase

amply-paced	* widely pacing or striding (D)
Anchisiades, Anchisia- den	a son of Anchises; especially Æneas
anchored	* held fast by an anchor (A)
angel	divine messenger
apaid	1) satisfied
	* 2) moved (as in 'apaid with greater spirit' (A) and 'all their hearts stood hatefully apaid' (D))
apart	apart from, out of
appal	shock, dismay
apparence	appearance, shape
appeasure	* action of appeasing (A)
appertain	belong to
applausive	* expressing approbation (A)
apply	(This word is used by Chapman in several senses, some of which vary somewhat from those given in the *NED:* 1) to manage (a horse), 2) to supply, 3) to put into action, 3) to lay at the door of, 4) to use)
appose	1) put in front of (applied to food, Chapman's seems to be the first use)
	* 2) oppose (A)
apprehensive	* capable of apprehending, perceptive
approve	prove, find, discover
arch	(As applied to a chariot seat, this word seems to have a special sense for Chapman)
ardent	fiery, strong (of wine)
areed	advise, admonish
Argicides	Mercury (who slew Argus)
armless	* without armour (B)
arms for, put on	* result in, lead to (as in 'that put on arms for death')
arrast	* covered with arras or tapestry (C)
arrive	bring someone to a destination, effect someone's arrival
arrogation	unwarrantable assumption; a thing arrogated
arted	* made by art (D)
artfully	* with skill (D)
artificial	made by art
artist	a person skilled in anything (hence applicable both to a poet and to a skilled charioteer)
artizan	artist
artship	artistry
arts-man	a person skilled in a profession

as	as if
ascension	ascent
ascentful	assentful (q.v.)
ascential	* ascending, aspiring (*B*)
aspire	1) inspire
	2) desire
	3) rise up to, reach
	4) aim at
assay	trial, attempt, endeavour
assay	1) try, test, make trial
	2) address oneself to
assentful	* ascentful, ascending, aspiring
assistful	* helpful, standing in aid (*C*)
assoyle	assoil, resolve, decide
assuage	mitigate, put a stop to
assume	adopt, accept
assumer	* a person who assumes to himself, who makes pretensions (*D*)
assumpt	assumption
atchieve	achieve
Atrides	a son of Atreus, especially Agamemnon but also used for Menelaus
attain	1) strike, touch, wound
	2) inflict
	('attain to' is used for 'arrive at')
attaint	touch, wound, process of wounding
attainted	touched, struck, wounded
attempt	endeavour, accomplishment
attend	1) wait, wait for
	2) be in attendance
attone	atone, unite
attraction	(This word Chapman seems to use in several peculiar senses: 1) 'attraction to society' in *B* may mean 'inclination'; 2) 'the scope of his attraction' in 21. 538 seems to signify that Achilles is edging Hector towards a certain point; 3) 'th' attraction of his love' in 11. 706 implies 'how far his love of you will allow him to be drawn towards accepting your counsel'; 4) 'according to Spondanus' attraction' in *A* appears to imply 'interpretation, opinion, judgment')
augment	increase, be added to
augurous	* presaging, reading omens (*D*)
austerity	harshness, severity
authentic	of authority; to be esteemed

authentical	authentic; valid, true
authentically	with validity, truly
author	one who originates anything
author	* originate (*A*)
authorise	give legal force to, make valid
authorised	endowed with authority
authority	* those in authority; the government or state (*C*) (See Commentary on 5. 165)
authress	1) authoress, originator
	* 2) mother (*C*)
auxiliary	* helpful, assistant (*A*)
avail	estimation
aversation	* turning away (*D*)
avert	turn aside or away
awry, look	look away or aside
axletree	axle
ayry	airy
azure	* blue-eyed (*A*)
balk	ridge of ground
bane	evil, injury
barbarism	barbarous condition
barbed	* fitted with barbs (*D*)
bastardise	bastardy, illegitimacy
battalia	* battle array (*A*)
battelous	* battling, drawn up in line of battle (*D*)
bavin	faggot
bawdrick	shoulder belt
bead-hook	* a kind of boat-hook (*D*)
beam	* pole of a chariot (*C*)
bear about	* be occupied with (*D*)
beastly	of or pertaining to a beast
beautified	made beautiful, handsome
beautify	make beautiful
becalm	* make calm, quiet (*D*)
beck	nod, bowing of the head
beechen tree	* axle made of beechwood (*C*)
beget	* put into, infuse (*D*)
belabouring	* laborious, toiling (*D*)
beldame	old woman (not in any derogatory sense)
belwether	leading sheep of a flock
bend	bow
bend to	incline, lean
bene	been
bent	1) inclination, bias (in 3. 406 'had the main bent

	of her will' seems to mean 'was most loved by her')
	2) bending, bowing
	3) intent, intention
bepinched	* pinched, grasped roughly (D)
berayed	befouled, defiled
bereft	* (in 20. 178 'thy knees bereft it' seems to mean 'you fled')
bernacle	wild goose
betray	* betrayal (D)
betray	* 1) reveal, show, demonstrate (C)
	* 2) discern (C)
betterness	superiority
bewray	reveal, exhibit
beyond-sea	outlandish, foreign
bid	challenge
billow	* pour as in billows (A)
bin	been
birth	offspring, child
bitten	* biting (D)
black	blacken
blackish	black, dark-coloured
blanch	whiten, give a fair appearance to anything
blaze	proclaim, make known
blind of	* unblest with (A)
blood	disposition
bloody	make bloody
blore	blast, gust
bluish	of a blue colour
boggle	* start with fright, shy (A)
boisterous	rough, tempestuous
boor	peasant
boot	* booty (A)
borne	born
boss	centre knob on a shield
boss-pikt	* fitted with a pike at the centre (A)
bostrous	boisterous
bosts	boasts
bow	bough
brackish	* belonging to the sea-shore (A)
braid	brayed
brake	thicket
branded	brindled
brass-hoved	* shod or hooved with brass (A)
brass-piled	* tipped with brass (C)

brast	covered with brass
brast	burst, shattered
brave	courageous, noble, outstanding
brave	bravely
brave	boast
brave	boasting speech
brawned	brawny
bray	break, shatter
breath	breathe
breath in	* inspire (C)
bred	* breeding, where one was bred (C)
bristle	* furnish with bristles (A)
bristle	* crested wave (C)
bristled	* 1) hairy, shaggy (A)
	* 2) bristling with spears (A)
broad	bold, rude, insulting
broken-hearted	* having one's heart broken, dead (D)
bruit	noise, tumult
buls	bulls
burbolt	birdbolt
burly	broad, extensive
bursten	* bursting (D)
burthen	* ship (A)
burthening	* manning a ship (A)
busle	* bustle, crash down (D)
but	without
caddesse	jackdaw
cald	called
call	caul
canapied	covered as with a canopy
capable of	having a legal right to
capriciously	* in a capricious manner (B)
careful	full of care, troubled, anxious ('careful of' is used in the sense of 'paying particular attention to')
careful, the	* those full of care, i.e. the living (D)
carquenet	necklace
carriage	a thing carried, burden
case	(There is a peculiar use in 22. 388, 'she little knew how much her cares lackt of his case,' i.e. 'she little knew how useless were her cares when he for whom she was concerned was lacking to her')

cask	casque, helmet
cast	pair (of vultures). (The word 'cast' is a hawking term, originally applied to the number of hawks, usually two, thrown into the air at one cast)
cast	cast down
caster	one who casts (a spear, etc.)
castigation	* emendation, adverse criticism (B)
castigatory	* fault-finding (B)
castrill	kestrel, kite
cates	delicacies
cease	put an end to
censure	opinion, judgment
censure	judge, pass an opinion on
centre	* surface of the earth (A)
centre	* stand in the centre of (D)
certesse	certainly, assuredly
ceston	* cestus, or girdle, of Venus (D)
chamber sted	(In 14. 286 this may mean 'chamber-place, i.e. room,' or 'sted' may be a verb meaning 'fitted up, placed')
champian	champain, open country
chance, make the	* (In 5. 593 this seems to mean 'be active'; in 15. 393 the sense rather is 'chance to fall on.' Neither significance is, apparently, listed in *NED*)
change	exchange (words)
channel-bone	collar-bone
charge	1) office or duty assigned to a person (hence 'thy charge' is used almost as 'Your Majesty')
	2) command, order
charge, have to	* have charge of (C)
chariot tree	* main pole of chariot (A)
charm the tongue	keep the tongue silent (in 5. 289 'his soul for ever charm'd his tongue' means 'he died')
chase, take the	* turn in flight (D)
chastly	chastely, in a chaste manner
cheard	cheered
check, take	* be checked, be made afraid (D)
chine	joint (of meat)
chinne	chin
choice, of	* (It seems as though this phrase has in Chapman's mind the sense of 'voluntarily'—a meaning not covered in the *NED*)
chuse	choose
Cimmerian	pitch-black
circle	encircle, make a circle round

circular	* perfect (with emphasis on moral and spiritual qualities)
cite	call, summon
clange	* trumpet call, shrill cry of a bird (*A*)
clear	brightness, clearness of the air or water
clear	fresh, bright
clear, bear on	* (In 20. 46 'He bore the iron streame on cleare' seems to mean 'He made the stream of armour dazzlingly-bright')
clime	climb
close	enclose
close	1) closing with an opponent, bout 2) enclosure, field
close	1) secret 2) secretly, by oneself
close to, come	* anger, vex, irritate (*D*)
close-fought	* closely fighting (*D;* this is apparently the sense, but 'close-fight' refers to a defensive part of a man-of-war)
closely	secretly
closure	* union, joining (*A*)
cloud	crowd, mass (as in 23. 121 'a cloude of infinite foote behind')
cloud-compelling	* that collects or controls clouds (*D*)
cloyd	1) cloyed, satiated * 2) wearied through excess (*D*)
cluster	crowd
clustering	crowding
coaugmented	* helped or added to by others (*D*)
coequal	equal
coherence	connection, state of agreement
coherent	* consistent or logical thought (*B*)
colour	put a gloss on, make plausible
coloured	specious, deceitful
combustion	* burning (of a corpse) (*D*)
come over	* (Apparently in the sense of 'get ill, collapse'; *D*)
comfort	inspiration
comfortable	inspiring
commend	recommend, praise
commender	one who commends
commentar, commenter	commentator
commercial	* of or pertaining to commerce (*A*)
commixed	mixed together, intertwined
compact	* framed, composed (*D*)
compel	* control, possess (*C*)

competent	sufficient
complement	* (The sense given in such a phrase as 'complements of field' i.e. martial endeavours (*A*) is hardly covered by the *NED;* nor is that in *D* 'with all their complements' i.e. all their endeavours)
complemental	* complimental (*A*)
comprehend	grasp, embrace (The phrase in *C* 'comprehend his likeness' seems to mean 'be like him')
comprehensible of	* able to comprehend (*B*)
compress	1) hold, grasp tightly
	* 2) embrace, get with child (*A*)
comprimise	compromise (q.v.)
comprobation	approbation, approval
compromise	* united promise (*B*)
concave	* (Seemingly in *A* this means 'concourse, area')
conceipt	conceit, idea, opinion
conceipt	* think, consider, regard (*A*)
conceipt, entertain	* decide, think (*A*)
conceited	* clever, fanciful (*A*)
conceited, be	* hold belief, think (*D*)
conceive	think
conclude	1) enclose
	2) include
concluse	* seclusion (*B*)
concoct	* make up, prepare (*A*)
concrete	congealed. (As applied to blood, this appears to be the sense, but what exactly is the significance of 'concrete crystal water' is doubtful)
conditioning	making the condition, stipulating
conduce	lead, bring
conducible	* expedient (*C*)
conduct of, in	* conducted or led by (*D*)
confect	prepare, concoct
confer	* 1) bring, bestow (*D*)
	* 2) bear, take to (*A*)
	3) collate, compare
conference	1) talk, conversation
	2) collation, comparing one thing with another
	3) consultation
confirmance	confirmation
confluent	* affluent (*A*)
conformable	disposed to conform, tractable
congression	* hostile encounter (*D*)
congruence	agreement, correspondence

[571]

conscionably	reasonably
consents	consent
consequently	subsequently
consort	consort with, join the company of
constraint	force, compulsion
consult	enter into consultation, hold a deliberative session
consult	* consultation (*A*)
consume	devour, spread destruction over
consummation	completion, carrying out
consumption, embrace	* be consumed (*D*)
contain	* 1) restrain oneself (*A*) 2) control
contemn	despise
content	(If, in 4. 473, 'both the foes her furie did content' means 'her fury did include both the foes,' there is an unrecorded meaning here; but 'content' may have the sense of 'satisfy')
contentious	prone to strife, warlike, contending
contexture	texture, composition
continent	* that which is contained or held, amount, possession (*D*)
contract	take on, acquire (*A*)
contract	* command, binding order (*A*)
contracted	* drawn together, frowning (*A*)
contrive into	* be summed up in (*C*)
control	rebuke
contumelious	insolent, humiliating
contumely	insolent abuse
convaid	conveyed
convenience, hold	* be proper, be appropriate (*D*)
convent	call together, assemble
conversion	translation
convert	1) turn 2) translate 3) turn round about in translation
convey	carry, bear
convince	1) overcome, defeat 2) prove
cookly	* after the manner of a cook (*D*)
cope	1) cloak, canopy 2) combat
copy	plenty, abundance
cost	(In 22. 209 'no more let's fear to lay cost on our lances' seems to mean 'no more let us fear to spare

	our lances'; in 22. 201 'costs me honor' evidently has the meaning of 'I have to honour you')
cote	pass by, outstrip
couched	* laid in layers (D)
counterflight	* flight backwards (A)
countermand	deny, take away
counterveiled	* balanced, made equal (D)
coopplets	couplets
course, give	* pass on (D)
course of, in	* in the way of (D)
court	pay courteous attention to
court-piece	* affair at court, palace intrigue (C; it is just possible this may mean 'court-peace' i.e. peaceful life at court)
cow-herd	coward
crased	damaged, unsound, cracked
cresset	lamp, torch
cround	crowned
crow	crowbar
crown	* fill to overflowing (A)
crown	* 1) circle of persons (D)
	* 2) completion, final end (D)
	* 3) king (C)
crowning	bringing to completion
crude	raw
cruent	bloody
cubit	forearm, elbow
cuff	* beat, strike, buffet (A)
cure-passing	* cure-surpassing, incurable (D)
curets	cuirass
curious	1) careful
	* 2) peculiar (D; with an anticipation of the modern sense)
curiously	carefully
current	* in progress, contemporary (B)
currie	quarry
curst	angry, wrathful
Dædalean	resembling the style of Dædalus, ingenious (B)
daies	days
daine	deign
dainty, make it	* hesitate (B)
damask	* inlaid (A)
dare	1) dare to meet (D)
	* 2) daunt, terrify (A)

dare	defiance, challenge (*D*)
date, take	* come to an end (*D*)
dead	* deep, deadly (*C;* as in 'with so dead a strength'; but perhaps the sense here is 'certain' as in *NED*, 31 b)
deadliest	implacable, bloody-minded
deadly	* terribly, loudly (*D*)
deal	engage in conflict
deathsman	slayer, murderer
deawd	dewed
debate	fight, conflict
deceived	deluded (peculiarly used in 10. 388, 'his head, deceiv'd, fell speaking on the ground')
decline	cast down, lower, depress
decysall	* decisal, cutting (*B*)
dedicatories	* dedicatory words (*B*)
deduce	bring
deduction	* derivation (*D*)
deed, out of	* not indulging in any action (*C*)
deedless	* without action, inactive, incapable of acting (*A*)
deep-growing	* deeply growing, thick (*D*)
deepness	* strength (*A;* as in 10. 43, 'the deepness of his hand')
deeps	* depths of the sea (*D*)
defame	dishonour, defamation
defect	want, lack
defend	protect, guard
defer	1) postpone
	* 2) hold back (*C*)
deferre	defer (q.v.)
degeneracy	* degenerate conditions or actions (*B*)
degree	position, status
deified	* belonging to a god (as in 3. 416, 'deified disguise')
deity	divine power, power of a god
dejected	* cast down (*A*)
delaid	delayed
delightsome	delightful, full of grace
deny	refuse (a challenge or order) (*A*)
depeople	* destroy, kill, the people of (*D*)
deplore	weep for
deploring	* lamentation (*D*)
depopulate	destroy, lay waste, massacre
depose	put or place aside
depravation	vilification
deprave	disparage, defame

deprehend	detect, catch
depress	crush down, subdue, conceal (*A*)
descent	offspring, son, sons
desert	deserted, desolate
desertful	deserving, meritorious
design	plan, enterprise
designment	plan, enterprise
desire	(Used almost in the sense of 'regret, grief' in *D*)
desire, in the	dearly loved (*D*)
desirous	eager, full of desire
desperate	* desperado (*D*)
despite	spite, anger
despite	vex, irk
destinate	decreed by destiny
destinate	doom, ordain
detracter	one who detracts, defamer
detraction	act of detraction
detriment	* destructive power (*C*; as in 12. 134, 'like Mars in detriment')
dexterous	* right-handed (with a peculiar sense in 21. 161, 'both his hands were dexterous')
difference	make a difference between, distinguish
difference	disagreement, controversy
differencing	* classifying, placing in different groups (*A*)
differing	* at variance, hostile (*A*)
digest	swallow, put up with
digressive	* 1) spoken by way of digression (*D*) 2) that turns any one out of his way (*D*)
diligent'st	diligentest, most diligent
diminution	* carping criticism (*B*; evidently an extension of the sense of 'depreciation')
director	guide
disanimate	deprive of spirit, dishearten
disaraid	* disarrayed, in disorder (*D*; in this same year, 1611, the word is also recorded in Speed)
discern	recognise
disclose	1) open up * 2) bring to birth (*D*) 3) reveal * 4) see, look upon (*D*; as in 21. 467)
discoloured	stained (as in 'discolour'd gore')
discountried	* alien (*B*)
discovery	declaration, disclosure
discrepance	distinction, difference
discursive	* 1) moving from one subject to another (*A*)

	* 2) having to do with discourse (*A*)
disdain	anger, grief
disdain	1) to be angry at or troubled by
	* 2) think unworthy, reject (*D*)
disease	trouble, awaken
disease	inconvenience, annoyance, bitterness
disengage	* liberate, hence protect (*A*)
disesteem	fail to esteem, disparage
disfurnish of	render destitute of
disinflamed	* made cool, deprived of ardour (*C*)
disjoin	undo, unharness
disjunction	* dissention, quarrel (*D*)
dislike	distaste, hatred (of something)
dismaied	dismayed
dismission	sending away or back
disparage	undervalue, vilify
disparent	* of various appearance, with diverse qualities (*D*)
dispense with	do away with, release
disperple	* stain with red (*A*)
dispersed	* troubled (*A;* as in 'dispersed heart')
display	see displayed, perceive
dispose	1) regulate, govern
	2) hand over, give
disposer	* one who disposes, applies precepts for another (*C*)
disposition	1) natural tendency of mind, character
	* 2) man of a certain character (*B*)
dispread	spread out
dissection	* analysis (*D*)
dissolve	1) soften (frequently in the sense of 'take away pain from, refresh')
	2) release, set free
dissolved	* 1) limp, wearied out (*A*)
	* 2) dissipated (*A*)
dissolving	* softening (*A*)
dissunder	cut off, sunder
disteine	dis-stain, stain, defile
distinct	divided
distinction	condition of being differenced
distinguished	* 1) separate, individual (*C*)
	* 2) divided, separated (*A*)
distorted	* twisted out of shape (*B*)
distract	distracted
dite	* dight, winnow (*C*)
diter	* dighter, winnower (*C*)

diverted	with attention drawn away from the main business
divine	* doom, prepare by divine power (*A*)
divined	* divine (*A*)
doom	judgment
dorp	* belonging to a village (*A*)
doter	* one who dotes on (followed by 'of' as in 'doters of their home'; *A*)
doterd	dotard
dotingly	foolishly
doubt	* redoubt (*C*; apparently this is the meaning, but in 12. 286 'This doubt downe that now betwixt us stands' might conceivably signify 'doubt or fear')
doubtless of	* not doubting or fearing (*B*)
doubt, out of	certainly, beyond all manner of doubt
dow	dough
drad	dread, dreadful
draught	(In 8. 282 'in his draught' seems to mean 'in his impulsive drive')
draught-tree	pole of a chariot
dreadless	fearless
drift	design, intention
drift	* wind that drives or impels (*C*)
drossy	made up of dross
dubd, dubt	* dubbed, smeared with fat (*D*)
durt	dirt
dust	* earth, firm ground (*D*; apparently an unrecorded sense)
dust	fling, knock
dutifully	* by duty (*A*)
eager	1) bitter
	* 2) sharp (*A*)
eagerly	bitterly, angrily
eagerly-fought	* fighting bitterly (*D*)
easely	* with ease, gladly (*D*)
easy	* weak, not vigorous (*D*; as in 17. 506, 'a passing easie souldier' where the Greek has the sense of 'unhardy' and Spondanus' version is 'mollis bellator')
edify	build
effect	accomplish, bring to realisation
effect	result, bringing to realisation, carrying out
effuse	* cast out (*A*)
egression	action of going out, departure from or entry into

[577]

elate	1) lift, raise
	* 2) raise the spirits of (*A*)
elated	* exalted, inspired, proud (*D*)
eld	old age, elders
elevate	* raise (one's spirits, etc.) (*C*)
Elisummes	* Elysiums (*A*)
elusive	* mocking (*A;* as in 11. 319 'elusive brave')
embattelling	drawing up in line of battle
embattled	drawn up in battle array
embost	* driven to extremity, foaming at the mouth (*A;* as in 4. 258; in 11. 421 'embost within a shadie hill' seems rather to be 'having taken shelter')
embrew	imbrue (q.v.)
empair	impair (q.v.)
empayr'd	empaired, impaired, injured
emperie	1) empire
	2) power
employ	put into action, encourage
emprese	* (In 11. 257 this appears to mean 'endeavour, effort')
emulate	strive to equal, aspire to rival
emulous	proceeding from rivalry (as in 'emulous affection')
enambush	* catch in an ambush (*D*)
enambusht	* lying in ambush (*A*)
enamoured	* of or pertaining to a nuptial feast (*B*)
enamouring	* of or pertaining to love (as in 5. 395, 'her enamouring fire')
enchac't	enchased, ornamented
enchase	1) ornament, decorate
	* 2) enshrine (*D*)
enchaste	enchased, ornamented
end	end someone's life, put an end **to**
endamaged	injured
endless	endlessly, finally
enflower	* make to flower, make full of flowers (*B*)
enforce	1) force, compel
	2) overcome by violence, take prisoner. (In addition *A* has the sense almost of 'carry out' and *B* has that of 'labour, dwell on')
enforced	* 1) taken by force (*C*)
	2) compelled
enforcive	* enforcing, forcible (*A*)
enfranchise	free, liberate
engaged	* in an engagement, in the thick of the fight (*C*)
engine	* cunning, hence means, device (*A*)

engored	1) covered with gore
	* 2) clotted (*A*)
engrailed	variegated, adorned
engross	1) seize upon, appropriate
	* 2) make thick or large (*D*)
engrost	* 1) engrossed, made thick (*D*)
	* 2) engrossed, absorbed (*A*)
enlarge	spread, extend
enlightened	light-giving, lighted up
enslumber	* put to sleep (*D*)
ensue	* strive, hasten (*A*)
ensulphured	* made sulphurous (*A*)
enthunder	* make to thunder (*A*)
entoiled	* toiling (*D*)
entomb	enclose in a tomb
envide	envied
envie	envy (q.v.)
envious	full of emulation
envy	desire to equal another, emulation. (In 13. 477 'then he lost his envie too' has a very peculiar sense, difficult to interpret: it seems to mean 'he failed in his malevolent aim')
enwrapped	* closely bound up (*D*)
epigraph	* title, name (*B*)
equal	* 1) level (*A*)
	2) impartial, balanced
equal	be equal to, match, rival
equalise	1) match, rival
	* 2) make equal, balance (*A*)
equipage	* equipping (*A*)
erne	earn
err	ramble, wander
errant	wandering
error	the action of wandering
escape	* escapade, intrigue (*C*)
escheat	* defeat and despoil (*A*)
eschew	avoid, keep out of the way of
estate	state, condition
estranged from	strange to, removed from
eternify	* make eternal (*A*)
eternise	1) make eternal
	* 2) immortalise (*A*)
event	1) result, resultant action
	* 2) fate (*C*)
event, take	* result, happen (*A*)

evermore	always
eversion	overthrow
evicke	(Translating αἶξ ἄγϱιος in *C*)
evulsion	* forcible extraction (*D*)
exaction	extortion, penalty
example	set an example of
exanimate	without life, dead
exceed	excel, surpass, assume greater stature
except against	take exception to
exception	formed objection
excess	preponderance, additional strength
excessive	* desiring to excel, desiring to surpass one's ordinary strength (*D*; as in 17. 398 'excessive spirit')
excitation	* 1) instigation, encouragement (*D*)
	* 2) exciting (of moral virtue) (*D*)
excite	incite, arouse
excitement	* exhortation (*D*)
exclaim	exclamation, outcry
execration	curse
exempt	* 1) choice, select, peerless (*A*)
	* 2) not subject to the control of (*D*)
exhale	* draw out (*A*)
exhaust	* (In 11. 230 the reference to a wound 'exhaust and crude' seems to give a peculiar sense—probably 'draining blood')
exhausture	* state of being exhausted, conclusion (*A*)
exhort	exhortation
exitial	deadly
expansure	expansion, extension
expect	wait for, await
expectance	* that which is expected or waited for (*D*)
expense	expenditure
expire	end, finish
expiscate	* fish out, find out (*A*)
expiscating	* enquiry into (*A*)
explode	thrust aside as useless
explore	* search out (*D*)
exposition	interpretation
exposure	* leaving without defence (*A*)
expressor	* one who has the power of expression, writer, poet (*D*)
expugn	overpower, wipe out
expugnance	* storming of a city (*A*)
expugned	wiped out
expulsion	process of expelling

expulsive	* tending to repel (C)
expulsure	* expulsion (A)
expunction	deletion, erasure
expunger	* one who deletes or cuts out something (D)
exquisite	elaborate, skilled
exsequies	exequies, funeral rites
extant	extant copy or version
extenuate	lessen, weaken (a blow)
extenuation	lessening, weakening
extirpate	extirpated, rooted out
extreme	extremity, extreme need
extrude	thrust out or away
eyeful	* plainly to be seen (A)
eyeshot	* range of the eye, view (A)
eyne	eyes
fabric	* manufactured object (D)
facilie	easily, with facility
fact	deed, action
factiously	in a factious manner
faculty	property
fadging	* labouring, wearying (D; the NED seems to be wrong in saying this means 'well-matched')
fained	feigned, deceptive, unreal
faining	feigning
fall	descent (of a bird)
falne	fallen, happened
false-heart	* false-hearted (D)
fantased	fantasied, created by the power of the fantasy
fantastical	resulting from fantasy, absurd
fantasy	mental apprehension, imagination. (Often used in a technical sense as 'the image impressed on the mind by an object of sense')
fare	condition (as in 22. 272, 'his mind's fare')
farre-fetcht	* deep, profound (C)
fatal	decreed or destined by fate
fausen	eel
fautor, fautour	protector, patron
fautress	patroness
favourer	friend, supporter
favourless	without favour
fear	peril, fearsomeness
fearful	timid
feast	* company at a feast (D)
feastfully	* in the manner of a banquet (B)

fell	fierce, bitter, dangerous
fell'ff	felloe or rim of a wheel
fellowless	without fellow, peerless
feltred	having shaggy hair
fere	mate, companion
ferrary	* the art of the smith, iron-work (B)
fervency	fiery quality
fervent	fiery (with various extensions of use)
fervour	fieriness
fetcher-in	* supplier, bringer in (D)
fetch-water	* fetcher of water (C)
field	battle, contest
fight	* breastwork on a rampart (C)
filchery	* theft (B)
fild	filled
filed	defiled
fillers	* those who fill up something, crowds (D)
filthily	in a filthy manner, venomously
fired	* eager, aroused (D)
fit	conflict
fixed	established, settled (as the Homeric original for 20. 425 indicates the sense of 'forceful,' some of this meaning may be implied here)
flame	* offspring (D)
flamie	1) flamy, flaming * 2) performed by the agency of flame (A)
flash	* weak, void of meaning (B)
flaw	gust of wind
fled	* that has fled (D)
fleer	laugh mockingly
fleet	float
flesh	* initiate (D)
flexible	able to be moved or appeased
flexure	action of bending or turning round
flockers	those who flock to a person or place
flown	* flying (D)
fluence	* flowing, flow, stream (D)
fluent	* that flows, flowing (B)
fluxure	* fluidity (B)
fly	1) flee, move away from 2) escape the notice of
foil	overthrow, defeat
foil	1) something that sets off another 2) overthrow
foiled	defeated, vanquished

foisting-hounds	* (A phrase based on 'foist,' meaning 'to break wind'; D)
foody	* 1) supplying food (A)
	* 2) of or pertaining to food (D)
foolery	foolish performance
force	force or carry away, despoil
forced	forced out
forechase	* foremost part of the chase or pursuit (D)
foredo	fordo, kill, put an end to
forefeel	feel beforehand
forefight	* 1) foremost rampart (C)
	* 2) front ranks of an army (D)
forego	go before, outstrip
foreignly	* in a foreign manner, influenced by foreign styles (B)
foreright	right forwards (of winds, 'favourable')
fore-run	run before
forespeak	predict, foretell one's fate
foreteam	* front part of chariot pole (D)
forgone	(The sense of 'men so long forgone' in 14. 421 is obscure. It may mean 'men who went forth so long ago')
form	1) shape, arrangement
	2) physical appearance
	3) lair of a hare
fortitude	strength (frequently used with a possessive adjective, as in 'Troyan fortitude')
forward	pressing forward, hence bold, impudent
fountain of the nerves	* nape of the neck (C)
fountful	* full of founts or springs (D)
frame	action of framing or shaping. (There are, besides, several rather strange uses of this word, such as 'surpassed for general frame' (A), 'in the frame of our Homer' (D), 'frame of all that skill' (C)— where 'principles, scope' seems to be the significance intended)
franchisement	liberation, fact of being freed
fray	frighten
freckled	marked in spots, bespattered
free	eager for action, willing
freight	load up, stock
frequent	crowded, assembled in great numbers
fret	fretted
friendless	* unfriendly (A)
frighted	* frightened away from (D)

froe	frow, drunken woman, Maenad (compare *The Shadow of Night, Hymnus in Cynthiam,* 189, 'That like loose froes at Bacchanalian feasts')
frontless	shameless, audacious
frugality	* barrenness, meagreness (B)
fruit	1) product
	2) offspring
fry	crowd of insignificant persons
fume	* smoke (D)
furnace	* exhale like a furnace (B)
furrow	* lair (A)
furrow	* furrow one's way, press through (A)
fury	inspired frenzy, poetic rage
fustian	inflated language, bombast
fustian	bombastic
futurely	* in the future (C)
gald	galled
galingale	aromatic spice
gals	galls
gasp	* cranny, rut (D)
gasping	* gaping (C; as in 'gasping cranny')
gat	got, reached
gavill	gavel, sheaf of corn
gavill, lie on the	* lie unbound (D)
gaze, at	(The phrase, as in 3. 149 and 4. 356, suggests a state of silent wonder or contemplation)
gears	horse collar, harness
gelid	* cold as ice (D; the first reference given in *NED* seems to be a different word)
generate	generated, born
generous	noble, valorous
get	* make pregnant (D)
gigot	* slice, piece of meat (A)
girdle-stead	place of the girdle, waist
gives	gyves
Glaucopides	(An invented word based on γλαυκῶπις, meaning 'the gray-eyed maid')
gleby	rich, fertile
glew	* fastened together, closely joined (D)
glorious	vain-glorious, boastful
gloriously	in glory, proudly
glory	1) honour, fame
	2) vainglory, boasting
gloryless	without glory

glose	conceal with specious comments
glose	gloss, commentary
glut	* flood, inundation (C)
gnash	* gnashing of teeth (D)
gobbit	gobbet, small piece
goddes	goddess
godlessly	* in a manner contemptuous of the will of the gods (A)
gold-affecting	* akin to gold, in appearance like gold (A)
golden	* golden-haired (D)
gold-locked	* with golden locks (D)
good, make	* hold on to, maintain possession of (D)
gracious	full of grace, graceful
grasier	grazier, one who grazes cattle
gratulate	1) welcome, hail
	* 2) show favour to, reward (A)
grave	bury
grave	heavy, ponderous
gravelled	cast into doubt or error
green	fresh
griev'd	greaved (i.e. wearing greaves)
groan under	* be oppressed by (D)
groght	growth
gross, in	in the mass, collectively
grudge	anger, annoyance
guard	protection
guard	keep, hold
guardiance, take to	take into one's protection
guide	guiding, guidance
guilt	gilt, gilded
guise	* prepare (A)
guise	custom
gulfy	* deep as an abyss (A)
gull	swallow, engulf
gyrlond-seller	garland-seller
hability	ability
habit	familiarity, experience, skill
hair	colour of hair (as in 'both of one hair')
hairpatch	haircloth
haleyard	halyard
halt	go haltingly, limp
hanch	haunch
hand, fill the	* occupy all the attention of, call forth all the strength of (D)

[585]

hant	(Apparently in 21. 82 'I should hant Jove with hate' means, 'if I were you, I should regard Jove with hate')
hapless	unhappy, ill-boding
hart	heart
hast	haste
hatched	* inlaid with silver (D)
hautie	haughty
hazardous	venturesome
headlong	* such as one might fall headlong into (D; as in 20. 289, 'headlong home')
health	welfare, safety
heard	herd
hearers	* ears (D)
heart	heartening, exhortation
heartening	exhortation
heartless	without heart, dispirited
heartquake	terror
hearty	coming from the heart, sincere
heat	pride, hot-headedness
heat	heated, aroused
heaven, all	* (There is some doubt as to what 'all heaven wide of his end,' in 23. 299, means. Hooper suggests that heaven is the past participle of 'heave,' but the phrase seems to mean 'utterly, completely')
height	1) prime quality 2) high place
helpless	* not granting help, unaiding (C)
help-tire	* something that helps one who is tired (C)
herby	full of herbs
hernshaw	heron
hid	(There is a peculiar phrase in 21. 140, 'with that long lance he hid,' where Homer's text suggests a far-shadowing spear)
high-flown	* high-flying (C)
high-haired	* high-branched (D)
hire	price, payment
hoast	host
hoice	hoise, hoist
hoise	hoist
holed	having a hole in it, pierced
holiness	(Peculiarly used in B; 'Homer's holiness of estimation')
home	of or pertaining to home, homeward
homicide	killer of men

hony	honey
horded	hoarded
horned	* hard, insensible (*A*)
horror	1) terror
	2) that which raises terror
horsed	covered by a horse
hospitious	hospitable
hot	heated, angry
hote	hot
hoves	hoofs
humorous	1) moist
	2) afflicted with (bad) humours
humour	1) moisture, dew
	2) disposition, mental or emotional inclination
hurl	action of hurling
hyperthetical	* superlative (*D*)
idol	image, figure
ignorant	ignorant person, ignoramus
illude	cheat, deceive
illustrate	resplendent, illustrious
illustrate	make light, make illustrious
illustration	1) lighting-up, illumination
	* 2) simile (*D*)
illustrious	shining, glorious
ils	ills
imaging	* imitating, acting as a copy of (*A*)
imbecility	* folly (*D*)
imbrew (embrew)	stain (with blood)
imitatory	* having an imitative manner (*D*)
immane	* monstrous, huge (*D*)
immartial	* inexperienced in war (*A*)
immetrical	* unmetrical (*C*)
impair (empair)	injure, harm in reputation
impair (empair)	injury, dishonour
impaired	injured
impalsied	* palsied (*B*)
impassion	make passionate
impeach	impeachment
impeach	challenge, dare
impierceable	that cannot be pierced
implied	* entangled (*C*)
imply	1) enfold, entangle
	* 2) encircle, fasten (as in 15. 18, 'on thy false wrists implied')

	3) involve
	4) employ, apply
import	importance
importance, bear no	* be of no value or significance (*D*)
importune	press, urge, hasten
importuned	* pressed on, urgent, hastening (*D*)
impose	place or put in
impress	1) imprint, inflict
	2) inflict a blow on
	* 3) fall upon (*A*)
impression	1) something impressed upon a person, exhortation
	2) force exerted by pressure
impressive place	* place suitable for creating an impression (*C*)
imprest	impressed, driven or urged by pressure
improve	reprove
impugn	resist, oppose
impulsion	* attack, blow (*A*)
impulsive	* governed by impulse, valiant, bold (*A*)
inaccessible	* resistless, invincible (*A*)
incense	set on fire, burn
incensory	* burnt offerings (*A*)
inchac't	chased into, enclosed
incitement	* incentive, process of arousing (*A*)
incline	1) bend, cause to bend
	2) dispose, bring one to
inclose	close up
inclusion	the state of being enclosed or shut in
income	coming in, entrance
incontinent	immediately
incorrupted	uncorrupted
incorruptible	that cannot decay or be destroyed
increase	growth in wealth or happiness
inculcate	(Used in *C* almost in sense of 'bring forward, demonstrate')
inculpable	blameless, innocent
indanger	endanger
indifferent	impartial
indifferently	without difference or distinction
indistinguished	* indistinguishable (*A*)
induce	bring in, introduce
indue (endue)	put on, dress
industrious	* full of toil or trouble (*A*)
inenarrable	that cannot be narrated or told
inevitable	* unending, endless (*D;* in 24. 494, where the

[588]

Homeric text has the sense of 'mourn not un-
abatingly,' Chapman writes 'mourne not inevi-
table things,' and in 14. 47 the phrase 'a most in-
evitable fight' has the meaning of 'endless')

inexpiate   * unappeased (*A*)

inexpugnable   that cannot be overthrown

inextricable   1) from which one cannot extricate oneself

     * 2) that cannot be untied or loosened (*C*)

inextricably   in an inextricable manner

infallibly   without doubt, inevitably

infer   1) bring about

     2) bestow

     * 3) confer (*A*)

infernal   of or belonging to the nether regions

infest   trouble, annoy

infestive   infesting, annoying

inflame   set on fire, burn

influence   spiritual aid

inform   animate, put spirit into

informed   formed, shaped

infortune   misfortune

infract   * unbreakable (*A*)

infuse   bring or pour into

ingenerate   born

ingenious   1) intelligent

     2) frank, open, sincere

ingenuously   frankly

ingored   engored (q.v.)

inject   * throw or cast in (*A*)

inkpot   ink-horn (used in *B* in sense of 'strained, of false
derivation')

innative   1) native

     * 2) natural (*C*)

innocence   * things innocently or unintentionally done (*A*)

innocent   good, doing no evil

innovation   * novelty, new interpretation (*D*)

innuate   * intimate, hint (*D*)

insea'd   * set in the midst of waters (*A*)

insecution   * close pursuit (*A*)

insensible   without sensibility, paying no attention

inspersion   sprinkling, application

instance   urgency, insistence

instinct   instigation, prompting

institute   1) set up, establish

     2) instruct

instruct	* put in order, equip (D)
instructed	drawn up in battle array
instruction	knowledge, information, news
insult	utter an insulting speech
insulting	* abuse (C)
integuments	* funeral clothes (D)
intellection	understanding
intelligencing	* deriving from the intellect, not from the imagination (D)
intendment	intention
intent	1) observe, pay attention to
	2) tend, try, endeavour
inter	bury, put in the grave
interest, for one's	in one's own favour
interest of, in	because of
interim	* intermission (D)
internunciess	* female messenger (D)
intervented	* seized upon (A)
intestine	internal, civil
intranced (entranced)	lying in a trance, dead
inundation	flowing in of waters
inure	* 1) impress as by burning (A)
	2) put into use
invade	* seize upon (D; as in 16. 312, 'invading him,' of a man defeated and taken alive)
invirond	environed, surrounded
invitement	invitation
inwall	* inner wall (D)
inward	intimate, attached in close spiritual intimacy
iron	weapon
irregularre	irregular
irrision	mockery, irony
issue	offspring
Italianist	* lover of Italy, one influenced by Italian speech and manners (B)
Ithacus	Ulysses
jacke	jack, jerkin
jeate	jet, colour of jet
jetty	black
jot	jog, bump
joynturelesse	jointureless, without jointure or marriage portion
just	joust, martial game
justifier	one who justifies or defends

keep, take	take possession
kel	* layer (of fat) (*D:* the word 'kel' does not seem to be recorded in this sense)
kelsine	kelson, structural timber of a ship
kerve	carve
kind	natural, lineal, proper to one's nature
kindly	natural
kind-worthy	* worthy of kindness (*A*)
knee	* leg, foot (*D*)
laborious	* 1) causing wearisome toil, or impelled by labour (*A*)
	2) toiling
labyrinthian	tortuous, difficult to find a passage through
lackeying	serving as a lackey, attending on foot
lackiest	lackeyest, attendest on foot
lancht	launched
large	generous, not keeping to an exact account
laterally	at the side
laughing game	object of laughter
lazy	sluggish
leavy	* 1) having leaves (of a gate) (*C*)
	2) covered with leaves (of branches)
	* 3) of or pertaining to leaves (*C*)
leer	* look eagerly on every side (*D*)
left	* that has left or departed (*D*)
legacy	action of a legate, embassy
lengthful	* lengthy, long (*A*)
let	prevent
liberal	free, ample
libertine	* one granted the freedom of a city (*D*)
licenst	licensed, permitted
lien	lain
lift	lifted
lightener	* one who sheds light (*C*)
lims	limbs
lineally	by lineal descent
lineaments	* limbs (*D*)
lingring	lingering, postponing
linne	flax, linen
liveries	allowances (peculiarly used in 5. 529, 'death fewer liveries gives')
lode	load
loose	* infirm, weak (*B*)
los'd	loosed

loser	destroyer
lote	lotus (strangely used in 21. 332, 'lote trees')
lover	a person who loves, husband, wife, friend
lucern	lynx
lumbering	moving ponderously
lust	desire, eagerness
lust	desire eagerly
lustration	* sacrifice (A)
luxurious	outrageous
luxury	* luxuriance (D)
lymne	limn
lynce	lynx
Mæonides	Homer
magnify	make glorious or powerful
mainly	with force
maistery	mastery
make in to	approach
manage	* skilful handling (D)
manager	* guide, charioteer (C)
mandilion	cassock
manless	* inhuman, brutal (A)
manly	befitting a man
maritimal	maritime, of the sea
martial	* soldier (D)
martialist	soldier, warrior
mask for, be the	* be the place of refuge for (D; as in 20. 178–9)
masking	wearing a mask, disguised
massie	massive
masterful	* characterised by the skill that constitutes a master (D)
mastife	mastiff
mate	fellow-soldier
material	full of good matter
matter	substance
mean	means, occasion
meaning	intention
meed	reward
meere	mere (q.v.)
melancholy	* pertaining to the melancholy humour (A)
memorise	make memorable
mere	pure, unadulterated
merit	reward, recompense
met	meted (past tense of mete, q.v.)
mete	measure

mettle	* encouragement (*D;* as it seems to be in 23. 561)
minion	* caress (*A*)
minion	servant
ministry	service
miraculously	wonderfully, greatly
misconceipt	* dislike, think badly of (*C*)
misease	distress, discomfiture, pain
misen	mizen
mist	missed
mitigatory	* alleviating pain (*A*)
moil	* maul, mangle (*D*)
monster	prodigy, marvel
moody	full of sad moods
morosity	moroseness
mould	earth, ground
movers	* legs, feet (*D*)
movingly	in a manner likely to move or attract
mowle	mole
moyle	moil (q.v.)
mucpits	* muck-pits, cesspools (*A*)
mulct	penalty, fine
munition	having a store of arms
murrion	morion, head-piece
muse	meuse, the 'run' of an animal (peculiarly used in 11. 368)
nail, to the	* exactly, to the last degree (*D*)
nailed	* pierced as with a nail (*D*)
nais	* river-nymph (*D*)
nation	* population (of animals) (*D*)
natural	1) legitimate
	2) born of the same father and mother
	3) belonging to by birth (opposed to adopted)
nature, in	by nature, naturally
naval	* of or pertaining to the navy (*D*)
nave	central block of a wheel
navil	navel
near	1) standing nearby
	2) nearer
near-fought	* fighting nearby (*A*)
neat	cattle
necessary	inevitably determined (as in 'necessary day')
neglective	* neglectful (*D*)
nerves	sinew
nervy .	sinewy

netify	* polish, make neat (*D*)
never so	ever so much
never to begin	(An obscure phrase in 16. 705, seeming to mean 'appear as though they would never cease')
new-eared	newly ploughed
nice, make	be shy
noblesse	nobility
nock	notch of a bow or arrow
noise	fame, reputation
nosthrills	nostrils
number	* numerous (*A*)
numerous	rhythmical, poetic
nummed	numbed
nutrition	* nourishment (in sense of son's aid to aged father) (*D*)
object	put over against or in way of
object	obstacle, something objected between one thing and another
objection	* something placed in opposition or between (*D*)
objector	* one who objects (*D*)
obscure	* conceal, hide (*B*)
obscurity	* quality of being insignificant (*B*)
observe	regard with attention
obtain	* be victorious, obtain the prize (*D*)
occurrent	occurrence
offend	strike, attack
officious	* official, ceremonial (*B*)
officiously	* in an unduly forward manner (*A*)
Olympius	Jove
ominous	full of omens, ill-boding
one-hoved	(Used in the sense of 'whole-hooved')
only	alone (as in 'his only presence')
op'd	opened
oppose	bring or put to a thing or person, set against
opposed	1) opposite, standing opposite
	* 2) pitted against one another (*C*)
opposite	opposed, hostile
opposite	opponent, adversary
oppressed	pressed down
optimate	* prince, potentate (*A*)
orbicular	round, circular
orbiguity	* roundness, circular shape (*B*)
orby	* circular (*C*)
orderer	one who orders, commander

[594]

original	original state
ornament	equipment (as in 11. 450, 'physicke ornaments')
Orthian	* high-pitched (*A*)
osspringer	* osprey (*D*)
ostent	prodigy, wonder
oth	oath
ought	owed
ougly	ugly
outrage	fury, passion
outraise	* raise or throw beyond (*D*)
outray	* 1) spread out in array (*C*)
	* 2) leave the course (of a chariot) (*D*)
outray	* deviation from a straight course, transgression (*D*)
outrun	* (A peculiar use in 24. 433, 'outrunne with some of my woes,' suggests a meaning such as 'oppress,' 'wear out.' This is slightly different from *NED*, 4)
outshew	* surpass in appearance (*D*)
outwrought	* worked more powerfully than (*D*)
overborne	* overwhelmed, trampled under-foot (*D*)
overdared	* daunted by great force against one (*D*)
overlaboured	worn out, excessively fatigued
overlay	1) lay over
	* 2) overwhelm, vex (*D*)
overlearnedness	* too meticulous study (*D*)
overlook	look over, be on top of
overpass	pass over, disregard
overplus	additional amount
overrun	run over or beyond
overseen	1) deceived, cheated
	2) looked over and hence below one's notice
overthwart	going crosswise (but for 21. 255, 'so overthwart his waves were,' Homer gives the sense of a violent current underneath)
overthwarts	athwart
owe	own
oyle	oil
paint	give a false colouring to
paise	peise (q.v.)
pale	barrier, rampart
pall	(It is difficult to say what is the significance of the phrase in 18. 155, 'he your pall will make his shoulders')
pallat	palate

pallesadoes	* palisades (*A*)
palm	spread of a deer's horns
pamphlet	* (The sense in *A*, 'pamphlet of errors' = 'list of errata,' is apparently unique)
pan	brain-pan, skull
paragon	equal, consort
paramour	lover (not necessarily in any bad sense)
parle	parley
part	take part in, share
partake	partake in or of
parted	* partial, i.e. with interest for diverse parts (*D*)
partie-coloured	parti-coloured, variegated
partless	* impartial (*A*; see Bartlett, *Poems,* p. 479)
partrich	partridge
pash	smash, knock violently
pass	1) surpass
	2) be accepted
	3) pass over, overlook
passage	exchange of blows
passing	1) surpassing
	2) surpassingly, very
passion	fit of passion
passport, give	permit to enter
pastern	part of horse's foot
patient of	enduring
peace, make	cause silence, make someone hold his peace
peares	peers
peece	piece
peecemeale	piecemeal
peise	1) weight
	2) balance
perfected	made perfect or ready
period	* 1) death (*D*)
	2) end, final point
perse	pierce
person	corpse (*D*)
personate	* personify (*D*)
persuade	urge
perswasion	persuasion, exhortation
pertinence	* the fact of pertaining or being attached (*D*)
perusal	* reading through (*B*)
pervial	* easily apprehended, shallow (*A*)
pervially	* at a casual glance (*D*)
pessant-common	* peasant-common, base, mean (*A*)
phane	fane

physically	* as regards the body (*A*)
physitian	physician
pickt	piked, set with a point or pike
piece, armed at every	fully armed
pile	point of a weapon
pinch	1) bite, snap at with the teeth
	* 2) afflict, harass (*A*)
pinch-in	* afflict, torment (*A*)
pine	exhaust through pining
pined	wearied out, worn out
pitching fields	* fields used for pitching or hurling (stones, etc.) (*C*)
pittance	allowance
plaguy	* vexatious (*A*)
plain	1) complain, bewail
	* 2) level with the plain (*C*)
planky	* composed of planks (*C*)
plant	1) planting (of anything, e.g. feet on ground)
	2) sole of foot
plash	* plashed thicket (*D*)
plat	plot
platane	plane tree
plausible	praiseworthy
play, show no	* (In 23. 622 seems to mean 'risked no fall [in wrestling]')
plight	bodily or physical condition
ply	1) apply
	2) use, keep at work
point	punctuate
poitril	breast-piece on harness
pold	polled, stripped off
politic	sagacious, wise
polity	* community of men (*A*)
portage	cargo, freight, luggage
pour	* cast, throw (missiles, etc.) (*C*)
powre	pour; power
practice	practical activity
praid	prayed
prairs	prayers
praiseful	praiseworthy
prease	press, fight, combat
prease	press, press on
predominant	predominating
prefer	1) put forward, advance the interests of
	2) put in front of

	3) proffer, present
	4) promote
preferd	1) preferred, put forward
	* 2) approved by preference (*D*)
prefigure	* show, outline (*D*)
prefixed	* previously fixed, foredoomed (*D*)
prejudicacy	* prejudice (*C*)
prejudicate	prejudiced, having preconceived opinions
prejudice	injury, harm
preposterously	upside down
presently	immediately
president	1) head, chief
	2) precedent
	3) example
presse	* pressing, forceful (*D*)
pressman	* man engaged in a wine-press (*D*)
prest	* ready, prepared (*D*)
presume	profess, dare to say
presume	presumption
pretermit	omit
prevent	1) anticipate
	2) interrupt
prey	booty
Priamides	son of Priam, especially Hector
Priamist	son of Priam
price	1) prize (q.v.)
	2) value
prise	1) prize, booty
	2) ransom
	3) price (q.v.)
prise	esteem
prison	pen up, hold
privity of sleight	secret or sly device
prize	prise (q.v.)
procinct	* preparation (*C*)
production	* treatment (*C*)
profuse	* pour forth (*D*)
proine	prune, strip off
project	* abject, base (*C;* already used in *Bussy D'Ambois*)
Promethean	like Prometheus, creative
prominent	* 1) promontory, hill-top (*A*)
	2) standing high
proof	trial, challenge to trial
prophane	profane
propitious	* favourable, advantageous (*B*)

proportionate	* corresponding, in proportion (*D*)
propose	1) hold or set before
	2) make a proposal
	3) put forward, exhibit
propt	* propped, held up (*D*)
prosecute	* put in one's hands (*A;* as in 11. 745, 'to thy honorable hands my ease I prosecute')
prosopopœia	personification
proud	stately, high
prove	suffer, endure
puff	braggart
puissant	strong, powerful
purchase	thing gained, reward
purchase	* get the attention of (*A*)
puritanical	* pretending to special grace (*B*)
purple	make purple
pursue	follow up
pusillanimous	* proceeding from want of courage (*D*)
put on	* advance, come or go forward (*A*)
putrify	putrefy, become putrid
qualified	* (There is a special sense in 19. 70, 'heart so qualified,' meaning 'with anger gone')
quench	act of quenching
quick	alive, living
quicken	1) bring to life
	* 2) enliven, amuse (*D*)
quit	release, pay up
quite	1) put an end to
	2) requite
quitture	* clotted blood (*D*)
rabid	* furious, raging (*D*)
rabidly	* madly, foolishly (*C*)
race	* offspring (*D*)
race	1) erase, raze
	2) scratch, tear
racer	* razer, one who razes (*A*)
rack	* motion of the clouds (*D*)
rac't	razed
raft	* stripped, torn or taken off (*A*)
raign	reign
ram up	fill or heap up
rammish	* having a rank smell (*C*)
Ramnusia	* vengeance (*A*)

ramp	rear up
rampire	rampart
rampired	equipped with ramparts
ranch	tear, wrench
rank-rode	* rank-riding (C)
ransomable	* capable of being ransomed (D)
rapping	action of knocking
rapture	* seizing or carrying away (C)
rare	1) excellent, admirable
	2) early
rarify	make rare or thin
rate	1) estimation
	* 2) qualification (D)
	* 3) ratification (D)
rate	1) estimate value of
	2) reckon, esteem, count
	* 3) be rated as (D)
	* 4) ratify (C)
ratl'd	rattled (see 'rattle')
rattle	* drive in a rattling manner (D)
raveling	ravelin, bulwark
receipt	act of receiving, welcome
receipt, stand at	* stand ready to answer (C)
receive	* 1) answer (D)
	2) welcome, greet
	* 3) interpret (D)
reciprocal	mutual (as in 18. 354–5, 'that to her father had reciprocall Oceanus,' meaning that 'he was her father as well as Thetis')
recoil	* resilience (A)
recomfort	inspire
recomforted	restored to life
recomforting	inspiring
reconcilement	reconciliation
recuile	recoil (q.v.)
recure	cure
recure	recovery, cure
recureless	incurable
reddition	application of a comparison
redemptory	* of or pertaining to redemption (A)
redress	redressing, satisfaction
redundant	* superfluous (C)
refell	repel, force back
refer	hand over, convey
reference	allusion, bringing forward

reflect	turn (back or round)
reflection	turning back, return
reft	took away
regiment	1) a body of soldiers
	2) rule
regress	return
religiously	faithfully, sincerely
remember	remind, tell in order to refresh memory
remission	1) letting go, abandonment
	2) forgiveness
remissness	* tardiness (A)
remit	let go, cease, give over
remorse	compassion
remorseful	compassionate
remove	removal, retiral
r'enforce	reinforce
renowme	renown
renowmed	renowned
rense	rinse, lave
renues	renews
repair	arrival
repeat	repetition
repel	stop, hinder
repent	sorrow over, regret
repercussive	reflected
repine	feel dissatisfaction or annoyance
report	resounding noise
reprehend	reprove, find fault with
reprehension	censure, reproof
reprise	gain afresh
repugn	resist, fight against
repugnant	hostile
repurchase	* recapture (D)
resail	* return voyage (A)
rescue	succour, reviving aid
reserve	1) keep back
	2) preserve
reserved	kept back, restrained
resignation	giving up, resigning
resist	* stop, rest (D)
resistless	irresistible
resolution	(The sense of 16. 524, 'that most had rate of resolutions,' seems to mean 'that was rated best for strength')
resolved	1) resolute, decided, fixed

	* 2) conscious of the fact, fully informed (*C*)
respect	regard. (Peculiarly used in 11. 365, 'truth puts no respect betwixt' and 11. 555, 'spite of his yeares' respect')
respectful	* mindful, careful (*D*)
respective	careful, heedful, respectful
respects	heed, care, attention
respiration	action of breathing
responsible	* corresponding, equal in power (*A*)
responsive	* corresponding, equal in power (*D*)
restore	carry back, convey back
rests	* (In 20. 199, 'to set up all rests for my life' seems to mean 'to recount my whole descent')
resty	restive
retain	keep in mind, remember
retire	1) retreat. (Maybe Chapman had no clear sense for the verb in 11. 519, 'retiring their retire,' which should mean 'aiding them in their retreat')
	* 2) cause to retire, recall (*D*)
retraite	retreat
reverse	* retreat (*A*)
revile	reviling
revoke	call back, summon again
revoluble	* revolving (*D*)
rew, on a	in a row
right, in	in fact, in deed, truly
ring	ring out, re-echo
robd	robed, wearing robes
rode	road; roadstead (for ships)
room, leave one's	leave one's place
rore	roar
rosine	* (In 11. 434 'rosine flowres' evidently means 'firs, pines')
rosy	fragrant
round-headed	* stupid (*B*)
rowting	routing, putting to rout
rub	obstacle
rub	annoy, irritate
ruff	excited state, disordered passion
ruffinous	* boisterous, ruffianly (*C*)
ruin	fall, destruction, death
ruinate	reduce to ruins
ruinated	ruined
ruinous	bringing ruin

Glossary

ruled	rightly judged, giving a precedent
run, fetch one's	* run into combat, make an attack (C)
rundled	* rounded, circular (A)
runnet	rennet
rusticly	* in a rustic manner (D)
ruth	1) pity, compassion
	2) sorrow
ruth, be in	feel grief
ruthful	sorrowful
sable	* dark-coloured (B; as in 'sable blood')
sad	heavy
sad	sadly, with vexation
sad, suffer	suffer under duress
safe	* save (A)
saft	* saved (A)
sail	ship
sallow-polished	(In 7. 4 it is uncertain whether the reading should be 'sallow polisht oares,' i.e. oars made of willow, or 'sallow-polisht' i.e. polished in a yellowish shade)
satiate	satiated
satiety	* sufficiency or abundance (D)
Saturnia	Juno
Saturnius	Jove
savage	* wild beast (C)
save	retain, preserve
scall'd	scaled, mounted
scandal	* slander (A)
scare	frighten away, drive off
scathe	harm, injury
scatter	* (There is a peculiar sense in the Commentarius to 24, 'I have scattered with my burden,' evidently meaning 'let my burden fall down at times')
scoles	scales
scoptical	* satirical (D)
scoptically	* in a satirical manner (D)
scuffle	fight at close quarters
seat	* court of justice (D)
second	* 1) follow (A)
	2) support a speaker in a debate
second sight	* (In 23. 414, eyes 'hold with the second sight,' seems to mean 'do not discern clearly' i.e. are weak because of age)

[603]

secure	having a feeling of security
secure of	secure from
secureful	* protecting (*A*)
seducement	* temptation (*A*)
seed	offspring
seele	seel, close eyes of
seen	skilled, experienced
senior	old man
sere	dry
sere	* talon (*A*)
set	seated
set gone	put to flight
several	separate, individual
several, in	separately
sey, take	assay, test
shady	* casting shade (*A*)
sharp-set	eager, hungry
sharply-bitten	* sharply biting (*D*)
shawm	a kind of oboe
sheaf	bundle of arrows
sheep-fels	sheep-skins
sherd	shard, broken fragment
shew, make	make show of, pretend
shift	* decline, shirk (a duty) (*C*)
shole	swim in a shoal
shoot	shooting
show	reveal the character of
shrewd	naughty, sly
shrewish	malignant, deceitful
shrike	shriek, shrill cry
shrill	* keen, sharp (*A*)
shrubby	covered with shrubs
side, pull down a	let one's companions down
sight	sigh'd
silly	weak, simple
simple	herb, drug
simplician	simple, ignorant fellow
since	because
singular	1) individual, of one person
	2) unique
sinister	1) portending misfortune
	2) appertaining to the left hand
sir-name	surname
sirnamed	surnamed
sise	**size**

Glossary

sit out	* endure (D)
skald	(Apparently in 21. 319 'scald')
skall	scale
skill	1) knowledge
	* 2) information from oracles (D)
skill, without one's	beyond one's knowledge
slack it	slacken one's efforts
sleight	slight
sleight	trick, trickery. (For the spelling see Bartlett, *Poems*, p. 448)
sleight	deceive
sleightly	carelessly, summarily
slick	sleek, smooth, glossy
slick-haired	sleek-haired
sloth	slothfulness
slue	slew
snore	snort
sod	seethed, boiled
sodaine	sudden
solicit	disturb, disquiet
soon-monied	* readily turned into money or sold (A)
sooth	truth
soothed	pampered, humoured
sorest	most sorely
sort	1) crowd, troop, herd, heap
	2) fate, lot
sorts it	it happens, or it applies
sound	resound
sounding	resounding
sowtedge	soutage, coarse cloth
sparse	sperse (q.v.)
speed	speeding, success
speedless	* without speed, moderate (A)
spent of	* emptied, deprived (as in 2. 96, 'of all her people spent')
sperse	disperse, spread
sphere	* encircle (D; already in *Bussy D'Ambois*)
spininess	* the quality of being spiny (C)
spiny	like spines or thorns
spiritful	full of spirit, lively
spiritless	deprived of spirit, lifeless
spleenful	full of spleen
splene	spleen
spoil	* 1) spoiler, destroyer (C)
	2) spoliation

[605]

spoken	speaking
spring	produce
spriteful	* full of spirit, animated (*D*)
sprout	* offspring (*C*)
spurrie	* radiating like the points of a spur-rowel (*D*)
square, upon the	* in square formation (*D*)
stagger	make to stagger, knock down
stale	stem of an arrow
stanch	stop, assuage
stand-fight	* single combat (*C*)
standing	* stagnant (*B*)
stare	starling
start	started
state	* 1) room or place of state (*D*)
	2) lord, king, man of power
state in, have	* join the company of (*D*)
station	harbour
station-fight	* standing fight, single combat (*A*)
stead	place (frequently used in such phrases as 'girdle-stead' = waist, or 'in his safety's stead' = for his safety's sake)
steep, laid in	steeped in
steep-up	precipitous, perpendicular
steer	stir
stentor	loud-voiced herald
stern part	* breastbone (*C;* translating στέρνον)
sterve	starve
stick	stay, remain, continue
stick by	cling to
stile	style
still	distil
sting	* spur, incitement (*D*)
stitch	turn of a furrow
stomach	pride, anger
stomach	* 1) show pride or anger (*C*)
	2) enrage
stomach, take	take courage
stooded	studded
stoop	1) swoop down at
	2) subdue, kill
stoop	descent
straight-lac't	grudging, excessively scrupulous
strain it	stretch it, exaggeratedly phrase it
strake	iron rim of a wheel
strange to, stand	* be a stranger to, avoid (*D*)

strapple	* bind, entangle (D)
stream, iron	* flow of battle (D)
stream to, give	* set in motion (D)
strength	army
strenuity	strenuous effort
strenuous	brave
stridulous	* shrill-toned (C)
strooke	struck
stroot	swell out
stroy	destroy
study	think anxiously
submiss	submissive
submit	place under
suborn	provide in a secret manner
subtile	of fine texture
subtly	craftily
subvert	overthrow
successless	unsuccessful
succour	ally
sufferance	suffering
suffering-minded	* (The Homeric original at 5. 276 calls for 'strong-souled'; Chapman uses the compound probably in this sense)
sufficiency	adequate capacity (but with a sense also of 'substantial quality' in B 'To the Reader')
suffisde	sufficed
suffrage	* approval, consent (A)
suite	suit, plea
suite, of a	* all shaped alike (of furniture) (D)
Sun	Apollo
superficies	* (Apparently used, in D, for the 'crests' of waves)
supple	1) mollify
	* 2) soften by pouring on (apparently the significance of 10. 469, 'she that supples earth with blood')
suppliance	* 1) supply, assistance (A)
	* 2) entreaty (D)
supplied	aided
supply	1) aid, assistance
	2) something to make up a deficiency
supportful	* affording support (A)
surcease	leave off, desist
surcuidrie	arrogance, overweening pride
surpassing	pre-eminent
surprised	* taken unawares (D)

surrebound	* resound once again (*D*)
survaid	surveyed, looked at
suspect	* suspicious thought (*A*)
suspend	* desist or refrain from temporarily (*A*)
sustain	1) maintain
	2) hold up, support
sustainer	one who sustains something
swaggering	quarreling, blustering
swinge	1) sway, free scope
	2) forcible movement
sylvan	* 1) a forest tree (*D*)
	2) covered with trees
symbolise	mix, unite
syre	sire
tail	* ordure (as in 23. 678)
taint	1) stroke, blow
	* 2) blame, censure (*D*)
taint	touch, strike
take	(See under 'town')
take down	* (Chapman's specific sense in *A* of 'defeat, cast down' seems slightly different from any in the *NED*)
take in	capture
tall	1) quick, active
	2) brave
tame-horse	* horse-tamer (*D*)
tamricke	tamarisk
tappish	tapis, hide, seek cover
targatier	targeteer, soldier with a shield
targe	shield
target	shield
Telamonius	son of Telamon, Ajax
tempt	* attempt, attack (*A*)
tendered	* held dear, esteemed (*D*)
term	end of service, time for being paid
terror, make	* feel fear (*D*)
theare	there
thickener	* something that thickens (*D*)
thirst	long for, desire vehemently
thirsted	* longed for (*C*)
threave	crowd
thrift	labour
throat	* shout, bellow (*D*)
throat	* shout (*D*)

throat, pour one's	* shout (D)
throwe	throe, pang
thrumb	thrum, tuft
thrust	crowd
timeless	untimely
timely	in good time
tire	feed on, prey on
tomb	entomb
tongue	talkativeness, use of the tongue
top-ayles	topmost ears of corn
touch	1) blow, injury
	2) mark, quality
touch at	* hear, make out (D)
toward	that is to come
towardness	good disposition
town, take the	* go into the town (D)
traditional	* customary, hackneyed (B)
traduction	translation
trail	* trail on, be dragged along (D)
transportance	transportation
transposed	changed from one's proper state, topsy-turvy
traverse	run through
treasurous	* full of treasure (C)
tress	trace (of a chariot)
tried	proved or tested by experience
trim	* state, order (C)
trim	polish, make ready
trim, in the	* in proper order (C)
trivet	tripod
troop, take	* return to the main body of the army (A)
troope-meale	in troops, troop by troop
trunk	corpse
truss	jacket, dress
truss	seize violently
trussed	* overwhelmed (C)
truss't	trussed (q.v.)
truth of, give a	* give a true account of or judgment on (D)
turning	* twisting in attempt to escape (D)
twibil	two-edged battle axe
twitch	act of twitching, wrenching
tyring	feeding greedily upon (see 'tire')
unappalled	without fear
uncontained	* uncontrolled (D)
undergo	go under

[609]

undergone	* gone under (*D*)
undergroan	* groan under (*A*)
under liquid	* under the waves (*A*)
undermine	* run under (*A*)
underput with	* with something put under (*D*)
understrife	* strife carried on upon the earth (*D*)
undertaking	ready to undertake an enterprise
underwent	went or passed under
undiscerned	* undiscernible (*A*)
undispersed	not scattered
unequal	uneven
ungear	* unharness (*A*)
ungracious in	* ungracious towards (*A*)
unhandsomely	* in an ugly or bad manner (*D*)
unimpeached	not accused or called in question
unimposed	* not put on (*B*)
uninvited	* unasked (*A*)
unless	if . . . not
unmanly	* brutal, inhuman (*D*)
unmatchedness	* unique quality (*D*)
unmeasured	immeasurable
unpainful	not causing pain
unpleased	* implacable (*A*)
unrac't	* unrazed (*C*)
unreacht	* unreached, unreachable (*D*)
unrecovered	* from which no recovery is or has been made (*A*)
unremorseful	* incompassionate (*A*)
unreproved	* irreproachable (*A*)
unresisted	* irresistible (*D*)
unrest	torment, trouble
unspeakable	inexpressible, ineffable
unsuffered	* unsufferable (*A*)
unthankful	* inconsiderate, not grateful (*C*)
untrussed	undone, slovenly
unturned	* without turning (*A*)
unvallued	unvalued, invaluable, priceless
upbraid	reproof, complaint
uplandish	belonging to the mountains
ure	use
use	1) be accustomed to
	2) put on (of dress)
use	custom, habit
useful	helpful
usually	according to custom
utmost	uttermost, furthest

Glossary

utter	1) uttermost
	2) outer
vail	bow down before
vainly	foolishly, thoughtlessly
vall	* valley (C)
valure	valour
vanity	vain, worthless thing
vant	vaunt
vaporous	having the nature of vapour
vaunt, make one's	* (In A evidently means 'make good one's boast')
vaunt-gard	vanguard
vein, prick a mad	* incline towards madness, behave madly (D)
Venerean	of or pertaining to love
vent	hole, exit
vent	* 1) relieve or unburden (one's feelings) (D)
	* 2) let loose, kill (D)
	* 3) cast out, avenge (D; as in 19. 199, 'venting infamie')
ventrous	venturesome, brave
verge	edge, rim
vertue	virtue, strength
vertuous	full of strength, courageous
vex	trouble, harass
viciously	* reprehensibly (D)
victles	victuals
victual	eat
villanizer	* reviler (A)
virtue	strength, power, valour
virtuous	full of vertù, pride, power
vitiate	impair, spoil
voiceful	* stentorian, with loud voices (A)
vow	make vows
wadl'd	(In 20. 162 this may be an error for 'swadl'd'; it evidently means 'lashed')
waist	girdle
wale (wal)	weal
walkers	* legs, feet (D)
wall	* blind (A)
wan	won
wanton	* extraordinary (A)
wantonness	1) lustfulness
	2) arrogance
wast	waste

wast costs	(See Commentary to 24. 576)
watching	vigil
weed	piece of clothing
weigh	count, esteem
well-arted	* artistically wrought (*D*)
well-coucht	* well ringed, with layers laid well on one another (*D*)
well-rode	* well riding, skilled in riding (*C*)
well-seen	skilled, experienced
well-written	* skilful in writing (*C*)
wether	sheep
wey	weigh
wheelband	tire of a wheel
whet	sharpen
whilome	once, some time ago
whirlpit	whirlpool
white	whiten
whitleather	a kind of leather
whoorlbat	whirlbat, hurling club
why	by which
win	persuade
wind to the stream	* (In 16. 262 'put his wind to the stream' seems to mean 'applied himself')
windfucker	a kind of kestrel, applied as a term of abuse (*C*)
wishfully	* longingly (*A*)
wishly	longingly
withdraw	draw out or off
without	outside of
withstand	keep away
witty	clever
wondrous	* wondering (*C*)
wonne	won
woo	* stand praising one another (*D*)
wool-bearer	sheep
wrack	suffer shipwreck
wrastle down	* suppress, quell (*D*)
wreak	vengeance
wreakful	vengeful
wreathe round	twist or turn round
wrest	strain the meaning of a passage
wright	write
writee	* one for whom something is written, reader (*D*)
yare	ready
yield	acknowledge

Glossary

yieldy	* yielding good crops (B)
ylles	ills
yokie sphere	* yoky circle, horse collar (D)
yong	young
zone	girdle